DEGENERATION

DEGENERATION

BY

MAX NORDAU

Translated from the Second Edition of the German Work

Introduction by George L. Mosse

University of Nebraska Press
Lincoln and London

Manufactured in the United States of America

First Bison Book printing: 1993
Most recent printing indicated by the last digit below:
10 9 8 7 6 5 4 3 2 1

Library of Congress Cataloging-in-Publication Data
Nordau, Max Simon, 1849–1923.
[Entartung. English]
Degeneration / by Max Nordau ; translated from the second edition of the German work; introduction by George L. Mosse.
p. cm.
Originally published: New York : D. Appleton, 1895.
Includes index.
ISBN 0-8032-8367-9 (pa)
1. Degeneration. 2. Europe—Intellectual life. 3. Literature, Comparative—History and criticism. I. Title.
CB417.N813 1993
809′.894—dc20
93-8474
CIP

Originally published in German in 1892. Reprinted from the English-language edition published in 1895 by D. Appleton & Co., New York; an index that was added to the 1900 reprint has been included.

The University of Nebraska Press is grateful to George L. Mosse and Howard Fertig for permission to reprint Dr. Mosse's introduction to the 1968 edition of *Degeneration,* published by Howard Fertig, Inc., New York.

∞

DEDICATED TO

CÆSAR LOMBROSO

PROFESSOR OF PSYCHIATRY AND FORENSIC MEDICINE
AT THE ROYAL UNIVERSITY OF TURIN

BY THE AUTHOR

TO

PROFESSOR CÆSAR LOMBROSO,

TURIN.

DEAR AND HONOURED MASTER,

I dedicate this book to you, in open and joyful recognition of the fact that without your labours it could never have been written.

The notion of degeneracy, first introduced into science by Morel, and developed with so much genius by yourself, has in your hands already shown itself extremely fertile in the most diverse directions. On numerous obscure points of psychiatry, criminal law, politics, and sociology, you have poured a veritable flood of light, which those alone have not perceived who obdurately close their eyes, or who are too short-sighted to derive benefit from any enlightenment whatsoever.

But there is a vast and important domain into which neither you nor your disciples have hitherto borne the torch of your method —the domain of art and literature.

Degenerates are not always criminals, prostitutes, anarchists, and pronounced lunatics; they are often authors and artists. These, however, manifest the same mental characteristics, and for the most part the same somatic features, as the members of the above-mentioned anthropological family, who satisfy their unhealthy impulses with the knife of the assassin or the bomb of the dynamiter, instead of with pen and pencil.

Some among these degenerates in literature, music, and painting have in recent years come into extraordinary prominence, and are revered by numerous admirers as creators of a new art, and heralds of the coming centuries.

This phenomenon is not to be disregarded. Books and works of art exercise a powerful suggestion on the masses. It is from these productions that an age derives its ideals of morality and beauty. If they are absurd and anti-social, they exert a disturbing and corrupting influence on the views of a whole generation. Hence the latter, especially the impressionable youth, easily excited to enthusiasm for all that is strange and seemingly new, must be warned and enlightened as to the real nature of the creations so blindly admired. This warning the ordinary critic does not give. Exclusively literary and æsthetic culture is, moreover, the worst preparation conceivable for a true knowledge of the pathological character of the works of degenerates. The verbose rhetorician exposes with more or less grace, or cleverness, the subjective impressions received from the works he criticises, but is incapable of judging if these works are the productions of a shattered brain, and also the nature of the mental disturbance expressing itself by them.

Now I have undertaken the work of investigating (as much as possible after your method) the tendencies of the fashions in art and literature; of proving that they have their source in the degeneracy of their authors, and that the enthusiasm of their admirers is for manifestations of more or less pronounced moral insanity, imbecility, and dementia.

Thus, this book is an attempt at a really scientific criticism, which does not base its judgment of a book upon the purely accidental, capricious, and variable emotions it awakens—emotions depending on the temperament and mood of the individual reader—but upon the psycho-physiological elements from which it sprang. At the same time it ventures to fill a void still existing in your powerful system.

I have no doubt as to the consequences to myself of my initiative. There is at the present day no danger in attacking the Church, for it no longer has the stake at its disposal. To write against rulers and governments is likewise nothing venturesome, for at the worst nothing more than imprisonment could follow, with compensating glory of martyrdom. But grievous is the fate of him who has the audacity to characterize æsthetic fashions as forms of mental decay.

The author or artist attacked never pardons a man for recognising in him a lunatic or a charlatan; the subjectively garrulous critics are furious when it is pointed out how shallow and incompetent they are, or how cowardly when swimming with the stream; and even the public is angered when forced to see that it has been running after fools, quack dentists, and mountebanks, as so many prophets. Now, the graphomaniacs and their critical body-guard dominate nearly the entire press, and in the latter possess an instrument of torture by which, in Indian fashion, they can rack the troublesome spoiler of sport, to his life's end.

The danger, however, to which he exposes himself cannot deter a man from doing that which he regards as his duty. When a scientific truth has been discovered, he owes it to humanity, and has no right to withhold it. Moreover, it is as little possible to do this as for a woman voluntarily to prevent the birth of the mature fruit of her womb.

Without aspiring to the most distant comparison of myself with you, one of the loftiest mental phenomena of the century, I may yet take for my example the smiling serenity with which you pursue your own way, indifferent to ingratitude, insult, and misunderstanding.

Pray remain, dear and honoured master, ever favourably disposed towards your gratefully devoted

MAX NORDAU.

CONTENTS.

BOOK I.

FIN-DE-SIÈCLE.

CHAPTER I.

CHAPTER II.

CHAPTER III.

CHAPTER IV.

BOOK II.

MYSTICISM.

CHAPTER I.

CHAPTER II.

CHAPTER III.

CHAPTER IV.

CHAPTER V.

CHAPTER VI.

BOOK III.

EGO-MANIA.

CHAPTER I.

CHAPTER II.

CHAPTER III.

CHAPTER IV.

CHAPTER V.

BOOK IV.

REALISM.

CHAPTER I.

CHAPTER II.

BOOK V.

THE TWENTIETH CENTURY.

CHAPTER I.

CHAPTER II.

Introduction

MAX NORDAU AND HIS DEGENERATION

by George L. Mosse

To generations of Europeans, man's fate rode on the spin of the wheel, at the mercy of Dame Fortune, who bestowed her favors on him one moment and dashed him to the ground the next. Max Nordau might well have been the child of capricious fortune. Today there is hardly an echo of the great fame that was his from 1883 until the beginning of the First World War. A literate public in Germany, France, Austria, England, and Eastern Europe regarded him as a pre-eminent journalist, literary critic, and iconoclast. A list of the editions of his books would fill several pages, and when he was won to the Zionist cause it was his international reputation that helped to make him a leader second only to Theodor Herzl himself. Nevertheless, after 1914 Max Nordau began to sink into obscurity, new editions of his books were no longer brought out, and by his death in 1923 the wheel of fortune had come full circle.

There was good reason for the fate that overtook him. Nordau had been typical of his age, and when that age died, he died with it. Born into a Hungarian rabbinical family in 1849, he escaped the narrowness of this Orthodox Jewish milieu by becoming a journalist. To symbolize his break with the past he changed his name from Südfeld (southern field) to Nordau (northern meadow). His work as a newspaper correspondent brought him to Germany and then to Paris, where he lived for most of his life. However, journalism was not, in itself, enough to satisfy his thirst for knowledge and experience. Nordau earned a medical degree and became a practicing physician. With that typical abundance of energy for which we might envy the men of his generation, he treated his patients, wrote some nine volumes of novels and short stories, seven plays, and fifteen works of essays and cultural criticism, some of them running to several volumes. Later in life he produced speeches and writings on behalf of the Zionist cause. Small wonder that Nordau consistently stressed intellectual discipline and power of will.

His pen, moreover, crossed national boundaries. While practicing medicine in Paris, he wrote the annual political review for the *Neue Freie Presse* of Vienna, Central Europe's most influential newspaper. At the time he wrote *Degeneration* (1892) he was also foreign correspondent for the important *Vossische Zeitung* of Berlin. For Nordau in those prewar decades the continent of Europe was still a true entity. His books caused a stir in all nations; *Degeneration* provoked replies by George Bernard Shaw in England, by Italian physicians, and by French philosophers. The book itself was translated into many languages and went through as many editions in Italian as it did in the original German. In the range of his activities, in the energy he poured into them, and in his cosmopolitanism, Nordau typifies one aspect of his age and the men who made it.

But these years also witnessed the beginning of a different cultural and national orientation. Nordau, in disillusionment, later called it the "spirit of churlishness and brutality."[1] The final years of the last century saw not only the birth of a new and aggressive nationalism but also the emergence of modern modes in art and literature. The time of Nordau's fame was also the seed time of Impressionism and Expressionism in art, of a new realism in literature, and of a drama that eventually led to the contemporary Theater of the Absurd. A young generation was engaged in a search for its own identity, and directly opposed all that Max Nordau stood for. Against this modernism Nordau struck back in his *Degeneration.*

The book can be read on two levels. There is the point of view from which Nordau criticizes modern writers whose fame has outlasted his own. But the goals and desires of the moderns themselves are also reflected in the bitter criticism that Nordau directs at their work. *Degeneration* is one of the most important documents of the *fin de siècle,* the years between the 1880s and 1900 when the robust views of the nineteenth century clashed with the heightened sensibilities of a searching and disillusioned generation. Thus it seems unimportant that the book proved a short-lived sensation. The last German and French editions had appeared by 1909, though the Italians reissued the work once more in 1925. But the memory of it lingered for many decades. Nordau's obituary in the London *Times* (1923) referred to him not only as "a writer of world fame" but also as the "philosopher of decadence." Yet by 1923 the moderns were in the ascendant, and nothing can demonstrate this better than an editorial which *The Times* devoted to the book a few weeks after its author's death. It still thought *Degeneration* important enough to merit discussion, but only so that the basic arguments of the book could be refuted. *The Times* insisted that real decadence was shown if "rash experiments" in art or life were rejected, if man was enslaved to the past and refused to think, experiment, or adventure[2]—this from a newspaper not especially noted for encouraging "rash experiments" in politics or social life.

The writers and artists against whom Nordau had fought won their victory, and so had the moderns who came after them. Yet it is still possible for the wheel of fortune to turn again and salvage much of relevance from Nordau's criticism. Contrary to what modern critics like to think, he was never irrelevant or cut off from the stream of modern culture. Indeed, it still remains to be seen just how close to the truth the English novelist Israel Zangwill was when he forecast, at the time of Nordau's death, that "whenever art goes crazy and letters loose touch with life, men will remember the prophet of *Degeneration*."[3]

The cornerstone of Nordau's world view was a belief in ordered progress based upon the potentialities of the natural sciences. Here he stood in the mainstream of European middle-class thought of the late nineteenth century. His most popular book, *Conventional Lies of Our Civilization* (1883), set the tone, which remained unchanged a decade later. The future of humanity lies in its elevation, not its degradation. Ideas based upon the natural sciences will enable humanity to see this distant development more clearly than will the fog of superstition.[4] Science and progress go together, and he who understands the workings of science will also have an unobstructed view of the future of mankind.

In *Degeneration,* Nordau explains that science operates through "irresistible and unchangeable" physical laws which apply to man as much as to nature itself. The law of cause and effect, one of the most important laws, is essential for the understanding of all others. Thus all relationships between things (including men) must be clearly formulated, for there is nothing vague or mystical about the law of causality. The absence of clear formulations in thought places a man like Tolstoi among the degenerates. But Nordau's world view involves a great deal more than mere clarity of formulation. For man can achieve clarity only through observation and knowledge, and both require a mental discipline which, at times, he calls "attention." This is crucial, for "whoever preaches absence of discipline is an enemy of progress."[5]

Nordau's elaboration of the qualities necessary for human progress increasingly reminds us of those very attributes that the bourgeois age prized so much. First there was strength of will, without which there can be no discipline. His major novel, *Malady of the Century* (1888), portrays a young man possessed of all the virtues except one: the power of will to make decisions. This "German Buddhist," despite his many good qualities, thus lives a futile existence. There was also the importance of duty and work, which were essential for observation and the acquisition of knowledge. Small wonder that Nordau has nothing but contempt for the artists who frequented the coffee houses of Vienna and Paris: they are vagabonds and prostitutes, incapable of performing any duty whatever. The truth about humanity could be discovered only through hard work. Thus, a retreat into metaphysics or "mysticism" was merely an evasion of duty.

The knowledge finally acquired through discipline and hard work was a knowledge of nature which would shape the future of the human species. This knowledge depended upon the recognition of irresistible organic laws. Most important, the law of cause and effect would permit man to understand the law that governed all living organisms: the law of evolution. Evolution is dominated by the struggle for existence and the survival of the fittest.[6] Here Nordau's acceptance of Darwinism, which first found expression in his *Conventional Lies of Our Civilization,* made him a true child of his age. Nordau remained a convinced Darwinian for the rest of his life.

In order to survive, the species must adapt to the total environment. Man must face the problems presented by existing reality, for to ignore reality leads to defeat in the struggle for existence. Nordau's basic objection to the "mystics" and "egomaniacs" (the chief categories in which he places his degenerates) rests upon these foundations. Both withdrew from the task at hand. Yet Nordau always remained an optimist. In *Paradoxes* (1885) he proclaims his great faith in the ability of organisms to adapt to their environment and grow according to the predetermined laws of nature.[7] As an organism, man cannot divorce his interior development from his environment. Knowledge of nature and the observation of facts must always be important in this context.

Thus Nordau criticizes Emile Zola for relying upon his imagination rather than observation. He accuses him of employing a false naturalism; after all, machines and streets have no fantastic life of their own. Later he criticized the sculptor Rodin for inventing human muscles where nature omitted them.[8] To our ears this may sound naive, but given Nordau's presuppositions, this kind of criticism is perfectly logical. "A clear-headed poet calls a cat a cat."[9] You cannot trifle with knowledge, for upon it depends the survival and the future of the human race. Consequently, all true knowledge becomes useful knowledge.

Nordau had a social aim: to create better conditions for the "human organism" by filling it with a greater number of pleasurable sensations. There is a mighty dose of utilitarianism in his thought; he did not need to go back to Jeremy Bentham for his inspiration, for it had become an accepted canon of the bourgeois way of life. Pleasure did not mean license. On the contrary, it was possible to attain it only within the framework of evolution—that is, disciplined progress. Whereas revolutions tend toward anarchy, true natural evolution is accompanied by a "philosophy of self-restraint."

This emphasis upon evolution explains much of Nordau's outlook. He opposed the "invention" of new artistic forms, for he believed that the ancient forms permitted enough flexibility for organic growth. He opposed political revolution as well: sudden breaks with the past were not in tune with evolutionary theory. A free republic might constitute the ideal form of government, but it could not be brought into being in any case until the people had learned to comprehend the universe from the standpoint of the natural sciences and swept out false transcendentalism.[10] This did not mean that Nordau rejected all political and social reform. He suggested an inheritance tax which would work to level property differences and make it possible for each man to get ahead through his own strength of will, dedication to duty, work, and discipline.[11] In addition, he was much concerned with the problem of workers displaced by modern technology. Displaced workers must settle on the soil, and if Europe lacked the space they must emigrate overseas. The emigrants would then take the place of the "lower races" who were not surviving in the struggle of evolution.

This notion seems as aggressive and imperialistic as the brutality of which Friedrich Nietzsche is accused in *Degeneration.* But Nordau softens its impact: he sees the struggle for survival as eternal; thus if the white race could not adapt in the tropics, it, in its turn, would be replaced.[12] These are familiar doctrines. Many of Nordau's contemporaries, including Nietzsche himself, believed that emigration would solve the problem of human obsolescence in an industrial society. During the last decades of the century, the preoccupation with land settlement was as common as the classification of higher and lower races according to the Darwinian doctrine of evolution.

A summary of Nordau's thought, up to this point, reads like that of the typical liberal of his age. Nineteenth-century liberalism, which was concerned with progress through order, will, and rationality, must not be equated with the "open-mindedness" of modern-day liberalism. Nordau deplored the *fin de siècle* contempt for accepted views of custom and morality and defended "traditional discipline." This was essential for the acquisition of knowledge and for progress within the scheme of evolution. Liberals believed in science and progress, but they also held that these were founded upon human attitudes formed by strict discipline and canons of morality which the middle classes had furthered long before Nordau wrote his book.

The liberal world view, in consequence, tended to deny progress to literature and art. The self-liberating attitudes of the moderns led to a "night of chaos," and from this point of view no distinctions were made between such disparate artists as Ibsen, Zola, Tolstoi, and Wilde. Liberals like Nordau advocated the emancipation of knowledge from "prejudice," whereas the emancipation of the modern writers menaced a world that had been built upon order, rationality, and progress. They were the opposite of Nordau's "normal" men upon whom human progress depended: those who rise early and are not weary before sunset, who have clear heads, solid stomachs, and hard muscles.[13] Is this not the stereotype of the "all-American boy" or of the "right-living Englishman" which has stayed with us until our own day?

Yet Nordau rises above this stereotype in his vision of the ideal society. He castigates not only the "mystics" but also the "ego-maniacs." For him the distinction between the ego and "non-ego" is an illusion, for every organism is related to the species and, ultimately, to the universe. Man and nature are governed by the same organic laws, and thus the larger unity of the whole implies unity among men. This unity produces a society which, far from being an artificial creation, is an evolutionary necessity, a necessity that has become instinctual among normal men. Human solidarity is part of nature's own morality.[14] The struggle for existence remains eternal, but it will become milder when a civilization based upon pessimism, lying, and egotism is replaced by one based upon truth, love of one's neighbor, and cheerfulness.[15]

If men could only discipline themselves to stay within the "truth" of natural evolution, a new civilization would develop, and Nordau attempted to help it along with his *Conventional Lies of Our Civilization* and *Degeneration.* The ordered progress he envisioned would lead to a time when evolution had advanced far enough for men to live together in solidarity without coercion by the state. For (and here Nordau is close, once again, to the liberals) the use of force and coercion might divert men from organic evolution, interfere with nature, and thus have devastating consequences. It would be better if the mass of men would follow the elite, who through superior knowledge and force of will could assume a natural leadership.[16]

The elite would have to act for the benefit of mankind, for action and thought were united. Nordau's organic view of the world certainly did not allow the divorce of one facet of human nature from another; as far as he was concerned, it was precisely Nietzsche's "ego-mania" which ruptured the relationship between will and judgment and led to unbridled excess. Nordau's concept of human solidarity was based upon his view of the unity of all living matter within a scientifically determined universe. It did not mean equality of functions or property.

This stress upon unity leads to an aspect of Nordau's thought that is so prominent in *Degeneration* and so difficult for us to accept today: his ideas on psychology. Nordau's psychology was meant to explain the actual functioning of the human organism within the larger physical laws which we have discussed. Nordau had studied in Paris under J. M. Charcot, who had also influenced Sigmund Freud. Indeed, when Freud came to study in Paris he presented a letter of introduction to his fellow student, but he never followed up the one brief meeting.[17] However, whereas Freud eventually freed himself from the physiological aspects of the current psychology, Nordau never did so. It is significant that the famous physician and psychologist Cesare Lombroso played no part in Freud's life but found a true disciple in Nordau. Lombroso's *Genius and Insanity* (*Genio e Follio,* 1863) was one of the principal sources of inspiration for *Degeneration.* It stressed that man's mode of feeling and his conduct of life are determined by his physical constitution which is reflected in his bodily structure. Moreover, in the formation of this constitution external factors meshed with those of man's own physical evolution. Here Darwinism played an important role for the Italian psychologist as it would for his admiring disciple. The human being was conceived as a unity—both in himself and with his environment—on the basis of physical, determinate factors.[18]

Much of Lombroso's work was based upon an analysis of criminals. He regarded their lack of altruistic feelings as a sign of their dominant atavism. Lombroso explained that, in evolutionary terms, their development had retrogressed. Nordau repeats these ideas in *Degeneration.* Lombroso also advocated the death penalty for criminals as part of the process of "deliberate selection" which would serve to supplement natural selection. Moreover, on the basis of a study of the nervous system, he believed that the line of distinction between genius and criminal was finely drawn. Nordau did not follow him here. His emphasis upon normality excluded any preoccupation with the nature of genius: in this he was more typical of his age and class than Lombroso was. Personally the two men were united by a deep friendship, and Lombroso hailed Nordau as the "true representative of a new humanity."[19] He might more accurately have said that Nordau was the representative of a century which at that very moment was being freely challenged by men and women who glorified precisely what the two friends castigated as criminal and degenerate. What were they to make of Henry Adams's exclamation in the 1870s: "Everything is respectable, and nothing amusing. There are no outlaws."

Through Lombroso, Max Nordau was part of that long tradition of psychology represented by the phrenology of Franz Joseph Gall (1758–1828), who sought to discover man's character structure through skull configuration, and by Francesco Giuseppe Broussais (1772–1838), for whom life's phenomena depended upon external stimuli (especially heat) while all pathology was based upon gastroenterites. Paul Broca's researches on the frontal lobe of the brain (1861) belong here as well. Broca's work climaxed in the attempt to cure mental disorder by operating on this part of the brain (lobotomy). For his time, Nordau's psychological explanations were not so farfetched as they might seem to us now in the post-Freudian age. To be sure, Charcot himself had already gone beyond this stage in his use of hypnotism in treating hysteria. And though Nordau, for a time, also used hypnotism, *Degeneration* remains one of the last examples of the application of the older and once dominant school of psychology.

Nordau's psychological studies confirmed him in his materialistic science, which looked upon all phenomena as "living matter." It should not surprise us that he thought all philosophy invalid except for psychology "in its scientific orientation."[20] The newly emerging psychoanalysis passed him by all his life, as did the new physics, which, shortly after the appearance of *Degeneration,* had already begun to destroy his all too mechanical and deterministic approach to scientific phenomena.

In choosing *Degeneration* as the title of his book, Nordau went back to another psychiatrist, the Frenchman B. A. Morel, who had popularized the catchword "degeneration" (1857) in order to describe human deviations. Nordau partially accepts Morel's physical reasons for human deviations: poisoning of the bodily system by alcohol, narcotics, stimulants, and the like; an unhealthy social environment; diseased nervous systems. In fact, in his book Nordau devotes several pages to an analysis of Morel's views. But Nordau soon returns to his own, more favored emphasis; the human organism itself has become fatigued with nervous excitement. The reasons he gives for this state of affairs constitute a criticism of industrial society. And again he links the external factors to the human organism itself. In an industrial society, not only does the individual have no time to assimilate new discoveries, but these discoveries themselves make increasing demands on his labor. Above all, residence in large towns leads to nervous excitement.

The victims of modern life suffer from decayed brain centers. They therefore lack all discipline; in them the aesthetic is allowed to prevail over the useful. Some of them register only nerve vibrations and become Impressionist painters. Others (like the naturalists) take to pessimism, exhibiting the exhaustion of old age.

Nordau here links himself with the literary use of the term "decadence," which was much narrower in scope than that current in psychology. For Anatole Baju, who founded *Le Décadent* in 1886, or for Paul Adam, in his journal *Décadence,* all faith has been lost and men can have no commitment.

Whatever the individual diagnosis, none of Nordau's degenerates are capable of "rational convictions arrived at by the sound labor of the intellect." They cannot perform such labor because, lacking the power of will, observation, and discipline, they fail to make clear and coherent connections. They are unable to grasp cause and effect. They can only associate ideas, throwing rational connections to the wind. This, as we shall see, was exactly the way in which such new artistic forms as Expressionism sought to give vent to the turmoil of men's souls. Against this Max Nordau quotes Kant: to think is to unite and to bind.[21] Nordau made such judgments not only from the conviction of a psychological theory but also from the fastness of an unshakable scientific truth from which such men were cut off.

Scientific truth is the basis of all morality. What startles us today is not only Nordau's psychology but also his use of moral judgments. Morality is not connected with metaphysical truth or an inner quest for sincerity, but rather with what is "useful" in terms of the progress of the species. In the same year that *Degeneration* appeared Nordau also published a novel, *The Right to Love,* in which he denies the rights of individuals when the survival of the species is involved. A husband and wife should live in an empty marriage rather than endanger the adaptability of their children. He wrote this novel to refute Ibsen's *Doll's House* with its portrayal of the free run of passions and man's selfishness. Indeed, his view of women was traditional, characteristic of his concept of sexual morality. At first he opposed the movement for woman's emancipation which was agitating the final decades of the century. Woman was not fit to endure the struggle for survival without the protection of man. Eventually he became convinced that emancipation would make little difference. Woman, by her very nature, was family-centered and would never abandon her proper tasks. Yet in the new century many women did compete professionally with men. Now Nordau urges the female to resume her "civilizing role": tempering the harshness of life by fulfilling her task as mother and home maker.[22] Nordau's own happy marriage may have reinforced these attitudes, but they were shared by most men of his class and generation.

He also linked sexual morality with the self-discipline that was essential for all progress. One must show a proper regard for one's neighbor. It was one thing to oppose the mass of men from the vantage of superior knowledge (which Nordau thought he had), but quite another to offend through eccentricity of behavior or dress, as Oscar Wilde was then doing. This morality, useful for the survival of the species, is identical with commonly accepted middle-class morality.

Those who do not share such a morality must be examined for signs of degeneracy. Nordau, in his unbounded optimism, believed that the instincts of all healthy men led down the path of successful survival and adaptation. A component of this instinct was the acceptance of morality. Both morality and the faculty of rational comprehension are part of the normal man's innermost being. Little wonder that he reserves some of his greatest scorn for the pessimists—those with no faith in life and the promise it holds. Pessimism is a physical sickness, caused by bad digestion or nervous exhaustion. As he wrote in *Paradoxes:* pessimistic philosophy cannot be taken seriously; it is merely a dissatisfaction with the limitations of rational comprehension. Instead of working hard to extend these limitations, the pessimist takes the short cut of despair. Through him men fall "into the tragic night of chaos."[23] Here was a man sure of himself and secure in his view of the world. Perhaps it is this sureness that we find most old-fashioned about Max Nordau, and yet it identifies him as a man of the last golden age known to the European middle classes.

Nordau wrote about literature and art. Yet it seems as if the creative artist could not play a meaningful part within his universe. In spite of the remark in *Degeneration* that literature will eventually be subordinated to science, Nordau did not really think so. But art cannot be the idiosyncratic creation of the artist, for it must find its place within the unity of all living matter. Art is work for the community.[24] One of the heroes in his novels exclaims that inner freedom is an illusory concept produced by sudden movements of the nerves, physical conditions, and what we wrongly see, hear, and learn.[25] Nevertheless, it will not do merely to reproduce an ugly and boring reality.[26] Art must give man back his dignity in industrial society and ennoble him.

The artist must make universally valid themes clear to the beholder. For if they are not clear there will be no emotional communication between artist and audience. Clarity demands a traditional form, which is connected with organic evolution. Words and music must not be mixed up (as was done by Wagner), for both have their separate tasks to perform. Moreover, meaning, not sound, determines the nature of words. In literature, Nordau was horrified by irrational associations, one of the sure marks of degeneracy. While clarity is essential, morality gives beauty to a work of art. Not by itself alone, but without it no beauty can exist. In this way the work of art is integrated into human solidarity and attains "usefulness." Nordau's own novels were highly didactic and conventional—they have not survived into the modern age. Action, so much prized, was another prerequisite, especially for the drama. To write a play one needs action and plot. The evolution of the modern theater, however, ignored the advice of the great proponent of scientific evolution.

George Bernard Shaw struck back on behalf of the "degenerates." Willfully he took a position directly opposed to Nordau's; no debate between them would have been possible, even had it been desired. To Shaw, passion was the steam in the engine of all moral and religious systems. Life was the fulfillment neither of moral law nor of deductions springing from reason, but of irrational passion. For Shaw most of the human race would share the features which Nordau calls degenerate. Nordau's great optimism is denounced as simple trust. Shaw does not criticize any of the basic scientific postulates upon which Nordau built his edifice.[27] Indeed, much of the attacks which converged upon *Degeneration* asserted the need for men "to believe" and saw in mysticism an eternal and therefore necessary trait of human nature.[28]

The cranks were not absent. A book published in England and the United States, entitled *Regeneration,* ridiculed any optimism that might be based upon Nordau's scientific "superstitions" or upon his views on human solidarity. All hope must come from the free institutions of England. The author of this book called Nordau both a "typical German" and a "free-thinking Jew."[29]

It was not the German but the Jew who dominated the second phase of Nordau's life. Nordau says nothing about his Jewishness or Judaism in *Degeneration.* But only one year after the book appeared he served as a newspaper correspondent at the trial of Captain Dreyfus in France. The proceedings rudely awakened the great optimist who had fled the narrowness of the Jewish milieu of Budapest so many years earlier. In 1895 his personal contact with Theodor Herzl proved decisive, and Nordau at once became a force in the new Zionist movement. As one of those who knew him in this period was to reminisce much later: "It was a revelation for Jewish youth that Max Nordau was a Jew; it was an inspiration to them to join the ranks of the Zionist movement."[30] After Herzl's death in 1904, it seemed likely that Nordau would assume the leadership, but being already under attack for his defense of political as opposed to a spiritually oriented Zionism, he stood aside. His influence within the movement vanished rapidly. By 1914 his stature in the eyes of most Zionists had shrunk almost to insignificance. With the outbreak of the First World War, Nordau, an Austrian subject, had to leave his beloved France for exile in Spain. Though he returned to Paris shortly before his death, his wartime isolation had separated him from the Zionist movement even further. Actually, the forces that had worked against Nordau's assumption of leadership in the Zionist movement were the same that had eroded his fame as a critic of contemporary culture. Had Theodor Herzl lived he might well have suffered the same fate.

Nordau and Herzl had come from the same background and shared identical attitudes toward Zionism and society. The Dreyfus affair had roused these "men of the world" to a sudden and unexpected awareness of the Jewish question. Both were liberals who saw their movement in political and sociological but not in spiritual terms. Nordau's speeches at various Zionist congresses stressed that the new wave of anti-Semitism made it necessary to find a home for the persecuted. Assimilation had not worked. Moreover, the assimilated Jew was unstable and, inwardly sick, acted the part of a hypocrite. As with everything not genuine, this kind of Jew was offensive to anyone with true aesthetic feeling.[31] These ideas, as well as the idea of solidarity, were echoes of *Degeneration.* Whereas a despised Jewish people was a burden to humanity, a strong people would perform useful work for the progress of all mankind.[32] Zionism, we hear, contained no mystical elements, only long, hard work.[33]

At times Nordau does speak of an essential ideal without which men cannot work, and refers to this as the Jewish messianic heritage. As a Zionist he had to reckon with the survival of the "eternal Jewish people," and it is interesting that as early as 1898 he connected this immortality with an undefined "secret."[34] Nothing is now said about science. However, despite such occasional writings in the service of his movement, Nordau always returned to the presuppositions which guided him all his life: the importance of the human will, of work, of duty, of order and self-restraint. Indeed, his last philosophical book, written in 1919–1920, pleads for an ascent from instinctive life to rational consciousness.[35]

Herzl was right when, commenting on his relationship to Nordau, he wrote: "I never felt so plainly that we belonged together. This has nothing to do with religion. He as much as said that there are no Jewish dogmas."[36] The new generation of "Cultural Zionists" which opposed him and Herzl within the movement would have agreed about dogmas but not about spirituality. Small wonder that Martin Buber as he matured confessed increasing disappointment with Nordau's Zionist speeches.[37]

As Nordau had struck out against the mystics in his work on cultural criticism, so now he began to wage a similar battle on the Zionist front. In 1902 he saw his friend Theodor Herzl attacked for concentrating upon the practical work of colonization rather than upon Jewish spiritual values. The leading critic was the Russian-Hebrew writer Asher Ginzberg, who styled himself Ahad Haam ("one of the people"), and it was to him that Nordau replied with singular bitterness. Ahad Haam first of all wanted to build a spiritual center in Palestine. Nordau, therefore, denounced him as a "dreamer of the ghetto." He countered the proposals of Ahad Haam with the ideas he had put forward ten years earlier, which emphasized the necessity for those who were displaced by industrialism to return to the soil. These ideas, he claimed, could now be transferred to the Jewish people. Typically enough, Nordau followed Herzl in his willingness to exchange Palestine for Uganda as the site for Jewish colonization. Such attitudes clearly estranged Nordau, the Western liberal, from a culture which he never understood as he rose up against it. Ahad Haam, in his turn, castigated the "European" rather than "Jewish" character of the society Herzl and Nordau wanted to build in the promised land.[38]

This was a perceptive criticism. Both Herzl and Nordau were children of the Western European middle classes, especially in their belief in the inevitability of progress through a tolerant secular society. Their Zionism had its roots in a realization of the failure of assimilation rather than in a deep spiritual conviction. Nordau regarded the Bible as good literature, but as no more than that.[39] Certainly it did not provide the basis for a nation. In fact, earlier he had believed that a common language was the only thing that formed men into nations (and he was a strong supporter of the modern Hebrew revival).[40] This then was the "European" who took up his pen against the man who had lived all his life within the closed society of Eastern European Jewry.

In the manner of *Degeneration,* Nordau ridicules the idea that "vacuities" such as the spirit of love could take the place of practical work. Those concepts of the Cultural Zionists seemed to him not merely devoid of logical, clear, and sharply defined ideas, but contained in addition a bigoted intolerance. Ahad Haam had indeed attacked Herzl's tolerance toward other peoples who were then living in or who might want to live in Palestine. Nordau praised his friend, for he saw the future of Palestine not as a ghetto but as a country of freedom where foreigners would be able to live without fear of discrimination.[41] The liberalism from which the Zionist movement in the West had sprung here asserted itself once again, but at the very moment when the secular and political form which Herzl and Nordau had given to it was already outdated. How telling that both Martin Buber, the philosopher of the new Jewish nationalism, and Chaim Weizmann, its future leader, sided against the elder statesman in his controversy with Ahad Haam.

Typically enough, within the Zionist movement itself Nordau enthusiastically encouraged sports and athletics. The thesis of *Degeneration* is reflected in his slogan: Jews must become men of muscle instead of remaining slaves to their nerves. Strengthening of muscle must go hand in hand with the building of character—that is, manliness, dignity, and self-respect. The argument that Nordau used to make his case demonstrates again the negative quality that runs through so much of his advocacy of Zionism. Jews cannot afford to be physically weak, for in such weakness the Gentile world sees proof of Jewish inferiority.[42] In contrast, a new generation of Zionists regarded their faith not merely as a reaction to a Gentile world, but, further, as a basic spiritual imperative. They were part and parcel of the reorientation of European thought at the *fin de siècle,* in which vocal and self-conscious intellectuals, Jewish and Gentile, rode roughshod over the confident liberalism and positivism of an older generation.

Youth took the offensive, trampling all that Nordau held clear. His book was rightly regarded as the most sensational attack upon the atmosphere of malaise which seemed to have engulfed so many of that generation. For them, life was a struggle for existence which was bound to end in defeat. Not the optimism for which Nordau stood, but the pessimism of the philosopher Schopenhauer seemed to triumph. To many a writer, "decadence" was not a sickness but the affirmation of a fatalistic outlook on the world which welcomed the individualism of symbolist poetry or the ecstatic selfishness of Nietzsche. Within the old order, pressed by the tensions of industrial civilization, all seemed to be decaying: "Everything around [the bourgeoisie] is uncertain and moving. They belong to a ruling class which no longer rules, and their incapacity and their egotism are marked with failure. They are part of an aristocracy that falls and rises according to its gain or loss of the money that is its sole reason for being. . . . They are themselves floating and abandoned."[43]

Anatole France was examining why modern youth in 1890 seemed to know that one can believe in nothing.[44] Some, however, did search for a way out of this emptiness: Maurice Barrès turned to the cult of energy, and in 1893 pleaded for a society based not on reason but on instinct. Others found their way back to religion or to the Christian mysticism of Tolstoi (as the Zionists did to their own spiritual imperative); occultism flourished both in France and in England.[45] Upon the road that Nordau traveled, the intellectuals refused to follow; and it was against the world he symbolized that the spirit of revolt was in the air.

Young playwrights heaped brutal scorn upon the rational, secure, and optimistic adult world, and it is typical that the most "advanced" writers stressed youth as the foil of oppressive society. Albert Jarry's *Ubu Roi* (1887) viewed adult society through the mind of a schoolboy, and what he saw was egotistical as well as barbaric. First performed in Paris, *Ubu Roi* focused upon the very atavism that was so repulsive to Max Nordau. In Franz Wedekind's *Rites of Spring* (1891) a sensitive schoolboy commits suicide because society wants to rob him of his inner sincerity. How different was Nordau's approach to the problem raised by such a suicide. In *Degeneration* he brushes off the description of a schoolboy's suicide in a novel by remarking that the boy thought himself too good to do his lessons. Discipline was the answer.

Vitally influenced by men Nordau called mystics or egomaniacs, the generation that came to maturity in the 1890s provides the link between the "degenerates" and our own time. But these young men searched and experimented much further than their elders had. As the new century opened, the Viennese critic Karl Kraus commented that Ibsen was not a degenerate (which

Nordau had called him), but rather a "soft-livered moralist" whose insipid bourgeois dramas the younger generation no longer understood.[46]

Many of the young writers never found any positive commitment, something that has left a deep mark on our own art and literature. Instead their revolt led them to search for truth within man's most basic, least civilized instincts. Theodore Däubler summarized their aim in *A New Point of View* (1919): "The return of man to animal as exemplified through art means a decision in favor of Expressionism."[47]

This movement was destined to prove a more decisive revolt in art and literature than had been foreshadowed by most of the men Nordau attacked in his book. Whereas *Degeneration* accused its subjects of perverting reality, now a young generation of writers and painters reversed the very concept of reality, plunging deep into the chaos that Nordau had feared so much. Yvan Goll summed it up in 1920: "The unreal becomes a fact." The use of the mask in drama symbolized this view.[48] The basic existential situation of man had to be expressed through allegory and symbol, for it was part of a dream world in which the only subjective truth was man's inner consciousness.

Here the influence of Sigmund Freud becomes obvious. His *Interpretation of Dreams* (1900) not only marked the end of the psychology in which Nordau had believed but also served to underwrite the Expressionist view of truth. Two years later August Strindberg, in the preface to his *Dream Play,* put the case squarely. "The laws of space and time have been abolished, reality contributes only a slight foundation upon which phantasy works and weaves new patterns . . . but one consciousness stands above all else: that of the dreamer. For there exist no secrets, no illogicalities, no scruples, no laws."[49] The certainty of Nordau's world had vanished. But the prophet of *Degeneration* was correct in his idea that a world of chaos would lead to pessimism. Strindberg's play pictures man imprisoned within a hopeless situation. Such then was the new reality which had replaced the old.

In attempting to break out of the old order, the moderns rejected literary and artistic convention together with traditional morality. Language no longer provided the chief expression of meaning; visual representation could make a more direct appeal to the understanding of nightmare reality. Language was made to depend upon the irrational associations that Nordau had deplored, rather than upon that clarity of argument which he had advocated but which now seemed merely another straitjacket for man's spirit. For some, action could serve to dispel the illusion that there could be clarity or certainty in this world. But they did not regard action as the rational goal which Nordau posited. Language, visual expression, and action were all part of the search for a new reality to be found solely within the irrational working of man's own inner world. "Uniformity, History"—so reads a short but telling entry in Franz Kafka's diary.[50]

The view began to spread that the artist could be truly creative only if he opposed himself to the norms of society. Gottfried Benn, whose early poetry offered such images as rats playing beneath the eardrum of a girl, mused that Nietzsche never paid his bills, Van Gogh needed twenty-eight cups of coffee a day, and Heinrich Mann lived in poverty.[51] This cultural pattern received increasing support from some schools of psychoanalysis, such as that of Carl Gustav Jung. Whereas Sigmund Freud shared with Nordau a vital concern with maintaining existing society and was aware of the need for discipline, Jung emphasized the eternal forces at play within the human archetypes. Man tended to become a self-contained island, feeding upon his complexes and his personal problems. Nordau would have called it the triumph of the egomaniac.

Art had lost contact with life in society. For some dramatists it was no longer possible to find motivations for human action except in the mystical constants of the psyche. Whether in Bertolt Brecht's early *Swamp of the Cities* (1921–1923) or in Pinter's recent play *Homecoming* (1964), the characters float upon a hate-love relationship which is assumed and does not have to be properly motivated. Moreover, the meaning of the proposition that "theater is action" was changed as action became an internalized psychological conflict. As Nordau might have put it: the sickness of the characters is talked out on the stage.

At the very time *Degeneration* was published, the concept of human nature on which it was based underwent a lasting change in the minds of many artists and writers. This change ran directly counter to the confident bourgeois world which Nordau himself symbolized. His degenerates, in reality, became the parents of a cultural shift which is still very much alive—carried through not merely by the egomaniacs, now supported by psychiatry, but also by the mystics who turned away from the individual and embraced the race or the nation conceived in spiritual terms. Nordau correctly regarded the Wagner cult as a religious act, but it was a religion which took a Christian framework and filled it with the idea of the "superior" Germanic race. Nordau's fight against cultural Zionism also encountered a mysticism linked to a national revival. As he wrote in *Degeneration,* the creative force capable of conceiving a universal normal life was denied to such men, whether mystics, egomaniacs, or indeed all those who in fact represented the wave of the future.

The creative force capable of conceiving a universal normal life—this was also the ambition of the "social realists" in the Communist camp and it is here that some of the essential features of Nordau's liberal world view were continued into our own time. Marxists also demanded that the artist "reproduce" reality "concretely" and clearly. Concepts of beauty and form were intimately related to the artist's role in society—namely, to transmit "progressive" ideas.[52] The French Communist newspaper *Humanité* must have felt the affinity between socialist realism and the ideals of the liberal cosmopolitan. For when Nordau died it praised his "noble love for mankind" and hatred of bourgeois ideas.[53]

The latter point seems puzzling, for Nordau, as we have seen, represented the perfect bourgeois in outlook and attitude. But the middle classes he typified had declined by 1923, and it was this "decay" which both Nordau and a Communist like Lenin linked with dissoluteness and lack of clarity. Both the liberal positivist and the Communist contrasted those who had succumbed to the disorder of their time (the "bourgeoisie" for Lenin) with those who had avoided unsettledness, organized their lives, and remained in control.[54]

Nordau himself had no use for socialism, though he acknowledged the usefulness of its criticism of contemporary society. The "progressive ideas" upon which he built took in all of mankind and not just the working classes. To derive a hatred of the possessing classes from a criticism of society was for him another example of "mysticism" which excluded reason.[55] Despite these objections, he shared a common ground of positivism and realism with these "mystics" and both could never resolve their common aesthetic dilemma. How could artistic creativity be confined to a plastic reproduction of concrete reality and at the same time rise above it as a work of art? The mid-twentieth-century dispute over social realism echoes problems that had already been set forth in Max Nordau's *Degeneration.* Nordau's own creative efforts failed, just as the artists he most admired are long forgotten.

The moderns found a mode of aesthetic expression that has been able to maintain a continuous audience in the West. But they never reached down to communicate with the mass of men. They failed to forge the link between artist and public which Nordau thought so important. Nonetheless, despite their intentions, these men did perform a useful function even in Nordau's pragmatic terms. Their protests helped loosen the hold of the conventions of bourgeois society; their experimentation, unhindered by traditionalism, opened up new perspectives of human creativity. And yet their protest did bog down in an unending vista of decay. Many of the most prominent of these writers, from Nordau's time to today, never progressed beyond their initial assertion of the world's absurdity. The denial of the idea of progress, of the relevance of society, meant that there could be no solutions, only an eternal imprisonment in Kafka's castle.

Nordau's criticism no longer seems as farfetched as it once did. Even the irrational can become boring. The intellectuals may still cling to what they praise as "modern," but popular culture has not followed in their footsteps. Here Nordau might almost seem vindicated. The good and the bad, the villain and the hero, are clearly distinguished from one another and are still related to a dominant morality which has never ceased to be middle-class. Action and plot have not been abandoned, cause and effect are not shrouded in mystery. During Nordau's lifetime, the optimistic works of Georges Courtline in France, the popular adventure stories of Karl May in Germany, and the new moral tone of the shilling shocker in England exemplified the continuing popularity of a literature he would have thought useful. In spite of the increasing intrusion of violence and the new psychology into this popular literature, it continued to transmit the values of Max Nordau's world.

In Nordau's terms, then, all is not lost. We may yet have confidence in the future. Nordau's science and his psychology are gone for good, but the values they supported probably have become more widely diffused, more basic to our society, than the custodians of cultural standards would have us believe. We are inclined to scoff at these values. But at one point in history, hard work, discipline, and attention to duty, combined with an unquenchable optimism, did help to build industrial Europe. This needs stressing, for the dark side of this liberal attitude toward life is familiar. It has been the theme of modern art and literature from the *fin de siècle* until our own time. This does not deny the validity of its criticism. Convention did crush those who had sensitivity, self-confidence turned into self-righteousness and led to brutality and egoism—no less so than with Max Nordau's Nietzsche.

The alienation from fruitful participation in society of so many intellectuals in the twentieth century, the very equation between creativity and opposition to the external world, betrays that all is not well. Moreover, the coexistence of two cultures in the West, lacking contact with each other, demonstrates the absence of those stable values which Nordau had assumed. The problem is not so much to reconcile the "scientific" with the "humanistic" culture, but rather to forge a meaningful connection between the isolated culture of the intellectuals and popular culture. Nordau's ideal of solidarity seems still meaningful in this context.

Man will solve such problems when he recognizes, as Nordau and his adversaries did not, that the real and the absurd do not necessarily exclude each other. More often than not in history men have transformed the essentially absurd or irrational into a living reality. The examples of fascism and National Socialism, so conspicuous in our century, spring to mind. Every human or social reality has some of the factors within it which Nordau brushed aside and condemned as shirking the issue. But this irrational, in order to become effective in history, needs a greater clarity and power of will than the moderns believed. The irrational is made concrete through rational acts within the terms of its own ideological framework: such an insight can help overcome the world of absolutes in which Nordau and his adversaries lived and whose frame of mind has continued to haunt us.

We now have a larger historical perspective than the age that assigned Nordau and his work to the curiosities of history. He was typical of much of his time, in success as well as in defeat. And indeed many of his attitudes have never been totally lost from the mainstream of Western civilization. His enemies also were symptomatic of the artistic revolt of many generations, and their ideas are with us still. *Degeneration* is a mirror of conflicting attitudes which are, in fact, contemporary with our present cultural dilemmas. But culture itself always reflects the state of society. Max Nordau presents us with a searchlight whose beams reflect the kind of world man has made for himself.

Madison, Wisconsin GEORGE L. MOSSE
July 1966

NOTES

1. Max Nordau, *Menschen und Menschliches* (Berlin, 1915), p. 30. The only biography of Nordau in English is Anna and Maxa Nordau, *Max Nordau* (New York, 1943), which is factual but is weak on analysis. Meir Ben-Horin, *Max Nordau: Philosopher of Human Solidarity* (London, 1956) is a detailed analysis of this part of Nordau's thought.

2. *The Times,* February 5, 1923, p. 11; January 23, 1923, p. 9.

3. Israel Zangwill, "The Martyrdom of Max Nordau" (1923), *Speeches, Articles and Letters of Israel Zangwill,* ed. by Maurice Simon (London, 1937), p. 142.

4. Max Nordau, *Conventional Lies of Our Civilization* (hereafter cited *Conventional Lies*), tr. from seventh German edition (London, 1906), p. 341. This book went through 71 editions. In the United States it became one of the Haldeman-Julius "Little Blue Books" in 1925.

5. See page 560.

6. *Conventional Lies,* pp. 113, 346.

7. Max Nordau, *Paradoxes* (Leipzig, 1885), p. 31.

8. Max Nordau, *Von Kunst und Künstlern* (Leipzig, 1905), p. 255.

9. See page 375.

10. *Conventional Lies,* pp. 77, 81.

11. The inheritance tax is one of the key ideas of *Conventional Lies.*

12. *Paradoxes,* pp. 406–409.

13. See page 541.

14. *Conventional Lies,* p. 344.

15. *Ibid.,* p. 346.

16. *Paradoxes,* p. 371; two years earlier he had still believed in hereditary elites because the qualities of the individual are inherited by his offspring. *Conventional Lies,* p. 113.

17. Ernest Jones, *The Life and Work of Sigmund Freud,* Vol. I (London, 1953), p. 205.

18. Hans Kurella, *Cesare Lombroso* (London, 1911), pp. 116, 137–138.

19. Cited in Domingo Mobac, *Genio, Scienza e Arte: il Positivismo di Max Nordau* (Turin, 1899), p. 1.

20. Max Nordau, *Die Krankheit des Jahrhunderts,* Vol. I (Leipzig, 1888), pp. 313–314.

21. See page 269.

22. *Conventional Lies,* p. 306; *Menschen und Menschliches,* pp. 39 ff, 351, 352.

23. *Paradoxes,* pp. 11, 13.

24. See Nordau, "Gesellschaftliche Aufgabe der Kunst" (1896), *Von Kunst und Künstlern, passim.* This was a lecture given at the request of Lombroso's daughters.

25. *Die Krankheit des Jahrhunderts,* Vol. I, p. 175.

26. *Von Kunst und Künstlern,* pp. 24, 25.

27. George Bernard Shaw, *The Sanity of Art: An Exposure of the Current Nonsense about Artists Being Degenerate* (London, 1908), pp. 43, 59, 73, 92. Shaw wrote this in 1895 at the request of the American philosophical anarchist Benjamin Tucker for his newspaper *Liberty.*

28. For example, Louis de Romain, *Médecin-Philosophe et Musicien-Poète: Etude sur Richard Wagner et Max Nordau* (Paris, 1895), p. 17.

29. [Alfred Egmont Hake], *Regeneration: A Reply to Max Nordau* (London, 1895), p. 25. The book of 315 pages appeared in the United States in 1896.

30. *Jewish Chronicle,* January 26, 1923, "Supplement No. xxv," p. 26.

31. Max Nordau, "I. Kongressrede" (1897), *Max Nordau Zionistische Schriften* (Cologne and Leipzig, 1909), p. 51.

32. Nordau, "Ein Tempelstreit" (1897), *ibid.,* p. 12.

33. Nordau, "Der Zionismus" (1902), *ibid.,* pp. 34, 35.

34. Nordau, "Das Unentbehrliche Ideal" (1898), *ibid.,* p. 284.

35. Max Nordau, *The Essence of Civilization* (published only in Spanish and not until 1932).

36. *The Diaries of Theodor Herzl,* ed. and tr. by Marvin Lowenthal (New York, 1956), p. 56 (entry for July 6, 1895).

37. Hans Kohn, *Martin Buber* (Cologne, 1961), p. 41.

38. For this controversy see Meir Ben-Horin, *Max Nordau,* pp. 203, ff.

39. *Conventional Lies,* p. 57.

40. *Paradoxes,* p. 384.

41. See Meir Ben-Horin, *Max Nordau, passim.*

42. Max Nordau quoted in *Körperliche Renaissance der Juden,* Festschrift zum 10 Jährigen bestehen des 'Bar Kochba' (Berlin, May 1909), p. 12; Max Nordau, "Jüdische Turner," *Jüdische Monatshefte für Turnen und Sport,* XIV, Heft 6 (August-September 1913), pp. 173, 174.

43. Quoted in Carter Jefferson, *Anatole France* (New Brunswick, 1965), p. 44.

44. *Ibid.,* p. 62.

45. I.e., the popularity of Theosophy in the last decades of the nineteenth century.

46. Karl Kraus, *Literatur und Lüge* (Collected Essays) (Vienna and Leipzig, 1929), pp. 23, 69.

47. Theodor Däubler, *Der neue Standpunkt* (Leipzig, 1919), p. 99.

48. Martin Esslin, *Das Theater des Absurden* (Hamburg, 1965), p. 288.

49. Quoted in *ibid.,* pp. 271–272.

50. *The Diaries of Franz Kafka,* ed. by Max Brod (New York, 1948), p. 213.

51. "Gottfried Benn an Paul Zech" (September 2, 1913), *Ausgewählte Briefe* (Wiesbaden, 1957), p. 12.

52. Wassili Iwanow, *Der sozialistiche Realismus* (Berlin, 1965), pp. 46, 56, 64, 65.

53. Quoted in *Jewish Chronicle*, January 26, 1923, "Supplement XXV," p. 26.

54. The analysis of Lenin has been suggested by Michael Walzer, *The Revolution of the Saints* (Cambridge, 1965), pp. 314–315.

55. *Die Krankheit des Jahrhunderts*, Vol. I, p. 210. Nordau, the liberal, had no use for modern racism either. David Starr Jordan, the first president of Stanford University, criticized him severely for ignoring race. I.e., *The Blood of the Nation* (Boston, 1912), pp. 18–19.

DEGENERATION

BOOK I.

FIN-DE-SIÈCLE.

CHAPTER I.

THE DUSK OF THE NATIONS.

FIN-DE-SIÈCLE is a name covering both what is characteristic of many modern phenomena, and also the underlying mood which in them finds expression. Experience has long shown that an idea usually derives its designation from the language of the nation which first formed it. This, indeed, is a law of constant application when historians of manners and customs inquire into language, for the purpose of obtaining some notion, through the origins of some verbal root, respecting the home of the earliest inventions and the line of evolution in different human races. *Fin-de-siècle* is French, for it was in France that the mental state so entitled was first consciously realized. The word has flown from one hemisphere to the other, and found its way into all civilized languages. A proof this that the need of it existed. The *fin-de-siècle* state of mind is to-day everywhere to be met with; nevertheless, it is in many cases a mere imitation of a foreign fashion gaining vogue, and not an organic evolution. It is in the land of its birth that it appears in its most genuine form, and Paris is the right place in which to observe its manifold expressions.

No proof is needed of the extreme silliness of the term. Only the brain of a child or of a savage could form the clumsy idea that the century is a kind of living being, born like a beast or a man, passing through all the stages of existence, gradually ageing and declining after blooming childhood, joyous youth, and vigorous maturity, to die with the expiration of the hundredth year, after being afflicted in its last decade with all the infirmities of mournful senility. Such a childish anthropomorphism or zoomorphism never stops to consider that the arbitrary division of time, rolling ever continuously along, is not identical amongst all civilized beings, and that while this nineteenth century of Christendom is held to be a creature reeling to its death presumptively in dire exhaustion, the fourteenth century of the Mahommedan world is tripping along in the baby-shoes of its first decade, and the fifteenth century of the Jews strides gallantly by in the full maturity of its fifty-second year. Every day on our globe 130,000 human beings are born, for whom the world begins with this same day, and the young citizen of the world is neither feebler nor fresher for leaping into life in the midst of the death-throes of 1900, nor on the birthday of the twentieth century. But it is a habit of the human mind to project externally its own subjective states. And it is in accordance with this naïvely egoistic tendency that the French ascribe their own senility to the century, and speak of *fin-de-siècle* when they ought correctly to say *fin-de-race*.*

But however silly a term *fin-de-siècle* may be, the mental constitution which it indicates is actually present in influential circles. The disposition of the times is curiously confused, a compound of feverish restlessness and blunted discouragement, of fearful presage and hang-dog renunciation. The prevalent feeling is that of imminent perdition and extinction. *Fin-de-siècle* is at once a confession and a complaint. The old Northern faith contained the fearsome doctrine of the Dusk of the Gods. In our days there have arisen in more highly-developed minds vague qualms of a Dusk of the Nations, in which all suns and all stars are gradually waning, and mankind with all its institutions and creations is perishing in the midst of a dying world.

It is not for the first time in the course of history that the horror of world-annihilation has laid hold of men's minds. A similar sentiment took possession of the Christian peoples at the approach of the year 1000. But there is an essential difference between chiliastic panic and *fin-de-siècle* excitement. The despair at the turn of the first millennium of Christian chronology proceeded from a feeling of fulness of life and joy of life. Men were aware of throbbing pulses, they were conscious of unweakened capacity for enjoyment, and found it unmitigatedly appalling to perish together with the world, when

* This passage has been misunderstood. It has been taken to mean that all the French nation had degenerated, and their race was approaching its end. However, from the concluding paragraph of this chapter, it may be clearly seen that I had in my eye only the upper ten thousand. The peasant population, and a part of the working classes and the *bourgeoisie*, are sound. I assert only the decay of the rich inhabitants of great cities and the leading classes. It is they who have discovered *fin-de-siècle*, and it is to them also that *fin-de-race* applies.

there were yet so many flagons to drain and so many lips to kiss, and when they could yet rejoice so vigorously in both love and wine. Of all this in the *fin-de-siècle* feeling there is nothing. Neither has it anything in common with the impressive twilight-melancholy of an aged Faust, surveying the work of a lifetime, and who, proud of what has been achieved, and contemplating what is begun but not completed, is seized with vehement desire to finish his work, and, awakened from sleep by haunting unrest, leaps up with the cry: 'Was ich gedacht, ich eil' es zu vollbringen.'*

Quite otherwise is the *fin-de-siècle* mood. It is the impotent despair of a sick man, who feels himself dying by inches in the midst of an eternally living nature blooming insolently for ever. It is the envy of a rich, hoary voluptuary, who sees a pair of young lovers making for a sequestered forest nook; it is the mortification of the exhausted and impotent refugee from a Florentine plague, seeking in an enchanted garden the experiences of a Decamerone, but striving in vain to snatch one more pleasure of sense from the uncertain hour. The reader of Turgenieff's *A Nest of Nobles* will remember the end of that beautiful work. The hero, Lavretzky, comes as a man advanced in years to visit at the house where, in his young days, he had lived his romance of love. All is unchanged. The garden is fragrant with flowers. In the great trees the happy birds are chirping; on the fresh turf the children romp and shout. Lavretzky alone has grown old, and contemplates, in mournful exclusion, a scene where nature holds on its joyous way, caring nought that Lisa the beloved is vanished, and Lavretzky, a broken-down man, weary of life. Lavretzky's admission that, amidst all this ever-young, ever-blooming nature, for him alone there comes no morrow; Alving's dying cry for 'The sun—the sun!' in Ibsen's *Ghosts*—these express rightly the *fin-de-siècle* attitude of to-day.

This fashionable term has the necessary vagueness which fits it to convey all the half-conscious and indistinct drift of current ideas. Just as the words 'freedom,' 'ideal,' 'progress' seem to express notions, but actually are only sounds, so in itself *fin-de-siècle* means nothing, and receives a varying signification according to the diverse mental horizons of those who use it.

The surest way of knowing what *fin-de-siècle* implies, is to consider a series of particular instances where the word has been applied. Those which I shall adduce are drawn from French books and periodicals of the last two years.†

* 'My thought I hasten to fulfil.'

† A four-act comedy, by H. Micard and F. de Jouvenot, named *Fin-de-Siècle*, which was played in Paris in 1890, hardly avails to determine the

A king abdicates, leaves his country, and takes up his residence in Paris, having reserved certain political rights. One day he loses much money at play, and is in a dilemma. He therefore makes an agreement with the Government of his country, by which, on receipt of a million francs, he renounces for ever every title, official position and privilege remaining to him. *Fin-de-siècle* king.

A bishop is prosecuted for insulting the minister of public worship. The proceedings terminated, his attendant canons distribute amongst the reporters in court a defence, copies of which he has prepared beforehand. When condemned to pay a fine, he gets up a public collection, which brings in tenfold the amount of the penalty. He publishes a justificatory volume containing all the expressions of support which have reached him. He makes a tour through the country, exhibits himself in every cathedral to the mob curious to see the celebrity of the hour, and takes the opportunity of sending round the plate. *Fin-de-siècle* bishop.

The corpse of the murderer Pranzini after execution underwent autopsy. The head of the secret police cuts off a large piece of skin, has it tanned, and the leather made into cigar-cases and card-cases for himself and some of his friends. *Fin-de-siècle* official.

An American weds his bride in a gas-factory, then gets with her into a balloon held in readiness, and enters on a honeymoon in the clouds. *Fin-de-siècle* wedding.

An *attaché* of the Chinese Embassy publishes high-class works in French under his own name. He negotiates with banks respecting a large loan for his Government, and draws large advances for himself on the unfinished contract. Later it comes out that the books were composed by his French secretary, and that he has swindled the banks. *Fin-de-siècle* diplomatist.

A public schoolboy walking with a chum passes the gaol where his father, a rich banker, has repeatedly been imprisoned for fraudulent bankruptcy, embezzlement and similar lucrative misdemeanours. Pointing to the building, he tells his friend with a smile: 'Look, that's the governor's school.' *Fin-de-siècle* son.

Two young ladies of good family, and school friends, are chatting together. One heaves a sigh. 'What's the matter?' asks the other. 'I'm in love with Raoul, and he with me.' 'Oh, that's lovely! He's handsome, young, elegant; and yet you're sad?' 'Yes, but he has nothing, and is nothing, and

sense of the word as the French use it. The authors were concerned, not to depict a phase of the age or a psychological state, but only to give an attractive title to their piece.

my parents want me to marry the baron, who is fat, bald, and ugly, but has a huge lot of money.' 'Well, marry the baron without any fuss, and make Raoul acquainted with him, you goose.' *Fin-de-siècle* girls.

Such test-cases show how the word is understood in the land of its birth. Germans who ape Paris fashions, and apply *fin-de-siècle* almost exclusively to mean what is indecent and improper, misuse the word in their coarse ignorance as much as, in a previous generation, they vulgarized the expression *demi-monde*, misunderstanding its proper meaning, and giving it the sense of *fille de joie*, whereas its creator Dumas intended it to denote persons whose lives contained some dark period, for which they were excluded from the circle to which they belong by birth, education, or profession, but who do not by their manner betray, at least to the inexperienced, that they are no longer acknowledged as members of their own caste.

Prima facie, a king who sells his sovereign rights for a big cheque seems to have little in common with a newly-wedded pair who make their wedding-trip in a balloon, nor is the connection at once obvious between an episcopal Barnum and a well-brought-up young lady who advises her friend to a wealthy marriage mitigated by a *cicisbeo*. All these *fin-de-siècle* cases have, nevertheless, a common feature, to wit, a contempt for traditional views of custom and morality.

Such is the notion underlying the word *fin-de-siècle*. It means a practical emancipation from traditional discipline, which theoretically is still in force. To the voluptuary this means unbridled lewdness, the unchaining of the beast in man; to the withered heart of the egoist, disdain of all consideration for his fellow-men, the trampling under foot of all barriers which enclose brutal greed of lucre and lust of pleasure; to the contemner of the world it means the shameless ascendency of base impulses and motives, which were, if not virtuously suppressed, at least hypocritically hidden; to the believer it means the repudiation of dogma, the negation of a super-sensuous world, the descent into flat phenomenalism; to the sensitive nature yearning for æsthetic thrills, it means the vanishing of ideals in art, and no more power in its accepted forms to arouse emotion. And to all, it means the end of an established order, which for thousands of years has satisfied logic, fettered depravity, and in every art matured something of beauty.

One epoch of history is unmistakably in its decline, and another is announcing its approach. There is a sound of rending in every tradition, and it is as though the morrow would not link itself with to-day. Things as they are totter and plunge, and they are suffered to reel and fall, because man is weary, and there is no faith that it is worth an effort to uphold them. Views that have hitherto governed minds are dead or driven hence like disenthroned kings, and for their inheritance they that hold the titles and they that would usurp are locked in struggle. Meanwhile interregnum in all its terrors prevails; there is confusion among the powers that be; the million, robbed of its leaders, knows not where to turn; the strong work their will; false prophets arise, and dominion is divided amongst those whose rod is the heavier because their time is short. Men look with longing for whatever new things are at hand, without presage whence they will come or what they will be. They have hope that in the chaos of thought, art may yield revelations of the order that is to follow on this tangled web. The poet, the musician, is to announce, or divine, or at least suggest in what forms civilization will further be evolved. What shall be considered good to-morrow—what shall be beautiful? What shall we know to-morrow—what believe in? What shall inspire us? How shall we enjoy? So rings the question from the thousand voices of the people, and where a market-vendor sets up his booth and claims to give an answer, where a fool or a knave suddenly begins to prophesy in verse or prose, in sound or colour, or professes to practise his art otherwise than his predecessors and competitors, there gathers a great concourse, crowding around him to seek in what he has wrought, as in oracles of the Pythia, some meaning to be divined and interpreted. And the more vague and insignificant they are, the more they seem to convey of the future to the poor gaping souls gasping for revelations, and the more greedily and passionately are they expounded.

Such is the spectacle presented by the doings of men in the reddened light of the Dusk of the Nations. Massed in the sky the clouds are aflame in the weirdly beautiful glow which was observed for the space of years after the eruption of Krakatoa. Over the earth the shadows creep with deepening gloom, wrapping all objects in a mysterious dimness, in which all certainty is destroyed and any guess seems plausible. Forms lose their outlines, and are dissolved in floating mist. The day is over, the night draws on. The old anxiously watch its approach, fearing they will not live to see the end. A few amongst the young and strong are conscious of the vigour of life in all their veins and nerves, and rejoice in the coming sunrise. Dreams, which fill up the hours of darkness till the breaking of the new day, bring to the former comfortless memories, to the latter high-souled hopes. And in the artistic products of the age we see the form in which these dreams become sensible.

Here is the place to forestall a possible misunderstanding.

The great majority of the middle and lower classes is naturally not *fin-de-siècle*. It is true that the spirit of the times is stirring the nations down to their lowest depths, and awaking even in the most inchoate and rudimentary human being a wondrous feeling of stir and upheaval. But this more or less slight touch of moral sea-sickness does not excite in him the cravings of travailing women, nor express itself in new æsthetic needs. The Philistine or the Proletarian still finds undiluted satisfaction in the old and oldest forms of art and poetry, if he knows himself unwatched by the scornful eye of the votary of fashion, and is free to yield to his own inclinations. He prefers Ohnet's novels to all the symbolists, and Mascagni's *Cavalleria Rusticana* to all Wagnerians and to Wagner himself; he enjoys himself royally over slap-dash farces and music-hall melodies, and yawns or is angered at Ibsen; he contemplates gladly chromos of paintings depicting Munich beer-houses and rustic taverns, and passes the open-air painters without a glance. It is only a very small minority who honestly find pleasure in the new tendencies, and announce them with genuine conviction as that which alone is sound, a sure guide for the future, a pledge of pleasure and of moral benefit. But this minority has the gift of covering the whole visible surface of society, as a little oil extends over a large area of the surface of the sea. It consists chiefly of rich educated people, or of fanatics. The former give the *ton* to all the snobs, the fools, and the blockheads; the latter make an impression upon the weak and dependent, and intimidate the nervous. All snobs affect to have the same taste as the select and exclusive minority, who pass by everything that once was considered beautiful with an air of the greatest contempt. And thus it appears as if the whole of civilized humanity were converted to the æsthetics of the Dusk of the Nations.

CHAPTER II.

THE SYMPTOMS.

LET us follow in the train frequenting the palaces of European capitals, the highways of fashionable watering-places, the receptions of the rich, and observe the figures of which it is composed.

Amongst the women, one wears her hair combed smoothly back and down like Rafael's Maddalena Doni in the Uffizi at Florence; another wears it drawn up high over the temples like Julia, daughter of Titus, or Plotina, wife of Trajan, in the busts in the Louvre; a third has hers cut short in front on the brow and long in the nape, waved and lightly puffed, after the fashion of the fifteenth century, as may be seen in the pages and young knights of Gentile Bellini, Botticelli and Mantegna. Many have their hair dyed, and in such a fashion as to be startling in its revolt against the law of organic harmony, and the effect of a studied discord, only to be resolved into the higher polyphony of the toilet taken as a whole. This swarthy, dark-eyed woman snaps her fingers at nature by framing the brown tones of her face in copper-red or golden-yellow; yonder blue-eyed fair, with a complexion of milk and roses, intensifies the brightness of her cheeks by a setting of artificially blue-black tresses. Here is one who covers her head with a huge heavy felt hat, an obvious imitation, in its brim turned up at the back, and its trimming of large plush balls, of the sombrero of the Spanish bull-fighters, who were displaying their skill in Paris at the exhibition of 1889, and giving all kinds of *motifs* to modistes. There is another who has stuck on her hair the emerald-green or ruby-red biretta of the mediæval travelling student. The costume is in keeping with the bizarre coiffure. Here is a mantle reaching to the waist, slit up on one side, draping the breast like a *portière*, and trimmed round the hem with little silken bells, by the incessant clicking of which a sensitive spectator would in a very short time either be hypnotized or driven to take frantic fright. There is a Greek peplos, of which the tailors speak as glibly as any venerable philologist. Next to the stiff monumental trim of Catharine de Medicis, and the high ruff of Mary, Queen of Scots, goes the flowing white raiment of the angel of the Annunciation in Memling's pictures, and, by way of antithesis, that caricature of masculine array, the fitting cloth coat, with widely opened lapels, waistcoat, stiffened shirt-front, small stand-up collar, and necktie. The majority, anxious to be inconspicuous in unimaginative mediocrity, seems to have for its leading style a laboured rococo, with bewildering oblique lines, incomprehensible swellings, puffings, expansions and contractions, folds with irrational beginning and aimless ending, in which all the outlines of the human figure are lost, and which cause women's bodies to resemble now a beast of the Apocalypse, now an armchair, now a triptych, or some other ornament.

The children, strolling beside their mothers thus bedecked, are embodiments of one of the most afflicting aberrations into which the imagination of a spinster ever lapsed. They are living copies of the pictures of Kate Greenaway, whose love of children, diverted from its natural outlet, has sought gratification in the most affected style of drawing, wherein the sacredness of childhood is profaned under absurd disguises. Here is an imp dressed from head to foot in the blood-red costume of a mediæval executioner; there a four-year-old girl wears a cabriolet bonnet of her great-grandmother's days and sweeps after her a court mantle of loud-hued velvet. Another wee dot, just able to keep on her tottering legs, has been arrayed in the long dress of a lady of the First Empire, with puffed sleeves and short waist.

The men complete the picture. They are preserved from excessive oddity through fear of the Philistine's laugh, or through some remains of sanity in taste, and, with the exception of the red dress-coat with metal buttons, and knee-breeches with silk stockings, with which some idiots in eye-glass and gardenia try to rival burlesque actors, present little deviation from the ruling canon of the masculine attire of the day. But fancy plays the more freely among their hair. One displays the short curls and the wavy double-pointed beard of Lucius Verus, another looks like the whiskered cat in a Japanese kakemono. His neighbour has the *barbiche* of Henri IV., another the fierce moustache of a lansquenet by F. Brun, or the chin-tuft of the city-watch in Rembrandt's 'Ronde de Nuit.'

The common feature in all these male specimens is that they do not express their real idiosyncrasies, but try to present something that they are not. They are not content to show their natural figure, nor even to supplement it by legitimate accessories, in harmony with the type to which they approximate, but they seek to model themselves after some artistic pattern which has no affinity with their own nature, or is even antithetical to it. Nor do they for the most part limit themselves to one pattern, but copy several at once, which jar one with another. Thus we get heads set on shoulders not belonging to them, costumes the elements of which are as disconnected as though they belonged to a dream, colours that seem to have been matched in the dark. The impression is that of a masked festival, where all are in disguises, and with heads too in character. There are several occasions, such as the varnishing day at the Paris Champs de Mars salon, or the opening of the Exhibition of the Royal Academy in London, where this impression is so weirdly intensified, that one seems to be moving amongst dummies patched together at haphazard, in a mythical mortuary, from fragments of bodies, heads, trunks, limbs, just as they came to hand, and which the designer, in heedless pell-mell, clothed at random in the garments of all epochs and countries. Every single figure strives visibly by some singularity in outline, set, cut, or colour, to startle attention violently, and imperiously to detain it. Each one wishes to create a strong nervous excitement, no matter whether agreeably or disagreeably. The fixed idea is to produce an effect at any price.

Let us follow these folk in masquerade and with heads in character to their dwellings. Here are at once stage properties and lumber-rooms, rag-shops and museums. The study of the master of the house is a Gothic hall of chivalry, with cuirasses, shields and crusading banners on the walls; or the shop of an Oriental bazaar with Kurd carpets, Bedouin chests, Circassian narghilehs and Indian lacquered caskets. By the mirror on the mantelpiece are fierce or funny Japanese masks. Between the windows are staring trophies of swords, daggers, clubs and old wheel-trigger pistols. Daylight filters in through painted glass, where lean saints kneel in rapture. In the drawing-room the walls are either hung with worm-eaten Gobelin tapestry, discoloured by the sun of two centuries (or it may be by a deftly mixed chemical bath), or covered with Morris draperies, on which strange birds flit amongst crazily ramping branches, and blowzy flowers coquet with vain butterflies. Amongst armchairs and padded seats, such as the cockered bodies of our contemporaries know and expect, there are Renaissance stools, the heart or shell-shaped bottoms of which would attract none but the toughened hide of a rough hero of the jousting lists. Startling is the effect of a gilt-painted couch between buhl-work cabinets and a puckered Chinese table, next an inlaid writing-table of graceful rococo. On all the tables and in all the cabinets is a display of antiquities or articles of vertù, big or small, and for the most part warranted not genuine; a figure of Tanagra near a broken jade snuff-box, a Limoges plate beside a long-necked Persian waterpot of brass, a *bonbonnière* between a breviary bound in carved ivory, and snuffers of chiselled copper. Pictures stand on easels draped with velvet, the frames made conspicuous by some oddity, such as a spider in her web, a metal bunch of thistle-heads, and the like. In a corner a sort of temple is erected to a squatting or a standing Buddha. The boudoir of the mistress of the house partakes of the nature of a chapel and of a harem. The toilet-table is designed and decorated like an altar, a *prie-Dieu* is a pledge for the piety of the inmate, and a broad divan, with an orgiastic *abandon* about the cushions, gives reassurance that things are not so bad. In the dining-room the walls are hung with the whole stock-in-trade of a porcelain shop, costly silver is displayed in an old farmhouse dresser, and on the table bloom aristocratic orchids, and proud silver vessels shine between rustic stone-ware plates and ewers. In the evening, lamps of the stature of a man illumine these rooms with light both subdued and tinted by sprawling shades, red, yellow or green of hue, and even covered by black lace. Hence the inmates appear, now bathed in variegated diaphanous mist, now suffused with coloured radiance, while the corners and backgrounds are shrouded in depths of artfully-effected *clair-obscur*, and the furniture and bric-à-brac are dyed in unreal chords of colour. Unreal, too, are the studied postures, by assuming which the inmates are enabled to reproduce on their faces the light effects of Rembrandt or Schalcken. Everything in these houses aims at exciting the nerves and dazzling the senses. The disconnected and antithetical effects in all arrangements, the constant contradiction between form and purpose, the outlandishness of most objects, is intended to be bewildering. There must be no sentiment of repose, such as is felt at any composition, the plan of which is easily taken in, nor of the comfort attending a prompt comprehension of all the details of one's environment. He who enters here must not doze, but be thrilled. If the master of the house roams about these rooms clothed after the example of Balzac in a white monk's cowl, or after the model of Richepin in the red cloak of the robber-chieftain of an operetta, he only gives expression to the admission that in such a comedy theatre a clown is in place. All is discrepant, indiscriminate jumble. The unity of abiding by one definite historic style counts as old-fashioned, provincial, Philistine, and the time has not yet produced a style of its own. An approach is, perhaps, made to one in the furniture of Carabin, exhibited in the salon of the Champs de Mars. But these balusters, down which naked furies and possessed creatures are rolling in mad riot, these bookcases, where base and pilaster consist of a pile of guillotined heads, and even this table, representing a gigantic open book borne by gnomes, make up a style that is feverish and infernal. If the director-general of Dante's 'Inferno' had an audience-chamber, it might well be furnished with such as these. Carabin's creations may be intended to equip a house, but they are a nightmare.

We have seen how society dresses and where it dwells. We shall now observe how it enjoys itself, and where it seeks stimulation and distraction. In the art exhibition it crowds, with proper little cries of admiration, round Besnard's women, with their grass-green hair, faces of sulphur-yellow or fiery-red, and arms spotted in violet and pink, dressed in a shining blue cloud resembling faintly a sort of nightdress; that is to say, it has a fondness for bold, revolutionary debauch of colour. But not exclusively so. Next to Besnard it worships with equal or greater rapture the works of Puvis de Chavannes, wan, and as though blotted out with a half-transparent wash of lime; or those of Carrière, suffused in a problematical vapour, reeking as if with a cloud of incense; or those of Roll, shimmering in a soft and silvery sheen. The purple of the Manet school, steeping the whole visible creation in bluish glamour, the half-tones, or, rather, phantom-colours of the 'Archaists,' that seem to have risen, faded and nebulous, out of some primeval tomb, and all these palettes of 'dead leaves,' 'old ivory,' evaporating yellows, smothered purple, attract on the whole more rapturous glances than the voluptuous 'orchestration' of the Besnard section. The subject of the picture leaves these select gazers apparently indifferent; it is only seamstresses and country-folk, the grateful *clientèle* of the chromo, who linger over the 'story.' And yet these as they pass stop by preference before Henry Martin's 'Every Man and his Chimæra,' in which bloated figures, in an atmosphere of yellow broth, are doing incomprehensible things that need profound explanation; or before Jean Béraud's 'Christ and the Adulteress,' where, in a Parisian dining-room, in the midst of a company in dress-coats, and before a woman in ball-dress, a Christ robed in correct Oriental gear, and with an orthodox halo, acts a scene out of the Gospel; or before Raffaelli's topers and cut-throats of the purlieus of Paris, drawn in high relief, but painted with ditch-water and dissolved clay. Steering in the wake of 'society' through a picture-gallery, one will be unalterably convinced that they turn up their eyes and fold their hands before pictures at which the commoner sort burst out laughing or pull the grimace of a man who believes he is made a fool of; and that they shrug their shoulders and hasten with scornful exchange of looks past such as the latter pause at in grateful enjoyment.

At opera and concert the rounded forms of ancient melody are coldly listened to. The translucent thematic treatment of classic masters, their conscientious observance of the laws of counterpoint, are reckoned flat and tedious. A coda graceful in cadence, serene in its 'dying fall,' a pedal-base with correct harmonization, provoke yawns. Applause and wreaths are reserved for Wagner's *Tristan and Isolde,* and especially the mystic *Parsifal,* for the religious music in Bruneau's *Dream,* or the symphonies of César Franck. Music in order to please must either counterfeit religious devotion, or agitate the mind by its form. The musical listener is accustomed involuntarily to develop a little in his mind every motive occurring in a piece. The mode in which the composer carries out his *motif* is bound, accordingly, to differ entirely from this anticipated development. It must not admit of being guessed. A dissonant interval must appear where a consonant interval was expected; if the hearer is hoping that a phrase in what is an obvious final cadence will be spun out to its natural end, it must be sharply interrupted in the middle of a bar. Keys and pitch must change suddenly. In the orchestra a vigorous polyphony must summon the attention in several directions at once; particular instruments, or groups of instruments, must address the listener simultaneously without heeding each other, till he gets as nervously excited as the man who vainly endeavours to understand what is being said in the jangle of a dozen voices. The theme, even if in the first instance it has a distinct outline, must become ever more indefinite, ever more dissolving into a mist, in which the imagination can see any forms it likes, as in driving clouds of night. The tide of sound must flow on without any perceptible limit or goal, surging up and down in endless chromatic passages of triplets. If now and then it delude the listener, borne along by it, and straining his eyes to see land with glimpses of a distant shore, this is soon discovered to be a fleeting mirage. The music must continually promise, but never perform; must seem about to tell some great secret, and grow dumb or break away ere to throbbing hearts it tells the word they wait for. The audience go to their concert-room in quest of Tantalus moods, and leave it with all the nervous exhaustion of a young pair of lovers, who for hours at the nightly tryst have sought to exchange caresses through a closely-barred window.

The books in which the public here depicted finds its delight or edification diffuse a curious perfume yielding distinguishable odours of incense, eau de Lubin and refuse, one or the other preponderating alternately. Mere sewage exhalations are played out. The filth of Zola's art and of his disciples in literary canal-dredging has been got over, and nothing remains for it but to turn to submerged peoples and social strata. The vanguard of civilization holds its nose at the pit of undiluted naturalism, and can only be brought to bend over it with sympathy and curiosity when, by cunning engineering, a drain from the boudoir and the sacristy has been turned into it. Mere sensuality passes as commonplace, and only finds admission when disguised as something unnatural and degenerate. Books treating of the relations between the sexes, with no matter how little reserve, seem too dully moral. Elegant titillation only begins where normal sexual relations leave off. Priapus has become a symbol of virtue. Vice looks to Sodom and Lesbos, to Bluebeard's castle and the servants' hall of the 'divine' Marquis de Sade's *Justine*, for its embodiments.

The book that would be fashionable must, above all, be obscure. The intelligible is cheap goods for the million only. It must further discourse in a certain pulpit tone—mildly unctuous, not too insistent; and it must follow up risky scenes by tearful outpourings of love for the lowly and the suffering, or glowing transports of piety. Ghost-stories are very popular, but they must come on in scientific disguise, as hypnotism, telepathy, somnambulism. So are marionette-plays, in which seemingly naïve but knowing rogues make used-up old ballad dummies babble like babies or idiots. So are esoteric novels, in which the author hints that he could say a deal about magic, kabbala, fakirism, astrology and other white and black arts if he only chose. Readers intoxicate themselves in the hazy word-sequences of symbolic poetry. Ibsen dethrones Goethe; Maeterlinck ranks with Shakespeare; Nietzsche is pronounced by German and even by French critics to be the leading German writer of the day; the *Kreutzer Sonata* is the Bible of ladies, who are amateurs in love, but bereft of lovers; dainty gentlemen find the street ballads and gaol-bird songs of Jules Jouy, Bruant, MacNab and Xanroff very *distingué* on account of 'the warm sympathy pulsing in them,' as the stock phrase runs; and society persons, whose creed is limited to baccarat and the money market, make pilgrimages to the Oberammergau Passion-play, and wipe away a tear over Paul Verlaine's invocations to the Virgin.

But art exhibitions, concerts, plays and books, however extraordinary, do not suffice for the æsthetic needs of elegant society. Novel sensations alone can satisfy it. It demands more intense stimulus, and hopes for it in spectacles, where different arts strive in new combinations to affect all the senses at once. Poets and artists strain every nerve incessantly to satisfy this craving. A painter, who for that matter is less occupied with new impressions than with old puffs, paints a picture indifferently well of the dying Mozart working at his *Requiem*, and exhibits it of an evening in a darkened room, while a dazzling ray of skilfully directed electric light falls on the painting, and an invisible orchestra softly plays the *Requiem*. A musician goes one step further. Developing to the utmost a Bayreuth usage, he arranges a concert in a totally darkened hall, and thus delights those of the audience who find opportunity, by happily chosen juxtapositions, to augment their musical sensations by hidden enjoyment of another sort. Haraucourt, the poet, has his paraphrase of the Gospel, written in spirited verse, recited on the stage by Sarah Bernhardt, while, as in the old-fashioned melodrama, soft music in unending melody accompanies the actress. Even the nose, hitherto basely ignored by the fine arts, attracts the pioneers, and is by them invited to take part in æsthetic delights. A hose is set up in the theatre, by which the spectators are sprayed with perfumes. On the stage a poem in approximately dramatic form is recited. In every division, act, scene, or however the thing is called, a different vowel-sound is made to preponderate; during each the theatre is illuminated with a differently tinted light, the orchestra discourses music in a different key, and the jet gives out a different perfume. This idea of accompanying verses with odours was thrown out years ago, half in jest, by Ernest Eckstein. Paris has carried it out in sacred earnest. The new school fetch the puppet theatre out of the nursery, and enact pieces for adults which, with artificial simplicity, pretend to hide or reveal a profound meaning, and with great talent and ingenuity execute a magic-lantern of prettily drawn and painted figures moving across surprisingly luminous backgrounds; and these living pictures make visible the process of thought in the mind of the author who recites his accompanying poem, while a piano endeavours to illustrate the leading emotion. And to enjoy such exhibitions as these society crowds into a suburban circus, the loft of a back tenement, a second-hand costumier's shop, or a fantastic artist's restaurant, where the performances, in some room consecrated to beery potations, bring together the greasy *habitué* and the dainty aristocratic fledgling.

CHAPTER III.

DIAGNOSIS.

THE manifestations described in the preceding chapter must be patent enough to everyone, be he never so narrow a Philistine. The Philistine, however, regards them as a passing fashion and nothing more; for him the current terms, caprice, eccentricity, affectation of novelty, imitation, instinct, afford a sufficient explanation. The purely literary mind, whose merely æsthetic culture does not enable him to understand the connections of things, and to seize their real meaning, deceives himself and others as to his ignorance by means of sounding phrases, and loftily talks of a 'restless quest of a new ideal by the modern spirit,' 'the richer vibrations of the refined nervous system of the present day,' 'the unknown sensations of an elect mind.' But the physician, especially if he have devoted himself to the special study of nervous and mental maladies, recognises at a glance, in the *fin-de-siècle* disposition, in the tendencies of contemporary art and poetry, in the life and conduct of the men who write mystic, symbolic and 'decadent' works, and the attitude taken by their admirers in the tastes and æsthetic instincts of fashionable society, the confluence of two well-defined conditions of disease, with which he is quite familiar, viz. degeneration (degeneracy) and hysteria, of which the minor stages are designated as neurasthenia. These two conditions of the organism differ from each other, yet have many features in common, and frequently occur together; so that it is easier to observe them in their composite forms, than each in isolation.

The conception of degeneracy, which, at this time, obtains throughout the science of mental disease, was first clearly grasped and formulated by Morel. In his principal work—often quoted, but, unfortunately, not sufficiently read*—the following definition of what he wishes to be understood by 'degeneracy' is given by this distinguished expert in mental pathology, who was, for a short time, famous in Germany, even outside professional circles.†

'The clearest notion we can form of degeneracy is to regard it as *a morbid deviation from an original type*. This deviation, even if, at the outset, it was ever so slight, contained transmissible elements of such a nature that anyone bearing in him the germs becomes more and more incapable of fulfilling his functions in the world; and mental progress, already checked in his own person, finds itself menaced also in his descendants.'

When under any kind of noxious influences an organism becomes debilitated, its successors will not resemble the healthy, normal type of the species, with capacities for development, but will form a new sub-species, which, like all others, possesses the capacity of transmitting to its offspring, in a continuously increasing degree, its peculiarities, these being morbid deviations from the normal form—gaps in development, malformations and infirmities. That which distinguishes degeneracy from the formation of new species (phylogeny) is, that the morbid variation does not continuously subsist and propagate itself, like one that is healthy, but, fortunately, is soon rendered sterile, and after a few generations often dies out before it reaches the lowest grade of organic degradation.‡

Degeneracy betrays itself among men in certain physical

* *Traité des Dégénérescences physiques, intellectuelles et morales de l'Espèce humaine et des Causes qui produisent ces Variétés maladives.* Par le Dr. B. A. Morel. Paris, 1857, p. 5.

† At the instigation of his mistress Ebergenyi, Count Chorinsky had poisoned his wife, previously an actress. The murderer was an epileptic, and a 'degenerate,' in the Morelian sense. His family summoned Morel from Normandy to Munich, for the purpose of proving to the jury, before whom the case (1868) was tried, that the accused was irresponsible. The latter was singularly indignant at this; and the Attorney-General also contradicted, in the most emphatic manner, the evidence of the French alienist, and supported himself by the approbation of the most prominent alienists in Munich. Chorinsky was pronounced guilty. Nevertheless, only a short time after his conviction, insanity developed itself in him, and a few months later he died, in the deepest mental darkness, thus justifying all the previous assertions of the French physician, who had, in the German tongue, demonstrated to a German jury the incompetence of his professional confrères in Munich.

‡ Morel, *op. cit.*, p. 683.

characteristics, which are denominated 'stigmata,' or brand-marks—an unfortunate term derived from a false idea, as if degeneracy were necessarily the consequence of a fault, and the indication of it a punishment. Such stigmata consist of deformities, multiple and stunted growths in the first line of asymmetry, the unequal development of the two halves of the face and cranium; then imperfection in the development of the external ear, which is conspicuous for its enormous size, or protrudes from the head, like a handle, and the lobe of which is either lacking or adhering to the head, and the helix of which is not involuted; further, squint-eyes, hare-lips, irregularities in the form and position of the teeth; pointed or flat palates, webbed or supernumerary fingers (syn- and poly-dactylia), etc. In the book from which I have quoted, Morel gives a list of the anatomical phenomena of degeneracy, which later observers have largely extended. In particular, Lombroso* has conspicuously broadened our knowledge of stigmata, but he apportions them merely to his 'born criminals'—a limitation which from the very scientific standpoint of Lombroso himself cannot be justified, his 'born criminals' being nothing but a subdivision of degenerates. Féré† expresses this very emphatically when he says, 'Vice, crime and madness are only distinguished from each other by social prejudices.'

There might be a sure means of proving that the application of the term 'degenerates' to the originators of all the *fin-de-siècle* movements in art and literature is not arbitrary, that it is no baseless conceit, but a fact; and that would be a careful physical examination of the persons concerned, and an inquiry into their pedigree. In almost all cases, relatives would be met with who were undoubtedly degenerate, and one or more stigmata discovered which would indisputably establish the diagnosis of 'Degeneration.' Of course, from human consideration, the result of such an inquiry could often not be made public; and he alone would be convinced who should be able to undertake it himself.

Science, however, has found, together with these physical stigmata, others of a mental order, which betoken degeneracy quite as clearly as the former; and they allow of an easy demonstration from all the vital manifestations, and, in particular, from all the works of degenerates, so that it is not necessary to measure the cranium of an author, or to see the lobe of a painter's ear, in order to recognise the fact that he belongs to the class of degenerates.

* *L'Uomo delinquente in rapporto all' Antropologia, Giurisprudenza e alle Discipline carcerarie.* 3a edizione. Torino, 1884, p. 147 *et seq.* See also Dr. Ch. Fére, 'La Famille nevropathique.' Paris, 1894, pp. 176-212.

† 'La Famille nevropathique,' *Archives de Nevrologie*, 1884, *Nos.* 19 *et* 20.

Quite a number of different designations have been found for these persons. Maudsley and Ball call them 'Borderland dwellers'—that is to say, dwellers on the borderland between reason and pronounced madness. Magnan gives to them the name of 'higher degenerates' (*dégénérés supérieurs*), and Lombroso speaks of 'mattoids' (from *matto*, the Italian for insane), and 'graphomaniacs,' under which he classifies those semi-insane persons who feel a strong impulse to write. In spite, however, of this variety of nomenclature, it is a question simply of one single species of individuals, who betray their fellowship by the similarity of their mental physiognomy.

In the mental development of degenerates, we meet with the same irregularity that we have observed in their physical growth. The asymmetry of face and cranium finds, as it were, its counterpart in their mental faculties. Some of the latter are completely stunted, others morbidly exaggerated. That which nearly all degenerates lack is the sense of morality and of right and wrong. For them there exists no law, no decency, no modesty. In order to satisfy any momentary impulse, or inclination, or caprice, they commit crimes and trespasses with the greatest calmness and self-complacency, and do not comprehend that other persons take offence thereat. When this phenomenon is present in a high degree, we speak of 'moral insanity' with Maudsley;* there are, nevertheless, lower stages in which the degenerate does not, perhaps, himself commit any act which will bring him into conflict with the criminal code, but at least asserts the theoretical legitimacy of crime; seeks, with philosophically sounding fustian, to prove that 'good' and 'evil,' virtue and vice, are arbitrary distinctions; goes into raptures over evildoers and their deeds; professes to discover beauties in the lowest and most repulsive things; and tries to awaken interest in, and so-called 'comprehension' of, every bestiality. The two psychological roots of moral insanity, in all its degrees of development, are, firstly, unbounded egoism,† and, secondly, impulsiveness‡—*i.e.*, in-

* See, on this subject, in particular, Krafft Ebing, *Die Lehre vom moralischen Wahnsinn*, 1871; H. Maudsley, *Responsibility in Mental Disease*, International Scientific Series; and Ch. Féré, *Dégénérescence et Criminalité*, Paris, 1888.

† J. Roubinovitch, *Hystérie mâle et Dégénérescence*; Paris, 1890, p. 62: 'The society which surrounds him (the degenerate) always remains strange to him. He knows nothing, and takes interest in nothing but himself.'

Legrain, *Du Délire chez les Dégénérés*; Paris, 1886, p. 10: 'The patient is . . . the plaything of his passions; he is carried away by his impulses, and has only one care—to satisfy his appetites.' P. 27: 'They are egoistical, arrogant, conceited, self-infatuated,' etc.

‡ Henry Colin, *Essai sur l'État mental des Hystériques*; Paris, 1890, p. 59: 'Two great facts control the being of the hereditary degenerate: obsession [the tyrannical domination of one thought from which a man cannot free

ability to resist a sudden impulse to any deed; and these characteristics also constitute the chief intellectual stigmata of degenerates. In the following sections of this work, I shall find occasion to show on what organic grounds, and in consequence of what peculiarities of their brain and nervous system, degenerates are necessarily egoistical and impulsive. In these introductory remarks I would wish only to point out the stigma itself.

Another mental stigma of degenerates is their emotionalism. Morel* has even wished to make this peculiarity their chief characteristic—erroneously, it seems to me, for it is present in the same degree among hysterics, and, indeed, is to be found in perfectly healthy persons, who, from any transient cause, such as illness, exhaustion, or any mental shock, have been temporarily weakened. Nevertheless it is a phenomenon rarely absent in a degenerate. He laughs until he sheds tears, or weeps copiously without adequate occasion; a commonplace line of poetry or of prose sends a shudder down his back; he falls into raptures before indifferent pictures or statues; and music especially,† even the most insipid and least commendable, arouses in him the most vehement emotions. He is quite proud of being so vibrant a musical instrument, and boasts that where the Philistine remains completely cold, he feels his inner self confounded, the depths of his being broken up, and the bliss of the Beautiful possessing him to the tips of his fingers. His excitability appears to him a mark of superiority; he believes himself to be possessed by a peculiar insight lacking in other mortals, and he is fain to despise the vulgar herd for the dulness and narrowness of their minds. The unhappy creature does not suspect that he is conceited about a disease and boasting of a derangement of the mind; and certain silly critics, when, through fear of being pronounced deficient in comprehension, they make desperate efforts to share the emotions of a degenerate in regard to some insipid or ridiculous production, or when they praise in exaggerated expressions the beauties which the degenerate asserts he finds therein, are unconsciously simulating one of the stigmata of semi-insanity.

Besides moral insanity and emotionalism, there is to be observed in the degenerate a condition of mental weakness and despondency, which, according to the circumstances of his life, assumes the form of pessimism, a vague fear of all men, and of

---

himself; Westphal has created for this the good term 'Zwangs-Vorstellung,' *i.e.*, coercive idea] and impulsion—both irresistible.'

* Morel, 'Du Délire émotif,' *Archives générales*, 6 série, vol. vii., pp. 385 and 530. See also Roubinovitch, *op. cit.*, p. 53.

† J. Roubinovitch, *op. cit.*, p. 68: 'Music excites him keenly

the entire phenomenon of the universe, or self-abhorrence. 'These patients,' says Morel,* 'feel perpetually compelled . . . to commiserate themselves, to sob, to repeat with the most desperate monotony the same questions and words. They have delirious presentations of ruin and damnation, and all sorts of imaginary fears.' 'Ennui never quits me,' said a patient of this kind, whose case Roubinovitch† describes, 'ennui of myself.' 'Among moral stigmata,' says the same author,‡ 'there are also to be specified those undefinable apprehensions manifested by degenerates when they see, smell, or touch any object.' And he further§ calls to notice 'their unconscious fear of everything and everyone.' In this picture of the sufferer from melancholia; downcast, sombre, despairing of himself and the world, tortured by fear of the Unknown, menaced by undefined but dreadful dangers, we recognise in every detail the man of the Dusk of the Nations and the *fin-de-siècle* frame of mind, described in the first chapter.

With this characteristic dejectedness of the degenerate, there is combined, as a rule, a disinclination to action of any kind, attaining possibly to abhorrence of activity and powerlessness to will (*aboulia*). Now, it is a peculiarity of the human mind, known to every psychologist, that, inasmuch as the law of causality governs a man's whole thought, he imputes a rational basis to all his own decisions. This was prettily expressed by Spinoza when he said: 'If a stone flung by a human hand could think, it would certainly imagine that it flew because it wished to fly.' Many mental conditions and operations of which we become conscious are the result of causes which do not reach our consciousness. In this case we fabricate causes *a posteriori* for them, satisfying our mental need of distinct causality, and we have no trouble in persuading ourselves that we have now truly explained them. The degenerate who shuns action, and is without will-power, has no suspicion that his incapacity for action is a consequence of his inherited deficiency of brain. He deceives himself into believing that he despises action from free determination, and takes pleasure in inactivity; and, in order to justify himself in his own eyes, he constructs a philosophy of renunciation and of contempt for the world and men, asserts that he has convinced himself of the excellence of Quietism, calls himself with consummate self-consciousness a Buddhist, and praises Nirvana in poetically eloquent phrases as the highest and worthiest ideal of the human mind. The degenerate and insane are the predestined disciples of Schopenhauer and Hartmann,

* Morel, 'Du Délire panophobique des Aliénés gémisseurs,' *Annales médico-psychologiques*, 1871.

† Roubinovitch, *op. cit.*, p. 28. ‡ *Ibid.*, p. 37. § *Ibid.*, p. 66.

and need only to acquire a knowledge of Buddhism to become converts to it.

With the incapacity for action there is connected the predilection for inane reverie. The degenerate is not in a condition to fix his attention long, or indeed at all, on any subject, and is equally incapable of correctly grasping, ordering, or elaborating into ideas and judgments the impressions of the external world conveyed to his distracted consciousness by his defectively operating senses. It is easier and more convenient for him to allow his brain-centres to produce semi-lucid, nebulously blurred ideas and inchoate embryonic thoughts, and to surrender himself to the perpetual obfuscation of a boundless, aimless, and shoreless stream of fugitive ideas; and he rarely rouses himself to the painful attempt to check or counteract the capricious, and, as a rule, purely mechanical associations of ideas and succession of images, and bring under discipline the disorderly tumult of his fluid presentations. On the contrary, he rejoices in his faculty of imagination, which he contrasts with the insipidity of the Philistine, and devotes himself with predilection to all sorts of unlicensed pursuits permitted by the unshackled vagabondage of his mind; while he cannot endure well-ordered civil occupations, requiring attention and constant heed to reality. He calls this 'having an idealist temperament,' ascribes to himself irresistible æsthetic propinquities, and proudly styles himself an artist.*

We will briefly mention some peculiarities frequently manifested by a degenerate. He is tormented by doubts, seeks for the basis of all phenomena, especially those whose first causes are completely inaccessible to us, and is unhappy when his inquiries and ruminations lead, as is natural, to no result.† He is ever supplying new recruits to the army of system-inventing metaphysicians, profound expositors of the riddle of the universe, seekers for the philosopher's stone, the squaring of the circle and perpetual motion.‡ These last three subjects have such a special attraction for him, that the Patent Office at Washington is forced to keep on hand printed replies to the numberless memorials in which patents are constantly

* Charcot, 'Leçons du Mardi à la Salpêtrière,' *Policlinique*, Paris, 1890, 2e partie, p. 392: 'This person [the invalid mentioned] is a performer at fairs; he calls himself "artist." The truth is that his art consists in personating a "wild man" in fair-booths.'

† Legrain, *op. cit.*, p. 73: 'The patients are perpetually tormented by a multitude of questions which invade their minds, and to which they can give no answer; inexpressible moral sufferings result from this incapacity. Doubt envelops every possible subject:—metaphysics, theology, etc.'

‡ Magnan, 'Considérations sur la Folie des Héréditaires ou Dégénerés,' *Progrès médical*, 1886, p. 1110 (in the report of a medical case): 'He also thought of seeking for the philosopher's stone, and of making gold.'

demanded for the solution of these chimerical problems. In view of Lombroso's researches,* it can scarcely be doubted that the writings and acts of revolutionists and anarchists are also attributable to degeneracy. The degenerate is incapable of adapting himself to existing circumstances. This incapacity, indeed, is an indication of morbid variation in every species, and probably a primary cause of their sudden extinction. He therefore rebels against conditions and views of things which he necessarily feels to be painful, chiefly because they impose upon him the duty of self-control, of which he is incapable on account of his organic weakness of will. Thus he becomes an improver of the world, and devises plans for making mankind happy, which, without exception, are conspicuous quite as much by their fervent philanthropy, and often pathetic sincerity, as by their absurdity and monstrous ignorance of all real relations.

Finally, a cardinal mark of degeneration which I have reserved to the last, is mysticism. Colin says:† 'Of all the delirious manifestations peculiar to the hereditarily-afflicted, none indicates the condition more clearly, we think, than mystical delirium, or, when the malady has not reached this point, the being constantly occupied with mystical and religious questions, an exaggerated piety, etc.' I will not here multiply evidence and quotations. In the following books, where the art and poetry of the times are treated of, I shall find occasion to show the reader that no difference exists between these tendencies and the religious manias observed in nearly all degenerates and sufferers from hereditary mental taint.

I have enumerated the most important features characterizing the mental condition of the degenerate. The reader can now judge for himself whether or not the diagnosis 'degeneration' is applicable to the originators of the new æsthetic tendencies. It must not for that matter be supposed that degeneration is synonymous with absence of talent. Nearly all the inquirers who have had degenerates under their observation expressly establish the contrary. 'The degenerate,' says Legrain,‡ 'may be a genius. A badly balanced mind is susceptible of the highest conceptions, while, on the other hand, one meets in the same mind with traits of meanness and pettiness all the more striking from the fact that they co-exist with the most brilliant qualities.' We shall find this reservation in all authors

* Lombroso, 'La Physionomie des Anarchistes,' *Nouvelle Revue*, May 15, 1891, p. 227: 'They [the anarchists] frequently have those characteristics of degeneracy which are common to criminals and lunatics, for they are anomalies, and bear hereditary taints.' See also the same author's *Pazzi ed Anomali*. Turin, 1884.

† Colin, *op. cit.*, p. 154.

‡ Legrain, *op. cit.*, p. 11.

who have contributed to the natural history of the degenerate. 'As regards their intellect, they can,' says Roubinovitch,* 'attain to a high degree of development, but from a moral point of view their existence is completely deranged. . . . A degenerate will employ his brilliant faculties quite as well in the service of some grand object as in the satisfaction of the basest propensities.' Lombroso† has cited a large number of undoubted geniuses who were equally undoubted mattoids, graphomaniacs, or pronounced lunatics; and the utterance of a French savant, Guérinsen, 'Genius is a disease of the nerves,' has become a 'winged word.' This expression was imprudent, for it gave ignorant babblers a pretext, and apparently a right, to talk of exaggeration, and to contemn experts in nervous and mental diseases, because they professedly saw a lunatic in everyone who ventured to be something more than the most ordinary, characterless, average being. Science does not assert that every genius is a lunatic; there are some geniuses of superabundant power whose high privilege consists in the possession of one or other extraordinarily developed faculty, without the rest of their faculties falling short of the average standard. Just as little, naturally, is every lunatic a genius; most of them, even if we disregard idiots of different degrees, are much rather pitiably stupid and incapable; but in many, nay, in abundant cases, the 'higher degenerate' of Magnan, just as he occasionally exhibits gigantic bodily stature or the disproportionate growth of particular parts, has some mental gift exceptionally developed at the cost, it is true, of the remaining faculties, which are wholly or partially atrophied.‡ It is this which enables the well-informed to distinguish at the first glance between the sane genius, and the highly, or even the most highly, gifted degenerate. Take from the former the special capacity through which he becomes a genius, and there still remains a capable, often conspicuously intelligent, clever, moral, and judicious man, who will hold his ground with propriety in our social mechanism. Let the same be tried in the case of a degenerate, and there remains only a criminal or madman, for whom healthy humanity can find no use. If

* Roubinovitch, *op. cit.*, p. 33.

† Lombroso, *Genie und Irrsinn;* German translation by A. Courth. Reclam's *Universal Bibliothek*, Bde. 2313-16. See also in particular, J. F. Nisbet, *The Insanity of Genius*. London, 1891.

‡ Falret, *Annales médico-psychologiques*, 1867, p. 76: 'From their childhood they usually display a very unequal development of their mental faculties, which, weak in their entirety, are remarkable for certain special aptitudes; they have shown an extraordinary gift for drawing, arithmetic, music, sculpture, or mechanics . . . and, together with those specially developed aptitudes, obtaining for them the fame of "infant phenomena," they for the most part give evidence of very great deficiencies in their intelligence, and of a radical debility in the remaining faculties.'

Goethe had never written a line of verse, he would, all the same, have still remained a man of the world, of good principles, a fine art connoisseur, a judicious collector, a keen observer of nature. Let us, on the contrary, imagine a Schopenhauer who had written no astounding books, and we should have before us only a repulsive *lusus naturæ*, whose morals would necessarily exclude him from all respectable society, and whose fixed idea that he was a victim of persecution would point him out as a subject for a madhouse. The lack of harmony, the absence of balance, the singular incapacity of usefully applying, or deriving satisfaction from, their own special faculty among highly-gifted degenerates, strikes every healthy censor who does not allow himself to be prejudiced by the noisy admiration of critics, themselves degenerates: and will always prevent his mistaking the mattoid for the same exceptional man who opens out new paths for humanity and leads it to higher developments. I do not share Lombroso's opinion* that highly-gifted degenerates are an active force in the progress of mankind. They corrupt and delude; they do, alas! frequently exercise a deep influence, but this is always a baneful one. It may not be at once remarked, but it will reveal itself subsequently. If cotemporaries do not recognise it, the historian of morals will point it out *a posteriori*. They, likewise, are leading men along the paths they themselves have found to new goals; but these goals are abysses or waste places. They are guides to swamps like will-o'-the-wisps, or to ruin like the ratcatcher of Hammelin. Observers lay stress on their unnatural sterility. 'They are,' says Tarabaud,† 'cranks; wrongheaded, unbalanced, incapable creatures; they belong to the class of whom it may not be said that they have no mind, but whose mind produces nothing.' 'A common type,' writes Legrain,‡ 'unites them:—weakness of judgment and unequal development of mental powers. . . . Their conceptions are never of a high order. They are incapable of great thoughts and prolific ideas. This fact forms a peculiar contrast to the frequently excessive development of their powers of imagination.' 'If they are painters,' we read in Lombroso,§ 'then their predominant attribute will be the colour-sense; they will be decorative. If they are poets, they will be rich in rhyme, brilliant in style, but barren of thought; sometimes they will be "decadents."'

Such are the qualities of the most gifted of those who are

* *Nouvelle Revue*, July 15, 1891.

† Tarabaud, *Des Rapports de la Dégénérescence mentale et de l'Hystérie*. Paris, 1888, p. 12.

‡ Legrain, *op. cit.*, pp. 24 and 26.

§ Lombroso, *Nouvelles recherches de Psychiatrie et d'Anthropologie criminelle*. Paris, 1892, p. 74.

discovering new paths, and are proclaimed by enthusiastic followers as the guides to the promised land of the future. Among them degenerates and mattoids predominate. The second of the above-mentioned diagnoses, on the contrary, applies for the most part to the multitude who admire these individuals and swear by them, who imitate the fashions they design, and take delight in the extravagances described in the previous chapter. In their case we have to deal chiefly with hysteria, or neurasthenia.

For reasons which will be elucidated in the next chapter, hysteria has hitherto been less studied in Germany than in France, where, more than elsewhere, it has formed a subject of earnest inquiry. We owe what we know of it almost exclusively to French investigators. The copious treatises of Axenfeld,* Richer,† and in particular Gilles de la Tourette,‡ adequately comprise our present knowledge of this malady; and I shall refer to these works when I enumerate the symptoms chiefly indicative of hysteria.

Among the hysterical—and it must not be thought that these are met with exclusively, or even preponderantly, among females. for they are quite as often, perhaps oftener, found among males§ —among the hysterical, as among the degenerate, the first thing which strikes us is an extraordinary emotionalism. 'The leading characteristic of the hysterical,' says Colin,‖ 'is the disproportionate impressionability of their psychic centres. . . . They are, above all things, impressionable.' From this primary peculiarity proceeds a second quite as remarkable and important—the exceeding ease with which they can be made to yield to suggestion.¶ The earlier observers always mentioned the boundless mendacity of the hysterical; growing, indeed, quite indignant at it, and making it the most prominent mark of the mental condition of such patients. They were mistaken. The hysterical subject does not consciously lie. He believes in the truth of his craziest inventions. The morbid mobility of his mind, the excessive excitability of his imagination, conveys to his consciousness all sorts of queer and senseless ideas. He suggests to himself that these ideas are founded on true perceptions, and believes in the truth of his foolish inventions until

* Axenfeld, *Des Névroses.* 2 vols., 2e édition, revue et complétée par le Dr. Huchard Paris, 1879.

† Paul Richer, *Études cliniques sur l'Hystéro-épilepsie ou Grande Hystérie.* Paris, 1891.

‡ Gilles de la Tourette, *Traité clinique et thérapeutique de l'Hystérie.* Paris, 1891.

§ Paul Michaut, *Contribution à l'Étude des Manifestations de l'Hystérie chez l'Homme.* Paris, 1890.

‖ Colin, *op. cit.*, p. 14.

¶ Gilles de la Tourette, *op. cit.*, p. 548 *et passim.*

a new suggestion—perhaps his own, perhaps that of another person—has ejected the earlier one. A result of the susceptibility of the hysterical subject to suggestion is his irresistible passion for imitation,* and the eagerness with which he yields to all the suggestions of writers and artists.† When he sees a picture, he wants to become like it in attitude and dress; when he reads a book, he adopts its views blindly. He takes as a pattern the heroes of the novels which he has in his hand at the moment, and infuses himself into the characters moving before him on the stage.

Added to this emotionalism and susceptibility to suggestion is a love of self never met with in a sane person in anything like the same degree. The hysterical person's own 'I' towers up before his inner vision, and so completely fills his mental horizon that it conceals the whole of the remaining universe. He cannot endure that others should ignore him. He desires to be as important to his fellow-men as he is to himself. 'An incessant need pursues and governs the hysterical—to busy those about them with themselves.'‡ A means of satisfying this need is the fabrication of stories by which they become interesting. Hence come the adventurous occurrences which often enough occupy the police and the reports of the daily press. In the busiest thoroughfare the hysterical person is set upon, robbed, maltreated and wounded, dragged to a distant place, and left to die. He picks himself up painfully, and informs the police. He can show the wounds on his body. He gives all the details. And there is not a single word of truth in the whole story; it is all dreamt and imagined. He has himself inflicted his wounds in order for a short time to become the centre of public attention. In the lower stages of hysteria this need of making a sensation assumes more harmless forms. It displays itself in eccentricities of dress and behaviour. 'Other hysterical subjects are passionately fond of glaring colours and extravagant forms; they wish to attract attention and make themselves talked about.'§

It is certainly unnecessary to draw the reader's attention in a special manner to the complete coincidence of this clinical picture of hysteria with the description of the peculiarities of the *fin-de-siècle* public, and to the fact that in the former we meet with all the features made familiar to us by the consideration of contemporary phenomena; in particular with the passion for imitating in externals—in dress, attitude, fashion of the hair and beard—the figures in old and modern pictures, and the feverish effort, through any sort of singularity, to make

* Colin, *op. cit.*, pp. 15 and 16.

† Gilles de la Tourette, *op. cit.*, p. 493.

‡ *Ibid.*, p. 303.

§ Legrain, *op. cit.*, p. 39.

themselves talked about. The observation of pronounced cases of degeneration and hysteria, whose condition makes them necessary subjects for medical treatment, gives us also the key to the comprehension of subordinate details in the fashions of the day. The present rage for collecting, the piling up, in dwellings, of aimless bric-à-brac, which does not become any more useful or beautiful by being fondly called *bibelots,* appear to us in a completely new light when we know that Magnan has established the existence of an irresistible desire among the degenerate to accumulate useless trifles. It is so firmly imprinted and so peculiar that Magnan declares it to be a stigma of degeneration, and has invented for it the name 'oniomania,' or 'buying craze.' This is not to be confounded with the desire for buying, which possesses those who are in the first stage of general paralysis. The purchases of these persons are due to their delusion as to their own greatness. They lay in great supplies because they fancy themselves millionaires. The oniomaniac, on the contrary, neither buys enormous quantities of one and the same thing, nor is the price a matter of indifference to him as with the paralytic. He is simply unable to pass by any lumber without feeling an impulse to acquire it.

The curious style of certain recent painters—'impressionists,' 'stipplers,' or 'mosaists,' 'papilloteurs' or 'quiverers,' 'roaring' colourists, dyers in gray and faded tints—becomes at once intelligible to us if we keep in view the researches of the Charcot school into the visual derangements in degeneration and hysteria. The painters who assure us that they are sincere, and reproduce nature as they see it, speak the truth. The degenerate artist who suffers from *nystagmus,* or trembling of the eyeball, will, in fact, perceive the phenomena of nature trembling, restless, devoid of firm outline, and, if he is a conscientious painter, will give us pictures reminding us of the mode practised by the draughtsmen of the *Fliegende Blätter* when they represent a wet dog shaking himself vigorously. If his pictures fail to produce a comic effect, it is only because the attentive beholder reads in them the desperate effort to reproduce fully an impression incapable of reproduction by the expedients of the painter's art as devised by men of normal vision.

There is hardly a hysterical subject whose retina is not partly insensitive.* As a rule the insensitive parts are connected, and include the outer half of the retina. In these cases the field of vision is more or less contracted, and appears to him not as it does to the normal man—as a circle—but as a picture bordered by whimsically zigzag lines. Often, however, the

* Dr. Emile Berger, *Les Maladies des Yeux dans leurs rapports avec la Pathologie général.* Paris, 1892, p. 129 *et seq.*

insensitive parts are not connected, but are scattered in isolated spots over the entire retina. Then the sufferer will have all sorts of gaps in his field of vision, producing strange effects, and if he paints what he sees, he will be inclined to place in juxtaposition larger or smaller points or spots which are completely or partially dissociated. The insensitiveness need not be complete, and may exist only in the case of single colours, or of all. If the sensitiveness is completely lost ('achromatopsy') he then sees everything in a uniform gray, but perceives differences in the degree of lustre. Hence the picture of nature presents itself to him as a copper-plate or a pencil drawing, where the effect of the absent colours is replaced by differences in the intensity of light, by greater or less depth and power of the white and black portions. Painters who are insensitive to colour will naturally have a predilection for neutral-toned painting; and a public suffering from the same malady will find nothing objectionable in falsely-coloured pictures. But if, besides the whitewash of a Puvis de Chavannes, obliterating all colours equally, fanatics are found for the screaming yellow, blue, and red of a Besnard, this also has a cause, revealed to us by clinical science. 'Yellow and blue,' Gilles de la Tourette* teaches us, 'are peripheral colours' (*i.e.*, they are seen with the outermost parts of the retina); 'they are, therefore, the last to be perceived' (if the sensitiveness for the remaining colours is destroyed). 'These are . . . the very two colours the sensations of which in hysterical amblyopia [dulness of vision] endure the longest. In many cases, however, it is the red, and not the blue, which vanishes last.'

Red has also another peculiarity explanatory of the predilection shown for it by the hysterical. The experiments of Binet† have established that the impressions conveyed to the brain by the sensory nerves exercise an important influence on the species and strength of the excitation distributed by the brain to the motor nerves. Many sense-impressions operate enervatingly and inhibitively on the movements; others, on the contrary, make these more powerful, rapid and active; they are 'dynamogenous,' or 'force-producing.' As a feeling of pleasure is always connected with dynamogeny, or the production of force, every living thing, therefore, instinctively seeks for dynamogenous sense-impressions, and avoids enervating and inhibitive ones. Now, red is especially dynamogenous. 'When,' says Binet,‡ in a report of an experiment on a female hysterical subject who was paralyzed in one half of her body, 'we place a dynamo-

* *Traité clinique et thérapeutique de l'Hystérie*, p. 339. See also Drs. A. Marie et J. Bonnet, *La Vision chez les Idiots et les Imbéciles*. Paris, 1892.

† Alfred Binet, 'Recherches sur les Altérations de la Conscience chez les Hystériques,' *Revue philosophique*, 1889, vol. xxvii.

‡ *Op. cit.*, p. 150.

meter in the anæsthetically insensible right hand of Amélie Cle...... the pressure of the hand amounts to 12 kilogrammes. If at the same time she is made to look at a red disc, the number indicating the pressure in kilogrammes is at once doubled.' Hence it is intelligible that hysterical painters revel in red, and that hysterical beholders take special pleasure in pictures operating dynamogenously, and producing feelings of pleasure.

If red is dynamogenous, violet is conversely enervating and inhibitive.* It was not by accident that violet was chosen by many nations as the exclusive colour for mourning, and by us also for half-mourning. The sight of this colour has a depressing effect, and the unpleasant feeling awakened by it induces dejection in a sorrowfully-disposed mind. This suggests that painters suffering from hysteria and neurasthenia will be inclined to cover their pictures uniformly with the colour most in accordance with their condition of lassitude and exhaustion. Thus originate the violet pictures of Manet and his school, which spring from no actually observable aspect of nature, but from a subjective view due to the condition of the nerves. When the entire surface of walls in salons and art exhibitions of the day appears veiled in uniform half-mourning, this predilection for violet is simply an expression of the nervous debility of the painter.

There is yet another phenomenon highly characteristic in some cases of degeneracy, in others of hysteria. This is the formation of close groups or schools uncompromisingly exclusive to outsiders, observable to-day in literature and art. Healthy artists or authors, in possession of minds in a condition of well-regulated equilibrium, will never think of grouping themselves into an association, which may at pleasure be termed a sect or band; of devising a catechism, of binding themselves to definite æsthetic dogmas, and of entering the lists for these with the fanatical intolerance of Spanish inquisitors. If any human activity is individualistic, it is that of the artist. True talent is always personal. In its creations it reproduces itself, its own views and feelings, and not the articles of faith learnt from any æsthetic apostle; it follows its creative impulses, not a theoretical formula preached by the founder of a new artistic or literary church; it constructs its work in the form organically necessary to it, not in that proclaimed by a leader as demanded by the fashion of the day. The mere fact that an artist or author allows himself to be

* Ch. Féré, 'Sensation et Mouvement,' *Revue philosophique*, 1886. See also the same author's *Sensation et Mouvement*, Paris, 1887; *Dégénérescence et criminalité*, Paris, 1888; and 'L'Énergie et la Vitesse des Mouvements volontaires,' *Revue philosophique*, 1889.

sworn in to the party cry of any 'ism,' that he perambulates with jubilations behind a banner and Turkish music, is complete evidence of his lack of individuality—that is, of talent. If the mental movements of a period—even those which are healthy and prolific—range themselves, as a rule, under certain main tendencies, which receive each its distinguishing name, this is the work of historians of civilization or literature, who subsequently survey the combined picture of an epoch, and for their own convenience undertake divisions and classifications, in order that they may more correctly find their way among the multifariousness of the phenomena. These are, however, almost always arbitrary and artificial. Independent minds (we are not here speaking of mere imitators), united by a good critic into a group, may, it is true, have a certain resemblance to each other, but, as a rule, this resemblance will be the consequence, not of actual internal affinity, but of external influences. No one is able completely to withdraw himself from the influences of his time, and under the impression of events which affect all contemporaries alike, as well as of the scientific views prevailing at a given time, certain features develop themselves in all the works of an epoch, which stamp them as of the same date. But the same men who subsequently appear so naturally in each other's company, in historical works, that they seem to form a family, went when they lived their separate ways far asunder, little suspecting that at one time they would be united under one common designation. Quite otherwise it is when authors or artists consciously and intentionally meet together and found an æsthetic school, as a joint-stock bank is founded, with a title for which, if possible, the protection of the law is claimed, with by-laws, joint capital, etc. This may be ordinary speculation, but as a rule it is disease. The predilection for forming societies met with among all the degenerate and hysterical may assume different forms. Criminals unite in bands, as Lombroso expressly establishes.* Among pronounced lunatics it is the *folie à deux*, in which a deranged person completely forces his insane ideas on a companion; among the hysterical it assumes the form of close friendships, causing Charcot to repeat at every opportunity: 'Persons of highly-strung nerves attract each other;'† and finally authors found schools.

The common organic basis of these different forms of one and the same phenomenon—of the *folie à deux*, the association of neuropaths, the founding of æsthetic schools, the banding of criminals—is, with the active part, viz., those who lead and inspire, the predominance of obsessions: with the

* Lombroso, *L'Uomo délinquente*, p. 524.

† 'Les Nerveux se recherchent,' Charcot, *Leçons du Mardi*, *passim*.

associates, the disciples, the submissive part, weakness of will and morbid susceptibility to suggestion.* The possessor of an obsession is an incomparable apostle. There is no rational conviction arrived at by sound labour of intellect, which so completely takes possession of the mind, subjugates so tyrannically its entire activity, and so irresistibly impels it to words and deeds, as delirium. Every proof of the senselesness of his ideas rebounds from the deliriously insane or half-crazy person. No contradiction, no ridicule, no contempt, affects him; the opinion of the majority is to him a matter of indifference; facts which do not please him he does not notice, or so interprets that they seem to support his delirium; obstacles do not discourage him, because even his instinct of self-preservation is unable to cope with the power of his delirium, and for the same reason he is often enough ready, without further ado, to suffer martyrdom. Weak-minded or mentally-unbalanced persons, coming into contact with a man possessed by delirium, are at once conquered by the strength of his diseased ideas, and are converted to them. By separating them from the source of inspiration, it is often possible to cure them of their transmitted delirium, but frequently their acquired derangement outlasts this separation.

This is the natural history of the æsthetic schools. Under the influence of an obsession, a degenerate mind promulgates some doctrine or other—realism, pornography, mysticism, symbolism, diabolism. He does this with vehement penetrating eloquence, with eagerness and fiery heedlessness. Other degenerate, hysterical, neurasthenical minds flock around him, receive from his lips the new doctrine, and live thenceforth only to propagate it.

In this case all the participants are sincere—the founder as well as the disciples. They act as, in consequence of the diseased constitution of their brain and nervous system, they are compelled to act. The picture, however, which from a clinical standpoint is perfectly clear, gets dimmed if the apostle of a craze and his followers succeed in attracting to themselves the attention of wider circles. He then receives a concourse of unbelievers, who are very well able to recognise the insanity of the new doctrine, but who nevertheless accept it, because they hope, as associates of the new sect, to acquire fame and money. In every civilized nation which has a developed art and literature there are numerous intellectual eunuchs, incapable of producing with their own powers a living mental work, but quite able to imitate the process of production. These cripples

* Legrain, *op. cit.*, p. 173: 'The true explanation of the occurrence of *folie à deux* must be sought for, on the one hand, in the predisposition to insanity, and, on the other hand, in the accompanying weakness of mind.' See also Régis, *La Folie à Deux*. Paris, 1880.

form, unfortunately, the majority of professional authors and artists, and their many noxious followers often enough stifle true and original talent. Now it is these who hasten to act as camp-followers for every new tendency which seems to come into fashion. They are naturally the most modern of moderns, for no precept of individuality, no artistic knowledge, hinders them from bunglingly imitating the newest model with all the assiduity of an artisan. Clever in discerning externals, unscrupulous copyists and plagiarists, they crowd round every original phenomenon, be it healthy or unhealthy, and without loss of time set about disseminating counterfeit copies of it. To-day they are symbolists, as yesterday they were realists or pornographists. If they can promise themselves fame and a good sale, they write of mysteries with the same fluency as if they were spinning romances of knights and robbers, tales of adventure, Roman tragedies, and village stories at a time when newspaper critics and the public seemed to demand these things in preference to others. Now these practitioners, who, let it be again asserted, constitute the great majority of the mental workers of the fashionable sects in art and literature, and therefore of the associates of these sects also, are intellectually quite sane, even if they stand at a very low level of development, and were anyone to examine them, he might easily doubt the accuracy of the diagnosis, 'Degeneration' as regards the confessors of the new doctrines. Hence some caution must be exercised in the inquiry, and the sincere originators be always distinguished from the aping intriguers, —the founder of the religion and his apostles from the rabble to whom the Sermon on the Mount is of less concern than the miraculous draught of fishes and the multiplication of loaves.

It has now been shown how schools originate. They arise from the degeneration of their founders and of the imitators they have convinced. That they come into fashion, and for a short time attain a noisy success, is due to the peculiarities of the recipient public, namely, to hysteria. We have seen that hypersusceptibility to suggestion is the distinguishing characteristic of hysteria. The same power of obsession with which the degenerate in mind wins imitators, gathers round him adherents. When a hysterical person is loudly and unceasingly assured that a work is beautiful, deep, pregnant with the future, he believes in it. He believes in everything suggested to him with sufficient impressiveness. When the little cow-girl, Bernadette, saw the vision of the Holy Virgin in the grotto of Lourdes, the women devotees and hysterical males of the surrounding country who flocked thither did not merely believe that the hallucinant maiden had herself seen the vision, but all of them saw the Holy Virgin with their own eyes. M. E. de

Goncourt* relates that in 1870, during the Franco-Prussian War, a multitude of men, numbering tens of thousands, in and before the Bourse in Paris, were convinced that they had themselves seen—indeed, a part of them had read—a telegram announcing French victories fastened to a pillar inside the Exchange, and at which people were pointing with their finger; but as a matter of fact it never existed. It would be possible to cite examples by the dozen, of illusions of the senses suggested to excited crowds. Thus the hysterical allow themselves without more ado to be convinced of the magnificence of a work, and even find in it beauties of the highest kind, unthought of by the authors themselves and the appointed trumpeters of their fame. If the sect is so completely established that, in addition to the founders, the priests of the temple, the paid sacristans and choir-boys, it has a congregation, processions, and far-sounding bells, it then attaches to itself other converts besides the hysterical who have accepted the new belief by way of suggestion. Young persons without judgment, still seeking their way, go whither they see the multitude streaming, and unhesitatingly follow the procession, because they believe it to be marching on the right road. Superficial persons, fearing nothing so much as to be thought behind the times, attach themselves to the procession, shouting 'Hurrah!' and 'All hail!' so as to convince themselves that they also are really dancing along before the latest conqueror and newest celebrity. Decrepit graybeards, filled with a ridiculous dread of betraying their real age, eagerly visit the new temple and mingle their quavering voices in the song of the devout, because they hope to be thought young when seen in an assembly in which young persons predominate.

Thus a regular concourse is established about a victim of degeneration. The fashionable coxcomb, the æsthetic 'gigerl,'† peeps over the shoulder of the hysterical whose admiration has been suggested to him; the intriguer marches at the heel of the dotard, simulating youth; and between all these comes pushing the inquisitive young street-loafer, who must always be in every place where 'something is going on.' And this crowd, because it is driven by disease, self-interest and vanity, makes very much more noise and bustle than a far larger number of sane men, who, without self-seeking after-thought, take quiet enjoyment in works of sane talent, and do not feel obliged to shout out their appreciation in the streets, and to threaten with death harmless passers-by who do not join in their jubilations.

* *Journal des Goncourt.* Dernière série, premier volume, 1870-71. Paris, 1890, p. 17.

† Viennese for 'fop.'—TRANSLATOR.

3

CHAPTER IV.

ETIOLOGY.

WE have recognised the effect of diseases in these *fin-de-siècle* literary and artistic tendencies and fashions, as well as in the susceptibility of the public with regard to them, and we have succeeded in maintaining that these diseases are degeneracy and hysteria. We have now to inquire how these maladies of the day have originated, and why they appear with such extraordinary frequency at the present time.

Morel,* the great investigator of degeneracy, traces this chiefly to poisoning. A race which is regularly addicted, even without excess, to narcotics and stimulants in any form (such as fermented alcoholic drinks, tobacco, opium, hashish, arsenic), which partakes of tainted foods (bread made with bad corn), which absorbs organic poisons (marsh fever, syphilis, tuberculosis, goitre), begets degenerate descendants who, if they remain exposed to the same influences, rapidly descend to the lowest degrees of degeneracy, to idiocy, to dwarfishness, etc. That the poisoning of civilized peoples continues and increases at a very rapid rate is widely attested by statistics.† The consumption of tobacco has risen in France from 0·8 kilogramme per head in 1841 to 1·9 kilogrammes in 1890. The corresponding figures for England are 13 and 26 ounces;‡ for Germany, 0·8 and 1·5 kilogrammes. The consumption of alcohol§ during

* *Traité des Dégénérescences, passim.*

† Personally communicated by the distinguished statistician, Herr Josef Körösi, Head of the Bureau of Statistics at Budapest.

‡ Speech of the Chancellor of the Exchequer, Mr. Goschen, in the House of Commons, April 11, 1892.

§ J. Vavasseur in the *Economiste français* of 1890. See also *Bulletin de Statistique* for 1891. The figures are uncertain, for they have been given differently by every statistician whom I have consulted. The fact of the increase in the consumption of alcohol alone stands out with certainty in all the publications consulted. Besides spirits, fermented drinks are consumed per head of the population, according to J. Körösi :

GREAT BRITAIN.

	Wine. Gall.	Beer and Cider. Gall.
1830—1850	0·2	26
1880—1888	0·4	27

FRANCE.

1840—1842	23	3
1870—1872	25	6

the same period has risen in Germany (1844) from 5·45 quarts to (1867) 6·86 quarts; in England from 2·01 litres to 2·64 litres; in France from 1·33 to 4 litres. The increase in the consumption of opium and hashish is still greater, but we need not concern ourselves about that, since the chief sufferers from them are Eastern peoples, who play no part in the intellectual development of the white races. To these noxious influences, however, one more may be added, which Morel has not known, or has not taken into consideration—residence in large towns. The inhabitant of a large town, even the richest, who is surrounded by the greatest luxury, is continually exposed to unfavourable influences which diminish his vital powers far more than what is inevitable. He breathes an atmosphere charged with organic detritus; he eats stale, contaminated, adulterated food; he feels himself in a state of constant nervous excitement, and one can compare him without exaggeration to the inhabitant of a marshy district. The effect of a large town on the human organism offers the closest analogy to that of the Maremma, and its population falls victim to the same fatality of degeneracy and destruction as the victims of malaria. The death-rate in a large town is more than a quarter greater than the average for the entire population; it is double that of the open country, though in reality it ought to be less, since in a large town the most vigorous ages predominate, during which the mortality is lower than in infancy and old age.* And the children of large towns who are not carried off at an early age suffer from the peculiar arrested development which Morel† has ascertained in the population of fever districts. They develop more or less normally until fourteen or fifteen years of age, are up to that time alert, sometimes brilliantly endowed, and give the highest promise; then suddenly there is a standstill, the mind loses its facility of comprehension, and the boy who, only yesterday, was a model scholar, becomes an obtuse, clumsy dunce, who can only be steered with the greatest

---

PRUSSIA.

	Quarts.
1839	13·48
1871	17 92

GERMAN EMPIRE.

	Litres.
1872	81·7
1889—1890	90·3

* In France the general mortality was, from 1886 to 1890, 22·21 per 1,000. But in Paris it rose to 23·4; in Marseilles to 34·8; in all towns with more than 100,000 inhabitants to a mean of 28·31; in all places with less than 5,000 inhabitants to 21·74. (*La Médecine moderne*, year 1891.)

† *Traité des Dégénérescences*, pp. 614, 615.

difficulty through his examinations. With these mental changes bodily modifications go hand in hand. The growth of the long bones is extremely slow, or ceases entirely, the legs remain short, the pelvis retains a feminine form, certain other organs cease to develop, and the entire being presents a strange and repulsive mixture of incompleteness and decay.*

Now we know how, in the last generation, the number of the inhabitants of great towns increased† to an extraordinary degree. At the present time an incomparably larger portion of the whole population is subjected to the destructive influences of large towns than was the case fifty years ago; hence the number of victims is proportionately more striking, and continually becomes more remarkable. Parallel with the growth of large towns is the increase in the number of the degenerate of all kinds—criminals, lunatics, and the 'higher degenerates' of Magnan; and it is natural that these last should play an ever more prominent part in endeavouring to introduce an ever greater element of insanity into art and literature.

The enormous increase of hysteria in our days is partly due to the same causes as degeneracy, besides which there is one cause much more general still than the growth of large towns—a cause which perhaps of itself would not be sufficient to bring about degeneracy, but which is unquestionably quite enough to produce hysteria and neurasthenia. This cause is the fatigue of the present generation. That hysteria is in reality a consequence of fatigue Féré has conclusively demonstrated by convincing experiments. In a communication to the Biological Society of Paris, this distinguished investigator says:‡ 'I have recently observed a certain number of facts which have made apparent the analogy existing between fatigue and the chronic condition of the hysterical. One knows that among the hysterical [involuntary!] symmetry of move-

* Brouardel, *La Semaine médicale.* Paris, 1887, p. 254. In this very remarkable study by the Parisian Professor, the following passage appears: 'What will these [those remaining stationary in their development] young Parisians become by-and-by? Incapable of accomplishing a long and conscientious work, they excel, as a rule, in artistic activities. If they are painters they are stronger in colour than in drawing. If they are poets, the flow of their verses assures their success rather than the vigour of the thought.'

† The 26 German towns which to-day have more than 100,000 inhabitants, numbered altogether, in 1891, 6,000,000, and in 1835 1,400,000. The 31 English towns of this category, in 1891, 10,870,000; in 1841, 4,590,000; the 11 French towns, in 1891, 4,180,000; in 1836, 1,710,000. It should be remarked that about a third of these 68 towns had not in 1840 as many generally as 100,000 inhabitants. To-day, in the large towns in Germany, France, and England, there reside 21,050,000 individuals, while in 1840 only 4,800,000 were living under these conditions. (Communicated by Herr Josef Körösi.)

‡ Féré, *La Semaine médicale.* Paris, 1890, p. 192.

ments frequently shows itself in a very characteristic manner. I have proved that in normal subjects this same symmetry of movements is met with under the influence of fatigue. A phenomenon which shows itself in a very marked way in serious hysteria is that peculiar excitability which demonstrates that the energy of the voluntary movements, through peripheral stimulations or mental presentations, suffers rapid and transitory modifications co-existing with parallel modifications of sensibility, and of the functions of nutrition. This excitability can be equally manifested during fatigue. . . . Fatigue constitutes a true temporary experimental hysteria. It establishes a transition between the states which we call normal and the various states which we designate hysteria. One can change a normal into a hysterical individual by tiring him. . . . All these causes (which produce hysteria) can, as far as the pathogenic part they play is concerned, be traced to one simple physiological process—to fatigue, to depression of vitality.'

Now, to this cause—fatigue—which, according to Féré, changes healthy men into hysterical, the whole of civilized humanity has been exposed for half a century. All its conditions of life have, in this period of time, experienced a revolution unexampled in the history of the world. Humanity can point to no century in which the inventions which penetrate so deeply, so tyrannically, into the life of every individual are crowded so thick as in ours. The discovery of America, the Reformation, stirred men's minds powerfully, no doubt, and certainly also destroyed the equilibrium of thousands of brains which lacked staying power. But they did not change the material life of man. He got up and laid down, ate and drank, dressed, amused himself, passed his days and years as he had been always wont to do. In our times, on the contrary, steam and electricity have turned the customs of life of every member of the civilized nations upside down, even of the most obtuse and narrow-minded citizen, who is completely inaccessible to the impelling thoughts of the times.

In an exceptionally remarkable lecture by Professor A. W. von Hofmann, in 1890, before the Congress of German Natural Science held in Bremen, he gave, in concluding, a short description of the life of an inhabitant of a town in the year 1822. He shows us a student of science who at that date is arriving with the coach from Bremen to Leipzig. The journey has lasted four days and four nights, and the traveller is naturally stiff and bruised. His friends receive him, and he wishes to refresh himself a little. But there is yet no Munich beer in Leipzig. After a short interview with his comrades, he goes in search of his inn. This is no easy task, for in the streets an Egyptian darkness reigns, broken only at long distances by the smoky flame of an oil-lamp. He at last finds his quarters, and wishes for a light. As matches do not yet exist, he is reduced to bruising the tips of his fingers with flint and steel, till he succeeds at last in lighting a tallow candle. He expects a letter, but it has not come, and he cannot now receive it till after some days, for the post only runs twice a week between Frankfort and Leipzig.*

But it is unnecessary to go back to the year 1822, chosen by Professor Hofmann. Let us stop, for purposes of comparison, at the year 1840. This year has not been arbitrarily selected. It is about the date when that generation was born which has witnessed the irruption of new discoveries in every relation of life, and thus personally experienced those transformations which are the consequences. This generation reigns and governs to-day; it sets the tone everywhere, and its sons and daughters are the youth of Europe and America, in whom the new æsthetic tendencies gain their fanatical partisans. Let us now compare how things went on in the civilized world in 1840 and a half-century later.†

In 1840 there were in Europe 3,000 kilometres of railway; in 1891 there were 218,000 kilometres. The number of travellers in 1840, in Germany, France and England, amounted to 2½ millions; in 1891 it was 614 millions. In Germany every inhabitant received, in 1840, 85 letters; in 1888, 200 letters. In 1840 the post distributed in France 94 millions of letters; in England, 277 millions; in 1881, 595 and 1,299 millions respectively. The collective postal intercourse between all countries, without including the internal postage of each separate country, amounted, in 1840, to 92 millions; in 1889, to 2,759 millions. In Germany, in 1840, 305 newspapers were published; in 1891, 6,800; in France, 776 and 5,182; in England (1846), 551 and 2,255. The German book trade produced, in 1840, 1,100 new works; in 1891, 18,700. The exports and imports of the world had, in 1840, a value of 28, in 1889 of 74, milliards of marks. The ships which, in 1840, entered all the ports of Great Britain contained 9½, in 1890 74½, millions of tons. The whole British merchant navy measured, in 1840, 3,200,000; in 1890, 9,688,000 tons.

* See, besides the lecture by Hofmann, the excellent book: *Eine deutsche Stadt vor 60 Jahren, Kulturgeschichtliche Skizze*, von Dr. Otto Bähr, 2 Auflage. Leipzig, 1891.

† In order not to make the footnotes too unwieldy, I state here that the following figures are borrowed in part from communications made by Herr Josef Körösi, in part from a remarkable study by M. Charles Richet: 'Dans Cent Ans,' *Revue scientifique*, 1891-92; and in a small degree from private publications (such as *Annuaire de la Presse*, *Press Directory*, etc.). For some of the figures I have also used, with profit, Mulhall, and the speech of Herr von Stephan to the Reichstag, February 4, 1892.

Let us now consider how these formidable figures arise. The 18,000 new publications, the 6,800 newspapers in Germany, desire to be read, although many of them desire in vain; the 2,759 millions of letters must be written; the larger commercial transactions, the numerous journeys, the increased marine intercourse, imply a correspondingly greater activity in individuals. The humblest village inhabitant has to-day a wider geographical horizon, more numerous and complex intellectual interests, than the prime minister of a petty, or even a second-rate state a century ago. If he do but read his paper, let it be the most innocent provincial rag, he takes part, certainly not by active interference and influence, but by a continuous and receptive curiosity, in the thousand events which take place in all parts of the globe, and he interests himself simultaneously in the issue of a revolution in Chili, in a bush-war in East Africa, a massacre in North China, a famine in Russia, a street-row in Spain, and an international exhibition in North America. A cook receives and sends more letters than a university professor did formerly, and a petty tradesman travels more and sees more countries and people than did the reigning prince of other times.

All these activities, however, even the simplest, involve an effort of the nervous system and a wearing of tissue. Every line we read or write, every human face we see, every conversation we carry on, every scene we perceive through the window of the flying express, sets in activity our sensory nerves and our brain centres. Even the little shocks of railway travelling, not perceived by consciousness, the perpetual noises, and the various sights in the streets of a large town, our suspense pending the sequel of progressing events, the constant expectation of the newspaper, of the postman, of visitors, cost our brains wear and tear. In the last fifty years the population of Europe has not doubled, whereas the sum of its labours has increased tenfold, in part even fifty-fold. Every civilized man furnishes, at the present time, from five to twenty-five times as much work as was demanded of him half a century ago.

This enormous increase in organic expenditure has not, and cannot have, a corresponding increase of supply. Europeans now eat a little more and a little better than they did fifty years ago, but by no means in proportion to the increase of effort which to-day is required of them. And even if they had the choicest food in the greatest abundance, it would do nothing towards helping them, for they would be incapable of digesting it. Our stomachs cannot keep pace with the brain and nervous system. The latter demand very much more than the former are able to perform. And so there follows what always happens if great expenses are met by small incomes; first the savings are consumed, then comes bankruptcy.

Its own new discoveries and progress have taken civilized humanity by surprise. It has had no time to adapt itself to its changed conditions of life. We know that our organs acquire by exercise an ever greater functional capacity, that they develop by their own activity, and can respond to nearly every demand made upon them; but only under one condition—that this occurs gradually, that time be allowed them. If they are obliged to fulfil, without transition, a multiple of their usual task, they soon give out entirely. No time was left to our fathers. Between one day and the next, as it were, without preparation, with murderous suddenness, they were obliged to change the comfortable creeping gait of their former existence for the stormy stride of modern life, and their heart and lungs could not bear it. The strongest could keep up, no doubt, and even now, at the most rapid pace, no longer lose their breath, but the less vigorous soon fell out right and left, and fill to-day the ditches on the road of progress.

To speak without metaphor, statistics indicate in what measure the sum of work of civilized humanity has increased during the half-century. It had not quite grown to this increased effort. It grew fatigued and exhausted, and this fatigue and exhaustion showed themselves in the first generation, under the form of acquired hysteria; in the second, as hereditary hysteria.

The new æsthetic schools and their success are a form of this general hysteria; but they are far from being the only one. The malady of the period shows itself in yet many other phenomena which can be measured and counted, and thus are susceptible of being scientifically established. And these positive and unambiguous symptoms of exhaustion are well adapted to enlighten the ignorant, who might believe at first sight that the specialist acts arbitrarily in tracing back fashionable tendencies in art and literature to states of fatigue in civilized humanity.

It has become a commonplace to speak of the constant increase of crime, madness and suicide. In 1840, in Prussia, out of 100,000 persons of criminally responsible age, there were 714 convictions; in 1888, 1,102 (from a letter communicated by the Prussian bureau of statistics). In 1865, in every 10,000 Europeans there were 63 suicides; in 1883, 109; and since that time the number has increased considerably. In the last twenty years a number of new nervous diseases have been discovered and named.* Let it not be believed that they always existed, and were merely overlooked. If they had been

* See G. André, *Les nouvelles maladies nerveuses.* Paris, 1892.

met with anywhere they would have been detected, for even if the theories which prevailed in medicine at various periods were erroneous, there have always been perspicacious and attentive physicians who knew how to observe. If, then, the new nervous diseases were not noticed, it is because they did not formerly appear. And they are exclusively a consequence of the present conditions of civilized life. Many affections of the nervous system already bear a name which implies that they are a direct consequence of certain influences of modern civilization. The terms 'railway-spine' and 'railway-brain,' which the English and American pathologists have given to certain states of these organs, show that they recognise them as due partly to the effects of railway accidents, partly to the constant vibrations undergone in railway travelling. Again, the great increase in the consumption of narcotics and stimulants, which has been shown in the figures above, has its origin unquestionably in the exhausted systems with which the age abounds. There is here a disastrous, vicious circle of reciprocal effects. The drinker (and apparently the smoker also) begets enfeebled children, hereditarily fatigued or degenerated, and these drink and smoke in their turn, because they are fatigued. These crave for a stimulus, for a momentary, artificial invigoration, or an alleviation of their painful excitability, and then, when they recognise that this increases, in the long-run, their exhaustion as well as their excitability, they cannot, through weakness of will, resist those habits.*

Many observers assert that the present generation ages much more rapidly than the preceding one. Sir James Crichton-Browne points out this effect of modern circumstances on contemporaries in his speech at the opening of the winter term, 1891, before the medical faculty of the Victoria University.† From 1859 to 1863 there died in England, of heart-disease, 92,181 persons; from 1884 to 1888, 224,102. Nervous complaints carried off from 1864 to 1868, 196,000 persons; from 1884 to 1888, 260,558. The difference of figures would have been still more striking if Sir James had chosen a more remote period for comparison with the present, for in 1865 the high pressure under which the English worked was already nearly as great as in 1885. The dead carried off by heart and nerve diseases are the victims of civilization. The heart and nervous system first break down under the overstrain. Sir James in his speech says further on: 'Men and women grow

* Legrain, *op. cit.*, p. 251: 'Drinkers are "degenerates";' and p. 258 (after four reports of invalids which serve as a basis to the following summary): 'Hence, at the base of all forms of alcoholism we find mental degeneracy.'

† *Revue scientifique*, year 1892; vol. xlix., p. 168 *et seq.*

old before their time. Old age encroaches upon the period of vigorous manhood. . . . Deaths due exclusively to old age are found reported now between the ages of forty-five and fifty-five. . . .' Mr. Critchett (an eminent oculist) says: 'My own experience, which extends now over a quarter of a century, leads me to believe that men and women, in the present day, seek the aid of spectacles at a less advanced period of life than their ancestors. . . . Previously men had recourse to spectacles at the age of fifty. The average age is now forty-five years.' Dentists assert that teeth decay and fall out at an earlier age than formerly. Dr. Lieving attests the same respecting the hair, and assures us that precocious baldness is to be specially observed 'among persons of nervous temperaments and active mind, but of weak general health.' Everyone who looks round the circle of his friends and acquaintances will remark that the hair begins to turn gray much sooner than in former days. Most men and women show their first white hairs at the beginning of the thirties, many of them at a very much younger age. Formerly white hair was the accompaniment of the fiftieth year.

All the symptoms enumerated are the consequences of states of fatigue and exhaustion, and these, again, are the effect of contemporary civilization, of the vertigo and whirl of our frenzied life, the vastly increased number of sense impressions and organic reactions, and therefore of perceptions, judgments, and motor impulses, which at present are forced into a given unity of time. To this general cause of contemporary pathological phenomena, one may be added special to France. By the frightful loss of blood which the body of the French people suffered during the twenty years of the Napoleonic wars, by the violent moral upheavals to which they were subjected in the great Revolution and during the imperial epic, they found themselves exceedingly ill-prepared for the impact of the great discoveries of the century, and sustained by these a more violent shock than other nations more robust and more capable of resistance. Upon this nation, nervously strained and predestined to morbid derangement, there broke the awful catastrophe of 1870. It had, with a self-satisfaction which almost attained to megalomania, believed itself the first nation in the world; it now saw itself suddenly humiliated and crushed. All its convictions abruptly crumbled to pieces. Every single Frenchman suffered reverses of fortune, lost some members of his family, and felt himself personally robbed of his dearest conceptions, nay, even of his honour. The whole people fell into the condition of a man suddenly visited by a crushing blow of destiny, in his fortune, his position, his family, his reputation, even in his self-respect. Thousands lost their reason. In

Paris a veritable epidemic of mental diseases was observed, for which a special name was found—*la folie obsidionale*, 'siege-madness.' And even those who did not at once succumb to mental derangement, suffered lasting injury to their nervous system. This explains why hysteria and neurasthenia are much more frequent in France, and appear under such a greater variety of forms, and why they can be studied far more closely in this country than anywhere else. But it explains, too, that it is precisely in France that the craziest fashions in art and literature would necessarily arise, and that it is precisely there that the morbid exhaustion of which we have spoken became for the first time sufficiently distinct to consciousness to allow a special name to be coined for it, namely, the designation of *fin-de-siècle*.

The proposition which I set myself to prove may now be taken as demonstrated. In the civilized world there obviously prevails a twilight mood which finds expression, amongst other ways, in all sorts of odd æsthetic fashions. All these new tendencies, realism or naturalism, 'decadentism,' neo-mysticism, and their sub-varieties, are manifestations of degeneration and hysteria, and identical with the mental stigmata which the observations of clinicists have unquestionably established as belonging to these. But both degeneration and hysteria are the consequences of the excessive organic wear and tear suffered by the nations through the immense demands on their activity, and through the rank growth of large towns.

Led by this firmly linked chain of causes and effects, everyone capable of logical thought will recognise that he commits a serious error if, in the æsthetic schools which have sprung up in the last few years, he sees the heralds of a new era. They do not direct us to the future, but point backwards to times past. Their word is no ecstatic prophecy, but the senseless stammering and babbling of deranged minds, and what the ignorant hold to be the outbursts of gushing, youthful vigour and turbulent constructive impulses are really nothing but the convulsions and spasms of exhaustion.

We should not allow ourselves to be deceived by certain catch-words, frequently uttered in the works of these professed innovators. They talk of socialism, of emancipation of the mind, etc., and thereby create the outward show of being deeply imbued with the thoughts and struggles of the times. But this is empty sham. The catch-words in vogue are scattered through the works without internal sequence, and the struggles of the times are merely painted on the outside. It is a phenomenon observed in every kind of mania, that it receives its special colouring from the degree of culture of the invalid, and from the views prevailing at the times in which he lived.

The Catholic who is a prey to megalomania fancies he is the Pope; the Jew, that he is the Messiah; the German, that he is the Emperor or a field-marshal; the Frenchman, that he is the President of the Republic. In the persecution-mania, the invalid of former days complained of the wickedness and knavery of magicians and witches; to-day he grumbles because his imaginary enemies send electric streams through his nerves, and torment him with magnetism. The degenerates of to-day chatter of Socialism and Darwinism, because these words, and, in the best case, the ideas connected with these, are in current use. These so-called socialist and freethinking works of the degenerate as little advance the development of society towards more equitable economic forms, and more rational views of the relations among phenomena, as the complaints and descriptions of an individual suffering from persecution-mania, and who holds electricity responsible for his disagreeable sensations, advance the knowledge of this force of nature. Those obscure or superficially verbose works which pretend to offer solutions for the serious questions of our times, or, at least, to prepare the way thereto, are even impediments and causes of delay, because they bewilder weak or unschooled brains, suggest to them erroneous views, and make them either more inaccessible to rational information or altogether closed to it.

The reader is now placed at those points of view whence he can see the new æsthetic tendencies in their true light and their real shape. It will be the task of the following books to demonstrate the pathological character of each one of these tendencies, and to inquire what particular species of degenerate delirium or hysterical psychological process they are related to or identical with.

BOOK II.

MYSTICISM.

CHAPTER I.

THE PSYCHOLOGY OF MYSTICISM.

We have already learnt to see in mysticism a principal characteristic of degeneration. It follows so generally in the train of the latter, that there is scarcely a case of degeneration in which it does not appear. To cite authorities for this is about as unnecessary as to adduce proof for the fact that in typhus a rise in the temperature of the body is invariably observed. I will therefore only repeat one remark of Legrain's:* 'Mystical thoughts are to be laid to the account of the insanity of the degenerate. There are two states in which they are observed—in epilepsy and in hysterical delirium.' When Federoff,† who makes mention of religious delirium and ecstasy as among the accompanying features of an attack of hysteria, puts them down as a peculiarity of women, he commits an error, since they are at least as common in male hysterical and degenerate subjects as in female.

What is really to be understood by this somewhat vague term 'mysticism'? The word describes a state of mind in which the subject imagines that he perceives or divines unknown and inexplicable relations amongst phenomena, discerns in things hints at mysteries, and regards them as symbols, by which a dark power seeks to unveil or, at least, to indicate all sorts of marvels which he endeavours to guess, though generally in vain. This condition of mind is always connected with strong emotional excitement, which consciousness conceives to be the result of its presentiments, although it is this excitement, on the contrary, which is pre-existent, while the presentiments are caused by it and receive from it their peculiar direction and colour.

* Legrain, *op. cit.*, p. 266.

† Quoted by J. Roubinovitch, *Hystérie mâle et Dégénérescence*, p. 18.

All phenomena in the world and in life present themselves in a different light to the mystic from what they do to the sane man. The simplest word uttered before the former appears to him an allusion to something mysteriously occult; in the most commonplace and natural movements he sees hidden signs. All things have for him deep backgrounds; far-reaching shadows are thrown by them over adjacent tracts; they send out wide-spreading roots into remote substrata. Every image that rises up in his mind points with mysterious silence, though with significant look and finger, to other images distinct or shadowy, and induces him to set up relations between ideas, where other people recognise no connection. In consequence of this peculiarity of his mind, the mystic lives as if surrounded by sinister forms, from behind whose masks enigmatic eyes look forth, and whom he contemplates with constant terror, since he is never sure of recognising any shapes among the disguises which press upon him. 'Things are not what they seem' is the characteristic expression frequently heard from the mystic. In the history of a 'degenerate' in the clinics of Magnan* it is written: 'A child asks drink of him at a public fountain. He finds this unnatural. The child follows him. This fills him with astonishment. Another time he sees a woman sitting on a curb-stone. He asks himself what that could possibly mean.' In extreme cases this morbid attitude amounts to hallucinations, which, as a rule, affect the hearing; but it can also influence sight and the other senses. When this is so, the mystic does not confine himself to conjectures and guesses at mysteries in and behind phenomena, but hears and sees as real, things which for the sane man are non-existent.

Pathological observation of the insane is content to describe this mental condition, and to determine its occurrence in the hysterical and degenerate. That, however, is not the end of the matter. We also want to know in what manner the degenerate or exhausted brain falls into mysticism. In order to understand the subject, we must refer to some simple facts in the growth of the mind.†

Conscious intellection is activity of the gray surface of the brain, a tissue consisting of countless nerve-cells united by nerve-fibres. In this tissue the nerves, both of the external bodily surface and of the internal organs, terminate. When one of these nerves is excited (the nerve of vision by a ray of

* Legrain, *op. cit.*, p. 200.

† The scientific psychologist will perhaps read with impatience expositions with which he is so familiar; but they are, unfortunately, not superfluous for a very numerous class of even highly educated persons, who have never had instruction in the laws of the operations of the brain.

light, a nerve in the skin by contact, an organic nerve by internal chemical action, etc.), it at once conveys the excitement to the nerve-cell in the cerebral cortex in which it debouches. This cell undergoes in consequence chemical changes, which, in a healthy condition of the organism, are in direct relation to the strength of the stimulus. The nerve-cell, which is immediately affected by the stimulus conveyed to it by the conducting nerve, propagates in its turn the stimulus received to all the neighbouring cells with which it is connected by fibrous processes. The disturbance spreads itself on all sides, like a wave-circle that is caused by any object thrown into water, and subsides gradually exactly as does the wave—more quickly or more slowly, with greater or less diffusion, as the stimulus that caused it has been stronger or weaker.

Every stimulus which reaches a place on the cerebral cortex results in a rush of blood to that spot,* by means of which nutriment is conveyed to it. The brain-cells decompose these substances, and transmute the stored-up energy in them into other forms of energy, namely, into ideas and motor impulses.† How an idea is formed out of the decomposition of tissues, how a chemical process is metamorphosed into consciousness, nobody knows; but the fact that conscious ideas are connected with the process of decomposition of tissues in the stimulated brain-cells is not a matter of doubt.‡

In addition to the fundamental property in the nerve-cells of responding to a stimulus produced by chemical action, they have also the capacity of preserving an image of the strength and character of this stimulus. To put it popularly, the cell is able to remember its impressions. If now a new, although it may be a weaker, disturbance reach this cell, it rouses in it an image of similar stimuli which had previously reached it, and this memory-image strengthens the new stimulus, making it more distinct and more intelligible to consciousness. If the cell could not remember, consciousness would be ever

* Mosso's experiments on, and observations of, the exposed surface of the brain during trepanning have quite established this fact.

† The experiments of Ferrier, it is true, have led him to deny that a stimulus which touches the cortex of the frontal lobes can result in movement. The case, nevertheless, is not so simple as Ferrier sees it to be. A portion of the energy which is set free by the peripheral stimulus in the cells of the cortex of the frontal lobes certainly transmutes itself into a motor impulse, even if the immediate stimulation of the anterior brain releases no muscular contractions. But this is not the place to defend this point against Ferrier.

‡ A. Herzen is the author of the hypothesis that consciousness is connected with the destruction of organic connections in the brain-cells, and the restoration of this connection with rest, sleep, and unconsciousness. All we know of the chemical composition of the secretions in sleeping and waking points to the correctness of this hypothesis.

incapable of interpreting its impressions, and could never succeed in attaining to a presentation of the outer world. Particular direct stimuli would certainly be perceived, but they would remain without connection or import, since they are by themselves, and without the assistance of earlier impressions, inadequate to lead to knowledge. Memory is therefore the first condition of normal brain activity.

The stimulus which reaches a brain-cell gives rise, as we have seen, to an expansion of this stimulus to the neighbouring cells, to a wave of stimulus proceeding in all directions. And since every stimulus is connected with the rise of conscious presentations, it proves that every stimulus calls a large number of presentations into consciousness, and not only such presentations as are related to the immediate external cause of the stimulation perceived, but also such as are only aroused by the cells that elaborate them happening to lie in the vicinity of that cell, or group of cells, which the external stimulus has immediately reached. The wave of stimulus, like every other wave-motion, is strongest at its inception; it subsides in direct ratio to the widening of its circle, till at last it vanishes into the imperceptible. Corresponding to this, the presentations, having their seat in cells which are in the immediate neighbourhood of those first reached by the stimulus, are the most lively, while those arising from the more distant cells are somewhat less distinct, and this distinctness continues to decrease until consciousness can no longer perceive them—until they, as science expresses it, sink beneath the threshold of consciousness. Each particular stimulus arouses, therefore, not only in the cell to which it was directly led, but also in countless other contiguous and connected cells, the activity which is bound up with presentation. Thus arise simultaneously, or, more accurately, following each other in an immeasurably short interval of time, thousands of impressions of regularly decreasing distinctness; and since unnumbered thousands of external and internal organic stimuli are carried to the brain, so continually thousands of stimulus-waves are coursing through it, crossing and intersecting each other with the greatest diversity, and in their course arousing millions of emerging, waning, and vanishing impressions. It is this that Goethe means when he depicts in such splendid language how

'. . . ein Tritt tausend Fäden regt,
Die Schifflein herüber, hinüber schiessen,
Die Fäden ungesehen fliessen,
Ein Schlag tausend Verbindungen schlägt.'*

* 'One tread moves a thousand threads,
The shuttles dart to and fro,
The threads flow on invisible,
One stroke sets up a thousand ties.'

Now, memory is a property not only of the nerve-cell, but also of the nerve-fibre, which is only a modification of the cell. The fibre has a recollection of the stimulus which it conveyed, in the same way as the cell has of that which it has transformed into presentation and motion. A stimulus will be more easily conducted by a fibre which has already conveyed it, than by one which propagates it for the first time from one cell to another. Every stimulus which reaches a cell will take the line of least resistance, and this will be set out for it along those nerve-tracks which it has already traversed. Thus a definite path is formed for the course of a stimulus-wave, a customary line of march; it is always the same nerve-cells which exchange mutually their stimulus-waves. Presentation always awakens the same resulting presentations, and always appears in consciousness accompanied by them. This procedure is called the association of ideas.

It is neither volition nor accident that determines to which other cells a disturbed cell habitually communicates its stimulus, which accompanying impressions an aroused presentation draws with it into consciousness. On the contrary, the linking of presentations is dependent upon laws which Wundt especially has well formulated.

Those who have not been born blind and deaf (like the unfortunate Laura Bridgman, cited by all psychologists) will never be influenced by one external stimulus only, but invariably by many stimuli at once. Every single phenomenon of the outer world has, as a rule, not only one quality, but many; and since that which we call a quality is the assumed cause of a definite sensation, it results that phenomena appeal at once to several senses, are simultaneously seen, heard, felt, and moreover are seen in different degrees of light and colour, heard in various nuances of timbre, etc. The few phenomena which possess only one quality and arouse therefore only one sense, *e.g.*, thunder, which is only heard, although with varying intensity, occur nevertheless in conjunction with other phenomena, such as, to keep to thunder, with a clouded sky, lightning and rain. Our brains are therefore accustomed to receive at once from every phenomenon several stimuli, which proceed partly from the many qualities of the phenomenon itself, and partly from the phenomena usually accompanying it. Now, it is sufficient that only one of these stimuli should reach the brain, in order to call into life, in virtue of the habitual association of the memory-images, the remaining stimuli of the same group as well. Simultaneity of impressions is therefore a cause of the association of ideas.

One and the same quality belongs to many phenomena. There is a whole series of things which are blue, round, and smooth. The possession of a common quality is a condition of similarity, which is greater in proportion to the number of common qualities. Every single quality, however, belongs to a habitually associated group of qualities, and can by the mechanism of simultaneity arouse the memory-image of this group. In consequence of their similarity, therefore, the memory-images can be aroused of all those groups, which resemble each other in some quality. The colour blue is a quality which belongs equally to the cheerful sky, the corn-flower, the sea, certain eyes, and many military uniforms. The perception of blue will awaken the memory of some or many blue things which are only related through their common colour. Similarity is therefore another cause of the association of ideas.

It is a distinctive characteristic of the brain-cell to elaborate at the same time both a presentation and its opposite. It is probable that what we perceive as its opposite is generally, in its original and simplest form, only the consciousness of the cessation of a certain presentation. As the fatigue of the optic nerve by a colour arouses the sensation of the complimentary colour, so, on the exhaustion of a brain-cell through the elaboration of a presentation, the contrary presentation appears in consciousness. Now, whether this interpretation be right or not, the fact itself is established through the 'contradictory double meaning of primitive roots,' discovered by K. Abel.* Contrast is the third cause of the association of ideas.

Many phenomena present themselves in the same place close to, or after, one another; and we associate there, presentation of the particular place with those objects, to which it is used to serve as a frame. Simultaneity, similarity, contrast, and occurrence in the same place (contiguity), are thus, according to Wundt, the four conditions under which phenomena will be connected in our consciousness through the association of ideas. To these James Sully† believes yet a fifth should be added: presentations which are rooted in the same emotion. Nevertheless all the examples cited by the distinguished English psychologist demonstrate without effort the action of one or more of Wundt's laws.

In order that an organism should maintain itself, it must be in a position to make use of natural resources, and protect itself from adverse conditions of every sort. It can accomplish this only if it possess a knowledge of these adverse conditions, and of such natural resources as it can use; and it can do this better and more surely the more complete this knowledge is.

* Karl Abel, *Ueber den Gegensinn der Urworte*. Leipzig, 1884.
† James Sully, *Illusions*. London, 1881.

In the more highly differentiated organism it devolves upon the brain and nervous system to acquire knowledge of the outer world, and to turn that knowledge to the advantage of the organism. Memory makes it possible for the brain to perform its task, and the mechanism by which memory is made to serve the purport of knowledge is the association of ideas. For it is clear that a brain, in which a single perception awakens through the operation of the association of ideas a whole train of connected representations, will recognise, conceive and judge far more rapidly than one in which no association of ideas obtains, and which therefore would form only such concepts as had for their content direct sense-perceptions and such representations as originated in those cells which, by the accident of their contiguity, happened to lie in the circuit of a stimulus-wave. For the brain which works with association of ideas, the perception of a ray of light, of a tone, is sufficient, in order instantly to produce the presentation of the object from which the sensation proceeds, as well as of its relations in time and space, to group these presentations as concepts, and from these concepts to arrive at a judgment. To the brain without association of ideas that perception would only convey the presentation of having something bright or sonant in front of it. In addition, presentations would be aroused which had nothing in common with this bright or sonant something; it could form no image of the exciter of the sense, but it would first have to receive a train of further impressions from several or all of the senses, in order to learn to recognise the various properties of the object, of which at first only a tone or a colour was perceived, and to unite them in a single presentation. Even then the brain would only know in what the object consisted, *i.e.*, what it had in front of it, but not how the object stood in relation to other things, where and when it had already been perceived, and by what phenomena it was accompanied, etc. Knowledge of objects thus acquired would be wholly unadapted to the formation of a right judgment. It can now be seen what a great advantage was given to the organism in the struggle for existence by the association of ideas, and what immense progress in the development of the brain and its activity the acquirement of it signified.

But this is only true with a limitation. The association of ideas as such does not do more to lighten the task of the brain in apprehending and in judging than does the uprising throng of memory-images in the neighbourhood of the excited centre. The presentations, which the association of ideas calls into consciousness, stand, it is true, in somewhat closer connection with the phenomenon which has sent a stimulus to the brain, and by the latter has been perceived, than do those occurring in the geometrical circuit of the stimulus-wave; but even this connection is so slight, that it offers no efficient help in the interpretation of the phenomenon. We must not forget that properly all our perceptions, ideas, and conceptions are connected more or less closely through the association of ideas. As in the example cited above the sensation of blue arouses the ideas of the sky, the sea, a blue eye, a uniform, etc., so will each of these ideas arouse in its turn, according to Wundt's law, ideas associated with them. The sky will arouse the idea of stars, clouds and rain; the sea, that of ships, voyages, foreign lands, fishes, pearls, etc.; blue eyes, that of a girl's face, of love and all its emotions; in short, this one sensation, through the mechanism of the association of ideas, can arouse pretty well almost all the conceptions which we have ever at any time formed, and the blue object which we have in fact before our eyes and perceive, will, through this crowd of ideas which are not directly related to it, be neither interpreted nor explained.

In order, however, that the association of ideas may fulfil its functions in the operations of the brain, and prove itself a useful acquisition to the organism, one thing more must be added, namely, attention. This it is which brings order into the chaos of representations awakened by the association of ideas, and makes them subserve the purposes of cognition and judgment.

What is attention? Th. Ribot* defines this attribute as 'a spontaneous or an artificial adaptation of the individual to a predominating thought.' (I translate this definition freely because too long an explanation would be necessary to make the uninitiated comprehend the expressions made use of by Ribot.) In other words, attention is the faculty of the brain to suppress one part of the memory-images which, at each excitation of a cell or group of cells, have arisen in consciousness, by way either of association or of stimulus-wave; and to maintain another part, namely, only those memory-images which relate to the exciting cause, *i.e.*, to the object just perceived.

Who makes this selection among the memory-images? The stimulus itself, which rouses the brain-cells into activity. Naturally those cells would be the most strongly excited which are directly connected with the afferent nerves. Somewhat weaker is the excitement of the cells to which the cell first excited sends its impulse by way of the customary nerve channels; still weaker the excitement of those cells which, by the same mechanism, receive their stimulus from the secondarily excited cell. That idea will be the most powerful, therefore,

* Th. Ribot, *Psychologie de l'Attention.* Paris, 1889.

which is awakened directly by the perception itself; somewhat weaker that which is aroused by the first impression through association of ideas; weaker still that which the association in its turn involves. We know further that a phenomenon never produces a single stimulus, but several at once. If, for example, we see a man before us, we do not merely perceive a single point in him, but a larger or smaller portion of his exterior, *i.e.*, a large number of differently coloured and differently illuminated points; perhaps we hear him as well, possibly touch him, and, at all events, perceive besides him somewhat of his environment, of his spacial relations. Thus, there arise in our brain quite a number of centres of stimulation, operating simultaneously in the manner described above. There awakes in consciousness a series of primary presentations, which are stronger, *i.e.*, clearer, than the associated or consequent representations, namely, just those presentations which the man standing before us has himself aroused. They are like the brightest light-spots in the midst of others less brilliant. These brightest light-spots necessarily predominate in consciousness over the lesser ones. They fill the consciousness, which combines them in a judgment. For what we call a judgment is, in the last resort, nothing else than a simultaneous lighting up of a number of presentations in consciousness, which we in truth only bring into relation with each other because we ourselves became conscious of them at one and the same moment. The ascendency which the clearer presentations acquire over the more obscure, the primary presentations over derived representations, in consciousness, enables them, with the help of the will, to influence for a time the whole brain-activity to their own advantage, viz., to suppress the weaker, *i.e.*, the derived, representations; to combat those which cannot be made to agree with them; to reinforce, to draw into their circuit of stimulation, or simply to arouse, others, through which they themselves are reinforced and secure some duration in the midst of the constant emergence and disappearance of representations in their pursuit of each other. I myself conceive the interference of the will in this struggle for life amongst representations as giving motor impulses (even if unconsciously) to the muscles of the cerebral arteries. By this means the bloodvessels are dilated or contracted as required,* and the consequent supply of blood becomes more or

* It is possible that an active expansion of the bloodvessels does not take place, but only a contraction. It has been lately denied that there are any nerves of vascular dilatation (*inter alia* by Dr. Morat, *La Semaine médicale*, 1892, p. 112). But the effect may be the same in both cases. For through the contraction of the vessels in a single brain-circuit, the dislodged blood would be driven to other portions of the brain, and these would experience a greater access of blood, just as if their vessels were actively dilated.

less copious.* The cells which receive no blood must suspend their action; those which receive a larger supply can, on the contrary, operate more powerfully. The will which regulates the distribution of blood, when incited by a group of presentations temporarily predominating, thus resembles a servant who is constantly occupied in a room in carrying out the behests of his master: to light the gas in one place, in another to turn it up higher, in another to turn it off partly or wholly, so that at one moment this, and at another that, corner of the room becomes bright, dim, or dark. The preponderance of a group of presentations allows them during their period of power to bring into their service, not only the brain-cells, but the whole organism besides; and not only to fortify themselves through the representations which they arouse by way of association, but also to seek certain new sense-impressions, and repress others, in order, on the one hand, to obtain new excitations favourable to their persistence—new original perceptions—and on the other hand, through the exclusion of the rest, to ward off such excitations as are adverse to their persistence.

For instance, I see in the street a passer-by who for some reason arouses my attention. The attention immediately suppresses all other presentations which, an instant before, were in my consciousness, and permits those only to remain which refer to the passer-by. In order to intensify these presentations I look after him, *i.e.*, the ciliary and ocular muscles, then the muscles of the neck, perhaps also the muscles of the body and of the legs, receive motor impulses, which serve the purpose only of keeping up continually new sense-impressions of the object of my attention, by means of which the presentations of him are continuously strengthened and multiplied. I do not notice other persons who for the time come into my field of vision, I disregard the sounds which meet my ears, if my attention is strong enough I do not perhaps even hear them; but I should at once hear them if they proceeded from the particular passer-by, or if they had any reference to him.

This is the 'adaptation of the whole organism to a pre-

* When I wrote these words I was under the impression that I was the sole originator of the physiological theory of attention therein set forth. Since the appearance of this book, however, I have read Alfred Lehmann's work, *Die Hypnose und die damit verwandten normalen Zustände*, Leipzig, 1890, and have there (pp. 27 *et seq.*) found my theory in almost identical words. Lehmann, then, published it two years before I did, which fact I here duly acknowledge. That we arrived at this conclusion independently of each other would testify that the hypothesis of vaso-motor reflex action is really explanatory. Wundt (*Hypnotismus und Suggestion*, Leipzig, 1892, pp. 27-30), it is true, criticises Lehmann's work, but he seems to agree with this hypothesis—which is also mine—or, at least, raises no objection to it.

dominant idea' of which Ribot speaks. This it is which gives us exact knowledge of the external world. Without it that knowledge would be much more difficult of attainment, and would remain much more incomplete. This adaptation will continue until the cells, which are the bearers of the predominating presentations, become fatigued. They will then be compelled to surrender their supremacy to other groups of cells, whereupon the latter will obtain the power to adapt the organism to their purposes.

Thus we see it is only through attention that the faculty of association becomes a property advantageous to the organism, and attention is nothing but the faculty of the will to determine the emergence, degree of clearness, duration and extinction of presentations in consciousness. The stronger the will, so much the more completely can we adapt the whole organism to a given presentation, so much the more can we obtain sense impressions which serve to enhance this presentation, so much the more can we by association induce memory-images, which complete and rectify the presentation, so much the more definitely can we suppress the presentations which disturb it or are foreign to it; in a word, so much the more exhaustive and correct will our knowledge be of phenomena and their true connection.

Culture and command over the powers of nature are solely the result of attention; all errors, all superstition, the consequence of defective attention. False ideas of the connection between phenomena arise through defective observation of them, and will be rectified by a more exact observation. Now, to observe means nothing else than to convey deliberately determined sense-impressions to the brain, and thereby raise a group of presentations to such clearness and intensity that it can acquire preponderance in consciousness, arouse through association its allied memory-images, and suppress such as are incompatible with itself. Observation, which lies at the root of all progress, is thus the adaptation through attention of the sense-organs and their centres of perception to a presentation or group of presentations predominating in consciousness.

A state of attention allows no obscurity to persist in consciousness. For either the will strengthens every rising presentation to full clearness and distinctness, or, if it cannot do this, it extinguishes the idea completely. The consciousness of a healthy, strong-minded, and consequently attentive man, resembles a room in the full light of day, in which the eye sees all objects distinctly, in which all outlines are sharp, and wherein no indefinite shadows are floating.

Attention, therefore, presupposes strength of will, and this, again, is the property only of a normally constituted and unexhausted brain. In the degenerate, whose brain and nervous system are characterized by hereditary malformations or irregularities; in the hysterical, whom we have learnt to regard as victims of exhaustion, the will is entirely lacking, is possessed only in a small degree. The consequence of weakness or want of will is incapacity of attention. Alexander Starr* published twenty-three cases of lesions, or diseases of the convolutions of the brain, in which 'it was impossible for the patients to fix their attention'; and Ribot† remarks: 'A man who is tired after a long walk, a convalescent who has undergone a severe illness—in a word, all weakened persons are incapable of attention. . . . Inability to be attentive accompanies all forms of exhaustion.'

Untended and unrestrained by attention, the brain activity of the degenerate and hysterical is capricious, and without aim or purpose. Through the unrestricted play of association representations are called into consciousness, and are free to run riot there. They are aroused and extinguished automatically; and the will does not interfere to strengthen or to suppress them. Representations mutually alien or mutually exclusive appear continuously. The fact that they are retained in consciousness simultaneously, and at about the same intensity, combines them (in conformity with the laws of conscious activity) into a thought which is necessarily absurd, and cannot express the true relations of phenomena.

Weakness or want of attention, produces, then, in the first place, false judgments respecting the objective universe, respecting the qualities of things and their relations to each other. Consciousness acquires a distorted and blurred view of the external world. And there follows a further consequence. The chaotic course of stimuli along the channels of association and of the adjacent structures arouses the activity both of contiguous, of further, and of furthest removed groups of cells, which, left to themselves, act only so long and with such varying intensity as is proportionate to the intensity of the stimulus which has reached them. Clear, obscure, and yet obscurer representations rise in consciousness, which, after a time, disappear again, without having attained to greater distinctness than they had when first appearing. The clear representations produce a thought, but such a one as cannot for a moment become firmer or clearer, because the definite representations of which it is composed are mingled with others which consciousness perceives indistinctly, or scarcely perceives at all. Such obscure ideas cross the threshold of even a healthy person's consciousness; but in that case attention intervenes

* *Brain*, January, 1886, quoted by Ribot, *Psychologie de l'Attention*, p. 68.

† Ribot, *op. cit.*, pp. 106 and 119.

at once, to bring them fully to the light, or entirely to suppress them. These synchronous over-tones of every thought cannot, therefore, blur the tonic note. The emergent thought-phantoms can acquire no influence over the thought-procedure because attention either lightens up their faces, or banishes them back to their under-world of the Unconscious. It is otherwise with the degenerate and debilitated, who suffer from weakness of will and defective attention. The faint, scarcely recognisable, liminal presentations are perceived at the same time as those that are well lit and centrally focussed. The judgment grows drifting and nebulous like floating fog in the morning wind. Consciousness, aware of the spectrally transparent shapes, seeks in vain to grasp them, and interprets them without confidence, as when one fancies in a cloud resemblances to creatures or things. Whoever has sought on a dark night to discern phenomena on a distant horizon can form an idea of the picture which the world of thought presents to the mind of an asthenic. Lo there! a dark mass! What is it? A tree? A hayrick? A robber? A beast of prey? Ought one to fly? Ought one to attack it? The incapacity to recognise the object, more guessed at than perceived, fills him with uneasiness and anxiety. This is just the condition of the mind of an asthenic in the presence of his liminal presentations. He believes he sees in them a hundred things at once, and he brings all the forms that he seems to discern into connection with the principal presentation which has aroused them. He has, however, a strong feeling that this connection is incomprehensible and inexplicable. He combines presentations into a thought which is in contradiction to all experience, but which he must look upon as equal in validity to all his remaining thoughts and opinions, because it originated in the same way. And even if he wishes to make clear to himself what is really the content of his judgment, and of what particular presentations it is composed, he observes that these presentations are, as a matter of fact, nothing but unrecognisable adumbrations of presentations, to which he vainly seeks to give a name. Now, this state of mind, in which a man is straining to see, thinks he sees, but does not see—in which a man is forced to construct thoughts out of presentations which befool and mock consciousness like will-o'-the-wisps or marsh vapours—in which a man fancies that he perceives inexplicable relations between distinct phenomena and ambiguous formless shadows—this is the condition of mind that is called Mysticism.

From the shadowy thinking of the mystic, springs his washed-out style of expression. Every word, even the most abstract, connotes a concrete presentation or a concept, which, inasmuch as it is formed out of the common attributes of different concrete presentations, betrays its concrete origin. Language has no word for that which one believes he sees as through a mist, without recognisable form. The mystic, however, is conscious of ghostly presentations of this sort without shape or other qualities, and in order to express them he must either use recognised words, to which he gives a meaning wholly different from that which is generally current, or else, feeling the inadequacy of the fund of language created by those of sound mind, he forges for himself special words which, to a stranger, are generally incomprehensible, and the cloudy, chaotic sense of which is intelligible only to himself; or, finally, he embodies the several meanings which he gives to his shapeless representations in as many words, and then succeeds in achieving those bewildering juxtapositions of what is mutually exclusive, those expressions which can in no way be rationally made to harmonize, but which are so typical of the mystic. He speaks, as did the German mystics of the seventeenth and eighteenth centuries, of the 'cold fire' of hell, and of the 'dark light' of Satan; or, he says, like the degenerate in the twenty-eighth pathological case of Legrain,* 'that God appeared to him in the form of luminous shadows;' or he remarks, as did another of Legrain's patients:† 'You have given me an immutable evening' (*soirée immuable*).‡

The healthy reader or listener who has confidence in his own judgment, and tests with lucidity and self-dependence, naturally discerns at once that these mystical expressions are senseless, and do but reflect the mystic's confused manner of thinking. The majority of mankind, however, have neither self-confidence nor the faculty of judging, and cannot throw off the natural inclination to connect some meaning with every word. And since the words of the mystic have no definite meaning in themselves, or in their juxtaposition, a certain meaning is arbitrarily imputed to them, is mysteriously conjured into them. The effect of the mystical method of expression on

* Legrain, *op. cit.*, p. 177. † *Ibid.*, p. 156.

‡ In the chapter which treats of French Neomystics, I shall give a cluster of such disconnected and mutually exclusive expressions, which are quite parallel with the instances cited by Legrain, of the manner of speech among those acknowledged to be of weak mind. In this place only one passage may be repeated from the Vte E. M. de Vogüé, *Le Roman Russe*, Paris, 1888, in which this mystical author, unconsciously and involuntarily, characterizes admirably the shadowiness and emptiness of mystic diction, while praising it as something superior. 'One trait,' he says (p. 215), 'they' (certain Russian authors) 'have in common, viz., the art of awakening series of feelings and thoughts by a line, a word, by endless re-echoings [*résonnances*]. . . . The words you read on this paper appear to be written, not in length, but in depth. They leave behind them a train of faint reverberations, which are gradually lost, no one knows where.' And p. 227: 'They see men and things in the gray light of earliest dawn. The weakly indicated outlines end in a confused and clouded "perhaps." . . .'

people who allow themselves to be bewildered is for this reason a very strong one. It gives them food for thought, as they call it; that is to say, it allows them to give way to all kinds of dream-fancies, which is very much easier, and therefore more agreeable, than the toil of reflecting on firmly outlined presentations and thoughts admitting of no evasions and extravagances.* It transports their minds to the same condition of mental activity determined by unbridled association of ideas that is peculiar to the mystic; it awakens in them also his ambiguous, unutterable presentations, and makes them divine the strangest and most impossible relations of things to each other. All the weak-headed appear therefore 'deep' to the mystic, and this designation has, from the constant use made of it by them, become almost an insult. Only very strong minds are really deep, such as can keep the processes of thought under the discipline of an extraordinarily powerful attention. Such minds are in a position to exploit the association of ideas in the best possible way, to impart the greatest sharpness and clearness to all representations which through them are called into consciousness; to suppress them firmly and rapidly if they are not compatible with the rest; to procure new sense-impressions, if these are necessary in order to make the presentations and judgments predominant at the time in their minds still more vivid and distinct; they gain in this way an incomparably clear picture of the world, and discover true relations among phenomena which, to a weaker attention, must always remain hidden. This true depth of strong select minds is wholly luminous. It scares shadows out of hidden corners, and fills abysses with radiant light. The mystic's pseudo-depth, on the contrary, is all obscurity. It causes things to appear deep by the same means as darkness, viz., by reason of its rendering their outlines imperceptible. The mystic obliterates the firm outlines of phenomena; he spreads a veil over them, and conceals them in blue vapour. He troubles what is clear, and makes the transparent opaque, as does the cuttle-fish the waters of the ocean. He, therefore, who sees the world through the eyes of a mystic, gazes into a black heaving mass, in which he can always find what he desires, although, and just because, he actually perceives nothing at all. To the weak-headed everything which is clearly, firmly defined, and which, therefore, has strictly but one meaning, is

* 'It is certain that the Beautiful never has such charms for us as when we read it attentively in a language which we only half understand. It is the ambiguity, the uncertainty, *i.e.*, the pliability of words, which is one of their greatest advantages, and renders it possible to make an exact [!] use of them.'—Joubert, quoted by Charles Morice, *La Littérature de tout-à-l'heure*. Paris, 1889, p. 171.

flat. To them everything is profound which has no meaning, and which, therefore, allows them to apply what meaning they please. To them mathematical analysis is flat; theology and metaphysics, deep. The study of Roman law is flat; the dream-book and the prophecies of Nostradamus are deep. The forms assumed by pouring molten lead on New Year's Eve are the true symbols of their depth.

The content of mystic thought is determined by the individual character and level of culture possessed by each degenerate and hysteric. For we should never forget that the morbidly-affected or exhausted brain is only the soil which receives the seed sown by nurture, education, impressions and experience of life, etc. The seed-grains do not originate in the soil; they only receive in and through it their special irregularities of development, their deformities, and crazy offshoots. The naturalist who loses the faculty of attention becomes the so-called 'Natural Philosopher,' or the discoverer of a fourth dimension in space, like the unfortunate Zöllner. A rough, ignorant person from the low ranks of the people falls into the wildest superstition. The mystic, nurtured in religion and nourished with dogma, refers his shadowy impressions to his beliefs, and interprets them as revelations of the nature of the Trinity, or of the condition of existence before birth or after death. The technologist who has fallen into mysticism worries over impossible inventions, believes himself to be on the track of the solution of the problem of a *perpetuum mobile,* devises communication between earth and stars, shafts to the glowing core of the earth, and what not. The astronomer becomes an astrologist, the chemist an alchemist and a seeker after the philosopher's stone; the mathematician labours to square the circle, or to invent a system in which the notion of progress is expressed by a process of integration, the war of 1870 by an equation, and so on.

As was set forth above, the cerebral cortex receives its stimuli, not only from the external nerves, but also from the interior of the organism, from the nerves of separate organs, and the nerve-centres of the spinal cord and the sympathetic system. Every excitement in these centres affects the brain-cells, and arouses in them more or less distinct presentations, which are necessarily related to the activity of the centres from which the stimulus proceeds. A few examples will make this clear, even to the uninitiated. If the organism feels the need of nourishment, and we are hungry, we shall not only be generally conscious of an indeterminate desire for food, but there will also arise in our minds definite representations of dishes, of served repasts, and of all the accessories of eating. If we, from some cause, maybe an affection of the heart or lungs, cannot breathe freely, we have not only a hunger for air, but also accompanying ideas of an uneasy nature, presentiments of unknown dangers, melancholy memories, etc., *i.e.*, representations of circumstances which tend to deprive us of breath or affect us oppressively. During sleep also organic stimuli exert this influence on the cerebral cortex, and to them we owe the so-called somatic dreams (*Leibesträume*), *i.e.*, dream-images about the functioning of any organs which happen not to be in a normal condition.

Now, it is known that certain organic nerve-centres, the sexual centres, namely, in the spinal cord and the medulla oblongata, are frequently malformed, or morbidly irritated among the degenerate. The stimuli proceeding from them therefore awaken, in the brain of patients of this sort, presentations which are more or less remotely connected with the sexual activity. In the consciousness, therefore, of such a subject there always exist, among the other presentations which are aroused by the varying stimuli of the external world, presentations of a sexual character, erotic thoughts being associated with every impression of beings and things. In this way he attains to a state of mind in which he divines mysterious relations among all possible objective phenomena, *e.g.*, a railway-train, the title of his newspaper, a piano on the one hand, and woman on the other; and feels emotions of an erotic nature at sights, words, odours, which would produce no such impression on the mind of a sound person, emotions which he refers to unknown qualities in those sights, words, etc. Hence it comes that in most cases mysticism distinctly takes on a decidedly erotic colouring, and the mystic, if he interprets his inchoate liminal presentations, always tends to ascribe to them an erotic import. The mixture of super-sensuousness and sensuality, of religious and amorous rapture, which characterizes mystic thought, has been noticed even by those observers who do not understand in what way it is brought about.

The mysticism which I have hitherto investigated is the incapacity, due to weakness of will, either innate or acquired, to guide the work of the association of ideas by attention, to draw shadowy liminal representations into the bright focal circle of consciousness, and to suppress presentations which are incompatible with those attended to. There exists, however, another form of mysticism, the cause of which is not defective attention, but an anomaly in the sensitivity of the brain and nervous system. In the healthy organism the afferent nerves convey impressions of the external world in their full freshness to the brain, and the stimulation of the brain-cell is in direct ratio to the intensity of the stimulus conducted to it. Not so is the deportment of a degenerate or exhausted organism.

Here the brain may have forfeited its normal irritability; it is blunted, and is only feebly excited by stimuli conveyed to it. Such a brain, as a rule, never succeeds in elaborating sharply-defined impressions. Its thoughts are always shadowy and confounded. There is, however, no occasion for me to depict in detail the characteristics of its mental procedure, for in the higher species of the degenerate a blunted brain is hardly ever met with, and plays no part in art or literature. To the possessor of a sluggishly-reacting brain it hardly ever occurs to compose or paint. He is of account only as forming the creative mystic's partial and grateful public. Inadequate excitability may moreover be a property of the sensory nerves. This irregularity leads to anomalies in mental life, with which I shall deal exhaustively in the next book. Finally, instead of slow reaction there may exist excessive excitability, and this may be peculiar to the whole nervous system and brain, or only to a portion of the latter. A generally excessive excitability produces those morbidly-sensitive natures in whom the most insignificant phenomena create the most astonishing perceptions; who hear the 'sobbing of the evening glow,' shudder at the contact of a flower; distinguish thrilling prophecies and fearful threatenings in the sighing of the wind, etc.* Excessive irritability of particular groups of cells of the cerebral cortex gives rise to other phenomena. In the affected part of the brain, stimulated either externally or by adjacent stimuli, in other words, by sense impressions or by association, the disturbance does not in this case proceed in a natural ratio to the strength of the exciting cause, but is stronger and more lasting than is warranted by the stimulus. The aroused group of cells returns to a state of rest either with difficulty or not at all. It attracts large quantities of nutriment for purposes of absorption, withdrawing them from the other parts of the brain. It works like a machine which an unskilful hand has set in motion but cannot stop. If the normal action of the brain-cells may be compared to quiet combustion; the action of a morbidly-irritable group of cells may be said to resemble an explosion, and one, too, which is both violent and persistent. With the stimulus there flames forth in consciousness a presentation, or train of presentations, conceptions and reasonings, which suffuse the mind as with the glare of a conflagration, outshining all other ideas.

* Gérard de Nerval, *Le Rêve et la Vie*, Paris, 1868, p. 53: 'Everything in Nature assumed a different aspect. Mysterious voices issued from plants, trees, animals, the smallest insects, to warn and to encourage me. I discerned mysterious turns in the utterances of my companions, and understood their purport. Even formless and inanimate things ministered to the workings of my mind.' Here is a perfect instance of that 'comprehension of the mysterious' which is one of the most common fancies of the insane.

The degree of exclusiveness and insistence in the predominance of any presentation is in proportion to the degree of morbid irritability in the particular tract of brain by which it is elaborated. Where the degree is not excessive there arise obsessions which the consciousness recognises as morbid. They do not preclude the coexistence of healthy functioning of the brain, and consciousness acquires the habit of treating these coexistent obsessions as foreign to itself, and of banishing them from its presentations and judgments. In aggravated cases these obsessions grow into fixed ideas. The immoderately excitable portions of the brain work out their ideas with such liveliness that consciousness is filled with them, and can no longer distinguish them from such as are the result of sense-impressions, the nature and strength of which they accurately reflect. Then we reach the stage of hallucinations and delirium. Finally, in the last stage, comes ecstasy, which Ribot calls 'the acute form of the effort after unity of consciousness.' In ecstasy the excited part of the brain works with such violence that it suppresses the functioning of all the rest of the brain. The ecstatic subject is completely insensible to external stimuli. There is no perception, no representation, no grouping of presentations into concepts, and of concepts into judgments and reasoning. A single presentation, or group of presentations, fills up consciousness. These presentations are of extreme distinctness and clearness. Consciousness is, as it were, flooded with the blinding light of mid-day. There therefore takes place exactly the reverse of what has been noticed in the case of the ordinary mystic. The ecstatic state is associated with extremely intense emotions, in which the highest bliss is mixed with pain. These emotions accompany every strong and excessive functioning of the nerve-cells, every extraordinary and violent decomposition of nerve-nutriment. The feeling of voluptuousness is an example of the phenomena accompanying extraordinary decompositions in a nerve-cell. In healthy persons the sexual nerve-centres are the only ones which, conformably with their functions, are so differentiated and so adapted that they exercise no uniform or lasting activity, but, for by far the greatest part of the time, are perfectly tranquil, storing up large quantities of nutriment in order, during very short periods, to decompose this suddenly and, as it were, explosively. Every nerve-centre which operates in this way would procure us voluptuous emotion; but precisely among healthy persons there are, except the sexual nerve-centres, none which are compelled to act in this manner, in order to serve the purpose of the organism. Among the degenerate, on the contrary, particular morbidly excited brain-centres operate in this way, and the emotions of delight which accompany their explosive activity are more powerful than sexual feelings, in proportion as the brain-centres are more sensitive than the subordinate and more sluggish spinal centres. One may completely believe the assurances of great ecstatics, such as a St. Theresa, a Mohammed, an Ignatius Loyola, that the bliss accompanying their ecstatic visions is unlike anything earthly, and almost more than a mortal can bear. This latter statement proves that they were conscious of the sharp pain which accompanies nerve-action in over-excited brain-cells, and which, on careful analysis, may be distinguished in every very strong feeling of pleasure. The circumstance that the only normal organic sensation known to us which resembles that of ecstasy is the sexual feeling, explains the fact that ecstatics connect their ecstatic presentations by way of association with the idea of love, and describe the ecstasy itself as a kind of supernatural act of love, as a union of an ineffably high and pure sort with God or the Blessed Virgin. This drawing near to God and the saints is the natural result of a religious training, which begets the habit of looking on everything inexplicable as supernatural, and of bringing it into connection with the doctrines of faith.

We have now seen that mysticism depends upon the incapacity to control the association of ideas by the attention, and that this incapacity results from weakness of will; while ecstasy is a consequence of the morbid irritability of special brain-centres. The incapacity of being attentive occasions, however, besides mysticism, other eccentricities of the intellect, which may here be briefly mentioned. In extreme stages of degeneration, *e.g.*, in idiocy, attention is utterly wanting. No stimulus is able to arouse it, nor is there any external means of making an impression on the brain of the idiot, and awakening his consciousness to definite presentations. In less complete degeneration, *i.e.*, in cases of mental debility, attention may exist, but it is extremely weak and fleeting. Imbeciles (weak minds) present, in graduated intensity, the phenomenon of fugitive thought (*Gedankenflucht*), *i.e.*, the incapacity to retain, or to unite in a concept or judgment, the representations automatically and reciprocally called into consciousness in conformity with the laws of association, and also that of reverie, which is another form of fugitive thought, but which differs from it in that the particular representations of which it is composed are feebly elaborated, and are therefore shadowy and undefined, sometimes so much so that an imbecile, who in the midst of his reveries is asked of what he is thinking, is not able to state exactly what happens to be present in his consciousness. All observers maintain that the 'higher degenerate' is frequently 'original, brilliant, witty,' and that whereas he is incapable of activity which demands attention and self-control, he has strong artistic inclinations. All these peculiarities are to be explained by the uncontrolled working of association.

The reader should recall the procedure of that brain which is incapable of attention. A perception arouses a representation which summons into consciousness a thousand other associated representations. The healthy mind suppresses the representations which are contradictory to, or not rationally connected with, the first perception. This the weak-minded cannot do. The mere similarity of sound determines the current of his thought. He hears a word, and feels compelled to repeat it, once or oftener, sometimes to the extent of 'Echolalia'; or it calls into his consciousness other words similar to it in sound, but not connected with it in meaning,* whereupon he thinks and talks in a series of completely disconnected rhymes; or else the words have, besides their similarity of sound, a very remote and weak connection of meaning; this gives rise to punning. Ignorant persons are inclined to call the rhyming and punning of imbeciles witty, not bearing in mind that this way of combining ideas according to the sound of the words frustrates the purposes of the intellect by obscuring the apprehension of the real connections of phenomena. No witticism has ever made easier the discovery of any truth. And whoever has tried to hold a serious conversation with a quibbling person of weak mind will have recognised the impossibility of keeping him in check, of getting from him a logical conclusion, or of making him comprehend a fact or a causal connection. When

* An imbecile degenerate, the history of whose illness is related by Dr. G. Ballet, said: 'Il y a mille ans que le monde est monde. Milan, la cathédrale de Milan' (*La Semaine médicale*, 1892, p. 133). 'Mille ans' (a thousand years) calls up in his consciousness the like-sounding word 'Milan,' although there is absolutely no rational connection between the two ideas. A graphomaniac named Jasno, whose case is cited by Lombroso, says 'la main se mène' (the hand guides itself). He then begins to speak of 'semaine' (week), and continues to play upon the like-sounding words 'se mène,' 'semaine,' and 'main' (*Genie und Irsinn*, p. 264). In the book of a German graphomaniac entitled *Rembrandt als Erzieher*, Leipzig, 1890 (a book which I shall have to refer to more than once, as an example of the lucubrations of a weak mind), I find, on the very first pages, the following juxtaposition of words according to their resemblance in sound: 'Sie verkünden eine Rückkehr . . . zur Einheit und Feinheit' (p. 3). 'Je ungeschliffener Jemand ist, desto mehr ist an ihm zu schleifen' (p. 4). 'Jede rechte Bildung ist bildend, formend, schöpferisch, und also künstlerisch' (p. 8). 'Rembrandt war nicht nur ein protestantischer Künstler, sondern auch ein künstlerischer Protestant' (p. 14). 'Sein Hundert guldenblatt allein könnte schon als ein Tausendgüldenkraut gegen so mancherlei Schäden . . . dienen' (p. 23). 'Christus und Rembrandt haben . . . darin etwas Gemeinsames, dass Jener die religiöse, dieser die künstlerische Armseligkeit—die Seligkeit der Armen—zu . . . Ehren bringt' (p. 25), etc.

5

presentations are connected, not merely according to auditory impressions of simple similarity of sound, but also according to the other laws of association, those juxtapositions of words are effected which the ignorant designate as 'original modes of expression,' and which confer upon their originator the reputation of a 'brilliant' conversationalist or author. Sollier* cites some characteristic examples of the 'original' modes of expression of imbeciles. One said to his comrade, 'You look like a piece of barley-sugar put out to nurse.' Another expresses the thought that his friend made him laugh so much he could not restrain his saliva, by saying, 'Tu me fais baver des ronds de chapeaux.' The junction of words which by their sense have little or no relation to each other is, as a rule, an evidence of imbecility, although it often enough is sensational and mirth-provoking. The cleverness which in Paris is called *blague*, or *boulevard-esprit*, the psychologist discerns as imbecility. That this condition goes hand-in-hand with artistic tendencies is easy to understand. All callings which require knowledge of fact, and adaptation to it, presuppose attention. This capacity is wanting in imbeciles; hence they are not fitted for serious professions. Certain artistic occupations, especially those of a subordinate kind, are, on the contrary, quite compatible with uncontrolled association of ideas, reverie, or fugitive thought, because they exact only a very limited adaptation to fact, and therefore have great attractions for persons of weak intellect.

Between the process of thought and movement there exists an exact parallelism explicable by the fact that the elaboration of presentations is nothing else than a modification of the elaboration of the motor impulses. The phenomena of movement make the mechanism of thought more easily apprehensible to the lay mind. The automatic association of muscular contractions corresponds to the association of ideas, their co-ordination to attention. As with defective attention there ensues no intelligent thought, so with faulty co-ordination there can be no appropriate movement. Palsy is equivalent to idiocy, St. Vitus's dance to obsessions and fixed ideas. The attempts at witticisms of the weak-minded are like beating the air with a sword; the notions and judgments of sound brains are like the careful thrust and parry of skilful fencing. Mysticism finds its reflected image in the aimless and powerless, often hardly discernible, movements of senile and paralytic trembling; and ecstasy is, for a brain-centre, the same state as a prolonged and violent tonic contraction for a muscle or group of muscles.

* Dr. Paul Sollier, *Psychologie de l'Idiot et de l'Imbécile*. Paris, 1891, p. 153.

CHAPTER II.

THE PRE-RAPHAELITES.

MYSTICISM is the habitual condition of the human race, and in no way an eccentric disposition of mind. A strong brain which works out every presentation to its full clearness—a powerful will, which sustains the toiling attention—these are rare gifts. Musing and dreaming, the free ranging of imagination, disporting itself at its own sweet will along the meandering pathways of association, demand less exertion, and will therefore be widely preferred to the hard labour of observation and intelligent judgment. Hence the consciousness of men is filled with a vast mass of ambiguous, shadowy ideas; they see, as a rule, in unmistakable clearness only those phenomena which are daily repeated in their most intimate personal experience, and, among these, those only which are the objects of their immediate needs.

Speech, that great auxiliary in the interchange of human thought, is no unmixed benefit. It brings to the consciousness of most men incomparably more obscurity than brightness. It enriches their memory with auditory images, not with well-defined pictures of reality. A word, whether written or spoken, excites a sense (sight or hearing), and sets up an activity in the brain. True; it always arouses presentation. A series of musical tones does the same. At an unknown word, at 'Abracadabra,' at a proper name, at a tune scraped on the fiddle, we also think of something, but it is either indefinite, or nonsensical, or arbitrary. It is absolute waste of labour to attempt to give a man new ideas, or to widen the circle of his positive knowledge, by means of a word. It can never do more than awaken such ideas as he already possesses. Ultimately everyone works only with the material for presentation which he has acquired by attentive personal observation of the phenomena of the universe. Nevertheless, he cannot do without the stimulus conveyed to him by speech. The desire for knowledge, without any hiatus, of all that is in the world, is irresistible; while the opportunities of perception at first hand, even in the most favourable circumstances, are limited. What we have not ourselves experienced we let others, the dead and the living, tell us. The word must take the place of the direct impressions of sense for us. And then it is itself an impression of sense, and our consciousness is accustomed to put this impression on a level with others, to estimate the idea aroused by this word equally with those ideas which have been acquired through the simultaneous co-operation of all the senses, through observations, and handling on every side, through moving and lifting, listening to, and smelling the object itself. This parity of values is an error of thought. It is false in any case if a word do more than call into consciousness a memory-image of a presentation, which it has acquired through personal experience, or a concept composed of such presentations. Nevertheless, we all of us commit this fallacy. We forget that language was only developed by the race as a means of communication between individuals, that it is a social function, but not a source of knowledge. Words are in reality much more a source of error. For a man can only actually know what he has directly experienced and attentively observed, not what he has merely heard or read, and what he repeats; and if he would free himself from the errors which words have led him into, he has no other means than the increase of his sterling representative material, through personal experience and attentive observation. And since man is never in a position to do this save within certain limits, everyone is condemned to carry on the operations of his consciousness with direct presentations, and at the same time with words. The intellectual structure which is built up with materials of such unequal solidity reminds one of those dilapidated Gothic churches which brainless masons used to patch up with a plaster of soot and cheese, giving it, by means of a wash, the appearance of stone. To the eye the frontage is irreproachable, but many parts of the building could not for one moment resist a vigorous blow of criticism.

Many erroneous explanations of natural phenomena, the majority of false scientific hypotheses, all religious and metaphysical systems, have arisen in such a way that mankind, in their thoughts and opinions, have interwoven, as equally valid components, ideas suggested by words only, together with such as were derived from direct perception. The words were either invented by mystics and originally indicated nothing beyond the unbalanced condition of a weak and diseased brain, or, whereas they at first expressed a definite, correct presentation, their proper meaning was not caught by those who repeated them, and by them was arbitrarily falsified, differently interpreted, or blurred. Innate or acquired weakness of mind and ignorance lead alike to the goal of mysticism. The brain of the ignorant elaborates presentations that are nebulous, because they are suggested by words, not by the thing itself, and the stimulus of a word is not strong enough to produce vigorous action in the brain-cells; moreover, the brain of the exhausted and degenerate elaborates nebulous presentations, because in any case it is not in a condition to respond to a stimulus by vigorous action. Hence ignorance is artificial weakness of mind, just as, conversely, weakness of mind is the natural organic incapacity for knowledge.

In one part or another of his mental field of vision each of us therefore is a mystic. From all the phenomena which he himself has not observed, everyone forms shadowy, unstable presentations. Nevertheless, it is easy to distinguish healthy men from those who deserve the designation of mystic. There is a sure sign for each. The healthy man is in a condition to obtain sharply-defined presentations from his own immediate perceptions, and to comprehend their real connection. The mystic, on the contrary, mixes his ambiguous, cloudy, half-formed liminal representations with his immediate perceptions, which are thereby disturbed and obscured. Even the most superstitious peasant has definite presentations of his field work, of the feeding of his cattle, and of looking after his landmark. He may believe in the weather-witch, because he does not know how the rain comes to pass, but he does not wait a moment for the angels to plough for him. He may have his field blessed, because the real conditions of the thriving or perishing of his seed are beyond his ken, but he will never so put his trust in supernatural favour as to omit sowing his grain. All the genuine mystic's presentations, on the contrary, even those of daily experience, are permeated and overgrown with that which is incomprehensible, because it is without form. His want of attention makes him incapable of apprehending the real connecting links between the simplest and most obviously related phenomena, and leads him to deduce them from one or another of the hazy, intangible presentations wavering and wandering in his consciousness.

There is no human phenomenon in the art and poetry of the century with whom this characteristic of the mystic so completely agrees as with the originators and supporters of the Pre-Raphaelite movement in England. It may be taken for granted that the history of this movement is known—at least, in its outlines—and that it will suffice here to recall briefly its principal features. The three painters, Dante Gabriel Rossetti, Holman Hunt, and Millais, in the year 1848, entered into a league which was called the Pre-Raphaelite Brotherhood. After the association was formed, the painters F. G. Stephens and James Collinson, and the sculptor Thomas Woolner, joined it. In the spring of 1849 they exhibited in London a number of pictures and statues, all of which, in addition to the signature of the artist, bore the common mark P.R.B. The result was crushing. Hitherto no hysterical fanatic had tyrannically forced on the public a belief in the beauty of these works, nor was it as yet under the domination of the fashion, invented by æsthetic snobs, of considering their admiration as a mark of distinction, and of membership of a narrow and exclusive circle of the aristocrats of taste. Hence it confronted them without prepossession, and found them incomprehensible and funny. The contemplation of them roused inextinguishable laughter among the good-humoured, and wrath among the morose, who are nettled when they think themselves made fools of. The brotherhood did not renew their attempt; the P.R.B. exhibition was never repeated; the league broke up of itself. Its members no longer added the shibboleth of initials after their names. They formed no longer a closed association, involving formal admission, but only a loosely-knit circle, consisting of friends having tastes in common, and who were perpetually modifying its character by their joining and retiring. In this way it was joined by Burne Jones and Madox Brown, who also passed for Pre-Raphaelites, although they had not belonged to the original P.R.B. Later on the designation was extended from painters to poets, and among the pre-Raphaelites, in addition to D. G. Rossetti (who soon exchanged the brush for the pen), were Algernon Charles Swinburne and William Morris.

What are the governing thoughts and aims of the Pre-Raphaelite movement? An Anglo-German critic of repute, F. Hüffer,* thinks that he answers this question when he says: 'I myself should call this movement the renaissance of mediæval feeling.' Apart from the fact that these words signify nothing, since every man may interpret 'mediæval feeling' as he pleases, the reference to the Middle Ages only emphasizes the most external accompanying circumstance of pre-Raphaelitism, leaving its essence entirely untouched.

It is true that the pre-Raphaelites with both brush and pen betray a certain, though by no means exclusive, predilection for the Middle Ages; but the mediævalism of their poems and paintings is not historical, but mythical, and simply denotes something outside time and space—a time of dreams and a place of dreams, where all unreal figures and actions may be conveniently bestowed. That they decorate their unearthly world with some features which may remotely recall mediævalism; that it is peopled with queens and knights, noble damozels with coronets on their golden hair, and pages with plumed caps—these may be accounted for by the prototypes which, perhaps unconsciously, hover before the eyes of the pre-Raphaelites.

Movements in art and literature do not spring up suddenly and spontaneously. They have progenitors from whom they descend in the natural course of generation. Pre-Raphaelitism

* *Poems by Dante Gabriel Rossetti.* With a memoir of the author by Franz Hüffer. Leipzig, 1873, p. viii.

is the grandson of German, and a son of French, Romanticism. But in its wanderings through the world Romanticism has suffered such alteration through the influence of the changing opinions of the times, and the special characteristics of various nations, that the English offspring bears scarcely any family resemblance to its German ancestor.

German romanticism was in its origin a reaction against the spirit of the French encyclopædists, who had held undisputed sway over the eighteenth century. Their criticism of ancient errors, their new systems which were to solve the riddles of the world and of the nature of man, had at first dazzled and nearly intoxicated mankind. They could not, however, satisfy in the long-run, for they committed a great fault in two respects. Their knowledge of facts was insufficient to enable them to explain the collective phenomenon of the universe, and they looked upon man as an intellectual being. Proud of their strictly logical and mathematical reasoning, they overlooked the fact that this is a method of knowledge, but not knowledge itself. The logical apparatus is a machine, which can manufacture only the material shot into it. If the machine is not fed, it runs on empty and makes a noise, but produces nothing. The condition of science in the eighteenth century did not allow the encyclopædists to make advantageous use of their logical machine. They did not take cognizance of this fact, however, and, with their limited material and much unconscious temerity, constructed a system which they complacently announced as a faithful representation of the system of the universe. It was soon discovered that the encyclopædists, for all their intellectual arrogance, were deluding both themselves and their followers. There were known facts which contradicted their hasty explanations, and there was a whole range of phenomena of which their system took no account, and failed to cover as if with too short a cloak, and which peeped out mockingly at all the seams. Hence the philosophy of the encyclopædists was kicked and abused, and the same faults were committed with respect to it which it had perpetrated; the methods of intelligent criticism were mistaken for the results obtained by them. Because the encyclopædists, from lack of knowledge and of natural facts, explained nature falsely and arbitrarily, those who were disappointed and thirsting for knowledge cried out, that intelligent criticism as such was a false method, that consistent reasoning led to nothing, that the conclusions of the 'Philosophy of Enlightenment' were just as unproven and unprovable as those of religion and metaphysics, only less beautiful, colder, and narrower; and mankind threw itself with fervour into all the depths of faith and superstition, where certainly the Tree of Knowledge did not grow, but where beautiful mirages charmed the eye, and the warm fragrant springs of all the emotions bubbled up.

And more fatal than the error of their philosophy was the false psychology of the encyclopædists. They believed that the thoughts and actions of men are determined by reason and the laws of consistency, and had no inkling that the really impelling force in thought and deed are the emotions, those disturbances elaborated in the depths of the internal organs, and the sources of which elude consciousness, but which suddenly burst into it like a horde of savages, not declaring whence they come, submitting to no police regulations of a civilized mind, and imperiously demanding lodgment. All that wide region of organic needs and hereditary impulses, all that E. von Hartmann calls the 'Unconscious,' lay hidden from the rationalists, who saw nothing but the narrow circle of the psychic life which is illumined by the little lamp of consciousness. Fiction which should depict mankind according to the views of this inadequate psychology would be absurdly untrue. It had no place for passions and follies. It saw in the world only logical formulæ on two legs, with powdered heads and embroidered coats of fashionable cut. The emotional nature took its revenge on this æsthetic aberration, breaking out in 'storm and stress,' and in turn attaching value only to the unconscious, the inherited impulse, and the organic appetites, while it neglected entirely reason and will, which are there none the less.

Mysticism, which rebelled against the application of the rationalistic methods to explain the universe, and the *Sturm und Drang*, which rebelled against their application to the psychical life of mankind, were the first-fruits of romanticism, which is nothing but the union and exaggeration of these two revolutionary movements. That it took up with fondness the form of mediævalism was due to circumstances and the sentiment of the age. The beginnings of romanticism coincide with the time of the deepest humiliation of Germany, and the suffering of young men of talent at the ignominy of foreign rule gave to the whole content of their thought a patriotic colouring. During the Middle Ages Germany had passed through a period of the greatest power and intellectual florescence; those centuries which were irradiated at one and the same time by the might of the world-empire of the Hohenstaufen, by the splendour of the poems of the Court Minnesingers, and by the vastness of the Gothic cathedrals, must naturally have attracted those spirits who, filled with disgust, broke out against the intellectual jejuneness and political abasement of the times. They fled from Napoleon to Frederick Barbarossa, and drew refreshment with Walter von der Vogelweide from their abhorrence of Voltaire. The foreign imitators of the German romanticists do not know that if in their flight from reality they come to a halt in mediævalism, they have German patriotism as their pioneer.

The patriotic side of romanticism was, moreover, emphasized only by the sanest talents of this tendency. In others it stands revealed most signally as a form of the phenomenon of degeneration. The brothers Schlegel, in their *Athenæum*, give this programme of romanticism: 'The beginning of all poetry is to suspend the course and the laws of rationally thinking reason, and to transport us again into the lovely vagaries of fancy and the primitive chaos of human nature. . . . The freewill of the poet submits to no law.' This is the exact mode of thought and expression of the weak-minded, of the imbecile, whose brain is incapable of following the phenomena of the universe with discernment and comprehension, and who, with the self-complacency which characterizes the weak-minded, proclaims his infirmity as an advantage, and declares that his muddled thought, the product of uncontrolled association, is alone exact and commendable, boasting of that for which the sane-minded are pitying him. Besides the unregulated association of ideas there appears in most romanticists its natural concomitant, mysticism. That which enchanted them in the idea of the Middle Ages was not the vastness and might of the German Empire, not the fulness and beauty of the German life of that period, but Catholicism with its belief in miracles and its worship of saints. 'Our Divine Service,' writes H. von Kleist, 'is nothing of the kind. It appeals only to cold reason. A Catholic feast appeals profoundly to all the senses.' The obscure symbolism of Catholicism, all the externals of its priestly motions, all its altar service so full of mystery, all the magnificence of its vestments, sacerdotal vessels and works of art, the overwhelming effect of the thunder of the organ, the fumes of incense, the flashing monstrance—all these undoubtedly stir more confused and ambiguous adumbrations of ideas than does austere Protestantism. The conversion of Friedrich Schlegel, Adam Müller, Zacharias Werner, Count Stolberg, to Catholicism is just as consistent a result as, to the reader who has followed the arguments on the psychology of mysticism, it is intelligible that, with these romanticists, the ebullitions of piety are accompanied by a sensuousness which often amounts to lasciviousness.

Romanticism penetrated into France a generation later than into Germany. The delay is easy of historical explanation. In the storms of the Revolution and the Napoleonic wars, the leading minds of the French people had no time to think of themselves. They had no leisure for testing the philosophy of their encyclopædists, to find it inadequate, reject it, and rise up against it. They devoted their whole energy to rough, big, muscular deeds of war, and the need for the emotional exercise afforded by art and poetry, asserted itself but feebly, being completely satisfied by the far stronger emotions of self-love and despair produced by their famous battles and cataclysmic overthrows. Æsthetic tendencies only reasserted their rights during the half-dormant period following the battle of Waterloo, and then the same causes led to the same results as in Germany. The younger spirits in this case also raised the flag of revolt against the dominating æsthetic and philosophic tendencies. They wished Imagination to grapple with Reason, and place its foot on its neck, and they proclaimed the martial law of passion against the sober procedure of discipline and morality. Through Madame de Staël and A. W. Schlegel, partly by the latter's personal intercourse with Frenchmen, and partly by his works, which were soon translated into French, they were in some measure made acquainted with the German movement. They joined it perhaps half unconsciously. Of the many impulses which were active among the German romanticists, patriotism and Catholic mysticism had no influence on the French mind, which only lent itself to the predilection for what was remote in time and space, and what was free from moral and mental restraints.

French romanticism was neither mediæval nor pious. It took up its abode rather in the Renaissance period as regards remoteness in time, and in the East or the realms of faerie, if it wished to be spacially remote from reality. In Victor Hugo's works the one drama of *Les Burgraves* takes place in the thirteenth century; but in all the others, *Cromwell*, *Maria Tudor*, *Lucrezia Borgia*, *Angelo*, *Ruy Blas*, *Hernani*, *Marion Delorme*, *Le Roi s'amuse*, the scenes were laid in the sixteenth and seventeenth centuries; and his one mediæval romance, *Notre Dame de Paris*, can be set over against all the rest, from *Han d'Islande*, which has for its scene of action a fancied Thule, to *Les Miserables* and *1793*, which take place in an apocalyptic Paris and in a history of the Revolution suited to the use of hashish-smokers. The bent of French romanticism towards the Renaissance is natural. That was the period of great passions and great crimes, of marble palaces, of dresses glittering with gold, and of intoxicating revels; a period in which the æsthetic prevailed over the useful, and the fantastic over the rational, and when crime itself was beautiful, because assassination was accomplished with a chased and damascened poniard, and the poison was handed in goblets wrought by Benvenuto Cellini.

The French romanticists made use of the unreality of their scene of action and costumes chiefly for the purpose of enabling them, without restraint, to attribute to their characters all the qualities, exaggerated even to monstrosity, that were dear to the French, not yet ailing with the pain of overthrow. Thus in the heroes of Victor Hugo, Alexandre Dumas, Théophile Gautier, Alfred de Musset, we become acquainted with the French ideal of man and woman. The subtle inquiries of Faust, the soliloquies of Hamlet, are not their affair. They talk unceasingly in dazzling witticisms and antitheses; they fight one against ten; they love like Hercules in the Thespidian night, and their whole life is one riot of fighting, wantoning, wine, perfume, and pageantry—a sort of magnificent illusion, with performance of gladiators, Don Juans, and Monte Christos; a crazy prodigality of inexhaustible treasures of bodily strength, gaiety and gold. These ideal beings had necessarily to wear doublets or Spanish mantles, and speak in the tongues of unknown times, because the tightness of the contemporary dress-coat could not accommodate all this wealth of muscle, and the conversation of the Paris salon did not admit of the candour of souls which their authors had turned inside out.

The fate of romanticism in England was exactly the reverse of that which befell it in France. Whereas the French had imitated chiefly, and even exclusively, in the German romanticists, their divergence from reality, and their declaration of the sovereign rights of the passions, the English just as exclusively elaborated their Catholic and mystical elements. For them the Middle Ages had a powerful attraction, inasmuch as it was the period of childlike faith in the letter, and of the revelling of simple piety in personal intercourse with the Trinity, the Blessed Virgin, and all the guardian saints.

Trade, industry, and civilization were nowhere in the world so much developed as in England. Nowhere did men work so assiduously, nowhere did they live under such artificial conditions as there. Hence the state of degeneration and exhaustion, which we observe to-day in all civilized countries as the result of this over-exertion, must of necessity have shown itself sooner in England than elsewhere, and, as a matter of fact, did show itself in the third and fourth decade of the century with continually increasing violence. In consequence, however, of the peculiarity of the English mind, the emotional factor in degeneration and exhaustion necessarily assumed with them a religious colouring.

The Anglo-Saxon race is by nature healthy and strong-minded. It has therefore, in a high degree, that strong desire for knowledge which is peculiar to normally-constituted persons. In every age it has inquired into the why and how of phenomena, and shown passionate sympathy with, and gratitude to, everyone who held out hopes of an explanation of them. The well-known and deeply thoughtful discourse of the Anglian noble concerning what precedes and follows man's life—a speech which Bede has preserved for us in his account of the conversion of Edwin to Christianity—has been cited by all authors (*e.g.*, by G. Freytag and H. Taine*) who have studied the origins of the English mental constitution. It shows that as early as the beginning of the seventh century the Anglo-Saxons were consumed by an ardent desire to comprehend the phenomenon of the universe. This fine and high-minded craving for knowledge has proved at once the strength and the weakness of the English. It led with them to the development along parallel lines of the natural sciences and theology. The scientific investigators contributed a store of facts won through toilsome observation ; the experts in divinity obtained theirs through systems compounded of notions arbitrarily conceived. Both claimed to explain the nature of things, and the people were deeply grateful to both, more so, it is true, to the theologians than to the scholars, because the former could afford to be more copious and confident in their teaching than the latter. The natural tendency to reckon words as equivalent to facts, assertions to demonstrations, always gives theologians and metaphysicians an immense advantage over observers. The craving of the English for knowledge has produced both the philosophy of induction and spiritualism. Humanity owes to them on the one hand Francis Bacon, Harvey, Newton, Locke, Darwin, J. S. Mill ; on the other, Bunyan, Berkeley, Milton, the Puritans, the Quakers, and all the religious enthusiasts, visionaries, and mediums of this century. No people has done so much for, and conferred such honour on, scientific investigators ; no people has sought with so much earnestness and devotion for instruction, especially in matters of faith, as have the English. Eagerness to know is, therefore, the main source of English religiousness. There is this also to be noticed, that among them the ruling classes never gave an example of indifference in matters of faith, but systematically made religiousness a mark of social distinction ; unlike France, where the nobility of the eighteenth century exalted Voltairianism into a symptom of good breeding. The evolution of history led in England to two results which apparently exclude each other—to caste-rule, and the liberty of the individual. The caste which is in possession of wealth and power naturally wishes to protect its possessions. The rigid independence of the English people precludes it from applying physical force. Hence it uses moral restraints to keep the lower ranks submissive and amenable, and, among these, religion is by far the most effective.

Herein lies the explanation both of the devoutness of the English and of the religious character of their mental degenera-

* Gustave Freytag, *Bilder aus der deutschen Vergangenheit*, Bd. I. : 'Aus dem Mittelalter.' Leipzig, 1872, § 266. H. Taine, *Histoire de la Littérature anglaise*. Paris, 1866, 2e édition, vol. i., p. 46.

tion. The first result of the epidemic of degeneration and hysteria was the Oxford Movement in the thirties and forties. Wiseman turned all the weaker heads. Newman went over to Catholicism. Pusey clothed the entire Established Church in Romish garb. Spiritualism soon followed, and it is worthy of remark that all mediums adopted theological modes of speech, and that their disclosures were concerned with heaven and hell. The 'revival meetings' of the seventies, and the Salvation Army of to-day, are the direct sequel of the Oxford stream of thought, but rendered turbid and foul in accordance with the lower intellectual grade of their adherents. In the world of art, however, the religious enthusiasm of degenerate and hysterical Englishmen sought its expression in pre-Raphaelitism.

An accurate definition of the connotation of this word is an impossibility, in that it was invented by mystics, and is as vague and equivocal as are all new word-creations of the feeble and deranged in mind. The first members of the Brotherhood believed that, in the artists of the fourteenth and fifteenth centuries, in the predecessors of the great geniuses of the Umbrian and Venetian schools, they had discovered minds congenial to their own. For a short time they took the methods of these painters for their models, and created the designation 'pre-Raphaelite.' The term was bound to approve itself to them, since the prefix 'pre' ('præ') arouses ideas of the primeval, the far-away, the hardly perceptible, the mysteriously shadowy. 'Pre-Raphaelite' calls up, through association of ideas, 'pre-Adamite,'* 'pre-historic,' etc.—in short, all that is opened to view by immeasurable vistas down the dusk of the unknown, and which allow the mind to wander dreamily beyond the limits of time and in the realms of myth. But that the pre-Raphaelites should have lit on the quattrocento painters for the embodiment of their artistic ideals is due to John Ruskin.

Ruskin is one of the most turbid and fallacious minds, and one of the most powerful masters of style, of the present century. To the service of the most wildly eccentric thoughts he brings the acerbity of a bigot and the deep sentiment of Morel's 'emotionalists.' His mental temperament is that of the first Spanish Grand Inquisitors. He is a Torquemada of æsthetics. He would liefest burn alive the critic who disagrees with him, or the dull Philistine who passes by works of art without a feeling of devout awe. Since, however, stakes do not stand within his reach, he can at least rave and rage in word, and annihilate the heretic figuratively by abuse and cursing. To his ungovernable irascibility he unites great knowledge of all the

* This is not an arbitrary assertion. One of D. G. Rossetti's most famous poems, of which further mention will be made, *Eden Bowers*, treats of the pre-Adamite Lilith.

minutiæ in the history of art. If he writes of the shapes of clouds he reproduces the clouds in seventy or eighty existing pictures, scattered amongst all the collections of Europe. And be it noted that he did this in the forties, when photographs of the masterpieces of art, which render the comparative study of them to-day so convenient, were yet unknown. This heaping up of fact, this toilsome erudition, made him conqueror of the English intellect, and explains the powerful influence which he obtained over artistic sentiment and the theoretic views concerning the beautiful of the Anglo-Saxon world. The clear positivism of the Englishman demands exact data, measures, and figures. Supplied with these he is content, and does not criticise starting-points. The Englishman accepts a fit of delirium if it appears with footnotes, and is conquered by an absurdity if it is accompanied by diagrams. Milton's description of hell and its inhabitants is as detailed and conscientious as that of a land-surveyor or a natural philosopher, and Bunyan depicts the *Pilgrim's Progress* to the mystical kingdom of Redemption in the method of the most graphic writer of travels—a Captain Cook or a Burton. Ruskin has in the highest conceivable degree this English peculiarity of exactness applied to the nonsensical, and of its measuring and counting applied to fevered visions.

In the year 1843, almost simultaneously with the outbreak of the great Catholicizing movement, Ruskin began to publish the feverish studies on art which were subsequently collected under the title of *Modern Painters*. He was then a young divinity student, and as such he entered upon the study of works of art. The old scholasticism wished to make philosophy the 'handmaid of godly learning.' Ruskin's mysticism had the same purpose with regard to art. Painting and sculpture ought to be a form of divine worship, or they ought not to exist at all. Works of art were valuable merely for the supersensuous thoughts that they conveyed, for the devotion with which they were conceived and which they revealed, not for the mastery of form.

From this point of view he was able to arrive at judgments among which I here quote a few of the most typical. 'It appears to me,' he says,* 'that a rude symbol is oftener more efficient than a refined one in touching the heart, and that as pictures rise in rank as works of art they are regarded with less devotion and more curiosity. . . . It is man and his fancies, man and his trickeries, man and his inventions, poor, paltry, weak, self-sighted man, which the connoisseur for ever seeks and worships. Among potsherds and dunghills, among drunken boors and withered beldames, through every scene of debauchery and degradation, we follow the erring artist, not to receive one wholesome lesson, not to be touched with pity, nor moved with

* J. Ruskin, *Modern Painters*, American edition, vol. i., pp. xxi. *et seq.*

indignation, but to watch the dexterity of the pencil, and gloat over the glittering of the hue. . . . Painting is nothing but a noble and expressive language, invaluable as the vehicle of thought, but by itself nothing. . . . It is not by the mode of representing and saying, but by what is represented and said, that the respective greatness either of the painter or the writer is to be finally determined. . . . The early efforts of Cimabue and Giotto are the burning messages of prophecy, delivered by the stammering lips of infants. . . . The picture which has the nobler and more numerous ideas, however awkwardly expressed, is a greater and a better picture than that which has the less noble and less numerous ideas, however beautifully expressed. . . . The less sufficient the means appear to the end the greater will be the sensation of power.' These propositions were decisive in determining the direction taken by the young Englishmen of 1843, who united artistic inclinations with the mysticism of the degenerate and hysterical. They comprise the æstheticism of the first pre-Raphaelites, who felt that Ruskin had expressed with clearness what was vaguely fermenting within them. Here was the art-ideal which they had presaged—form as indifferent, idea as everything; the clumsier the representation, the deeper its effect; the devotion of faith as the only worthy import of a work of art. They reviewed the history of art for phenomena agreeing with the theories of Ruskin, which they had taken up with enthusiasm, and they found what they sought in the archaic Italian school, in which the London National Gallery is extraordinarily rich. There they had perfect models to imitate; they were bound to take for their starting-point these Fra Angelicos, Giottos, Cimabues, these Ghirlandajos and Pollajuolos. Here were paintings bad in drawing, faded or smoked, their colouring either originally feeble or impaired by the action of centuries; pictures executed with the awkwardness of a learner representing events in the Passion of Christ, in the life of the Blessed Virgin, or in the Golden Legend, symbolizing childish ideas of hell and paradise, and telling of earnest faith and fervent devotion. They were easy of imitation, since, in painting pictures in the style of the early masters, faulty drawing, deficient sense of colour, and general artistic incapacity, are so many advantages. And they constituted a sufficiently forcible antithesis to all the claims of the artistic taste of that decade to satisfy the proclivity for contradiction, paradox, negation and eccentricity which we have learned to recognise as a special characteristic of the feeble-minded.

Ruskin's theory is in itself delirious. It mistakes the fundamental principles of æsthetics, and, with the unconsciousness of a saucy child at play, muddles and entangles the boundary lines of the different arts. It holds of account in plastic art only the conception. A picture is valuable only in so far as it is a symbol giving expression to a religious idea. Ruskin does not take into consideration, or deliberately overlooks the fact, that the pleasurable feelings which are produced by the contemplation of a picture are not aroused by its intellectual import, but by it as a sensuous phenomenon. The art of painting awakens through its media of colour and drawing (*i.e.*, the exact grasp and reproduction of differences in the intensity of light), firstly, a purely sensuously agreeable impression of beautiful single colours and happily combined harmonies of colour; secondly, it produces an illusion of reality and, together with this, the higher, more intellectual pleasures arising from a recognition of the phenomena depicted, and from a comprehension of the artist's intention; thirdly, it shows these phenomena as seen with the eye of the artist, and brings out details or collective traits, which until then the inartistic beholder had not been by himself able to perceive. The painter therefore influences, through the medium of his art, only so far as he agreeably excites the sense of colour, gives to the mind an illusion of reality, together with the consciousness that it is an illusion, and, through his deeper, more penetrating vision, discloses to the spectator the hidden treasures of the phenomenal world. If, in addition to the presentation of the picture, 'its story' also affects the beholder, it is no longer the merit of the painter as such, but of his not exclusively pictorial intelligence in making choice of a subject, and in committing its portrayal to his specific pictorial abilities. The effect of the story is not called forth through the media of painting; it is not based on the pleasure of the spectator in colour, on the illusion of reality, or on a better grasp of the phenomenon, but on some pre-existing inclination, some memory, some prejudice. A purely painter's picture, such as Leonardo's *Mona Lisa*, charms everyone whose eye has been sufficiently trained. A picture which tells a story, but is not distinguished for its purely pictorial qualities, leaves everyone unappreciative to whom the story in itself is uninteresting, *i.e.*, to whom it would in any case have been uninteresting, had it not been executed by the instrumentality of pictorial art, but simply narrated. A Russian eikon affects a moujik, and leaves the Western art connoisseur cold. A painting which represents a French victory over Russian troops would excite and please a French Philistine, even if it were painted in the style of an Épinal. It is true, no doubt, that there is a sort of painting which does not seek to seize and awaken visual impressions in the spectator, together with the emotions which they directly arouse, but to express ideas, and in which the picture is intended to affect the mind, not by itself and its own consummate art, but by its spiritual significance. But this kind of painting has a special name: we call it writing. The signs, which are meant to have no pictorial, but only symbolic value, where we turn away from the form in order to dwell upon their meaning, we call 'letters,' and the art which makes use of such symbols for the expression of mental processes is not painting, but poetry. Originally, pictures were actually, no doubt, a means of symbolizing thoughts, and their value as things of beauty was considered of secondary importance in relation to their value as means of expression. On the other hand, æsthetic impressions still play in these days a subdued accompaniment to our writing, and a beautiful handwriting, quite apart from its import, affects us more agreeably than one that is ugly. At the very beginning of their evolution, however, the kind of painting which satisfied only æsthetic needs separated itself from that of writing, which serves to render ideas perceptible to the senses. Descriptive drawing became the hieroglyph, the demotic writing, the letter; and it was reserved for Ruskin to be the first to try to annul a distinction which the scribes of Thebes had learnt to make six thousand years before him.

The pre-Raphaelites, who got all their leading principles from Ruskin, went further. They misunderstood his misunderstandings. He had simply said that defectiveness in form can be counter-balanced by devotion and noble feeling in the artist. They, however, raised it to the position of a fundamental principle, that in order to express devotion and noble feeling, the artist must be defective in form. Incapable, like all the weak-minded, of observing any process and of giving a clear account of it to themselves, they did not distinguish the real causes of the influence exercised over them by the old masters. The pictures touched and moved them; the most striking distinction between such pictures and others, to which they were indifferent, was their awkward stiffness; they did not look further, however, than this awkward stiffness for the source of what touched and moved them, and imitated with great care and conscientiousness the bad drawing of the old masters.

Now, the clumsiness of the old masters is certainly touching; but why? Because these Cimabues and Giottos were sincere. They wished to get closer to nature, and to free themselves from the thraldom of the Byzantine school, which had become entirely unreal. They struggled with vehement endeavour against the bad habits of hand and eye which they had acquired from the teachers of their guilds, and the spectacle of such a conflict, like every violent effort of an individuality which sets itself to rend fetters of any sort and save its own soul from bondage, is the most attractive thing possible to observe. The whole difference between the old masters and the pre-Raphaelites is, that the former had first to find out how to draw and paint correctly, while the latter wished to forget it. Hence, where the former fascinate, the latter must repel. It is the contrast between the first babbling of a thriving infant and the stammering of a mentally enfeebled gray-beard; between child-like and childish. But this retrogression to first beginnings, this affectation of simplicity, this child's play in word and gesture, is a frequent phenomenon amongst the weak-minded, and we shall often meet with it among the mystic poets.

According to the doctrine of their master in theory, Ruskin, the decline of art for pre-Raphaelites begins with Raphael—and for obvious reasons. To copy Cimabue and Giotto is comparatively easy. In order to imitate Raphael it is necessary to be able to draw and paint to perfection, and this was just what the first members of the Brotherhood could not do. Moreover, Raphael lived in the most glorious period of the Renaissance. The rosy dawn of the New Thought shone in his being and his work. With the liberal-mindedness of an enlightened Cinquecentist, he no longer painted only religious subjects, but mythological and historical, or, as the mystics say, profane, subjects as well. His paintings appealed not only to the devotion of faith, but also to the sense of beauty. They are no longer exclusively divine worship; consequently, as Ruskin says, and his disciples repeat, they are devil-worship, and therefore to be rejected. Finally, it is consistent with the tendency to contradiction, and to the repudiation of what is manifest, which governs the thoughts of the weak-minded, that they should declare as false those tenets in the history of art which others than themselves deemed the most incontestable. The whole world for three hundred years had said, 'Raphael is the zenith of painting.' To this they replied, 'Raphael is the nadir of painting.' Hence it came about that, in the designation which they appropriated, they took up a direct allusion to Raphael, and to no other master or other portion of the history of art.

Consistency of sequence and unity are not to be expected from mystical thought. It proceeds after its kind in perpetual self-contradiction. In one place Ruskin says:* 'The cause of the evil lies in the painter's taking upon him to modify God's works at his pleasure, casting the shadow of himself on all he sees. Every alteration of the features of nature has its origin either in powerless indolence or blind audacity.' Thus the painter should reproduce the phenomenon exactly as he sees it, and not suffer himself to make the smallest alteration in it. And a few pages further on:† 'There is an ideal form of every herb, flower, and tree; it is that form to which every individual of the species has a tendency to attain, freed from the influence

* Ruskin, *op. cit.*, p. 24.

† *Ibid.*, p. 26.

of accident or disease.' And, he continues, to recognise and to reproduce this ideal form is the one great task of the painter.

That one of these propositions completely nullifies the other it is hardly necessary to indicate. The 'ideal form' which every phenomenon strives after does not stand before the bodily eyes of the painter. He reads it, according to some preconceived notion, into the phenomenon. He has to deal with individual forms which, through 'accident or disease,' have diverged from the 'ideal form.' In order to bring them back in painting to their ideal form, he must alter the object given by nature. Ruskin demands that he should do this, but at the same time says that every alteration is an act of 'powerless indolence or blind audacity.' Naturally, only one of these mutually exclusive statements can be true. Unquestionably it is the former. The 'ideal form' is an assumption, not a perception. The separation of the essential from the accidental, in the phenomenon, is an abstraction—the work of reason, not of the eye or æsthetic emotion. Now, the subject-matter of painting is the visible, not the conjectural; the real, not the possible or probable; the concrete, not the abstract. To exclude individual features from a phenomenon as unessential and accidental, and to retain others as intrinsic and necessary, is to reduce it to an abstract idea. The work of art, however, is not to abstract, but to individualize. Firstly, because abstraction presupposes an idea of the law which determines the phenomenon, because this idea may be erroneous, because it changes with the ruling scientific theories of the day, whereas the painter does not reproduce changing scientific theories, but impressions of sense. Secondly, because the abstraction rouses the working of thought, and not emotion, while the task of art is to excite emotion.

Nevertheless, the pre-Raphaelites had no eye for these contradictions, and followed blindly all Ruskin's injunctions. They typified the human form, but they rendered all accessories truthfully, and had neither 'the blind audacity nor powerless indolence' to change any of them. They painted with the greatest precision the landscape in which their figures stood, and the objects with which they were surrounded. The botanist can determine every kind of grass and flower painted; the cabinet-maker can recognise the joining and glueing in every footstool, the kind of wood and varnish in the furniture. Moreover, this conscientious distinctness is just the same in the foreground as in the extreme background, where, according to the laws of optics, things should be scarcely perceptible.

This uniformly clear reproduction of all the phenomena in the field of vision is the pictorial expression of the incapacity for attention. In intellection, attention suppresses a portion of that which is presented to consciousness (through association or perception), and suffers only a dominant group of the latter to remain. In sight, attention suppresses a portion of the phenomena in the field of vision in order distinctly to perceive only that part which the eye can focus. To look at a thing is to see one object intently, and to disregard others. The painter must observe if he wishes to make clear to us what phenomenon has engrossed him, and what his picture is to show us. If he does not dwell observantly on a definite point in the field of vision, but represents the whole field of view with the same proportion of intensity, we cannot divine what he wishes particularly to tell us, and on what he wishes to direct our attention. Such a style of painting may be compared to the disconnected speech of a weak mind, who chatters according to the current of the association of ideas, wanders in his talk, and neither knows himself what he wishes to arrive at, nor is able to make it clear to us; it is painted drivelling, echolalia of the brush.

But it is just this manner of painting which has gained for itself an influence on contemporary art. It is the pre-Raphaelite contribution to its evolution. The non-mystical painters have also learnt to observe accessories with precision, and to reproduce them faithfully; but they have prudently avoided falling into the faults of their models, and nullifying the unity of their work by filling the most distant backgrounds with still life, painted with painful accuracy. The lawns, flowers and trees, which they render with botanical accuracy, the geologically correct rocks, surfaces of soil, and mountain structures, the distinct patterns of carpets and wall-papers, which we find in the new pictures, are traceable to Ruskin and the pre-Raphaelites.

These mystics believed themselves to be mentally affiliated with the Old Masters, because, like the latter, they painted religious pictures. But in this they deceive themselves. Cimabue, Giotto and Fra Angelico were no mystics, or, to put it more precisely, they are to be classed as mystics because of their ignorance, and not because of organic weakness of mind. The mediæval painter, who depicted a religious scene, was convinced that he was painting something perfectly true. An Annunciation, a Resurrection, an Ascension, an event in the lives of the saints, a scene of life in paradise or in hell, possessed for him the same incontestable character of reality as drinking bouts in a soldier's tavern, or a banquet in a ducal palace. He was a realist when he was painting the transcendental. To him the legend of his faith was related as a fact; he was penetrated with a sense of its literal truth, and reproduced it exactly as he would have done any other true story. The spectator approached the picture with the same conviction. Religious art was the Bible of the poor. It had for the mediæval man the same importance as the illustrations in the works on the history of civilization, and on natural science, have in our day. Its duty was to narrate and to teach, and hence it had to be exact. We know from the touching stanza of Villon* how the illiterate people of the Middle Ages regarded church pictures. The dissolute poet makes his mother say to the Virgin Mary:

> 'A pitiful poor woman, shrunk and old,
> I am, and nothing learn'd in letter-lore;
> Within my parish-cloister I behold
> A painted Heaven where harps and lutes adore,
> And eke an Hell whose damned folk seethe full sore:
> One bringeth fear, the other joy to me.
> That joy, great Goddess, make thou mine to be—
> Thou of whom all must ask it even as I;
> And that which faith desires, that let it see,
> For in this faith I choose to live and die.'

With this sober faith a mystic mode of painting would be quite incompatible. The painter then avoided all that was obscure or mysterious; he did not paint nebulous dreams and moods, but positive records. He had to convince others, and could do so, because he was convinced himself.

It was quite otherwise with the pre-Raphaelites. They did not paint sober visions, but emotions. They therefore introduced into their pictures mysterious allusions and obscure symbols, which have nothing to do with the reproduction of visible reality. I need cite only one example—Holman Hunt's *Shadow of the Cross*. In this picture Christ is standing in the Oriental attitude of prayer with outstretched arms, and the shadow of his body, falling on the ground, shows the form of a cross. Here we have a most instructive pattern of the processes of mystic thought. Holman Hunt imagines Christ in prayer. Through the association of ideas there awakes in him simultaneously the mental image of Christ's subsequent death

* 'BALLADE QUE VILLON FEIT À LA REQUESTE DE SA MÈRE POUR PRIER NOSTRE DAME.

> 'Femme je suis povrette et ancienne.
> Que riens ne scay, oncques lettres ne leuz,
> Au Monstier voy (dont suis parroissienne)
> Paradis painct, ou sont harpes et luz,
> Et ung enfer, où damnez sont boulluz,
> L'ung me faict paour, l'autre joye et liesse,
> La joye avoir faictz moy (haulte deesse)
> A qui pecheurs doivent tous recourir
> Combley de foy, sans faincte ne paresse,
> En ceste foy je vueil vivre et mourir.'

It is significant that the pre-Raphaelite Rossetti has translated this very poem of Villon, *His Mother's Service to Our Lady*. *Poems*, p. 180.

on the cross. He wants, by the instrumentality of painting, to make the association of these ideas visible. And hence he lets the living Christ throw a shadow which assumes the form of a cross, thus foretelling the fate of the Saviour, as if some mysterious, incomprehensible power had so posed his body with respect to the rays of the sun that a wondrous annunciation of his destiny must needs write itself on the floor. The invention is completely absurd. It would have been childish trifling if Christ had drawn his sublime death of sacrifice, whether in jest or in vanity, in anticipation, by his shadow on the ground. Neither would the shadow-picture have had any object, for no contemporary of Christ's would have understood the significance of the shadowed cross before he had suffered death by crucifixion. In Holman Hunt's consciousness, however, emotion simultaneously awakened the form of the praying Christ and of the cross, and he unites both presentations anyhow, without regard to their reasonable connection. If an Old Master had had to paint the same idea, namely, the praying Christ filled with the presentiment of his impending death, he would have shown us in the picture a realistic Christ in prayer, and in a corner an equally realistic crucifixion; but he would never have sought to blend both these different scenes into a single one by a shadowy connection. This is the difference between the religious painting of the strong healthy believer and of the emotional degenerate mind.

In the course of time the pre-Raphaelites laid aside many of their early extravagances. Millais and Holman Hunt no longer practise the affectation of wilfully bad drawing and of childish babbling in imitation of Giotto's language. They have only retained, of the leading principles of the school, the careful reproduction of the unessential and the painting of the idea. A benevolent critic, Edward Rod,* says of them: 'They were themselves writers, and their painting is literature.' This speech is still applicable to the school.

A few of the earliest pre-Raphaelites have understood it. They have recognised in time that they had mistaken their vocation, and have gone over, from a style of painting which was merely thought-writing, to genuine writing. The most notable among them is Dante Gabriel Rossetti, who, though born in England, was the son of an Italian Carbonaro, and a scholar of Dante. His father gave him the name of the great poet at his entrance into the world, and this expressive baptismal name became a constant suggestion, which Rossetti felt, and has, perhaps half unconsciously, admitted.† He is the most instructive example of the often-quoted assertion of Balzac, of the

* Edward Rod, *Études sur le XIX. Siècle.* Paris et Lausanne, 1888, p. 89.

† Rossetti, *Poems*, p. 277.

determining influence of a name on the development and destiny of its bearer. Rossetti's whole poetical feeling was rooted in Dante. His theory of life bears an indistinct cast of that of the Florentine. Through all his ideas there runs a reminiscence, faint or strong, of the *Divina Commedia* or the *Vita Nuova*.

The analysis of one of his most celebrated poems, *The Blessed Damozel*, will show this parasitic battening on the body of Dante, and at the same time disclose some of the most characteristic peculiarities of the mental working of a mystic's brain. The first strophe runs thus:

> 'The blessed damozel leaned out
> From the gold bar of Heaven;
> Her eyes were deeper than the depth
> Of waters stilled at even;
> She had three lilies in her hand,
> And the stars in her hair were seven.'

The whole of this description of a lost love, who looks down upon him from a heaven imagined as a palace, with paradisiacal decorations, is a reflection of Dante's *Paradiso* (Canto iii.), where the Blessed Virgin speaks to the poet from the moon. We even find details repeated, *e.g.*, the deep and still waters (. . . '*ver per acque nitide e tranquille Non sì profonde, che i fondi sien persi* . . .'). The 'lilies in her hand' he gets from the Old Masters, yet even here there is a slight ring of the morning greeting from the *Purgatorio* (Canto xxx.), '*Manibus o date lilia plenis*.' He designates his love by the Anglo-Norman word 'damozel.' By this means he makes any clear outlines in the idea of a girl or lady artificially blurred, and shrouds the distinct picture in a veil of clouds. By the word 'girl' we should just think of a girl and nothing else. 'Damozel' awakens in the consciousness of the English reader obscure ideas of slim, noble ladies in the tapestries of old castles, of haughty Norman knights in mail, of something remote, ancient, half forgotten; 'damozel' carries back the contemporary beloved into the mysterious depths of the Middle Ages, and spiritualizes her into the enchanted figure of a ballad. This one word awakens all the crepuscular moods which the body of romantic poets and authors have bequeathed as a residuum in the soul of the contemporary reader. In the hand of the 'damozel' Rossetti places three lilies, round her head he weaves seven stars. These numbers are, of course, not accidental. From the oldest times they have been reckoned as mysterious and holy. The 'three' and the 'seven' are allusions to something unknown, and of deep meaning, which the intuitive reader may try to understand.

It must not be said that my criticism of the means by which Rossetti seeks to express his own dreamy states of mind, and to arouse similar states in the reader, applies equally to all lyrics and poetry generally, and that I condemn the latter when I adduce the former as the emanations of the mystic's weakness of mind. All poetry no doubt has this peculiarity, that it makes use of words intended not only to arouse the definite ideas which they connote, but also to awaken emotions that shall vibrate in consciousness. But the procedure of a healthy-minded poet is altogether different from that of a weak-minded mystic. The suggestive word employed by the former has in itself an intelligible meaning, but besides this it is adapted to excite emotions in every healthy-minded man ; and finally the emotions excited have all of them reference to the subject of the poem. One example will make this clear. Uhland sings the *Praise of Spring* in these words :

'Saatengrün, Veilchenduft,
Lerchenwirbel, Amselschlag
Sonnenregen, linde Luft
Wenn ich solche Worte singe,
Braucht es dann noch grosse Dinge,
Dich zu preisen, Frühlingstag ?'*

Each word of the first three lines contains a positive idea. Each of them awakens glad feelings in a man of natural sentiment. These feelings, taken together, produce the mood with which the awakening of spring fills the soul, to induce which was precisely the intention of the poet. When, on the other hand, Rossetti interweaves the mystical numbers 'three' and 'seven' in the description of his 'damozel,' these numbers signify nothing in themselves ; moreover, they will call up no emotion at all in an intellectually healthy reader, who does not believe in mystical numbers; but even in the case of the degenerate and hysterical reader, on whom the cabbala makes impression, the emotions excited by the sacred numbers will not involve a reference to the subject of the poem, viz., the apparition of one loved and lost, but at best will call up a general emotional consciousness, which may perhaps tell in a remote way to the advantage of the 'damozel.'

But to continue the analysis of the poem. To the maiden in bliss it appears that she has been a singer in God's choir for only one day; to him who is left behind this one day has been actually a matter of ten years. 'To one it is ten years of years.' This computation is thoroughly mystical. It means, that is, absolutely nothing. Perhaps Rossetti imagined that there may

* 'The springing green, the violet's scent,
The trill of lark, the blackbird's note,
Sunshowers soft, and balmy breeze :
If I sing such words as these,
Needs there any grander thing
To praise thee with, O day of spring?'

exist a higher unity to which the single year may stand as one day does to a year; that therefore 365 years would constitute a sort of higher order of year. The words 'year of years' therefore signified 365 years. But as Rossetti portrays this thought vaguely and imperfectly, he is far from expressing it as intelligibly as this.

> 'It was the rampart of God's house
> That she was standing on;
> By God built over the sheer depth
> The which is space begun;
> So high that, looking downward, thence
> She scarce could see the sun.
>
> 'It lies in heaven, across the flood
> Of ether, as a bridge.
> Beneath, the tides of day and night
> With flame and darkness ridge
> The void, as low as where this earth
> Spins like a fretful midge.
>
> 'Heard hardly, some of her new friends,
> Amid their loving games,
> Spake evermore among themselves
> Their virginal chaste names,
> And the souls mounting up to God
> Went by her like thin flames.
>
> 'From the fixed place of Heaven she saw
> Time like a pulse shake fierce
> Through all the worlds. . . .'

I leave it to the reader to imagine all the details of this description and unite them into one complete picture. If he fail in this in spite of honest exertion, let him comfort himself by saying that the fault is not his, but Rossetti's.

The damozel begins to speak. She wishes that her beloved were already with her. For come he will.

> '"When round his head the aureole clings,
> And he is clothed in white,
> I'll take his hand and go with him
> To the deep wells of light.
> We will step down as to a stream,
> And bathe there in God's sight."'

It is to be observed how, in the midst of the turgid stream of these transcendental senseless modes of speech, the idea of bathing together takes a definite shape. Mystical reverie never fails to be accompanied by sensuality.

> '"We two," she said, "will seek the groves
> Where the Lady Mary is,
> With her five handmaidens, whose names
> Are five sweet symphonies—
> Cecily, Gertrude, Magdalen,
> Margaret, and Rosalys."'

The enumeration of these five feminine names, occupying two lines of the stanza, is a method of versification characteristic of the mystic. Here the word ceases to be the symbol of a distinct presentation or concept, and sinks into a meaningless vocal sound, intended only to awaken divers agreeable emotions through association of ideas. In this case the five names arouse gliding shadowy ideas of beautiful young maidens, 'Rosalys' those of roses and lilies as well; and the two verses together diffuse a glamour of faerie, as if one were roaming at ease in a garden of flowers, where between lilies and roses slender white and rosy maidens pace to and fro.

The maiden in paradise goes on picturing to herself the union with her beloved, and then:

> 'she cast her arms along
> The golden barriers,
> And laid her face between her hands
> And wept—I heard her tears.'

These tears are incomprehensible. The blessed maiden after her death lives in the highest bliss, in a golden palace, in the presence of God and the Blessed Virgin. What pains her now? That her beloved is not yet with her? Ten years of mortal men are to her as a single day. Even if it be her beloved's destiny to live to be a very old man, she will at most have to wait only five or six of her days until he appears at her side, and after this tiny span of time there blossoms for them both an eternity of joy. It is not, therefore, obvious why she is distressed and sheds tears. This can only be attributed to the bewildered thoughts of the mystic poet. He imagines to himself a life of happiness after death, but at the same time there dawn in his consciousness dim pictures of the annihilation of individuality, and of final separation through death, and those painful feelings are excited which we are accustomed to associate with ideas of death, decay, and separation from all we love. Hence it is that he comes to close an ecstatic hymn of immortality with tears, which have a meaning only if one does not believe in the continuation of life after death. In other respects also there are contradictions in the poem which show that Rossetti had not formed any one of his ideas so clearly as to exclude the opposite and incompatible. Thus, at one time the dead are dressed in white, and adorned with a galaxy of stars; they appear in pairs and call each other by caressing names; they must also be thought of as resembling human beings in appearance, while on another occasion their souls are 'thin flames' which rustle past the damozel. Every single idea in the poem, when we try soberly to follow it out, infallibly takes refuge after this manner in darkness and intangibility.

In the 'Divine Comedy,' echoes of which are ever humming in Rossetti's soul, we find nothing of this kind. This was because Dante, like the Old Masters, was a mystic from ignorance, not from the weak-mindedness of degeneration. The raw material of his thought, the store of facts with which he worked, was false, but the use his mind made of it was true and consistent. All his ideas were clear, homogeneous, and free from internal contradictions. His hell, his purgatory, his paradise, he built up on the science of his times, which based its knowledge of the world exclusively on dogmatic theology. Dante was familiar with the system of his contemporary, Thomas Aquinas (he was nine years old when the Doctor Angelicus died), and permeated by it. To the first readers of the *Inferno* the poem must have appeared at least as well founded on fact and as convincing as, let us say, Häckel's *Natural History of Creation* does to the public of to-day. In coming centuries our ideas of an atom as merely a centre of force, of the disposition of atoms in the molecule of an organic combination, of ether and its vibrations, will perhaps be discerned to be just as much poetical dreams as the ideas of the Middle Ages concerning the abode of the souls of the dead appear to us. But that is no reason why anyone should claim the right to designate Helmholtz or William Thompson as mystics, because they base their work upon those notions which even to their minds do not to-day represent anything definite. For the same reason no one ought to call Dante a mystic like a Rossetti. Rossetti's *Blessed Damozel* is not based upon the scientific knowledge of his time, but upon a mist of undeveloped germs of ideas in constant mutual strife. Dante followed the realities of the world with the keenly penetrating eyes of an observer, and bore with him its image down to his hell. Rossetti is not in a condition to understand, or even to see the real, because he is incapable of the necessary attention; and since he feels this weakness he persuades himself, in conformity with human habit, that he does not wish to do what in reality he cannot do. 'What is it to me,' he once said,* 'whether the earth revolves around the sun or the sun around the earth?' To him it is of no importance, because he is incapable of understanding it.

It is, of course, impossible to go so deeply into all Rossetti's poems as into the *Blessed Damozel;* but it is also unnecessary, since we should everywhere meet with the same mixture of transcendentalism and sensuality, the same shadowy ideation, the same senseless combinations of mutually incompatible ideas. Reference, however, must be made to some of the peculiarities of the poet, because they characterize the brain-work of weak degenerate minds.

* Rod, *op. cit.*, p. 67.

The first thing that strikes us is his predilection for refrains. The refrain is an excellent artistic medium for the purpose of unveiling the state of a soul under the influence of a strong emotion. It is natural that, to the lover yearning for his beloved, the recurring idea of her should be ever thrusting itself among all the other thoughts in which he temporarily indulges. It is equally comprehensible that the unhappy being who is made miserable by thoughts of suicide should be unable to free himself from an idea which is in harmony with his mental condition, say of an *Armensünderblum*, or 'flower of the doomed soul,' which he sees when walking at night. (See Heine's poem, *Am Kreuzweg wird begraben,* in which the line *die Armensünderblum* is repeated at the end of both strophes with peculiarly thrilling effect.)

Rossetti's refrains, however, are different from this, which is natural and intelligible. They have nothing to do with the emotion or action expressed by the poem. They are alien to the circle of ideas belonging to the poem. In a word, they possess the character of an obsession, which the patient cannot suppress, although he recognises that they are in no rational connection with the intellectual content of his consciousness. In the poem *Troy Town* it is related how Helen, long before Paris had carried her off, kneels in the temple of Venus at Sparta, and, drunken with the luxuriant beauty of her own body, fervently implores the Goddess of Love to send her a man panting for love, where or whoever he might be, to whom she might give herself. The absurdity of this fundamental idea it is sufficient to indicate in passing. The first strophe runs thus:

'Heaven-born Helen, Sparta's Queen
(O Troy town!),
Had two breasts of heavenly sheen,
The sun and the moon of the heart's desire.
All Love's lordship lay between.
(O Troy's down,
Tall Troy's on fire!)

'Helen knelt at Venus' shrine
(O Troy town!)
Saying, "A little gift is mine,
A little gift for a heart's desire.
Hear me speak and make me a sign!
(O Troy's down,
Tall Troy's on fire!)" '*

And thus through fourteen strophes there constantly recurs, after the first line, 'O Troy town!' at the end of the third line, 'heart's desire'; and after the fourth line, 'O Troy's down, tall Troy's on fire!' It is easy to discern what Rossetti wishes. In him there is repeated the mental process which we recognised

* *Poems*, p. 16.

in Holman Hunt's picture, *The Shadow of the Cross*. As by association of ideas, in thinking of Helen at Sparta, he hits upon the idea of the subsequent fate of Troy, so shall the reader, while he sees the young queen in Sparta intoxicated by her own beauty, be simultaneously presented with the picture of the yet distant tragical consequences of her longing desire. But he does not seek to connect these two trains of thought in a rational way. He is ever muttering as he goes, monotonously as in a litany, the mysterious invocations to Troy, while he is relating the visit to the temple of Venus at Sparta. Sollier* remarks this peculiarity among persons of feeble intellect. 'Idiots,' he says, 'insert words which have absolutely no connection with the object.' And further on: 'Among idiots constant repetition [*le rabâchage*] grows into a veritable *tic*.'

In another very famous poem, *Eden Bower*,† which treats of the pre-Adamite woman Lilith, her lover the serpent of Eden, and her revenge on Adam, the litany refrain of 'Eden Bower's in flower,' and 'And O the Bower and the hour,' are introduced alternately after the first line in forty-nine strophes. As a matter of course, between these absolutely senseless phrases and the strophe which each interrupts, there is not the remotest connection. They are strung together without any reference to their meaning, but only because they rhyme. It is a startling example of echolalia.

We frequently find this peculiarity of the weak and deranged mind, *i.e.*, echolalia, in Rossetti. Here are a few proofs:

> 'So wet she comes to wed' (*Stratton Water*).

Here the sound 'wed' has called up the sound 'wet.' In the poem *My Sister's Sleep*, in one place where the moon is spoken of, it is said:

> 'The hollow halo it was in
> Was like an icy crystal cup.'

It is stark nonsense to qualify a plane surface such as a halo by the adjective 'hollow.' The adjective and noun mutually exclude each other, but the rhyming assonance has joined 'hollow' to 'halo.' With this we may also compare the line:

> 'Yet both were ours, but hours will come and go'
> (*A New Year's Burden*),

and

> 'Forgot it not, nay, but got it not' (*Beauty*).

---

* Sollier, *Psychologie de l'Idiot et de l'Imbécile*, p. 184. See also Lombroso, *The Man of Genius* (Contemporary Science Series), London, 1891, p. 216. A special characteristic found in literary mattoids, and also, as we have already seen, in the insane, is that of repeating some words or phrases hundreds of times in the same page. Thus, in one of Passanante's chapters the word *riprovate* (blame) occurs about 143 times.

† *Poems*, p. 31.

Many of Rossetti's poems consist of the stringing together of wholly disconnected words, and to mystic readers these absurdities seem naturally to have the deepest meaning. I should like to cite but one example. The second strophe of the *Song of the Bower* says:

> '. . . My heart, when it flies to thy bower,
> What does it find there that knows it again?
> There it must droop like a shower-beaten flower,
> Red at the rent core and dark with the rain.
> Ah! yet what shelter is still shed above it—
> What waters still image its leaves torn apart?
> Thy soul is the shade that clings round it to love it,
> And tears are its mirror deep down in thy heart.'*

The peculiarity of such series of words is, that each single word has an emotional meaning of its own (such as 'heart,' 'bower,' 'flies,' 'droop,' 'flower,' 'rent,' 'dark,' 'lone,' 'tears,' etc.), and that they follow each other with a cradled rhythm and ear-soothing rhyme. Hence they easily arouse in the emotional and inattentive reader a general emotion, as does a succession of musical tones in a minor key. And the reader fancies that he understands the strophe, while he, as a matter of fact, only interprets his own emotion according to his own level of culture, his character, and his recollections of what he has read.

Besides Dante Gabriel Rossetti, it has been customary to include Swinburne and Morris among the pre-Raphaelite poets. But the similarity between these two and the head of the school is remote. Swinburne is, in Magnan's phrase, a 'higher degenerate,' while Rossetti should be counted among Sollier's imbeciles. Swinburne is not so emotional as Rossetti, but he stands on a much higher mental plane. His thought is false and frequently delirious, but he has thoughts, and they are clear and connected. He is mystical, but his mysticism partakes more of the depraved and the criminal than of the paradisiacal and divine. He is the first representative of 'Diabolism' in English poetry. This is because he has been influenced, not only by Rossetti, but also and especially by Baudelaire. Like all 'degenerates,' he is extraordinarily susceptible to suggestion, and, consciously or unconsciously, he has imitated, one after another, all the strongly-marked poetic geniuses that have come under his notice. He was an echo of Rossetti and Baudelaire, as he was of Gautier and Victor Hugo, and in his poems it is possible to trace the course of his reading step by step.

Completely Rossettian, for example, is *A Christmas Carol*:†

* *Poems*, p. 247.

† Algernon Charles Swinburne, *Poems and Ballads*. London: Chatto and Windus, 1889, p. 247.

'Three damsels in the queen's chamber,
The queen's mouth was most fair;
She spake a word of God's mother,
As the combs went in her hair.
"Mary that is of might,
Bring us to thy Son's sight."'

Here we find a mystical content united to the antiquarianism and childish phraseology of genuine pre-Raphaelitism. *The Masque of Queen Bersabe* is worked out on the same model, being an imitation of the mediæval miracle-play, with its Latin stage directions and puppet-theatre style. This, in its turn, has become the model of many French poems, in which there is only a babbling and stammering and a crawling on all fours, as if in a nursery.

Where he walks in Baudelaire's footsteps, Swinburne tries to distort his face to a diabolical mien, and makes the woman say (in *Anactoria*) to the other unnaturally loved woman:

'I would my love could kill thee. I am satiated
With seeing thee live, and fain would have thee dead.
I would earth had thy body as fruit to eat,
And no mouth but some serpent's found thee sweet.
I would find grievous ways to have thee slain,
Intense device, and superflux of pain;
. . . O! that I
Durst crush thee out of life with love, and die—
Die of thy pain and my delight, and be
Mixed with thy blood and molten unto thee.'

Or, when he curses and reviles, as in *Before Dawn:*

'To say of shame—what is it?
Of virtue—we can miss it,
Of sin—we can but kiss it,
And it's no longer sin.'

One poem deserves a more detailed analysis, because it contains unmistakably the germ of the later 'symbolism,' and is an instructive example of this form of mysticism. The poem is *The King's Daughter*. It is a sort of ballad, which in fourteen four-lined stanzas relates a fairy story about the ten daughters of a king, of whom one was preferred before the remaining nine, was beautifully dressed, pampered with the most costly food, slept in a soft bed, and received the attentions of a handsome prince, while her sisters remained neglected; but instead of finding happiness at the prince's side, she became deeply wretched and wished she were dead. In the first and third lines of every stanza the story is rehearsed. The second line speaks of a mythical mill-stream, which comes into the ballad one knows not how, and which always, by some mysterious influence, symbolically reflects all the changes that take place as the action of the ballad progresses; while the fourth line contains a litany-like exclamation, which likewise makes a running reference to the particular stage reached in the narrative.

'We were ten maidens in the green corn,
  Small red leaves in the mill-water:
Fairer maidens never were born,
  Apples of gold for the King's daughter.

'We were ten maidens by a well-head,
  Small white birds in the mill-water:
Sweeter maidens never were wed,
  Rings of red for the King's daughter.'

In the following stanzas the admirable qualities of each of the ten princesses are portrayed, and the symbolical intermediate lines run thus:

'Seeds of wheat in the mill-water— . . . White bread and brown for the King's daughter— . . . Fair green weed in the mill-water— . . . White wine and red for the King's daughter— . . . Fair thin reeds in the mill-water— . . . Honey in the comb for the King's daughter— . . . Fallen flowers in the mill-water— . . . Golden gloves for the King's daughter— . . . Fallen fruit in the mill-water— . . . Golden sleeves for the King's daughter— . . .'

The King's son then comes, chooses the one princess and disdains the other nine. The symbolical lines point out the contrast between the brilliant fate of the chosen one and the gloomy destiny of the despised sisters:

'A little wind in the mill-water; A crown of red for the King's daughter— A little rain in the mill-water; A bed of yellow straw for all the rest; A bed of gold for the King's daughter— Rain that rains in the mill-water; A comb of yellow shell for all the rest,— A comb of gold for the King's daughter— Wind and hail in the mill-water; A grass girdle for all the rest, A girdle of arms for the King's daughter— Snow that snows in the mill-water; Nine little kisses for all the rest, An hundredfold for the King's daughter.'

The King's daughter thus appears to be very fortunate, and to be envied by her nine sisters. But this happiness is only on the surface, for the poem now suddenly changes:

'Broken boats in the mill-water;
Golden gifts for all the rest,
Sorrow of heart for the King's daughter.

'"Ye'll make a grave for my fair body,"
Running rain in the mill-water;
"And ye'll streek my brother at the side of me,"
The pains of hell for the King's daughter.'

What has brought about this change in her fate the poet purposely leaves obscure. Perhaps he wishes to have us understand that the King's son has no right to sue for her hand, being her brother, and that the chosen princess for shame at the incest perishes. This would be in keeping with Swinburne's childish devilry. But I am not dwelling on this aspect of the poem, but on its symbolism.

It is psychologically justifiable that a subjective connection should be set up between our states of mind for the time being and phenomena; that we should perceive in the external world a reflection of our moods. If the external world shows a well-marked emotional character, it awakens in us the mood corresponding to it; and conversely, if we are under the influence of some pronounced feeling, we notice, in accordance with the mechanism of attention, only those features of nature which are in harmony with our mood, which intensify and sustain it, while the opposing phenomena we neither observe nor even perceive. A gloomy ravine overhung by a cloudy sky makes us sad. This is one form of associating our humour with the outer world. But if we from any cause are already sad, we find some corresponding sadness in all the scenes around us—in the streets of the metropolis ragged, starved-looking children, thin, miserably kept cab-horses, a blind beggar-woman; in the woods withered, mouldering leaves, poisonous fungi, slimy slugs, etc. If we are joyous, we see just the same objects, but take no notice of them, perceiving only beside them, in the street, a wedding procession, a fresh young maiden with a basket of cherries on her arm, gaily-coloured placards, a funny fat man with his hat on the back of his head; in the woods, birds flitting by, dancing butterflies, little white anemones, etc. Here we have the other form of that association. The poet has a perfect right to make use of both these forms. If Heine sings:

> 'Es ragt ins Meer der Runenstein,
> Da sitz ich mit meinen Träumen;
> Es pfeift der Wind, die Möwen schrein,
> Die Wellen, die wandern und schäumen.
>
> 'Ich habe geliebt manch schönes Kind
> Und manchen guten Gesellen—
> Wo sind sie hin?—Es pfeift der Wind,
> Es schäumen und wandern die Wellen,'*

he brings his own mournful, melancholy frame of mind with him. He bemoans the fleetingness of man's life, the impermanence of the feelings, the shadowy passing by and away of beloved companions. In this state he looks out over the sea from the shore where he sits, and perceives only those objects

* 'The Runic stone stands out in the sea,
There sit I with my dreams,
'Mid whistling winds and wailing gulls,
And wandering, foaming waves.
I have loved many a lovely child,
And many a good comrade—
Where are they gone? The wind whistles,
The waves wander foaming on.'

that are in keeping with his humour and give it embodiment: the driving gust of wind, the hurrying gulls, now seen, now lost to sight, the rolling in and trackless ebbing of the surf. These features of an ocean scene become symbols of what is passing through the poet's mind, and this symbolism is sound and founded on the laws of thought.

Swinburne's symbolism is of quite another kind. He does not let the external world express a mood, but makes it tell a story; he changes its appearance according to the character of the event he is describing. Like an orchestra, it accompanies all events which somewhere are taking place. Here nature is no longer a white wall on which, as in a game of shadows, the varied visions of the soul are thrown; but a living, thinking being, which follows the sinful love-romance with the same tense sympathy as the poet, and which, with its own media, expresses just as much as he does—complacency, delight, or sorrow—at every chapter of the story. This is a purely delirious idea. It corresponds in art and poetry to hallucination in mental disease. It is a form of mysticism, which is met with in all the degenerate. Just as in Swinburne the mill-water drives 'small red leaves,' and, what is certainly more curious, 'little white birds,' when everything is going on well, and on the other hand is lashed by snow and hail, and tosses shattered boats about, if things take an adverse turn; so, in Zola's *Assommoir*, the drain from a dyeing factory carries off fluid of a rosy or golden hue on days of happiness, but a black or gray-coloured stream if the fates of Gervaise and Lantier grow dark with tragedy. Ibsen, too, in his *Ghosts*, makes it rain in torrents if Frau Alving and her son are in sore trouble, while the sunshine breaks forth just as the catastrophe is about to occur. Ibsen, moreover, goes farther in this hallucinatory symbolism than the others, since with him Nature not only plays an active part, but shows scornful malice—she not only furnishes an expressive accompaniment to the events, but makes merry over them.

William Morris is intellectually far more healthy than Rossetti and Swinburne. His deviations from mental equilibrium betray themselves, not through mysticism, but through a want of individuality, and an overweening tendency to imitation. His affectation consists in mediævalism. He calls himself a pupil of Chaucer.* He artlessly copies whole stanzas also from Dante, *e.g.*, the well-known Francesca and Paolo episode from Canto V. of the *Inferno*, when he writes in his *Guenevere*:

* William Morris, *Poems* (Tauchnitz edition), p. 169:

'And if it hap that . . .
My master, Geoffrey Chaucer, thou do meet,
Then speak . . . the words:
"O master! O thou great of heart and tongue!"' . . .

> 'In that garden fair
> Came Lancelot walking ; this is true, the kiss
> Wherewith we kissed in meeting that spring day,
> I scarce dare talk of the remembered bliss.'

Morris persuades himself that he is a wandering minstrel of the thirteenth or fourteenth century, and takes much trouble to look at things in such a way, and express them in such language, as would have befitted a real contemporary of Chaucer. Beyond this poetical ventriloquism, so to speak, with which he seeks so to alter the sound of his voice that it may appear to come from far away to our ear, there are not many features of degeneracy in him to notice. But he sometimes falls into outspoken echolalia, *e.g.*, in a stanza of the *Earthly Paradise :*

> 'Of Margaret sitting glorious there,
> In glory of gold and glory of hair,
> And glory of glorious face most fair'—

where 'glory' and 'glorious' are repeated five times in three lines. His emotional activity in recent years has made him an adherent of a vague socialism, consisting chiefly of love and pity for his fellow-men, and which has an odd effect when expressed artistically in the language of the old ballads.

The pre-Raphaelites have for twenty years exercised a great influence on the rising generation of English poets. All the hysterical and degenerate have sung with Rossetti of 'damozels' and of the Virgin Mary, have with Swinburne eulogized unnatural license, crime, hell, and the devil. They have, with Morris, mangled language in bardic strains, and in the manner of the *Canterbury Tales ;* and if the whole of English poetry is not to-day unmitigatedly pre-Raphaelite, it is due merely to the fortunate accident that, contemporaneously with the pre-Raphaelites, so sound a poet as Tennyson has lived and worked. The official honours bestowed on him as Poet Laureate, his unexampled success among readers, pointed him out to a part at least of the petty strugglers and aspirants as worthy of imitation, and so it comes about that among the chorus of the lily-bearing mystics there are also heard other street-singers who follow the poet of the *Idylls of the King*.

In its further development pre-Raphaelitism in England degenerated into 'æstheticism,' and in France into 'symbolism.' With both of these tendencies we must deal more fully.

CHAPTER III.

SYMBOLISM.

A SIMILAR phenomenon to that which we observed in the case of the pre-Raphaelites is afforded by the French Symbolists. We see a number of young men assemble for the purpose of founding a school. It assumes a special title, but in spite of all sorts of incoherent cackle and subsequent attempts at mystification it has, beyond this name, no kind of general artistic principle or clear æsthetic ideal. It only follows the tacit, but definitely recognisable, aim of making a noise in the world, and by attracting the attention of men through its extravagances, of attaining celebrity and profit, and the gratification of all the desires and conceits agitating the envious souls of these filibusters of fame.

Shortly after 1880 there was, in the Quartier Latin in Paris, a group of literary aspirants, all about the same age, who used to meet in an underground café at the Quai St. Michel, and, while drinking beer, smoking and quibbling late into the night, or early hours of the morning, abused in a scurrilous manner the well-known and successful authors of the day, while boasting of their own capacity, as yet unrevealed to the world.

The greatest talkers among them were Emile Goudeau, a chatterbox unknown save as the author of a few silly satirical verses; Maurice Rollinat, the author of *Les Névroses;* and Edmond Haraucourt, who now stands in the front rank of French mystics. They called themselves the 'Hydropaths,' an entirely meaningless word, which evidently arose out of an indistinct reminiscence of both 'hydrotherapy' and 'neuropath,' and which was probably intended, in the characteristic vagueness of the mystic thought of the weak-minded, to express only the general idea of people whose health is not satisfactory, who are ailing and under treatment. In any case there is, in the self-chosen name, a suggestion of shattered nervous vitality vaguely felt and admitted. The group, moreover, owned a weekly paper *Lutèce,* which ceased after a few issues.*

About 1884 the society left their paternal pot-house, and pitched their tent in the Café François I., Boulevard St. Michel. This *café* attained a high renown. It was the cradle of Symbolism. It is still the temple of a few ambitious youths, who hope, by joining the Symbolist school, to acquire that

* A history of the commencement of this society has been written by one of the members, Mathias Morhardt. See 'Les Symboliques,' *Nouvelle Revue* du 15 Février, 1892, p. 765.

advancement which they could not expect from their own abilities. It is, too, the Kaaba to which all foreign imbeciles make a pilgrimage, those, that is, who have heard of the new Parisian tendency, and wish to become initiated into its teachings and mysteries. A few of the Hydropaths did not join in the change of quarters, and their places were taken by fresh auxiliaries—Jean Moréas, Laurent Tailhade, Charles Morice, etc. These dropped the old name, and were known for a short time as the 'Décadents.' This had been applied to them by a critic in derision, but just as the 'Beggars' of the Netherlands proudly and truculently appropriated the appellation bestowed in contempt and mockery, so the 'Décadents' stuck in their hats the insult, which had been cast in their faces, as a sign of mutiny against criticism. Soon, however, these original guests of the François I. became tired of their name, and Moréas invented for them the designation of 'Symbolistes,' under which they became generally known, while a special smaller group, who had separated themselves from the Symbolists, continued to retain the title of 'Décadents.'

The Symbolists are a remarkable example of that group-forming tendency which we have learnt to know as a peculiarity of 'degenerates.' They had in common all the signs of degeneracy and imbecility: overweening vanity and self-conceit, strong emotionalism, confused disconnected thoughts, garrulity (the 'logorrhœa' of mental therapeutics), and complete incapacity for serious sustained work. Several of them had had a secondary education, others even less. All of them were profoundly ignorant, and being unable, through weakness of will and inability to pay attention, to learn anything systematically, they persuaded themselves, in accordance with a well-known psychological law, that they despised all positive knowledge, and held that only dreams and divinings, only 'intuitions,' were worthy of human beings. A few of them, like Moréas and Guaita, who afterwards became a 'magian,' read in a desultory fashion all sorts of books which chanced to fall into their hands at the *bouquinistes* of the Quais, and delivered themselves of the snatched fruits of their reading in grandiloquent and mysterious phrases before their comrades. Their listeners thereupon imagined that they had indulged in an exhausting amount of study, and in this way they acquired that intellectual lumber which they peddled out in such an ostentatious display in their articles and pamphlets, and in which the mentally sane reader, to his amused astonishment, meets with the names of Schopenhauer, Darwin, Taine, Renan, Shelley and Goethe; names employed to label the shapeless, unrecognisable rubbish-heaps of a mental dustbin, filled with raw scraps of uncomprehended and insolently mutilated propositions and fragments of thought, dishonestly extracted and appropriated. This ignorance on the part of the Symbolists, and their childish flaunting of a pretended culture, are openly admitted by one of them. 'Very few of these young men,' says Charles Morice,* 'have any exact knowledge of the tenets of religion or philosophy. From the expressions used in the Church services, however, they retain some fine terms, such as "monstrance," "ciborium," etc.; several have preserved from Spencer, Mill, Shopenhauer (*sic!*), Comte, Darwin, a few technical terms. Few are those who know deeply what they talk about, or those who do not try to make a show and parade of their manner of speaking, which has no other merit than that of being a conceit in syllables.' (Charles Morice naturally is responsible for this last unmeaning phrase, not I.)

The original guests of the François I. made their appearance at one o'clock in the day at their café, and remained there till dinner-time. Immediately after that meal they returned, and did not leave their headquarters till long after midnight. Of course none of the Symbolists had any known occupation. These 'degenerates' are no more capable of regularly fulfilling any duty than they are of methodical learning. If this organic deficiency appears in a man of the lower classes, he becomes a vagabond; in a woman of that class it leads to prostitution; in one belonging to the upper classes it takes the form of artistic and literary drivel. The German popular mind betrays a deep intuition of the true connection of things in inventing such a word as 'day-thief' (*Tagedieb*) for such æsthetic loafers. Professional thieving and the unconquerable propensity to busy, gossiping, officious idleness flow from the same source, to wit, inborn weakness of brain.

It is true that the boon companions of the café are not conscious of their mentally-crippled condition. They find pet names and graceful appellations for their inability to submit themselves to any sort of discipline, and to devote persistent concentration and attention to any sort of work. They call it 'the artist nature,' 'genius roaming at large,' 'a soaring above the low miasma of the commonplace.' They ridicule the dull Philistine, who, like the horse turning a winch, performs mechanically a regular amount of work; they despise the narrow-minded loons who demand that a man should either pursue a circumscribed bourgeois trade or possess an officially acknowledged status, and who profoundly distrust impecuniary professions. They glory in roving folk who wander about singing and carelessly begging, and they hold up as their ideal the 'commoner of air,' who bathes in morning dew, sleeps under flowers, and gets his clothing from the same firm as the lilies of the field in the Gospel. Richepin's *La Chanson des Gueux* is the most typical expression

* Charles Morice, *La Littérature de tout-à-l'heure*. Paris, 1889, p. 274.

of this theory of life. Baumbach's *Lieder eines fahrenden Gesellen* and *Spielmannslieder* are analogous specimens in German literature, but of a less pronounced character. Schiller's *Pegasus im Joch* seems to be pulling at the same rope as these haters of the work society expects of them, but it is only apparently so. Our great poet sides not with the impotent sluggard, but with that overflowing energy which would fain do greater things than the work of an office-boy or a night-watchman.

Moreover, the pseudo-artistic loafer, in spite of his imbecility and self-esteem, cannot fail to perceive that his mode of life runs contrary to the laws on which the structure of society and civilization are based, and he feels the need of justifying himself in his own eyes. This he does by investing with a high significance the dreams and chatter over which he wastes his time, calculated to arouse in him the illusion that they rival in value the most serious productions. 'The fact is, you see,' says M. Stéphane Mallarmé, 'that a fine book is the end for which the world was made.'* Morice complains † touchingly that the poetic mind 'should be bound to suffer the interruption of a twenty-eight days' army drill between the two halves of a verse.' 'The excitement of the streets,' he goes on, 'the jarring of the Governmental engine, the newspapers, the elections, the change of the Ministry, have never made so much noise; the stormy and turbulent autocracy of trade has suppressed the love of the beautiful in the thoughts of the multitude, and industry has killed as much silence as politics might still have permitted to survive.' In fact, what are all these nothings — commerce, manufactures, politics, administration—against the immense importance of a hemistich?

The drivelling of the Symbolists was not entirely lost in the atmosphere of their café, like the smoke of their pipes and cigarettes. A certain amount of it was perpetuated, and appeared in the *Revue Indépendante*, the *Revue Contemporaine*, and other fugitive periodicals, which served as organs to the round table of the François I. These little journals and the books published by the Symbolists were not at first noticed outside the café. Then it happened that *chroniqueurs* of the Boulevard papers, into whose hands these writings chanced to fall, devoted an article to them on days when 'copy' was scanty, but only to hold them up to ridicule. That was all the Symbolists wanted. Mockery or praise mattered little so long as they got noticed. Now they were in the saddle, and showed at once what unparalleled circus-riders they were. They themselves used every effort to get into the larger newspapers, and when one of them succeeded, like the smith of Jüterbock in the familiar fairy tale,

* Jules Huret, *Enquête sur l'Évolution littéraire*. Paris, 1891, p. 65.
† Charles Morice, *op. cit.*, p. 271.

in throwing his cap into an editor's office through the crack of the door incautiously put ajar, he followed it neck and crop, took possession of the place, and in the twinkling of an eye transformed it into the citadel of the Symbolist party. In these tactics everything served their turn—the dried-up scepticism and apathy of Parisian editors, who take nothing seriously, are capable neither of enthusiasm nor of repugnance, and only know the cardinal principle of their business, viz., to make a noise, to arouse curiosity, to forestall others by bringing out something new and sensational; the uncritical gaping attitude of the public, who repeat in faith all that their newspaper gossips to them with an air of importance; the cowardice and cupboard-love of the critics who, finding themselves confronted by a closed and numerous band of reckless young men, got nervous at the sight of their clenched fists and angry threatening glances, and did not dare to quarrel with them; the low cunning of the ambitious, who hoped to make a good bargain if they speculated on the rise of shares in Symbolism. Thus the very worst and most despicable characteristics of editors, critics, aspiring authors, and newspaper readers, co-operated to make known, and, in part, even famous, the names of the original habitués of the François I., and to awaken the conviction in very many weak minds of both hemispheres that their tendency governed the literature of the day, and included all the germs of the future. This triumph of the Symbolists marks the victory of the gang over the individual. It proves the superiority of attack over defence, and the efficacy of mutual-admiration-insurance, even in the case of the most beggarly incapacity.

With all their differences, the works of the Symbolists have two features in common. They are vague often to the point of being unintelligible, and they are pious. Their vagueness is only to be expected, after all that has been said here about the peculiarities of mystic thought. Their piousness has attained to an importance which makes it necessary to consider it more in detail.

When, in the last few years, a large number of mysteries, passion plays, golden legends, and cantatas appeared, when one dozen after another of new poets and authors, in their first poems, novels, and treatises, made ardent confessions of faith, invoked the Virgin Mary, spoke with rapture of the sacrifice of the Mass, and knelt in fervent prayer, the cry arose amongst reactionists, who have a vested interest in diffusing a belief in a reversion of cultured humanity to the mental darkness of the past: 'Behold, the youth, the hope, the future of the French people is turning away from science; "emancipation" is becoming bankrupt; souls are opening again to religion, and the Holy Catholic Church steps anew into its lofty office, as the teacher, comforter, and guide of civilized mankind.' The Symbolistic tendency is designedly called 'neo-Catholic,' and certain critics pointed to its appearance and success as a proof that freethought was overthrown by faith. 'Even the most superficial glance at the state of the world,' writes Edouard Rod,* 'shows us that we are on all sides in the full swing of reaction.' And, further, 'I believe in reaction in every sense of the word. How far this reaction will go is the secret of to-morrow.'

The jubilant heralds of the new reaction, in inquiring into the cause of this movement, find, with remarkable unanimity, this answer, viz.: The best and most cultivated minds return to faith, because they found out that science had deceived them, and not done for them what it had promised to do. 'The man of this century,' says M. Melchior de Vogüé,† 'has acquired a very excusable confidence in himself. . . . The rational mechanism of the world has been revealed to him. . . . In the explanation of things the Divine order is wholly eliminated. . . . Besides, why follow after doubtful causes, when the operations of the universe and of humanity had become so clear to the physicist and physiologist? . . . The least wrong God ever wrought was that of being unnecessary. Great minds assured us of this, and all mediocre spirits were convinced of it. The eighteenth century had inaugurated the worship of Reason. The rapture of that millennium lasted but a moment. Then came eternal disillusion, the regularly recurring ruin of all that man had built upon the hollow basis of his reason. . . . He had to admit that, beyond the circle of acquired truths, the abyss of ignorance appeared again just as deep, just as disquieting.'

Charles Morice, the theorist and philosopher of the Symbolists, arraigns Science on almost every page of his book, *La Littérature de tout-à-l'heure*, for her great and divers sins. 'It is lamentable,' he says in his apocalyptic phraseology,‡ 'that our learned men have no idea how, in popularizing science, they were disorganizing it (?). To entrust principles to inferior memories, is to expose them to the uncertainty of unauthorized interpretations, of erroneous commentaries and heterodox hypotheses. For the word that the books contain is a dead letter, and the books themselves may perish, but the impact which they leave behind them, the breath going forth from them, survives. And what if they have breathed out storm and unloosed (!) darkness? But this is just what all this chaos of vulgarization has as its most patent result. . . . Is not such the natural consequence of a century of psychological investigation, which was a good training for the reason, but whose immediate and actual

* Huret, *op. cit.*, p. 14. † Vte E. M. de Vogüé, *op. cit.*, p. xix *et seq.*
‡ Morice, *op. cit.*, pp. 5, 103, 177.

consequences must inevitably be weariness, and disgust, ay, and despair of reason? . . . Science had erased the word mystery. With the same stroke of the pen she had expunged the words beauty, truth, joy, humanity. . . . And now mysticism takes from Science, the intruder and usurper, not only all that she had stolen, but something also, it may be, of her own property. The reaction against the shameless and miserable negations of scientific literature . . . has taken the form of an unforeseen poetical restoration of Catholicism.'

Another graphomaniac, the author of that imbecile book, *Rembrandt as Educator*, drivels in almost the same way. 'Interest in science, and especially in the once so popular natural science, has widely diminished of late in the German world. . . . There has been to a certain extent a surfeit of induction; there is a longing for synthesis; the days of objectivity are declining once more to their end, and, in its place, subjectivity knocks at the door.'*

Edouard Rod† says: 'The century has advanced without keeping all its promises'; and further on he speaks again of 'this ageing and deluded century.'

In a small book, which has become a sort of gospel to imbeciles and idiots, *Le Devoir présent*, the author, M. Paul Desjardins,‡ makes continual attacks on 'so-called scientific empiricism,' and speaks of the 'negativists, the empiricists, and the mechanists, whose attention is wholly taken up with physical and inexorable forces,' boasting of his intention 'to render invalid the value of the empirical methods.'

Even a serious thinker, M. F. Paulhan,§ in his investigation of the basis of French neo-mysticism, comes to the conclusion that natural science has shown itself powerless to satisfy the needs of mankind. 'We feel ourselves surrounded by a vast unknown, and demand that at least access to it should be permitted to us. Evolution and positivism have blocked the way. . . . For these reasons evolution could not but show itself incapable of guiding the mind, even if it left us great thoughts.'

Overwhelming as may appear this unanimity between strong minds commanding respect and weak graphomaniacs, it does not, nevertheless, contain the slightest spark of truth. To assert that the world turns away from science because the 'empirical,' which means the scientific, method of observation and registration has suffered shipwreck, is either a conscious lie or shows lack of mental responsibility. A healthy-minded and honourable man must almost feel ashamed to have still to

* *Rembrandt als Erzieher.* Leipzig, 1890, p. 2.

† Edouard Rod, *Les Idées morales du Temps présent.* Paris, 1892, p. 66.

‡ Paul Desjardins, *Le Devoir présent.* Paris, 1892, pp. 5, 8, 39.

§ F. Paulhan, *Le nouveau Mysticisme.* Paris, 1891, p. 120.

demonstrate this. In the last ten years, by means of spectrum-analysis, science has made disclosures in the constitution of the most distant heavenly bodies, their component matter, their degree of heat, the speed and direction of their motions; it has firmly established the essential unity of all modes of force, and has made highly probable the unity of all matter; it is on the track of the formation and development of chemical elements, and it has learnt to understand the building up of extremely intricate organic combinations; it shows us the relations of atoms in molecules, and the position of molecules in space; it has thrown wonderful light on the conditions of the action of electricity, and placed this force at the service of mankind; it has renewed geology and palæontology, and disentangled the concatenation of animal and vegetable forms of life; it has newly created biology and embryology, and has explained in a surprising manner, through the discovery and investigation of germs, some of the most disquieting mysteries of perpetual metamorphosis, illness, and death; it has found or perfected methods which, like chronography, instantaneous photography, etc., permit of the analysis and registration of the most fleeting phenomena, not immediately apprehensible by human sense, and which promise to become extremely fruitful for the knowledge of nature. And in the face of such splendid, such overwhelmingly grand results, the enumeration of which could easily be doubled and trebled, does anyone dare to speak of the shipwreck of science, and of the incapacity of the empirical method?

Science is said not to have kept what she promised. When has she ever promised anything else than honest and attentive observation of phenomena and, if possible, establishment of the conditions under which they occur? And has she not kept this promise? Does she not keep it perpetually? If anyone has expected of her that she would explain from one day to another the whole mechanism of the universe, like a juggler explains his apparent magic, he has indeed no idea of the true mission of science. She denies herself all leaps and flights. She advances step by step. She builds slowly and patiently a firm bridge out into the Unknown, and can throw no new arch over the abyss before she has sunk deep the foundations of a new pier in the depths, and raised it to the right height.

Meanwhile, she asks nothing at all about the first cause of phenomena, so long as she has so many more proximate causes to investigate. Many of the most eminent men of science go so far, indeed, as to assert that the first cause will never become the object of scientific investigation, and call it, with Herbert Spencer, 'the Unknowable,' or exclaim despondingly with Du Bois-Reymond, *Ignorabimus*. Both of them in this respect are completely unscientific, and only prove that even clear thinkers like Spencer, and sober investigators like Du Bois Reymond, stand yet under the influence of theological dreams. Science can speak of no Unknowable, since this would presuppose that she is able to mark exactly the boundaries of the Knowable. This, however, she cannot do, since every new discovery thrusts back that boundary. Moreover, the acceptance of an Unknowable involves the acknowledgment that there is something which we cannot know. Now, in order to be able seriously to assert the existence of this Something, either we must have acquired some knowledge of it, however slight and indistinct, and this, therefore, would prove that it cannot be unknowable, since we actually know it, and nothing then would justify us in declaring beforehand that our present knowledge of it, however little it may be, will not be extended and deepened ; or else we have no knowledge, even of the minutest character, of the philosopher's Unknowable, in which case it cannot exist for us. The whole conception is based upon nothing, and the word is an idle creation of a dreaming imagination. The same thing can be said of *Ignorabimus*. It is the opposite of science. It is not a correct inference from well-founded premises, it is not the result of observation, but a mystical prophecy. No one has the right to make communications with respect to the future as matters of fact. Science can announce what she knows to-day ; she can also mark off exactly what she does not know ; but to say what she will or will not at any time know is not her office.

It is true that whoever asks from Science that she should give an answer to all the questions of idle and restless minds with unshaken and audacious certainty must be disappointed by her ; for she will not, and cannot, fulfil his desires. Theology and metaphysics have an easier task. They devise some fable, and propound it with overwhelming earnestness. If anyone does not believe in them, they threaten and insult the intractable client ; but they can prove nothing to him, they cannot force him to take their chimeras for cash. Theology and metaphysics can never be brought into a dilemma. It costs them nothing to add to their words more words, to unite to one voluntary assertion another, and pile up dogma upon dogma. It will never occur to the serious sound mind, which thirsts after real knowledge, to seek it from metaphysics or theology. They appeal only to childish brains, whose desire for knowledge, or, rather, whose curiosity, is fully satisfied with the cradling croon of an old wife's tale.

Science does not compete with theology and metaphysics. If the latter declare themselves able to explain the whole phenomenon of the universe, Science shows that these pretended explanations are empty chatter. She, for her part, is naturally on her guard against putting in the place of a proved absurdity another absurdity. She says modestly: 'Here we have a fact, here an assumption, here a conjecture. 'Tis a rogue who gives more than he has.' If this does not satisfy the neo-Catholics, they should sit down and themselves investigate, themselves find out new facts, and help to make clear the weird obscurity of the phenomenon of the universe. That would be a proof of a true desire for knowledge. At the table of Science there is room for all, and every fellow-observer is welcome. But this does not enter into even the dreams of these poor creatures, who drivel about the 'bankruptcy of science.' Talk is so much easier and more comfortable than inquiry and discovery!

True, science tells us nothing about the life after death, of harp-concerts in Paradise, and of the transformation of stupid youths and hysterical geese into white-clad angels with rainbow-coloured wings. It contents itself, in a much more plain and prosaic manner, with alleviating the existence of mankind on earth. It lessens the average of mortality, and lengthens the life of the individual through the suppression of known causes of disease; it invents new comforts, and makes easier the struggle against Nature's destructive powers. The Symbolist, who is preserved after surgical interference through asepsy from suppuration, mortification, and death; who protects himself by a Chamberland filter from typhus; who by the careless turning of a button fills his room with electric light; who through a telephone can converse with someone beloved in far-distant countries, has to thank this alleged bankrupt science for it all, and not the theology to which he maintains that he wants to return.

The demand that science should give not only true, if limited, conclusions, and offer not only tangible benefits, but also solve all enigmas to-day and at once, and make all men omniscient, happy, and good, is ridiculous. Theology and metaphysics have never fulfilled this demand. It is simply the intellectual manifestation of the same foolish conceit, which in material concerns reveals itself in hankering after pleasure and in shirking work. The man who has lost his social status, who craves for wine and women, for idleness and honours, and complains of the constitution of society because it offers no satisfaction to his lusts, is own brother to the Symbolist who demands truth, and reviles science because it does not hand it to him on a golden platter. Both betray a similar incapacity to grasp the reality of things, and to understand that it is not possible to acquire goods without bodily labour, or truth without mental exertion. The capable man who wrests her gifts from Nature, the industrious inquirer who in the sweat of his brow bores into the sources of knowledge, inspires respect and cordial sympathy. On the other hand, there can be but little esteem for the discontented idlers who look for riches from a lucky lottery ticket, or a rich uncle, and for enlightenment from a revelation which is to come to them without trouble on their part over the slovenly beer-drinking at their favourite café.

The dunces who abuse science, reproach it also for having destroyed ideals, and stolen from life all its worth. This accusation is just as absurd as the talk about the bankruptcy of science. A higher ideal than the increase of general knowledge there cannot be. What saintly legend is as beautiful as the life of an inquirer, who spends his existence bending over a microscope, almost without bodily wants, known and honoured by few, working only for his own conscience' sake, without any other ambition than that perhaps one little new fact may be firmly established, which a more fortunate successor will make use of in a brilliant synthesis, and insert as a stone in some monument of natural science? What religious fable has inspired with a contempt of death sublimer martyrs than a Gehlen, who sank down poisoned while preparing the arsenious hydrogen which he had discovered; or a Crocé-Spinelli, who was overtaken by death in an over-rapid ascent of his balloon while observing the pressure of the atmosphere; or an Ehrenberg, who became blind over his life's work; or a Hyrtl, who almost entirely destroyed his eyesight by his anatomical corrosive preparations; or the doctors, who inoculate themselves with some deadly disease—not to speak of the innumerable crowd of discoverers travelling to the North Pole, and to the interior of dark continents? And did Archimedes really feel his life to be so worthless when he entreated the pillaging bands of Marcellus, 'Do not disturb my circles'? Genuine healthy poetry has always recognised this, and finds its most ideal characters, not in a devotee, who murmurs prayers with drivelling lips, and stares with distorted eyes at some visual hallucination, but in a Prometheus and a Faust, who wrestle for science, *i.e.*, for exact knowledge of nature.

The assertion that science has not kept its promises, and that, therefore, the rising generation is turning away from it, does not for a moment resist criticism, and is entirely without foundation. It is a senseless premise of neo-Catholicism, were the Symbolists to declare a hundred times over that disgust with science had made them mystics. The explanations which even a healthy-minded man makes with respect to the true motives of his actions are only to be accepted with the most cautious criticism; those proffered by the degenerate are completely useless. For the impulse to act and to think originate, for the degenerate, in the unconscious, and consciousness finds subsequent, and in some measure plausible, reasons for the thoughts and deeds, the real source of which is unknown to itself. Every book on suggestion gives illustrations of Charcot's typical case: a hysterical female is sent into hypnotic sleep, and it is suggested to her that on awaking she is to stab one of the doctors present. She is then awakened. She grasps a knife and makes for her appointed victim. The blade is wrenched from her, and she is asked why she wishes to murder the doctor. She answers without hesitation, 'Because he has done me an injury.' Note that she had seen him that day for the first time in her life. This person felt when in a waking condition the impulse to kill the doctor. Her consciousness had no presentiment that this impulse had been suggested to her in a hypnotic state. Consciousness knows that a murder is never committed without some motive. Forced to find a motive for the attempted murder, consciousness falls back upon the only one reasonably possible under the circumstances, and fancies that it got hold of the idea of murder in order to avenge some wrong.

The brothers Janet* offer, as an explanation of this psychological phenomenon, the hypothesis of dual personality. 'Every person consists of two personalities, one conscious and one unconscious. Among healthy persons both are alike complete, and both in equilibrium. In the hysteric they are unequal, and out of equilibrium. One of the two personalities, usually the conscious, is incomplete, the other remaining perfect.' The conscious personality has the thankless task of inventing reasons for the actions of the unconscious. It resembles the familiar game where one person makes movements and another says words in keeping with them. In the degenerate with disturbed equilibrium consciousness has to play the part of an ape-like mother finding excuses for the stupid and naughty tricks of a spoiled child. The unconscious personality commits follies and evil deeds, and the conscious, standing powerless by, and unable to hinder it, seeks to palliate them by all sorts of pretexts.

The cause of the neo-Catholic movement, then, is not to be sought in any objection felt by younger minds to science, or in their having any complaint to make against it. A De Vogüé, a Rod, a Desjardins, a Paulhan, who impute such a basis to the mysticism of the Symbolists, arbitrarily attribute to it an origin which it never had. It is due solely and alone to the degenerate condition of its inventors. Neo-Catholicism is rooted in emotivity and mysticism, both of these being the most frequent and most distinctive stigmata of the degenerate.

That the mysticism of the degenerate, even in France, the

* Pierre Janet, 'Les Actes inconscients et le Dédoublement de la Personalité,' *Revue philosophique*, December, 1886. Paul Janet, 'L'Hystérie et l'Hypnotisme d'après la Théorie de la double Personnalité,' *Revue scientifique*, 1888, 1er vol., p. 616.

land of Voltaire, has frequently taken the form of religious enthusiasm might at first seem strange, but will be understood if we consider the political and social circumstances of the French people during the last decade.

The great Revolution proclaimed three ideals: Liberty, Equality, and Fraternity. Fraternity is a harmless word which has no real meaning, and therefore disturbs nobody. Liberty, to the upper classes, is certainly unpleasant, and they lament greatly over the sovereignty of the people and universal suffrage, but still they bear, without too much complaint, a state of things which, after all, is sufficiently mitigated by a prying administration, police supervision, militarism, and gendarmerie, and which will always be sufficient to keep the mob in leash. But equality to those in possession is an insufferable abomination. It is the one thing won by the great Revolution, which has outlasted all subsequent changes in the form of government, and has remained alive in the French people. The Frenchman does not know much about fraternity; his liberty in many ways has a muzzle as its emblem; but his equality he possesses as a matter of fact, and to it he holds firmly. The lowest vagabond, the bully of the capital, the rag-picker, the hostler, believes that he is quite as good as the duke, and says so to his face without the smallest hesitation if occasion arises. The reasons of the Frenchman's fanaticism for equality are not particularly elevated. The feeling does not spring from a proud, manly consciousness and the knowledge of his own worth, but from low envy and malicious intolerance. There shall be nothing above the dead level! There shall be nothing better, nothing more beautiful or even more striking, than the average vulgarity! The upper classes struggle against this rage for equalization with passionate vehemence, especially and precisely those who have reached their high position through the great Revolution.

The grandchildren of the rural serfs, who plundered and destroyed the country seats of noblemen, basely murdered the inmates, and seized upon their lands; the descendants of town grocers and cobblers, who waxed rich as politicians of street and club, as speculators in national property and assignats, and as swindlers in army purveyance, do not want to become identified with the mob. They want to form a privileged class. They want to be recognised as belonging to a more honourable caste. They sought, for this purpose, a distinguishing mark, which would make them at once conspicuous as members of a select class, and they found it in belonging to the Church.

This choice is quite intelligible. The mass of the people in France, especially in towns, is sceptical, and the aristocracy of the *ancien régime*, who in the eighteenth century bragged about free thought, had come out of the deluge of 1789 as very pious persons, comprehending or divining the inner connection between all the old ideas and emblems of the Faith, of the Monarchy, and of feudal nobility. Hence, through their clericalism, the parvenus at once established a contrast between themselves and the multitude from whom they wanted to keep distinct, and a resemblance with the class into which they would like to smuggle or thrust themselves.

Experience teaches that the instinct of preservation is often the worst adviser in positions of danger. The man who cannot swim, falling into the water, involuntarily throws up his arms, and thus infallibly lets his head be submerged and himself be drowned; whereas his mouth and nose would remain above water if he held his arms and hands quietly under the surface. The bad rider, who feels his seat insecure, usually draws up his legs, and then comes the certainty of a fall; whereas he would probably be able to preserve his equilibrium if he left his legs outstretched. Thus the French *bourgeoisie*, who knew that they had snatched for themselves the fruits of the great upheaval, and let the Fourth Estate, who alone had made the Revolution, come out of it empty-handed, chose the worst means for retaining their unjustly-acquired possessions and privileges, and for escaping unnatural equalization when they made use of their clericalism for the establishment of their social status. They alienated, in consequence, the wisest, strongest, and most cultivated minds, and drove over to socialism many young men who, though intellectually radical, were yet economically conservative, and little in favour of equality, and who would have become a strong defence for a free-thinking *bourgeoisie*, but who felt that socialism, however radical its economic doctrines and impossible its theories of equality, represented emancipation.

But I have not to judge here whether the religious mimicry of the French *bourgeoisie*, which was to make them resemble the old nobility, exerts the protection expected of it or not; I only set down the fact of this mimicry. It is a necessary consequence that all the rich and snobbish parvenus send their sons to the Jesuit middle and high schools. To be educated by the Jesuits is regarded as a sign of caste, very much as is membership of the Jockey Club. The old pupils of the Jesuits form a 'black freemasonry,' which zealously advances their protégés in every career, marries them to heiresses, hurries to their assistance in misfortune, hushes up their sins, stifles scandal, etc. It is the Jesuits who for the last decade have made it their care to inculcate their own habits of thinking into the rich and high-born youth of France entrusted to them. These youths brought brains of hereditary deficiency, and therefore mystically disposed, into the clerical schools, and these then gave to the mystic thoughts of the degenerate pupils a religious content.

This is not an arbitrary assumption, but a well-founded fact. Charles Morice, the æsthetic theorist and philosopher of the Symbolists, received his education from the Jesuits, according to the testimony of his friends.* So did Louis le Cardonnel, Henri de Régnier, and others. The Jesuits invented the phrase 'bankruptcy of science,' and their pupils repeat it after them, because it includes a plausible explanation of their pietistic mooning, the real organic causes of which are unknown to them, and for that matter would not be understood if they were known. 'I return to faith, because science does not satisfy me,' is a possible statement. It is even a superior thing to say, since it presupposes a thirst for truth and a noble interest in great questions. On the contrary, a man will hardly be willing to confess, 'I am an enthusiastic admirer of the Trinity and the Holy Virgin because I am degenerate, and my brain is incapable of attention and clear thought.'

That the Jesuitical argument as reported by MM. de Vogüé, Rod, etc., can have found credit beyond clerical circles and degenerate youth, that the half-educated are heard repeating to-day, 'Science is conquered, the future belongs to religion,' is consistent with the mental peculiarities of the million. They never have recourse to facts, but repeat the ready-made propositions with which they have been prompted. If they would have regard to facts, they would know that the number of faculties, teachers and students of natural science, of scientific periodicals and books, of their subscribers and readers, of laboratories, scientific societies and reports to the academies increases year by year. It can be shown by figures that science does not lose, but continually gains ground.† But the million does not care about exact statistics. In France it accepts without resistance the suggestion, that science is retreating before religion, from a few newspapers, written mainly for clubmen and gilded courtezans, into the columns of which the pupils of the clerical schools have found an entrance. Of science itself, of its hypotheses, methods, and results, they have never known anything. Science was at one time the fashion. The daily press of that date said, 'We live in a scientific age'; the news of the day reported the travels and marriages of scientists; the feuilleton-novels contained witty allusions to Darwin; the inventors of elegant walking-sticks and perfumes called their productions 'Evolution Essence' or 'Selection Canes'; those who

* Morhardt, *op. cit.*, p. 769.

† See the Catalogue of Scientific Papers compiled and published by the Royal Society. The first series of this catalogue, covering the time from 1800 to 1863, comprises six volumes; the second, dealing with the decade from 1864 to 1873, comprises two volumes, equivalent to at least three of the first series (1047 and 1310 pages); of the third series (1874 to 1883) only one volume has been issued as yet, but it promises to outrun the second by at least one half.

affected culture took themselves seriously for the pioneers of progress and enlightenment. To-day those social circles which set the fashions, and the papers which seek to please these circles, decree that, not science is *chic*, but faith, and now the paragraphs of the boulevard papers relate small piquant sayings of preachers ; in the feuilleton-novels there are quotations from the *Imitation of Christ ;* inventors bring out richly-mounted prie-dieus and choice rosaries, and the Philistine feels with deep emotion the miraculous flower of faith springing up and blossoming in his heart. Of real disciples science has scarcely lost one. It is only natural, on the contrary, that the plebs of the salons, to whom it has never been more than a fashion, should turn their backs on it at the mere command of a tailor or a modiste.

Thus much on the neo-Catholicism which, partly for party reasons, partly from ignorance, partly from snobbishness, is mistaken for a serious intellectual movement of the times.

The pretension of Symbolism to be, not only a return to faith, but a new theory of art and poetry, is what we must now proceed to test.

If we wish to know at the outset what Symbolists understand by symbol and symbolism, we shall meet with the same difficulties we encountered in determining the precise meaning of the name pre-Raphaelitism, and for the same reason, viz., because the inventors of these appellations understood by them hundreds of different mutually contradictory, indefinite things, or simply nothing at all. A skilled and sagacious journalist, Jules Huret,* instituted an inquiry about the new literary movement in France, and from its leading representatives acquired information, by which he has furnished us with a trustworthy knowledge of the meaning which they connect, or pretend to connect, with the expressions and phraseology of their programme. I will here adduce some of these utterances and declarations. They will not tell us what Symbolism is. But they may afford us some insight into symbolist methods of thought.

M. Stéphane Mallarmé, whose leadership of the Symbolist band is least disputed among the disciples, expresses himself as follows: 'To name an object means to suppress three-quarters of the pleasure of a poem—*i.e.*, of the happiness which consists in gradually divining it. Our dream should be to suggest the object. The symbol is the perfected use of this mystery, viz., to conjure up an object gradually in order to show the condition of a soul; or, conversely, to choose an object, and out of it to reveal a state of the soul by a series of interpretations.'

If the reader does not at once understand this combination of vague words, he need not stop to solve them. Later on I will translate the stammerings of this weak mind into the speech of sound men.

* Jules Huret, *Enquête sur l'Évolution littéraire.* Paris, 1891.

M. Paul Verlaine, another high-priest of the sect, expresses himself as follows: 'It was I who, in the year 1885, laid claim to the name of Symbolist. The Parnassians, and most of the romanticists, in a certain sense lacked symbols. . . . Thence errors of local colouring in history, the shrinking up of the myth through false philosophical interpretations, thought without the discernment of analogies, the anecdote emptied of feeling.'

Let us listen to a few second-rate poets of the group. 'I declare art,' says M. Paul Adam, 'to be the enshrining of a dogma in a symbol. It is a means of making a system prevail, and of bringing truths to the light of day.' M. Rémy de Gourmont confesses honestly: 'I cannot unveil the hidden meaning of the word "symbolism," since I am neither a theorist nor a magician.' And M. Saint-Pol-Roux-le-Magnifique utters this profound warning: 'Let us take care! Symbolism carried to excess leads to *nombrilisme*, and to a morbid mechanism. . . . This symbolism is to some extent a parody of mysticism. . . . Pure symbolism is an anomaly in this remarkable century, remarkable for militant activities. Let us view this transitional art as a clever trick played upon naturalism, and as a precursor of the poetry of to-morrow.'

We may expect from the theorists and philosophers of the group more exhaustive information concerning their methods and aims. Accordingly, M. Charles Morice instructs us how 'the symbol is the combination of the objects which have aroused our sensations, with our souls, in a fiction [*fiction*]. The means is suggestion; it is a question of giving people a remembrance of something which they have never seen.' And M. Gustav Kahn says: 'For me personally, symbolic art consists in recording in a cycle of works, as completely as possible, the modifications and variations of the mind of the poet, who is inspired by an aim which he has determined.'

In Germany there have already been found some imbeciles and idiots, some victims of hysteria and graphomania, who affirm that they understand this twaddle, and who develop it further in lectures, newspaper articles and books. The cultured German Philistine, who from of old has had preached to him contempt for 'platitude,' *i.e.*, for healthy common-sense, and admiration for 'deep meaning,' which is as a rule only the futile bubbling of soft and addled brains incapable of thought, becomes visibly uneasy, and begins to inquire if there may not really be something behind these senseless series of words. In France people have not been caught on the limed twigs of these poor fools and cold-blooded jesters, but have considered Symbolism to be what in fact it is, madness or humbug. We shall meet with these words in the writings of noted representatives of all shades of literary thought.

'The Symbolists!' exclaims M. Jules Lemaître, 'there are

none. . . . They themselves do not know what they are or what they want. There is something stirring and heaving under the earth, but unable to break through. Do you understand? When they have painfully produced something, they would like to build formulæ and theories around it, but fail in doing so, because they do not possess the necessary strength of mind. . . . They are jesters with a certain amount of sincerity—that I grant them—but nevertheless jesters.' M. Josèphin Péladan describes them as 'whimsical pyrotechnists of metrics and glossaries, who combine in order to get on, and give themselves odd names in order to get known.' M. Jules Bois is much more forcible: 'Disconnected action, confused clamour, such are the Symbolists. Cacophony of savages who have been turning over the leaves of an English grammar, or a glossary of obsolete words. If they have ever known anything, they pretend to have forgotten it. Indistinct, faulty, obscure, they are nevertheless as solemn as augurs. . . . You, decadent Symbolists, you deceive us with childish and necromantic formulæ.' Verlaine himself, the co-founder of Symbolism, in a moment of sincerity, calls his followers a 'flat-footed horde, each with his own banner, on which is inscribed *Réclame!*' M. Henri de Régnier says apologetically: 'They feel the need of gathering round a common flag, so that they may fight more effectually against the contented.' M. Zola speaks of them as 'a swarm of sharks who, not being able to swallow us, devour each other.' M. Joseph Caraguel designates symbolical literature as 'a literature of whining, of babbling, of empty brains, a literature of Sudanese Griots [minstrels].' Edmond Haraucourt plainly discerns the aims of the Symbolists: 'They are discontented, and in a hurry. They are the Boulangists of literature. We must live! We would take a place in the world, become notorious or notable. We beat wildly on a drum which is not even a kettledrum. . . . Their true symbol is "Goods by express." Everyone goes by express train. Their destination—Fame.' M. Pierre Quillard thinks that under the title of Symbolists 'poets of rare gifts and unmitigated simpletons have been arbitrarily included.' And M. Gabriel Vicaire sees in the manifestoes of Symbolists 'nothing but school-boy jokes.' Finally, M. Laurent Tailhade, one of the leading Symbolists, divulges the secret: 'I have never attached any other value to this performance than that of a transient amusement. We took in the credulous judgment of a few literary beginners with the joke of coloured vowels, Theban love, Schopenhauerism, and other pranks, which have since made their way in the world.' Quite so; just, as we have already said, in Germany.

To abuse, however, is not to explain, and although summary justice is fit in the case of deliberate swindlers, who, like quack-dentists, play the savage in order to entice money from market-folk, yet anger and ridicule are out of place in dealing with honest imbeciles. They are diseased or crippled, and as such deserve only pity. Their infirmities must be disclosed, but severity of treatment has been abolished even in lunatic asylums since Pinel's time.

The Symbolists, so far as they are honestly degenerate and imbecile, can think only in a mystical, *i.e.*, in a confused way. The unknown is to them more powerful than the known ; the activity of the organic nerves preponderates over that of the cerebral cortex ; their emotions overrule their ideas. When persons of this kind have poetic and artistic instincts, they naturally want to give expression to their own mental state. They cannot make use of definite words of clear import, for their own consciousness holds no clearly-defined univocal ideas which could be embodied in such words. They choose, therefore, vague equivocal words, because these best conform to their ambiguous and equivocal ideas. The more indefinite, the more obscure a word is, so much the better does it suit the purpose of the imbecile, and it is notorious that among the insane this habit goes so far that, to express their ideas, which have become quite formless, they invent new words, which are no longer merely obscure, but devoid of all meaning. We have already seen that, for the typical degenerate, reality has no significance. On this point I will only remind the reader of the previously cited utterances of D. G. Rossetti, Morice, etc. Clear speech serves the purpose of communication of the actual. It has, therefore, no value in the eyes of a degenerate subject. He prizes that language alone which does not force him to follow the speaker attentively, but allows him to indulge without restraint in the meanderings of his own reveries, just as his own language does not aim at the communication of definite thought, but is only intended to give a pale reflection of the twilight of his own ideas. That is what M. Mallarmé means when he says: 'To name an object means to suppress three quarters of the pleasure. . . . Our dream should be to suggest the object.'

Moreover, the thought of a healthy brain has a flow which is regulated by the laws of logic and the supervision of attention. It takes for its content a definite object, manipulates and exhausts it. The healthy man can tell what he thinks, and his telling has a beginning and an end. The mystic imbecile thinks merely according to the laws of association, and without the red thread of attention. He has fugitive ideation. He can never state accurately what he is thinking about ; he can only denote the emotion which at the moment controls his consciousness. He can only say in general, 'I am sad,' 'I am merry,' 'I am fond,' 'I am afraid.' His mind is filled with evanescent, floating, cloudy ideas, which take their hue from the reigning emotion, as the vapour hovering above a crater flames red from the glow at the bottom of the volcanic caldron. When he poetizes, therefore, he will never develop a logical train of thought, but will seek by means of obscure words of distinctly emotional colouring to represent a feeling, a mood. What he prizes in poetical works is not a clear narrative, the exposition of a definite thought, but only the reflected image of a mood, which awakens in him a similar, but not necessarily the same, mood. The degenerate are well aware of this difference between a work which expresses strong mental labour and one in which merely emotionally coloured fugitive ideation ebbs and flows; and they eagerly ask for a distinguishing name for that kind of poetry of which alone they have any understanding. In France they have found this designation in the word 'Symbolism.' The explanations which the Symbolists themselves give of their cognomen appear nonsensical; but the psychologist gathers clearly from their babbling and stammering that under the name 'symbol' they understand a word (or series of words) expressing, not a fact of the external world, or of conscious thought, but an ambiguous glimmer of an idea, which does not force the reader to think, but allows him to dream, and hence brings about no intellectual processes, but only moods.

The great poet of the Symbolists, their most admired model, from whom, according to their unanimous testimony, they have received the strongest inspiration, is Paul Verlaine. In this man we find, in astonishing completeness, all the physical and mental marks of degeneration, and no author known to me answers so exactly, trait for trait, to the descriptions of the degenerate given by the clinicists—his personal appearance, the history of his life, his intellect, his world of ideas and modes of expression. M. Jules Huret* gives the following account of Verlaine's physical appearance: 'His face, like that of a wicked angel grown old, with a thin, untrimmed beard, and abrupt (?) nose; his bushy, bristling eyebrows, resembling bearded wheat, hiding deep-set green eyes; his wholly bald and huge long skull, misshapen by enigmatic bumps—all these give to his physiognomy a contradictory appearance of stubborn asceticism and cyclopean appetites.' As appears in these ludicrously laboured and, in part, entirely senseless expressions, even the most unscientific observer has been struck with what Huret calls his 'enigmatic bumps.' If we look at the portrait of the poet, by Eugène Carrière, of which a photograph serves as frontispiece in the *Select Poems* of Verlaine,† and still more at that by M. Aman-Jean, exhibited in the Champs de Mars Salon in 1892, we instantly remark the great asymmetry of the head, which Lombroso‡ has pointed out

* Huret, *op. cit.*, p. 65.

† Paul Verlaine, *Choix de Poësies.* Paris, 1891.

‡ Lombroso, *L'Uomo delinquente*, p. 184.

among degenerates, and the Mongolian physiognomy indicated by the projecting cheek-bones, obliquely placed eyes, and thin beard, which the same investigator* looks upon as signs of degeneration.

Verlaine's life is enveloped in mystery, but it is known, from his own avowals, that he passed two years in prison. In the poem *Écrit en* 1875† he narrates in detail, not only without the least shame, but with gay unconcern, nay, even with boasting, that he was a true professional criminal:

> 'J'ai naguère habité le meilleur des châteaux
> Dans le plus fin pays d'eau vive et de coteaux:
> Quatre tours s'élevaient sur le front d'autant d'ailes,
> Et j'ai longtemps, longtemps habité l'une d'elles . . .
> Une chambre bien close, une table, une chaise,
> Un lit strict où l'on pût dormir juste à son aise, . . .
> Tel fut mon lot durant les longs mois là passés . . .
> . . . J'étais heureux avec ma vie,
> Reconnaissant de biens que nul, certes, n'envie.'

And in the poem *Un Conte* he says:

> . . . 'ce grand pécheur eut des conduites
> Folles à ce point d'en devenir trop maladroites,
> Si bien que les tribunaux s'en mirent—et les suites!
> Et le voyez-vous dans la plus étroite des boîtes?
>
> Cellules! prison humanitaires! Il faut taire
> Votre horreur fadasse et ce progrès d'hypocrisie' . . .

It is now known that a crime of a peculiarly revolting character led to his punishment; and this is not surprising, since the special characteristic of his degeneration is a madly inordinate eroticism. He is perpetually thinking of lewdness, and lascivious images fill his mind continually. I have no wish to quote passages in which this unhappy slave of his morbidly excited senses has expressed the loathsome condition of his mind, but the reader who wishes to become acquainted with them may be referred to the poems *Les Coquillages*, *Fille*, and *Auburn*.‡ Sexual license is not his only vice. He is also a dipsomaniac, and (as may be expected in a degenerate subject) a paroxysmal dipsomaniac, who, awakened from his debauch, is seized with deep disgust of the alcoholic poison and of himself, and speaks of 'les breuvages exécrés' (*La Bonne Chanson*), but succumbs to the temptation at the next opportunity.

Moral insanity, however, is not present in Verlaine. He sins through irresistible impulse. He is an Impulsivist. The difference between these two forms of degeneration lies in the fact that the morally insane does not look upon his crimes as bad, but commits them with the same unconcern as a sane man would

* Lombroso, *op. cit.*, p. 276. † Verlaine, *op. cit.*, p. 272.
‡ Verlaine, *op. cit.*, pp. 72, 315, 317.

perform any ordinary or virtuous act, and after his misdeed is quite contented with himself; whereas the Impulsivist retains a full consciousness of the baseness of his deeds, hopelessly fights against his impulse until he can no longer resist it, and after the performance* suffers the most terrible remorse and despair. It is only an Impulsivist who speaks in execration of himself as a reprobate (' Un seul Pervers,' in *Sagesse*), or strikes the dejected note which Verlaine touches in the first four sonnets of *Sagesse:*

> 'Hommes durs ! Vie atroce et laide d'ici bas !
> Ah ! que du moins, loin des baisers et des combats,
> Quelque chose demeure un peu sur la montagne,
>
> 'Quelque chose du cœur enfantin et subtil,
> Bonté, respect ! car qu'est-ce qui nous accompagne,
> Et vraiment quand la mort viendra que reste-l-il ? . . .
>
> 'Ferme les yeux, pauvre âme, et rentre sur-le-champ :
> Une tentation des pires. Fuis l'infâme . . .
> Si la vieille folie était encore en route ?
>
> 'Ces souvenirs, va-t-il falloir les retuer ?
> Un assaut furieux, le suprême, sans doute !
> O va prier contre l'orage, va prier ! . . .
>
> 'C'est vers le Moyen-Age énorme et delicat
> Qu'il faudrait que mon cœur en panne naviguât,
> Loin de nos jours d'esprit charnel et de chair triste . . .
>
> 'Et là que j'eusse part . . .
> . . . à la chose vitale,
> Et que je fusse un saint, actes bons, pensers droits,
>
> 'Haute théologie et solide morale,
> Guidé par la folie unique de la Croix
> Sur tes ailes de pierre, ô folle Cathédrale !'

This example serves to show that there is not wanting in Verlaine that religious fervour which usually accompanies morbidly intensified eroticism. This finds a much more decided expression in several other poems. I should wish to quote only from two.†

> 'O mon Dieu, vous m'avez blessé d'amour,
> Et la blessure est encore vibrante,
> O mon Dieu, vous m'avez blessé d'amour.
>
> 'O mon Dieu, votre crainte m'a frappé,
> Et la brûlure est encore là qui tonne
> O mon Dieu, votre crainte m'a frappé.

(Observe the mode of expression and the constant repetitions.)

> 'O mon Dieu, j'ai connu que tout est vil,
> Et votre gloire en moi s'est installée,
> O mon Dieu, j'ai connu que tout est vil.

---

* Shortly, but not immediately after, the immediate result being a sense of great relief and satisfaction.

† Verlaine, *op. cit.*, pp. 175, 178.

'Noyez mon âme aux flots de votre vin,
Fondez ma vie au pain de votre table,
Noyez mon âme aux flots de votre vin.

'Voici mon sang que je n'ai pas versé,
Voici ma chair indignée de souffrance,
Voici mon sang que je n'ai pas versé.'

Then follows the ecstatic enumeration of all the parts of his body, which he offers up in sacrifice to God; and the poem closes thus:

'Vous connaissez tout cela, tout cela,
Et que je suis plus pauvre que personne,
Vous connaissez tout cela, tout cela,
Mais ce que j'ai, mon Dieu, je vous le donne.'

He invokes the Virgin Mary as follows:

'Je ne veux plus aimer que ma mère Marie.
Tous les autres amours sont de commandement,
Nécessaires qu'ils sont, ma mère seulement
Pourra les allumer aux cœurs qui l'ont chérie.

'C'est pour Elle qu'il faut chérir mes ennemis,
C'est pour Elle que j'ai voué ce sacrifice,
Et la douceur de cœur et le zèle au service.
Comme je la priais, Elle les a permis.

'Et comme j'étais faible et bien méchant encore,
Aux mains lâches, les yeux éblouis des chemins,
Elle baissa mes yeux et me joignit les mains,
Et m'enseigna les mots par lesquels on adore.'

The accents here uttered are well known to the clinics of psychiatry. We may compare them to the picture which Legrain* gives of some of his patients. 'His speech continually reverts to God and the Virgin Mary, his cousin.' (The case in question is that of a degenerate subject who was a tramway conductor.) 'Mystical ideas complete the picture. He talks of God, of heaven, crosses himself, kneels down, and says that he is following the commandments of Christ.' (The subject under observation is a day labourer.) 'The devil will tempt me, but I see God who guards me. I have asked of God that all people might be beautiful,' etc.

The continual alternation of antithetical moods in Verlaine—this uniform transition from bestial lust to an excess of piety, and from sinning to remorse—has struck even observers who do not know the significance of such a phenomenon. 'He is,' writes M. Anatole France,* 'alternately devout and atheistical, orthodox and sacrilegious.' These he certainly is. But why? Simply because he is a *circulaire*. This not very happy expression, invented by French psychiatry, denotes that form

* Legrain, *Du délire chez les dégénéres*, pp. 135, 140, 164.
† Huret, *op. cit.*, p. 8.

of mental disease in which states of excitement and depression follow each other in regular succession. The period of excitement coincides with the irresistible impulses to misdeeds and blasphemous language; that of dejection with the paroxysms of contrition and piety. The *circulaires* belong to the worst species of the degenerate. 'They are drunkards, obscene, vicious, and thievish.'* They are also in particular incapable of any lasting, uniform occupation, since it is obvious that in such a condition of mental depression they cannot accomplish any work which demands strength and attention. The *circulaires* are, by the nature of their affliction, condemned to be vagabonds or thieves, unless they belong to rich families. In normally constituted society there is no place for them. Verlaine has been a vagabond the whole of his life. He has loafed about all the highways of France, and roamed as well through Belgium and England. Since his release from prison he has spent most of his time in Paris, where, however, he has no residence, but resorts to the hospitals under the pretext of rheumatism, which for that matter he may easily have contracted during the nights which, as a tramp, he has spent under the open sky. The administration winks at his doings, and grants him food and shelter gratis, out of regard for his poetical capacity. Conformably with the constant tendency of the human mind to beautify what cannot be altered, he persuades himself that his vagrancy, which was forced upon him by his organic vice, is a glorious and enviable condition; he prizes it as something beautiful, artistic, and sublime, and looks upon vagabonds with especial tenderness. Speaking of them he says (*Grotesques*):

'Leur jambes pour toutes montures,
Pour tous biens l'or de leurs regards,
Par le chemin des aventures
Ils vont haillonneux et hagards.

'Le sage, indigné, les harangue;
Le sot plaint ces fous hasardeux;
Les enfants leur tirent la langue
Et les filles se moquent d'eux.'

We find in every lunatic and imbecile the conviction that the rational minds who discern and judge him are 'blockheads.'

'. . . Dans leurs prunelles
Rit et pleure—fastidieux—
L'amour des choses éternelles,
Des vieux morts et des anciens dieux!

'Donc, allez, vagabonds sans trêves,
Errez, funestes et maudits,
Le long des gouffres et des grèves,
Sous l'œil fermé des paradis!

* E. Marandon de Montyel, 'De la Criminalité et de la Dégénérescence,' *Archives de l'Anthropologie criminelle*, Mai, 1892, p. 287.

'La nature à l'homme s'allie
Pour châtier comme il le faut
L'orgueilleuse mélancolie
Qui vous fait marcher le front haut.'

In another poem (*Autre*) he calls to his chosen mates:

'Allons, frères, bons vieux voleurs,
Doux vagabonds
Filous en fleur
Mes chers, mes bons,

'Fumons philosophiquement,
Promenons nous
Paisiblement:
Rien faire est doux.'

As one vagabond feels himself attracted by other vagabonds, so does one deranged mind feel drawn to others. Verlaine has the greatest admiration for King Louis II. of Bavaria, that unhappy madman in whom intelligence was extinct long before death, in whom only the most abominable impulses of foul beasts of the most degraded kind had survived the perishing of the human functions of his disordered brain. He apostrophizes him thus:

'Roi, le seul vrai Roi de ce siècle, salut, Sire,
Qui voulûtes mourir vengeant votre raison
Des choses de la politique, et du délire
De cette Science intruse dans la maison,

'De cette Science assassin de l'Oraison
Et du Chant et de l'Art et de toute la Lyre,
Et simplement et plein d'orgueil et floraison
Tuâtes en mourant, salut, Roi, bravo, Sire!

'Vous fûtes un poète, un soldat, le seul Roi
De ce siècle . . .
Et le martyr de la Raison selon la Foi. . . .'

Two points are noticeable in Verlaine's mode of expression. First, we have the frequent recurrence of the same word, of the same turn of phrase, that chewing the cud, or *rabâchage* (repetition), which we have learnt to know as the marks of intellectual debility. In almost every one of his poems single lines and hemistiches are repeated, sometimes unaltered, and often the same word appears instead of one which rhymes. Were I to quote all the passages of this kind, I should have to transcribe nearly all his poems. I will therefore give only a few specimens, and those in the original, so that their peculiarity will be fully apparent to the reader. In the *Crépuscule du soir mystique* the lines, 'Le souvenir avec le crépuscule,' and 'Dahlia, lys, tulipe et renoncules,' are twice repeated without any internal necessity. In the poem *Promenade sentimentale* the adjective *blême* (wan) pursues the poet in the manner of an obsession or 'onomatomania,' and he applies it to water-lilies and waves ('wan waves'). The *Nuit du Walpurgis classique* begins thus:

> 'Un rythmique sabbat, rythmique, extrêmement
> Rythmique.' . . .

In the *Sérénade* the first two lines are repeated *verbatim* as the fourth and eighth. Similarly in *Ariettes oubliées*, VIII.:

> 'Dans l'interminable
> Ennui de la plaine,
> La neige incertaine
> Luit comme du sable.
>
> 'Le ciel est de cuivre,
> Sans lueur aucune.
> On croirait voir vivre
> Et mourir la lune.
>
> 'Comme des nuées
> Flottent gris les chênes
> Des forêts prochaines
> Parmi les buées.
>
> 'Le ciel est de cuivre,
> Sans lueur aucune.
> On croirait voir vivre
> Et mourir la lune.
>
> 'Corneille poussive,
> Et vous, les loups maigres,
> Par ces bises aigres
> Quoi donc vous arrive?
>
> 'Dans l'interminable
> Ennui de la plaine,
> La neige incertaine
> Luit comme du sable.'

The *Chevaux de bois* begins thus:

> 'Tournez, tournez, bons chevaux de bois,
> Tournez cent tours, tournez mille tours,
> Tournez souvent et tournez toujours,
> Tournez, tournez au son des hautbois.'

In a truly charming piece in *Sagesse* he says:

> 'Le ciel est, par-dessus le toit,
> Si bleu, si calme!
> Un arbre, par dessus le toit
> Berce sa palme.
>
> 'La cloche, dans le ciel qu'on voit,
> Doucement tinte.
> Un oiseau, sur l'arbre qu'on voit,
> Chante sa plainte.'

In the passage in *Amour*, 'Les fleurs des champs, les fleurs innombrables des champs . . . les fleurs des gens,' 'champs' and 'gens' sound somewhat alike. Here the imbecile repetition of similar sounds suggests a senseless pun to the poet, and as for this stanza in *Pierrot gamin :*

'Ce n'est pas Pierrot en herbe
Non plus que Pierrot en gerbe,
C'est Pierrot, Pierrot, Pierrot.
Pierrot gamin, Pierrot gosse,
Le cerneau hors de la cosse,
C'est Pierrot, Pierrot, Pierrot !'

it is the language of nurses to babies, who do not care to make sense, but only to twitter to the child in tones which give him pleasure. The closing lines of the poem *Mains* point to a complete ideational standstill, to mechanical mumbling :

'Ah ! si ce sont des mains de rêve,
Tant mieux, ou tant pis, ou tant mieux.'*

The second peculiarity of Verlaine's style is the other mark of mental debility, viz., the combination of completely disconnected nouns and adjectives, which suggest each other, either through a senseless meandering by way of associated ideas, or through a similarity of sound. We have already found some examples of this in the extracts cited above. In these we find the 'enormous and tender Middle Ages' and the 'brand which thunders.' Verlaine writes also of 'feet which glide with a pure and wide movement,' of 'a narrow and vast affection,' of 'a slow landscape,'† of 'a slack liqueur' ('jus flasque'), 'a gilded perfume,' a 'condensed' or 'terse contour' ('galbe succinct'), etc. The Symbolists admire this form of imbecility, as 'the research for rare and precious epithets' (la recherche de l'epithète rare et précieuse).

Verlaine has a clear consciousness of the vagueness of his thoughts, and in a very remarkable poem from the psychological point of view, *Art poétique,* in which he attempts to give a theory of his lyric creation, he raises nebulosity to the dignity of a fundamental method :

'De la musique avant toute chose
Et pour cela préfère l'Impair
Plus vague et plus soluble dans l'air,
Sans rien en lui qui pèse ou qui pose.'

The two verbs 'pèse' and 'pose' are juxtaposed merely on account of their similarity of sound.

'Il faut aussi que tu n'ailles point
Choisir les mots sans quelque méprise ;
Rien de plus cher que la chanson grise
Où l'Indécis au Précis se joint.

---

* Ah ! if these are dream hands,
So much the better, or so much the worse, or so much the better.

† Virgil's 'lentus,' when applied to aspects of nature, conveys a very different meaning.

'C'est des beaux yeux derrière des voiles,
C'est le grand jour tremblant de midi,
C'est par un ciel d'automne attiédi,
Le bleu fouillis des claires étoiles !

'Car nous voulons la Nuance encor,
Pas la Couleur, rien que la nuance !
Oh ! la nuance seule fiance
Le rêve au rêve et la flûte au cor !'

(This stanza is completely delirious ; it places 'nuance' and 'colour' in opposition, as though the latter were not contained in the former. The idea of which the weak brain of Verlaine had an inkling, but could not bring to a complete conception, is probably that he prefers subdued and mixed tints, which lie on the margin of several colours, to the full intense colour itself.)

'Fuis du plus loin la Pointe assassine,
L'esprit cruel et le Rire impur,
Qui font pleurer les yeux de l'Azur,
Et tout cet ail de basse cuisine !'

It cannot be denied that this poetical method in the hands of Verlaine often yields extraordinarily beautiful results. There are few poems in French literature which can rival the *Chanson d'Automne* :

'Les sanglots longs
Des violons
De l'automne
Blessent mon cœur
D'une langueur
Monotone.

'Tout suffocant
Et blême, quand
Sonne l'heure,
'Je me souviens
Des jours anciens,
Et je pleure.

'Et je m'en vais
Au vent mauvais
Qui m'emporte
Deçà, delà,
Pareil à la
Feuille morte.'

Even if literally translated, there remains something of the melancholy magic of the lines, which in French are richly rhythmical and full of music. *Avant que tu ne t'en ailles* (p. 99) and *Il pleure dans mon cœur* (p. 116) may also be called pearls among French lyrics.

This is because the methods of a highly emotional, but intellectually incapable, dreamer suffice for poetry which deals exclusively with moods, but this is the inexorable limit of his power. Let the true meaning of mood be always present with us. The word denotes a state of mind, in which, through organic excitations which it cannot directly perceive, consciousness is filled with presentations of a uniform nature, which it elaborates with greater or less clearness, and one and all of which relate to those organic excitations inaccessible to consciousness. The mere succession of words, giving a name to these presentations, the roots of which are in the unknown, expresses the mood, and is able to awaken it in another. It has no need of a fundamental thought, or of a progressive exposition to unfold it. Verlaine often attains to astonishing effects in such poetry of moods. Where, however, distinct vision, or a feeling the motive of which is clear to consciousness, or a process well delimitated in time and space, is to be poetically rendered, the poetic art of the emotional imbecile fails utterly. In a healthy and sane poet even the mood pure and simple is united to clear presentations, and is not a mere undulation of fragrance and rose-tinted mist. Poems like Goethe's *Ueber allen Gipfeln ist Ruh*, *Der Fischer*, or *Freudvoll und leidvoll*, can never be created by the emotionally degenerate; but, on the other hand, the most marvellous of Goethe's poems are not so utterly incorporeal, not such mere sighs, as three or four of the best of a Verlaine.

We have now the portrait of this most famous leader of the Symbolists clearly before us. We see a repulsive degenerate subject with asymmetric skull and Mongolian face, an impulsive vagabond and dipsomaniac, who, under the most disgraceful circumstances, was placed in gaol; an emotional dreamer of feeble intellect, who painfully fights against his bad impulses, and in his misery often utters touching notes of complaint; a mystic whose qualmish consciousness is flooded with ideas of God and saints, and a dotard who manifests the absence of any definite thought in his mind by incoherent speech, meaningless expressions and motley images. In lunatic asylums there are many patients whose disease is less deep-seated and incurable than is that of this irresponsible *circulaire* at large, whom only ignorant judges could have condemned for his epileptoid crimes.

A second leader among the Symbolists, whose prestige is in no quarter disputed, is M. Stéphane Mallarmé. He is the most curious phenomenon in the intellectual life of contemporary France. Although long past fifty years of age, he has written hardly anything, and the little that is known of him is, in the opinion of his most unreserved admirers, of no account; and yet he is esteemed as a very great poet, and the utter infertility of his pen, the entire absence of any single work which he can produce as evidence of his poetical capacity, is prized as his greatest merit, and as a most striking proof of his intellectual importance. This statement must appear so fabulous to any reader not deranged in mind, that he may rightly demand proofs of these statements. M. Charles Morice* says of Mallarmé: 'I am not obliged to unveil the secrets of the works of a poet who, as he has himself remarked, is excluded from all participation in any official exposition of the beautiful. The fact itself that these works are still unknown . . . would seem to forbid our associating the name of M. Mallarmé with those of men who have given us books. I let vulgar criticism buzz without replying to it, and state that M. Mallarmé, without having given us books . . . is famous—a fame which, of course, has not been won without arousing the laughter of stupidity in both petty and important newspapers, but which does not offer public and private . . . ineptitude that opportunity for showing its baseness which is provoked by the advent of a new wonder. . . . The people, in spite of their abhorrence of the beautiful, and especially of novelty in the beautiful, have gradually, and in spite of themselves, come to comprehend the prestige of a legitimate authority. They themselves, even they, feel ashamed of their foolish laughter; and before this man, whom that laughter could not tear from the serenity of his meditative silence, laughter became dumb, and itself suffered the divine contagion of silence. Even for the million this man, who published no books, and whom, nevertheless, all designated "a poet," became, as it were, the very symbol of a poet, seeking, where possible, to draw near to the absolute. . . . By his silence he has signified that he . . . cannot yet realize the unprecedented work of art which he wishes to create. Should cruel life refuse to support him in his effort, our respect—nay, more, our veneration—can alone give an answer worthy of a reticence thus conditioned.'

The graphomaniac Morice (of whose crazy and distorted style of expression this literally translated example gives a very good idea) assumes that perhaps Mallarmé will yet create his 'unprecedented work.' Mallarmé himself, however, denies us the right to any such hope. 'The delicious Mallarmé,' Paul Hervieu relates,† 'told me one day . . . he could not understand that anyone should let himself appear in print. Such a proceeding gave him the impression of an indecency, an aberration, resembling that form of mental disease called "exhibitionism." Moreover, no one has been so discreet with his soul as this incomparable thinker.'‡

So, then, this 'incomparable thinker' shows 'a complete discretion as regards his soul.' At one time he bases his silence on a sort of shamed timidity at publicity; at another, on the

* Charles Morice, *La Littérature de tout-à-l'heure*, p. 238.

† Huret, *op. cit.*, p. 33.

‡ Since these words were written, M. Mallarmé has decided to publish his poems in one volume. This, far from invalidating what has been said, is its best justification.

fact that he 'cannot yet realize the unprecedented work of art which he wishes to create,' two reasons for that matter reciprocally precluding each other. He is approaching the evening of his life, and beyond a few brochures, such as *Les Dieux de la Grèce* and *L'après-midi d'un Faune,* together with some verses and literary and theatrical criticisms, scattered in periodicals, the lot barely sufficing for a volume, he has published nothing but some translations from the English and a few school-books (M. Mallarmé is a teacher of English in a Parisian lycée), and yet there are some who admire him as a great poet, as the one exclusive poet, and they overwhelm the 'blockheads' and the 'fools' who laugh at him with all the expressions of scorn that the force of imagination in a diseased mind can display. Is not this one of the wonders of our day? Lessing makes Conti, in *Emilia Galotti,* say that 'Raphael would have been the greatest genius in painting, even if he had unfortunately been born without hands.' In M. Mallarmé we have a man who is revered as a great poet, although 'he has unfortunately been born without hands,' although he produces nothing, although he does not pursue the art he professes. During the period when in London a great number of bubble-company swindles were being promoted, when all the world went mad for the possession of the least scrap of Stock Exchange paper, it happened that a few sharp individuals advertised in the newspapers, inviting people to subscribe for shares in a company of which the object was kept a secret. There really were men who brought their money to these lively promoters, and the historian of the City crisis regards this fact as inconceivable. Inconceivable as it is, Paris sees it repeated. Some persons demand unbounded admiration for a poet whose works are his own secret, and will probably remain such, and others trustingly and humbly bring their admiration as required. The sorcerers of the Senegal negroes offer their congregation baskets and calabashes for veneration, in which they assert that a mighty fetich is enclosed. As a matter of fact they contain nothing; but the negroes regard the empty vessels with holy dread, and show them and their possessors divine honours. Exactly thus is empty Mallarmé the fetich of the Symbolists, who, it must be admitted, are intellectually far below the Senegal negroes.

This position of a calabash worshipped on bended knees he has attained by oral discourse. Every week he gathers round him embryonic poets and authors, and develops his art theories before them. He speaks just as Morice and Kahn write. He strings together obscure and wondrous words, at which his disciples become as stupid 'as if a mill-wheel were going round in their heads,' so that they leave him as if intoxicated, and with the impression that incomprehensible, superhuman disclosures have been made to them. If there is anything comprehensible in the incoherent flow of Mallarmé's words, it is perhaps his admiration for the pre-Raphaelites. It was he who drew the attention of the Symbolists to this school, and enjoined imitation of it. It is through Mallarmé that the French mystics received their English mediævalism and neo-Catholicism. Finally, it may be mentioned that among the physical features of Mallarmé are 'long pointed faun-like ears.'* After Darwin, who was the first to point out the apish character of this peculiarity, Hartmann,† Frigerio,‡ and Lombroso,§ have firmly established the connection between immoderately long and pointed external ears and atavism and degeneration; and they have shown that this peculiarity is of especially frequent occurrence among criminals and lunatics.

The third among the leading spirits of the Symbolists is Jean Moréas, a Franco-Greek poet, who at the completion of his thirty-sixth year (his friends assert, it may be in friendly malice, that he makes himself out to be very much younger than he is) has produced *in toto* three attenuated collections of verses, of hardly one hundred to one hundred and twenty pages, bearing the titles, *Les Syrtes*, *Les Cantilènes*, and *Le Pélerin passionné*. The importance of a literary performance does not, of course, depend upon its amplitude, if it is otherwise unusually significant. When, however, a man cackles during interminable café séances of the renewal of poetry and the unfolding of a new art of the future, and finally produces three little brochures of childish verses as the result of his world-stirring effort, then the material insignificance of the performance also becomes a subject for ridicule.

Moréas is one of the inventors of the word 'Symbolism.' For some few years he was the high-priest of this secret doctrine, and administered the duties of his service with requisite seriousness. One day he suddenly abjured his self-founded faith, and declared that 'Symbolism' had always been meant only as a joke, to lead fools by the nose withal; and that the true salvation of poetry was in Romanism (*romanismè*). Under this new word he affirms a return to the language, versification and mode of feeling of the French poets at the close of the Middle Ages, and of the Renaissance period; but it were well to adopt his declarations with caution, since in two or three years he may be proclaiming his 'romanisme' as much a tap-room joke as his 'symbolism.' The appearance of the *Pélerin passionné* in 1891 was celebrated by the Symbolists as an event which was to be the beginning of a new era in

* Huret, *op. cit.*, p. 55.

† Hartmann, *Der Gorilla.* Leipzig, 1881, p. 34.

‡ Dr. L. Frigerio, *L'Oreille externe: Étude d'Anthropologie criminelle* Lyon, 1889, pp. 32 and 40.

§ Lombroso, *L'Uomo delinquente*, p. 255.

poetry. They arranged a banquet in honour of Moréas, and in the after-dinner speeches he was worshipped as the deliverer from the shackles of ancient forms and notions, and as the saviour who was bringing in the kingdom of God of true poetry. And the same poets who sat at the table with Moréas, and delivered to him rapturous addresses or joined in the applause, a few weeks after this event overwhelmed him with contumely and contempt. 'Moréas a Symbolist!' cried Charles Vignier.* 'Is he one through his ideas? He laughs at them himself! His thoughts! They don't weigh much, these thoughts of Jean Moréas!' 'Moréas?' asks Adrien Remacle,† 'we have all been laughing at him. It is that which has made him famous.' René Ghil calls his *Pélerin passionné* 'doggerel written by a pedant,' and Gustav Kahn‡ passes sentence on him thus: 'Moréas has no talent. . . . He has never done anything worth mentioning. He has his own particular jargon.' These expressions disclose to us the complete hollowness and falseness of the Symbolistic movement, which outside France is obstinately proclaimed as a serious matter by imbeciles and speculators, although its French inventors make themselves hoarse in trying to convince the world that they merely wanted to banter the Philistine with a tap-room jest and advertise themselves.

After the verdict of his brethren in the Symbolist Parnassus, I may really spare myself the trouble of dwelling longer on Moréas; I will, however, cite a few examples from his *Pélerin passionné*, in order that the reader may form an idea of the softness of brain which displays itself in these verses.

The poem *Agnes*§ begins thus:

'Il y avait des arcs où passaient des escortes
Avec des bannières de deuil et du fer
Lacé (?) des potentats de toutes sortes
—Il y avait—dans la cité au bord de la mer.
Les places étaient noires, et bien pavées, et les portes,
Du côté de l'est et de l'ouest, hautes; et comme en hiver
La forêt, dépérissaient les salles de palais, et les porches,
Et les colonnades de belvéder.
C'était (tu dois bien t'en souvenir) c'était aux plus beaux jours de ton adolescence.

'Dans la cité au bord de la mer, la cape et la dague lourdes
De pierres jaunes, et sur ton chapeau des plumes de perroquets,
Tu t'en venais, devisant telles bourdes,
Tu t'en venais entre tes deux laquais
Si bouffis et tant sots—en verité, des happelourdes!—
Dans la cité au bord de la mer tu t'en venais et tu vaguais
Parmi de grands vieillards qui travaillaient aux felouques,
Le long des môles et des quais.
C'était (tu dois bien t'en souvenir) c'était aux plus beaux jours de ton adolescence.

---

* Huret, *op. cit.*, p. 102. † *Ibid.*, p. 106. ‡ *Ibid.*, p. 401.

§ Jean Moréas, *Le Pélerin passionné.* Paris, 1891, p. 3.

And thus the twaddle goes on through eight more stanzas, and in every line we find the characteristics of the language used by imbeciles and made notorious by Sollier (*Psychologie de l'Idiot et de l'Imbécile*), the 'ruminating,' as it were, of the same expressions, the dreamy incoherence of the language, and the insertion of words which have no connection with the subject.

Two *Chansons** run thus :

'Les courlis dans les roseaux !
(Faut-il que je vous en parle,
Des courlis dans les roseaux ?)
O vous joli' Fée des eaux.

'Le porcher et les pourceaux !
(Faut-il que je vous en parle,
Du porcher et des pourceaux ?)
O vous joli' Fée des eaux.

'Mon cœur pris en vos réseaux !
(Faut-il que je vous en parle,
De mon cœur en vos réseaux ?)
O vous joli' Fée des eaux.

'On a marché sur les fleurs au bord de la route,
Et le vent d'automne les secoue si fort, en outre.

'La malle-poste a renversé la vieille croix au bord de la route ;
Elle était vraiment si pourrie, en outre.

'L'idiot (tu sais) est mort au bord de la route,
Et personne ne le pleurera, en outre.'

The stupid artifice with which Moréas here seeks to produce a feeling of wretchedness by conjuring up the three associated figures of crushed flowers, dishevelled by the wind, an overturned and mouldering cross, and a dead, unmourned idiot, makes this poem a model of the would-be profound production of a mad-house !

When Moréas is not soft of brain, he develops a rhetorical turgidity which reminds us of Hofmann von Hofmannswaldau in his worst efforts. Only one example† of this kind, and we have done with him :

'J'ai tellement soif, ô mon amour, de ta bouche,
Que j'y boirais en baisers le cours detourné
Du Strymon, l'Araxe et le Tanaïs farouche ;
Et les cent méandres qui arrosent Pitané,
Et l'Hermus qui prend sa source où le soleil se couche,
Et toutes les claires fontaines dont abonde Gaza,
Sans que ma soif s'en apaisât.'

Behind the leaders Verlaine, Mallarmé, and Moréas a troop of minor Symbolists throng, each, it is true, in his own eyes the one great poet of the band, but whose illusions of greatness do not entitle them to any special observation. Sufficient justice

* Moréas, *op. cit.*, pp. 21 and 2.

† *Ibid.*, p. 43.

is dealt them if the spirit they are made of be characterized by quoting a few lines of their poetry. Jules Laforgue, 'unique not only in his generation, but in all the republic of literature,'* cries: 'Oh, how daily [*quotidienne*] is life!' and in his poem *Pan et la Syrinx* we come upon lines like the following:

'O Syrinx! voyez et comprenez la Terre et la merveille de cette matinée et la circulation de la vie.
Oh, vous là! et moi, ici! Oh vous! Oh, moi! Tout est dans Tout!'†

Gustav Kahn, one of the æstheticists and philosophers of Symbolism, says in his *Nuit sur la Lande:* 'Peace descends from thy lovely eyes like a great evening, and the borders of slow tents descend, studded with precious stones, woven of far-off beams and unknown moons.'

In German, at least, 'borders of slow tents which descend' is completely unintelligible nonsense. In French they are also unintelligible; but in the original their meaning becomes apparent. 'Et des pans de tentes lentes descendent,' the line runs, and betrays itself as pure echolalia, as a succession of similar sounds, as it were, echoing each other.

Charles Vignier, 'the beloved disciple of Verlaine,' says to his mistress:

'Là-bas c'est trop loin,
Pauvre libellule,
Reste dans ton coin
Et prends des pilules . . .

'Sois Edmond About
Et d'humeur coulante,
Sois un marabout
Du Jardin des Plantes.'

Another of his poems, *Une Coupe de Thulé*, runs thus:

'Dans une coupe de Thulé
Où vient pâlir l'attrait de l'heure,
Dort le sénile et dolent leurre
De l'ultime rêve adulé.

'Mais des cheveux d'argent filé
Font un voile à celle qui pleure,
Dans une coupe de Thulé
Où s'est éteint l'attrait de l'heure.

'Et l'on ne sait quel jubilé
Célèbre une harpe mineure
Que le hautain fantôme effleure
D'un lucide doigt fuselé! . . .
Dans une coupe de Thulé!'

---

* Moréas, *op. cit.*, p. 311.

† 'O Syrinx! do you see and understand the Earth, and the wonder of this morning, and the circulation of life!
O thou, there! and I, here! O thou! O me! All is in All!'

These poems remind us so forcibly of those doggerel rhymes at which in Germany jovial students are often wont to try their skill, and which are known as 'flowery [*lit.* blooming] nonsense,' that, in spite of the solemn assurance of French critics, I am convinced that they were intended as a joke. If I am right in my supposition, they are really evidences, not of the mental status of Vignier, but of his readers, admirers, and critics.

Louis Dumur addresses the Neva in the following manner :

> 'Puissante, magnifique, illustre, grave, noble reine !
> O Tsaristsa [*sic !*] de glace et de fastes Souveraine !
> Matrone hiératique et solennelle et vénérée ! . . .
> Toi qui me forces à rêver, toi qui me deconcertes,
> Et toi surtout que j'aime, Émail, Beauté, Poème, Femme.
> Néva ! j'évoque ton spectacle et l'hymne de ton âme !'

And René Ghil, one of the best-known Symbolists (he is chief of a school entitled 'évolutive-instrumentiste'), draws from his lyre these tones, which I also quote in French ; in the first place because they would lose their ring in a translation, and, secondly, because if I were to translate them literally, it is hopeless to suppose that the reader would think I was serious :

> 'Ouïs ! ouïs aux nues haut et nues où
> Tirent-ils d'aile immense qui vire . . .
> et quand vide
> et vers les grands pétales dans l'air plus aride—
>
> '(Et en le lourd venir grandi lent stridule, et
> Titille qui n'alentisse d'air qui dure, et !
> Grandie, erratile et multiple d'éveils, stride
> Mixte, plainte et splendeur ! la plénitude aride)
>
> 'et vers les grands pétales d'agitations
> Lors évanouissait un vol ardent qui stride. . . .
>
> '(des saltigrades doux n'iront plus vers les mers. . . .)'

One thing must be acknowledged, and that is, the Symbolists have an astonishing gift for titles. The book itself may belong to pure mad-house literature ; the title is always remarkable. We have already seen that Moréas names one of his collection of verses *Les Syrtes*. He might in truth just as well call it the *North Pole*, or *The Marmot*, or *Abd-el-Kader*, since these have just as much connection with the poems in the little volume as *Syrtes ;* but it is undeniable that this geographical name calls up the lustre of an African sun, and the pale reflection of classic antiquity, which may well please the eye of the hysteric reader. Edouard Dubus entitles his poem, *Quand les Violons sont partis ;* Louis Dumur, *Lassitudes ;* Gustave Khan, *Les Palais nomades ;* Maurice du Plessis, *La Peau de Marsyas ;* Ernest Raynaud, *Chairs profanes* and *Le Signe;* Henri de Régnier, *Sites et*

Episodes; Arthur Rimbaud, *Les Illuminations;* Albert Saint Paul, *L'Echarpe d'Iris;* Viélé-Griffin, *Ancæus;* and Charles Vignier, *Centon.*

Of the prose of the Symbolists, I have already given some examples. I should further like to cite only a few passages from a book which the Symbolists declare to be one of their most powerful mental manifestations, *La Littérature de tout-à-l'heure,* by Charles Morice. It is a sort of bird's-eye view of the development of literature up to the present time, a rapid critique of the more and most recent books and authors, a kind of programme of the literature of the future. This book is one of the most astonishing which exists in any language. It strongly resembles *Rembrandt as Educator,* but is far beyond that book in the utter senselessness of its concatenations of words. It is a monument of pure literary insanity, of 'graphomania'; and neither Delepierre in his *Littérature des Fous,* nor Philomnestes (Gustave Brunet) in his *Fous Littéraires,* quotes examples of more complete mental dislocation than are visible in every page of this book. Notice the following confession of faith by Morice :* 'Although in this book treating only of æsthetics—although of æsthetics based upon metaphysics—we shall remember to refrain, as far as possible, from pure philosophizing, we must approximately paraphrase a word which will more than once be made use of, and which, in the highest sense here put upon it, is not incapable of being paraphrased. God is the first and universal cause, the final and universal end; the bond between spirits; the point of intersection where two parallels would meet; the fulfilment of our inclinations; the fruition which accords with the glories of our dreams; the abstraction itself of the concrete; the unseen and unheard and yet certain ideal of our demands for beauty in truth. God is, par excellence, THE very word—the very word, that is to say, that unknown certain word of which every author has the incontrovertible, but undiscernible idea, the self-evident but hidden goal which he will never reach, and which he approaches as near as possible. In, so to say, practical æsthetics He is the atmosphere of joy in which the mind revels victorious, because it has reduced irreducible mystery to imperishable symbols.' I do not for a moment doubt that this incomparable jumble will be quite intelligible to theologians. Like all mystics, they discover a sense in every sound; that is, they persuade themselves and others that the nebulous ideas which the sound awakens in their brains by association are the meaning of that sound. But anyone who demands of words that they should be the media of definite thoughts, will perceive in the face of this twaddle that the author was not thinking anything at all

* Morice, *op. cit.,* p. 30.

when he wrote, although he was dreaming of many things. 'Religion' is for Morice (p. 56), 'the source of art, and art in its essence is religious'—an affirmation which he borrows from Ruskin, although he does not acknowledge it. 'Our scholars, our thinkers . . . the luminous heads of the nineteenth century,' are 'Edgar Poe, Carlyle, Herbert Spencer, Darwin, Auguste Comte, Claude Bernard, Berthelot' (p. 57). Edgar Poe by the side of Spencer, Darwin, and Claude Bernard! never have ideas danced a crazier fools' quadrille in a disordered brain.

And this book, of which the passages we have cited give a sufficiently correct idea, was, in France (just as *Rembrandt as Educator* was in Germany), pronounced by thoroughly responsible critics to be 'strange, but interesting and suggestive.' A poor degenerate devil who scribbles such stuff, and an imbecile reader who follows his twaddle like passing clouds, are simply to be pitied. But what words of contempt are strong enough for the sane intellectual tatterdemalions who, in order not to offend or else to give themselves the appearance of possessing a remarkable faculty of comprehension, or to affect fairness and benevolence even towards those whose opinions they in part do not share, insist that they discover in books of this kind many a truth, much wit along with peculiar whims, an ideal of fervour and frequent lightnings of thought?

The word 'Symbolism' conveys, as we have seen, no idea to its inventors. They pursue no definite artistic tendency; hence it is not possible to show them that their tendency is a false one. It is otherwise with some of their disciples, who joined their ranks, partly through a desire to advertise themselves, partly because they thought that, in the conflicts between literary parties, they were fighting on the side which was the stronger and the more sure of victory, and partly, also, through the folly of fashion, and through the influence exerted by any noisy novelty over uncritical minds. Less weak-brained than the leaders, they felt the need of giving the word 'Symbolism' a certain significance, and, in fact, drew up a number of axioms which, according to their profession, serve to guide them in their creations. These axioms are sufficiently defined to allow of discussion.

The Symbolists demand greater freedom in the treatment of French verse. They fiercely rebel against the old alexandrines, with the cæsura in the middle, and the necessary termination of the sentence at the end; against the prohibition of the hiatus; against the law of a regular alternation of masculine and feminine rhymes. They make defiant use of the 'free verse,' with length and rhythm *ad libitum*, and false rhymes. The foreigner can only smile at the savage gestures with which this conflict is carried on. It is a schoolboys' war against some hated book, which is solemnly torn in pieces, trodden under foot, and burned. The whole dispute concerning prosody and the rules of rhyme is, so to speak, an inter-Gallic concern, and is of no consequence to the literature of the world. We have long had everything which the French poets are only now seeking to obtain by barricades and street massacres. In Goethe's *Prometheus*, *Mahomet's Gesang*, *Harzreise im Winter*, in Heine's *Nordsee Cyklus*, etc., we possess perfect models of free verse; we alternate the rhymes as we will; we allow masculine and feminine rhymes to follow one another as seems good to us; we do not bind ourselves to the rigid law of old classic metres, but suffer, in the cradling measure of our verse, anapæsts to alternate with iambics and spondees, according to our feeling for euphony. English, Italian and Sclavonic poetry have gone equally far, and if the French alone have remained behind, and have at last found a need for casting aside their old matted, moth-eaten periwig, this is quite reasonable; but to anyone but a Frenchman they merely make themselves ridiculous when they trumpet their painful hobbling after the nations who are far in front of them, as an unheard-of discovery of new paths and opening up of new roads, and as an advance inspired by the ideal into the dawn of the future.

Another æsthetic demand of the Symbolists is that the line should, independently of its sense, call forth an intended emotion merely by its sound. A word should produce an effect, not through the idea which it embodies, but as a tone, language becoming music. It is noteworthy that many of the Symbolists have given their books titles which are intended to awaken musical ideas. We find *Les Gammes* (The Scales), by Stuart Merrill; *Les Cantilènes*, by Jean Moréas; *Cloches dans la Nuit*, by Adolphe Retté; *Romances sans Paroles*, by Paul Verlaine, etc. To make use of language as a musical instrument for the production of pure tone effects is the delirious idea of a mystic. We have seen that the pre-Raphaelites demand of the fine arts that they should not represent the concrete plastically or optically, but should express the abstract, and therefore simply undertake the *rôle* of alphabetic writing. Similarly, the Symbolists displace all the natural boundary lines of art, and impose upon the word a task which belongs to musical signs only. But while the pre-Raphaelites wish to raise the fine arts to a higher rank than is suited to them, the Symbolists greatly degrade the word. In its origin sound is musical. It expresses no definite idea, but only a general emotion of the animal. The cricket fiddles, the nightingale trills, when sexually excited. The bear growls when stirred by the rage of conflict; the lion roars in his pleasure when tearing a living prey. In proportion as the brain develops in the animal kingdom, and mental life becomes richer, the means of vocal expression are evolved and differentiated, and become capable of making perceptible to the senses not only simple generic emotions, but also presentative complexes of a more restricted and definitely delimitated nature—nay, if Professor Garner's observations concerning the language of apes are accurate, even tolerably distinct single presentations. Sound, as a means of expressing mental operations, reaches its final perfection in cultivated, grammatically articulated language, inasmuch as it can then follow exactly the intellectual working of the brain, and make it objectively perceptible in all the minutest details. To bring the word, pregnant with thought, back to the emotional sound is to renounce all the results of organic development, and to degrade man, rejoicing in the power of speech, to the level of the whirring cricket or the croaking frog. The efforts of the Symbolists, then, result in senseless twaddle, but not in the word-music they intend, for this simply does not exist. No word of any single human language is, as such, musical. Many languages abound in consonants; in others vowels predominate. The former require more dexterity in the muscles employed in speaking; their pronunciation, therefore, counts as more difficult, and they seem less agreeable to the ears of foreigners than the languages which are rich in vowels. But this has nothing to do with the musical side of the question. What remains of the phonetic effect of a word if it is whispered, or if it is only visible as a written character? And yet in both cases it is able to awaken the same emotions, as if it had reached consciousness full-toned through the sense of hearing. Let anyone have read aloud to him the most cleverly chosen arrangement of words in a language completely unknown to him, and try to produce in himself a definite emotion through the mere phonetic effect. In every case it will be found impossible. The meaning of a word, and not its sound, determines its value. The sound is as such neither beautiful nor ugly. It becomes so only through the voice which gives it life. Even the first soliloquy in Goethe's *Iphigenie* would be ugly coming from the throat of a drunkard. I have had the opportunity of convincing myself that even the Hottentot language, spoken in a mellow, agreeable contralto voice, could be pleasing.

Still more cracked is the craze of a sub-section of the Symbolists, the 'Instrumentalists,' whose spokesman is René Ghil. They connect each sound with a definite feeling of colour, and demand that the word should not only awaken musical emotion, but at the same time operate æsthetically in producing a colour-harmony. This mad idea has its origin in a much-quoted sonnet by Arthur Rimbaud, *Les Voyelles* (Vowels), of which the first line runs thus:

'A black, e white, i red, u green, o blue.'

Morice declares* explicitly (what in any case no one in a sane state of mind would have doubted) that Rimbaud wished to make one of those silly jokes which imbeciles and idiots are in the habit of perpetrating. Some of his comrades, however, took the sonnet in grim earnest, and deduced from it a theory of art. In his *Traité du Verbe* René Ghil specifies the colour-value, not only of individual vowels, but of musical instruments. 'Harps establish their supremacy by being white. And violins are blue, often softened by a shimmer of light, to subdue paroxysms.' (It is to be hoped the reader will duly appraise these combinations of words.) 'In the exuberance of ovations, brass instruments are red, flutes yellow, allowing the childlike to proclaim itself astonished at the luminance of the lips. And the organ, synthesis of all simple instruments, bewails deafness of earth and the flesh all in black. . . .' Another Symbolist, who has many admirers, M. Francis Poictevin, teaches us, in *Derniers Songes*, to know the feelings corresponding to colours. 'Blue goes—without more of passion—from love to death; or, more accurately, it is a lost extreme. From turquoise blue to indigo, one goes from the most shame-faced influences to final ravages.'

Wiseacres were, of course, at once to the fore, and set up a quasi-scientific theory of 'colour-hearing.' Sounds are said to awaken sensations of colour in many persons. According to some, this was a gift of specially finely organized nervous natures; according to others, it was due to an accidental abnormal connection between the optic and acoustic brain-centres by means of nerve filaments. This anatomical explanation is entirely arbitrary, and has not been substantiated by any facts. But 'colour-hearing' itself is by no means confirmed. The most complete book hitherto published on this subject, the author of which is the French oculist, Suarez de Mendoza,† collects all the available observations on this alleged phenomenon, and deduces from them the following definition: 'It is the faculty of associating tones and colours, by which every objective acoustic perception of sufficient intensity, nay, even the memory-image of such a perception, arouses in certain persons a luminous or non-luminous image, which is always the same for the same letters, the same tone of voice or instrument, and the same intensity or pitch of tone.' Suarez well hits the truth when he says, 'Colour-hearing' (he calls it *pseudo-photesthésie*) 'is often a consequence of an association of ideas established in youth . . . and often of a special action of the brain, the particular nature of which is unknown to us, and may have a certain similarity to sense-illusion and hallucination.' For my part, I have no

* Morice, *op. cit.*, p. 321.

† Dr. F. Suarez de Mendoza, *L'Audition colorée: Étude sur les fausses Sensations secondaires physiologiques.* Paris, 1892.

doubt that colour-hearing is always the consequence of association of ideas, the origins of which must remain obscure, because the combination of certain presentations of colour with certain sensations of sound may possibly depend upon the very evanescent perceptions of early childhood, which were not powerful enough to arouse the attention, and have therefore remained undiscerned in consciousness. That it is a question of purely individual associations brought about by the accident of associated ideas, and not of organic co-ordinations depending upon definite abnormal nervous connections, is made very probable by the fact that every colour-hearer ascribes a different colour to the same vowel or instrument. We have seen that to Ghil the flute is yellow, to L. Hoffmann (whom Goethe cites in his *Farbenlehre*) this instrument is scarlet. Rimbaud calls the letter 'a' black. Persons whom Suarez mentions heard this vowel as blue, and so on.

The relation between the external world and the organism is originally very simple. Movements are continually occurring in nature, and the protoplasm of living cells perceives these movements. Unity of effect corresponds to unity of cause. The lowest animals perceive of the outer world only this, that something in it changes, and possibly, also, whether this change is marked or slight, sudden or slow. They receive sensations differing quantitatively, but not qualitatively. We know, for example, that the proboscis, or syphon, of the *Pholas dactylus*, which contracts more or less vigorously and quickly at every excitation, is sensitive to all external impressions—light, noise, touch, smell, etc. This mollusc sees, hears, feels and smells, therefore, with this simple organ; his proboscis is to him at once eye, ear, nose, finger, etc. In the higher animals the protoplasm is differentiated. Nerves, ganglia, brain and sense-apparatus are formed. The movements of nature are now perceived in a variety of ways. The differentiated senses transform the unity of the phenomenon into the diversity of the percept. But even in the highest and most differentiated brain there still remains something like a very distant and very dim remembrance that the cause which excites the different senses is one and the same movement, and there are formed presentations and conceptions which would be unintelligible if we could not concede this vague intuition of the fundamental unity of essence in all perceptions. We speak of 'high' and 'deep' tones, and thus give to sound-waves a relationship in space which they cannot have. In the same way we speak of tone-colour, and, conversely, of colour-tones, and thus confound the acoustic and optic properties of the phenomena. 'Hard' and 'soft' lines or tones, 'sweet' voices, are frequent modes of expression, which depend on a transference of the perception of one sense to the impressions of another. In many cases this method of speech may no doubt be traced to mental inertia. It is more convenient to designate a sense-perception by a word which is familiar, though borrowed from the province of another sense, than to create a special word for the particular percept. But even this loan for convenience' sake is possible and intelligible only if we admit that the mind perceives certain resemblances between the impressions of the different senses—resemblances which, although they are often to be explained by conscious or unconscious association of ideas, are oftener quite inexplicable objectively. It only remains for us to assume that consciousness, in its deepest substrata, neglects the differentiation of phenomena by the various senses, passes over this perfection attained very late in organic evolution, and treats impressions only as undifferentiated material for the acquirement of knowledge of the external world without reference to their origin by way of this or that sense. It thus becomes intelligible that the mind mingles the perceptions attained through the different senses, and transforms them one into another. Binet* has established, in his excellent essays, this transposition of the senses in hysterical persons. A female patient, whose skin was perfectly insensible on one half of her body, took no notice when, unseen by herself, she was pricked with a needle. But at the moment of puncture there arose in her consciousness the image of a black (in the case of another invalid, of a bright) point. Consciousness thus transposed an impression of the nerves of the skin, which, as such, was not perceived, into an impression of the retina, of the optic nerve.

In any case, it is an evidence of diseased and debilitated brain-activity, if consciousness relinquishes the advantages of the differentiated perceptions of phenomena, and carelessly confounds the reports conveyed by the particular senses. It is a retrogression to the very beginning of organic development. It is a descent from the height of human perfection to the low level of the mollusc. To raise the combination, transposition and confusion of the perceptions of sound and sight to the rank of a principle of art, to see futurity in this principle, is to designate as progress the return from the consciousness of man to that of the oyster.

Moreover, it is an old clinical observation that mental decay is accompanied by colour mysticism. One of Legrain's† mental invalids 'endeavoured to recognise good and evil by the difference of colour, ascending from white to black; when he was reading, words had (according to their colour) a hidden meaning, which he understood.' Lombroso‡ cites 'eccentric

* Alfred Binet, 'Recherche sur les altérations de la conscience chez les hystériques,' *Revue philosophique*, 1889, 27e vol., p. 165.

† Legrain ,*op. cit.*, p. 162.

‡ Lombroso *Genie und Irrsinn.* German edition, p. 233.

persons' who, 'like Wigman, had the paper for their books specially manufactured with several colours on each page. . . . Filon painted each page of the books he wrote in a different colour.' Barbey d'Aurevilly, whom the Symbolists venerate as a pioneer, used to write epistles in which each letter of a word was coloured with a different tint. Most alienists know similar cases in their experience.

The more reliable Symbolists proclaim their movement as 'a reaction against naturalism.' Such a reaction was certainly justified and necessary; for naturalism in its beginnings, as long as it was embodied in De Goncourt and Zola, was morbid, and, in its later development in the hands of their imitators, vulgar and even criminal, as will be proved further on. Nevertheless Symbolism is not in the smallest degree qualified to conquer naturalism, because it is still more morbid than the latter, and, in art, the devil cannot be driven out by Beelzebub.

Finally, it is affirmed that Symbolism connotes 'the inscribing of a symbol in human form.' Expressed unmystically, this means that in the poems of the Symbolists the particular human form should not only exhibit its special nature and contingent destiny, but also represent a general type of humanity, and embody a universal law of life. This quality, however, is not the monopoly of Symbolistic poetry, but belongs to all kinds of poetry. No genuine poet has yet been impelled to deal with an utterly unprecedented and unique case, or with a monstrous being whose likeness is not to be found in mankind. That which interests him in men and their destiny is just the intimate connection between the two and the universal laws of human life. The more the government of universal laws is made apparent in the fate of the individual, the more there is embodied in him that which lives in all men, so much the more attractive will this destiny and this man be to the poet. There is not in all the literature of humanity a single work of recognised importance which in this sense is not symbolic, and in which the characters, their passions and fortunes, have not a typical significance, far transcending the particular circumstances. It is, therefore, a piece of foolish arrogance in the Symbolists to lay claim to the sole possession of this quality in the works of their school. They show, moreover, that they do not understand their own formulæ; for those theorists of the school who demand of poetry that it should be 'a symbol inscribed in human form,' assert at the same time that only the 'rare and unique case' (*le cas rare et unique*) deserves the attention of the poet, *i.e.*, the case which is significant of nothing beyond itself, and consequently the opposite of a symbol.*

* I may here be allowed to remind my readers that in the year 1885, and, accordingly, before the promulgation of the professed symbolistic programme, I laid down in my *Paradoxe* (popular edition, part ii., p. 253) the principle

We have now seen that Symbolism, like English pre-Raphaelitism (from which it borrowed its catch-words and opinions), is nothing else than a form of the mysticism of weak-minded and morbidly emotional degeneration. The efforts of some followers of the movement to import a meaning into the stammering utterances of their leaders, and falsely to ascribe to them a sort of programme, do not for a moment withstand criticism, but show themselves to be graphomaniac and delirious twaddle, without the smallest grain of truth or sound reason. A young Frenchman, who is certainly not adverse to rational innovation, Hugues Le Roux,* describes the group of Symbolists quite correctly in saying of them: 'They are ridiculous cripples, each intolerable to the other; they live uncomprehended by the public, several by their friends as well, and a few by themselves. As poets or prose writers they proceed in the same way: no material, no sense, and only juxtapositions of loud-sounding musical (?) words; teams of strange rhymes, groupings of unexpected colours and tones, swaying cadences, hurtlings, hallucinations and evoked suggestions.'

CHAPTER IV.

TOLSTOISM.

COUNT LEO TOLSTOI has become in the last few years one of the best-known, and apparently, also, of the most widely-read authors in the world. Every one of his words awakens an echo among all civilized nations on the globe. His strong influence over his contemporaries is unmistakable. But it is no artistic influence. No one has yet imitated him—at least, for the present. He has formed no school after the manner of the pre-Raphaelites and Symbolists. The already large number of writings to which he has given occasion are explanatory or critical. There are no poetical creations modelled upon his own. The influence which he exercises over contemporary thoughts and feelings is a moral one, and applies far more to the great bulk of his readers than to the smaller circle of struggling authors who are on the look-out for a leader. What

---

that the poet must 'to the majority of his readers utter the deep saying, "*Tat twam asi!*"—"That art thou!" of the Indian sage,' and 'must be able, with the ancient Romans, to repeat to the sound and normally developed man, "*Of thee is the fable related.*" In other words, the poem must be "symbolical" in the sense that it brings into view characters, destinies, feelings and laws of life which are universal.'

* Hugues Le Roux, *Portraits de Cire.* Paris, 1891, p. 129.

we, then, can call Tolstoism is no æsthetic theory, but rather a conception of life.

In order to bring forward the proof that Tolstoism is a mental aberration, that it is a form of the phenomenon of degeneration, it will be necessary to look critically first at Tolstoi himself, and then at the public which is inspired by his thoughts.

Tolstoi is at once a poet and a philosopher, the latter in the widest sense—*i.e.*, he is a theologian, a moralist, and a social theorist. As the author of works of imagination he stands very high, even if he does not equal his countryman Tourgenieff, whom he at present appears in the estimation of most people to have thrown into the shade. Tolstoi does not possess the splendid sense of artistic proportion of Tourgenieff, with whom there is never a word too much, who neither protracts his subject nor digresses from his point, and who, as a grand and genuine creator of men, stands Prometheus-like over the figures he has inspired with life. Even Tolstoi's greatest admirers admit that he is long-winded, loses himself in details, and does not always know how to sacrifice the unessential in order, with sure judgment, to enhance the indispensable. Speaking of the novel *War and Peace*, M. de Vogüé* says: 'Is this complicated work properly to be termed a novel? . . . The very simple and very loose thread of the plot serves to connect chapters on history, politics, philosophy, which are all crammed promiscuously into this polygraphy of Russian life. . . . Enjoyment has here to be purchased in a manner resembling a mountain ascent. The way is often wearisome and hard; at times one goes astray; effort is necessary and toil. . . . Those who only seek diversion in fiction are by Tolstoi driven from their wonted ways. This close analyst does not know, or else disdains, the first duty of analysis, which is so natural to the French genius; we desire that the novelist should select; that he should set apart a person, a fact, out of the chaos of beings and things, in order to observe the objects of his choice. The Russian, governed by the feeling of universal interdependence, cannot make up his mind to cut the thousand cords which unite a man, a fact, a thought, to the whole course of the world.'

Vogüé sees rightly that these facts are deserving of notice, but he cannot explain them. Unconsciously he has clearly characterized the method with which a mystical degenerate looks upon the world, and depicts its phenomena. We know that it is lack of attention which constitutes the peculiarity of mystical thought. It is attention which selects from the chaos of phenomena, and so groups what it selects as to illustrate the predominating thought in the mind of the beholder. If atten-

* Vte E. M. de Vogüé, *Le Roman russe*. Paris, 1888, p. 293 *et seq.*

tion fails, the world appears to the beholder like a uniform stream of enigmatic states, which emerge and disappear without any connection, and remain completely without expression to consciousness. These primary facts of mental life must ever be kept in view by the reader. The attitude of the attentive man in the face of external phenomena is one of activity; that of the inattentive man is passive; the former orders them according to a plan which he has worked out in his mind; the latter receives the turmoil of their impress without attempting to organize, separate, or co-ordinate. The difference is the same as that between the reproduction of the scenes of nature by a good painter and a photographic plate. The painting suppresses certain features in the world's phenomena, and brings others into prominence, so that it at once permits a distinct external incident, or a definite internal emotion of the painter, to be recognised. The photograph reflects the whole scene with all its details indiscriminately, so that it is without meaning, until the beholder brings into play his attention, which the sensitive plate could not do. At the same time it is to be observed that even the photograph is not a true impression of reality, for the sensitive plate is only sensitive to certain colours; it records the blue and violet, and receives from yellow and red either a weak impression or none at all. The sensitiveness of the chemical plate corresponds to the emotionalism of the degenerate mind. The latter also makes a choice among phenomena, not, however, according to the laws of conscious attention, but according to the impulse of unconscious emotionalism. He perceives whatever is in tune with his emotions; what is not consonant with them does not exist for him. Thus arises the method of work which Vogüé has pointed out in Tolstoi's novels. The details are perceived equally, and placed side by side, not according to their importance for the leading idea, but according to their relation with the emotions of the novelist. For that matter, there is scarcely any leading idea, or none at all. The reader must first carry it into the novel, as he would carry it into Nature herself, into a landscape, into a crowd of people, into the course of events. The novel is only written because the novelist felt certain strong emotions, and certain features of the world's panorama as it unrolled before his eyes intensified these emotions. Thus, the novel of Tolstoi resembles the picture of the pre-Raphaelites: an abundance of amazingly accurate details,* a mystically blurred, scarcely recognisable,

* See, in *War and Peace* (Leo. N. Tolstoi's collected works, published, with the author's sanction, by Raphael Löwenfeld, Berlin, 1892, vols. v.—viii.), the soldiers' talk, part i., p. 252; the scene at the outposts, p. 314 *et seq.;* the description of the troops on the march, p. 332; the death of Count Besuchoi, pp. 142-145; the coursing, part ii., pp. 383-407, etc.

leading idea,* a deep and strong emotion.† This is also distinctly felt by M. de Vogüé, but again without his being able to explain it. He says:‡ 'Through a peculiar and frequent contradiction, this troubled, vacillating mind, steeped as it is in the mists of Nihilism, is endowed with an incomparable clearness and power of penetration for the scientific (?) study of the phenomena of life. He sees distinctly, rapidly, analytically, everything on earth. . . . One might say, the mind of an English chemist in the soul of an Indian Buddhist. Let anyone who can explain this singular union; whoever succeeds will be able to explain Russia. . . . These phenomena, which offer so firm a basis to him when he observes them singly, he wishes to know in their universal relations, and to arrive at the definite laws governing these relations, and at their inaccessible causes. Then it is that this clear vision darkens, the intrepid inquirer loses his footing, he falls into the abyss of philosophical contradictions; in him and around him he feels only nothingness and night.'

M. de Vogüé wishes for an explanation of this 'singular union' between great clearness in apprehension of details, and complete incapacity of understanding their relations to each other. The explanation is now familiar to my readers. The mystical intellect, the intellect without attention, of the *émotif* conveys to his consciousness isolated impressions, which can be very distinct if they relate to his emotions; but it is not in the condition to connect these isolated impressions intelligibly, just because it is deficient in the attention necessary to this object.

Grand as are the qualities which Tolstoi's works of fiction possess, it is not them he has to thank for his world-wide fame, or his influence on his contemporaries. His novels were recognised as remarkable works, but for decades of years neither *Peace and War*, nor *Anna Karenina*, nor his short stories, had very many readers outside Russia; and the critics bestowed upon their author only a guarded commendation. In Germany, as recently as 1882, Franz Bornmüller said of Tolstoi in his *Biographical Dictionary of Authors of the Present Time:* 'He possesses no ordinary talent for fiction, but one devoid of due artistic finish, and which is influenced by a certain one-sidedness in his views of life and history.' This was the opinion until a few years ago of the not very numerous non-Russian readers who knew him at all.

* See, in *War and Peace*, the thoughts of the wounded Prince Andrej, part i., p. 516; Count Peter's conversation with the freemason and Martinief Basdjejeff, part ii., pp. 106-114, etc.

† *War and Peace*, the episode of Princess Maria and her suitor, part i., pp. 420-423; the confinement of the little Princess, part ii., pp. 58-65; and all the passages where Count Rostoff sees the Emperor Alexander, or where the author speaks of the Emperor Napoleon I., etc.

‡ Vogüé, *op. cit.*, p. 282.

In 1889 his *Kreutzer Sonata* appeared, and was the first of his works to carry his name to the borders of civilization. This little tale was the first to be translated into all cultivated languages. It was disseminated in hundreds of thousands of copies, and was read by millions with lively emotion. From this time onward the public opinion of the Western nations placed him in the first rank of living authors: his name was in everyone's mouth, and universal sympathy turned not only towards his early writings (which had remained unnoticed for decades), but also to his person and his career, and he became, as it were, in a night what he unquestionably is now in the evening of his life—one of the chief representative figures of the departing century. Yet the *Kreutzer Sonata* stands, as a poetic creation, not so high as most of his older works. A fame which was not gained by *War and Peace*, *The Cossacks*, *Anna Karenina*, etc., nor, indeed, until long after the appearance of these rich creations, but came at one stroke through the *Kreutzer Sonata*, cannot therefore depend either solely or principally on æsthetic excellence. The history of this fame shows consequently that Tolstoi the novelist is not the cause of Tolstoism.

In fact, the tendency of mind so named is far more—perhaps wholly and entirely—traceable to Tolstoi the philosopher. The philosopher is, therefore, incomparably more important to our inquiry than the novelist.

Tolstoi has formed certain views on the position of man in the world, on his relation to collective humanity, and on the aim of his life, which are visible in all his creations, but which he has also set forth connectedly in several theoretic works, especially in *My Confession*, *My Faith*, *A Short Exposition of the Gospel*, and *About my Life*. These views are but little complicated, and can be condensed in a few words: the individual is nothing; the species is everything; the individual lives in order to do his fellow-creatures good; thought and inquiry are great evils; science is perdition; faith is salvation.

How he arrived at these results is related in *My Confessions*: 'I lost my faith early. I lived for a long time like everyone else, in the frivolities of life. I wrote books, and taught, like everyone else, what I did not know. Then the Sphinx began to follow me more and more ruthlessly: "Guess my problem or I will tear thee to pieces." Science has explained absolutely nothing to me. In answer to my everlasting question, the only one which means anything, "Wherefore am I alive?" Science replied by teaching me things that were indifferent to me. Science only said . . .: "Life is a senseless evil." I wanted to kill myself. Finally I had a fancy to see how the vast majority of men lived who, unlike us of the so-called upper classes, who give ourselves up to pondering and investigation, work and suffer, and are, nevertheless, quiet and clear in their minds over the aim of life. I understood that to live like these men one must return to their simple beliefs.'

If this train of thought is seriously considered, it will be recognised at once as nonsensical. The question, 'Wherefore am I alive?' is incorrectly and superficially put. It tacitly presupposes the idea of finality in nature, and it is just upon this presupposition that the mind, thirsting earnestly for truth and knowledge, has to exercise its criticism.

In order to ask, 'What is the aim of our life?' we must take for granted, above all, that our life has a definite aim, and since it is only a particular phenomenon in the universal life of nature, in the evolution of our earth, of our solar system, of all solar systems, this assumption includes in itself the wider one, that the universal life of Nature has a definite aim. This assumption, again, necessarily presupposes the rule of a conscious, prescient, and guiding mind over the universe. For what is an aim? The fore-ordained effect in the future of forces active in the present. The aim exercises an influence on these forces in pointing out to them a direction, and is thus itself a force. It cannot, however, exist objectively, in time and space, because then it would cease to be an aim and become a cause, *i.e.*, a force fitting in with the general mechanism of the forces of nature, and all the speculation concerning the aim would fall to the ground. But if it is not objective, if it does not exist in time and space, it must, in order to be conceivable, exist somewhere, virtually, as idea, as a plan and design. But that which contains a design, a thought, a plan, we name consciousness; and a consciousness that can conceive a plan of the universe, and for its realization designedly uses the forces of nature, is synonymous with God. If a man, however, believes in a God, he loses at once the right to raise the question, 'Wherefore am I alive?' Since it is in that case an insolent presumption, an effort of small, weak man to look over God's shoulder, to spy out God's plan, to aspire to the height of omniscience. But neither is it in such a case necessary, since a God without the highest wisdom cannot be conceived, and if He has devised a plan for the world, this is certain to be perfect, all its parts are in harmony, and the aim to which every co-operator, from the smallest to the greatest, will devote himself is the best conceivable. Thus, man can live in complete rest and confidence in the impulses and forces implanted in him by God, because he, in every case, fulfils a high and worthy destiny by co-operating in a, to him, unknown Divine plan of the world.

If, on the other hand, there is no belief in a God, it is also impossible to form a conception of the aim, for then the aim, existing in consciousness only as an idea, in the absence of a universal consciousness, has no locus for its existence; there is no place for it in Nature. But if there is no aim, then one cannot ask the question, 'Wherefore am I alive?' Then life has not a predetermined aim, but only causes. We have then to concern ourselves only with these causes—at least, with the more proximate, and which are accessible to our examination, since the remote, and especially the first, causes elude our cognition. Our question must then run, 'Why do we live? and we find the answer to it without difficulty. We live, because we stand, like the rest of cognizable Nature, under the universal law of causality. This is a mechanical law, which requires no predetermined plan, and no design, consequently also no universal consciousness. According to this law present phenomena are grounded on the past, not on the future. We live because we are engendered by our parents, because we have received from them a definite measure of force, which makes it possible for us to resist for a given time the influence upon us of Nature's forces of dissolution. How our life is shaped is determined by the constant interaction of our inherited organic forces and of our environment. Our life is, therefore, objectively viewed, the necessary result of the law-governed activity of the mechanical forces of Nature. Subjectively it includes a quantity of pleasures and pains. We feel as pleasure the satisfaction of our organic impulses, as pain their fruitless struggles for satisfaction. In a sound organism, possessing a high capacity for adaptation, those appetites only attain development, the satisfaction of which is possible—at least, to a certain degree—and is accompanied by no bad consequences for the individual. In such a life pleasure consequently prevails decidedly over pain, and he looks upon existence, not as an evil, but as a great good. In the organism deranged by disease degenerate appetites exist which cannot be satisfied, or of which the gratification injures or destroys the individual, or the degenerate organism is too weak or too inapt to gratify the legitimate impulses. In his life pain necessarily predominates, and he looks upon existence as an evil. My interpretation of the riddle of life is nearly related to the well-known theory of eudæmonism, but it is founded on a biological, not a metaphysical, basis. It explains optimism and pessimism simply as an adequate or inadequate vitality, as the existence or absence of adaptability, as health or illness. Unprejudiced observation of life shows that the whole of mankind stands knowingly or unknowingly at the same philosophical standpoint. Men live willingly, and rather quietly happy than sadly, so long as existence affords them gratification. If the sufferings are stronger than the feeling of pleasure conferred by the satisfaction of the first and most important of all organic impulses—the impulse of life or self-preservation—then they do not hesitate to kill themselves. When Prince Bismarck once said, 'I do not know why I should bear all the troubles of life, if I were not able to believe in a God and a future life,' it only shows that he is insufficiently acquainted with the progress of human thought since Hamlet, who raised somewhat the same question. He bears the troubles of life because, and as long as, he can bear them, and he throws them down infallibly at the moment in which his strength is no longer adequate to carry them. The unbeliever lives and is happy, so long as the sweets of life weigh down the scale, and for this reason also the believer, as experience daily teaches, will commit suicide if he sees his balance of life's account yielding a deficit of satisfaction. The arguments of religion have undoubtedly in the mind of the believer, as have the arguments of duty and honour in the mind of the unbeliever, a convincing force, and must likewise be taken into account as so many assets. Nevertheless they have only a limited, if high value, and can counterbalance their own equivalent of suffering only, and no more.

From these considerations it follows that the terrible question—'Wherefore am I alive?'—which nearly drove Tolstoi to suicide, is to be answered satisfactorily and without difficulty. The believer, who accepts the fact that his life must have an aim, will live according to his inclinations and powers, and tell himself that he performs correctly, in this way, his allotted portion of the world's work without knowing its final aim; as also a soldier, at that point of the field of battle where he is placed, does his duty willingly, without having any notion of the general progress of the fight, and of its significance for the whole campaign. The unbeliever, who is convinced that his life is a particular instance of the universal life of Nature, that his individuality has blossomed into existence as a necessary law-governed operation of eternal organic forces, knows also very well not only 'wherefore,' but also 'what for,' he is alive; he lives because, and as long as, life is to him a source of gratification—that is to say, of joy and happiness.

Has Tolstoi found any other answer by his desperate seeking? No. The explanation which his pondering and searching did not offer him was, as we have seen in the above-quoted passage in *My Confessions,* given him by 'the enormous majority of mankind, who . . . labour and suffer, and, nevertheless, are quiet and clear in their minds as to the aim of life.' 'I understood,' he adds, 'that one must return to their simple faith to live as these men do.' The conclusion is arbitrary, and is a *saltum* of mystic thought. 'The masses live quietly, and are clear in their minds as to the aim of life,' not because they have a 'simple faith,' but because they are healthy, because they like to feel themselves alive, because life gives them, in every organic function, in every manifestation of their powers, at every moment, some gratification. The 'simple faith' is the accidental accompanying phenomenon of this natural optimism. No doubt the majority of the uneducated classes, who represent the healthy portion of mankind, and therefore certainly rejoice in life, receive, during childhood, instruction in religious faith, and afterwards only rarely rectify through their own thought the errors which, for state reasons, have been imparted to them; but their unthinking belief is a consequence of their poverty and ignorance, like their bad clothing, insufficient food, and insanitary dwellings. To say that the majority 'live quietly, and are clear in their minds as to the aim of life,' because they 'have simple faith,' is quite as logical a sequitur as the assertion that this majority 'live quietly, and are clear in their minds as to the aim of life' because they chiefly eat potatoes, or because they live in cellars, or because they seldom take baths.

Tolstoi has rightly noticed the fact that the majority do not share his pessimism, and rejoice in their life, but he has explained it mystically. Instead of recognising that the optimism of the masses is simply a sign of their vitality, he traces it to their belief, and then seeks in faith the clue to the aim of his existence. 'I was led to Christianity,' he writes in another book,* 'neither through theological nor historical research, but by the circumstance that when, at fifty years of age, I asked myself and the wise among my acquaintance what myself and my life might signify, and received the answer: "You are an accidental concatenation of parts; there is no significance in life; life as such is an evil"—I was then brought to despair, and wished to kill myself. Remembering, however, that formerly, in childhood, when I believed, life had a meaning for me, and that the people about me who believe—the greater number being men unspoilt by riches—both believe and lead real lives, I doubted the accuracy of the answer which had been given me by the wisdom of my circle, and endeavoured to understand that answer which Christianity gives to men who lead a real life.'†

He found this answer 'in the Gospels, that source of light.' 'It was quite the same thing to me,' he goes on to say, 'whether Jesus was God or not God; whether the Holy Ghost proceeded from the one or the other. It was likewise neither necessary nor important for me to know when and by whom the Gospel, or any one of the parables, was composed, and whether they could be ascribed to Christ or not. What to me was important

* Count Leo Tolstoi, *A Short Exposition of the Gospel.* From the Russian, by Paul Lauterbach. Leipzig: Reclam's Universal-Bibliothek, p. 13.

† L. Tolstoi, *Short Exposition of the Gospel*, p. 13.

was that Light, which for eighteen hundred years was the Light of the World, and is that Light still, but what name was to be given to the source of this Light, or what were its component parts, and by whom it was lighted, was quite indifferent to me.'

Let us appraise this process of thought in a mystical mind. The Gospel is the source of truth ; it is, however, quite the same thing whether the Gospel is God's revelation or man's work, and whether it contains the genuine tradition of the life of Christ, or whether it was written down hundreds of years after his death on the basis of obscured and distorted traditions. Tolstoi himself feels that he here makes a great error of thought, but he deceives himself over and out of it in genuine mystical fashion, in that he makes use of a simile, and pretends that his image was the matter-of-fact truth. He speaks, namely, of the Gospel as a light, and says it is indifferent to him what that light is called, and of what it consists. This is correct if it concerns a real, material light, but the Gospel is only figuratively a light, and can obviously, therefore, be compared to a light only if it contains the truth. Whether it does contain the truth should first be decided by inquiry. Should inquiry result in establishing that it is man's work, and consists only in unauthenticated traditions, then it would evidently be no receptacle of truth, and one could not any longer compare it with light, and the magnificent image with which Tolstoi cuts short inquiry into the source of the light would vanish into air. While, therefore, Tolstoi calls the Gospel a light, and denies the necessity of following up its origin, he forthwith takes as proven the very thing which is to be proved, namely, that the Gospel is a light. We know already, however, the peculiarity of mystics to found all their conclusions on the most senseless premises, alleging contempt of reality and resisting all reasonable verification of their starting-point. I only remind the reader of Rossetti's sentence, 'What does it matter to me whether the sun revolves round the earth, or the earth round the sun?' and of Mallarmé's expression, 'The world is made in order to lead to a beautiful book.'

One can read for one's self in his *Short Exposition* how Tolstoi handles the Gospel, so that it may give him the required explanation. He does not trouble himself in the least about the literal sense of the Scriptures, but puts into them what is in his own head. The Gospel which he has so recast has about as much resemblance to the canonical Scriptures as the *Physiognomische Fragmente*, which Jean Paul's 'merry little schoolmaster, Maria Wuz in Auenthal,' 'drew out of his own head,' had with Lavater's work of the same title. This Gospel of his taught him concerning the importance of life as follows :* 'Men imagine

* Tolstoi, *Short Exposition*, etc., p. 172.

that they are isolated beings, each one shaping his own life as he wills. This, however, is a delusion. The only true life is that which acknowledges the will of the Father as the source of life. This unity of life my teaching reveals, and represents that life, not as separate shoots, but as a single tree on which all the shoots grow. He only who lives in the will of the Father, like a shoot on the tree, has life; but he who would live according to his own will, like a severed shoot, dies.' He has already said that the Father is synonymous with God, and that God, who 'is the eternal origin of all things,' is synonymous with 'Spirit.' If, then, this passage has any sense at all, it can only be that the whole of Nature is a single living being, that every single living being, therefore also every human being, is a portion of universal life, and that this universal life is God. This teaching is, however, not invented by Tolstoi. It has a name in the history of philosophy, and is called Pantheism. It is shadowed forth in Buddhism* and Greek Hylozoism, and was elaborated by Spinoza. It is certainly not contained in the Gospel, and it is a definite denial of Christianity which, let its dogmas be ever so rationalistically interpreted and tortured, can never give up its doctrine of a personal God and the Divine nature of Christ without ridding itself of its whole religious import and its vitally important organs, and ceasing to be a creed.

Thus we see that, though Tolstoi supposes he has succeeded in his attempt to explain life's problems by the Christian faith of the masses, he has, on the contrary, fallen into its very opposite, namely, Pantheism. The reply of the 'wise,' that he 'is an accidental concatenation of parts, and that there is no significance in life,' 'drove him almost to suicide'; he is, on the contrary, quite tranquil in the knowledge that† 'the true life is . . . not the life which is past, nor that which will be, but is the life which now is, that which confronts everyone at the present minute'; he expressly denies in *My Religion* the resurrection of the body and the individuality of the soul, and does not notice that the teaching which contents him is quite the same as that of the 'wise,' who 'almost drove him into suicide.' For if life exists only in the present, it can have no aim, since this would refer to the future; and if the body does not rise again, and the soul has no individual existence, then the 'wise' are quite right to call the human being (certainly not accidental, but necessary, because causally conditioned) 'a concatenation of parts.'

Tolstoi's theory of life, the fruit of the despairing mental labour of his whole life, is therefore nothing but a haze, a failure to comprehend his own questions and answers, and hollow

* More accurately, in Vedântism.—TRANSLATOR.

† Tolstoi, *Short Exposition*, etc., p. 128.

verbiage. His ethics—on which he himself lays a far greater stress than on his philosophy—is not in much better case than the latter. He comprises them* in five laws, of which the fourth is the most important: 'Do not resist evil; suffer wrong, and do more than men ask; and so judge not, nor suffer to be judged. . . .' To avenge one's self only teaches to avenge one's self. His admirer, M. de Vogüé, expresses Tolstoi's moral philosophy in this form:† 'Resist not evil, judge not, kill not. Consequently no courts of justice, no armies, no prisons, no public or private reprisals. No wars nor judgments. The world's law is the struggle for existence; the law of Christ is the sacrifice of one's own existence for others.'

Is it still necessary to point out the unreasonableness of these ethics? It is obvious to sound common-sense without saying any more. If the murderer had no longer to fear the gallows, and the thief the prison, throat-cutting and stealing would be soon by far the most generally adopted trade. It is so much more convenient to filch baked bread and ready-made boots than to rack one's self at the plough and in the workshop. If society should cease to take care that crime should be a dangerous risk, what would there be, forsooth, to deter wicked men, who certainly exist, according to Tolstoi's assumption, from surrendering themselves to their basest impulses; and how could the great mass of indifferent people be restrained, who have no pronounced leaning either for good or for evil, from imitating the example of the criminal? Certainly not Tolstoi's own teaching that 'the true life is life in the present.' The first active measures of society, for the sake of which individuals originally formed themselves into a society, is the protection of their members against those who are diseased with homicidal mania, and against the parasites—another unhealthy variation from the normal human type—who can only live by the work of others, and who, to appease all their lusts, unscrupulously overpower every human being who crosses their path. Individuals with anti-social impulses would soon be in the majority if the healthy members did not subdue them, and make it difficult for them to thrive. Were they once to become the stronger, society, and soon mankind itself, would of a necessity be devoted to destruction.

In addition to the negative precept that one should not resist evil, Tolstoi's moral philosophy has yet a positive precept, viz.: we ought to love all men; to sacrifice everything, even one's own life, for them; to do good to them where we can. 'It is necessary to understand that man, if he does good, only does that to which he is bound—what he cannot leave undone. . . . If he gives up his carnal life for the good, he does nothing for

* *Short Exposition*, p. 60. † De Vogüé, *op. cit.*, p. 333.

which he need be thanked and praised. . . . Only those live who do good' (*Short Exposition of the Gospel*). 'Not is alms-giving effectual, but brotherly sharing. Whoever has two cloaks should give one to him who has none' (*What ought one to Do?*). This distinction between charity and sharing cannot be maintained in earnest. Every gift that a man receives from some other man without work, without reciprocal service, is an alms, and as such is deeply immoral. The sick, the old, the weak, those who cannot work, must be supported and tended by their fellow-creatures; it is their duty, and it is also their natural impulse. But to give to men capable of working is under all circumstances a sin and a self-deception. If men capable of work find no work, this is obviously attributable to some defect in the economical structure of society; and it is the duty of each individual to assist earnestly in removing this defect, but not to facilitate its continuance by pacifying for awhile the victim of the defective circumstances by a gift. Charity has in this case merely the aim of deadening the conscience of the donor, and furnishing him with an excuse why he should shirk his duty of curing recognised evils in the constitution of society. Should, however, the capable man be averse to labour, then charity spoils him completely, and kills in him entirely any inclination to put his powers into action, which alone keeps the organism healthy and moral. Thus alms, extended to an able-bodied man, degrades both the donor and the recipient, and operates like poison on the feeling of duty and the morality of both.

But the love of our neighbour which exhibits itself in alms-giving, or even brotherly sharing, is, properly speaking, no such love if we look at it closely. Love in its simplest and most original form (I speak here not of sexual love, but of general sympathy for some other living being, and that need not even be a human being) is a selfish impulse, which seeks only its own gratification, not that of the beloved being; in its higher development, on the contrary, it is principally, or wholly, bent upon the happiness of the beloved being, and forgets itself. The healthy man, who has no anti-social impulses, enjoys the company of other men; he therefore avoids almost unconsciously those actions which would cause his fellow-creatures to avoid him, and he does that which, without costing himself too much effort, is sufficiently pleasant to his fellows to attract them to him. In the same healthy man the idea of sufferings, even when they are not his own, produces pain, which is always greater or less according to the degree of excitability of his brain; the more active the idea of suffering, the more violent is the accompanying feeling of pain. Because the ideas excited by direct sense-impressions are the most vivid, the sufferings which he sees with his own eyes cause him the sharpest pain, and in order to escape from this, he makes suitable efforts to put an end to this extraneous suffering, or often, it is true, only not to witness it. This degree of love to our neighbour is, as was said above, pure self-love; it merely aims at averting pain from self, and at increasing one's own feelings of pleasure. The love of our neighbour, on the contrary, which Tolstoi obviously wishes to preach, claims to be unselfish. It contemplates the diminution of the sufferings, and the increase of the happiness, of others; it can no longer be exercised instinctively, for it demands an exact knowledge of the conditions of life, and the feelings and wishes of others, and the acquisition of this knowledge presupposes observation, reflection, and judgment. One must earnestly consider what is really needful and good for one's neighbour. One must come out of one's self, must set aside one's own habits and ideas completely, and strive to slip into the skin of him to whom one would show love. One must regard the intended benefit with the other's eyes, and feel with his nature, and not with one's own. Does Tolstoi do this? His novels, in which he shows his alleged love between fellow-men living and working, prove the exact contrary.

In the tale *Albert** Delessow takes up a sickly, strolling violin-player out of admiration for his great talent, and out of pity for his poverty and helplessness. But the unhappy artist is a drunkard. Delessow locks him up in his dwelling, places him under the care of his servant Sachar, and keeps him from intoxicating drinks. On the first day Albert the artist submits, but is very depressed and out of temper. On the second day he is already casting 'malignant glances' at his benefactor. 'He seemed to fear Delessow, and whenever their eyes met a deadly terror was depicted on his face. . . . He did not answer the questions which were put to him.' Finally, on the third day Albert rebels against the restraint to which he believes himself subjected. 'You have no right to shut me up here,' he cries. 'My passport is in order. I have stolen nothing from you; you can search me. I will go to the superintendent of police.' The servant Sachar tries to appease him. Albert becomes more and more enraged, and suddenly 'shrieks out at the top of his voice: "Police!"' Delessow allows him to depart. Albert 'goes out of the door without taking leave, and constantly muttering to himself incomprehensible words.'

Delessow had taken Albert home, because the sight was painful to him of the poorly-clad, sickly, pale artist, trembling in the cold of a Russian winter. When he saw him in his warm house, before a well-spread table, in his own handsome dressing-gown,

* L. Tolstoi, *Gesammelte Werke*, Berlin, 1891, Band II.: *Novels and Short Tales*, part i.

Delessow felt contented and happy. But was Albert also contented? Tolstoi testifies that Albert feels himself much more unhappy in the new position than in the old—so unhappy that very soon he could not bear it, and freed himself from it with an outburst of fury. To whom, then, had Delessow done good, to himself or to Albert?

In this narrative a mentally diseased man is depicted, and, it must be admitted, upon such a one a benefit has frequently to be forcibly pressed, which he does not understand or appreciate as such, though, of course, in a manner more consistent, persistent, and prudent than Delessow's. In another story in the same volume, however, *From the Diary of the Prince Nechljudow, Lucerne*, the absurdity of love for one's fellow-creature which does not trouble itself about the real needs of the fellow-creature is brought out more vividly and without any excuse.

One glorious evening in July, in front of the Schweizer-Hof, in Lucerne, Prince Nechljudow heard a street-singer whose songs touched and enraptured him deeply. The singer is a poor, small, hump-backed man, insufficiently clad and looking half starved. On all the balconies of the sumptuous hotel rich Englishmen and their wives are standing; all have enjoyed the glorious singing of the poor cripple, but when he takes off his hat and begs a small reward for his artistic performance, not one person throws even the smallest coin to him. Nechljudow falls into the most violent excitement. He is beside himself over the fact that 'the singer could beg three times for a gift, and no one gave him the smallest thing, while the greater number laughed at him.' It seems to him 'an event which the historian of our times should inscribe in the pages of history with indelible letters of fire.' He, for his part, will not be a participator in this unprecedented sin. He hastens after the poor devil, overtakes him and invites him to drink a bottle of wine with him. The singer accepts. 'Close by is a small café,' says he; 'we can go in there—it is a cheap one,"' he continued. 'The words, "a cheap one," involuntarily suggested the idea,' relates Nechljudow in his diary, 'not to go to a cheap café, but into the Schweizer-Hof, where were the people who had listened to his singing. Although he refused the Schweizer-Hof several times in timid agitation, because he thought it was much too grand there, I persisted in it.'

He leads the singer into the splendid hotel. Although he appears in the company of the princely guest, the servants look at the badly dressed vagabond with hostile and comtemptuous glances. They show the pair into the 'saloon on the left, the drinking-bar for the people.' The singer is very much embarrassed, and wishes himself far away, but he conceals his feelings.

The Prince orders champagne. The singer drinks without any real pleasure and without confidence. He talks about his life, and says suddenly: 'I know what you wish. You want to make me drunk, and then see what can be got out of me.' Nechljudow, annoyed by the scornful and insolent demeanour of the servants jumps up and goes with his guest into the handsome dining-room on the right hand, which is set apart for the visitors. He will be served here and nowhere else. The English, who are present, indignantly leave the room; the waiters are dismayed, but do not venture to oppose the angry Russian Prince. 'The singer drew a very miserable, terrified face, and begged me, as soon as possible, to go away, evidently not understanding why I was angry and what I wished.' The little mannikin 'sat more dead than alive' near the Prince, and was very happy when Nechljudow finally dismissed him.

It must be noticed how extremely absurdly Prince Nechljudow behaves from beginning to end. He invites the singer to a bottle of wine, although, if he had possessed the faintest glimmer of sound common-sense, he might have said to himself that a hot supper, or, still better, a five-franc piece, would be far more necessary and useful to the poor devil than a bottle of wine. The singer proposes to go to a modest restaurant, where he himself would feel comfortable. The Prince pays not the smallest attention to this natural, reasonable desire, but drags the poor devil into a leading hotel, where he feels extremely uncomfortable in his bad clothing, under the cross-fire of the waiters' insolent and scornful looks. The Prince does not care about this, but orders champagne, to which the singer is not accustomed, and which gives him so little pleasure that the thought occurs to him that his noble host desires to make sport of him by seeing him drunk. Nechljudow begins to squabble with the waiters, proceeds to the finest saloon of the hotel, scares away the remaining guests, who do not desire to sit at supper with the street-singer, and does not concern himself during the whole of this time about the feelings of his guest, who sits on hot coals, and would far rather sink into the floor, and who only breathes again when his terrible benefactor lets him escape out of his fangs.

Did Nechljudow exercise neighbourly love? No. He did nothing pleasant to the singer. He tormented him. He only satisfied himself. He wished to revenge himself on the hard-hearted English people, with whom he was furious, and he did so at the expense of the poor devil. Nechljudow calls it an unheard-of occurrence that the wealthy Englishmen should give nothing to the singer, but what he did to the latter is worse. The odious niggardliness of the English people annoyed the singer for a quarter of an hour, perhaps; Nechljudow's foolish entertainment tortured him for an hour. The Prince never took the trouble to consider, even for a moment, what would be agreeable and useful to the singer; he thought always of himself only, of his own feelings, his anger, his indignation. This tender-hearted philanthropist is a dangerous, depraved egoist.

The irrational neighbourly love of the emotional mystic fails necessarily in its ostensible aim, because it does not arise from a knowledge of the true needs of the neighbour. The mystic practises a sentimental anthropomorphism. He transfers his own feelings, without more ado, to other beings, who feel quite differently from himself. He is in a condition bitterly to commiserate the moles because they are condemned to brood in perpetual darkness in their underground passages, and dreams, perhaps with tears in his eyes, of introducing electric light into their burrows. Because he, as seeing, would suffer severely under the conditions of a mole's life, therefore this animal is naturally to be pitied also, although it is blind and so does not miss the light. An anecdote relates that a child poured some hot water into the drawing-room aquarium one winter's day because it must have been so intolerably cold for the gold-fish; and in comic papers there is frequently a hit at the benevolent societies which bestow warm winter clothing on the negroes at the equator. This is Tolstoi's love of one's neighbour put into practice.

One especial point of his moral doctrine is the mortification of the flesh. All sexual intercourse is for him unchaste; marriage is quite as impure as the loosest tie. The *Kreutzer Sonata* is the most complete, and at the same time most celebrated, embodiment of these propositions. Pozdnyscheff, the murderer from motives of jealousy, says:* 'There is nothing pleasant in the honeymoon; on the contrary, it is a period of continual embarrassment, a shame, a profound depression, and, above all, boredom—fearful boredom! I can only compare the situation to that of a youth who is beginning to smoke: he feels sick, swallows his saliva, and pretends to like it very much. If the cigar is to give him any pleasure, it can only be later on, as it is with marriage. In order to enjoy it, the married couple must first accustom themselves to the vice.'

'How do you mean—to the vice? You are speaking of one of the most natural things—of an instinct.'

'Natural thing? An instinct? Not in the least. Allow me to tell you that I have been brought to, and maintain, the opposite conviction. I, the depraved and dissolute, assert that it is something unnatural. . . . It is an entirely unnatural treatment for any pure girl, just as it would be for a child.'

* Léon Tolstoi, *La Sonate à Kreutzer.* Traduit du Russe par E. Halpérine-Kaminsky. Paris: Collection des auteurs célèbres, p. 72.

Further on Pozdnyscheff develops the following crazy theory of the law of life: 'The object of man, as of humanity in general, is happiness, and to attain it humanity has a law which must be carried out. This law consists in the union of the individual beings which compose humanity. Human passions only impede this union, particularly the strongest and worst of all, sensual love, sexual pleasures. When human passions, especially the most violent, sensuality, shall have been suppressed, the union will be accomplished, and humanity, having attained its end, will have no further reason for existing.' And his last words are: 'People should understand that the true meaning of the words of St. Matthew, "Whosoever looketh on a woman to lust after her hath committed adultery with her already in his heart," applies to one's sister, and not only to a strange woman, but also, and above all, to one's own wife.'

Tolstoi, in whom, as in every 'higher degenerate,' two natures co-exist, of whom the one notices and judges the follies of the other, has yet a distinct feeling of the senselessness of his *Kreutzer Sonata* theory, and he makes his mouthpiece, Pozdnyscheff, declare* that he 'was looked upon as cracked.' But in the *Short Exposition*, where Tolstoi speaks in his own name, he develops, if with somewhat more reserve, the same philosophy.† 'The temptation to break the seventh commandment is due to the fact that we believe woman to have been created for carnal pleasure, and that, if a man leave one wife and take another, he will have more pleasure. Not to fall into this temptation, we must remember that it is not the will of the Father that the man should have pleasure through feminine charms. . . .' In the story *Family Happiness*‡ he likewise explains that a husband and wife, even if they have married from love, must become enemies in their wedded life, and it is quite purposeless to attempt a lasting cultivation of the original feelings.

It is not indeed necessary to refute a theory which pours contempt on all experience, all observations of nature, all institutions and laws that have been historically developed, and the known aim of which is the destruction of humanity. The thought of assailing it with zeal could only occur to men who were themselves more or less deranged. It is sufficient for the healthy minded to state it in distinct language; it is at once recognisable, then, for what it is—insanity.

For Tolstoi the great enemy is science. In *My Confession* he is never tired of accusing and abusing it. It is of no use to the people, but only to governments and to capitalists. It

* P. 119. † *Short Exposition of the Gospel*, p. 140.

‡ *Le Roman du Mariage.* Traduit du Russe par Michel Delines. Paris. *Auteurs célèbres.*

occupies itself with idle and vain things, such as the inquiries into protoplasm and spectrum analysis, but has never yet thought of anything useful, *e.g.*, 'how an axe and an axe-handle can best be manufactured; how a good saw ought to be fashioned; how good bread can be baked, which species of flour is best adapted for the purpose, how to manage the yeast, construct and heat the baking-oven; what foods and beverages are the most wholesome; what mushrooms are edible,' etc.

He is, be it noted, particularly unfortunate in his examples, since, as a matter of fact, every beginner takes up all the subjects he enumerates in the scientific study of hygiene and mechanics. In accordance with his poetic nature, he has had a strong desire to embody his views on science artistically. This he has done in the comedy *The Fruits of Enlightenment.* What does he scoff at in that? At the pitiable blockheads who believe in spirits and, in dread of death, hunt after bacteria. Spiritualism, and the opinions created in uneducated men of the world by the imperfectly understood news of the day, conveyed in political papers, respecting infectious micro-organisms, are what he takes for science, and against them he directs the arrows of his satire.

Real science does not need to be protected against attacks of this sort. I have already proved, in estimating the value of the reproaches which the neo-Catholic Symbolists and their critical patrons raised against natural science, that all those phrases were either childish or dishonest. The accusation of dishonesty cannot be brought against Tolstoi. He believes what he says. But childish his complaints and his mockery certainly are. He speaks of science as a blind man of colour. He has evidently no suspicion of its essence, its mission, its methods and the subjects with which it deals. He resembles Bouvard and Pécuchet, Flaubert's two idiots, who, completely ignorant, without teachers or guides, skim through a number of books indiscriminately, and fancy themselves in this sportive manner to have gained positive knowledge; this they seek to apply with the candour of a trained Krooboy, commit, self-evidently, one hair-raising stupidity after another, and then believe themselves justified in sneering at science, and declaring it a vain folly and deception. Flaubert avenged himself on the absurdity of his own efforts to conquer science as a lieutenant conquers a music-hall singer, by tarring and feathering Bouvard and Pécuchet. Tolstoi exploded his little fuss and fume on Science, that proud, disdainful beauty, who is only to be won by long, earnest, unselfish service, by lampooning the blockheads of his *Fruits of Enlightenment.* The degenerate Flaubert and the degenerate Tolstoi meet here in the same frenzy.

The way to happiness is, according to Tolstoi, the turning away from science, the renunciation of reason, and the return to the life of Nature ; that is, to agriculture. 'The town must be abandoned, the people must be sent away from the factories and into the country to work with their hands ; the aim of every man should be to satisfy all his wants himself' (*What ought one to Do?*).

How oddly is reason mixed with nonsense even in these economic demands! Tolstoi has rightly discerned the evils which follow the uprooting of the people from fostering Mother Earth, and the incubation of a day-wage-earning, urban industrial proletariate. It is true, also, that agriculture could employ very many more men healthily and profitably than at present if the land were the property of the community, and each one received only such a share, and that only for his lifetime, as he could himself cultivate thoroughly. But must industry on this account be destroyed? Would not that mean the destruction of civilization itself? Is it not rather the duty of intelligent philanthropy and justice carefully to maintain the division of labour, this necessary and profitable result of a long evolution, but at the same time, through a better system of economy, to transform the artisan from a factory convict, condemned to misery and ill-health, into a free producer of wealth, who enjoys the fruits of his labour himself, and works no more than is compatible with his health and his claims on life?

It is vain to seek for even the slightest hint of such a solution in Tolstoi. He contents himself with a barren enthusiasm for country life, which, if beautiful in Horace, has become annoying and ridiculous in Rousseau ; and he garrulously plagiarizes the hollow phrases about the worthlessness of civilization of the eloquent Genevese, who, smitten with the mania of persecution, could only have led a sentimental century like his own by the nose. Return to nature! It is not possible to compress more absurdity into fewer words. On our earth Nature is our enemy, whom we must fight, before whom we dare not lay down our weapons. In order to maintain our span of life we must create endlessly complicated artificial conditions ; we must clothe our bodies, build a roof over our heads, and store up provisions for many months, during which Nature denies us every nourishment. There is only one very narrow strip of our planet where mankind can live without exertion, without inventions and arts, like the beast in the forest and the fish in the water, and that is on some of the South Sea islands. There, in perpetual spring, he certainly needs no clothes and no dwelling, or only some palm-leaves as a shelter from occasional rain. There, at all seasons of the year, he finds food constantly prepared for him in the cocoa-nut palm, the bread-fruit tree, the banana, in some domestic animals, in fish and mussels. No beast of prey threatens his safety, and forces on him the development of strength and contempt of death. But how many men can this earthly paradise maintain? Perhaps a hundredth part of present humanity. The remaining ninety-nine hundredths have only the alternative either of perishing, or of settling in regions of our planet where the table is not spread, and the pillow of delight is not prepared, but in which everything which life demands for its sustenance must be procured artificially and laboriously. The 'return to Nature' means, in our degrees of latitude, the return to hunger, to freezing, to being devoured by wolves and bears. Not in the impossible 'return to Nature' lies healing for human misery, but in the reasonable organization of our struggle with Nature, I might say, in universal and obligatory service against it, from which only the crippled should be exempted.

We have now learnt to know the particular ideas which together constitute Tolstoism. As a philosophy it gives explanations of the world and of life, with unmeaning or contradictory paraphrases of some intentionally misunderstood Bible verses. As ethics, it prescribes the renunciation of resistance against vice and crime, the distribution of property, and the annihilation of mankind by complete abstinence. As sociological and economic doctrine it preaches the uselessness of science, the happiness of becoming stupid, the renunciation of manufactured products, and the duty of agriculture, though without betraying from whence the farmer is to get the necessary soil for cultivation. The remarkable thing in this system is, that it does not notice its own superfluity. If it understood itself, it would restrict itself to one single point—abstinence—since it is evident that it is unnecessary to break one's head over the aim and import of human life, over crime and love of your neighbour, and particularly over country or town life, if in any case through abstinence humanity is to die out with the present generation.

Rod* denies that Tolstoi is a mystic. 'Mysticism was always, as the word indicates, a transcendental doctrine. The mystics, especially the Christian mystics, have always sacrificed the present to the future life. . . . What, on the contrary, astonishes an unprejudiced mind in Tolstoi's books is the almost complete absence of all metaphysics, his indifference to the so-called questions of the other world.'

Rod simply does not know what mysticism is. He unduly restricts the sense of the word, if he only uses it to mean the investigation of 'other-world questions.' If he were less superficial he would know that religious enthusiasm is only one special instance of a general mental condition, and that mysticism is any morbid obscuration and incoherence of thought which is accompanied by emotionalism, and therefore includes that thought, the fruit of which is the system at once Materialistic, Pantheistic,

* Ed. Rod, *Les Idées morales du Temps présent.* Paris, 1892, p. 241.

Christian, Ascetic, Rousseauistic and Communistic, of Leo Tolstoi.

Raphael Löwenfeld, whom we have to thank for the first complete German edition of Tolstoi's works, has also written a very commendable biography of the Russian novelist, yet in which he feels himself obliged, not only to take sides vehemently with his hero, but also to assure that hero's possible critics beforehand of his deep contempt for them. 'Want of comprehension,' he says,* 'calls them (the "independent phenomena" of Tolstoi's sort) eccentrics, unwilling to allow that anyone should be a head taller than the rest. The unprejudiced man, who is capable of admiring greatness, sees in their independence the expression of an extraordinary power which has outgrown the possibilities of the time, and, leading on, points out the paths to those coming after.' It is indeed hazardous forthwith to accuse all who are not of his opinion of 'want of comprehension.' One who judges so autocratically will have to put up with the answer, that he is guilty of 'want of comprehension' who, without the most elementary training, enters upon the criticism of a phenomenon, to the understanding of which some degree of æsthetical and literary so-called 'knowledge' and personal feeling are very far from sufficient. Löwenfeld boasts of his capacity to admire greatness. He is possibly wrong not to presuppose this capacity in others also. What he precisely has to prove is this, that what he admires deserves in truth the designation of greatness. His assertion, however, is the only proof he brings on this most important point. He calls himself unprejudiced. It may be admitted that he is free from prejudices, but then he is free also from the preliminary knowledge that alone entitles anyone to form an opinion on psychological phenomena, which strike even the uninitiated as extraordinary, and to present them with self-assurance. Did he possess this preliminary knowledge he would know that Tolstoi, who, 'leading, is to point out the paths to those coming after,' is a mere copy of a class of men who have had their representatives in every age. Lombroso† instances a certain Knudsen, a madman, who lived in Schleswig about 1680, and asserted that there was neither a God nor a hell; that priests and judges were useless and pernicious, and marriage an immorality; that men ceased to exist after death; that everyone must be guided by his own inward insight,' etc. Here we have the principal features of Tolstoi's cosmology and moral philosophy. Knudsen has, however, so little 'pointed out, leading, the way to those coming after,' that he still only exists as an instructive case of mental aberration in books on diseases of the mind.

* Raphael Löwenfeld, *Leo N. Tolstoi, sein Leben, seine Werke, seine Weltanschauung.* Erster Theil. Berlin, 1892, Introd., p. 1.

† Lombroso, *Genie und Irrsinn*, p. 256, foot-note.

The truth is that all Tolstoi's idiosyncrasies could be traced to the best-known and most often observed stigmata of higher degeneration. He even relates of himself:* 'Scepticism brought me at one time to a condition nearly bordering on frenzy. I had the idea that besides myself nobody and nothing existed in the whole world; that things were not things, but presentations, which only became phenomenal at what time I directed my attention to them, and that these presentations disappeared at once when I ceased to think of them. . . . There were hours when, under the influence of this fixed idea, I came to such a pitch of mental bewilderment that I at times looked quickly the other way, in the hope that in the place where I was not, I might be surprised by nothingness.' And in his *Confession* he says explicitly: 'I felt that I was not quite mentally sound.'† His feeling was correct. He was suffering from a mania of brooding doubt, observable in many of the 'higher degenerates.' Professor Kowalewski‡ explains the mania of doubt straight away as exclusively a psychosis of degeneration. Griesinger§ relates the case of a patient who continually brooded over the notions of beauty, existence, etc., and put endless questions about them. Griesinger, however, was less familiar with the phenomena of degeneration, and therefore held his case as 'one little known.' Lombroso‖ mentions in the enumeration of the symptoms of his maniacs of genius: 'Almost all are taken up, in the most painful manner, with religious doubts, which disturb the mind and oppress the timid conscience and sick heart, like a crime.' It is not, then, the noble desire for knowledge which forces Tolstoi to be ceaselessly occupied with questions concerning the aim and meaning of life, but the degeneration-mania of doubt and brooding thought, which is barren, because no answer, no explanation can satisfy them. For it is obvious that be the 'therefore' never so clear, never so exhaustive, it can never silence the mechanically impulsive 'wherefore' proceeding from the Unconscious.

A special form of the phenomenon of scepticism and brooding thought is a rage for contradiction, and the inclination to bizarre assertions, as is noted by many clinicists—*e.g.*, Sollier¶—as a special stigma of degeneration. It has appeared very strongly in Tolstoi at certain times. 'In the struggles for independence,' relates Löwenfeld,** 'Tolstoi frequently overstepped the limits of good taste, while he combated tradition only because it was tradition. Thus he called . . . Shakespeare a scribbler by the dozen,

* Löwenfeld, *op. cit.*, p. 39. † *Ibid.*, p. 276.

‡ Professor Kowalewski, in *The Journal of Mental Science*, January, 1888.

§ Griesinger, 'Ueber einen wenig bekannten psychopathischen Zustand,' *Archiv für Psychiatrie*, Band I.

‖ Lombroso, *Genie und Irrsinn*, p. 324.

¶ Sollier, *Psychologie de l'Idiot et de l'Imbécile*.

** Löwenfeld, *op. cit.*, p. 100.

and asserted that the admiration . . . for the great Englishman . . . has properly no other origin than the custom of echoing strange opinions with thoughtless obsequiousness.'

What one finds most touching and most worthy of admiration in Tolstoi is his boundless spirit of fraternity. I have already shown above that it is foolish in its starting-points and manifestations. Here, however, I may have to point out that it is likewise a stigma of degeneration. Though he has not the experience of an alienist, the clear-minded, healthy Tourgenieff has, by his own common-sense, 'scoffingly' called Tolstoi's fervent love for the oppressed people 'hysterical,' as Löwenfeld* says. We shall find it again in many degenerate subjects. 'In contrast to the selfish imbecile,' Legrain† teaches, 'we have the imbeciles who are good to excess, who are philanthropic, who set up a thousand absurd systems in order to advance the happiness of humanity.' And further on: 'Full of his love for humanity, the imbecile patient, without reflection, takes up the social question on its most difficult side, and settles it confidently in a series of grotesque inventions.' This irrational philanthropy, untutored by judgment, which Tourgenieff, with just surmise if incorrect designation, called 'hysterical,' is nothing else than a manifestation of that emotionalism which constitutes for Morel the fundamental character of degeneration. Nothing in this diagnosis is altered by the fact that Tolstoi had the good fortune, during the recent famine, of being able to develop the most highly effective and most devoted helpfulness for the alleviation of the misery of his countrymen. The case happened to be very simple. The need of his fellow-creatures was of the most primitive form, want of bodily food. Fraternal love could likewise set to work in its most primitive form, in the distribution of food and clothing. A special power of judgment, a deep comprehension of the need of his fellow-creatures, was here unnecessary. And that Tolstoi's preparations for the relief of the sufferers were more effective than those of the proper authorities only proved the stupidity and incapacity of the latter.

Tolstoi's attitude towards women also, which must remain incomprehensible to a healthy human understanding, will, in the light of clinical experience, forthwith be understood. It has been repeatedly pointed out in these pages that the emotionalism of the degenerate has, as a rule, an erotic colouring, because of the pathological alteration in their sexual centres. The abnormal excitability of these parts of the nervous system can have as a consequence both an especial attraction towards woman and an especial antipathy to her. The common

* Löwenfeld, *op. cit.*, p. 47.

† Legrain, *Du Délire chez les Dégénérés*, pp. 28, 195.

element connecting these opposing effects of one and the same organic condition is the being constantly occupied with woman, the being constantly engrossed with presentations in consciousness from the region of sexuality.*

In the mental life of a sane man, woman is far from filling the part she plays in that of the degenerate. The physiological relation of man to woman is that of desire for the time being toward her, and of indifference when the state of desire is not present. Antipathy, let alone violent enmity, to woman, the normal man never feels. If he desires the woman, he loves her; if his erotic excitement is appeased, he becomes cool and more distant in his attitude, though without feeling aversion or fear. The man, from his purely subjective, physiological necessities and inclinations, would certainly never have invented marriage, the persistent alliance with woman. This is not a sexual but a social arrangement. It does not rest on the organic instincts of the individual man, but on the need of collectivity. It depends on the existing economic order and the dominant opinions about the State, its problems and its relations to the individual, and changes its form with these. A man may—or at least should—choose a certain woman for his consort out of love; but what holds him fast married, after a suitable choice and successful courtship, is no longer physiological love, but a complex mixture of habit, gratitude, unsexual friendship, convenience, the wish to obtain for himself social advantages (to which must naturally be added an ordered household, social representation, etc.), considerations of duty towards children and State; more or less, also, unthinking imitation of a universal observance. But feelings such as are described in the *Kreutzer Sonata* and in *Family Happiness* the normal man never experiences towards his wife, even if he has ceased to love her in the natural sense of the word.

These relations are quite otherwise in the degenerate. The morbid activity of his sexual centres completely rules him. The thought of woman has for him the power of an 'obsession.' He feels that he cannot resist the exciting influences proceeding from the woman, that he is her helpless slave, and would commit any folly, any madness, any crime, at her beck and call. He necessarily, therefore, sees in woman an uncanny, overpowering force of nature, bestowing supreme delights or dealing

* It is not my object, in a book intended primarily for the general educated reader, to dwell on this delicate subject. Anyone wishing to be instructed more closely in the morbid eroticism of the degenerate may read the books of Paul Moreau (of Tours) *Des Aberrations du Sens génésique*, 2e édition, Paris, 1883; and Krafft-Ebing's *Psychopathia sexualis*, Stuttgart, 1886. Papers on this subject by Westphal (*Archiv für Psychiatrie*, 1870 and 1876), by Charcot and Magnan (*Archives de Neurologie*, 1882), etc., are scarcely accessible to the general public.

destruction, and he trembles before this power, to which he is defencelessly exposed. If, then, besides this, the almost never-failing aberrations set in, if he, in fact, commits things for woman for which he must condemn and despise himself; or if woman, without its coming to actual deeds, awakens in him emotions and thoughts before whose baseness and infamy he is horrified, then, in the moment of exhaustion, when judgment is stronger than impulse, the dread which woman inspires him withal will be suddenly changed into aversion and savage hatred. The erotomaniac 'degenerate' stands in the same position to the woman as a dipsomaniac to intoxicating drinks. Magnan* has given an appalling picture of the struggles waged in the mind of a dipsomaniac by the passionate eagerness for the bottle, and the loathing and horror of it. The mind of an erotomaniac presents a similar spectacle, but probably still stronger struggles. These frequently lead the unhappy creature, who sees no other means of escaping from his sexual obsession, to self-mutilation. There are in Russia, as is well known, a whole sect of 'degenerates,' the Skoptzi, by whom this is systematically exercised, as the only effective treatment to escape the devil and be saved. Pozdnyscheff, in the *Kreutzer Sonata*, is a Skopetz without knowing it, and the sexual morality which Tolstoi teaches in this narrative and in his theoretic writings is the expression in literature of the sexual psychopathy of the Skoptzi.

The universal success of Tolstoi's writings is undoubtedly due in part to his high literary gifts. But that part is not the greatest; for, as we have seen in the beginning of this chapter, it was not his artistically most important creations, the works of his best years, but his later mystical works, which have won for him his body of believers. This effect is to be explained, not on æsthetical, but on pathological grounds. Tolstoi would have remained unnoticed, like any Knudsen of the seventeenth century, if his extravagances as a degenerate mystic had not found his contemporaries prepared for their reception. The wide-spread hysteria from exhaustion was the requisite soil in which alone Tolstoism could flourish.

That the rise and expansion of Tolstoism is to be traced, not to the intrinsic merit of Tolstoi's writings, but to the mental condition of his readers, is made clear in the most significant manner by the difference in those parts of his system which have made an impression in various countries. In every nation just such tones awakened an echo as were attuned with its own nervous system.

In England it was Tolstoi's sexual morality that excited the

* V. Magnan, *Leçons cliniques sur la Dipsomanie, faites à l'asile Sainte-Anne.* Recueillies et publiées par M. le Dr. Marcel Briand. Paris, 1884.

greatest interest, for in that country economic reasons condemn a formidable number of girls, particularly of the educated classes, to forego marriage; and, from a theory which honoured chastity as the highest dignity and noblest human destiny, and branded marriage with gloomy wrath as abominable depravity, these poor creatures would naturally derive rich consolation for their lonely, empty lives, and their cruel exclusion from the possibility of fulfilling their natural calling. The *Kreutzer Sonata* has, therefore, become the book of devotion of all the spinsters of England.

In France Tolstoism is particularly valued for the way in which it casts out science, deposes the intellect from all offices and dignities, preaches the return to implicit faith, and praises the poor in spirit as alone happy. This is water to the mill of neo-Catholics, and those mystics, from political motives, or from degeneration, who erect a cathedral to pious symbolism, raise up also a high altar to Tolstoi in their church.

In Germany, on the whole, but little enthusiasm is evinced for the abstinence-morality of the *Kreutzer Sonata*, and the intellectual reaction of *My Confession*, *My Religion*, and *Fruits of Enlightenment*. On the other hand, his followers in that country exalt Tolstoi's vague socialism and his morbid fraternal love into their dogma. All the muddle-headed among our people who, not from sober scientific conviction, but from hysterical emotionalism, feel a leaning towards a sickly, impotent socialism, which tends principally towards ministering cheap broth to proletarians, and towards revelling in sentimental romances and melodramas from the pretended life of the city worker, naturally discovered in Tolstoi's 'give-me-something-communism,' with its scorn for all economic and moral laws, the expression of their —very platonic!—love for the disinherited. And in the circles in which Herr von Egidy's watery rationalism (at least a hundred years behind time) could rise into notoriety, and in which his first writing could call forth nearly a hundred replies, assents, and explanations, Tolstoi's *Short Exposition of the Gospel*, with its denial of the divine nature of Christ, and of existence after death, with its effusions of a superabundance of feelings of aimless love, its incomprehensible personal sanctification and rhetoric morality, and especially with its astounding misinterpretation of the clearest passages from Scripture, must indeed have been an event. All the adherents of Herr von Egidy are predestined followers of Tolstoi, and all Tolstoi's admirers perpetrate an inconsistency if they do not enter into the new Salvation Army of Herr von Egidy.

By the special *timbre* of the echo which Tolstoism calls forth in different countries, he has become an instrument which is better fitted than any other tendency of degeneration in contemporary literature for the determination, measurement, and comparison, in kind and degree, of degeneration and hysteria among those civilized nations in which the phenomenon of the Dusk of the Nations has been observed.

CHAPTER V.

THE RICHARD WAGNER CULT.

We have seen in a previous chapter that the whole mystic movement of the period has its roots in romanticism, and hence originally emanates from Germany. In England German romanticism was metamorphosed into pre-Raphaelitism, in France the latter engendered, with the last remains of its procreative strength, the abortions of symbolism and neo-Catholicism, and these Siamese twins contracted with Tolstoism a mountebank marriage such as might take place between the cripple of a fair and the wonder of a show-booth. While the descendants of the emigrant (who on his departure from his German home already carried in him all the germs of subsequent tumefactions and disfigurements), so changed as to be almost unrecognisable, grew up in different countries, and set about returning to their native land to attempt the renewal of family ties with their home-staying connections, Germany gave birth to a new prodigy, who was in truth only reared with great trouble to manhood, and for long years received but little notice or appreciation, but who finally obtained an incomparably mightier attractive force over the great fools' fair of the present time than all his fellow-competitors. This prodigy is 'Wagnerism.' It is the German contribution to modern mysticism, and far outweighs all that the other nations combined have supplied to that movement. For Germany is powerful in everything, in evil as in good, and the magnitude of its elementary force manifests itself in a crushing manner in its degenerate, as well as in its ennobling, efforts.

Richard Wagner is in himself alone charged with a greater abundance of degeneration than all the degenerates put together with whom we have hitherto become acquainted. The stigmata of this morbid condition are united in him in the most complete and most luxuriant development. He displays in the general constitution of his mind the persecution mania, megalomania and mysticism ; in his instincts vague philanthropy, anarchism, a craving for revolt and contradiction ; in his writings all the signs of graphomania, namely, incoherence, fugitive ideation, and a tendency to idiotic punning, and, as the groundwork of his being, the characteristic emotionalism of a colour at once erotic and religiously enthusiastic.

For Wagner's persecution mania, we have the testimony of his most recent biographer and friend, Ferdinand Praeger, who relates that for years Wagner was convinced that the Jews had conspired to prevent the representation of his operas—a delirium inspired by his furious anti-Semitism. His megalomania is so well known through his writings, his verbal utterances, and the whole course of his life, that a bare reference to it is sufficient. It is to be admitted that this mania was essentially increased by the crazy procedure of those who surrounded Wagner. A much firmer equilibrium than that which obtained in Wagner's mind would have been infallibly disturbed by the nauseous idolatry of which Bayreuth was the shrine. The *Bayreuther Blätter* is a unique phenomenon. To me, at least, no other instance is known of a newspaper which was founded exclusively for the deification of a living man, and in every number of which, through long years, the appointed priests of the temple have burned incense to their household god, with the savage fanaticism of howling and dancing dervishes, bent the knee, prostrated themselves before him, and immolated all opponents as sacrificial victims.

We will take a closer view of the graphomaniac Wagner. His *Collected Writings and Poems* form ten large thick volumes, and among the 4,500 pages which they approximately contain there is hardly a single one which will not puzzle the unbiased reader, either through some nonsensical thought or some impossible mode of expression. Of his prose works (his poems will be treated of further on), the most important is decidedly *The Art-work of the Future*.* The thoughts therein expressed —so far as the wavering shadows of ideas in a mystically emotional degenerate subject may be so called—occupied Wagner during his whole life, and were again and again propounded by him in ever new terms and phraseology. *The Opera and the Drama*, *Judaism in Music*, *On the State and Religion*, *The Vocation of the Opera*, *Religion and Art*, are nothing more than amplifications of single passages of *The Art-work of the Future*. This restless repetition of one and the same strain of thought is itself characteristic in the highest degree. The clear, mentally sane author, who feels himself impelled to say something, will once for all express himself as distinctly and impressively as it is possible for him to do, and have done with it. He may, perhaps, return to the subject, in order to clear up misconceptions, repel attacks, and fill up lacunæ; but he will

* Richard Wagner, *Das Kunstwerk der Zukunft*. Leipzig, 1850. The numbering of the pages given in quotations from this work refers to the edition here indicated.

never wish to rewrite his book, wholly or in part, two or three times in slightly different words, not even if in later years he attains to the insight that he has not succeeded in finding for it an adequate form. The crazed graphomaniac, on the contrary, cannot recognise in his book, as it lies finished before him, the satisfying expression of his thoughts, and he will always be tempted to begin his work afresh, a task which is endless, because it must consist in giving a fixed linguistic form to ideas which are formless.

The fundamental thought of the *Art-work of the Future* is this : The first and most original of the arts was that of dancing ; its peculiar essence is rhythm, and this has developed into music; music, consisting of rhythm and tone, has raised (Wagner says 'condensed') its phonetic element to speech, and produced the art of poetry ; the highest form of poetry is the drama, which for the purpose of stage-construction, and to imitate the natural scene of human action, has associated itself with architecture and painting respectively ; finally, sculpture is nothing but the giving permanence to the appearance of the actor in a dead rigid form, while acting is real sculpture in living, flowing movement. Thus all the arts group themselves around the drama, and the latter should unite them naturally. Nevertheless they appear at present in isolation, to the great injury of each and of art in general. This reciprocal estrangement and isolation of the different arts is an unnatural and decadent condition, and the effort of true artists must be to win them back to their natural and necessary conjunction with each other. The mutual penetration and fusion of all arts into a single art will produce the genuine work of art. Hence the work of art of the future is a drama with music and dance, which unrolls itself in a landscape painting, has for a frame a masterly creation of architectural art designed for the poetico-musical end, and is represented by actors who are really sculptors, but who realize their plastic inspirations by means of their own bodily appearance.

In this way Wagner has set forth for himself the evolution of art. His system calls for criticism in every part. The historical filiation of the arts which he attempts to establish is false. If the original reciprocal connections of song, dance and poetry be granted, the development of architecture, painting and sculpture is certainly independent of poetry in its dramatic form. That the theatre employs all the arts is true, but it is one of those truths which are so self-evident that it is generally unnecessary to mention them, and least of all with profound prophetic mien and the grand priestly gestures of one proclaiming surprising revelations. Everyone knows from experience that the stage is in a theatrical building, that it displays painted decorations which represent landscapes or buildings, and that on it there is speaking, singing and acting. Wagner secretly feels that he makes himself ridiculous when he strains himself to expound this trite matter of first experience in the Pythian mode, with an enormous outlay of gush and exaltation . . . ; hence he exaggerates it to such a degree as to turn it into an absurdity. He not only asseverates that in the drama (more correctly speaking, the opera, or the musical drama, as Wagner prefers to call it) different arts co-operate, but he asserts that it is only through this co-operation that each individual art is advanced to its highest capacity of expression, and that the individual arts must and will surrender their independence as an unnatural error, in order to continue to exist only as collaborators of the musical drama.

The first asseveration is at least doubtful. In the cathedral of Cologne architecture produces an impression without the representation of a drama; the accompaniment of music would add nothing whatever to the beauty and depth of Faust and Hamlet; Goethe's lyric poetry and the *Divina Commedia* need no landscape-painting as a frame and background; Michael Angelo's *Moses* would hardly produce a deeper impression surrounded by dancers and singers; and the *Pastoral Symphony* does not require the accompaniment of words in order to exercise its full charm. Schopenhauer, although Wagner admired him as the greatest thinker of all time, expresses himself very decidedly on this point. 'The grand opera,' he says,* 'is, properly speaking, no product of pure artistic sense, but rather of the somewhat barbaric conception of elevating æsthetic enjoyment through accumulation of means, simultaneity of quite different impressions, and intensification of the effect through the multiplication of the operating masses and forces; while, on the other hand, music, as the mightiest of all arts, is able by itself alone completely to occupy the mind which is susceptible to it; indeed, its loftiest productions, to be appropriately grasped and enjoyed, demand a mind wholly undivided and undiverted, so that it may yield itself up to them, and lose itself in them, in order completely to understand their incredible inwardness of language. Instead of this, in highly complicated operatic music the mind is besieged at the same time by way of the eye, by means of the most variegated pomp, the most fantastic pictures, and the liveliest impressions of light and colour; while over and above this it is occupied with the story of the piece. . . . Strictly speaking, then, one may call opera an unmusical invention for the benefit of unmusical minds, into which music must only be smuggled by means of a medium

* Arthur Schopenhauer, *Parerga und Paralipomena, Kurze Phil. Schriften.* Leipzig, 1888, Band II., p. 465.

foreign to it, that is, as a sort of accompaniment to a long spun-out, insipid love-story, and its poetical thin broth; for the libretto of an opera does not tolerate concise poetry, full of genius and thought.' This is an absolute condemnation of the Wagnerian idea of the musical drama as the collective art-work of the future. It might seem, it is true, that certain recent experiments in psychophysics had come to the help of Wagner's theory of the reciprocal enhancement of the simultaneous effects of different arts. Charles Féré* has, in fact, shown that the ear hears more keenly when the eye is simultaneously stimulated by an agreeable (dynamogenous) colour; but, in the first place, this phenomenon may also be interpreted thus: that the keenness of hearing is enhanced not by the visual impression as such, not simply as sense excitation, but only through its dynamogenous quality, which arouses the whole nervous system as well to a more lively activity. And then the question in Féré's experiments is merely one of simple sense-perceptions, whereas the musical drama is supposed to awaken a higher cerebral activity, to produce presentations and thoughts, together with direct emotions; in which case each of the arts acting in concert will produce, in consequence of the necessary dispersion of the attention to it, a more feeble effect than if it appealed by itself alone to sense and intellect.

Wagner's second assertion, that the natural evolution of each art necessarily leads it to the surrender of its independence and to its fusion with the other arts,† contradicts so strongly all experience and all the laws of evolution, that it can at once be characterized as delirious. Natural development always proceeds from the simple to the complex—not inversely; progress consists in differentiation, *i.e.*, in the evolution of originally similar parts into special organs of different structure and independent functions, and not in the retrogression of differentiated beings of rich specialization to a protoplasm without physiognomy.

* Charles Féré, *Sensation et Mouvement.* Paris, 1887.

† *Das Kunstwerk der Zukunft*, p. 169: 'It is only when the desire of the artistic sculptor has passed into the soul of the *dancer*, of the *mimic interpreter*, of him who sings and speaks, that this desire can be conceived as satisfied. It is only when the art of sculpture no longer exists, or has followed another tendency than that of representing human bodies—when it has passed, as sculpture, into *architecture*—when the rigid solitude of this *one* man carved in stone will have been resolved into the infinitely flowing plurality of veritable, living men . . . it is only then, too, that *real plastic* will exist.' And on p. 182: 'That which it [painting] *honestly* exerts itself to attain, it attains in . . . greatest perfection . . . when it descends from canvas and chalk to ascend to the *tragic stage*. . . . But landscape-painting will become, as the last and most finished conclusion of all the fine arts, the life-giving soul, properly speaking, of architecture; it will teach us thus to organize the *stage* for works of the dramatic art of the future, in which, itself living, it will represent the warm *background* of *nature* for the use of the *living*, and not for the imitated *man*.'

The arts have not arisen accidentally; their differentiation is the consequence of organic necessity; once they have attained independence, they will never surrender it. They can degenerate, they can even die out, but they can never again shrink back into the germ from which they have sprung. The effort to return to beginnings is, however, a peculiarity of degeneration, and founded in its deepest essence. The degenerate subject is himself on the downward road from the height of organic development which our species has reached; his imperfect brain is incapable of the highest and most refined operations of thought; he has therefore a strong desire to lighten them, to simplify the multifariousness of phenomena and make them easier to survey; to drag everything animate and inanimate down to lower and older stages of existence, in order to make them more easy of access to his comprehension. We have seen that the French Symbolists, with their colour-hearing, wished to degrade man to the indifferentiated sense-perceptions of the pholas or oyster. Wagner's fusion of the arts is a pendant to this notion. His *Art-work of the Future* is the art-work of times long past. What he takes for evolution is retrogression, and a return to a primeval human, nay, to a pre-human stage.

Still more extraordinary than the fundamental idea of the book is its linguistic form. For example, let us estimate the following remarks on musical art (p. 68): 'The sea separates and unites countries; thus musical art separates and unites the two extreme poles of human art, dancing and poetry. It is the heart of man; the blood which takes its circulation from it gives to the outward flesh its warm living colour; but it nourishes with an undulating, elastic force the nerves of the brain which are directed inward' [!!]. 'Without the activity of the heart, the activity of the brain would become a piece of mechanical skill [!], the activity of the external limbs an equally mechanical, emotionless procedure.' 'By means of the heart the intellect feels itself related to the entire body [!]; the mere sensuous man rises to intellectual activity' [!]. 'Now, the organ of the heart [!] is *sound*, and its artistic language is music.' What here floated before the mind of Wagner was a comparison, in itself senseless, between the function of music as the medium of expression for the feelings, and the function of the blood as the vehicle of nutritive materials for the organism. But as his mystically-disposed brain was not capable of clearly grasping the various parts of this intricate idea, and of arranging them in parallel lines, he entangled himself in the absurdity of an 'activity of the brain without activity of the heart'; of a 'relation between the intellect and the whole body through the heart,' etc., and finally attains to the pure twaddle of calling 'sound' the 'organ of the heart.'

He wishes to express the very simple thought that music cannot communicate definite images and judgments, but merely feelings of a general character; and for this purpose devises the following rigmarole (p. 88): 'It is never able . . . of itself alone to bring the human individual, determined as to sensation and morals, to an exactly perceptible, distinctive representation; it is in its infinite involution always and only feeling; it appears as an *accompaniment* of the moral deed, not as the *deed itself;* it can place feelings and dispositions side by side, not develop in necessary sequence one disposition from another; it is lacking in *moral will*' [!].

Let the reader further bury himself in this passage (p. 159): 'It is only and exactly in the degree to which the woman of perfected womanliness, in her love for the man, and through her absorption into his being, shall have developed the masculine element as well as this womanliness, and brought it with the purely womanly element in herself to a complete consummation; in other words, in the degree in which she is not only the man's mistress, but also his friend, is the man able to find perfect satisfaction in a woman's love.'

Wagner's admirers asseverate that they understand this string of words thrown together at random. Indeed, they find them remarkably clear! This, however, should not surprise us. Readers who through weakness of mind or flightiness of thought are incapable of attention always understand everything. For them there exists neither obscurity nor nonsense. They seek in the words over which their absent gaze flits superficially, not the author's thoughts, but a reflection of their own rambling dreams. Those who have lived lovingly observant in children's nurseries must have frequently seen the game in which a child takes a book, or printed paper, and, holding it before his face, generally upside down, begins gravely to read aloud, often the story told him by his mamma yesterday before he dropped asleep, or, more frequently, the fancies which at the moment are buzzing in his little head. This is somewhat the procedure of these blessed readers who understand everything. They do not read what is in the books, but what they put into them; and as far as the process and result of this mental activity are concerned, it is certainly very much a matter of indifference what the author has actually thought and said.

The incoherence of Wagner's thought, determined as it is by the excitations of the moment, manifests itself in his constant contradictions. At one time (p. 187) he asserts, 'The highest aim of mankind is the artistic; the most highly artistic is the drama;' and in a footnote (p. 194) he exclaims, 'These easy-going creatures are fain to see and hear everything, except *the real, undisfigured human being* who stands exhorting at the exit of their dreams. *But it is exactly this very human being whom we must now place in the foreground.*' It is evident that one of these affirmations is diametrically opposed to the other. The 'artistic' 'dramatic' man is not the 'real' man, and it will be impossible for him, who looks upon it as his task to occupy himself with the real man, to recognise art as 'the highest aim of man,' and to regard his 'dreams' as the most distinguished of his activities.

In one passage (p. 206) he says: 'Who, therefore, will be *the artist of the future?* Unquestionably the poet. But *who* will be the poet? Incontestably the *interpreter*. Again, however, *who* will be the interpreter? Necessarily the *association of all artists*.' If this has any sense at all, it can only be that in the future the people will jointly write and act their dramas; and that Wagner really meant this he proves in the passage (p. 225) where he meets the objection he anticipated, that therefore the mob is to be the creator of the art-work of the future, with the words, 'Bear in mind that this mob is in no way a normal product of real human nature, but rather the artificial result of your unnatural civilization; that all the devices and abominations which disgust you in this mob are only the desperate movements of the fight which real human nature is carrying on against its cruel oppressor, modern civilization.' Let us contrast with these expressions the following passage from the treatise, *What is German?** : 'The fact that from the bosom of the German race there have sprung Goethe and Schiller, Mozart and Beethoven, too easily seduces the greater number of persons of mediocre gifts into regarding these great minds as belonging by right to them, and to attempt, with the complacency of a demagogue, to persuade the masses that they themselves are Goethe and Schiller, Mozart and Beethoven.' But who, if not Wagner himself, has thus persuaded the masses, proclaiming them to be the 'artists of the future'? And this very madness, which he himself recognises as such in the remark quoted, has made a great impression on the multitude. They have taken literally what Wagner, with the 'complacency of a demagogue,' has persuasively said to them. They have really imagined themselves to be the 'artists of the future,' and we have lived to see societies formed in many places in Germany who wanted to build theatres of the future, and themselves to perform works of the future in them! And these societies were joined not only by students or young commercial employés in whom a certain propensity for acting plays comes as a malady of adolescence, and who persuade themselves that they are serving the 'ideal' when with childish vanity and in grotesque

* Richard Wagner, *Gesammelte Schriften und Dichtungen*. Leipzig, 1883, Band X., p. 68.

theatrical costume they gesticulate and declaim before their touched and admiring relatives and acquaintances. Nay, old burgesses, bald and bulky, abandoned their sacred *skat*, and even the thrice-holy morning tankard, and prepared themselves devoutly for noble dramatic achievements! Since the memorable occasion on which Quince, Snug, Bottom, Flute, Snout, and Starveling rehearsed their admirable *Pyramus and Thisbe*, the world has seen no similar spectacle. Emotional shopkeepers and enthusiastic counter-jumpers got Wagner's absurdities on the brain, and the provincials and Philistines whom his joyful message had reached actually set about with their united strength to carry on the work of Goethe and Schiller, Mozart and Beethoven.

In the passages quoted, in which, in the most used-up style of Rousseau, he glorifies the masses, speaks of 'unnatural culture,' and calls 'modern civilization' 'the cruel oppressor of human nature,' Wagner betrays that mental condition which the degenerate share with enlightened reformers, born criminals with the martyrs of human progress, namely, deep, devouring discontent with existing facts. This certainly shows itself otherwise in the degenerate than in reformers. The latter grow angry over real evils only, and make rational proposals for their remedy which are in advance of the time: these remedies may presuppose a better and wiser humanity than actually exists, but, at least, they are capable of being defended on reasonable grounds. The degenerate subject, on the other hand, selects among the arrangements of civilization such as are either immaterial or distinctly suitable, in order to rebel against them. His fury has either ridiculously insignificant aims or simply beats the air. He either gives no earnest thought to improvement, or hatches astoundingly mad projects for making the world happy. His fundamental frame of mind is persistent rage against everything and everyone, which he displays in venomous phrases, savage threats, and the destructive mania of wild beasts. Wagner is a good specimen of this species. He would like to crush 'political and criminal civilization,' as he expresses it. In what, however, does the corruption of society and the untenableness of the condition of everything reveal themselves to him? In the fact that operas are played with tripping airs, and ballets are performed! And how shall humanity attain its salvation! By performing the musical drama of the future! It is to be hoped that no criticism of this universal plan of salvation will be demanded of me.

Wagner is a declared anarchist. He distinctly develops the teaching of this faction in the *Art-work of the Future* (p. 217): '*All* men have but *one* common *need* . . . the need of *living* and *being happy*. Herein lies the natural bond between all men. . . . It is only the special needs which, according to time, place, and individuality, make themselves known and increase, which in the rational condition of future humanity can serve as a basis for special associations. . . . These associations will change, will take another form, dissolve and reconstitute themselves according as those needs change and reappear.'* He does not conceal the fact that this 'rational condition of future humanity 'can be brought about only by force' (p. 228). 'Necessity must force us, too, through the Red Sea if we, purged of our shame, are to reach the Promised Land. We shall not be drowned in it; it is destructive only to the *Pharaohs* of this world, who have once already been swallowed up—man and horse . . . the arrogant, proud Pharaohs who then forgot that once a poor shepherd's son with his shrewd advice had saved their land from starvation.'

Together with this anarchistic acerbity, there is another feeling that controls the entire conscious and unconscious mental life of Wagner, viz., sexual emotion. He has been throughout his life an erotic (in a psychiatric sense), and all his ideas revolve about woman. The most ordinary incitements, even those farthest removed from the province of the sexual instinct, never fail to awaken in his consciousness voluptuous images of an erotic character, and the bent of the automatic association of ideas is in him always directed towards this pole of his thought. In this connection let this passage be read from the *Art-work of the Future* (p. 44), where he seeks to demonstrate the relation between the art of dancing, music, and poetry: 'In the contemplation of this ravishing dance of the most genuine and noblest muses, of the artistic man [?], we now see the three arm-in-arm lovingly entwined up to their necks; then this, then that one, detaching herself from the entwinement, as if to display to the others her beautiful form in complete separation, touching the hands of the others only with the extreme tips of her fingers; now the one, entranced by a backward glance at the twin forms of her closely entwined sisters, bending towards them; then two, carried away by the allurements of the one [!] greeting her in homage; finally all, in close embrace, breast to breast, limb to limb, in an ardent kiss of love, coalescing in one blissfully living shape. This is the love and life, the joy and wooing of art,' etc. (Observe the word-play: *Lieben und Leben, Freuen und Freien!*) Wagner here visibly loses the thread of his argument; he neglects what he really wishes to say, and revels in the picture of the three dancing

* Compare also, in *Das Bühnenweihfestspiel in Bayreuth*, 1882 (*Gesammelte Schriften*, Band X., p. 384): 'This [the 'sure rendering of all events on, above, under, behind, and before the stage'] anarchy accomplishes, because each individual does what he *wishes* to do, namely (?), what is right.'

maidens, who have arisen before his mind's eye, following with lascivious longing the outline of their forms and their seductive movements.

The shameless sensuality which prevails in his dramatic poems has impressed all his critics. Hanslick* speaks of the 'bestial sensuality' in *Rheingold*, and says of *Siegfried:* 'The feverish accents, so much beloved by Wagner, of an insatiable sensuality, blazing to the uttermost limits—this ardent moaning, sighing, crying, and sinking to the ground, move us with repugnance. The text of these love-scenes becomes sometimes, in its exuberance, sheer nonsense.' Compare in the first act of the *Walküre*,† in the scene between Siegmund and Sieglinde, the following stage directions: 'Hotly interrupting'; 'embraces her with fiery passion'; 'in gentle ecstasy'; 'she hangs enraptured upon his neck'; 'close to his eyes'; 'beside himself'; 'in the highest intoxication,' etc. At the conclusion, it is said, 'The curtain falls quickly,' and frivolous critics have not failed to perpetrate the cheap witticism, 'Very necessary, too.' The amorous whinings, whimperings and ravings of *Tristan und Isolde*, the entire second act of *Parsifal*, in the scene between the hero and the flower-girls, and then between him and Kundry in Klingsor's magic garden, are worthy to rank with the above passages. It certainly redounds to the high honour of German public morality, that Wagner's operas could have been publicly performed without arousing the greatest scandal. How unperverted must wives and maidens be when they are in a state of mind to witness these pieces without blushing crimson, and sinking into the earth for shame! How innocent must even husbands and fathers be who allow their womankind to go to these representations of 'lupanar' incidents! Evidently the German audiences entertain no misgivings concerning the actions and attitudes of Wagnerian personages; they seem to have no suspicion of the emotions by which they are excited, and what intentions their words, gestures and acts denote; and this explains the peaceful artlessness with which these audiences follow theatrical scenes during which, among a less childlike public, no one would dare lift his eyes to his neighbour or endure his glance.

With Wagner amorous excitement assumes the form of mad delirium. The lovers in his pieces behave like tom-cats gone mad, rolling in contortions and convulsions over a root of valerian. They reflect a state of mind in the poet which is well known to the professional expert. It is a form of Sadism. It is the love of those degenerates who, in sexual transport, become like wild

* Edward Hanslick, *Musikalische Stationen.* Berlin, 1880, pp. 220, 243.
† Wagner, *Gesammelte Schriften und Dichtungen*, Band VI., p. 3 *ff.*

beasts.* Wagner suffered from 'erotic madness,' which leads coarse natures to murder for lust, and inspires 'higher degenerates' with works like *Die Walküre*, *Siegfried*, and *Tristan und Isolde*.

Wagner's graphomania is shown not only by the substance, but also by the outward form of his writings. The reader will have been able to remark in the quotations given what a misuse Wagner makes of italics. He often has whole half-pages printed in spaced letters. Lombroso expressly establishes this phenomenon among graphomaniacs.† It is sufficiently explained by the peculiarity of mystical thought, so often set forth in this work. No linguistic form which the mystically degenerate subject can give to his thought-phantoms satisfies him; he is always conscious that the phrases he is writing do not express the mazy processes of his brain; and as he is forced to abandon the attempt to embody these in words, he seeks, by means of notes of exclamation, dashes, dots, and blanks, to impart to his writings more of mystery than the words themselves can express.

The irresistible propensity to play on words—another peculiarity of graphomaniacs and imbeciles—is developed to a high degree in Wagner. I will here give only a few examples from the *Art-work of the Future*—p. 56: 'Thus it [the science of music] acquires through sound, which has become speech . . . its most *exalted satisfaction*, and at the same time its most *satisfying exaltation*.' P. 91: 'Like a second Prometheus, who from *Thon* (clay) formed men, Beethoven had striven to form them from *Ton* (music). Not from clay or music (*Thon* or *Ton*), but from both of these substances, should man, the image of Zeus, the dispenser of life, be created.' Special attention may, however, be called to the following astounding passage (p. 103): 'If fashion or custom permitted us again to adopt, in speech and writing, the genuine and true use of

* In a book on degeneration it is not possible wholly to avoid the subject of eroticism, which includes precisely the most characteristic and conspicuous phenomena of degeneration. I dwell, however, on principle as little as possible on this subject, and will, therefore, in reference to the characterization of Wagner's erotic madness, quote only one clinical work: Dr. Paul Aubry, 'Observation d'Uxoricide et de Libéricide suivis du Suicide du Meurtrier,' *Archives de l'Anthropologie criminelle*, vol. vii., p. 326: 'This derangement [erotic madness] is characterized by an inconceivable fury of concupiscence at the moment of approach.' And in a remark on the report of a murder perpetrated on his wife and children by an erotic maniac—a professor of mathematics in a public school—whom Aubrey had under his observation, he says, 'Sa femme qui parlait facilement et à tous des choses que l'on tient ordinairement le plus secrètes, disait que son mari était comme un furieux pendant l'acte sexuel.' See also Ball, *La Folie érotique*. Paris, 1891, p. 127.

† Lombroso, *Genie und Irrsinn*, p. 229: 'When the expression of their ideas eludes their grasp . . . they resort . . . to the continual italicizing of words and sentences,' etc.

Tichten for *Dichten* (to compose poetry), we should thus obtain, in the united names of the three primitive human arts, *Tanz-*, *Ton-*, and *Tichtkunst* (dancing, music, and poetry), a beautifully significant, sensuous image of the essence of this trinity of sisters, viz., a perfect alliteration. . . . This alliteration would, moreover, be peculiarly characteristic, on account of the position held in it by *Tichtkunst* (poetry), for only as its last member would *Tichtkunst* transform the alliteration into rhyme,' etc.

We now come to the mysticism of Wagner, which permeates all his works, and has become one of the chief causes of his influence over his contemporaries—at least, outside Germany. Although he is irreligious through and through, and frequently attacks positive religions, their doctrines and their priests, there have, nevertheless, remained active in him from childhood (passed in an atmosphere of Christian Protestant views and religious practices) ideas and sentiments which he subsequently transformed so strangely in his degenerate mind. This phenomenon, viz., the persistence, in the midst of later doubts and denials, of early-acquired Christian views, operating as an ever-active leaven, singularly altering the whole mind, and at the same time themselves suffering manifold decomposition and deformation—may be frequently observed in confused brains. We shall meet it, for example, in Ibsen. At the foundation of all Wagner's poems and theoretical writings there is to be found a more or less potent sediment of the Catechism, distorted as to its doctrines ; and in his most luxuriant pictures, between the thick, crude colours, we get glimpses of strange and hardly recognisable touches, betraying the fact that the scenes are brutally daubed on the pale background of Gospel reminiscences.

One idea, or, more accurately, one word, has remained especially deeply fixed in his mind, and pursued him throughout his whole life as a real obsession, viz., the word 'redemption.' True, it has not with him the value it possesses in the language of theology. To the theologian 'redemption,' this central idea of the whole Christian doctrine, signifies the sublime act of superhuman love, which freely takes upon itself the greatest suffering, and gladly bears it, that it may free from the power of evil those whose strength is insufficient for such a task. So understood, redemption presupposes three things. Firstly, we must assume a dualism in nature, most distinctly developed in the Zend religion ; the existence of a first principle of good and one of evil, between which mankind is placed, and becomes the cause of their strife. Secondly, the one who is to be redeemed must be free from all conscious and wilful fault ; he must be the victim of superior forces which he is himself incapable of warding off. Thirdly, in order that the redeemer's act may be a true act of salvation and acquire power to deliver, he must, in the fulfilment of a clearly recognised and purposed mission, offer himself in sacrifice. It is true that a tendency has often asserted itself to think of redemption as an act of grace, in which not only the victims, but also sinners, may participate; but the Church has always recognised the immorality of such a conception, and has expressly taught that, in order to receive redemption, the guilty must himself strive for it, through repentance and penance, and not passively await it as a completely unmerited gift.

This theological redemption is not redemption in Wagner's sense. With him it has never any clearly recognisable import, and serves only to denote something beautiful and grand, which he does not more closely specify. At the outset the word has evidently made a deep impression on his imagination, and he subsequently uses it like a minor chord, let us say *a*, *c*, *e*, which is likewise without definite significance, but, nevertheless, awakens emotion and peoples consciousness with floating presentations. With Wagner someone is constantly being 'redeemed.' If (in the *Art-work of the Future*) the art of painting ceases to paint pictures, and produces thenceforth only decorations for the theatre, this is its 'redemption.' In the same way the music accompanying a poem is a 'redeemed' music. Man is 'redeemed' when he loves a woman, and the people is 'redeemed' when it plays at the drama. His compositions also turn upon 'redemption. Nietsche* has already remarked this, and makes merry over it, if with repulsively superficial witticisms. 'Wagner,' he says, 'has meditated on nothing so much as on redemption' (a wholly false assertion, since Wagner's redemption-twaddle is certainly no result of meditation, but only a mystical echo of childish emotions); 'his opera is the opera of redemption. With him someone is always wanting to be redeemed—now a male, now a female. . . . Who, if not Wagner, teaches us that innocence has a predilection for redeeming interesting sinners (the case of *Tannhäuser*)? Or that even the Wandering Jew will be redeemed and become sedentary when he marries (the case of *The Flying Dutchman*)? Or that depraved old wantons prefer to be redeemed by chaste youths (the case of *Kundry*)? Or that beauteous maidens like best to be redeemed by a knight who is a Wagnerian (the case in *Meistersinger*)? Or that even married women like to be redeemed by a knight (the case of *Isolde*)? Or that the ancient god, after having morally compromised himself in every respect, is redeemed by a free-thinker and an immoral character (the case in the *Niebelungen*)? How particularly admirable is this last profundity! Do you understand it? As for me, defend me from understanding it.'

The work of Wagner which may be truly termed 'the opera

* Friedrich Nietsche, *Der Fall Wagner*. Leipzig, 1889.

of redemption' is *Parsifal.* Here we may catch Wagner's mind in its most nonsensical vagaries. In *Parsifal* two persons are redeemed: King Amfortas and Kundry. The King has allowed himself to become infatuated with the charms of Kundry, and has sinned in her arms. As a punishment, the magic spear which had been entrusted to him has been taken from him, and he wounded by this sacred weapon. The wound gapes and bleeds unceasingly, and causes him dreadful suffering. Nothing can heal it but the spear itself which gave it. But 'the pure fool who through compassion knows' can alone wrest the spear from the wicked magician, Klingsor. Kundry, when a young maiden, had seen the Saviour on the path of his Passion, and had laughed at him. As a penalty for her act she is doomed to live for ever, longing in vain for death, and seducing to sin all men who approach her. Only if a man is able to resist her allurements can she be redeemed from her curse. (One man has, in fact, resisted her, the magician Klingsor. Yet this victorious resistance has not redeemed her as it ought. Why? Wagner does not reveal this by a single syllable.) It is Parsifal who brings redemption to the two accursed ones. The 'pure fool' has no inkling that he is predestined to redeem Amfortas and Kundry, and he neither undergoes any suffering nor exposes himself to any serious danger in accomplishing the act of salvation. It is true that, in forcing his way into the enchanted garden, he is obliged to have a small bout with its knights, but this skirmish is far more a pleasure than an effort for him, for he is far stronger than his adversaries, and, after some playful passes, puts them to flight, bleeding and beaten. He certainly resists the beauty of Kundry, and this is meritorious, yet it hardly constitutes an act of deadly self-sacrifice. He obtains the magic spear without any effort. Klingsor hurls it at him to slay him, but the weapon 'remains floating above his head,' and Parsifal has only to stretch out his hand to take it at his convenience, and then to fulfil his mission.

Every individual feature of this mystical piece is in direct contrast to the Christian idea of redemption, which has nevertheless inspired it. Amfortas is in need of redemption through his own weakness and guilt, not on account of an invincible fate, and he is redeemed without any assistance on his part beyond whining and moaning. The salvation he is awaiting and ultimately obtains has its source completely outside his will and consciousness. He has no part in its attainment. Another effects it for him, and bestows it on him as a gift. The redemption is a purely external affair, a lucky windfall, and not the reward of an inward moral struggle. Still more monstrous are the conditions of Kundry's redemption. Not only is she not allowed to labour for her own salvation, but she is compelled to employ all her strength to prevent it; for her redemption depends on her being despised by a man, and the task to which she has been condemned is to turn to account all the seductive power of beauty and passionate solicitation to win over the man. She must by all possible means thwart the man by whom her redemption is to come, from becoming her redeemer. If the man yields to her charms, then the redemption is frustrated, not through her fault, though by her action; if the man resists the temptation, she obtains redemption without deserving it, because in spite of her opposing effort. It is impossible to concoct a situation more absurd and at the same time more immoral. Parsifal the redeemer is, in fine, from beginning to end, a mystic re-incarnation of 'Hans in Luck' in the German fairy-tale. He succeeds in everything without personal effort. He sets out to kill a swan, and finds the Grail and the royal crown. His redeemership is no self-sacrifice, but a benefice. The favour of Heaven has called him to an enviable, honourable office—on what powerful recommendation Wagner does not disclose. But a closer examination reveals worse things. Parsifal, the 'pure fool,' is simply a precipitate of confused reminiscences of Christology. Powerfully struck by the poetical elements of the Saviour's life and sufferings, Wagner has been impelled to externalize his impressions and emotions, and has created Parsifal, whom he causes to experience some of the most affecting scenes of the Gospel, and who in his hands becomes (partly, perhaps, without his being aware of it) at once a foolish and frivolous caricature of Jesus Christ. In the mystical work, the temptation of the Saviour in the desert is transformed into the temptation of Parsifal by Kundry. The scene in the Pharisee's house, where the Magdalene anoints the Saviour's feet, is reproduced exactly: Kundry bathes and anoints Parsifal's feet, and dries them with her unbound hair; and the 'pure fool' plagiarizes the words of Christ, 'Thy sins be forgiven thee,' in this exclamation: 'Thus I accomplish my first office; be baptized and believe on the Redeemer.' That the ordinary theatre-goer is not shocked by this misused application of the Christ legend—nay, that in the distorted fragments of the Gospel he is able to revive some of the emotions it perhaps at one time excited in him—is conceivable. But it is incomprehensible that earnest believers, and especially zealous fanatics, have never perceived what a profanation of their most sacred ideas is perpetrated by Wagner, when he endows his Parsifal with traits of the Christ Himself.

We may mention only one of the other absurd details of the *Parsifal*. The aged Titurel has succumbed to the earthly penalty of death, but through the Saviour's mercy continues to live in the grave. The sight of the Grail continually renews for a time his waning vital strength. Titurel seems to attach a great value to this comfortless life-in-death existence. 'By the mercy of the Saviour I live in the tomb,' he joyously cries from his coffin, demanding with impetuous vehemence that the Grail be shown him, in order that his life may thereby be prolonged. 'Am I to-day to see once more the Grail and live?' he asks in anguish, and because he receives no immediate answer thus laments, 'Must I die unaccompanied by the Deliverer?' His son, Amfortas, hesitates, whereupon the old man gives his orders: 'Unveil the Grail! The benediction!' And when his wishes are complied with, he exults: 'Oh, sacred bliss! How bright the Lord doth greet us to-day!' Subsequently Amfortas has for some time neglected the unveiling of the Grail, and hence Titurel has had to die. Amfortas is in despair. 'My father! highly blessed of heroes! . . . I, who alone was fain to die, to thee have I given death!' From all this it undoubtedly results that all the persons concerned see in life, even if it be the shadowy and empty life of a being already laid in his coffin, an exceedingly precious possession, and in death a bitter misfortune. And this takes place in the same piece in which Kundry endures eternal life as a frightful curse, and passionately longs for death as a most delicious salvation! Is a more ridiculous contradiction conceivable? Moreover, the Titurel episode is a denial of all the premises of *Parsifal*, constructed as it is on the foundation of the religious idea of personal persistence after death. How can death frighten the man who is convinced that the bliss of paradise awaits him? We are here in the presence of the same non-comprehension of his own assumptions which has already struck us in Dante Gabriel Rossetti and Tolstoi. But this is precisely the peculiarity of morbidly mystic thought. It unites mutually exclusive ideas; it shuns the law of consistency, and imperturbably combines details which are dumfounded at finding themselves in company. We do not observe this phenomenon in one who is a mystic through ignorance, mental indolence, or imitation. He may take an absurd idea as a point of departure for a train of thought; but the latter unrolls itself rationally and consistently, and suffers no gross contradiction among its particular members.

As Christology inspired Wagner with the figures of *Parsifal*, so did the Eucharist inspire him with the most effective scene of the piece—the love-feast of the Grail. It is the *mise-en-scène* of the Catholic Mass, with the heretical addition of one Protestant feature—the partaking by the communicants of the elements in both kinds. The unveiling of the Grail corresponds to the elevation of the Host. The acolytes take the form of the choir of boys and youths. In the antiphonal songs and the actions of Amfortas, we find approximations to all four parts of the Mass. The knights of the Grail intone a sort of stunted introit, the long plaint of Amfortas: 'No! Let it not be unveiled! Oh, may no one, no one, fathom the depths of this torment!' etc., may be regarded as a *Confiteor*. The boys sing the offertory ('Take ye my blood for the sake of our love!' etc.). Amfortas proceeds to the consecration; all partake in the Communion, and there is even a parodied reminiscence of the 'Ite, missa est' in Gurnemanz's exclamation, 'Go out hence upon thy way!' Since Constantine the Great, since the elevation of Christianity to the rank of a State religion, no poet has dared do what Wagner has done; he has drawn theatrical effects from the incomparable rich emotional content of the function of the Mass. He felt profoundly the symbolism of the Lord's Supper; it provoked in him a powerful mystical excitement, and the need arose in him of endowing the symbolical event with a dramatic form, and of sensuously experiencing in all its details and in its entirety that which in the sacrifice of the Mass is only indicated, condensed, and spiritualized. He wished to see and feel in his own person how the elect enjoy, amid violent emotions, the body of Christ and His redeeming blood; and how super-terrestrial phenomena, the purple gleaming of the Grail and the downward hovering dove (in the final scene), etc., make palpable the real presence of Christ and the divine nature of the Eucharist. Just as Wagner has borrowed from the Church his inspiration for the scenes in the Grail, and then for his own purposes has popularized the liturgy in the style of the *Biblia Pauperum*, so does the audience find again the cathedral and high mass on his stage, and import into the piece all the emotions left in their soul by Church ceremonies. The real priest in his sacerdotal robes, the remembrance of his gestures, of the hand-bell and the genuflexions of the servers, the blue reek and perfume of the incense, the pealing of the organ and the play of chequered sunlight through the stained windows of the church—these are, in the heart of the public, Wagner's collaborators; and it is not his art which lulls them into mystic ecstasy, but the fundamental mood inculcated in the vast majority of white races by two centuries of Christian sentiment.

Mysticism is, as we know, always accompanied by eroticism, especially in the degenerate, whose emotionalism has its chief source in morbidly excited states of the sexual centres. Wagner's imagination is perpetually occupied with woman. But he never sees her relation to man in the form of healthy and natural love, which is a benefit and satisfaction for both lovers. As with all morbid erotics (we have already remarked this in Verlaine and Tolstoi), woman presents herself to him as a terrible force of nature, of which man is the trembling, helpless victim. The woman that he knows is the gruesome Astarté of the Semites, the frightful man-eating Kali Bhagawati of the Hindoos, an apocalyptic vision of smiling blood-thirstiness, of eternal perdition and infernal torment, in demoniacally beautiful embodiment. No poetical problem has so profoundly moved him as the relation between man and this his ensnaring destroyer. He has approached this problem from all sides, and has given it different solutions corresponding to his instincts and views of morality. The man frequently succumbs to the temptress, but Wagner revolts against this weakness, of which he is himself only too conscious, and in his chief works makes the man offer a desperate, but finally victorious, resistance. Not, however, by his own strength does man tear himself from the paralyzing charm of woman. He must receive supernatural aid. This proceeds most frequently from a pure and unselfish virgin, who forms the antithesis to the sphinx with soft woman's body and lion's paws. In conformity with the psychological law of contrast, Wagner invents as a counterpart to the terrible woman of his inmost perception an angelic woman, who is all love, all devotion, all celestial mildness; a woman who asks for nothing and gives all; a woman soothing, caressing and healing; in a word, a woman for whom an unhappy creature pants as he writhes, consumed by flames, in the white-hot flames of Belit. Wagner's Elizabeth, Elsa, Senta, and Gertrude are extremely instructive manifestations of erotic mysticism, in which the half-unconscious idea is struggling for form, viz., that the safety of the sexually crazy degenerate lies in purity, continence, or in the possession of a wife having no sort of individuality, no desire and no rights, and hence incapable of ever proving dangerous to the man.

In one of his first compositions, as in his last, in *Tannhäuser* as in *Parsifal*, he treats of the combat between man and his corruptress, the fly versus the spider, and in this way testifies that for thirty-three years, from youth to old age, the subject has never been absent from his mind. In *Tannhäuser* it is the beautiful devil Venus herself who ensnares the hero, and with whom he has to wage a desperate conflict for the salvation of his soul. The pious and chaste Elizabeth, this dream-being, woven of moonlight, prayer, and song, becomes his 'redeemer.' In *Parsifal* the beautiful devil is named Kundry, and the hero escapes the danger with which she threatens his soul only because he is 'the pure fool,' and is in a state of grace.

In the *Walküre* Wagner's imagination surrenders itself to unbridled passion. He here represents the ardent man wildly and madly abandoning himself to his appetite, without regard to the dictates of society, and without attempting to resist the furious impetuosity of his instinct. Siegmund sees Sieglinde, and thenceforth has but one idea—to possess her. That she is another's wife—nay, that he recognises her as his own sister—does not check him for a moment. Those considerations are as feathers before the storm. He pays for his night of pleasure by his death the following morning. For with Wagner love is always a fatality, and ever round its pillow blaze the flames of hell. And as he has not made manifest in Sieglinde the images of carnage and annihilation evoked in him by his idea of woman, he personifies these separately in the *Walküre.* Their appearance in the drama is for him a psychological need. The traits inseparable in his mind from his conception of woman, and ordinarily united by him in a single figure, are here separated and raised to the dignity of independent types. Venus, Kundry, are seducer and destroyer in one person. In the *Walküre* Sieglinde is only the seducer, but the destroyer grows into a horde of gruesome Amazons, who drink the blood of battling men, revel in the spectacle of murderous blows, and rush with wild, exulting cries across the corpse-strewn waste.

Siegfried, Götterdämmerung, Tristan und Isolde are exact repetitions of the essential content of the *Walküre.* It is always the dramatic embodiment of the same obsession of the terrors of love. Siegfried sees Brunhilde in the midst of her fire-circle, and both instantly fall into each other's arms in a rage of love; but Siegfried must expiate his happiness with his life, and falls under the steel of Hagen. The mere death of Siegfried does not suffice for Wagner's imagination as the inevitable consequence of love; destiny must show itself more terribly. The castle of Asgard itself breaks out in flames, and the slave of love in dying drags to his own perdition all the gods of heaven along with him. *Tristan und Isolde* is the echo of this tragedy of passion. Here also is the complete annihilation of the sentiment of duty and self-conquest, by the springing up of love both in Tristan and Isolde; and here also is death as the natural end towards which love is hurried. To express his fundamental mystic thought, that love is an awful fatality wherewith the unapproachable powers of destiny visit the poor mortal incapable of resistance, he has resort to a childishly clumsy device; he introduces into his compositions love-philtres of potent spell, now to explain the birth of the passion itself, and to indicate its superhuman nature, as in *Tristan und Isolde;* now to withdraw all the moral life of the hero from the control of his will, and show him as the plaything of super-terrestrial forces, as in the *Götterdämmerung.*

Thus Wagner's poems give us a deep insight into the world of ideas of an erotically emotional degenerate nature. They reveal the alternating mental conditions of a most reckless sensuality, of a revolt of moral sentiment against the tyranny of appetite, of the ruin of the higher man and his despairing repentance. As has already been said, Wagner is an admirer of Schopenhauer and his philosophy. Like his master, he persuaded himself that life is a misfortune, and non-existence salvation and happiness. Love, as the constantly active incitement to the maintenance of the species and continuance of life, with all its accompanying sufferings, was bound to seem to him the source of all evil; and, on the other hand, the highest wisdom and morality, to consist in the victorious resistance of this incitement, in chastity, sterility, the negation of the will to perpetuate the species. And while his judgment bound him to these views, his instincts attracted him irresistibly to woman, and forced him during his whole life to do all that flouted his convictions and condemned his doctrine. This discord between his philosophy and his organic inclinations is the inner tragedy of his mental life, and his poems form a unique whole, recounting the process of the internal conflict. He sees a woman, at once loses himself, and is absorbed in her charms (Siegmund and Sieglinde, Siegfried and Brunhilde, Tristan and Isolde). This is a great sin, demanding expiation; death alone is an adequate punishment (final scenes in the *Walküre*, *Götterdämmerung*, *Tristan und Isolde*). But the sinner has a timid and feeble excuse: 'I could not resist. I was the victim of superhuman powers. My seducer was of the race of the gods' (Sieglinde, Brunhilde). 'Magic philtres deprived me of my reason' (Tristan, Siegfried in his relations with Gutrune). How glorious to be strong enough to vanquish the devouring monster of appetite within! How radiant and exalted the figure of a man able to plant his foot on the neck of the demon woman! (Tannhäuser and Parsifal). And, on the other hand, how beautiful and adorable the woman who should not set ablaze the hell-fire of passion in man, but aid him in quenching it; who should not exact of him a revolt against reason, duty, and honour, but be an example to him of renunciation and self-discipline; who, instead of enslaving him, should, as his loving handmaid, divest herself of her own nature, to blend herself with his; in a word, a woman who would leave him safe in his defencelessness, because she herself would be unarmed! (Elizabeth, Elsa, Senta, Gutrune). The creation of these forms of woman is a sort of *De Profundis* of the timid voluptuary, who feels the sting of the flesh, and implores aid to protect him from himself.

Like all the degenerates, Wagner is wholly sterile as a poet, although he has written a long series of dramatic works. The creative force capable of reproducing the spectacle of universal normal life is denied him. He has recourse to his own mystico-erotic emotions for the emotional content of his pieces, and the external incidents forming their skeleton are purely the fruits of reading, the reminiscences of books which have made an impression on him. This is the great difference between the healthy and the degenerate poet who receives his sentiments at second-hand. The former is able to 'plunge into full human life,' as Goethe says; to seize it, and either make it enter all breathing and palpitating into a poem which itself thus becomes a part of natural life, or else remould it with idealizing art, suppressing its accidental, accessory features, so as to make prominent the essential; and in this way convincingly to reveal law behind enigmatically bewildering phenomena. The degenerate subject, on the contrary, can do nothing with life; he is blind and deaf to it. He is a stranger in the midst of healthy men. He lacks the organs necessary for the comprehension of life—nay, even for its perception. To work from a model does not lie within his powers. He can only copy existing sketches, and then colour them subjectively with his own emotions. He can see life only when it lies before him on paper in black and white. While the healthy poet resembles the chlorophyllic plant, which dives into the soil, and, by the honest labour of its own roots, procures for itself the nutritive materials out of which it constructs its blossoms and fruit, the degenerate poet has the nature of a parasitic plant, which can only live on a host, and receives its nutriment exclusively from the juices already elaborated by the latter. There are modest parasites and proud parasites. Their range extends from the insignificant lichen to the wondrous rafflesia, the flower of which, a yard in breadth, illumines the sombre forests of Sumatra with the wild magnificence of its blood-red colour. Wagner's poems have in them something of the carrion stench and uncanny beauty of this plant of rapine and corruption. With the single exception of the *Meistersinger*, they are grafted on the Icelandic sagas, the epics of Gottfried of Strassburg, Wolfram of Eschenbach, and the singer of the Wartburg war in the Manessian manuscript, as on so many trunks of half-dead trees, and they draw their strength from these. *Tannhäuser*, the *Niebelungen Tetralogy*, *Tristan und Isolde*, *Parsifal*, and *Lohengrin*, are constructed entirely from materials supplied him by ancient literature. *Rienzi* he derives from written history, and the *Fliegender Holländer* from the tradition already utilized a hundred times. Among popular legends, that of the Wandering Jew has made the deepest impression on his mind, on account of its mysticism. He has elaborated it once in the *Fliegender Holländer*; a second time transposed it feature for feature into a feminine form in the person of Kundry, not without weaving into this inversion some reminiscences of the legend of Herodias. All this is patchwork and dilettantism. Wagner deceives himself (probably unconsciously) as to his incapacity for creating human beings, representing, not men, but gods and demigods, demons and spectres, whose deeds are not to be explained by human motives, but by mysterious destinies, curses and prophecies, fatal and magic forces. That which passes before our eyes in Wagner's pieces is not life, but spectres, witches' sabbaths, or dreams. He is a dealer in old clothes, who has bought at second-hand the cast-off garments of fairy-tales, and makes of them (often not without clever tailoring) new costumes, in which we may recognise, strangely jumbled and joined, rags of ancient gala stuffs and fragments of damascened suits of armour. But these masquerading suits do not serve for clothes to a single being of flesh and blood. Their apparent movements are produced exclusively by the hand of Wagner, who has slipped into the empty doublets and sleeves, and behind the flowing trains and dangling robes, and kicks about in them with epileptic convulsions, that he may awaken in the spectator the impression of a ghostly animation in this obsolete wardrobe.

Healthy geniuses have also, no doubt, allied themselves with popular tradition or history, like Goethe in *Faust* and *Tasso*. But what a difference between the respective treatment by a healthy poet and a degenerate one of that which they find, of that which is given! To the former it is a vessel which he fills with genuine, fresh life, so that the new contents become the essential part; to the latter, on the contrary, the outside is and remains the chief thing, and his own activity consists at best in choking the receptacle with the chaff of nonsensical phrases. The great poets, too, lay claim to the cuckoo's privilege of laying their egg in a strange nest. But the bird which issues from the egg is so much larger, handsomer and stronger than the original denizens, that the latter are mercilessly driven from their home and the former remains the sole possessor. When the great poet puts his new wine into old bottles, he doubtless shows a little indolence, a little poverty of invention and a not very high-minded reckoning on the reader's pre-existing emotions. But he cannot be held too rigorously accountable for this small amount of stinginess, because, after all, he gives us so much that is his own. Imagine *Faust* deprived of all the portions drawn from old popular books; there would still remain nearly everything; there would remain all of the man who thirsts for knowledge and seeks for it; all the struggle between his baser instincts craving for satisfaction, and the higher morality rejoicing in renunciation; in brief, just that which makes the work one of the loftiest poems of humanity. If, on the other hand, Wagner's old ancestral marionettes are stripped of their armour and brocades, there remains nothing, or, at best, only air and a musty smell. Assimilating minds have hundreds of times felt tempted to modernize *Faust*. The undertaking is so sure of success that it is superfluous; Faust in dress-coat would be no other than the unaltered embodiment of Goethe's own

Faust. But imagine Lohengrin, Siegmund, Tristan, Parsifal, as contemporaries! They would not even serve for burlesque, in spite of the Tannhäuser lampoon by the old Viennese poet Nestroy.

Wagner swaggered about the art-work of the future, and his partisans hailed him as the artist of the future. He the artist of the future! He is a bleating echo of the far-away past. His path leads back to deserts long since abandoned by all life. Wagner is the last mushroom on the dunghill of romanticism. This 'modern' is the degraded heir of a Tieck, of a La Motte-Fouqué—nay more, sad to say, of a Johann Friedrich Kind. The home of his intellect is the Dresden evening paper. He derives his subsistence from the legacy of mediæval poems, and dies of starvation when the remittance from the thirteenth century fails to arrive.

The subject alone of the Wagnerian poems can raise a claim to serious consideration. As for their form, it is beneath criticism. The absurdity of his style, his shallowness, the awkwardness of his versification, his complete inability to clothe his feelings and thoughts in anything like adequate language—these have been so often pointed out and exposed in detail that I may spare myself the trouble of dwelling on these points. But one faculty among the essential constituents of dramatic endowment cannot be denied him—that of picturesque imagination. It is developed in him to the point of genius. Wagner as a dramatist is really a historical painter of the highest rank. Nietzsche (in his skit, *Der Fall Wagner**) perhaps means the same when, without stopping at this important assertion, he calls Wagner, not only 'magnetizer' and 'collector of gew-gaws,' but also a 'fresco-painter.' This he is in a degree never yet attained by any other dramatic author in the whole world of literature. Every action embodies itself for him in a series of most imposing pictures, which, when they are composed as Wagner has seen them with his inner eye, must overwhelm and enrapture the beholder. The reception of the guests in the hall of the Wartburg; the arrival and departure of Lohengrin in the boat drawn by the swan; the gambols of the Rhine maidens in the river; the defiling of the gods over the rainbow-bridge towards the castle of Asgard; the bursting of the moonlight into Hunding's hut; the ride of the Walküre over the battlefield; Brunhilde in the circle of fire; the final scene in *Götterdämmerung*, where Brunhilde flings herself on to her horse and leaps into the midst of the funeral-pyre, while Hagen throws himself into the surging Rhine, and the heavens are aflame with the glow from the burning palace of the gods; the love-feast of the knights in the castle of the Grail; the obsequies of Titurel and the healing of Amfortas—these are pictures to

* *Der Fall Wagner. Ein Musikanten-Problem.* 2[te] Auflage. Leipzig, 1889.

which nothing hitherto in art approaches. It is on account of this gift for inventing incomparably imposing spectacles that Nietzsche has termed Wagner a 'comedian.' The word signifies nothing, and, in so far as it may contain a tinge of contempt, is unjust. Wagner is no comedian, but a born painter. If he had been a healthy genius, endowed with intellectual equilibrium, that is what he would undoubtedly have become. His inner vision would have forced the brush into his hand, and constrained him to realize it on canvas, by means of colour. Leonardo da Vinci had the same gift. It made him the greatest painter the world had yet known, and at the same time the unsurpassed deviser and organizer of fêtes, pageants, triumphs, and allegorical plays, which, perhaps more than his genius as a painter, won for him the admiration of his princely patrons Ludovico Moro, Isabella of Aragon, Cæsar Borgia, Charles VIII., Louis XII., Francis I. But Wagner, as is the case with all the degenerate, did not see clearly into his own nature. He did not understand his natural impulses. Perhaps also, with the feeling of his own deep organic feebleness, he dreaded the heavy labour of drawing and painting, and, conformably with the law of least effort, his instinct sought vent in the theatre, where his inner visions were embodied by others—the decorative painters, machinists, and actors—without requiring him to exert himself. His pictures have unquestionably a large share in the effect produced by his pieces. They are admired without an inquiry into how far their introduction is warranted by the rational course of the drama. However nonsensical as part of an action, they justify their appearance, from an artistic standpoint, by their intrinsic beauty, which makes of them independent æsthetical phenomena. Through their enormous aggrandizement by the media of the stage, their pictorial allurements are perceptible even to the eye of the most crass Philistine, whose sense were otherwise dead to them.

Of Wagner the musician, more important to all appearance than Wagner the author, dramatic poet and fresco-painter, I treat lastly, because this task will give us a clear proof of his degeneration, although this is very much more evident in his writings than in his music, where certain stigmata of degeneration are not so prominent, and where others appear as its unmistakable advantages. The incoherence in words, noticeable at once to an attentive person, does not exhibit itself in music unless it is excessively strongly marked ; the absurdity, the contradictions, the twaddle, are hardly apparent in the language of tones, because it is not the function of music to express an exact meaning, and emotionalism is not in it an indication of disease, since emotion is music's proper essence.

We know, moreover, that high musical talent is compatible

with a very advanced state of degeneration—nay, even with pronounced delusion, illusion, and idiocy. Sollier* says: 'We have to deal with certain aptitudes very often manifested with great intensity by idiots and imbeciles. . . . That for music especially is often met with. . . . Although this may seem disagreeable to musicians, it nevertheless proves that music is the least intellectual of all the arts.' Lombroso† remarks: 'It has been observed that the aptitude for music has been displayed almost involuntarily and unexpectedly among many sufferers from hypochondria and mania, and even among the really insane.' He cites, with other cases, a mathematician attacked with melancholia, who improvised on the piano; a woman seized with megalomania, who 'sang very beautiful airs, at the same time improvising two different themes on the piano'; a patient 'who composed very beautiful new and melodious tunes,' etc.; and he adds in explanation that those who are afflicted with megalomania and general paralysis surpass other mental invalids in musical talent, 'and from the very same cause as that of their unusual aptitude for painting, viz., their violent mental excitation.'

Wagner the musician encounters his most powerful attacks from musicians themselves. He himself bears witness to it:‡ 'Both my friends (Ferd. Hiller and Schumann) believed that they very soon discovered me to be a musician of no remarkable endowment. My success also has seemed to them to be due to the libretti written by myself.' In other language, the same old story—musicians regarded him as a poet, and poets as a musician. It is of course convenient to explain *a posteriori* the decisive judgments of men who were at once prominent professionals and sincere friends of Wagner by saying (after he had attained success) that his tendency was too novel to be immediately appreciated, or even understood, by them. This solution, however, hardly applies to Schumann, as he was a friend to all innovations, and audacities, even differing from his own, rather attracted than shocked him. Rubinstein § still makes important reservations in regard to Wagner's music; and among serious contemporary musical critics who have witnessed the birth, development and triumph of the Wagner cult, Hanslick remained a long time recalcitrant, until at last, though not very valiantly, he struck his colours in face of the overpowering fanaticism of hysterical Wagnerphiles. What Nietzsche (in his *Der Fall Wagner*) says against Wagner as a musician is unimportant, since the brochure of abjuration is quite as insanely delirious as

* Sollier, *op. cit.*, p. 101.

† Lombroso, *Genie und Irrsinn*, p. 214 *et seq.*

‡ Wagner, *Ges. Schriften*, Band X., p. 222.

§ Rubinstein, *Musiciens modernes.* Traduit du russe par M. Delines. Paris, 1892.

the brochure of deification (*Wagner in Bayreuth*) written twelve years before.

In spite of the unfavourable judgments of many of his professional brethren, Wagner is incontestably an eminently gifted musician. This coolly-expressed recognition will certainly seem grotesque to Wagnerian fanatics, who place him above Beethoven. But a serious inquirer into truth need not trouble himself about the impressions provoked by Wagner among these persons. In the first period of his productivity Wagner much oftener achieved compositions of beauty than subsequently, and among these many may be termed pearls of musical literature, and will for a long time enjoy even the esteem of serious and rational people. But Wagner the musician had to confront a life-long enemy, who forcibly prevented the full unfolding of his gifts, and this enemy was Wagner the musical theorist.

In his graphomaniacal muddle he concocted certain theories, which represent so many fits of æsthetic delirium. The most important of these are the dogmas of the *leit-motif* and of the unending melody. Everyone now undoubtedly knows what Wagner understood by the former. The expression has passed into all civilized languages. The *leit-motif*, in which the threshed-out discarded 'programme music' was bound logically to culminate, is a sequence of tones supposed to express a definite conception, and appears in the orchestration whenever the composer intends to recall to the auditor the corresponding conception. By the *leit-motif* Wagner transforms music into dry speech. The orchestration, leaping from *leit-motif* to *leit-motif*, no longer embodies general emotions, but claims to appeal to memory and to reason, and communicate sharply defined presentations. Wagner combines a few notes into a musical figure, as a rule not even distinct or original, and makes this arrangement with the auditor :—'This figure signifies a combat, that a dragon, a third a sword,' etc. If the auditor does not agree to the stipulation, the *leit-motifs* lose all significance, for they possess in themselves nothing which compels us to grasp the meaning arbitrarily lent them; and they cannot have anything of this kind in them, because the imitative powers of music are by its nature limited to purely acoustical phenomena, or at most to those optical phenomena ordinarily accompanied by acoustical phenomena. By imitating thunder, music can express the notion of a thunderstorm ; by the imitation of the tones of a bugle, it can call up that of an army in such a way that the listener can hardly have a doubt as to the significance of the corresponding sequences of tones. On the other hand, it is absolutely denied to music, with the means at its disposal, to produce an unequivocal embodiment of the visible and tangible world, let alone that of abstract thought. Hence the *leit-motifs* are at best cold symbols, resembling written characters, which in themselves say nothing, and convey to the initiated and the learned alone the given import of a presentation.

Here again is found the phenomenon already repeatedly indicated by us as a mark of the mode of thought among the degenerate—the unconscious moon-struck somnambulous way in which they transgress the most firmly-established limits of the particular artistic domain, annul the differentiation of the arts arrived at by long historical evolution, and lead them back to the period of the lacustrines, nay, of the most primitive troglodytes. We have seen that the pre-Raphaelites reduce the picture to a writing which is no longer to produce its effect by its pictorial qualities, but must express an abstract idea ; and that the Symbolists make of the word, that conventional vehicle of a conception, a musical harmony, by whose aid they endeavour to awaken not an idea, but a phonetic effect. In precisely the same way Wagner wishes to divest music of its proper essence, and to transform it from a vehicle of emotion into a vehicle of rational thought. The disguise produced by this interchange of costumes is in this way complete. Painters proclaim themselves writers; poets behave like the composers of symphonies; the musician plays the poet. Pre-Raphaelites wishing to record a religious apothegm do not make use of writing, which leaves nothing to be desired in the way of convenience, and by which they would be distinctly understood, but plunge into the labour of a highly-detailed painting, costing them much time, and which, in spite of its wealth of figures, is far from speaking so clearly to the intelligence as a single line of rational writing. Symbolists desirous of awakening a musical emotion do not compose a melody, but join meaningless, though ostensibly musical words, capable, perhaps, of provoking amusement or vexation, but not the intended emotion. When Wagner wishes to express the idea of 'giant,' 'dwarf,' 'tarn-cap which makes the wearer invisible,' he does not say in words universally understood 'giant,' 'dwarf,' 'tarn-cap' (which makes the wearer invisible), but replaces these excellent words by a series of notes, the sense of which no one will divine without a key. Is anything more needed to expose the complete insanity of this confusion of all the means of expression, this ignorance of what is possible to each art ?

It is Wagner's ambition to imitate those facetious students who teach their dog to say 'papa.' He wants to perform the trick of making music say the names 'Schulze' and 'Müller' (=Smith and Jones). The score should, when necessary, supply the place of the directory. Language does not suffice him. He creates for himself a *volapük*, and demands that his hearers should learn it. No admission without hard work ! Those who have not assimilated the vocabulary of the Wagnerian *volapük* cannot understand his operas. It is useless to go to the trouble of a journey to Bayreuth if one cannot talk fluently in *leit-motifs.* And how pitiable after all is the result of this delirious effort! H. von Wolzogen, the writer of the *Thematische Leitfaden* (Thematic Guide) to the Niebelungen Tetralogy, finds in all these four prodigious works only ninety *leit-motifs.* A language of ninety words, however inflated they may be, such as 'motif of the weary Siegmund,' 'motif of the mania for vengeance,' 'motif of bondage,' etc.! with such a vocabulary it would be impossible even to exchange ideas about the weather with a native of Tierra del Fuego. A page of Sanders' lexicon contains more means of expression than Wolzogen's entire dictionary of the Wagnerian *leit-motif* language. The history of art knows no more astounding aberration than this *leit-motif* craze. To express ideas is not the function of music; language provides for that as completely as could be desired. When the word is accompanied by song or orchestra it is not to make it more definite, but to re-enforce it by the intervention of emotion. Music is a kind of sounding-board, in which the word has to awake something like an echo from the infinite. But such an echo of presentiment and mystery does not ring out from *leit-motifs* coldly pasted together, as if by the labour of a conscientious registrar.

With the 'unending melody,' the second of Wagner's tenets, it is the same as with the *leit-motif.* It is a product of degenerate thought; it is musical mysticism. It is the form in which incapacity for attention shows itself in music. In painting, attention leads to composition; the absence of it to a uniformly photographic treatment of the whole field of vision as with the pre-Raphaelites. In poetry, attention results in clearness of ideas, consistency of statement, the suppression of the unimportant, and the giving emphasis to the essential; its absence leads to twaddle as with the graphomaniacs, and to a painful prolixity in consequence of the indiscriminate recording of all perceptions as with Tolstoi. Finally, in music attention expresses itself in completed forms, *i.e.*, in well-defined melodies; its absence, on the contrary, by the dissolution of form, the obliteration of its boundary lines, and thus by unending melodies as with Wagner. This parallelism is not an arbitrary play of ideas, but an exact picture of the corresponding mental processes among the different groups of degenerate subjects, producing in the different arts different manifestations according to their specific means and aims.

Let us grasp what melody is. It is the regular grouping of notes in a highly expressive series of tones. Melody in music corresponds to what in language is a logically-constructed sentence, distinctly presenting an idea, and having a clearly-marked beginning and ending. The dreamy rambling of half-formed nebulous thoughts as little allows the mintage of sentences of this kind, as does the fleeting agitation of the vague bewildered emotion lead to the composition of a melody. The emotions, too, have their own grades of distinctness. They, too, can appear as chaotic, or as well-regulated states. In the one case they stand out in the consciousness which grasps their composition and their purpose as discriminable modes strongly illuminated by the attention; in the other case they are a disturbing enigma to consciousness, and perceived by it merely as a generic excitement, as a sort of subterranean trembling and rumbling of unknown origin and tendency. If the emotions are intelligible, they will be fain to manifest themselves in a form at once the most expressive and most easily grasped. If, on the contrary, they are a generic continuous state, without determined cause and discoverable aim, the music presenting them to the senses will be as blurred and as nebulously fluctuating in form as themselves. Melody may be said to be an effort of music to say something definite. It is clear that an emotion unconscious of its cause and its aims, and unilluminated by attention, will not raise its musical expression to the height of melody, precisely because it has nothing definite to say.

A completed melody is a late acquisition of music, obtained by it only after long evolution. In its historic, and still more in its prehistoric, beginnings, the art of music knew it not. Music springs originally from song, and the rhythmic noise (*i.e.*, noise repeated in equal or regular intervals of time) of accompanying stamping, knocking, or clapping of the hands; and song is nothing but speech grown louder and moving in wider intervals through emotional excitement. I should like to cite only one passage from the almost unlimited literature on this hackneyed subject. Herbert Spencer, in his well-known treatise on *The Origin and Function of Music*,* says: 'All music is originally vocal. . . . The dance-chants of savage tribes are very monotonous, and in virtue of their monotony are much more nearly allied to ordinary speech than are the songs of civilized races. . . . The early poems of the Greeks, which, be it remembered, were sacred legends embodied in that rhythmical, metaphorical language which strong feeling excites, were not recited, but chanted; the tones and the cadences were made musical by the same influences which made the speech poetical. . . . This chanting is believed to have been not what we call singing, but nearly allied to our recitative; far simpler, indeed, if we may judge from the fact that the early Greek lyre, which had but

* *The Origin and Function of Music: Essays, Scientific, Political and Speculative.* London: Williams and Norgate, 1883; vol. i., p. 213 *et seq.*

four strings, was played in *unison* with the voice, which was therefore confined to four notes. . . . That recitative—beyond which, by the way, the Chinese and Hindoos seem never to have advanced—grew naturally out of the modulations and cadences of strong feeling, we have, indeed, still current evidence. There are even now to be met with occasions on which strong feeling vents itself in this form. Whoever has been present when a meeting of Quakers was addressed by one of their preachers (whose practice it is to speak only under the influence of religious emotion) must have been struck by the quite unusual tones, like those of a subdued chant, in which the address was made.'

Recitative, which is nothing but speech intensified, and allows no recognition of completed forms of melody, is therefore the most ancient form of music; it is the degree of development reached by the art of music among savages, the ancient Greeks, and contemporary races in Eastern Asia. Wagner's 'unending melody' is nothing but recitative, richly harmonized and animated, but, nevertheless, recitative. The name bestowed by him on his pretended invention must not mislead us. In the mouth of the degenerate a word has never the meaning ascribed to it by universal language. Wagner calmly applies the term 'melody'—with a distinguishing adjective—to a form which is actually the negation and suppression of melody. He designates unending melody as an advance in music, while it is really a return to its primeval starting-point. Here there recurs in Wagner what we have so often laid stress upon in the preceding chapters, viz., that by a strange optical illusion the degenerate regard their atavism, their morbid reversion to the most remote and lowest grades of evolution, as an ascent into the future.

Wagner was led to his theory of unending melody by his limited capacity for the invention of finite, that is of real, melodies. His weakness in melodic creation has struck all impartial musicians. In youth his power in this direction was more abundant, and he succeeded in creating some superb melodies (in *Tannhäuser*, *Lohengrin*, *Fliegender Höllander*). With increasing age this power became more and more impoverished, and in proportion as the torrent of melodic invention dried up in him, he accentuated his theory of unending melody with ever more obstinacy and asperity. Always there reappears the well-known device of concocting a theory *a posteriori* as a plausible ground for, and palliation of, what is done through unconscious organic necessity. Wagner was incapable of distinguishing the individual personages of his operas by a purely musical characterization, and therefore he invented the *leit-motif*.* Experiencing a great difficulty, especially with

* E. Hanslick, *op. cit.*, p. 233: 'As the dramatis personæ in "music-drama" are not distinguished by the character of the melodies they sing, as

advancing age, in creating true melodies, he set up the postulate of the unending melody.

All the other crotchets of his musical theory also find their explanation in this clear consciousness of definite incompetency. In the *Art-work of the Future* he overwhelms the theory of counterpoint and the contrapuntists—those dull pedants who abase the most vital of all arts to a desiccated, dead mathematics—with a scorn intended to be biting, but producing the effect of an echo of Schopenhauer's invectives against the German philosophers. Why? Because, as an inattentive mystic, abandoned to amorphous dreams, he must feel intolerably oppressed by the severe discipline and fixed rules of the theory of composition, which gave a grammar to the musical babbling of primeval times, and made of it a worthy medium for the expression of the emotions of civilized men. He asserts that pure instrumental music ended with Beethoven; that progress after him is impossible; that 'musical declamation' is the only path along which the art of music can further develop itself. It may be that, after Beethoven, instrumental music will make no progress for decades, or for centuries. He was such a stupendous genius that it is, in fact, difficult to imagine how he can be surpassed, or even equalled. Leonardo da Vinci, Shakespeare, Cervantes, Goethe, produce a similar impression; and, in truth, these geniuses have not yet been surpassed. It is also conceivable that there are limits which it is impossible for any given art to pass at all, so that a very great genius says the last word for it, and after that no progress can be made in it. In such a case, however, the aspirant should humbly say: 'I know that I cannot do better than the supreme master of my art; I am therefore contented to labour as one of the *epigoni* in the shadow of his greatness, content if my work expresses some peculiarities of my individuality.' He ought not in presumptuous self-conceit to affirm: 'There is no sense in emulating the eagle-flight of the mighty one; progress now lies alone in the flapping of my bats'-wings.' But this is exactly what Wagner does. Not being himself endowed with any great gift for pure instrumental music, as his few symphonic works suffice to prove, he decrees in the tone of infallibility: 'Instrumental music ended with Beethoven. It is an error to seek for anything on this well-browsed field. The future of music lies in the accompaniment of the word, and I am he who is to show you the way into that future.'

Here Wagner simply makes a virtue of his necessity, and of

in ancient opera (Don Juan and Leporello, Donna Anna and Zerlina, Max and Caspar), but all resemble each other in the physiognomic pathos of the tones of their speech, Wagner aims at replacing this characteristic by so-called *leit motifs* in the orchestra.'

his weakness a title of glory. The symphony is the highest differentiation of musical art. In it music has wholly discarded its relationship with words, and attained its highest independence. Hence the symphony is the most musical of all that music can produce. To disown it is to disown that music is a special, differentiated art. To place above the symphony music as an accompaniment of words is to raise the handmaiden to a higher rank than her free-born mistress. It will never occur to a composer, whose inmost being is charged with musical feeling and thought, to seek words instead of musical themes for the expression of that in him which is yearning for embodiment. For if it does occur to him, it is a proof that in his inmost being he is a poet or an author, and not a musician. The choruses in the Ninth Symphony are not to be cited as proof of the inaccuracy of this assertion. In that case Beethoven was overmastered by an emotion so powerful and univocal, that the more general and equivocal character of purely musical expression could no longer suffice for him, and he was unconditionally compelled to call in the aid of words. In the deeply significant Biblical legend, even Balaam's ass acquired the power of speech when he had something definite to say. The emotion which becomes clearly conscious of its content and aim ceases to be a mere emotion, and transforms itself into presentation, notion and judgment, but these express themselves, not in music, but in articulate language. When Wagner, as a fundamental principle, placed music as an accompaniment to words above that which is purely instrumental, and not as a medium for the expression of thought—for in regard to that there can be no difference of opinion—but as a musical form properly so called, he only proved that, in the inmost depths of his nature, and by virtue of his organic disposition, he was not a musician, but a confused mixture of a poet feeble in style, and a painter lazy of brush, with a Javanese 'gamelang' accompaniment buzzing in between. This is the case with most 'higher degenerates,' except that the separate fragments of their strangely intermingled hybrid talent are not so strong and great as Wagner's.

The musical productions in which Wagner has been most successful—the Venusberg music; the E flat, G, B flat, 'Wigala-Weia' of the Rhinemaidens, repeated one hundred and thirty-six times; the Walküre ride; the fire incantation; the murmur of the forest; the Siegfried idyl; the Good-Friday spell; magnificent compositions, and highly praised with justice—show precisely the peculiarly unmusical character of his genius. All these pieces have one thing in common that they depict. They are not an inner emotion crying out from the soul in music, but the mental vision of the gifted eye of a painter, which Wagner, with gigantic power, but also with gigantic aberration, strives to fix in tones instead of lines and colours. He avails himself of natural sounds or noises, either imitating them directly, or awakening ideas of them through association, reproducing the ripple and roar of waves, the sough of the tree-top and the song of wild birds, which are in themselves acoustic; or, by an acoustic parallelism, the optical phenomena of the movements in the dance of voluptuous female forms, the tearing along of fiercely snorting steeds, the blazing and flickering of flames, etc. These creations are not the outgrowth of emotional excitement, but have been produced by external impressions conveyed through the senses; they are not the utterance of a feeling but a reflection—*i.e.*, something essentially optical. I might compare Wagner's music, at its very best, to the flight of flying-fishes. It is an astonishing and dazzling spectacle, and yet unnatural. It is a straying from a native to an alien element. Above all, it is something absolutely barren and incapable of profiting either normal fishes or normal birds.

Wagner has felt this himself very forcibly; he was quite clear on the point that no one could build further on the foundation of his tone-paintings; for with reference to the efforts of musicians eagerly desirous of founding a Wagner school, he complains* that 'younger composers were most irrationally putting themselves to trouble in imitating him.'

A searching examination has thus shown us that this pretended musician of the future is an out-and-out musician of long-ago. All the characteristics of his talent point not forward, but far behind us. His *leit-motif*, abasing music to a conventional phonetic symbol, is atavism; his unending melody is atavism, leading back the fixed form to the vague recitative of savages; atavism, his subordination of highly differentiated instrumental music to music-drama, which mixes music and poetry, and allows neither of the two art-forms to attain to independence; even his peculiarity of almost never permitting more than one person on the stage to sing and of avoiding vocal polyphony is atavism. As a personality he will occupy an important place in music; as an initiator, or developer of his art, hardly any, or a very narrow one. For the only thing that musicians of healthy capacity can learn from him is to keep song and accompaniment in opera closely connected with the words, to declaim with sincerity and propriety, and to suggest pictorial ideas to the imagination by means of orchestral effects. But I dare not decide whether the latter is an enlargement or an upheaval of the natural boundaries of musical art, and in any event disciples

* Wagner, *Ueber die Anwendung der Musik auf das Drama. Ges. Schriften*, Band X., p. 242.

of Wagner must use his rich musical palette with caution if they are not to be led astray.

Wagner's mighty influence on his contemporaries is to be explained, neither by his capacities as author and musician, nor by any of his personal qualities, with the exception, perhaps, of that 'stubborn perseverance in one and the same fundamental dea' which Lombroso* cites as a characteristic of graphomaniacs, but by the peculiarities in the life of the present nervous temperament. His earthly destiny resembles that of those strange Oriental plants known as 'Jericho roses' (*Anastatica asteriscus*), which, dingy-brown in colour, leathery and dry, roll about, driven by every wind, until they reach a congenial soil, when they take root and blossom into full-blown flowers. To the end of his life Wagner's existence was conflict and bitterness, and his boastings had no other echo than the laughter not only of rational beings, but, alas! of fools also. It was not until he had long passed his fiftieth year that he began to know the intoxication of universal fame; and in the last decade of his life he was installed among the demi-gods. It had come to this, that the world had, in the interval, become ripe for him—and for the madhouse. He had the good fortune to endure until the general degeneration and hysteria were sufficiently advanced to supply a rich and nutritious soil for his theories and his art.

The phenomenon repeatedly established and verified in these pages, that lunatics fly to each other as iron filings to the magnet, is quite strikingly observable in Wagner's life. His first great patroness was the Princess Metternich, daughter of the well-known eccentric Count Sandor, and whose own eccentricities formed material for the chronicle of the Napoleonic Court. His most enthusiastic disciple and defender was Franz Liszt, whom I have elsewhere characterized (see my *Ausgewählte Pariser Briefe*; 2te Auflage; Leipzig, 1887, p. 172), and of whom I will therefore only briefly remark that he bore in his nature the greatest resemblance to Wagner. He was an author (his works, filling six thick volumes, have an honourable place in the literature of graphomaniacs), composer, erotomaniac and mystic, all in an incomparably lower degree than Wagner, whom he surpassed only in a prodigiously developed talent for pianoforte-playing. Wagner was an enthusiastic admirer of all graphomaniacs who came in his way—*e.g.*, of that A. Gleizès expressly cited by Lombroso† as a lunatic, but whom Wagner praises in most exuberant terms;‡

* Lombroso, *Genie und Irrsinn*, p. 225.

† *Ibid.*, *op. cit.*, p. 226.

‡ Wagner, *Religion und Kunst*. *Ges. Schr.*, Band X., p. 307, note: 'The author here expressly refers to A. Gleizès' book, *Thalysia oder das Heil der Menschheit*. . . . Without an exact knowledge of the results, recorded in this book, of the most careful investigations, which seem to have absorbed the entire life of one of the most amiable and profound of Frenchmen, it might be difficult to gain attention for . . . the regeneration of the human race.'

and he even gathered round him a court of select graphomaniacs, among whom may be mentioned Nietzsche, whose insanity compelled his confinement in a madhouse; H. von Wolzogen, whose *Poetische Laut-Symbolik* might have been written by the most exquisite of French 'Symbolists' or 'Instrumentists';* Henri Porges, E. von Hagen, etc. But the most important relations of this kind were with the unhappy King Louis II. In him Wagner found the soul he needed. In him he met with a full comprehension of all his theories and his creations. It may be safely asserted that Louis of Bavaria created the Wagner Cult. Only when the King became his protector did Wagner and his efforts become of importance for the history of civilization; not, perhaps, because Louis II. offered Wagner the means of realizing the boldest and most sumptuous of his artistic dreams, but chiefly because he placed the prestige of his crown in the service of the Wagnerian movement. Let us for a moment consider how deeply monarchical is the disposition of the vast majority of the German people; how the knees of the beery Philistine tremble as he reverentially salutes even an empty court carriage; and how the hearts of well-bred maidens flutter with ineffable inspiration at the sight of a prince! And here was a real king, handsome as the day, young, surrounded by legends, whose mental infirmity was at that time regarded by all sentimentalists as sublime 'idealism,' displaying unbounded enthusiasm for an artist, and reviving on a far larger scale the relations between Charles Augustus and Goethe! From that moment it was natural that Wagner should become the idol of all loyal hearts. To share in the royal taste for the 'ideal' was a thing to be proud of. Wagner's music became provisionally a royal Bavarian music, adorned with crown and escutcheon, till it should subsequently become an imperial German music. At the head of the Wagnerian movement there walks, as is fit, an insane king. Louis II. was able to bring Wagner into vogue with the entire German nation (excepting, of course, those Bavarians who were revolted by the King's prodigalities); nevertheless, no amount of grovelling obsequiousness could by itself have produced a fanaticism for Wagner. That the mere Wagner-fashion might attain to this height another factor was necessary—the hysteria of the age.

Although not so widespread as in France and England, this

* 'Alberich's seductive appeal to the water-sprites makes prominent the hard, mordant sound of *N*, so well corresponding in its whole essence to the negative power in the drama, inasmuch as it forms the sharpest contrast to the soft *W* of the water-spirits. Then when he prepares to climb after the maidens, the alliance of the *Gl* and *Schl* with the soft, gliding *F* marks most forcibly the gliding off the slippery rock. In the appropriate *Pr* (*Fr*), Woglinde as it were shouts "Good luck to you!" (*Prosit*) when Alberich sneezes.'—Cited by Hanslick, *Musikalische Stationen*, p. 255.

hysteria is not wanting in Germany, where during the last quarter of a century it has continued to gain ground. Germany has been longer protected from it than the civilized nations of the West by the smaller development of large industry and by the absence of large cities properly so called. In the last generation, however, both of these gifts have been abundantly accorded her, and two great wars have done the rest to make the nervous system of the people susceptible to the pernicious influences of the city and the factory system.

The effect of war on the nerves of the participants has never been systematically investigated; and yet how highly important and necessary a work this would be! Science knows what disorders are produced in man by a single strong moral shock, *e.g.*, a sudden mortal danger; it has recorded hundreds and thousands of cases in which persons saved from drowning, or present at a fire on shipboard, or in a railway accident, or who have been threatened with assassination, etc., have either lost their reason, or been attacked by grave and protracted, often incurable, nervous illnesses. In war hundreds of thousands are exposed to all these fearful impressions at the same time. For months cruel mutilation or sudden death menaces them at every step. They are frequently surrounded by the spectacle of devastation, conflagration, the most appalling wounds, and heaps of corpses frightful to behold. Moreover, the greatest demands are made on their strength; they are forced to march until they break down, and cannot count on having adequate nourishment or sufficient sleep. And shall there not appear among these hundreds of thousands the effect which is proved to result from a single one of the occurrences which take place by thousands during war? Let it not be said that in a campaign a soldier becomes callous to the horrors encompassing him. That merely signifies that they cease to excite the attention of his consciousness. They are nevertheless perceived by the senses and their cerebral centres, and therefore leave their traces in the nervous system. That the soldier does not at the moment notice the deep shock —nay, even shattering—he has experienced, equally proves nothing. 'Traumatic hysteria,' 'railway spine,' the nervous maladies consequent on a moral shock, are also frequently unobserved until months after the event occasioning them.

In my belief, it can scarcely be doubted that every great war is a cause of hysteria among multitudes, and that far the larger number of soldiers, even completely unknown to themselves, bring home from a campaign a somewhat deranged nervous system. Of course this is much less applicable to the conquerors than to the conquered, for the feeling of triumph is one of the most pleasurable the human brain can experience, and the force-producing ('dynamogenous') effect of this pleasurable feeling is well qualified to counteract the destructive influences of the impressions produced by war. But it is difficult for it to entirely annul these impressions, and the victors, like the vanquished, no doubt leave a large part of their nervous strength and moral health on the battle-field and in the bivouac.

The brutalization of the masses after every war has become a commonplace. The expression originates in the perception that after a campaign the tone of the people becomes fiercer and rougher, and that statistics show more acts of violence. The fact is correctly stated, but the interpretation is superficial. If the soldier on returning home becomes more short-tempered, and even has recourse to the knife, it is not because the war has made him rougher, but because it has made him more excitable. This increased excitability is, however, only one of the forms of the phenomenon of nervous debility.

Hence under the action of the two great wars in connection with the development of large industries and the growth of large towns, hysteria among the German people has, since 1870, increased in an extraordinary manner, and we have very nearly overtaken the unenviable start which the English and French had over us in this direction. Now, all hysteria, like every form of insanity, and for that matter like every disease, receives its special form from the personality of the invalid. The degree of culture, the character, propensities and habits of the deranged person give the derangement its peculiar colour. Among the English, always piously inclined, degeneration and hysteria were bound to appear both mystical and religious. Among the French, with their highly developed taste and widespread fondness for all artistic pursuits, it was natural that hysteria should take an artistic direction, and lead to the notorious extravagances in their painting, literature and music. We Germans are in general neither very pious nor very cultivated in matters of art. Our comprehension of the beautiful in art expresses itself, for the most part, in the idiotic '*Reizend!*' (charming), and '*Entzückend!*' (ravishing), squeaked in shrill head-tones and with upturned eyes by our well-bred daughters at the sight of a quaintly-shaved poodle, and before the Darmstadt Madonna by Holbein, indiscriminately; and in the grunts of satisfaction with which the plain citizen pumps in his beer at a concert of his singing club. Not that we are by nature devoid of a sense of the beautiful—I believe, on the contrary, that in our deepest being we have more of it than most other nations—but owing to unfavourable circumstances this sense has not been able to attain development. Since the Thirty Years' War we have been too poor, we have had too hard a combat with the necessities of life, to have anything over for any sort of luxury; and our ruling classes, profoundly

Latinized and slaves to French fashion, were so estranged from the masses, that for the last two centuries the latter could have no part in the culture, taste, or æsthetic satisfactions of the upper strata of society, separated from them by an impassable gulf. As, therefore, the large majority of the German people had no interest in art, and troubled themselves little about it, German hysteria could not assume an artistic, æsthetic form.

It assumed other forms, partly abominable, partly ignoble and partly laughable. German hysteria manifests itself in anti-Semitism, that most dangerous form of the persecution-mania, in which the person believing himself persecuted becomes a savage persecutor, capable of all crimes (the *persécuté persécuteur* of the French mental therapeutics).* Like hypochondriacs and 'hémorroïdaires,' the German hysterical subject is anxiously concerned about his precious health. His crazes hinge on the exhalations of his skin and the functions of his stomach. He becomes a fanatic for Jaeger vests, and for the groats which vegetarians grind for themselves. He gets vehemently affected over Kneipp's douches and barefoot perambulations on wet grass. At the same time, he excites himself with morbid sentimentalism (the 'Zoophilia' of Magnan) concerning the sufferings of the frog, utilized in physiological experiments, and through all this anti-Semitic, Kneippish, Jaegerish, vegetarian, and anti-vivisection insanity, there rings out the fundamental note of a megalomaniacal, Teutonomaniacal Chauvinism, against which the noble Emperor Frederick vainly warned us. As a rule, all these derangements appear simultaneously, and in nine out of ten cases it is safe to take the proudly strutting wearer of Jaeger's garments for a Chauvinist, the Kneipp visionary for a groats-dieted maniac, and the defender of the frog, thirsting for the professor's blood, for an anti-Semitist.

Wagner's hysteria assumed the collective form of German hysteria. With a slight modification of Terence's *Homo sum*, he could say of himself, 'I am a deranged being, and no kind of derangement is a stranger to me.' He could as an anti-Semitist give points to Stoecker.† He has an inimitable mastery of Chauvinistic phraseology.‡ Was he not able to convince his hypnotized hysterical following that the heroes of his pieces were primeval German figures—these Frenchmen and Brabanters, these Icelanders and Norwegians, these women of Palestine—all the fabulous beings he had fetched from the

* Legrand du Saulle terms the persecutor who believes himself persecuted, 'persécuté actif.' See his fundamental work: *Le Délire des Persécutions*. Paris, 1871, p. 194.

† Wagner, *Das Judenthum in der Musik*. *Ges. Schr.* Band V., p. 83. *Aufklärungen über das Judenthum in der Musik*. Band VIII., p. 299.

‡ Wagner, *Deutsche Kunst und Deutsche Politik*. *Ges. Schr.* Band VIII., p. 39. *Was ist Deutsche?* Band X., p. 51 *et passim*.

poems of Provence and Northern France, and from the Northern saga, who (with the exception of *Tannhäuser* and the *Meistersinger*) have not a single drop of German blood or a single German fibre in their whole body? It is thus that, in public exhibitions, a quack hypnotist persuades his victims that they are eating peaches instead of raw potatoes. Wagner became an advocate for vegetarianism, and as the fruit needed for the nourishment of the people in accordance with this diet exists in abundance only in warm regions of the earth, he promptly advised 'the direction of a rational emigration to lands resembling the South American peninsula, which, it has been affirmed, might, through its superabundant productivity, supply nourishment for the present population of the entire globe.'* He brandishes his knightly sword against the physiologists who experiment on animals.† He was not an enthusiast for wool, because personally he preferred silk; and this is the only hiatus in the otherwise complete picture. He did not live to witness the greatness of the reverend Pastor Kneipp, otherwise he probably would have found words of profound significance for the primitive German sanctity of wet feet, and the redeeming power vested in the knee-douche.

When, therefore, the enthusiastic friendship of King Louis had given Wagner the necessary prestige, and directed the universal attention of Germany to him; when the German people had learned to know him and his peculiarities, then all the mystics of the Jewish sacrifice of blood, of woollen shirts, of the vegetable *menu*, and sympathy cures, were compelled to raise their pæans in his honour, for he was the embodiment of all their obsessions. As for his music, they simply threw that into the bargain. The vast majority of Wagner fanatics understood nothing of it. The emotional excitement which the works of their idol made them experience did not proceed from the singers and the orchestra, but in part from the pictorial beauty of the scenic tableaux, and in a greater measure from the specific craze each brought with him to the theatre, and of which each worshipped Wagner as the spokesman and champion.

I do not, however, go so far as to assert that *skat*‡ patriotism, and the heroic idealism of natural cures, rice with fruit, 'away with the Jews!' and flannel, alone made the hearts of Wagner-bigots beat faster in blissful emotion when they were listening to his music. This music was certainly of a nature to fascinate the hysterical. Its powerful orchestral effects produced in them hypnotic states (at the Salpêtrière hospital in Paris the

* Wagner, *Religion und Kunst*. *Ges. Schr.* Band X., p. 311.

† *Offenes Schreiben au Herrn Ernst von Weber, Verfasser der Schrift: 'Die Folterkammern der Wissenschaft.' Ges. Schr.* Band X., p. 251.

‡ A game of cards to which Teutomaniacs are much addicted.

hypnotic state is often induced by suddenly striking a gong), and the formlessness of the unending melody was exactly suited to the dreamy vagaries of their own thought. A distinct melody awakens and demands attention, and is hence opposed to the fugitive ideation of the weak brains of the degenerate. A flowing recitative, on the contrary, without beginning or end, makes no sort of demand on the mind—for most auditors trouble themselves either not at all, or for a very short time, about the hide-and-seek play of the *leit-motif*—one can allow one's self to be swayed and carried along by it, and to emerge from it at pleasure, without any definite remembrance, but with a merely sensual feeling of having enjoyed a hot, nervously exciting tone-bath. The relation of true melody to the unending melody is the same as that of a genre or historical painting to the wayward arabesques of a Moorish mural decoration, repeated a thousand times, and representing nothing definite ; and the Oriental knows how favourable the sight of his arabesques is to 'Kef'—that dreamy state in which Reason is lulled to sleep, and crazy Imagination alone rules as mistress of the house.

Wagner's music initiated hysterically-minded Germans into the mysteries of Turkish Kef. Nietzsche may make sport of this subject with his idiotic play on words '*Sursum*—bum-bum,' and with his remarks about the German youth who seeks for 'Ahnung' (presentiments) ; but the fact is not to be denied that a part of Wagner's devotees—those who brought a diseased mysticism with them to the theatre—found in him their satisfaction ; for nothing is so well qualified to conjure up 'presentiments,' *i.e.*, ambiguous, shadowy border-land presentations, as a music which is itself born of nebulous adumbrations of thought.

Hysterical women were won over to Wagner chiefly by the lascivious eroticism of his music, but also by his poetic representation of the relation of man to woman. Nothing enchants an 'intense' woman so much as demoniacal irresistibleness on the part of the woman, and trembling adoration of her supernatural power on the part of the man. In contrast to Frederick William I., who cried in anger, 'You should not fear, but love me,' women of this sort would rather shout to every man, 'You are not to love me, but to lie, full of dread and terror, in the dust at my feet.' 'Frau' Venus, Brunhilde, Isolde, and Kundry have won for Wagner much more admiration among women than have Elizabeth, Elsa, Senta, and Gudrune.

After Wagner had once conquered Germany, and a fervent faith in him had been made the first article in the catechism of German patriotism, foreign countries could not long withstand his cult. The admiration of a great people has an extraordinary power of conviction. Even its aberrations it forces with irresistible suggestion on other nations. Wagner was one of the foremost conquerors in the German wars. Sadowa and Sedan were fought in his behalf. The world, *nolens volens*, had to take up its attitude with regard to a man whom Germany proclaimed its national composer. He began his triumphal march round the globe draped in the flag of Imperial Germany. Germany's enemies were his enemies, and this forced even such Germans as withstood his influence to take his side against foreign lands. 'I beat my breast: I, too, have fought for him against the French in speech and writing. I also have defended him against the pastrycooks who hissed his *Lohengrin* in Paris.' How was one to get off this duty? Hamlet thrusts at the arras, well knowing that Polonius stands there; hence any son or brother of Polonius is bound resolutely to attack Hamlet. Wagner had the good fortune to play the part of the tapestry to the French Hamlets, giving them the pretext for thrusting at the Polonius of Germany. As a result, the attitude in the Wagner question of every German was rigidly prescribed for him.

To the zeal of Germans all manner of other things added their aid in favouring the success of Wagner abroad. A minority, composed in part of really independent men of honorably unprejudiced minds, but in part also of degenerate minds with a morbid passion for contradiction, took sides with him just because he was blindly and furiously maligned by the Chauvinist majority, who were a prey to national hatred. 'It is contemptible,' cried the minority, 'to condemn an artist because he is a German. Art has no fatherland. Wagner's music should not be judged with the memory of Alsace-Lorraine.' These views are so reasonable and noble, that those who entertained them must have rejoiced in them and been proud of them. On listening to Wagner, they had the clear feeling, 'We are better and cleverer than the Chauvinists,' and this feeling necessarily placed them at the outset in such an agreeable and benevolent mood, that his music seemed much more beautiful than they would have found it if they had not been obliged first to stifle their vulgar and base instincts, and fortify those which were more elevated, free and refined. They erroneously ascribed to Wagner's music the emotions produced by their self-satisfaction.

The fact that only in Bayreuth could this music be heard, unfalsified and in its full strength, was also of great importance for the esteem in which it was held. If it had been played in every theatre, if, without trouble and formalities, one could have gone to a representation of Wagner as to one of *Il Trovatore*, Wagner would not have obtained his most enthusiastic public from foreign countries. To know the real Wagner it was necessary to journey to Bayreuth. This could be done only at long intervals and at specified times ; seats and lodgings had to be obtained long in advance, and at great expenditure of trouble. It was a pilgrimage requiring much money and leisure ; hence 'hoi polloi' were excluded from it. Thus, the pilgrimage to Bayreuth became a privilege of the rich and well-bred, and to have been to Bayreuth came to be a great social distinction among the snobs of both worlds. The journey was a thing to make a great parade of and be haughty over. The pilgrim no longer belonged to the vulgar crowd, but to the select few ; he became a hadji! Oriental sages so well know the peculiar vanity of the hadjis, that one of their proverbs contains an express warning against the pious man who has been thrice to Mecca.

Hence the pilgrimage to Bayreuth became a mark of aristocracy, and an appreciation of Wagner's music, in spite of his nationality, was regarded as evidence of intellectual pre-eminence. The prejudice in his favour was created, and provided one went to him in this mood, there was no reason why Wagner should not have the same influence on hysterical foreigners as on hysterical Germans. *Parsifal* was especially fitted completely to subjugate the French neo-Catholics and Anglo-American mystics who marched behind the banner of the Salvation Army. It was with this opera that Wagner chiefly triumphed among his non-German admirers. Listening to the music of *Parsifal* has become the religious act of all those who wish to receive the Communion in musical form.

These are the explanatory causes of Wagner's conquest, first of Germany, and then of the world. The absence of judgment and independence among the multitude, who chant the antiphony in the Psalter ; the imitation of musicians possessed of no originality, who witnessed his triumph, and, like genuine little boys wanting 'to be taken,' clung to his coat-tails—these did what was still needed to lay the world at his feet. As it is the most widely diffused, so is Wagnerism the most momentous aberration of the present time. The Bayreuth festival theatre, the *Bayreuther Blätter*, the Parisian *Revue Wagnérienne*, are lasting monuments by which posterity will be able to measure the whole breadth and depth of the degeneration and hysteria of the age.

CHAPTER VI.

PARODIES OF MYSTICISM.

THE artistic and poetic forms of mysticism, which we have studied hitherto, might perhaps inspire doubts in superficial or insufficiently instructed minds as to their origin in degeneration, and present themselves as manifestations of a genuine and fertile talent. But beside them appear others, in which a state of mind reveals itself which suddenly arrests and perplexes any reader, however credulous, and however accessible to the suggestion of printed words, and to self-puffing charlatanism. Books and theories find publication, in which even the unlearned observe the deep intellectual degradation of their authors. One pretends to be able to initiate the reader into the black art, and enable him to practise magic himself; another gives a poetical form to definitely insane ideas, such as have been classified by mental therapeutics; a third writes books as if prompted by thoughts and feelings worthy of little children or idiots. A great part of the works I have in view would justify, without further consideration, the placing of their authors under constraint. As, however, in spite of their manifest craziness, well-known critics are bent upon discovering in them 'the future,' 'fresh nerve-stimulations,' and beauties of a mysterious kind, and to puff them by their chatter to gaping simpletons as revelations of genius, it is not superfluous to devote some brief consideration to them.

A not very large amount of mysticism leads to belief; a larger amount leads necessarily to superstition, and the more confused, the more deranged, the mind is, so much the crazier will be the kind of superstition. In England and America this most frequently takes the form of spiritualism and the founding of sects. The hysterical and deranged receive spiritual inspirations, and begin to preach and prophesy, or they conjure up spirits and commune with the dead. In English fiction ghost-stories have begun to occupy a large place, and in English newspapers to act glibly as stopgaps, as was done formerly in the Continental press by the sea-serpent and the Flying Dutchman. A society has been formed which has for its object the collecting of ghost-stories, and testing their authenticity; and even literary men of renown have been seized with the vertigo of the supernatural, and condescend to serve as vouchers for the most absurd aberrations.

In Germany, too, spiritualism has found an entrance, although, on the whole, it has not gained much ground. In the large towns there may be some small spiritualist bodies. The English expression *trance* has become so familiar to some deranged persons that they have adopted it in German as *trans*, imagining apparently, with the popular etymology, that it means 'beyond' instead of 'ecstasy,' or, in other words, the state in which, according to the spiritualist hypothesis, the medium ought to find himself who enters into communication with the world of spirits. Nevertheless, spiritualism has as yet exerted little influence on our literature. Excluding the later romanticists who have fallen into childishness, notably the authors of tragedies based on the idea of 'fatality' (*Schicksalstragödien*), few writers have dared to introduce the supernatural into their creations otherwise than allegorically. At most in Kleist and Kerner it attains a certain importance, and healthy readers do not consider that as a merit in the dramas of the unfortunate author of the *Hermannsschlacht*, and in the *Seer of Prevorst* of the Swabian poet. On the other hand, it must certainly be noted that it is the ghost element precisely which has brought to these two writers, in recent times, a renewal of youth and popularity among degenerate and hysterical Germans. Maximilian Perty, who was evidently born too soon, met with but rare and even rather derisive notice from the less soft-headed generation which preceded ours, for his bulky books on apparitions. And, among contemporaries, none but Freiherr Karl du Prel has chosen the spirit world as the special subject of his theoretic writings and novels. After all, our plays, our tales, are very little haunted, scarcely enough to make a schoolgirl shiver; and even among the eminent foreign authors best known in Germany, such, for example, as Tourgenieff, it is not the world of apparitions which attracts German readers.

The few ghost-seers whom we have at present in Germany endeavour naturally to give their mental derangement a scientific colouring, and appeal to individual professors of mathematics and natural science who happen entirely to agree with them, or are supposed to be partially inclined to do so. However, their one sheet-anchor is Zöllner, who is simply a sad proof of the fact that a professorship is no protection from madness; and they can besides, at any rate, point to opportune remarks of Helmholtz and other mathematicians on *n* dimensions, which they, either intentionally or from mystical weakness of mind, have misunderstood. In an analytical problem the mathematician, instead of one, two, or three dimensions, may place *n* dimensions without altering thereby the law of the problem and its legitimately resulting corollaries, but it does not occur to him to imagine, under the geometrical expression, '*n*th dimension,' something given in space, and capable of being apprehended by the senses. When Zöllner gives the well-known example of the inversion of the india-rubber ring which, because only possible in the third dimension, necessarily appeared quite inconceivable and supernatural to a bi-dimensional being, he believes that he facilitates the comprehension of the formation of a knot in a closed ring as an operation practicable in the fourth dimension. In doing this he simply offers one more example of the known tendency of the mystic to delude himself, as he does others, with words which seem to signify something, and which a simpleton is convinced oftener than not that he understands, but which in reality express no idea, and are, therefore, empty sound, void of import.

France is about to become the promised land of believers in ghosts. Voltaire's countrymen have already got the start of the pious Anglo-Saxons in dealings with the supernatural. I am not now thinking of the lower ranks of the people, among whom the book of dreams (*La Clé des Songes*) has never ceased to constitute the family library, together with the Calendar, and, perhaps, the 'Paroissien' (missal); nor of the fine ladies who at all times have ensured excellent incomes to clairvoyantes and fortune-tellers; but only of the male representatives of the educated classes. Dozens of spiritualist circles count their numbers by thousands. In numerous drawing-rooms of the best (even in the opinion of the 'most cultured'!) society, the dead are called up. A monthly publication, *L'Initiation*, announces, in weighty tones, and with a prodigality of philosophical and scientific technicalities, the esoteric doctrine of the marvels of the unearthly. A bi-monthly publication, *Annales des Sciences Psychiques*, terms itself a 'collection of observations and researches.' Next to these two most important periodicals, a whole series of others exist, similar in tendency, and all having a wide circulation. Strictly technical works on hypnotism and suggestion run through edition after edition, and it has become a profitable speculation for doctors without practice, who do not attach much importance to the opinions of their colleagues, to compile so-called manuals and text-books on these subjects, which scientifically are completely worthless, but which are bought up by the public like hot rolls. Novels have, with rare exceptions, no longer any sale in France, but works on obscure phenomena of nerve function go off splendidly, so that sagacious publishers give their discouraged authors this advice: 'Leave novels for a time, and write on magnetism.'

Some of the books on magic which have appeared of late years in France connect their subject directly with the phenomena of hypnotism and suggestion; for example, A. De Rochas' *Les États profonds de l'Hypnose*, and C. A. de Bodisco's *Traits de Lumière*, or 'physical researches dedicated to unbelievers and egoists.' This has brought many observers to the idea that the works and discoveries of the Charcot school in general have given the impulse to the whole of this movement. Hypnotism, say the representatives of this opinion, has brought such remarkable facts to light that the accuracy of certain traditions, popular beliefs and old records can no longer be doubted, though hitherto they have been generally considered inventions of superstition; possession, witch-spells, second-sight, healing by imposition of hands, prophecy, mental communication at the remotest distance without the intervention of words, have received a new interpretation and have been recognised as possible. What, then, more natural than that minds weak in balance, and of insufficient scientific training, should become accessible to the marvellous (against which they had shielded themselves, as long as they considered it to be all old nurses' fables), when they saw it appear in the garb of science, and found themselves in the best society by believing in it?

Plausible as this opinion is, it is not the less false. It puts the cart before the horse. It confounds cause with effect. No completely sound mind has been led by the experiences of the new hypnotic science into a belief in the marvellous. In former times no attention was paid to obscure phenomena, or they were passed by with eyes intentionally closed, because they could not be fitted in to the prevailing system, and were consequently held to be chimæras or frauds. For the last twelve years official science has taken cognizance of them, and Faculties and Academies are engaged upon them. But no one thinks of them for a moment as supernatural, or supposes the working of unearthly forces behind them. They class them with all other natural phenomena which are accessible to the observation of the senses, and are determined by the ordinary laws of nature. Our knowledge has simply enlarged its frame, and admitted an order of facts which in former times had remained beyond its pale. Many processes of hypnosis are more or less satisfactorily explained; others as yet not at all. But an earnest and healthy mind attaches no great importance to this, for he knows that the pretended explanation of phenomena does not go very far, and that we have mostly to be satisfied to determine them with certainty, and to know their immediate conditions. I do not say that the new science has exhausted its subject and has reached its limits. But whatever it may bring to light of the unknown and the unexpected, it is not a matter of doubt to the healthy mind that it will be accounted for by natural means, and that the simple, ultimate laws of physics, chemistry and biology cannot be shaken by these discoveries.

If, therefore, so many people now interpret the phenomena of hypnosis as supernatural, and indulge the hope that the conjuration of the spirits of the dead, aerial voyages on Faust's magic cloak, omniscience, etc., will soon be arts as common as reading and writing, it is not the discoveries of science which have brought them to this delusion, although the existing delusion is happy to be able to pass itself off for science. Far from concealing itself, as formerly, it exhibits itself proudly in the streets on the arms of professors and academicians. Paulhan understands the matter very well: 'It is not the love of positive facts,' he says,* 'which has carried minds away; there has been a certain kind of return for the love of the marvellous in desires formerly satisfied, and which, now repressed, slumbered unacknowledged in a latent condition. Magic, sorcery, astrology, divination, all these ancient beliefs correspond to a need of human nature; that of being able easily to act upon the external world and the social world; that of possessing, by means relatively easy, the knowledge requisite to make this action possible and fruitful.' The stormy outburst of superstition has by no means been let loose through hypnological researches; it merely launches itself into the channels they have dug. We have here already repeatedly drawn attention to the fact that unbalanced minds always adapt their crazes to the prevailing views, and usurp by predilection the most recent discoveries of science to explain them. The physicists were still far from occupying themselves with magnetism and electricity, when the persons attacked by persecution-mania were already referring their own unpleasant sensations and hallucinations to the electric currents or sparks which their persecutors were supposed to cast on them through walls, ceilings and floors; and in our days the degenerate were equally the first to appropriate to themselves the results of hypnological researches, and to employ them as 'scientific' proofs of the reality of spirits, angels and devils. But the degenerate started with the belief in miracles; it is one of their peculiar characteristics,† and it was not first called forth by the observations of Parisian and Nancy hypnologists.

If another proof were needed in support of this affirmation, it could be found in the fact that the greater number of 'occultists,' as they call themselves, in their treatises on occult arts and magic sciences, scorn to fall back on the results of hypnological experiments, and, without any pretext of 'modernity,' without any concession to honest investigation of nature, have direct recourse to the most ancient traditions. Papus (the pseudonym of a physician, Dr. Encausse) writes a *Traité méthodique de Science occulte*, an enormous large-octavo volume of 1,050 pages, with 400 illustrations, which introduces the reader to the cabala, magic, necromancy and

* F. Paulhan, *Le nouveau Mysticisme.* Paris, 1891, p. 104.

† Legrain, *op. cit.*, p. 175: 'The need for the marvellous is almost always inevitable among the weak-minded.'

cheiromancy, astrology, alchemy, etc., and to which an old, not undeserving savant, Adolf Franck, of the Institute of France, was imprudent enough to write a long eulogistic preface, presumably without having even opened the book himself. Stanislaus de Guaita, revered with awe by the adepts as past master in the Black Art, and arch-magician, gives two treatises, *Au Seuil du Mystère* and *Le Serpent de la Genèse,* so darkly profound that, in comparison, Nicolas Flamel, the great alchemist, whom no mortal has ever comprehended, seems clear and transparent as crystal. Ernest Bosc confines himself to the theory of the sorcery of the ancient Egyptians. His book, *Isis dévoilée, ou l'Egyptologie sacrée,* has for the sub-title: 'Hieroglyphics, papyri, hermetic books, religion, myths, symbols, psychology, philosophy, morals, sacred art, occultism, mysteries, initiation, music.' Nehor has likewise his speciality. If Bosc unveils Egyptian mysteries, Nehor reveals the secrets of Assyria and Babylonia. *Les Mages et le Secret magique* is the name of the modest pamphlet in which he initiates us into the profoundest magic arts of the Chaldean Mobeds, or Knights Templars.

If I do not enter more fully into these books, which have found readers and admirers, it is because I am not quite certain that they are intended to be in earnest. Their authors read and translate so fluently Egyptian, Hebraic and Assyriac texts, which no professional Orientalist has yet deciphered; they quote so frequently and so copiously from books which are found in no library in the world; they give with such an imperturbable air exact instructions how to resuscitate the dead, how to preserve eternal youth, how to hold intercourse with the inhabitants of Sirius, how to divine beyond all the limits of time and space, that one cannot get rid of the impression that they wished, in cold blood, to make fun of the reader.

Only one of all these master-sorcerers is certainly to be taken in good faith, and as he is at the same time intellectually the most eminent among them, I will deal with him somewhat more in detail. This is M. Joséphin Péladan. He has even arrogated to himself the Assyrian royal title of 'Sar,' under which he is generally known. The public authorities alone do not give him his Sar title; but then they do not usually recognise any titles of nobility in France. He maintains he is the descendant of the old Magi, and the possessor of all the mental legacies of Zoroaster, Pythagoras and Orpheus. He is, moreover, the direct heir of the Knights Templars and Rosicrucians, both of which orders he has amalgamated and revived under a new form as the 'Order of the Rosy Cross.' He dresses himself archaically in a satin doublet of blue or black; he trims his extremely luxuriant blue-black hair and beard into the shape in use among the Assyrians; he affects a large upright hand, which might be taken for mediæval character, writes by preference with red or yellow ink, and in the corner of his letter-paper is delineated, as a distinctive mark of his dignity, the Assyrian king's cap, with the three serpentine rolls opening in front. As a coat of arms he has the device of his order; on an escutcheon divided by sable and argent a golden chalice surmounted by a crimson rose with two outspread wings, and overlaid with a Latin cross in sable. The shield is surmounted by a coronet with three pentagrams as indents. M. Péladan has appointed a series of commanders and dignitaries of his order ('grand-priors,' 'archons,' 'æsthetes'), which numbers, besides, 'postulants' and 'grammarians' (scholars). He possesses a special costume as grand-master and Sar (in which his life-sized portrait has been painted by Alexandre Séon), and a composer, who belongs to the order, has composed for him a special fanfare, which on solemn occasions is to be played by trumpets at his entrance. He makes use of extraordinary formulæ. His letters he calls 'decrees,' or commands (*mandements*). He addresses the persons to whom they are directed either as 'magnifiques,' or 'peers,' sometimes also 'dearest adelphe,' or 'synnoède.' He does not call them 'sir,' but 'your lordship' (*seigneurie*). The introduction is: 'Health, light and victory in Jesus Christ, in the only God, and in Peter, the only king'; or '*Ad Rosam per Crucem, ad Crucem per Rosam, in eâ, in eis gemmatus resurgam.*' This is at the same time the heraldic motto of the Order of the Rosy Cross. At the conclusion is usually, '*Amen. Non nobis, Domine, non nobis, sed nominis tui gloriæ solæ.*' He writes the name of his order, with a cross inserted in the middle, thus: '*Rose* ✠ *Croix.*' His novels he calls '*éthopées*,' himself as their author '*éthopoète*,' his dramas '*wagneries*,' their table of contents '*éumolpées*.'

Every one of his books is ornamented with a large number of symbols. That which appears the most often is a vignette showing on a column a cowering form with the head of a woman breathing flames, and with a woman's breast, lion's paws, and the lower part of the body of a wasp or dragon-fly, terminating in an appendage similar to the tail of a fish. The work itself is always preceded by some prefaces, introductions and invocations, and is often followed by pages of the same nature. I take as an example the book entitled, *Comment on devient Mage*.* After the two title-pages adorned with a great number of symbolical images (winged Assyrian bulls, the mystic rose cross, etc.), comes a long dedication 'to Count Antoine de la Rochefoucauld, grand-prior of the temple, archon of the

* Sar Mérodack J. Péladan, *Amphithéatre des Sciences mortes. Comment on devient Mage.* Éthique. Avec un portrait pittoresque gravé par G. Poirel. Paris, 1892.

Rose ✠ Cross.' Then follows in Latin a 'prayer of St. Thomas Aquinas, well suited to warn the reader against the possible errors of this book'; after this, an *élenctique* (counter-demonstration) containing a sort of profession of Catholic faith; next, an 'invocation to ancestors' in the style of the Chaldean prayers; lastly, a long allocution 'to the contemporary young man,' after which the book properly begins.

At the head of every chapter appear nine mysterious formulæ. Here are two examples: 'I. The Neophyte. Divine Name: Jud (the Hebrew letter so called). Sacrament: Baptism. Virtue: Faith. Gift: Fear of God. Beatitude: Poor in spirit. Work: Teaching. Angel: Michael. Arcanum: Unity. Planet: Samas. II. Society. Divine Name: Jah—El (in Hebrew characters, which Péladan evidently cannot read, for he turns it into El-lah). Sacrament: Consecration. Virtue: Hope. Gift: Pity. Beatitude: Gentleness. Work: Counsel. Angel: Gabriel. Arcanum: Duality. Planet: Sin.'

Of the further contents of this mighty volume I think no examples need be given. They correspond exactly with the headings of these chapters.

The novels or 'éthopées' of M. Péladan, of which nine have appeared hitherto, but of which the author has announced fourteen, are arranged in groups of seven, the mystical number. He has even established a *Schéma de Concordance*,* which claims to give a synopsis of their leading ideas. Let us hear how he explains his works:

'First series of seven: I. The supreme vice. Moral and mental Diathesis of the Latin decline—Merodach, summit of conscious will, type of absolute entity; Alta, prototype of the monk in contact with the world; Courtenay, inadequate man-of-fate, bewitched by social facts; L. d'Este, extreme pride, the grand style in evil; Coryse, the true young maiden; La Nine, the wicked Androgyne, or, better, Gynander; Dominicaux, conscious reprobate, character of the irremediable, resulting from a specious æsthetic theory for every vice, which kills consciousness and, in consequence, conversion. Every novel has a Merodach, that is, an abstract Orphic principle, as opposed to an ideal enigma.

'II. Inquisitive. Parisian clinical collective-phenomenism. Ethics: Nebo; the systematic, sentimental will. Erotics: Paula, passionate with Androgynous Prism. The great horror, the Beast with two backs, in Gynander (IX.), metamorphosing itself into unisexual corruption. Inquisitive, that is the everyday and the everybody of instinct. Gynander, the Goethesque midnight, and the exceptional,' etc.

* Joséphin Péladan, *La Décadence latine*. Ethopée IX.: 'La Gynandre.' Couverture de Séon, eau-forte de Desboutins. Paris, 1891, p. xvii.

I have taken pains to reproduce faithfully all M. Péladan's whimsical methods of expression. That his *Concordance* can give even the slightest idea of the contents of his novels, I do not for a moment believe. I will, therefore, say a few words about these in non-magian language.

They all move in the three following circles of ideas, variously penetrating and intersecting each other: The highest intellectual aim of man is to hear and thoroughly to appreciate Wagnerian music; the highest development of morality consists in renouncing sexuality and in transforming one's self into a hybrid hermaphrodite (Androgyne and Gynander); the higher man can quit and retake his body at pleasure, soar into space as an 'astral being,' and subject to his will the entire supernatural power of the world of spirits, of the good as well as the bad.

Accordingly, in every romance a hero appears who unites in himself the distinctive marks of both sexes, and resists with horror the ordinary sexual instincts, who plays or enjoys the music of Wagner, enacts in his own life some scene from the Wagnerian drama, and conjures up spirits or has to repel their attacks.

If anyone wishes to trace the origin of all these delirious ideas, it will not be difficult to discover how they arose. One day while reading the Bible Péladan alighted on the name of the Babylonian king, Merodach Baladan. The similarity of sound between 'Baladan' and 'Péladan' gave an impulse to his imagination to establish relations between himself and the Biblical Babylonian king. Once he began to reflect on this, he found a resemblance, in the cast of his features, the colour of his hair, and the growth of his beard, to the heads of Assyrian kings on the alabaster casts from the palace at Nineveh. Thus he easily arrived at the idea that he was possibly a descendant of Baladan, or of other Assyrian kings, or, at least, that it would be a curious thing if he were. And he continued to work out this thought, until one day he resolutely took the title of Sar. If he were descended from the kings of Babylon, he could also be the heir of the wisdom of the Magi. So he began to proclaim the Magian esoteric doctrine. To these musings were added afterwards the impressions he received on a pilgrimage to Bayreuth, from *Tristan*, and especially from *Parsifal*. In fancy he wrought his own life into the legend of the Grail, looked upon himself as a knight of the Grail, and created his order of the 'Rose Croix,' which is entirely composed of reminiscences of *Parsifal*. His invention of the asexual hybrid being shows that his imagination is actively preoccupied with presentations of a sexual character, and unconsciously seeks to idealize the 'contrary sexual feelings.'

The mental life of Péladan permits us to follow, in an extremely well-marked instance, the ways of mystic thought. He is wholly dominated by the association of ideas. A fortuitous assonance awakens in him a train of thought which urges him irresistibly to proclaim himself an Assyrian king and Magus, without his attention being in a condition to make him realize the fact that a man can be called Péladan without being, therefore, necessarily descended from a Biblical Baladan. The meaningless flow of words of the mediæval scholastics misleads him, because he is continually thinking by way of analogy, that is to say, because he follows exclusively the play of the association of ideas provoked by the most secondary and superficial resemblances. He receives every artistic suggestion with the greatest ease. If he hears Wagner's operas, he believes himself to be a Wagnerian character; if he reads of the Knights Templars and Rosicrucians, he becomes the Grand-Master of the Temple, and of all other secret orders. He has the peculiar sexual emotionalism of the 'higher degenerates,' and this endows him with a peculiar fabulous shape, which, at once chaste and lascivious, embodies, in curiously demonstrative manner, the secret conflicts which take place in his consciousness between unhealthily intensified instincts, and the judgment which recognises their dangerous character.

Does Péladan believe in the reality of his delusions? In other words, does he take himself seriously? The answer to this question is not so simple as many perhaps think. The two beings which exist in every human mind are, in a nature such as Péladan's, a prey to a strange conflict. His unconscious nature is quite transfused with the *rôle* of a Sar, a Magus, a Knight of the Holy Grail, Grand-Master of the Order, etc., which he has invented. The conscious factor in him knows that it is all nonsense, but it finds artistic pleasure in it, and permits the unconscious life to do as it pleases. It is thus that little girls behave who play with dolls, caressing or punishing them, and treating them as if they were living beings, all the time well aware that in reality they have before them only an object in leather and porcelain.

Péladan's judgment has no power over his unconscious impulses. It is not in his power to renounce the part of a Sar or a Magus, or no longer to pose as grand-master of an order. He cannot abstain from perpetually returning to his 'Androgynous' absurdity. All these aberrations, as well as the invention of neologisms and the predilection for symbols, the prolix titles, and the casket-series of prefaces, so characteristic of the 'higher degenerates,' proceed from the depths of his organic temperament, and evade the influence of his higher centres. On its conscious side Péladan's cerebral activity is rich and beautiful. In his novels there are pages which rank among the most splendid productions of a contemporary pen. His moral ideal is high and noble. He pursues with ardent hatred all that is base and vulgar, every form of egoism, falsehood, and thirst for pleasure; and his characters are thoroughly aristocratic souls, whose thoughts are concerned only with the worthiest, if somewhat exclusively artistic, interests of humanity. It is deeply to be regretted that the overgrowth of morbidly mystic presentations should render his extraordinary gifts completely sterile.

Far below Péladan stands Maurice Rollinat, who ought, nevertheless, to be mentioned first, because he embodies in a very instructive manner a definite form of mystic degeneration, and next because all French, and many foreign, hysterical persons honour in him a great poet.

In his poems, which with characteristic self-knowledge he entitles *Les Névroses** (Nervous Maladies) he betrays all the stigmata of degeneration, which by this time ought to be familiar enough to the reader for me to content myself with a brief notice of them.

He feels in himself criminal impulses (*Le Fantôme du Crime*):

'Wicked thoughts come into my soul in every place, at all hours, in the height of my work. . . . I listen in spite of myself to the infernal tones which vibrate in my heart where Satan knocks; and although I have a horror of vile saturnalias, of which the mere shadow suffices to anger me, I listen in spite of myself to the infernal tones. . . . The phantom of crime across my reason prowls around (in my skull). . . . Murder, rape, robbery, parricide, pass through my mind like fierce lightnings. . . .'

The spectacle of death and corruption has a strong attraction for him. He delights in putrefaction and revels in disease.

'My ghostly belovèd, snatched by death, played before me livid and purple. . . . Bony nakedness, chaste in her leanness! Hectic beauty as sad as it is ardent! . . . Near her a coffin . . . greedily opened its oblong jaws, and seemed to call her. . . .' (*L'Amante macabre*).

'Mademoiselle Squelette!
Je la surnommais ainsi:
Elle était si maigrelette!

'Crachant une gouttelette
De sang très peu cramoisi . . .
Elle était si maigrelette! . . .

'Sa phthisie étant complète; . . .
Sa figure verdelette . . .
Un soir, à l'espagnolette
Elle vint se pendre ici.

* Maurice Rollinat, *Les Névroses* (Les Ames—Les Suaires—Les Refuges—Les Spectres—Les Ténèbres). Avec un portrait de l'auteur par F. Desmoulin. Paris, 1883. Quite as striking is his later collection of poems, *L'Abîme*. Paris, 1891.

'Horreur ! une cordelette
Décapitait sans merci
Mademoiselle Squelette :
Elle était si maigrelette !'
Mademoiselle Squelette.

'That I might rescue the angelically beautiful dead from the horrible kisses of the worm I had her embalmed in a strange box. It was on a winter's night. From the ice-cold, stiff and livid body were taken out the poor defunct organs, and into the open belly, bloody and empty, were poured sweet-smelling salves. . . .' (*La Morte embaumée*).

'Flesh, eyebrows, hair, my coffin and my winding-sheet, the grave has eaten them all ; its work is done. . . . My skull has attested its shrinking, and I, a scaling, crumbling residue of death, have come to look back with regret upon the time when I was rotting, and the worm yet fasted not. . . .' (*Le mauvais Mort*).

This depravity of taste will not seldom be observed among the deranged. In Rollinat it merely inspires loathsome verses ; among others it leads them to the eager devouring of human excretions, and, in its worst forms, to being enamoured of a corpse (*Necrophilia*).

Violent erotomaniacal excitement expresses itself in a series of poems (*Les Luxures*), which not only celebrate the most unbridled sensuality, but also all the aberrations of sexual psychopathy.

But the most conspicuous are the sensations of undefined horrors which continually beset him. Everything inspires him with anguish ; all the sights of Nature appear to him to enclose some frightful mystery. He is always expecting, in trembling, some unknown terror.

'I always shudder at the strange look of some boot and some shoe. Ay, you may shrug your shoulders mockingly, I do shudder ; and suddenly, on thinking of the foot they cover, I ask myself : "Is it mechanical, or living ?" . . .' (*Le Maniaque*).

'My room is like my soul. . . . Heavy curtains, very ancient, cling round the deep bed ; long fantastic insects dance and crawl on the ceiling. When my clock strikes the hour it makes an appalling noise ; every swing of the pendulum vibrates, and is strangely prolonged. . . . Furniture, pictures, flowers, even the books, all smell of hell and poison ; and the horror, which loves me, envelops this prison like a pall. . . .' (*La Chambre*).

'The library made me think of very old forests ; thirteen iron lamps, oblong and spectral, poured their sepulchral light day and night on the faded books full of shadow and secrets. I always shuddered when I entered. I felt myself in the midst of fogs and death-rattles, drawn on by the arms of thirteen pale armchairs, and scanned by the eyes of thirteen great portraits. . . .' (*La Bibliothèque*).

'In the swamp full of malice, which clogs and penetrates his stockings, he hears himself faintly called by several voices making but one. He finds a corpse as sentinel, which rolls its dull eyeballs, and moves its corruption with an automatic spring. I show to his dismayed eyes fires in the deserted houses, and in the forsaken parks beds full of green rose . . . . And the old cross on the calvary hails him from afar, and curses him, crossing its stern arms as it stretches out and brandishes them. . . .' (*La Peur*).

I will not weary by multiplying examples, and will only quote the titles of a few more poems: *The Living Grave; Troppmann's Soliloquy* (a well-known eight-fold murderer); *The Crazy Hangman; The Monster; The Madman; The Headache* (*La Céphalalgie*); *The Disease; The Frenzied Woman; Dead Eyes; The Abyss; Tears; Anguish; The Slow Death-struggle; The Interment; The Coffin; The Death-knell; Corruption; The Song of the Guillotined*, etc.

All these poems are the production of a craze, which will be frequently observed among degenerates. Even Dostojevski, who is known to have been mentally afflicted, suffered from it also. 'As soon as it grew dusk,' he relates of himself,* 'I gradually fell into that state of mind which so often overmasters me at night since I have been ill, and which I shall call mystic fright. It is a crushing anxiety about something which I can neither define nor even conceive, which does not actually exist, but which perhaps is about to be realized suddenly, at this very moment, to appear and rise up before me like an inexorable, horrible, unshapen fact.' Legrain† quotes a degenerate lunatic whose mania began 'with feelings of fear and anguish at some fancy.' Professor Kowalewski ‡ indicates as degrees of mental derangement in degeneration—first, neurasthenia; secondly, impulses of 'obsession' and feelings of morbid anguish. Legrand du Saulle § and Morel ‖ describe this state of groundless, undefined fear, and coin for it the not very happy word 'Panophobia.' Magnan calls it more correctly 'Anxiomania'—frenzied anguish—and speaks of it as a very common stigma of degeneration. The anguish mania is an error of consciousness, which is filled with presentations of fear, and transfers their cause into the external world, while, as a matter of fact, they are stimulated by pathological processes within the organism. The invalid feels oppressed and uneasy, and imputes

* *Humiliés et Offensés*, p. 55; quoted by De Vogüé, *Le Roman russe*, p. 222, foot-note.

† Legrain, *op. cit.*, p. 246.

‡ *Journal of Mental Science*, January, 1888.

§ *Le Délire des Persécutions*. Paris, 1871, p. 512.

‖ Morel, 'Du Délire panophobique des Aliénés gémisseurs.' *Annales médico-psychologiques*, 1871, 2e vol., p. 322.

to the phenomena which surround him a threatening and sinister aspect, in order to explain to himself his dread, the origin of which escapes him, because it is rooted in the unconscious.

As in Rollinat we have learnt to know the poet of anxiomania, so shall we find in another author, whose name has become widely known in the last two years, in the Belgian, Maurice Maeterlinck, an example of an utterly childish idiotically-incoherent mysticism. He reveals the state of his mind most characteristically in his poems,* of which I will give a few examples. Here is the first of the collection—*Serres chaudes*:

'O hot-house in the middle of the woods. And your doors ever closed! And all that is under your dome! And under my soul in your analogies!

'The thoughts of a princess who is hungry; the tedium of a sailor in the desert; a brass-band under the windows of incurables.

'Go into the warm moist corners! One might say, 'tis a woman fainting on harvest-day. In the courtyard of the infirmary are postilions; in the distance an elk-hunter passes by, who now tends the sick.

'Examine in the moonlight! (Oh, nothing there is in its place!) One might say, a madwoman before judges, a battle-ship in full sail on a canal, night-birds on lilies, a death-knell towards noon (down there under those bells), a halting-place for the sick in the meadows, a smell of ether on a sunny day.

'My God! my God! when shall we have rain and snow and wind in the hot-house?'

These idiotic sequences of words are psychologically interesting, for they demonstrate with instructive significance the workings of a shattered brain. Consciousness no longer elaborates a leading or central idea. Representations emerge just as the wholly mechanical association of ideas arouses them. There is no attention seeking to bring order into the tumult of images as they come and go, to separate the unconnected, to suppress those that contradict each other, and to group those which are allied into a single logical series.

A few more examples of these fugitive thoughts exclusively under the rule of unbridled association. Here is one entitled *Bell-glasses* (*Cloches de verre*):

'O bell-glasses! Strange plants for ever under shelter! While the wind stirs my senses without! A whole valley of the soul for ever still! And the enclosed lush warmth towards noon! And the pictures seen through the glass!

'Never remove one of them! Several have been placed on old moonlight. Look through their foliage. There is perhaps a vagabond on a throne; one has the impression that corsairs

* Maurice Maeterlinck, *Serres chaudes*. Nouvelle édition. Bruxelles, 1890.

are waiting on the pond, and that antediluvian beings are about to invade the towns.

'Some have been placed on old snows. Some have been placed on ancient rains. (Pity the enclosed atmosphere!) I hear a festival solemnized on a famine Sunday; there is an ambulance in the middle of the house, and all the daughters of the king wander on a fast-day across the meadows.

'Examine specially those of the horizon! They cover carefully very old thunderstorms. Oh, there must be somewhere an immense fleet on a marsh! And I believe that the swans have hatched ravens. (One can scarcely distinguish through the dampness.)

'A maiden sprinkles the ferns with hot water; a troop of little girls watch the hermit in his cell; my sisters have fallen asleep on the floor of a poisonous grotto!

'Wait for the moon and the winter, among these bells, scattered at last on the ice.'

Another called *Soul* (*Ame*):

'My soul! O my soul truly too much sheltered! And these flocks of desires in a hot-house! Awaiting a storm in the meadows! Let us go to the most sickly: they have strange exhalations. In the midst of them I cross a battlefield with my mother. They are burying a brother-in-arms at noon, while the sentries take their repast.

'Let us go also to the weakest; they have strange sweats: here is a sick bride, treachery on Sunday, and little children in prison. (And further across the mist.) Is it a dying woman at the door of a kitchen? Or a nun, who cleans vegetables at the foot of the bed of an incurable?

'Let us go lastly to the saddest: (at the last because they have poisons). O my lips accept the kisses of one wounded!

'All the ladies of the castle are dead of hunger this summer in the towers of my soul! Here is the dawn, which enters into the festival! I have a glimpse of sheep along the quays, and there is a sail at the windows of the hospital!

'It is a long road from my heart to my soul! And all the sentries are dead at their posts!

'One day there was a poor little festival in the suburbs of my soul! They mowed the hemlock there one Sunday morning; and all the convent virgins saw the ships pass by on the canal one sunny fast-day. While the swans suffered under a poisonous bridge. The trees were lopped about the prison; medicines were brought one afternoon in June, and meals for the patients were spread over the whole horizon!

'My soul! And the sadness of it all, my soul! and the sadness of it all!'

I have translated with the greatest exactness, and not omitted one word of the three 'poems.' Nothing would be easier than to compose others on these models, overtrumping even those of Maeterlinck—*e.g.*, 'O Flowers! And we groan so heavily under the very old taxes! An hour-glass, at which the dog barks in May; and the strange envelope of the negro who has not slept. A grandmother who would eat oranges and could not write! Sailors in a ballroom, but blue! blue! On the bridge this crocodile and the policeman with the swollen cheek beckons silently! O two soldiers in the cowhouse, and the razor is notched! But the chief prize they have not drawn. And on the lamp are ink-spots!' etc. But why parody Maeterlinck? His style bears no parody, for it has already reached the extreme limits of idiocy. Nor is it quite worthy of a mentally sound man to make fun of a poor devil of an idiot.

Certain of his poems consist simply of assonances, linked together without regard to sense and meaning, *e.g.*, one which is entitled *Ennui:*

'The careless peacocks, the white peacocks have flown, the white peacocks have flown from the tedium of awaking; I see the white peacocks, the peacocks of to-day, the peacocks that went away during my sleep, the careless peacocks, the peacocks of to-day, reach lazily the pond where no sun is, I hear the white peacocks, the peacocks of ennui, waiting lazily for the times when no sun is.'

The French original reveals why these words were chosen; they contain almost all the nasal sounds, 'en,' or 'an,' or 'aon': '*Les paons nonchalants, les paons blancs ont fui, les paons blancs ont fui l'ennui du réveil; je vois les paons blancs . . . atteindre indolents l'étang sans soleil*,' etc. This is a case of that form of echolalia which is observed not seldom among the insane. One patient says, *e.g.*, '*Man kann dann ran Mann wann Clan Bann Schwan Hahn*,' and he continues to grind similar sounds till he is either tired, or takes a word spoken before him as a starting-point for a new series of rhymes.

If Maeterlinck's poems are read with some attention, it is soon seen that the muddled pictures which follow each other pell-mell as in a dream, are borrowed from a very limited circle of ideas, which have either generally, or only for him, an emotional content. 'Strange,' 'old,' 'distant,' are the adjectives he constantly repeats; they have this in common that they indicate something indistinct, not definitely recognisable, away on the bounds of the distant horizon, corresponding, therefore, to the nebulous thought of mysticism. Another adjective which sets him dreaming is 'slow' (*lent*). It also influences the French Symbolists, and hence their fondness for it. They evidently associated it with the idea of the movements of the priest reading the Mass, and it awakens in them the emotions of the mysticism of faith. They betray this association of ideas by this, that they frequently use *lent* together with *hiératique* (sacerdotal). Maeterlinck, moreover, is constantly thinking of hospitals with their sick, and of everything connected with them (nuns, invalids' diet, medicines, surgical operations, bandages, etc.), of canals with ships and swans, and of princesses. The hospitals and the canals, which are a feature in the Belgian landscape, may be connected with the first impressions of his childhood, and therefore produce emotions in him. The princesses, on the contrary, shut up in towers, suffering hunger, going astray, wading through swamps, etc., have evidently remained fixed in his imagination from the childish ballads of the pre-Raphaelites, one of which, by Swinburne, was given above as an example. Hospitals, canals, princesses, these are the pictures which always recur with the obstinacy of obsessions, and in the midst of the nebulous chaos of his jargon, alone show some sort of firm outline.

A few of his poems are written in the traditional poetical form ; others, on the contrary, have neither measure nor rhyme, but consist of lines of prose, arbitrarily changing in length, not according to the style of Goethe's free poems, or of Heine's *North Sea Songs*, which ripple by with very strongly marked rhythmic movement, but deaf, jolting and limping, as the items of an inventory. These pieces are a servile imitation of the effusions of Walt Whitman, that crazy American to whom Maeterlinck was necessarily strongly attracted, according to the law I have repeatedly set forth—that all deranged minds flock together.

I should like here to interpolate a few remarks on Walt Whitman, who is likewise one of the deities to whom the degenerate and hysterical of both hemispheres have for some time been raising altars. Lombroso ranks him expressly among 'mad geniuses.'* Mad Whitman was without doubt. But a

* Lombroso, *Genie und Irrsinn*, p. 322 : 'Walt Whitman, the poet of the modern Anglo-Americans, and assuredly a mad genius, was a typographer, teacher, soldier, joiner, and for some time also a bureaucrat, which, for a poet, is the queerest of trades.'

This constant changing of his profession Lombroso rightly characterizes as one of the signs of mental derangement. A French admirer of Whitman, Gabriel Sarrazin (*La Renaissance de la Poésie anglaise*, 1798—1889 ; Paris, 1889, p. 270, footnote), palliates this proof of organic instability and weakness of will in the following manner : 'This American facility of changing from one calling to another goes against our old European prejudices, and our unalterable veneration for thoroughly hierarchical, bureaucratic routine-careers. We have remained in this, as in so many other respects, essentially narrow-minded, and cannot understand that diversity of capacities gives a man a very much greater social value.' This is the true method of the æsthetic windbag, who for every fact which he does not understand finds roundly-turned phrases with which he explains and justifies everything to his own satisfaction.

genius? That would be difficult to prove. He was a vagabond, a reprobate rake, and his poems* contain outbursts of erotomania so artlessly shameless that their parallel in literature could hardly be found with the author's name attached. For his fame he has to thank just those bestially sensual pieces which first drew to him the attention of all the pruriency of America. He is morally insane, and incapable of distinguishing between good and evil, virtue and crime. 'This is the deepest theory of susceptibility,' he says in one place, 'without preference or exclusion; the negro with the woolly head, the bandit of the highroad, the invalid, the ignorant—none are denied.' And in another place he explains he 'loves the murderer and the thief, the pious and good, with equal love.' An American driveller, W. D. O'Connor, has called him on this account 'The good gray Poet.' We know, however, that this 'goodness,' which is in reality moral obtuseness and morbid sentimentality, frequently accompanies degeneration, and appears even in the cruellest assassins, for example, in Ravachol.

He has megalomania, and says of himself:

'From this hour I decree that my being be freed from all restraints and limits.

'I go where I will, my own absolute and complete master.

'I breathe deeply in space. The east and the west are mine.

'Mine are the north and south. I am greater and better than I thought myself.

'I did not know that so much boundless goodness was in me. . . .

'Whoever disowns me causes me no annoyance.

'Whoever recognises me shall be blessed, and will bless me.'

He is mystically mad, and announces: 'I have the feeling of all. I am all, and believe in all. I believe that materialism is true, and that spiritualism is also true; I reject nothing.' And in another still more characteristic passage:

'Santa Spirita [*sic!*], breather, life,
Beyond the light, lighter than light,
Beyond the flames of hell, joyous, leaping easily above hell,
Beyond Paradise, perfumed solely with mine own perfume,
Including all life on earth, touching, including God, including Saviour and Satan,
Ethereal, pervading all, for without me what were all? what were God?
Essence of forms, life of the real identities . . .
Life of the great round world, the sun and stars, and of man, I, the general soul.'

In his patriotic poems he is a sycophant of the corrupt American vote-buying, official-bribing, power-abusing, dollar-democracy, and a cringer to the most arrogant Yankee conceit.

* Walt Whitman, *Leaves of Grass;* a new edition. Glasgow, 1884.

His war-poems—the much renowned *Drum Taps*—are chiefly remarkable for swaggering bombast and stilted patter.

His purely lyrical pieces, with their ecstatic 'Oh!' and 'Ah!' with their soft phrases about flowers, meadows, spring and sunshine, recall the most arid, sugary and effeminate passages of our old Gessner, now happily buried and forgotten.

As a man, Walt Whitman offers a surprising resemblance to Paul Verlaine, with whom he shared all the stigmata of degeneration, the vicissitudes of his career, and, curiously enough, even the rheumatic ankylosis. As a poet, he has thrown off the closed strophe as too difficult, measure and rhyme as too oppressive, and has given vent to his emotional fugitive ideation in hysterical exclamations, to which the definition of 'prose gone mad' is infinitely better suited than it is to the pedantic, honest hexameters of Klopstock. Unconsciously, he seemed to have used the parallelism of the Psalms, and Jeremiah's eruptive style, as models of form. We had in the last century the *Paramythien* of Herder, and the insufferable 'poetical prose' of Gessner already mentioned. Our healthy taste soon led us to recognise the inartistic, retrogressive character of this lack of form, and that error in taste has found no imitator among us for a century. In Whitman, however, his hysterical admirers commend this *réchauffé* of a superannuated literary fashion as something to come; and admire, as an invention of genius, what is only an incapacity for methodical work. Nevertheless, it is interesting to point out that two persons so dissimilar as Richard Wagner and Walt Whitman have, in different spheres, under the pressure of the same motives, arrived at the same goal—the former at 'infinite melody,' which is no longer melody; the latter at verses which are no longer verses, both in consequence of their incapacity to submit their capriciously vacillating thoughts to the yoke of those rules which in 'infinite' melody, as in lyric verse, govern by measure and rhyme.

Maeterlinck, then, in his poems is a servile imitator of crazy Walt Whitman, and carries his absurdities still further. Besides his poems he has written things to which one cannot well refuse the name of plays, since they are cast in the form of dialogues. The best known of them is *The Princess Maleine*.*

The 'dramatis personæ,' as he, true to the romantic and mystical practice of the pre-Raphaelites and Symbolists, entitles the list of his characters, are as follows: Hjalmar, King of one part of Holland; Marcellus, King of another part of Holland; Prince Hjalmar, son of King Hjalmar; little Allan, son of Queen Anne; Angus, friend to Prince Hjalmar; Stephano and

* Maurice Maeterlinck, *The Princess Maleine and the Intruder*. London: W. Heinemann, 1892.

Vanox, officers of Marcellus ; Anne, Queen of Jutland ; Godeliva, wife of King Marcellus ; Princess Maleine, daughter of Marcellus and Godeliva ; Maleine's nurse ; Princess Uglyane, daughter of Queen Anne. With them come all the old well-known jointed dolls and puppets out of the dustiest corners of the old lumber-rooms of romance—a fool, three poor people, two old peasants, courtiers, pilgrims, a cripple, beggars, vagabonds, an old woman, seven (the mystic number !) nuns, etc.

The names which Maeterlinck gives to his figures should be noted. As a Fleming, he knows very well that Hjalmar is not Dutch, but Scandinavian ; that Angus is Scotch. But he makes this confusion intentionally, in order to obliterate the distinct outlines with which he appears to surround his figures, when he calls them 'Kings of Holland'; in order again to detach them from the firm ground on which he pretends to place them and to suppress their co-ordinates, which assign them a place in space and time. They may wear clothes, have names and take a human rank, but all the while they are only shadows and clouds.

King Hjalmar comes with Prince Hjalmar to the castle of Marcellus in order to ask for the hand of the Princess Maleine. The two young people see each other for the first time, and only for a few minutes, but they instantly fall in love with each other. At the banquet in honour of the King a quarrel breaks out, about which we learn no particulars ; King Hjalmar is seriously offended, swears revenge, and leaves the castle in a rage. In the interlude Hjalmar wages war against Marcellus, kills him and his wife, Godeliva, and at once razes his castle and town to the ground. Princess Maleine and her nurse were on this occasion — how, why and by whom is not explained — immured in a vaulted room in a tower ; then the nurse, after three' days work with her finger-nails, loosens a stone in the wall, and the two women obtain their liberty.

Since Maleine loves Hjalmar and cannot forget him, they make their way towards his father's castle. Things are going very badly in Hjalmar's castle. There Queen Anne of Jütland resides, who has been driven away by her subjects, and with her grown-up daughter Uglyane and her little son Allan (here also the Dane is systematically given a Scottish name), has found hospitality with King Hjalmar. Queen Anne has turned the head of the old man. She has become his mistress, rules him completely, and makes him ill in body and soul. She wishes that his son should marry her daughter. Hjalmar is in despair about his father's collapse. He detests his morganatic step-mother, and shudders at the thought of a marriage with Uglyane. He believes Maleine to have been slain with her parents in the war, but he cannot yet forget her.

Maleine has in the meantime been wandering with her nurse

through a kind of enchanted forest, and through an incomprehensible village, where she has uncanny meetings with all sorts of people, beggars, vagabonds, peasants, old women, etc., interchanging odd talk, and reaches Hjalmar's castle, where no one knows her. She is, however, in spite of this, at once appointed as lady-in-waiting to the Princess Uglyane.

One evening Prince Hjalmar decides to make advances to Uglyane, and with that object he gives her a nocturnal rendezvous in the park of the castle, not a secret, but, so to speak, an official, lovers' tryst, to which he, with his father's consent, and she, with her mother's, is to go. Maleine hinders it by telling Uglyane, who is splendidly attiring and adorning herself, that Prince Hjalmar has gone into the forest and will not come. She then goes herself into the park, and makes herself known to Hjalmar, who arrives punctually. He leads her in great delight to his father, who receives her as his future daughter-in-law, and there is no further talk of his betrothal to Uglyane. Queen Anne determines to get rid of the intruder. She behaves at first in a friendly manner, assigns her a beautiful room in the castle, then in the night she forces the King, who for a long time resists her, to penetrate into Maleine's room, where she puts a cord round the Princess's neck and strangles her. Signs and wonders accompany the deed : a tempest forces open a window, a comet appears, a wing of the castle falls in ruins, a forest bursts into flames, swans fall wounded out of the air, etc., etc.

Next morning the body of the Princess Maleine is discovered. King Hjalmar, whom the night's murder has robbed of the last remnant of reason, betrays the secret of the deed. Prince Hjalmar stabs Queen Anne, and then plunges the dagger into his own heart. Thereupon the piece closes thus :

NURSE. Come away, my poor lord.

KING. Good God ! good God ! She is waiting now on the wharf of hell !

NURSE. Come away ! come away !

KING. Is there anybody here that fears the curses of the dead?

ANGUS. Ay, my lord, I do.

KING. Well, you close their eyes, and let us be gone.

NURSE. Ay, ay. Come hence ! come hence !

KING. I will ; I will. Oh, oh ! how lonely I shall feel hereafter ! I am steeped in misery up to my ears at seventy-seven years of age. But where are you ?

NURSE ! Here, here !

KING. You will not feel angry with me? Let us go to breakfast. Will there be salad for breakfast ? I should like a little salad.

NURSE. Yes, yes. You shall have some, my lord.

KING. I do not know why ; I feel somewhat melancholy to-day. Good God ! good God ! How unhappy the dead do look ! [*Exit with* NURSE.

ANGUS. Another night such as this, and all our heads will have turned white.

[*Exeunt all save the* NUNS, *who begin singing the Miserere while conveying the corpses towards the bed. The church bells cease sounding. Nightingales are heard warbling without. A cock jumps on the window-sill, and crows.*

When we begin to read this piece we are startled, and ask: 'Why is all this so familiar to me? Of what does it remind me?' After a few pages it all at once becomes clear: the whole thing is a kind of cento from Shakespeare! Every character, every scene, every speech in any way essential to the piece! King Hjalmar is put together out of King Lear and Macbeth; Lear in his madness and manner of expressing himself, Macbeth in his share in the murder of the Princess Maleine. Queen Anne is patched up out of Lady Macbeth and Queen Gertrude; Prince Hjalmar is unmistakably Hamlet, with his obscure speeches, his profound allusions and his inner struggles between filial duty and morality; the nurse is from Romeo and Juliet; Angus is Horatio; Vanox and Stephano are Rosenkranz and Guildenstern, with an admixture of Marcellus and Bernardo, and all the subordinate characters, the fool, the doctor, the courtiers, etc., bear the physiognomy of Shakespeare's characters.

The piece begins in the following manner:

The Gardens of the Castle.

Enter STEPHANO *and* VANOX.

VANOX. What o'clock is it?
STEPHANO. Judging from the moon, it should be midnight.
VANOX. I think 'tis going to rain.

Let us compare this with the first scene in *Hamlet:*

A platform before the Castle.

FRANCISCO . . . BERNARDO.

FRANCISCO. You come most carefully upon your hour.
BERNARDO. 'Tis now struck twelve. . . .
FRANCISCO. . . . 'Tis bitter cold, and I am sick at heart, etc.

One could, if it were worth while, trace scene for scene, word for word, from some passage in Shakespeare. In the *Princesse Maleine* we find in succession the fearfully stormy night from *Julius Cæsar* (Act I., Scene 3); the entrance of King Lear into the palace of Albany (Act I., Scene 4 . . . 'LEAR: Let me not stay a jot for dinner; go, get it ready,' etc.); the night scene in *Macbeth,* where Lady Macbeth induces her husband to commit murder; the thrice-repeated 'Oh! oh! oh!' of Othello which Queen Anne here utters; Hamlet's conversation with Horatio, etc. The death of the Princess Maleine has been inspired by memories both of Desdemona suffocated and of Cordelia hanged.. All this is jumbled up in the craziest manner, and often distorted almost beyond recognition, or given the opposite meaning; but, with a little attention, one can always find one's way.

Let us imagine a child, at the age when he is able to follow the conversation of grown-up people, attending a performance or a reading of *Hamlet, Lear, Macbeth, Romeo and Juliet* and *Richard II.*, and who on his return to the nursery should relate in his own way to his little brothers and sisters what he had heard. We should in this way get a correct idea of the composition of *Princesse Maleine.* Maeterlinck has crammed himself with Shakespeare, and reproduces the pieces undigested, yet repulsively altered and with the beginnings of foul decomposition. This is an unappetizing picture, but it alone can serve to illustrate the mental process which goes on in the so-called 'creations' of the degenerate. They read greedily, receive a very strong impression in consequence of their emotionalism; this pursues them with the force of an 'obsession,' and they do not rest till they have reproduced, sadly travestied, what they have read. Thus their works resemble the coins of the barbarians, which are imitations of Roman and Greek models, while betraying that their artificers could not read or understand the letters and symbols inscribed on them.

Maeterlinck's *Princesse Maleine* is a Shakespearian anthology for children or Tierra del Fuegians. The characters of the British poet have gone to make parts for the actors in a theatre of monkeys. They still remind us more or less of the attitudes and movements of the persons whom they ape, but they have not a human brain in their heads, and cannot say two connected and rational words. Here are a few examples of the manner in which Maeterlinck's people converse:

King Marcellus in the First Act (Scene 2) endeavours to dissuade the Princess Maleine from loving Hjalmar.

MARCELLUS. Well, Maleine!

MALEINE. My lord?

MARCELLUS. Do you not understand?

MALEINE. What, my lord?

MARCELLUS. Will you promise me to forget Hjalmar?

MALEINE. My lord! . . .

MARCELLUS. What say you? Do you still love Hjalmar?

MALEINE. Ay, my lord.

MARCELLUS. Ay, my lord. Oh, devils and tempests! she coolly confesses it. She dares to tell me this without shame. She has seen Hjalmar once only, for one single afternoon, and now she is hotter than hell.

GODELIVA. My lord! . . .

MARCELLUS. Be silent, you. "Ay, my lord!" and she is not yet fifteen! Ha! it makes one long to kill them then and there. . . .

GODELIVA. My lord. . . .

NURSE. Isn't she free to love, just like anyone else? Do you mean to put her under a glass case? Is this a reason to bully a poor child? She has done no harm. . . .

MARCELLUS. Oh, she has done no harm! . . . Now, in the first place, hold your peace, you. . . . I am not addressing you; and it is doubtless at your prompting, you procuress. . . .

GODELIVA. My lord! . . .

NURSE. A procuress! I a procuress!

MARCELLUS. Will you let me speak? Begone! begone, both of you! Oh! I know well enough you have put your heads together, and that the season of scheming and plotting has set in; but wait awhile. . . . Now, Maleine, . . . you should be reasonable. Will you promise to be reasonable?

MALEINE. Ay, my lord.

MARCELLUS. There! come now. Therefore you will not think any more of this marriage? . . .

MALEINE. Ay.

MARCELLUS. Ay? You mean you will forget Prince Hjalmar?

MALEINE. No.

MARCELLUS. You do not yet give up Prince Hjalmar?

MALEINE. No.

MARCELLUS. Now, supposing I compel you? Ay, I! and supposing I have you put under lock and key? and supposing I separate you for evermore from your Hjalmar with his puny, girlish face? What say you? (*She weeps.*) Ha! that's it—is 't? Begone, and we shall see about that—begone!

Next, the scene in the second act, where Maleine and Hjalmar meet in the gloomy park of the castle:

HJALMAR. . . . Come!

MALEINE. Not yet.

HJALMAR. Uglyane! Uglyane!

[*Kisses her. Here the waterfall, blown about by the wind, collapses and splashes them.*

MALEINE. Oh! what have you done?

HJALMAR. It is the fountain.

MALEINE. Oh, oh!

HJALMAR. It's the wind.

MALEINE. I am afraid.

HJALMAR. Think not of that any longer. Let us get further away. Let us not think of that any more. Ah, ah, ah! I am wet all over.

MALEINE. There is somebody weeping, close by us.

HJALMAR. Somebody weeping?

MALEINE. I am afraid.

HJALMAR. But cannot you hear that it's only the wind?

MALEINE. What are all those eyes on the tree, though?

HJALMAR. Where? Ha! those are the owls. They have returned. I will put them to flight. (*Throws earth at them.*) Away! away!

MALEINE. There is yonder one that will not go.

HJALMAR. Where is it?

MALEINE. On the weeping willow.

HJALMAR. Away!

MALEINE. He is not gone.

HJALMAR. Away, away! [*Throws earth at the owl.*

MALEINE. Oh! you have thrown earth on me.

HJALMAR. Thrown earth on you?

MALEINE. Ay, it fell on me.

HJALMAR. Oh, my poor Uglyane!

MALEINE. I am afraid.

HJALMAR. Afraid—at my side?

MALEINE. There are flames amid the trees.

HJALMAR. That is nothing—mere lightning. It has been very sultry to-day.

MALEINE. I am afraid. Oh! who can be digging so at the ground around us?

HJALMAR. That is nothing. 'Tis but a mole—a poor little mole at work.

(The mole in Hamlet! To our old acquaintance greeting!)

MALEINE. I am afraid.

After some more conversation in the same style:

HJALMAR. What are you thinking of?
MALEINE. I feel sad.
HJALMAR. Sad? Now, what are your sad thoughts about, Uglyane?
MALEINE. I am thinking of Princess Maleine.
HJALMAR. What do you say?
MALEINE. I am thinking of Princess Maleine.*
HJALMAR. Do you know Princess Maleine?
MALEINE. I am Princess Maleine.
HJALMAR. You are not Uglyane?
MALEINE. I am Princess Maleine.
HJALMAR. What! you Princess Maleine? Dead! But Princess Maleine is dead!
MALEINE. I am Princess Maleine.

Has anyone anywhere in the poetry of the two worlds ever seen such complete idiocy? These 'Ahs' and 'Ohs,' this want of comprehension of the simplest remarks, this repetition four or five times of the same imbecile expressions, gives the truest conceivable clinical picture of incurable cretinism. These parts are precisely those most extolled by Maeterlinck's admirers. According to them, all has been chosen with a deep artistic intention. A healthy reader will scarcely swallow that. Maeterlinck's puppets say nothing, because they have nothing to say. Their author has not been able to put a single thought into their hollow skulls, because he himself possesses none. The creatures moving on his stage are not thinking and speaking human beings, but tadpoles or slugs, considerably more stupid than trained fleas at a fair.

Moreover, *Princesse Maleine* is not altogether a Shakespearian dream. The 'seven nuns,' *e.g.*, belong to Maeterlinck. They are an astounding invention. They are ever marching like demented geese through the piece, winding in and out, with their psalm-singing, through all the rooms and corridors of the King's castle, through the court, through the park, through the forest, coming unexpectedly round a corner in the middle of a scene, trotting across the stage and off at the other side without anyone understanding whence they come, whither they go, or for what purpose they are brought on at all. They are a living 'obsession,' mixing itself irresistibly in all the incidents of the piece. Here also we find all the intellectual fads which we noticed in the *Serres Chaudes*. The Princess Maleine is herself the embodiment of the hungry, sick, strayed princesses, wandering over the meadows, who haunt these poems, and undoubtedly sprang from Swinburne's ballad of *The King's Daughters*. The canals also play their part (p. 18). 'And the expression of her eyes! It seemed as though one were all of a sudden in a great stream [Fr. *canal*] of fresh water. . . .' (p. 110). 'We have been to look at the windmills along the canal,' etc.

* Omitted in the English translation.—TRANSLATOR.

And sick people and illness are mentioned on almost every page (p. 110):

> ANNE. I was fever-stricken myself.
> THE KING. Everyone is fever-stricken on arriving here.
> HJALMAR. There is much fever in the village, etc.

Besides *Princesse Maleine,* Maeterlinck has written some other pieces. One, *L'Intruse* (The Intruder), deals with the idea that in a house where a sick person lies *in extremis,* Death intrudes towards midnight, that he walks audibly through the garden, makes at first a few trial strokes with his scythe on the grass before the castle, then knocks at the door, forces it open because they will not admit him, and carries off his victim. In a second, *Les Aveugles* (The Blind), we are shown how a number of blind men, the inmates of a blind asylum, were led by an old priest into a forest, how the priest died suddenly without a sound, how the blind men did not at first notice this, but becoming at length uneasy, groped about, succeeded in touching the corpse, already growing cold, assured themselves by questioning each other that their leader was dead, and then in terrible despair awaited death by hunger and cold. For this charming story takes place on a wild island in the far north; and between the wood and the asylum lies a river, crossed by only one bridge, which the blind cannot find without a guide. It never occurs either to Maeterlinck or to his inconsolable blind men as possible that in the asylum, where, as is expressly mentioned, there are attendant nuns, the long absence of the whole body of blind men would be noticed, and someone sent out to look for them. The reader will not expect me to point out in detail the craziness of the assumption in both these pieces, or that, after these examples, I should relate and analyze two other pieces of Maeterlinck's, *Les Sept Princesses* ('seven,' of course!) and *Pelléas et Mélisande.*

The Intruder has been translated into several languages, and performed in many towns. The Viennese laughed at its imbecility. In Paris and London men shook their heads. In Copenhagen an audience of appreciators of the 'poetry of the future' was touched, enraptured and inspired. This demonstrates the hysteria of to-day quite as much as the piece itself.

The history of Maeterlinck's celebrity is especially remarkable and instructive. This pitiable mental cripple vegetated for years wholly unnoticed in his corner in Ghent, without the Belgian Symbolists, who outbid even the French, according him the smallest attention; as to the public at large, no one had a suspicion of his existence. Then one fine day in 1890 his writings fell accidentally into the hands of the French novelist, Octave Mirbeau. He read them, and whether he desired to make fun of his contemporaries in grand style, or whether he obeyed some morbid 'impulsion' is not known; it is sufficient to say that he published in *Le Figaro* an article of an unheard-of extravagance, in which he represented Maeterlinck as the most brilliant, sublime, moving poet which the last three hundred years had produced, and assigned him a place near—nay, above Shakespeare. And then the world witnessed one of the most extraordinary and most convincing examples of the force of suggestion. The hundred thousand rich and cultivated readers to whom the *Figaro* addresses itself immediately took up the views which Mirbeau had imperiously suggested to them. They at once saw Maeterlinck with Mirbeau's eyes. They found in him all the beauties which Mirbeau asserted that he perceived in him. Andersen's fairy-tale of the invisible clothes of the emperor repeated itself line for line. They were not there, but the whole court saw them. Some imagined they really saw the absent state robes; the others did not see them, but rubbed their eyes so long that they at least doubted whether they saw them or not; others, again, could not impose upon themselves, but dared not contradict the rest. Thus Maeterlinck became at one stroke, by Mirbeau's favour, a great poet, and a poet of the 'future.' Mirbeau had also given quotations which would have completely sufficed for a reader who was not hysterical, not given over irresistibly to suggestion, to recognise Maeterlinck for what he is, namely, a mentally debilitated plagiarist; but these very quotations wrung cries of admiration from the *Figaro* public, for Mirbeau had pointed them out as beauties of the highest rank, and one knows that a decided affirmation is sufficient to compel hypnotic subjects to eat raw potatoes as oranges, and to believe themselves to be dogs or other quadrupeds.

Everywhere apostles were quickly at hand to proclaim, interpret and extol the new master. The 'mashers' of the critic world, whose ambition is set on being the first to assume—nay, where it is possible, to foretell—the very latest fashions, the fashion of to-morrow, as much in the styles of literature, as in the colour and shape of neckties, vied with each other in deifying Maeterlinck. Ten editions of his *Princesse Maleine* have been sold out since Mirbeau's suggestion, and, as I have said before, his *Aveugles* and *Intruse* have been performed in various places.

We now know the different forms under which the mysticism of degeneration manifests itself in contemporary literature. The magism of a Guaita and a Papus, the Androgyne of a Péladan, the anxiomania of a Rollinat, the idiotic drivelling of a Maeterlinck, may be regarded as its culminating aberrations. At least I cannot myself imagine that it would be possible for mysticism to go beyond, even by the thickness of a hair, these extreme points without even the hysterical, the devotees and the snobs of fashion, who are still in some degree capable of discernment, recognising in it a profound and complete intellectual darkness.

BOOK III.

EGO-MANIA.

CHAPTER I.

THE PSYCHOLOGY OF EGO-MANIA.

HOWEVER dissimilar such individualities as Wagner and Tolstoi, Rossetti and Verlaine, may at first sight appear, we have, nevertheless, encountered in all of them certain common traits, to wit, vague and incoherent thought, the tyranny of the association of ideas, the presence of obsessions, erotic excitability, religious enthusiasm, by which we may recognise them as members of one and the same intellectual family, and justify their union into one single group—that of mystics.

We must go a step farther and say that not only the mystics among the degenerate, but in the main all the degenerate, of whatever nature they may be, are moulded from the same clay. They all show the same lacunæ, inequalities, and malformations in intellectual capacity, the same psychic and somatic stigmata. If, then, anyone, having a certain number of degenerate subjects to judge from, were to bring into prominence and represent as their exclusive peculiarity merely mystical thought in some, merely erotic emotionalism in others, merely vague, barren, fraternal love and a mania for regenerating the world, or else merely an impulsion to commit acts of a criminal nature, etc., he would manifestly be seeing only one side of the phenomenon, and taking no account of the rest. One or another stigma of degeneration may, in a given case, be especially apparent; but, on duly careful inspection, the presence of all the others, or, at least, indications of them, will be discerned.

To the celebrated French alienist, Esquirol, is due the signal merit of having discovered that there are forms of mental derangement in which thought proceeds apparently in a perfectly rational manner, but in which, in the midst of intelligent and logical cerebral activity, some insane presentations appear, like erratic boulders, thus enabling us to recognise the subject as mentally diseased. But Esquirol has committed the fault of not digging deep enough; his observation is too much on the surface. It was through this that he came to introduce into science the notion of 'monomania,' that is, of well-delimitated, partial madness, of an isolated, fixed idea beside which all the rest of the intellectual life operates with sanity. This was an error. There is no monomania. Esquirol's own pupil, the elder Falret, has sufficiently proved it, and our Westphal, from whose other merits I have no wish to detract, was far from standing in the forefront of research, when, half a century after Esquirol, and thirty years after Falret, he still described the 'fear of space,' or agoraphobia, as a special mental malady, or kind of monomania. What is apparently monomania is in reality an indication of a profound organic disorder which never reveals itself by one single phase of folly. A fixed idea never exists in isolation.* It is always accompanied by other irregularities of thought and feeling, which, it is true, at a cursory glance, may not be so distinctly remarked as the more strongly developed insane idea. Recent clinical observation has discovered a long series of similar fixed ideas or 'monomanias,' and recognised the fact that they are one and all the consequence of a fundamental disposition of the organism, viz., of its degeneration. It was unnecessary for Magnan to give a special name to each symptom of degeneration, and to draw up in array, with almost comical effect, the host of 'phobias' and 'manias.' Agoraphobia (fear of open space), claustrophobia (fear of enclosed space), rupophobia (fear of dirt), iophobia (fear of poison), nosophobia (fear of sickness), aichmophobia (fear of pointed objects), belenophobia (fear of needles), cremnophobia (fear of abysses), trichophobia (fear of hair), onomatomania (folly of words or names), pyromania (incendiary madness), kleptomania (madness for theft), dipsomania (madness for drink), erotomania (love madness), arithmomania (madness of numbers), oniomania (madness for buying), etc. This list might be lengthened at pleasure, and enriched by nearly all the roots of the Greek dictionary. It is simply philologico-medical trifling. None of the disorders discovered and described by Magnan and his pupils, and decorated with a sonorous Greek name, forms an independent entity, and appears separately; and Morel is right in disregarding as unessential all these varied manifestations of a morbid cerebral activity, and adhering to the principal phenomenon which lies at the base of all the 'phobias'

* Lisandro Reyes has clearly seen this in his useful sketch entitled *Contribution à l'Etude de l'État mental chez les Enfants dégénérés;* Paris, 1890, p. 8. He affirms expressly that among degenerate children there is no really exclusive 'monomania.' 'Among them an isolated delirious idea may endure for some time, but it is most frequently replaced all at once by a new conception.'

and 'manias,' namely, the great emotionalism of the degenerate.* If to emotionalism, or an excessive excitability, he had added the cerebral debility, which implies feebleness of perception, will, memory, judgment, as well as inattention and instability, he would have exhaustively characterized the nature of degeneration, and perhaps prevented psychiatry from being stuffed with a crowd of useless and disturbing designations. Kowalewski approached much nearer to the truth in his well-known treatise,† where he has represented all the mental disorders of the degenerate as one single malady, which merely presents different degrees of intensity, and which induces in its mildest form neurasthenia; under a graver aspect impulsions and groundless anxieties; and, in its most serious form, the madness of brooding thought or doubt. Within these limits may be ranged all the particular 'manias' and 'phobias' which at present swarm in the literature of mental therapeutics.

But if it be untenable to make a particular malady out of every symptom in which the fundamental disorder (*i.e.*, degeneration) shows itself, it should not, on the other hand, be ignored that among certain of the degenerate a group of morbid phenomena distinctly predominates, without involving the absence of the other groups. Thus, it is permissible to distinguish among them certain principal species, notably, beside the mystics, of whom we have studied the most remarkable representatives in contemporary art and poetry, the ego-maniacs (*Ichsüchtigen*). It is not from affectation that I use this word instead of the terms 'egoism' (*Selbstsucht*) and 'egoist,' so generally employed. Egoism is a lack of amiability, a defect in education, perhaps a fault of character, a proof of insufficiently developed morality, but it is not a disease. The egoist is quite able to look after himself in life, and hold his place in society; he is often also, when the attainment of low ends only is in view, even more capable than the superior and nobler man, who has inured himself to self-abnegation. The ego-maniac, on the contrary, is an invalid who does not see things as they are, does not understand the world, and cannot take up a right attitude towards it. The difference I make in German between *Ichsucht* and *Selbstsucht*, the French also make in their language, where a careful writer will never confound the word 'egotisme,' borrowed from the English, with 'egoisme'—that is, selfishness.

Of course the reader to whom the mental physiognomy of ego-maniacs is shown ought always to remember that, if the principal representatives of this species and of that of the mystics are

* Legrain (*Du Délire chez les Dégénérés*, Paris, 1886) merely expresses this in somewhat different words, when he says (p. 68), 'Obsession, impulsion, these are to be found at the base of all monomania.'

† Analyzed in the *Journal of Mental Science*, January, 1888.

characterized with sufficient clearness, the confines of the latter type are fluctuating. The ego-maniacs are, on the one hand, at once mystics, erotics, and, though it seems paradoxical, even affect occasionally an appearance of philanthropy ; among the mystics, on the other hand, we frequently meet with a strongly-developed ego-mania. There are certain specimens among the degenerate in whom all the disorders are produced to such an equal degree that it is doubtful whether they ought to be classed with the mystics or the ego-maniacs. As a general rule, however, co-ordination under one class or the other will not be very difficult.

That egoism is a salient feature in the character of the degenerate has been unanimously confirmed by all observers. 'The degenerate neither knows nor takes interest in anything but himself,' says Roubinovitch ;* and Legrain† asserts that he 'has . . . only one occupation, that of satisfying his appetites.' This peculiarity establishes a bond which unites the highest of the degenerate to the lowest, the insane genius to the feeble mental cripple. 'All delirious geniuses,' remarks Lombroso, 'are very much captivated by, and preoccupied with, their own selves,'‡ and Sollier writes on the subject of their antipodes, the imbeciles: 'Undisciplined as they are, they obey only through fear, are often violent, especially to those who are weaker than themselves, humble and submissive towards those they feel to be stronger. They are without affection, egoistic in the highest degree, braggarts.'§

The clinicist is satisfied with indicating the fact of this characteristic egoism, but for ourselves we wish further to investigate what are its organic roots, why the degenerate must be more than egoistic, why he must be an ego-maniac, and cannot be otherwise.

In order to understand how the consciousness of the 'I' (morbidly exaggerated and frequently increasing to megalomania) originates, we must recall how the healthy consciousness of the 'I' is formed.

It is, of course, not my intention here to treat of the whole theory of cognition. It is only the most important results of this science, so highly developed in the present day, that can find place in this work.

It has become a philosophical commonplace that we know directly only those changes which take place in our own organism. If, in spite of this, we are able to form an image of the external world surrounding us, from perceptions derived

* J. Roubinovitch, *Hystérie mâle et Dégénérescence.* Paris, 1890, p. 62.

† Legrain, *op. cit.*, p. 10.

‡ Lombroso, *Genie und Irrsinn* (German edition cited in vol. i.), p. 325.

§ Dr. Paul Sollier, *Psychologie de l'Idiot et de l'Imbécile.* Paris, 1890, p. 174.

only from within, it is because we trace the changes in our organism which we have perceived to causes exterior to it; and from the nature and force of the changes taking place in our organism draw conclusions as to the nature and force of the external events causing them.

How we come in general to assume that there is something exterior, and that changes perceived by us only in our organism can have causes which are not in the organism itself, is a question over which metaphysics has cudgelled its brain for centuries. So little has it found an answer, that, in order to put an end to this difficulty anyhow, it has simply denied the very question, and jumped to the conclusion that the 'I' has actually no knowledge of a 'not-I,' of an external world, and cannot have it because there is no external world at all, that what we so call is a creation of our mind, and exists only in our thought as a presentation, but not outside our 'I' as a reality.

It is a fact characteristic of the soporific action exercised by the sound of a word on the human mind that this wholly senseless cackle, glib, well arranged and formed into the philosophical system of idealism, should have thoroughly satisfied for nearly eight generations the greater number of professional metaphysicians, from Berkeley to Fichte, Schelling and Hegel. These wise men repeated, in a tone of conviction, the doctrine of the non-existence of the 'not-I,' and it did not trouble them that they themselves contradicted constantly, in all their actions, their own fustian; that they devoted themselves from their birth to their death to an uninterrupted series of absolutely absurd actions, if there were no objective external world; that therefore they themselves recognised their system to be but wind and shadow, a childish game with words devoid of sense. And the most logical among these grave drivellers, Bishop Berkeley, did not even observe that after all he had not obtained, even at the price of the total abdication of common sense, the answer he sought to the fundamental question of knowledge, for his dogmatic idealism denies, it is true, the reality of the external world, but admits with frivolous thoughtlessness that there are other minds outside of him, Berkeley, and even a universal mind. Thus, then, even according to him, the 'I' is not all; there is still something outside of the 'I,' a 'not-I'; there does exist an external world, if only under the form of immaterial spirits. This, however, brings up the question, How does Berkeley's 'I' come to conceive the existence of something outside of itself, the existence of a 'not-I'? That was the question which had to be answered, and, in spite of its sacrificing the whole world of phenomena, Berkeley's idealism, like the idealism of every one of his successors, makes no reply to it whatsoever.

Metaphysics could find no answer to the question, because the latter, as stated by the former, does not admit of an answer. Scientific psychology—*i.e.*, psycho-physiology—does not encounter the same difficulties. It does not take the finished 'I' of the adult, clearly conscious of himself, feeling himself distinctly opposed to the 'not-I' to the entire external world, but it goes back to the beginnings of this 'I,' investigates in what manner it is formed, and then finds that, at a time when the idea of the existence of a 'not-I,' would be really inexplicable, this idea, in fact, was absolutely non-existent, and that, when we do meet it, the 'I' has already had experiences which completely explain how it could and must arrive at the formation of the idea of a 'not-I.'

We may assume that a certain degree of consciousness is the accompanying phenomenon of every reaction of the protoplasm on external action—*i.e.*, is a fundamental quality of living matter. Even the simplest unicellular living organisms move with obvious intention towards certain goals, and away from certain points; they distinguish between foods and such materials as are unfit for nutrition; thus they have a species of will and judgment, and these two activities presuppose consciousness.* What may be the nature of this consciousness localized in protoplasm not yet even differentiated into nerve-cells, is a thing of which it is impossible for the human mind to form a definite idea. The only thing we can presuppose with any certainty is that in the crepuscular consciousness of a unicellular organism, the notion of an 'I' and a 'not-I,' which is opposed to it, does not exist. The cell feels changes in itself, and these changes provoke others, in accordance with established biochemical or bio-mechanical laws; it receives an impression to which it responds by a movement, but it has certainly no idea that the impression is caused by a process in the external world, and that its movement reacts on the external world.

Even among animals very much higher in the scale, and considerably more advanced in differentiation, a consciousness of the 'Ego,' properly so called, is inconceivable. How can the ray of a star-fish, the bud of a tunicate, of a botryllus, the half of a double animal (diplozoon), the tube of an actinia, or of some other coral polypus, be aware of itself as a separate 'I,' seeing that, though it is an animal, it is at the

* See on this subject the remarkable treatise of Alfred Binet, 'On the Psychic Life of Micro-organisms,' contained in the volume of extracts: '*Le Fétichisme dans l'Amour* (*Etudes de Psychologie expérimentale*). *La Vie psychique des Micro-organismes*, *l'Intensité des Images mentales*, *le Problème hypnotique*, *Note sur l'Écriture hystérique*.' Paris, 1890.—A short time before Binet, this same subject was treated by Verworn in a very deserving manner, at once original and suggestive, in his *Psycho-physiologische Protisten-Studien.* Jena, 1889.

same time a portion of a composite animal, of a colony of animals, and must perceive impressions which strike it directly, as well as those experienced by a companion of the same colony? Or can certain large worms, many of the species of Eunice, for example, have an idea of their 'Ego,' when they neither feel nor recognise portions of their own bodies as constituent parts of their individuality, and begin to eat their tails when, by any accident in coiling themselves, it happens to lie in front of their mouths?

The consciousness of the 'Ego' is not synonymous with consciousness in general. While the latter is probably an attribute of all living matter, the former is the result of the concordant action of a nervous tissue highly differentiated and 'hierarchized,' or brought into a relation of mutual dependence. It appears very late in the series of organic evolution, and is, up to the present, the highest vital phenomenon of which we have knowledge. It arises little by little from experiences which the organism acquires in the course of the natural activity of its constituent parts. Every one of our nerve-ganglia, every one of our nerve-fibres, and even every cell, has a subordinate and faint consciousness of what passes in it. As the whole nervous system of our body has numerous communications between all its parts, it perceives in its totality something of all the stimulations of its parts, and the consciousness which accompanies them. In this manner there arises in the centre where all the nerve ducts of the whole body meet, *i.e.*, in the brain, a total consciousness composed of innumerable partial consciousnesses, having evidently for its object only the processes of its own organism. In the course of its existence, and that at a very early period, consciousness distinguishes two kinds of wholly different perceptions. Some appear without preparation, others accompanied and preceded by other phenomena. No act of will precedes the stimulation of the senses, but such an act does precede every conscious movement. Before our senses perceive anything, our consciousness has no notion of what they will perceive; before our muscles execute a movement, an image of this movement is elaborated in the brain, or spinal marrow (in the case of a reflex action). There exists then, beforehand, a presentation of the movement which the muscles will execute. We feel clearly that the immediate cause of the movement lies in ourselves. On the other hand, we have no similar feelings in regard to sense-impressions. Again, we learn by the muscular sense the realization of motor images elaborated by our consciousness; on the other hand, we experience nothing similar when we elaborate a motor image not having our own muscles exclusively for its object. We wish, for example, to raise our arm. Our consciousness elaborates this image, the brachial muscles obey, and consciousness receives the communication that the image has been realized by the brachial muscles. Next, we wish to raise or throw a stone with our arm. Our consciousness elaborates a motor image, involving our own muscles and the stone. When we are executing the desired and meditated movement, our consciousness receives sensations from the muscles in activity, but not from the stone. Thus it perceives the movements which are accompanied by muscular sensations, and others which appear without this accompaniment.

In order thoroughly to comprehend the formation of our consciousness of the 'Ego,' and the presentation of the existence of a 'non-Ego,' we must consider a third point. All the parts, all the cells of our body, have their own separate consciousness, which accompanies every one of their excitations. These excitations are occasioned partly by the activity of nutrition, of assimilation, of the cleavage of the nucleus—that is to say, by the vital processes of the cell itself, and partly by action of the environment. The excitations which proceed from the interior, the bio-chemical and bio-mechanical processes of the cell, are continued, and endure as long as the life of the cell itself. The stimulations which are the result of the action of the environment only appear, of course, with this action, *i.e.*, not continuously, but intermittently. The vital processes in the cell have direct value and significance only for the cell itself, not for the whole organism; actions of the environment may become important for the whole organism. The principal organ, the brain, acquires the habit of neglecting the excitations relating to the interior vital activity of the cell—first, because they are continuous, and we perceive distinctly only a change of state, not a state itself; and then, because the cell accomplishes its own functions by its own energy, which renders the interference of the brain useless. The brain takes notice, on the contrary, of excitations which are produced by action *ab extra*—first, because they appear with interruptions; and, secondly, because they may necessitate an adaptation of the whole organism, which could only take place through the intervention of the brain.

It cannot be doubted that the brain has knowledge also of the internal excitations of the organism, and only for the reasons already stated is not, as a general rule, distinctly conscious of them. If through illness a disturbance is produced in the functions of the single cell, we at once become conscious of the processes in the cell—we feel the diseased organ, it stimulates our attention; the whole organism is uncomfortable and out of tune. It is sensations of this kind, which, in a healthy state, do not distinctly reach our consciousness, that make up the sensation of our body, our organic 'I,' the so-called cœnæsthesis or general sensibility.

Cœnæsthesis, the organic dimly-conscious 'I,' rises into the clear consciousness of the 'Ego,' by excitations of the second order, reaching the brain from the nerves and muscles, for they are stronger and more distinct than the others, and are interrupted. The brain learns the changes produced in the nervous system by external causes, and the contraction of the muscles. How it has knowledge of the latter is still obscure. It has been recently asserted that the muscular sense has for its seat the nerves of the joints. This is certainly false. We have distinct sensations of the contractions of muscles which put no joint in movement—for example, of the orbicular and constrictor muscles. Then there are the cramps and spasms even of isolated muscular fibres, which likewise do not produce a change of position in the joints. But in any case the perceptions of muscular sense exist, however they are or are not produced.

Thus consciousness very soon learns that the muscular movements it perceives are preceded by certain acts accomplished by itself, namely, the elaboration of motor images, and the despatch of impulses to the muscles. It receives knowledge of these movements twice, one after the other—it perceives them, first, directly as its own presentation and act of volition, as a motor image elaborated in the nerve-centres; and immediately afterwards as an impression arising from the muscular nerves as accomplished movement. It acquires the habit of connecting its own acts—those previously elaborated motor images—with the muscular movements, and of regarding the latter a consequence of the former—in short, of thinking causally. If consciousness has adopted the habit of causality, it seeks a cause in all its perceptions, and can no longer imagine a perception without a cause. The cause of muscular perceptions—that is, of movements consciously willed—it finds in itself. The cause of nervous perceptions—that is, the information reported by the nervous system concerning the excitations which it experiences—it does not find in itself. But the latter must have a cause. Where is it? As it is not in consciousness, it must necessarily exist somewhere else; there must then be something else outside consciousness, and so consciousness comes, through the habit of causal thought, to assume the existence of something outside itself, of a 'not-I,' of an external world, and to project into it the cause of the excitations which it perceives in the nervous system.

Experience teaches that the distinction between the 'I' and the 'not-I' is really only a question of a habit of thought, of a form of thought, and not of an effective, certain knowledge, which carries in itself the criteria of its accuracy and certitude.

When, in consequence of a morbid disturbance, our sensory nerves or their centres of perception are excited, and consciousness acquires knowledge of this excitation, it imputes to it without hesitation, according to its habit, an external cause existing in the 'not-I.' Hence arise illusions and hallucinations, which the patient takes for realities, and that so positively that there is absolutely no means of convincing him that he perceives facts passing within him, not outside of him. In the same manner consciousness concludes that the movements executed unconsciously are occasioned by an extraneous will. It perceives the movement, but it has not noticed that the habitual internal cause, viz., a motor image and an act of the will, has preceded it; hence it places the cause of the movement without hesitation in the 'not-I,' although it resides in the 'I,' and is only occasioned by subordinate centres, the activity of which remains concealed from consciousness. This it is which gives rise to spiritualism, which, in so far as it is in good faith and not openly a hocus-pocus, is simply a mystical attempt to explain movements, the real cause of which consciousness does not find in itself, and which it places, in consequence, in the 'not-I.'

In ultimate analysis, the consciousness of the 'Ego,' and notably the opposition of the 'Ego' and the 'non-Ego,' is an illusion of the senses and a fallacy of thought. Every organism is related to a species, and, over and above that, to the universe. It is the direct material continuation of its parents; it is itself continued directly and materially in its descendants. It is composed of the same materials as the whole environing world; these materials are constantly penetrating into it, transforming it, producing in it all the phenomena of life and consciousness. All the lines of action of the forces of nature are prolonged in its interior; it is the scene of the same physical and chemical processes in action throughout the universe. What pantheism divines and clothes in needlessly mystic words is clear, sober fact, namely, the unity of nature, in which each organism is also a part related to the whole. Certain parts are more nearly connected; others are more separated from one another. Consciousness perceives only the closely-knit parts of its physical basis, not those more remote. Thus it falls into the illusion that the parts near together alone belong to it, and that the more distant are strangers to it, and to consider itself as an 'individuum,' confronting the world as a separate world or microcosm. It does not observe that the 'I,' so rigidly posited, has no fixed limits, but continues and spreads beneath the threshold of consciousness, with an ever-diminishing distinctness of separation, to the extreme depths of nature, till it blends there with all the other constituents of the universe.

We may now resume much more briefly the natural history of

the 'I' and the 'not-I,' and present it in a few formulæ. Consciousness is a fundamental quality of living matter. The highest organism itself is only a colony of the simplest organisms—that is to say, of living cells—differentiated diversely in order to qualify the colony for higher functions than the simple cell can accomplish. The collective or ego-consciousness of the colony is composed of the individual consciousness of the parts. The ego-consciousness has an obscure and disregarded part which relates to the vital functions of the cells, or the cœnæsthesis, and a clear, privileged part which is attentive to the excitations of the sensory nerves, and to the voluntary activity of the muscles, and which recognises them. Clear consciousness learns from experience that acts of will precede voluntary movements. It arrives at the assumption of causality. It observes that the sensorial excitations are not caused by anything contained in itself. It is compelled, in consequence, to transfer this cause, the assumption of which it cannot renounce, elsewhere, and is necessarily first brought by this to the presentation of a 'not-I,' and afterwards to the development of this 'not-I' into an apparent universe.

The old spiritualistic psychology, which regards the 'Ego' as something entirely different from the body, as a special unitary substance, maintains that this 'Ego' considers its own body as something not identical with it, as opposed to the 'Ego' properly so called, as something external—in fact, as 'non-Ego.' Thus, it denies cœnæsthesis—that is to say, an absolutely certain empirical fact. We constantly have an obscure sensation of the existence of all parts of our body, and our ego-consciousness immediately experiences a change if the vital functions of any one of our organs or tissues suffers a disturbance.*

Development advances from the unconscious organic 'I' to the clear conscious 'I,' and to the conception of the 'not-I.' The infant probably has cœnæsthesis even before, in any case after, its birth, for it feels its vital internal processes, shows satisfaction when they are in healthy action, manifests its discomfort by movements and cries, which are also only a movement of the respiratory and laryngeal muscles, when any dis-

* 'Certain [sick] persons enjoy keenly a sense of the lightness of their body, feel themselves hovering in the air, believe they could fly; or else they have a feeling of weight either in the whole body, in many limbs, or in one single limb, which seems to them huge and heavy. A young epileptic sometimes felt his body so extraordinarily heavy that he could scarcely raise it. At other times he felt himself so light that he believed he did not touch the ground. Sometimes it seemed to him that his body had assumed such proportions that it was impossible for him to pass through a door. In this last illusion . . . the patient feels himself very much smaller or very much larger than he really is.'—Th. Ribot, *Les Maladies de la Personnalité.* 3e édition. Paris, 1889, p. 35.

turbances appear there, perceives and expresses general states of the organism, such as hunger, thirst and fatigue. But clear consciousness does not yet exist for it ; the brain has not yet taken command over the inferior centres. Sense-impressions are perhaps perceived, but certainly not yet grouped into ideas ; the greater part of the movements are preceded by no conscious act of will, and are only reflex actions—that is, manifestations of those local consciousnesses which later become so obscure as to be imperceptible, when the cerebral consciousness has attained its full clearness. Little by little the higher centres develop ; the child begins to give heed to its sense-impressions, to form from its perceptions ideas, and to make voluntary movements adapted to an end. With the awakening of its conscious will the birth of the consciousness of its 'Ego' is linked. The child apprehends that it is an individual. But its internal organic processes occupy it very much more than does the procedure of the external world, transmitted to it by the sensory nerves, and its own states fill up its consciousness more or less completely. The child is, for this reason, a model of egoism, and, until it reaches a more advanced age, is wholly incapable of displaying either attention or interest in anything at all which is not directly connected with itself, its needs and inclinations. By the continued culture of his brain man finally arrives at that degree of maturity in which he acquires a just idea of his relations to other men and to Nature. Then consciousness pays less and less regard to the vital processes in its own organism, and more and more to the stimulations of its senses. It only notices the former when they reveal pressing necessities ; it is, on the contrary, always concerned with the latter when in a waking state. The 'I' retires decidedly behind the 'not-I,' and the image of the world fills the greater part of consciousness.

As the formation of an 'I,' of an individuality clearly conscious of its separate existence, is the highest achievement of living matter, so the highest degree of development of the 'I' consists in embodying in itself the 'not-I,' in comprehending the world, in conquering egoism, and in establishing close relations with other beings, things and phenomena. Auguste Comte, and after him Herbert Spencer, have named this stage 'altruism,' from the Italian word *altrui*, 'others.' The sexual instinct which forces an individual to seek for another individual is as little altruism as the hunger which incites the hunter to follow an animal in order to kill and eat it. There can be no question of altruism until an individual concerns himself about another being from sympathy or curiosity, and not in order to satisfy an immediate, pressing necessity of his body, the momentary hunger of some organ.

Not till he attains to altruism is man in a condition to maintain himself in society and in nature. To be a social being, man must feel with his fellow-creatures, and show himself sensitive to their opinion about him. Both the one and the other presuppose that he is capable of so vividly representing to himself the feelings of his fellow-creatures as to experience them himself. He who is not capable of imagining the pain of another with sufficient clearness to suffer the same himself will not have compassion, and he who cannot exactly feel for himself what impression an action or an omission on his part will make on another will have no regard for others. In both cases he will soon see himself excluded from the human community as the enemy of all, and treated as such by all, and very probably he will perish. And to defend himself against destructive natural forces and turn them to his advantage, man must know them intimately—that is, he must be able distinctly to picture their effects. A clear presentation of the feelings of others, and of the effects of natural forces, presupposes the faculty of occupying himself intensively with the 'not-I.' While a man is attending to the 'not-I,' he is not thinking of his 'Ego,' and the latter descends below the level of consciousness. In order that the 'not-I' should in this way prevail over the 'I,' the sensory nerves must properly conduct the external impressions, the cerebral centres of perception must be sensitive to the excitations of the sensory nerves, the highest centres must develop, in a sure, rapid and vigorous manner, the perceptions into ideas, unite these into conceptions and judgments, and, on occasion, transform them into acts of volition and motor impulses. And as the greatest part of these different activities is accomplished by the gray cortex of the frontal lobes, this means that this gray cortex must be well developed and work vigorously.

It is thus that a sane man appears to us. He perceives little and rarely his internal excitations, but always and clearly his external impressions. His consciousness is filled with images of the external world, not with images of the activity of his organs. The unconscious work of his inferior centres plays an almost vanishing part by the side of the fully conscious work of the highest centres. His egoism is no stronger than is strictly necessary to maintain his individuality, and his thoughts and actions are determined by knowledge of Nature and his fellow-creatures, and by the consideration he owes to them.

Quite otherwise is the spectacle offered by the degenerate person. His nervous system is not normal. In what the digression from the norm ultimately consists we do not know. Very probably the cell of the degenerate is formed a little differently from that of sane men, the particles of the protoplasm are otherwise and less regularly disposed; the molecular movements take place, in consequence, in a less free and rapid, less rhythmic and vigorous, manner. This is, however, a mere undemonstrable hypothesis. Nevertheless, it cannot reasonably be doubted that all the bodily signs or 'stigmata' of degeneration, all the arrests and inequalities of development that have been observed, have their origin in a bio-chemical and bio-mechanical derangement of the nerve-cell, or, perhaps, of the cell in general.

In the mental life of the degenerate the anomaly of his nervous system has, as a consequence, the incapacity of attaining to the highest degree of development of the individual, namely, the freely coming out from the factitious limits of individuality, *i.e.*, altruism. As to the relation of his 'Ego' to his 'non-Ego,' the degenerate man remains a child all his life. He scarcely appreciates or even perceives the external world, and is only occupied with the organic processes in his own body. He is more than egoistical, he is an ego-maniac.

His ego-mania may spring directly from different circumstances of his organism. His sensory nerves may be obtuse, are, in consequence, but feebly stimulated by the external world, transmit slowly and badly their stimuli to the brain, and are not in a condition to incite it to a sufficiently vigorous perceptive and ideational activity. Or his sensory nerves may work moderately well, but the brain is not sufficiently excitable, and does not perceive properly the impressions which are transmitted to it from the external world.

The obtuseness of the degenerate is attested by almost all observers. From the almost illimitable number of facts which could be adduced on this point, we will only give a very concise, but sufficiently characteristic selection. 'Among many idiots,' says Sollier, 'there is no distinction between sweet and bitter. When sugar and colocynth are administered to them alternately, they manifest no change of sensation. . . . Properly speaking, taste does not exist among them. . . . Besides this, there are perversions of taste. We are not speaking here of complete idiots . . . but even of imbeciles who eat ordure or repulsive things . . . even their own excrements. . . . The same remarks apply to smell. Perhaps sensibility appears still more absolutely obtuse for smells than for taste. . . . Tactile sensibility is very obtuse in general, but it is always uniformly so. . . . Sometimes it might be a question whether there is not complete anæsthesia.'* Lombroso has examined the general sensitiveness of skin in sixty-six criminals, and has found it obtuse in thirty-eight among them, and unequal in the two halves of the body in forty-six.† In a later work he sums up in

* Sollier, *Psychologie de l'Idiot et de l'Imbécile*, p. 52 *et seq.*

† Lombroso, *L'Uomo delinquente.* 3ª edizione. Torino, 1884, p. 329 *et seq.*

these words his observations of sensorial acuteness in the degenerate: 'Inaccessible to the feeling of pain, themselves without feeling, they never understand pain even in others.'* Ribot traces the 'diseases of personality' (that is, the false ideas of the 'I') to 'organic disturbances, of which the first result is to depress the faculty of feeling in general; the second, to pervert it.' 'A young man whose conduct had always been excellent suddenly gave himself up to the worst inclinations. It was ascertained that in his mental condition there was no sign of evident alienation, but it could be seen that the whole outer surface of the skin had become absolutely insensible.' 'It may seem strange that weak and false sensitivity . . . that is, that simple disturbances or sensorial alterations should disorganize the "Ego." Nevertheless, observation proves it.'† Maudsley‡ describes some cases of degeneration among children whose skin was insensible, and remarks: 'They cannot feel impressions as they naturally should feel them, nor adjust themselves to their surroundings, with which they are in discord; and the motor outcomes of the perverted affections of self are accordingly of a meaningless and destructive character.'§

The defective sensibility of the degenerate, confirmed by all observers, is, moreover, susceptible of different interpretations. Whereas many consider it a consequence of the pathological condition of the sensory nerves, others believe that the perturbation has its seat, not in these nerves, but in the brain; not in the ducts, but in the centres of perception. To quote one of the most eminent among the psycho-physiologists of the new school, Binet‖ has proved that, 'if a portion of the body of a person is insensible, he is ignorant of what passes there; but, on the other hand, the nervous centres in connection with this insensible

* Lombroso, *Les Applications de l'Anthropologie criminelle.* Paris, 1892, p. 179.

† Th. Ribot, *Les Maladies de la Personnalité*, pp. 61, 78, 105.

‡ Maudsley, *The Pathology of Mind.* London, 1879, p. 287.

§ See also Alfred Binet, *Les Altérations de la Personnalité*, Paris, 1892, p. 39: 'His senses close to outside stimulation; for him, the external world ceases to exist; he lives no more than his exclusively personal life; he acts only through his own stimuli, with the automatic movement of his brain. Although he receives nothing more from outside, and his personality is completely isolated from the surroundings in which he is placed, he may be seen to go, come, do, act, as if he had his senses and intelligence in full exercise.' This, it is true, is the description of a patient, but what he says of the latter applies equally, with a difference of degree only, to the ego-maniac. Féré has communicated to the Biological Society of Paris, in the seánce of November 12, 1892, the results of a great number of experiments made by him, whence it appears 'that among the greater part of epileptics, hysterical and degenerate subjects, cutaneous sensibility is diminished.' See *La Semaine médicale*, 1892, p. 456.

‖ Alfred Binet, *Les Altérations de la Personnalité.* Paris, 1892, pp. 83, 85, *et seq.*

region can continue to act; the result is that certain acts, often simple, but sometimes very complicated, can be accomplished in the body of a hysterical subject, without his knowledge; much more, these acts can be of a psychical nature, and manifest an intelligence which will be distinct from that of the subject, and will constitute a second "I" co-existent with the first. For a long time there was a misconception of the true nature of hysterical anæsthesia, and it was compared to a common anæsthesia from organic causes, due, for example, to the interruption of afferent nerves. This view must be wholly abandoned, and we know now that hysterical anæsthesia is not a true insensibility; it is insensibility from unconsciousness from mental disaggregation; in a word, it is psychical insensibility.'

Most frequently it is not a question of simple cases, where it is the sensory nerves alone, or only the cerebral centres which work badly, but of mixed cases, where the two apparatuses have a diversely varying part in the disturbance. But whether the nerves do not conduct the impressions to the brain, or the brain does not perceive, or does not raise the impressions brought to it into consciousness, the result is always the same, viz., the external world will not be correctly and distinctly grasped by consciousness, the 'not-I' will not be suitably represented in consciousness, the 'I' will not experience the necessary derivation of the exclusive preoccupation with the processes taking place in its own organism.

The natural healthy connection between organic sensations and sense-perceptions is much more strongly displaced when to the insensibility of the sensory nerves, or of the centres of perception, or both, is added an unhealthily modified and intensified vital activity of the organs. Then the organic ego-sensibility, or cœnæsthesis, advances irrepressibly into the foreground, overshadowing in great part or wholly the perceptions of the external world in consciousness, which no longer takes notice of anything but the interior processes of the organism. In this way there originates that peculiar hyper-stimulation or emotionalism constituting, as we have seen, the fundamental phenomenon of the intellectual life of the degenerate. For the fundamental emotional tone, despairing or joyful, angry or tearful, which determines the colour of his presentations as well as the course of his thoughts, is the consequence of phenomena taking place in his nerves, vessels and glands.* The consciousness of the emotionally degenerate subject is filled with obsessions which

* 'The organic, cardiac, vaso-motor, secretory, etc., phenomena accompanying almost all, if not all, affective states . . . far from following the conscious phenomenon, precede it; none the less they remain in many cases unconscious.'—Gley, quoted by A. Binet, *Les Altérations de la Personnalité*, p. 208.

are not inspired by the events of the external world, and by impulsions which are not the reaction against external stimulation. To this is added next the unfailing weakness of will of the degenerate person, which makes it impossible for him to suppress his obsessions, to resist his impulsions, to control his fundamental moods, to keep his higher centres to the attentive pursuit of objective phenomena. According to the saying of the poet, the necessary result of these conditions is that the work must be differently reflected in such heads than it is in normal ones. The external world, the 'not-I,' either does not exist at all in the consciousness of an emotionally degenerate subject, or it is merely represented there as on a faintly reflecting surface, by a scarcely recognisable, wholly colourless image, or, as in a concave or convex mirror, by a completely distorted, false image; consciousness, on the other hand, is imperiously monopolized by the somatic 'I,' which does not permit the mind to be occupied with anything but the painful or tumultuous processes taking place in the depths of the organs.

Badly-conducting sensory nerves, obtuse perceptive centres in the brain, weakness of will with its resulting incapacity of attention, morbidly irregular and violent vital processes in the cells, are therefore the organic basis on which ego-mania develops.

The ego-maniac must of necessity immensely over-estimate his own importance and the significance of all his actions, for he is only engrossed with himself, and but little or not at all with external things. He is therefore not in a position to comprehend his relation to other men and the universe, and to appreciate properly the part he has to play in the aggregate of social institutions. There might at this juncture be an inclination to confound ego-mania with megalomania, but there is a characteristic difference between the two states. Megalomania, it is true, is itself, like its clinical complement, the delusion of persecution, occasioned by morbid processes within the organism obliging consciousness perpetually to be attending to its own somatic 'Ego.' More especially the unnaturally increased bio-chemical activity of the organs gives rise to the pleasantly extravagant presentations of megalomania, while retarded or morbidly aberrant activity gives rise to the painful presentations of the delusion of persecution.* In megalomania, however, as in the delusion of persecution, the patient is constantly engrossed with the external

* This is not merely a simple hypothesis, but a well-demonstrated fact. Hundreds of experiments by Boeck, Weill, Moebius, Charrin, Mairet, Bosc, Slosse, Laborde, Marie, etc., have established that among the deranged, during periods of excitation and afterwards, the urine is more toxic, *i.e.*, more full of waste and excreted organic matter, while after the periods of depression it is less toxic, *i.e.*, poorer in disaggregated matter, than among sane individuals, which proves that, among the former, the nutrition of the tissues is morbidly increased or retarded.

world and with men ; in ego-mania, on the contrary, he almost completely withdraws himself from them. In the systematically elaborated delirium of the megalomaniac and persecution-maniac, the 'not-I' plays the most prominent part. The patient accounts for the importance his 'Ego' obtains in his own eyes by the invention of a grand social position universally recognised, or by the inexorable hostility of powerful persons, or groups of persons. He is Pope, or Emperor, and his persecutors are the chief men in the State, or great social powers, the police, the clergy, etc. His delirium, in consequence, takes account of the State and society ; he admits their importance, and attaches the greatest value, in one case, to the homage, in the other to the enmity, of his neighbours. The ego-maniac, on the contrary, does not regard it as necessary to dream of himself as occupying some invented social position. He does not require the world or its appreciation to justify in his own eyes himself as the sole object of his own interest. He does not see the world at all. Other people simply do not exist for him. The whole 'non-Ego' appears in his consciousness merely as a vague shadow or a thin cloud. The idea does not even occur to him that he is something out of the common, that he is superior to other people, and for this reason either admired or hated ; he is alone in the world ; more than that, he alone is the world and everything else, men, animals, things are unimportant accessories, not worth thinking about.

The less diseased are the conducting media, the centres of nutrition, perception and volition, so much the weaker naturally will the ego-mania be, and so much the more harmlessly will it be manifested. Its least objectionable expression is the comic importance which the ego-maniac often attributes to his sensations, inclinations and activities. Is he a painter? he has no doubt that the whole history of the universe only hinges on painting, and on his pictures in particular. Is he a writer of prose or verse? he is convinced that humanity has no other care, or at least no more serious care, than for verses and books. Let it not be objected that this is not peculiar to ego-maniacs, but is the case with the vast majority of mankind. Assuredly everyone thinks what he is doing is important, and that man would not be worth much who performed his work so heedlessly and so superficially, with so little pleasure and conscientiousness, that he himself could not look upon it with respect. But the great difference between the rational and sane man and the ego-maniac is, that the former sees clearly how subordinate his occupation is to the rest of humanity, although it fills his life and exacts his best powers, while the latter can never imagine that any exertion to which he devotes his time and efforts can appear to others as unimportant and even puerile.

An honest cobbler, resoleing an old boot, gives himself up heart and soul to his work, nevertheless he admits that there are far more interesting and important things for humanity than the repairing of damaged sole-leather. The ego-maniac, on the contrary, if he is a writer, does not hesitate to declare, like Mallarmé, 'The world was made to lead up to a fine book.' This absurd exaggeration of one's own occupations and interests produces in literature the Parnassians and the Æsthetes.

If degeneration is deeper, and ego-mania is stronger, the latter no longer assumes the comparatively innocent form of total absorption in poetic and artistic cooings, but manifests itself as an immorality, which may amount to moral madness. The tendency to commit actions injurious to himself or society is aroused now and then even in a sane man when some obnoxious desire demands gratification, but he has the will and the power to suppress it. The degenerate ego-maniac is too feeble of will to control his impulsions, and cannot determine his actions and thoughts by a regard to the welfare of society, because society is not at all represented in his consciousness. He is a solitary, and is insensible to the moral law framed for life in society, and not for the isolated individual. It is evident that for Robinson Crusoe the penal code did not exist. Alone on his island, having only Nature to deal with, it is obvious he could neither kill, steal, nor pillage in the sense of the penal code. He could only commit misdemeanours against himself. Want of insight and of self-control are the only immoralities possible to him. The ego-maniac is a mental Robinson Crusoe, who in his imagination lives alone on an island, and is at the same time a weak creature, powerless to govern himself. The universal moral law does not exist for him, and the only thing he may possibly see and avow, perhaps also regret a little, is that he sins against the moral law of the solitary, *i.e.*, against the necessity of controlling instincts in so far as they are injurious to himself.

Morality—not that learnt mechanically, but that which we feel as an internal necessity—has become, in the course of thousands of generations, an organized instinct. For this reason, like all other organized instincts, it is exposed to 'perversion,' to aberration. The effect of this is that an organ, or the whole organism, works in opposition to its normal task and its natural laws, and cannot work otherwise.* In perversion of taste the

* Dr. Paul Moreau, of Tours, describes perversion (*l'aberration*) in these somewhat obscure terms: 'Perversion constitutes a deviation from the laws which rule the proper sensibility of the organs and faculties. By this word we mean to designate those cases in which observation testifies to an unnatural, exceptional, and wholly pathological change, a change carrying palpable disturbance into the regular working of a faculty.'—*Des Aberrations du Sens génésique.* 4e édition. Paris, 1887, p. 1.

patient seeks greedily to swallow all that ordinarily provokes the deepest repugnance, *i.e.*, is instinctively recognised as noxious, and rejected for that reason—decaying organic matter, ordure, pus, spittle, etc. In perversion of smell he prefers the odours of putrefaction to the perfume of flowers. In perversion of the sexual appetite he has desires which are directly contrary to the purpose of the instinct, *i.e.*, the preservation of the species. In perversion of the moral sense the patient is attracted by, and feels delight in, acts which fill the sane man with disgust and horror. If this particular perversion is added to ego-mania, we have before us not merely the obtuse indifference towards crime which characterizes moral madness, but delight in crime. The ego-maniac of this kind is no longer merely insensible to good and evil, and incapable of discriminating between them, but he has a decided predilection for evil, esteems it in others, does it himself every time he can act according to his inclination, and finds in it the peculiar beauty that the sane man finds in good.

The moral derangement of an ego-maniac, with or without perverted moral instincts, will naturally manifest itself in ways varying according to the social class to which he belongs, as well as according to his personal idiosyncrasies. If he is a member of the disinherited class, he is simply either a fallen or degraded being, whom opportunity has made a thief, who lives in horrible promiscuity with his sisters or daughters, etc., or is a criminal from habit and profession. If he is cultivated and well-to-do, or in a commanding position, he commits misdemeanours peculiar to the upper classes which have as their object not the gratification of material needs, but of other kinds of craving. He becomes a Don Juan of the drawing-room, and carries shame and dishonour without hesitation into the family of his best friend. He is a legacy-hunter, a traitor to those who trust in him, an intriguer, a sower of discord, and a liar. On the throne he may even develop into a rapacious animal, and to a universal conqueror. With a limited tether he becomes Charles the Bad the Count d'Evreux and King of Navarre, Gilles de Rais, the prototype of Blue Beard, or Cæsar Borgia ; and, with a wider range, Napoleon I. If his nervous system is not strong enough to elaborate imperious impulsions, or if his muscles are too feeble to obey such impulsions, all these criminal inclinations remain unsatisfied, and only expend themselves by way of his imagination. The perverted ego-maniac is then only a platonic or theoretic malefactor, and if he embraces the literary career, he will concoct philosophic systems to justify his depravity, or will employ an accommodating rhetoric in verse and prose to celebrate it, bedizen it and present it under as seductive a form as possible. We then find ourselves in the presence of the literary phases called Diabolism and Decadentism. 'Diaboliques' and 'décadents' are distinguished from ordinary criminals merely in that the former content themselves with dreaming and writing, while the latter have the resolution and strength to act. But they have this bond in common, of being both of them 'antisocial beings.'*

A second characteristic which is shared by all ego-maniacs is their incapacity to adapt themselves to the conditions in which they live, whether they assert their anti-social inclinations in thought or action, in writings or as criminals. This want of adaptability is one of the most striking peculiarities of the degenerate, and it is to them a source of constant suffering, and finally of ruin. It is a necessary result, however, of the constitution of his central nervous system. The indispensable premise of adaptation is the having an exact presentation of the facts to which a man must adapt himself.† I cannot avoid the ruts

* 'The vices of the psycho-physical organization manifesting themselves by acts prohibited, not only by morality—that aggregate of necessary rules elaborated by the secular experience of peoples—but also by their penal codes, are in discord with life in society, in the midst of which humanity can alone make progress. . . . A man, from his birth adapted to social life, can only acquire such vices as a consequence of certain pernicious conditions, through which his psycho-physical powers are set in opposition to the necessary exigencies of social life.'—Drill, *Les Criminels mineurs*, quoted by Lombroso in *Les Applications de l'Anthropologie criminelle.* Paris, 1892, p. 94. See also G. Tarde, *La Philosophie pénale*, Lyon, 1890, *passim*: 'The morally deranged are not true lunatics. A Marquise de Brinvilliers, a Troppmann, a being born without either compassion or sense of shame—can it be said of such an one that he is not himself when he commits his crime? No. He is only too much himself. But his existence, his person, are hostile to society. He does not feel the same sentiments which we civilized people regard as indispensable. It is useless to think of curing him or of reforming him.'

† Darwinism explains adaptation only as the result of the struggle for existence, and of selection which is a form of this struggle. In one individual a quality appears accidentally, which makes it more capable of preserving itself and of conquering its enemies than those individuals not born with this quality. It finds more favourable conditions of existence, leaves behind it more numerous descendants inheriting this advantageous quality, and by the survival of the fittest and the disappearance of the less fit, the whole species comes into the possession of this advantageous quality. I do not at all deny that an accidental individual deviation from the type of the species, which proves an advantage in the struggle for existence, can be a source of transformations having as their result a better adaptation of the species to given and unmodifiable circumstances. But I do not believe that such an accident is the only source, or even the most frequent source, of such transformations. The process of adaptation appears to me to be quite otherwise, viz., the living being experiences in some situation feelings of discomfort from which he wishes to escape, either by change of situation (movement, flight), or by trying to act vigorously on the causes of these feelings of discomfort (attack, modification of natural conditions). If the organs possessed by the living being, and the aptitude these organs have acquired, are not sufficient to furnish the counteractions felt and wished for as necessary to those feelings

in the road if I do not see them; I cannot ward off the blow I do not see coming; it is impossible to thread a needle if its eye is not seen with sufficient clearness, and if the thread is not carried with steady hand to the right spot. All this is so elementary it is scarcely necessary to say it. What we term power over Nature is, in fact, adaptation to Nature. It is an inexact expression to say we make the forces of Nature subject to us. In reality we observe them, we learn to know their peculiarities, and we manage so that the tendencies of natural forces and our own desires coincide. We construct a wheel at the point where the water power, by natural law, must fall, and we have then the advantage that the wheel turns according to our needs. We know that electricity flows along copper wire, and so, with cunning submission to its peculiar ways, we lay down copper lines to the place where we want it, and where its action would be useful to us. Without knowledge of Nature,

---

of discomfort, the weaker creatures submit to their destiny, and suffer or even perish. More vigorous individuals, on the contrary, make violent and continuous efforts in order to attain their design, of flight, defence, attack, suppression of natural obstacles; they give strong nervous impulses to their organs to increase to the highest degree their functional capacity, and these nervous impulses are the immediate cause of transformations, giving to the organs new qualities, and rendering them more fit to make the living creature thrive. That the nervous impulse produces, as a consequence, an increase in the flow of blood, and a better nutrition for the organ in play, is a positive biological fact. In my opinion, then, adaptation is most frequently an act of the will, and not the result of qualities accidentally acquired. It has as premise the clear perception and representation of the external causes of the feelings of discomfort, and a keen desire to escape from them, or, again, that of procuring feelings of pleasure, *i.e.*, an inorganic appetite. Its mechanism consists in the elaboration of an intense representation of serviceable acts of certain organs, and in the sending of adequate impulses to these organs. That such impulses can modify the anatomical structure of the organs, Kant already anticipated when he wrote his treatise, *Von der Macht des Gemüthes;* and modern therapeutics has fully confirmed this, by showing that the stigmata of a Louise Lateau, the healing of tumours on the tomb of the Deacon Paris, the modifications induced by suggestion on the skin of hysterical subjects, the formation of birth-marks by eventualities and emotions, are the effect of presentations on the bodily tissues. It was wrong to laugh at Lamarck for teaching that the giraffe has a long neck because it has continually stretched it in order to be able to feed off the topmost foliage of plants with tall stems. When the animal elaborates the clear idea that he ought to elongate his neck as much as possible in order to reach the elevated foliage, this presentation will influence in the strongest manner the circulation of the blood in all the tissues of the neck; these will be quite differently nourished from what they would be without this presentation, and the changes desired by the animal will certainly take place little by little, if his general organization makes them possible. Knowledge and will are therefore causes of adaptation—not the will in the mystical sense of Schopenhauer, but the will that is the dispenser of nervous impulses. This summary must suffice for the reader; this is not the place to develop it more, and to demonstrate in detail how fertile these ideas are for the theory of evolution.

therefore, no adaptation, and without adaptation no possibility of profiting by its forces. Now, the degenerate subject cannot adapt himself, because he has no clear idea of the circumstances to which he ought to adapt himself, and he does not obtain from them any clear idea, because, as we know, he has bad nerve-conductors, obtuse centres of perception, and feeble attention.

The active cause of all adaptation, as of all effort in general—and adaptation is nothing else than an effort of a particular kind—is the wish to satisfy some organic necessity, or to escape from some discomfort. In other words, the aim of adaptation is to give feelings of pleasure, and to diminish or suppress the feelings of discomfort. The being incapable of self-adaptation is for this reason far less able to procure agreeable, and avoid disagreeable, sensations than the normal being; he runs up against every corner, because he does not know how to avoid them; and he longs in vain for the luscious pear, because he does not know how to catch hold of the branch on which it hangs. The ego-maniac is a type of such a being. He must, therefore, necessarily suffer from the world and from men. Hence at heart he is bad-tempered, and turns in wrathful discontent against Nature, society and public institutions, irritated and offended by them, because he does not know how to accommodate himself to them. He is in a constant state of revolt against all that exists, and contrives how he may destroy it, or, at least, dreams of destruction. In a celebrated passage Henri Taine indicates 'exaggerated self-esteem' and 'dogmatic argument' as the roots of Jacobinism.* This leads to contempt for and rejection of institutions already established, and hence

* H. Taine, *Les Origines de la France contemporaine: La Révolution*, vol. ii., 'La Conquête jacobine,' Paris, 1881, pp. 11-12: 'Neither exaggerated self-esteem nor dogmatic argument is rare in the human species. In every country these two roots of the Jacobin spirit subsist indestructible beneath the surface. Everywhere they are kept in check by established society, and everywhere they try to upheave the old historical structure which presses on them with all its weight. . . . At twenty years old, when a young man enters the world, his reason is hurt at the same time as his pride. In the first place, of whatever society he may be a member, it is a scandal to pure reason, for it has not been constructed on a simple principle by a philosophical legislator; it has been arranged by successive generations according to their multiple and varying needs. . . . In the second place, however perfect institutions, laws, and manners may be, since they have preceded him he has not assented to them at all; others, his predecessors, have chosen for him, and have enclosed him, in advance, in a moral, political, and social mould which pleased them. It matters little if it displeases him; he is forced to submit to it, and, like a harnessed horse, he must walk between the shafts in the harness put on him. . . . It is not surprising, then, if he is tempted to kick against the framework in which, *nolens volens*, he is enclosed, and in which subordination will be his lot. Thence it comes that the majority of young men—above all, those who have their careers to make—are more or less Jacobins on leaving college; it is *an infirmity of growth*.'

not invented or chosen by himself. He considers the social edifice absurd because it is not 'a work of logic,' but of history.

Besides these two roots of Jacobinism which Taine has brought to light, there is yet another, and the most important, that has escaped his attention, viz., the inability of the degenerate to adapt himself to given circumstances. The ego-maniac is condemned by his natural organization to be a pessimist and a Jacobin. But the revolutions he wishes for, preaches, and perhaps effectively accomplishes, are barren as regards progress. He is, as a revolutionary, what an inundation or cyclone would be as a street-sweeper. He does not clear the ground with conscious aim, but blindly destroys. This distinguishes him from the clear-minded innovator, the true revolutionary, who is a reformer, leading suffering and stagnating humanity from time to time by toilsome paths into a new Canaan. The reformer hurls down with pitiless violence, if violence is necessary, the ruins which have become obstacles, in order to make way for useful constructions; the ego-maniac raves against everything that stands upright, whether useful or useless, and does not think of clearing the building-ground after the devastation; his pleasure consists in seeing heaps of rubbish overgrown by noxious weeds where once walls and gables reared themselves.

There is an impassable gulf between the sane revolutionary and the ego-maniac Jacobin. The former has positive ideals, the latter has not. The former knows what he is striving for; the latter has no conception how that which irritates him could be changed for the better. His thoughts do not reach so far; he never troubles himself to question what will replace the things destroyed. He knows only that everything frets him, and he desires to vent his muddled and blustering ill-humour on all around him. Hence it is characteristic that the foolish necessity to revolt of this kind of revolutionary frequently turns against imaginary evils, follows puerile aims, or even fights against those laws which are wise and beneficent. Here they form a 'league against lifting the hat in saluting'; there they oppose compulsory vaccination; another time they rise in protest against taking the census of the population; and they have the ridiculous audacity to conduct these silly campaigns with the same speeches and attitudes that the true revolutionaries assume—for example, in the service of suppression of slavery, or liberty of thought.

To the ego-maniac's incapacity for adaptation is often added the mania for destruction, or clastomania, which is so frequently observed among idiots and imbeciles, and in some forms of insanity.* In a child the instinct of destruction is normal. It

* Dr. Paul Sollier, *Psychologie de l'Idiot et de l'Imbécile*, p. 109 *et seq.*: There exists among idiots another instinct which is met with, nevertheless,

is the first manifestation of the desire to exert muscular strength. Very soon, however, the desire is aroused to exert its strength, not in destroying, but in creating. Now, the act of creating has a psychic premise, viz., attention. This being absent in the degenerate, the impulse to destroy, which can be gratified without attention, by disorderly and casual movements, does not rise in them to the instinct of creation.

Hence, discontent as the consequence of incapacity of adaptation, want of sympathy with his fellow-creatures arising from weak representative capacity, and the instinct of destruction, as the result of arrested development of mind, together constitute the anarchist, who, according to the degree of his impulsions, either merely writes books and makes speeches at popular meetings, or has recourse to a dynamite bomb.

Finally, in its extreme degree of development, ego-mania leads to that folly of Caligula in which the unbalanced mind boasts of being 'a laughing lion,' believes himself above all restraints of morality or law, and wishes the whole of humanity had one single head that he might cut it off.

The reader who has hitherto followed me will now, I hope, quite comprehend the psychology of ego-mania. As I have stated above, consciousness of the 'Ego' originates from the sensations of the vital processes in all parts of our body, and the conception of the 'non-Ego' from changes in our organs of special sense. How, generally speaking, we arrive at the assumption of the existence of a 'not-I,' I have explained above in detail, hence it is unnecessary to repeat it here. If we wish to leave the firm soil of positively established facts, and risk ourselves on the somewhat shaky ground of probable assumptions, we may say that consciousness of the 'Ego' has its anatomical basis in the sympathetic system, and the conception of the 'not-I' in the cerebro-spinal system. In a healthy man the perception of vital internal facts does not rise above the level of consciousness. The brain receives its stimulations far more from the sensory, than from the sympathetic nerves. In consciousness the presentation of the external world greatly outweighs the consciousness of the 'Ego.' In the degenerate, either (1) vital internal facts are morbidly intensified, or proceed abnormally, and are therefore constantly perceived by consciousness; or (2) the sensory nerves are obtuse, and the perceptional centres weak

---

to a certain degree among normal children. This is destructiveness, which shows itself among all children as a first manifestation of their powers of movement, under the form of a desire to strike, break, and destroy. . . . This tendency is much more pronounced among idiots. . . . It is not the same with imbeciles. Their malicious and mischievous spirit drives them to destroy, not only for the purpose of expending their strength, but with the object of injuring. It is an unwholesome gratification which they seek.'

and sluggish; or (3) perhaps these two deviations from the norm co-exist. The result in all three cases is that the notion of the 'Ego' is far more strongly represented in consciousness than the image of the external world. The ego-maniac, consequently, neither knows nor grasps the phenomenon of the universe. The effect of this is a want of interest and sympathy, and an incapacity to adapt himself to nature and humanity. The absence of feeling, and the incapacity of adaptation, frequently accompanied by perversion of the instincts and impulses, make the ego-maniac an anti-social being. He is a moral lunatic, a criminal, a pessimist, an anarchist, a misanthrope, and he is all these, either in his thoughts and his feelings, or also in his actions. The struggle against the anti-social ego-maniac, his expulsion from the social body, are necessary functions of the latter; and if it is not capable of accomplishing it, it is a sign of waning vital power or serious ailment. Toleration, and, above all, admiration, of the ego-maniac, be he one in theory or in practice, is, so to speak, a proof that the kidneys of the social organism do not accomplish their task, that society suffers from Bright's disease.

In the following chapters we shall study the forms under which ego-mania manifests itself in literature, and we shall find occasion to treat in detail of many points to which at this stage mere allusion has been sufficient.

CHAPTER II.

PARNASSIANS AND DIABOLISTS.

It has become the custom to designate the French Parnassians a school, but those who are comprised under this denomination have always refused to allow themselves to be included under a common name. 'The Parnassus?' . . . exclaimed one of the most undoubted Parnassians, M. Catulle Mendès.* 'We have never been a school! . . . The Parnassus! We have not even written a preface! . . . The Parnassus originated from the necessity of reaction against the looseness of poetry issuing from the adherents of Murger, Charles Bataille, Amédée Rolland, Jean du Boys; then it became a league of minds, who sympathized in matters of art. . . .'

The name 'Parnassiens' was, in fact, applied to a whole series of poets and writers who have scarcely a point in common between them. They are united by a purely external bond; their works have been brought out by the Parisian editor

* Jules Huret, *Enquête sur l'Évolution littéraire*, p. 288.

Alphonse Lemerre, who was able to make Parnassians, as the editor Cotta, in the first half of this century, made German classics. The designation itself emanates from a sort of almanac of the Muses, which Catulle Mendès published in 1860 under the title, *Le Parnasse contemporain: recueil de vers nouveaux*, and which contains contributions from almost all the poets of the period.

With most of the names of this numerous group I do not need to concern myself, for those who bear them are not degenerate, but honest average men, correctly twittering what others have first sung to them. They have exercised no sort of direct influence on contemporary thought, and have only indirectly contributed to strengthen the action of a few leaders by grouping themselves around them in the attitude of disciples, and in permitting them thus to present themselves with an imposing retinue, which always makes an impression on vacuous minds.

The leaders alone are of importance in my inquiries. It is of them we think when we speak of the Parnassians, and it is from their peculiarities that the artistic theory attributed to *Le Parnasse* has been derived. Embodied most completely in Théophile Gautier, it can be summed up in two words: perfection of form and *impassibilité*, or impassiveness.

To Gautier and his disciples the form is everything in poetry; the substance has no importance. 'A poet,' says he,* 'say what you will, is a labourer; he ought not to have more intelligence than a labourer, or know any other trade than his own, otherwise he will do it badly. I hold the mania that there is for putting them on an ideal pedestal is perfectly absurd; nothing is less ideal than a poet. . . . The poet is a keyboard [*clavecin*], and nothing more. Every idea in passing lays its finger on a key; the key vibrates and gives its note, that is all.' In another place he says: 'For the poet, words have in themselves, and outside the sense they express, a beauty and value of their own, like precious stones as yet uncut, and set in bracelets, necklaces, or rings; they charm the connoisseur who looks at them, and sorts them with his finger in the little bowl where they are stored.'† Gustave Flaubert, another worshipper of words, takes entirely this view of the subject when he exclaims:‡ 'A beautiful verse meaning nothing, is superior to a verse less beautiful meaning something.' By the words 'beautiful' and 'less beautiful,' Flaubert here understands

* Théophile Gautier, *Les Grotesques*. 3me édition. Paris, 1856.

† *Les Fleurs du Mal*, par Charles Baudelaire, précédées d'une notice par Théophile Gautier. 2e édition. Paris, 1869, p. 46.

‡ M. Guyau, 'L'Esthétique du Vers moderne,' *Revue philosophique*, vol. xvii., p. 270.

'names with triumphant syllables, sounding like the blast of clarions,' or 'radiant words, words of light.'* Gautier only credited Racine, for whom he, a romanticist, naturally had a profound contempt, with one verse of any value:

'La fille de Minos et de Pasiphae.'

The most instructive application of this theory is found in a piece of poetry by Catulle Mendès, entitled *Récapitulation,* which begins as follows:

'Rose, Emmeline,
Margueridette,
Odette,
Alix, Aline.

'Paule, Hippolyte,
Lucy, Lucile,
Cécile,
Daphné, Mélite.

'Artémidore,
Myrrha, Myrrhine,
Périne,
Naïs, Eudore.'

Eleven stanzas of the same sort follow, which I will dispense with reproducing, and then this final strophe:

'Zulma, Zélie,
Régine, Reine,
Irène! . . .
Et j'en oublie.'†

'And I forget the rest'—this is the only one of the sixty lines of the piece which has any sense, the fifty-nine others being composed of women's names only.

What Catulle Mendès intends here is clear enough. He wishes to show the state of a libertine's soul, who revels in the remembrance of all the women he has loved, or with whom he has flirted. In the mind of the reader the enumeration of their names is to give rise to voluptuous images of a troop of young girls, ministrants of pleasure, of pictures of a harem or of the paradise of Mahomet. But apart from the length of the list, which makes the piece insupportably wearisome and chilling, Mendès does not attain the desired effect for yet a second reason—because his artificiality betrays at the first glance the profound insincerity of his pretended emotion. When before the mind of a gallant the figures of the Phyllises of his pastoral idylls present themselves, and he really feels the necessity of tenderly murmuring their names, he certainly does not think of arranging these names as a play on words (Alix—

* Th. Gautier, quoted by M. Guyau, *loc. cit.*, p. 270.
† Printed in *L'Écho de Paris*, No. 2,972, July 8, 1892.

Aline, Lucy—Lucile, Myrrha—Myrrhine, etc.). If he is cold-blooded enough to give himself up to this barren desk-work, he cannot possibly find himself in the lascivious ecstasy which the piece is supposed to express and impart. This emotion, immoral and vulgar in its boasting, would still have the right, like every genuine affection of the soul, of being lyrically expressed. But a list of unmeaning names, artificially combined, and arranged according to their assonance, implies nothing. According to the art theory of the Parnassians, however, *Récapitulation* is poetry—nay, the ideal of poetry—for it 'ne signifie rien,' as Flaubert requires, and is wholly composed of words which, according to Th. Gautier, 'ont en eux-mêmes une beauté et une valeur propres.'

Another eminent Parnassian, Théodore de Banville,* without pushing to its extreme limits, with the intrepid logic of Catulle Mendès, the theory of verbal resonance bare of all meaning, has professed it with a sincerity to which homage is due. 'I charge you,' he exclaims to poets in embryo, 'to read as much as possible, dictionaries, encyclopædias, technical works treating of all the professions, and of all the special sciences, catalogues of libraries and of auctions, handbooks of museums—in short, all the books which can increase your stock of words, and give you instruction on their exact sense, proper or figurative. Directly your head is thus furnished you will be already well prepared to find rhymes.' The only essential thing in poetry, according to Banville, is to catch rhymes. To compose a piece of poetry on any subject, he teaches his disciples: 'All the rhymes on this subject must first of all be known. The remainder, the soldering, that which the poet must add to stop up the holes with the hand of an artist and workman—these are called the plugs. I should like to see those who counsel us to avoid the plugs bind two planks together with the help of thought.' The poet—Banville thus sums up his doctrine—has no ideas in his brain; he has only sounds, rhymes, and play on words (*calembours*). This play on words inspires his ideas, or his simulacra of ideas.

Guyau rightly uses this criticism with regard to the æsthetic theory of the Parnassians established by Banville.† 'The search for rhyme, pushed to the extreme, tends to make the poet lose the habit of logically connecting his ideas—that is to say, in reality to think—for to think, as Kant has said, is to unite and to bind. To rhyme, on the contrary, is to place in juxtaposition words necessarily unconnected. . . . The cult of rhyme for rhyme's sake introduces into the brain itself of the poet, little

* Théodore de Banville, *Petit Traité de Poésie française.* 2e édition revue. Paris, 1880, pp. 54, 64.

† M. Guyau, *loc. cit.*, pp. 264, 265.

by little, a kind of disorder and permanent chaos; all the usual laws of association, all the logic of thought is destroyed in order to be replaced by the chance encounter of sounds. . . Periphrasis and metaphor are the only resources for good rhyming. . . . The impossibility in seeking for rich rhymes, of remaining simple, involves in its turn a consequent risk of a certain lack of sincerity. Freshness of spontaneous feeling will disappear in the too consummate artist in words; he will lose that respect for thought as such which ought to be the first quality of the writer.'

Where Guyau commits an error is when he says that the cult of rhyme for rhyme's sake 'introduces into the brain even of the poet a kind of disorder and permanent chaos.' The proposition must be reversed. 'Permanent chaos' and 'disorder' in the brain of the poet are there already; the exaggeration of the importance of rhyme is only a consequence of this state of mind. Here we have again to deal with a form of that inaptitude for attention, well known to us, which is a peculiarity of the degenerate subject. The course of his ideas is determined, not by a central idea round which the will groups all other ideas, suppressing some and strengthening others with the help of attention; but by the wholly mechanical association of ideas, awakened in the case of the Parnassians by a similar or identical verbal sound. His poetical method is pure echolalia.

The Parnassian theory of the importance of form, notably of rhyme, for poetry, of the intrinsic value of beauty in the sound of words, of the sensuous pleasure to be derived from sonorous syllables without regard to their sense, and of the uselessness, and even harmfulness, of thought in poetry, has become decisive in the most recent development of French poetry.* The Symbolists, whom we have studied in an earlier chapter, hold closely to this theory. These poor in spirit, who only babble 'sonorous syllables' without sense, are the direct descendants of the Parnassians.

The Parnassian theory of art is mere imbecility. But the egomania of the degenerate minds who have concocted it reveals itself in the enormous importance they attribute to their hunt for rhymes, to their puerile pursuit of words which are 'tonitruants' and 'rayonnants.' Catulle Mendès ends a poem (*La seule Douceur*), where he describes in the most fulsome manner a series of the pleasures of life, with this envoi: 'Prince, I lie.

* Compare with the above Tolstoi's opinion on the same subject: 'He is violently hostile to all rhymed verse. Rhythm and rhyme chain down thought, and all that is opposed to the most complete formation possible of the idea is an evil. . . . Tolstoi . . . regards the decline in our esteem for poetry in verse as a progress.'—Raphael Löwenfeld, *Gespräche über und mit Tolstoi.* Berlin, 1891, p. 77.

Beneath the Twins or the Urn (? Aquarius) to make noble words rhyme together in one's book, this is the sole joy of life.'* He who is not of this opinion is simply said to forfeit his humanity. Thus it is that Baudelaire calls Paris 'a Capernaum, a Babel peopled by the imbecile and useless, not over-fastidious in their ways of killing time, and wholly inaccessible to literary pleasures.'† To treat as imbecile those who look upon a senseless jumble of rhymes and a litany of so-called beautiful proper names as of no value, is a stupid self-conceit at which one might well laugh. But Baudelaire goes so far as to speak of the 'useless.' No one has a right to live who is inaccessible to what he calls 'literary pleasures'—that is, an idiotic echolalia! Because he cultivates the art of playing on words with a puerile seriousness, everyone must place the same importance as he does on his infantile amusements, and whoever does not do so is not simply a Philistine or an inferior being, without susceptibility or refinement—no, he is a 'useless creature.' If this simpleton had the power, he would no doubt wish to pursue his idea to the end and sweep the 'useless' out of the ranks of the living, as Nero put to death those who did not applaud his acting in the theatre. Can the monstrous ego-mania of one demented be more audaciously expressed than in this remark of Baudelaire's?

The second characteristic of the Parnassians, after their insane exaggeration of the value for humanity of the most external form for poetry and rhyming, is their 'impassibility,' or impassivity. They themselves, of course, will not admit that this term is applicable to them. 'Will they ever have done with this humbug!' angrily cried Leconte de Lisle, when interrogated on the subject of 'impassibility,' and Catulle Mendès says, 'Because Glatigny has written a poem entitled *Impassible*, and because I myself wrote this line, the avowed pose in which is belied in the course of the poem,

'"Pas de sanglots humains dans le chant des poètes!"‡

it has been concluded that the Parnassians were or wished to be "impassive." Where do they find it, where do they see it, this icy equanimity, this dryness which they have ascribed to us?'§

Criticism, in sooth, has chosen its word badly. 'Impassi-

* 'Prince, je mens. Sous les Gémeaux
Ou l'Amphore, faire en son livre
Rimer entre eux de noble mots,
C'est la seule douceur de vivre.'

† Eugène Crépet, *Les Poètes français*, vol. iv., p. 536: study by Charles Baudelaire of Théodore de Banville.

‡ 'No human sobs in the poets' song!'

§ Jules Huret, *op. cit.*, pp. 283, 297.

bility' in art, in the sense of complete indifference to the drama of nature and of life, there cannot be. It is psychologically impossible. All artistic activity, in so far as it is not the mere imitation of disciples, but flows from an original necessity, is a reaction of the artist upon received impressions. Those which leave him completely indifferent inspire the poet with no verse, the painter with no picture, the musician with no tone composition. Impressions must strike him in some way or other, they must awaken in him some emotion, in order that he may have the idea at all of giving them an objective artistic form. In the infinite volume of phenomena flowing uniformly past his senses, the artist has distinguished the subject he treats with the peculiar methods of his art; he has exercised a selective activity, and has given the preference to this subject over others. This preference presupposes sympathy or antipathy; the artist, therefore, must have felt something on perceiving his subject. The sole fact that an author has written a poem or a book testifies that the subject treated of has inspired him with curiosity, interest, anger, an agreeable or disagreeable emotion, that it has compelled his mind to dwell upon it. This is, therefore, the contrary of indifference.

The Parnassians are not impassive. In their poems there is whimpering, cursing and blasphemy, and the utterance of joy, enthusiasm and sorrow. But what tortures them or enchants them is exclusively their own states, their own experiences. The only foundation of their poetry is their 'Ego.' The sorrow and joy of other men do not exist for them. Their 'impassibilité' is, therefore, not impassivity, but rather a complete absence of sympathy. The 'tower of ivory' in which, according to the expression of one of them, the poet lives and proudly withdraws himself from the indifferent mob, is a pretty name given to his obtuseness in regard to the being and doing of his fellow-creatures. All this has been well discerned by that beneficently clear-minded critic, M. Ferdinand Brunetière. 'One of the worst consequences,' he writes, 'that they [the theories of the Parnassians, and, in particular, those of Baudelaire] may involve, is, by isolating art, to isolate the artist as well, making him an idol to himself, and as it were enclosing him in the sanctuary of his "Ego." Not only, then, does his work become a question merely concerned with himself—of his griefs and his joys, his loves and his dreams—but, in order to develop himself in the direction of his aptitudes, there is no longer anything which he respects or spares, there is nothing he will not subordinate to himself; which is, to speak by the way, the true definition of immorality. To make one's self the centre of things, from a philosophical point of view, is as puerile an illusion as to see in man "the king of creation," or in the earth what the ancients called "the navel of the world"; but, from the purely human point of view, it is the glorification of egoism, and, consequently, the negation itself of solidarity.'*

Thus Brunetière notices the ego-mania of the Parnassians, and affirms their anti-social principles, their immorality; he believes, however, that they have freely chosen their point of view. This is his only error. They are not ego-maniacs by free choice, but because they must be, and cannot be otherwise. Their ego-mania is not a philosophy or a moral doctrine; it is their malady.

The impassivity of the Parnassians is, as we have seen, a callousness with regard, not to everything, but only to their fellow-creatures, united to the tenderest love for themselves. But their 'impassibility' has yet another aspect, and those who have found the term have probably thought above all of this, without having given themselves a complete account of it. The indifference which the Parnassians display, and of which they are particularly proud, applies less to the joys and sufferings of their fellow-creatures than to the universally recognised moral law. For them there is neither virtue nor vice, but only the beautiful and the ugly, the rare and the commonplace. They took their point of view 'beyond good and evil,' long before the moral madness of Frederick Nietzsche found this formula. Baudelaire justifies it in the following terms: 'Poetry . . . has no other aim than itself; it cannot have any other, and no poem will be so great, so noble, so truly worthy of the name of poem, as that which will have been written only for the pleasure of writing a poem. I do not wish to say—be it well understood—that poetry may not ennoble morals, that its final result may not be to raise man above vulgar interests. This would evidently be an absurdity. I say that, if the poet has pursued a moral aim he has diminished his poetical power, and it is not imprudent to wager that his work will be bad. Poetry cannot, under pain of death or degradation, assimilate itself to science or morals. It has not truth for its object, it has only itself.' And Th. Gautier, who records this remark, wholly approves of it. 'On the high summits he [the poet] is at peace: *pacem summa tenent*,' he says,† in employing an image which occurs dozens of times in Nietzsche.

Let us nail here first of all a current sophistical artifice employed by Baudelaire. The question to which he wishes to reply is this: Is poetry to be moral or not? Suddenly he smuggles science, with which it has nothing to do, into his

* F. Brunetière, 'La Statue de Baudelaire,' *Revue des deux Mondes*, September 1, 1892, vol. cxiii., p. 221.

† *Les Fleurs du Mal*, par Charles Baudelaire, précédées d'une notice par Théophile Gautier. 2e édition. Paris, 1869, p 22.

demonstration, names it in the same breath with morality, shows triumphantly that science has nothing in common with poetry, and then acts as though he had demonstrated the same thing on the subject of morality. Now, it does not occur to any reasonable man of the present day to demand of poetry the teaching of scientific truths, and for generations no serious poet has thought of treating of astronomy or physics in a didactic poem. The only question which some minds would wish to consider as an open one is that of knowing if we may, or may not, exact of poetry that it be moral, and it is this question that Baudelaire answers by an unproven affirmative, and by a crafty shuffling.

I have no wish to linger here on this question, not because it embarrasses me and I should like to avoid it, but because it seems to me more in place to discuss it when considering the disciples of the 'Parnassus,' the 'Décadents,' and the Æsthetes, who have pushed the doctrine to its extreme. I will for the present leave uncontradicted the assertion of the Parnassians, that poetry has not to trouble itself about morality. The poet ought to stand 'beyond good and evil.' But that could only reasonably signify an absolute impartiality; it can only amount to this—that the poet, in considering some action or aspect, simply aspires to find himself confronted by a drama, which he judges only for its beauty or ugliness, without even asking if it is moral or not. A poet of this kind must necessarily see, then, as many beautiful as ugly things, as many moral as immoral. For, taking all in all, moral and beautiful things in humanity and Nature are at least as frequent as the contrary, and must even preponderate. For we consider as ugly, either what presents a deviation from laws which are familiar to us, and to which we have adapted ourselves, or that in which we recognise the manifestation of anything prejudicial to us; and we regard as immoral all that is contrary to the prosperity, or even the maintenance, of society. Now, the mere fact that we have looked to find laws is a proof that phenomena corresponding to recognised laws, and consequently agreeable to us, must be far more numerous than the phenomena in contradiction to those laws, and therefore repulsive; and so, too, the maintenance of society is a proof that conservative and favourable, *i.e.*, moral, forces must be more vigorous than destructive, *i.e.*, immoral, forces. Hence, in a poem which while it did not trouble itself about morals, was nevertheless truly impartial, as it pretended to be, morality would be represented on a scale at least as large as, and even somewhat larger than, immorality. But in the poetry of the Parnassians this is not the case. It delights almost exclusively in depravity and ugliness. Théophile

Gautier extols, in *Mademoiselle de Maupin*, the basest sensuality, which, if it should become the general rule, would carry humanity back to the condition of savages living in sexual promiscuousness without individual love, and without any family institutions whatever; Sainte-Beuve, in other respects more romanticist than Parnassian, builds in his novel *Volupté* an altar to sexual pleasure, at which the ancient Asiatic adorers of Ashtaroth could, without hesitation, have performed their worship; Catulle Mendès, who began his literary career by being condemned for a moral outrage (brought upon himself by his play *Le Roman d'une Nuit*) exalts in his later works, of which I will not quote the titles, one of the most abominable forms of unnatural license; Baudelaire sings of carrion, maladies, criminals and prostitutes; in short, if one contemplates the world in the mirror of Parnassian poetry, the impression received is that it is composed exclusively of vices, crimes and corruption without the smallest intermixture of healthy emotions, joyous aspects of Nature and human beings feeling and acting honestly. In perpetual contradiction to himself, as becomes a truly degenerate mind, the same Baudelaire, who in one place does not wish poetry to be confounded with morality, says in another place: 'Modern art has an essentially devilish [*démoniaque*] tendency. And it seems that this infernal side of his nature, which man takes a pleasure in explaining to himself, increases daily, as if the devil amused himself by magnifying it through artificial processes, in imitation of the poultry-farmers, patiently cramming the human species in his hen-yards to prepare for himself a more succulent nourishment.'*

There is no indifference here to virtue or vice; it is an absolute predilection for the latter, and aversion for the former. Parnassians do not at all hold themselves 'beyond good or evil,' but plunge themselves up to the neck in evil, and as far as possible from good. Their feigned 'impartiality' with regard to the drama of morality or immorality is in reality a passionate partisanship for the immoral and the disgusting. It was wrong, therefore, to think of characterizing them by 'impassibility.' Just as they lack feeling only towards their fellow-creatures, and not towards themselves, so they are only cold and indifferent towards good, not towards evil; the latter attracts them, on the contrary, as forcibly, and fills them as much with feelings of pleasure, as the good attracts and rejoices the sane majority of men.

This predilection for evil has been discerned by many observers, and a good number have endeavoured to explain it

* Baudelaire, in the work quoted by Eugène Crépet, *Les Poètes français*, vol. iv., pp. 541, 542.

philosophically. In a lecture on 'Evil as the Object of Poetical Representation,' Franz Brentano says :*

'Since what is presented in tragedy appears so little desirable and cheerful, it suggests the idea that these explanations (of the pleasure we find in it) are less to be sought in the excellence of the subject than in some peculiar need of the public, which finds a response alone in the things thus exhibited. . . . Can it be that man feels, from time to time, the need of a melancholy emotion, and longs for tragedy as for something which satisfies this need in the most efficacious way, assisting him, so to speak, to weep heartily for once? . . . If for a long time no passions, such as tragedies excite, have had sway in us, the power to experience them demands anew, in some way, to manifest itself, and it is tragedy which comes to our aid ; we feel the emotions painfully, it is true, but at the same time we experience a beneficial alleviation of our need. I think I have observed similar facts a hundred times—less in myself than in others, in those, for example, who devour with avidity the newspaper report of the "latest murder."'

Professor Brentano here confounds first of all, with a lamentable levity, what is evil and what is saddening — two wholly different concepts. The death of a beloved being, for example, is saddening, but there is nothing evil in it, *i.e.*, immoral, unless, by a subtle quibble, it is proposed to interpret as an immorality the action of natural forces in the dissolution of the individual. Further, he gives as an explanation what is only a perfectly superficial paraphrase—Why do we take pleasure in evil? Because . . . we have evidently in us a tendency to take pleasure in evil! *Opium facit dormire quia est in eo virtus dormitiva.* M. Fr. Paulhan has treated the question more seriously, but neither do we get very far with him. 'A contemplative, broad, inquisitive, penetrating mind,' he says,† 'with profound moral tendencies, which can nevertheless sink into oblivion in great part during scientific research or æsthetic contemplation ; sometimes also with a slight natural perversion, or simply a marked tendency towards certain pleasures, whatever they may be, which are not an evil in themselves, and may even be a good, but of which the abuse is an evil—such are the foundations of the sentiment (love of evil) which is occupying us. The idea of evil, by flattering a taste, finds a solid point of support ; and there is one reason more why it is agreeable—in that it satisfies, ideally, an inclination which reason hinders from being satisfied really to satiety.'

* Franz Brentano, *Das Schlechte als Gegenstand dichterischer Darstellung.* Vortrag gehalten in der Gesellschaft der Litteraturfreunde zu Wien. Leipzig, 1892, p. 17.

† Fr. Paulhan, *Le nouveau Mysticisme.* Paris, 1891, p 94. See, in addition, all the chapter 'L'amour du mal,' pp. 57-99.

Here again is this sequence of ideas revolving in a circle, like a cat at play biting its tail: we have a taste for evil, because we find a taste for evil. The intellectual ineptitude which M. Paulhan here reveals is so much the more surprising in that, some pages above, he came very near the true solution of the enigma. 'There are morbid states,' he there says, 'where the appetites are depraved; the patient eagerly swallows coal, earth, or things still worse. There are others in which the will is vitiated, and the character warped in some point. The pathological examples are striking, and the case of the Marquis de Sade is one of the most characteristic. . . . One sometimes finds enjoyment in the evils suffered by one's self, just as in those of others. The sentiments of voluptuousness, sorrow and pity, which psychology has studied, appear to betray sometimes a veritable perversion, and to contain as elements the love of sorrow for sorrow itself. . . . Often one has to do with people who desire their own weal primarily, and then the woe of others. One or other of these psychical states is visible in many cases of wickedness; for example, in the fact of a rich manufacturer falsely accusing a young man, who is going to marry, of being affected by a venereal disease, and maintaining his assertion *for the pleasure* of doing so . . . or, again, of a young villain who relishes the pleasure of theft to the point of crying: "Even if I were rich, I should always like to steal." Even the sight of physical suffering is not always disagreeable; many people seek it. . . . This perversion is probably of all times and of all countries. . . . It would seem that into the mind of a man of our times there might enter a certain enjoyment in upsetting the order of nature, which does not appear to have been manifested before with a similar intensity. It is one of the thousand forms of recoiling on one's self which characterizes our advanced civilization.' Here M. Paulhan touches the kernel of the question, without remarking it or being arrested by it. The love of evil is not a universally human attribute; it is an 'aberration' and a 'perversion,' and 'one of the thousand forms of recoiling on one's self,' otherwise more briefly and more clearly expressed as ego-mania.

The literature of penal legislation and mental therapeutics has registered hundreds of cases of aberration in which the patient has felt a passionate predilection for the evil and horrible, for sorrow and death. I should like to quote only one characteristic example: 'In the autumn of 1884 there died, in a Swiss prison, Marie Jeanneret, a murderess. After having received a good education she devoted herself to the care of the sick, not for the love of doing good, but to satisfy a mad passion. The sufferings, groans and distorted features of the sick filled her with secret voluptuousness. She implored the doctors, on her knees and with tears, to allow her to assist in dangerous operations, in order to be able to gratify her cravings. The death-agony of a human being afforded her the height of enjoyment. Under the pretext of a disease of the eyes, she had consulted several oculists, and had obtained from them belladonna and other poisons. Her first victim, a woman, was her friend; others followed; the doctors, to whom she had recommended herself as nurse, having no suspicions, the less so because she frequently changed her residence. An attempt failing in Vienna led to discovery; she had poisoned not less than nine persons, but felt neither repentance nor shame. In prison her most ardent wish was to fall dangerously ill, in order to satiate herself in the looking-glass with the contortions of her own features.'*

Thus we recognise, in the light of clinical observation, the true nature of the Parnassians. Their impassivity, in so far as it is mere indifference to the sufferings of others, and to virtue and vice, proceeds from their ego-mania, and is a consequence of their obtuseness, which makes it impossible for them to receive a sufficiently keen presentation of the external world, hence also of sorrow, vice, or ugliness, so as to be able to respond by normal reactions, by aversion, indignation, or pity. But in cases where impassivity constitutes a declared predilection for what is evil and disgusting, we can see the same aberration which makes of the imbecile a cruel torturer of animals,† and of Marie Jeanneret, cited above, a tenfold poisoner. The whole difference consists in the degree of impulsion. If it is strong enough, its consequences are heartless acts and crimes. If it is elaborated by diseased centres with insufficient force, it can be satisfied by imagination alone, by poetic or artistic activity.

Of course there have been attempts made to defend aberration as something justified and voluntary, and even to erect it

* Oswald Zimmermann, *Die Wonne des Leids. Beiträge zur Erkenntniss des menschlichen Empfindens in Kunst und Leben.* 2te umgearbeitete Auflage. Leipzig, 1885, p. 111. This book is without value in point of ideas, for it reproduces, in language deliberately inflated, and visibly aspiring to 'depth,' the most imbecile drivel of the trio, Edward von Hartmann, Nietzsche and Gustave Jäger. But the author, who is well read, has carefully compiled some useful materials in certain chapters, particularly in that entitled, 'Association of Voluptuousness and Cruelty' (p. 107 *et seq.*). (The case of Jeanneret, first published by Chatelain in the *Annales médico-psychologiques*, has also been quoted by Krafft-Ebing, *Lehrbuch der gerichtlichen Psychopathologie.* 3te Auflage. Stuttgart, 1892, p. 248.

† Sollier, *op. cit.*, p. 123: 'The imbecile is refined in his persecutions, and that knowingly. He loves to see suffering. He skins a bird alive, laughs on hearing its cries and seeing its struggles. He tears off the feet of a frog, looks at its suffering for a moment, then abruptly crushes it, or kills it in some other way, as one of the imbeciles at Bicêtre does. . . . The imbecile is as cruel to his fellow-creature as to animals, and that even in his jesting. Thus he will laugh maliciously and mock at a comrade who has become crippled.'

into an intellectual distinction. Thus it is that M. Paul Bourget* puts into the mouth of the 'Décadents,' with little artifices of style which do not permit a moment's doubt that he is expressing his own opinion, the following argument: 'We delight in what you call our corruptions of style, and we delight at the same time the refined people of our race and our time. It remains to be seen whether our exception is not an aristocracy, and whether, in the æsthetic order, the majority of suffrages represents anything else than the majority of ignorances. . . . It is a self-deception not to have the courage of one's intellectual pleasure. Let us delight, therefore, in our singularities of ideal and of form, even if we must shut ourselves up in a solitude without visitors.'

It seems scarcely necessary to show that by these arguments, in which M. Bourget anticipates the whole delirious 'philosophy' of Nietzsche, every crime can be glorified as an 'aristocratic' action. The assassin has 'the courage of his intellectual pleasure,' the majority which does not approve of him is a majority of the 'ignorant,' he delights in the 'singularity' of his 'ideal,' and for this reason must at the most allow himself to be shut up in 'a solitude without visitors,' *i.e.*, to speak plainly, in a reformatory, if 'the majority of ignorances' does not have him hanged or guillotined. Has not the 'Décadent' Maurice Barrès defended and justified Chambige, a specimen of the murderer for love of murder, with Bourget's theory?

This same repulsive theorist of the most abandoned anti-social ego-mania denies also that one can speak of a mind as diseased or healthy. 'There is,' he says,† 'from the metaphysical observer's point of view, neither disease nor health of the soul; there are only psychological states, for he perceives in our sufferings and in our faculties, in our virtues and in our vices, in our volitions and in our renunciations, only changing combinations, inevitable, and therefore normal, subject to the known laws of the association of ideas. Only prejudice, in which the ancient doctrine of final causes and the belief in the definite aim of the universe reappear, can make us consider the loves of Daphnis and Chloë in the valley as natural and healthy, and the loves of a Baudelaire as artificial and unwholesome.'

To bring this silly sophistry down to its just value, common-sense has only to recollect the existence of lunatic asylums. But common-sense has not the right of suffrage among the rhetoricians of M. Paul Bourget's stamp. We reply to him, then, with a seriousness he does not merit, that in fact every vital manifestation, those of the brain as of any other organ, is the

* Paul Bourget, *Essais de Psychologie contemporaine.* Paris, 1883, p. 28.
† *Ibid.*, pp. 12, 13.

necessary and only possible effect of the causes which occasion them, but that, according to the state of the organ and of its elementary parts, its activity, necessary and natural as such, can be useful or hurtful to the whole organism. Whether the world has a purpose is a question that can altogether be left indecisive, but the activity of each part of the organism has nevertheless, if not the aim, at least unquestionably the effect, of preserving the whole organism; if it does not produce this effect, and if, on the contrary, it thwarts it, it is injurious to the whole organism, and for such an injurious activity of any particular organ language has coined the word 'disease.' The sophist who denies that there may be disease and health must also logically deny that there may be life and death, or, at least, that death may have some sort of importance. For, as a matter of fact, given a certain activity of its parts which we call morbid, the organism perishes, while with an activity of another nature, which we qualify as healthy, it lives and thrives. As long, then, as Bourget does not lay down the dogma that pain is as agreeable as pleasure, decrepitude as satisfactory as vigour, and death as desirable as life, he proves that he does not know, or dares not draw from his premise, the just conclusion which would immediately make the absurdity of it apparent.

The whole theory which must explain and justify the predilection for evil has, besides, been invented as an after-thought. The inclination for what is evil and disgusting existed first, and was not a consequence of philosophical considerations and self-persuasion. We have here merely another case of that method of our consciousness, so often attested in the course of these inquiries, which consists of inventing rational causes for the instincts and acts of the unconscious.

In the predilection of the Parnassians for the immoral, criminal and ugly, we have to deal merely with an organic aberration, and with nothing else. To pretend that inclinations of this kind exist in all men, even in the best and sanest, and are merely stifled by him, while the Parnassians give the rein to theirs, is an arbitrary and unproved assertion. Observation and the whole march of the historical development of humanity contradict it.

There may be repulsion and attraction in nature—no one denies it. A glance at the magnetic poles, at the positive and negative electrodes, suffices to establish this fact. We find this phenomenon again among the lowest forms of life. Certain materials attract, others repel them. There is no question here of an inclination or an expression of the will. We must rather consider the process as purely mechanical, having its reason probably in molecular relations which are still unknown to us. Microbiology gives to the attitude of micro-organisms towards attractive and repulsive matter the name of 'chemotaxis' or chimiotaxia, invented by Pfeffer.* In higher organisms the conditions are naturally not so simple. Among them also, it is true, the ultimate cause of inclinations and aversions is certainly chimiotactic, but the effect of chimiotaxia must necessarily manifest itself under another form. A simple cell such as a bacillus, for example, is repelled directly when it penetrates into the radius of a chimic body which repels it. But the cell constituting a portion of a higher organism has not this liberty of movement. It cannot change its place independently. If it is now chimiotactically repelled, it cannot escape from the pernicious action, but must remain exposed to it, and submit to the disturbances in its vital activity. If these are sufficiently serious to injure the functions of the whole organism, the latter obtains knowledge of it, endeavours to perceive their cause, discovers it also, as a general rule, and does for the suffering cell what the latter cannot do alone, namely, shields it from the repelling action. The organism necessarily acquires experience in its defence against pernicious influences. It learns to know the circumstances in which they appear, and no longer permits matters to reach the stage of the really chimiotactic effect, but for the most part evades disturbing matters before they can exert a really direct repulsion. The knowledge acquired by the individual becomes hereditary, transforms itself into an organized faculty of the species, and the organism feels subjectively, as a discomfort which may amount to pain, the warning that a pernicious influence is acting upon it, and that it has to avoid it. To escape from pain becomes one principal function of the organism, which it cannot insufficiently provide against or neglect without expiating that negligence by its ruin.

In the human being processes take place not otherwise than as they have been here described. The hereditary organized experience of the species warns him of the noxiousness of influences to which he is frequently exposed. His outposts against naturally hostile forces are his senses. Taste and smell give him, as to repulsive chimiotactic matter, the impressions of nausea and of stench; the different kinds of skin-sensations make him aware, through sensations of pain, heat, or cold, that a given contact is unfavourable to him; eye and ear place him on his guard, by loud, shrill, discordant sensations, against the mechanical effects of certain physical phenomena. Finally, the higher cerebral centres respond to recognised noxious influences of a composite nature, or to the representation of them by an equally composite reaction of aversion in different degrees of intensity, from simple discomfort to horror, indignation, dismay, or fury.

The vehicle of this hereditary, organized, racial experience

* Verworn employs the word 'chemotropism.'

is the unconscious life ; to it is confided defence against simple, frequently recurring noxious influences. Nausea at intolerable tastes, repugnance to insufferable smells, the fear of dangerous animals, natural phenomena, etc., have become for it an instinct to which the organism abandons itself without reflection—*i.e.*, without the intervention of consciousness. But the human organism learns to distinguish and avoid not only all that is directly prejudicial to itself; it acts in the same way with regard to that which menaces it not as an individual, but as a racial being, as a member of an organized society; antipathy to influences injurious to the maintenance or prosperity of the society becomes in him an instinct. But this enriching of organized unconscious cognition represents a higher degree of development than many human beings attain to. The social instincts are those that a man acquires last of all, and, in conformity to a known law, he loses them first when he retrogrades in his organic development.

Consciousness has occasion to declare the dangerous nature of phenomena, and to defend the organism against it, only if these phenomena are either quite new, or very rare, so that they cannot be hereditarily recognised and dreaded; or if they enclose in themselves many different elements, and do not act directly, but only by their more or less remote consequences, so that to know them exacts a complex activity of representation and judgment.

Thus aversion is always the instinctive, or conscious cognition of a noxious influence. Pleasure, its opposite, is not merely, as has been sometimes maintained, the absence of discomfort—*i.e.*, a negative state—but something positive. Every part of the organism has definite needs which assert themselves as a conscious or unconscious tendency, as an inclination or appetite; the satisfaction of these needs is felt as a pleasure which can rise to a feeling of bliss. The first need of each organ is to manifest itself in activity. Its simple activity is a source of pleasure to it, so long as it does not go beyond its powers. The activity of the cerebral centres consists in receiving impressions, and in transforming them into representations and movements. This activity produces in them feelings of pleasure ; they have in consequence a strong desire to receive impressions so as to be put into activity by them, and experience feelings of pleasure.

This, broadly sketched, is the natural history of the feelings of pleasure and pain. The reader who has mastered it will experience no difficulty in comprehending the nature of aberration.

Unconscious life is subject to the same biological laws as conscious life. The vehicle of the unconscious is the same nervous tissue—although, it may be, another portion of the system—in which consciousness is also elaborated, The unconscious is just as little infallible as consciousness. It can be more highly developed or retarded in its development; it can be more or less stupid or intelligent. If the unconscious is incompletely developed, it distinguishes badly and judges falsely, it deceives itself in the knowledge of what is prejudicial or favourable to it, and instinct becomes unreliable or obtuse. Then we get the phenomenon of indifference to what is ugly, loathsome, immoral.

We know that among the degenerate divers arrested developments and malformations appear. Particular organs or entire systems of organs are arrested at a degree of development which corresponds to infancy, or even to the fœtal life. If the highest cerebral centres of the degenerate stop in their development at a very low stage, they become imbeciles or idiots. If the arrest of development strikes the nervous centres of unconscious life, the degenerate lose the instincts which, in normal beings, find expression in nausea and disgust at certain noxious influences; I might say, their unconscious life suffers from imbecility or idiocy.

Again, we have seen in the preceding chapter that the impressionability of the nerves and brain in the degenerate subject is blunted. Hence he only perceives strong impressions, and it is only these which excite his cerebral centres to that intellectual and motor activity which produces in them feelings of pleasure. Now, disagreeable impressions are naturally stronger than agreeable or indifferent impressions, for if they were not stronger we should not feel them as painful, and they would not induce the organism to make efforts to defend itself. To procure, then, the feelings of pleasure which are linked with the activity of the cerebral centres, to satisfy the need of functioning which is peculiar to the cerebral centres as to all the other organs, the degenerate person seeks impressions which are strong enough to excite to activity his obtuse and inert centres. But such impressions are precisely those which the healthy man feels as painful or repugnant. Thus, the aberrations or perversions of the degenerate find explanation. They have a longing for strong impressions, because these only can put their brains into activity, and this desired effect on their centres is only exercised by impressions that sane beings dread because of their violence, *i.e.*, painful, repugnant and revolting impressions.

To say that every human being has secretly a certain predilection for the evil and the abominable is absurd: the only little spark of truth contained in this foolish assertion is, that even the normal human being becomes obtuse when fatigued, or exhausted by illness; *i.e.*, he falls into the state which, in the degenerate, is chronic. Then he presents naturally the same phenomena as we have attested in the case of the latter, although in a much lower degree. He may find pleasure, then, in crime and ugliness, and in the former rather than in the latter; for crimes are social injuries, while uglinesses are the visible form of forces unfavourable to the individual; but social instincts are feebler than the instincts of self-preservation. Consequently they are sooner put to sleep, and for this reason the repulsion against crime disappears more quickly than that against ugliness. In any case, this state is also an aberration in the normal being, but imputable to fatigue, and in him is not chronic, as in the degenerate, nor does it amount to the hidden fundamental character of his being, as the sophists who calumniate him pretend.

An uninterrupted line of development leads from the French romantic school to the Parnassians, and all the germs of the aberrations which confront us in full expansion among the latter can be distinguished in the former. We have seen in the preceding book how superficial and poor in ideas their poetry is, how they exalt their imagination above the observation of reality, and what importance they assign to their world of dreams. Sainte-Beuve, who at first joined their group, says on this subject, with a complacency which proves he was not conscious of expressing any blame: 'The Romance School . . . had a thought, a cult, viz., love of art and passionate inquisitiveness for a vivid expression, a new turn, a choice image, a brilliant rhyme: they wished for every one of their frames a peg of gold. [A remarkably false image, let it be said in passing. A rich frame may be desired for a picture, but as to the nail which supports it, regard will be had to its solidity and not to its preciousness.] Children if you will, but children of the Muses, who never sacrifice to ordinary grace [*grâce vulgaire*].'*

Let us hold this admission firmly, that the romantic writers were children; they were so in their inaptitude to comprehend the world and men, in the seriousness and zeal with which they gave themselves up to their game of rhymes, in the artlessness with which they placed themselves above the precepts of morality and good sense in use among adults. Let us exaggerate this childishness a little (without allying with it the wild and exuberant imagination of a Victor Hugo, and his gift of lightning-like rapidity of association, evoking the most startling antitheses), and we obtain the literary figure of Théophile Gautier, whom the imbecile Barbey d'Aurevilly could name in the same breath with Goethe,† evidently for the sole reason that the sound of the great German poet's name in French pronunciation has a certain resemblance to that of Gautier, but of whom one of his admirers,

* Sainte-Beuve, *Causeries du Lundi*, vol. xiv., p. 70. Article on the complete poems of Théodore de Banville, October 12th, 1857.

† Barbey d' Aurevilly, *Goethe et Diderot*. Paris, 1882.

M. J. K. Huysmans, says:* 'Des Esseintes [the hero of his novel] became gradually indifferent to Gautier's work; his admiration for that incomparable painter had gone on diminishing from day to day, and now he was more astonished than delighted by his indifferent descriptions. The impression left by the objects was fixed on his keenly observant eye, but it was localized there, and had not penetrated further into his brain and flesh [?]; like a monstrous reflector, he was constantly limited to reverberate his environment with an impersonal distinctness.'

When M. Huysmans regards Gautier as an impersonal mirror of reality, he is the victim of an optical illusion. In verse as in prose, Gautier is a mechanical worker, who threads one line of glittering adjectives after another, without designing anything particular. His descriptions never give a clear outline of the object he wishes to depict. They recall some crude mosaic of the later Byzantine decadence, the different stones of which are lapis-lazuli, malachite, chrysoprase and jasper, and which yield, for this reason, an impression of barbarous splendour, while scarcely any design is discernible. In his ego-mania, lacking all sympathy with the external world, he does not suspect what sorrows and joys its drama encloses, and just as he feels nothing in the prospect before him, so neither can he awaken in the reader emotion of any sort by his listless and affected attempts to render it. The only emotions of which he is capable, apart from his arrogance and vanity, are those connected with sex; hence, in his works we merely find alternations between glacial coldness and lubricity.

If we exaggerate Théophile Gautier's worship of form and lasciviousness, and if to his indifference towards the world and men we associate the aberration which caused it to degenerate into a predilection for the bad and the loathsome, we have before us the figure of Baudelaire. We must stop there awhile, for Baudelaire is—even more than Gautier—the intellectual chief and model of the Parnassians, and his influence dominates the present generation of French poets and authors, and a portion also of English poets and authors, to an omnipotent degree.

It is not necessary to demonstrate at length that Baudelaire was a degenerate subject. He died of general paralysis, after he had wallowed for months in the lowest depths of insanity. But even if no such horrible end had protected the diagnosis from all attack, there would be no doubt as to its accuracy, seeing that Baudelaire showed all the mental stigmata of degeneration during the whole of his life. He was at once a mystic and an

* J. K. Huysmans, *A Rebours*. 4ème mille. Paris, 1892, p. 251.

erotomaniac,* an eater of hashish and opium;† he felt himself attracted in the characteristic fashion by other degenerate minds, mad or depraved, and appreciated, for example, above all authors, the gifted but mentally-deranged Edgar Poe, and the opium-eater Thomas de Quincey. He translated Poe's tales, and devoted to them an enthusiastic biography and critique, while from the *Confessions of an Opium-Eater*, by De Quincey, he compiled an exhaustive selection, to which he wrote extravagant annotations.

The peculiarities of Baudelaire's mind are revealed to us in the collection of his poems, to which he has given a title betraying at once his self-knowledge and his cynicism: *Les Fleurs du Mal*—'The Flowers of Evil.' The collection is not complete. There lack some pieces which only circulate in manuscript, because they are too infamous to bear the full publicity of a marketable book. I will take my quotations, however, from the printed verses only, which are quite sufficient to characterize their author.

Baudelaire hates life and movement. In the piece entitled *Les Hiboux*, he shows us his owls sitting in a row, motionless, under the black yews, and continues:

'Leur attitude au sage enseigne
Qu'il faut en ce monde qu'il craigne
Le tumulte et le mouvement.

L'homme ivre d'une ombre qui passe
Porte toujours le châtiment
D'avoir voulu changer de place.'

Beauty says of herself, in the piece of that name:

'Je hais le mouvement qui déplace les lignes;
Et jamais je ne pleure et jamais je ne ris.'

---

* Paul Bourget, *op. cit.*, p. 6: 'He is a libertine, and depraved visions amounting to Sadism disturb the very man who comes to worship the raised finger of his Madonna. The morose orgies of the vulgar Venus, the heady fumes of the black Venus, the refined delights of the learned Venus, the criminal audacity of the bloodthirsty Venus, have left their memories in the most spiritualized of his poems. 'An offensive odour of vile alcoves escapes from these . . . verses. . . .' And p. 19: '. . . It is not so with the mystic soul—and that of Baudelaire's was one. For this soul did not content itself with a faith in an idea. It *saw* God. He was for it not a word, not a symbol, not an abstraction, but a Being, in whose company the soul lived as we live with a father who loves us.'

† Théophile Gautier, who was himself a member of a hashish club, tries to make us believe (*Les Fleurs du Mal*, p. 57 *et seq.*), that Baudelaire was addicted to the use of narcotic poisons only with the object of 'physiological experiment'; but we know the tendency of the degenerate to represent the impulsions of which they are ashamed as acts of free will, for which they have all sorts of palliating explanations.

He abhors the natural as much as he loves the artificial. Thus he depicts his ideal world (*Rêve Parisien*):

'De ce terrible paysage
Que jamais œil mortel ne vit,
Ce matin encore l'image,
Vague et lointaine, me ravit . . .

'J'avais banni de ces spectacles
Le végétal irrégulier . . .

'Je savourais dans mon tableau
L'enivrante [!] monotonie
Du métal, du marbre et de l'eau.

'Babel d'escaliers et d'arcades
C'était un palais infini,
Plein de bassins et de cascades
Tombant dans l'or mat ou bruni;

'Et des cataractes pesantes,
Comme des rideaux de cristal,
Se suspendaient, éblouissantes,
A des murailles de métal.

'Non d'arbres, mais de colonnades
Les étangs dormants s'entouraient,
Où de gigantesques naïades,
Comme des femmes, se miraient.

'Des nappes d'eau s'epanchaient, bleues,
Entre des quais roses et verts,
Pendant des millions de lieues,
Vers les confins de l'univers;

'C'étaient des pierres inouïes
Et des flots magiques; c'étaient
D'immenses glaces éblouies
Par tout ce qu'elles reflétaient.

'Et tout, même la couleur noire,
Semblait fourbi, clair, irisé . . .

'Nul astre d'ailleurs, nuls vestiges
De soleil, même au bas du ciel,
Pour illuminer ces prodiges,
Qui brillaient d'un feu personnel (!)

'Et sur ces mouvantes merveilles
Planait (terrible nouveauté!
Tout pour l'œil, rien pour les oreilles!)
Un silence d'eternité.'

Such is the world he represents to himself, and which fills him with enthusiasm: not an 'irregular' plant, no sun, no stars, no movement, no noise, nothing but metal and glass, *i.e.*, something like a tin landscape from Nuremberg, only larger and of more costly material, a plaything for the child of an American millionaire suffering from the wealth-madness of parvenus, with a little electric lamp in the interior, and a mechanism which slowly turns the glass cascades, and makes the glass sheet of water slide. Such must necessarily be the aspect of the ego-maniac's ideal world. Nature leaves him cold or repels him, because he neither perceives nor comprehends her ; hence, where the sane man sees the picture of the external world, the ego-maniac is surrounded by a dark void in which, at most, uncomprehended nebulous forms are hovering. To escape the horror of them he projects, as from a magic-lantern, coloured shadows of the images which fill his consciousness ; but these representations are rigid, inert, uniform and infantile, like the morbid and weak cerebral centres by which they are elaborated.

The incapacity of the ego-maniac to feel aright external impressions, and the toil with which his brain works, are also the key of the frightful tedium of which Baudelaire complains, and of the profound pessimism with which he contemplates the world and life. Let us hear him in *Le Voyage :*

> 'Nous avons vu partout . . .
> Le spectacle ennuyeux de l'immortel péché :
>
> 'La femme, esclave vile, orgueilleuse et stupide,
> Sans rire s'adorant et s'aimant sans dégôut ;
> L'homme, tyran goulu, paillard, dur et cupide,
> Esclave de l'esclave et ruisseau dans l'égout ;
>
> 'Le bourreau qui jouit, le martyr qui sanglote ;
> La fête qu'assaisonne et parfume le sang ; . . .
>
> 'Et les moins sots, hardis amants de la démence,
> Fuyant le grand troupeau parqué par le Destin,
> Et se réfugiant dans l'opium immense [!].
> — Tel est du globe entier l'éternel bulletin . . .
>
> 'O Mort, vieux capitaine, il est temps ! levons l'ancre !
> Ce pays nous ennuie, O Mort ! Appareillons !
>
> 'Nous voulons . . .
> Plonger au fond du gouffre, Enfer ou Ciel, qu'importe ?
> Au fond de l'Inconnu pour trouver du nouveau !'

This desperate cry towards the 'new' is the natural complaint of a brain which longs to feel the pleasures of action, and greedily craves a stimulation which his powerless sensory nerves cannot give him. Let a sane man imagine the state of mind into which he would fall if he were imprisoned in a cell where no ray of light, no noise, no scent from the outer world would reach him. He would then have an accurate idea of the chronic state of mind in the ego-maniac, eternally isolated by the imperfection of his nervous system from the universe, from its joyous sounds, from its changing scenes and from its captivating movement. Baudelaire cannot but suffer terribly from ennui, for his mind really learns nothing new and amusing, and is forced constantly to indulge in the contemplation of his ailing and whimpering self.

The only pictures which fill the world of his thought are sombre, wrathful and detestable. He says (*Un Mort joyeux*):

> 'Dans une terre grasse et pleine d'escargots
> Je veux creuser moi-même une fosse profounde
> Où je puisse à loisir étaler mes vieux os
> Et dormir dans l'oubli comme un requin dans l'onde . . .
> Plutôt que d'implorer une larme du monde
> Vivant, j'aimerais mieux inviter les corbeaux
> A saigner tous les bouts de ma carcasse immonde.
>
> 'O vers ! noir compagnons sans oreille et sans yeux,
> Voyez venir à vous un mort libre et joyeux !'

In *La Cloche fêlée*, he says of himself:

> '. . . Mon âme est fêlée, et lorsqu'en ses ennuis
> Elle veut de ses chants peupler l'air froid des nuits
> Il arrive souvent que sa voix affaiblie
>
> Semble le râle épais d'un blessé qu'on oublie
> Au bord d'un lac de sang, sous un grand tas de morts.'

Spleen:

> '. . . Mon triste cerveau . . .
> C'est . . . un immense caveau
> Qui contient plus de morts que la fosse commune.
> — Je suis un cimetière abhorré de la lune
> Où, comme des remords, se traînent de longs vers. . . .

Horreur sympathique:

> 'Cieux déchirés comme des grèves,
> En vous se mire mon orgueil !
> Vos vastes nuages en deuil.
>
> 'Sont les corbillards de mes rêves,
> Et vos lueurs sont le reflet,
> De l'Enfer où mon cœur se plaît !'

Le Coucher du Soleil romantique:

> 'Une odeur de tombeau dans les ténèbres nage,
> Et mon pied peureux froisse, au bord du marécage,
> Des crapauds imprévus et de froids limaçons.'

Dance macabre: The poet speaking to a skeleton:

> 'Aucuns t'appelleront une caricature,
> Qui ne comprennent pas, amants ivres de chair,
> L'élégance sans nom de l'humaine armature.
> Tu réponds, grand squelette, à mon goût le plus cher ! . . .'

Une Charogne:

> 'Rappelez-vous l'objet que nous vîmes, mon âme,
> Ce beau matin d'été si doux:
> Au détour d'un sentier une charogne infâme
> Sur un lit semé de cailloux,

'Les jambes en l'air, comme une femme lubrique
Brûlante et suant les poisons,
Ouvrait d'une façon nonchalante et cynique
Son ventre plein d'exhalaisons . . .

'Et le ciel regardait la carcasse superbe [!]
Comme une fleur s'epanouir.
La puanteur était si forte, que sur l'herbe
Vous crûtes vous évanouir . . .

'Et pourtant vous serez semblable à cette ordure,
A cette horrible infection,
Étoile de mes yeux, soleil de ma nature,
Vous, mon ange et ma passion !

'Oui ! telle vous serez, ô la reine des grâces,
Après les derniers sacrements,
Quand vous irez, sous l'herbe et les floraisons grasses,
Moisir parmi les ossements. . . .'

That which pleases Baudelaire most are these pictures of death and corruption which I could quote in still greater numbers if I did not think that these examples sufficed. However, next to the frightful and the loathsome it is the morbid, the criminal and the lewd, which possess the strongest attraction for him.

Le Rêve d'un Curieux :

'Connais-tu, comme moi, la douleur savoureuse? . . .'

Spleen :

'Mon chat sur le carreau cherchant une litière
Agite sans repos son corps maigre et galeux. . . .

Le Vin du Solitaire :

'Un baiser libertin de la maigre Adeline. . . .'

Le Crépuscule du Soir :

'Voici le soir charmant, ami du criminel ; . . .
Et l'homme impatient se change en bête fauve. . . .

La Destruction :

'Sans cesse à mes côtés s'agite le Démon . . .
Je l'avale et le sens qui brûle mon poumon
Et l'emplit d'un désir éternel et coupable . . .

'Il me conduit . . .
Haletant et brisé de fatigue, au milieu
Des plaines de l'Ennui, profondes et désertes,

'Et jette dans mes yeux . . .
Des vêtements souillés, des blessures ouvertes,
Et l'appareil sanglant de la Destruction !'

In *Une Martyre* he describes complacently and in detail a bedroom in which a young, presumably pretty courtesan has been murdered ; the assassin had cut off her head and carried it away. The poet is only curious to know one thing :

'L'homme vindicatif que tu n'as pu, vivante,
Malgré tant d'amour, assouvir,
Combla-t-il sur ta chair inerte et complaisante
L'immensité de son désir ?'

Femmes damnées, a piece dedicated to the worst aberration of degenerate women, terminates with this ecstatic apostrophe to the heroines of unnatural vice :

'O vierges, ô démons, ô monstres, ô martyres,
De la réalité grands esprits contempteurs,
Chercheuses d'infini, dévotes et satyres,
Tantôt pleines de cris, tantôt pleines de pleurs,

Vous que dans votre enfer mon âme a poursuivies,
Pauvres sœurs, je vous aime autant que je vous plains. . . .'

Préface :

'Si le viol, le poison, le poignard, l'incendie,
N'ont pas encore brodé de leurs plaisants dessins
Le canevas banal de nos piteux destins,
C'est que notre âme, hélas ! n'est pas assez hardie. . . .'

But if he is not bold enough to commit crimes himself, he does not leave a moment's doubt that he loves them, and much prefers them to virtue, just as he prefers the 'end of autumns, winters, springs steeped in mud,' to the fine season of the year (*Brumes et Pluies*). He is 'hostile to the universe rather than indifferent' (*Les sept Vieillards*). The sight of pain leaves him cold, and if tears are shed before him they only evoke in his mind the image of a landscape with running waters.

Madrigal triste :

'Que m'importe que tu sois sage ?
Sois belle ! et sois triste ! Les pleurs
Ajoutent un charme au visage,
Comme le fleuve au paysage.'

In the struggle between *Abel et Caïn* he takes the part of the latter without hesitation :

'Race d'Abel, dors, bois et mange ;
Dieu te sourit complaisamment.

'Race de Caïn, dans la fange
Rampe et meurs misérablement.

'Race d'Abel, ton sacrifice
Flatte le nez du Séraphin.

'Race de Caïn, ton supplice
Aura-t-il jamais une fin ?

'Race d'Abel, vois tes semailles
Et ton bétail venir à bien ;

'Race de Caïn, tes entrailles
Hurlent la faim comme un vieux chien.

'Race d'Abel, chauffe ton ventre
A ton foyer patriarchal ;

'Race de Caïn, dans ton antre
Tremble de froid, pauvre chacal !

'Ah ! race d'Abel, ta charogne
Engraissera le sol fumant !

'Race de Caïn, ta besogne
N'est pas faite suffisamment.

'Race d'Abel, voici ta honte :
Le fer est vaincu par l'épieu ! [?]

'Race de Caïn, au ciel monte
Et sur la terre jette Dieu !'

If he prays it is to the devil (*Les Litanies de Satan*):

'Gloire et louange à toi, Satan, dans les hauteurs
Du Ciel, où tu régnas, et dans les profondeurs
De l'Enfer, où, vaincu, tu rêves en silence !
Fais que mon âme un jour, sous l'Arbre de Science,
Prés de toi se repose. . . .'

Here there mingles with the aberration that mysticism which is never wanting in the degenerate. Naturally, the love of evil can only take the form of devil-worship, or diabolism, if the subject is a believer, if the supernatural is held to be a real thing. Only he who is rooted with all his feelings in religious faith will, if he suffers from moral aberration, seek bliss in the adoration of Satan, in impassioned blasphemy of God and the Saviour, in the violation of the symbols of faith, or will wish to incite unnatural voluptuousness by mortal sin and infernal damnation, though humouring it in the *messe noir*, in the presence of a really consecrated priest, and in a hideous travesty of all the forms of the liturgy.

Besides the devil, Baudelaire adores only one other power, viz., voluptuousness. He prays thus to it (*La Prière d'un Païen*):

'Ah ! ne ralentis pas tes flammes !
Réchauffe mon cœur engourdi,
Volupté, torture des âmes ! . . .
Volupté, sois toujours ma reine !'

To complete the portrait of this mind, let us cite two more of his peculiarities. He suffers first from images of perpetual anguish, as his piece testifies (*Le Gouffre*), which is valuable as a confession :

'. . . Tout est abîme,—action, désir, rêve,
Parole ! et sur mon poil qui tout droit se relève
Mainte fois de la peur je sens passer le vent.

'En haut, en bas, partout, la profondeur, la grève,
Le silence, l'espace affreux et captivant . . .
Sur le fonde de mes nuits, Dieu, de son doigt savant,
Dessine un cauchemar multiforme et sans trêve.

'J'ai peur du sommeil comme on a peur d'un grand trou,
Tout plein de vague horreur, menant on ne sait où ;
Je ne vois qu' infini par toutes les fenêtres,

'Et mon esprit, toujours du vertige hanté,
Jalouse du néant l'insensibilité.'

Baudelaire describes here accurately enough that obsession of degenerates which is called 'fear of abysses' (cremnophobia).* His second peculiarity is his interest in scents. He is attentive to them, interprets them ; they provoke in him all kinds of sensations and associations. He expresses himself thus on this subject in *Correspondances :*

'Les parfums, les couleurs, et les sons se répondent.

'Il est des parfums frais comme des chairs d'enfants,
Doux comme les hautbois, verts comme les prairies,
— Et d'autres, corrumpus, riches et triomphants,

'Ayant l'expansion des choses infinies,
Comme l'ambre, le muse, le benjoin et l'encens,
Qui chantent les transports de l'esprit et des sens.'

He loves woman through his sense of smell . . . ('Le parfum de tes charmes étranges,' *A une Malabaraise*), and never fails, in describing a mistress, to mention her exhalations.

Parfum exotique :

'Quand les deux yeux fermés, en un soir chaud d'automne,
Je respire l'odeur de ton sein chaleureux,
Je vois se dérouler des rivages heureux
Qu'eblouissent les feux d'un soleil monotone.'

La Chevelure :

'O toison, moutonnant jusque sur l'encolure !
O boucles ! O parfum chargé de nonchaloir ! . . .

'La langoureuse Asie et la brûlante Afrique,
Tout un monde lointain, absent, presque défunt,
Vit dans tes profondeurs, forêt aromatique !'

Naturally, instead of good odours, he prefers the perfumes which affect the healthy man as stinks. Putrefaction, decomposition and pestilence charm his nose.

Le Flacon :

'Il est de forts parfums pour qui toute matière
Est poreuse. On dirait qu'ils pénètrent le verre . . .
Parfois on trouve un vieux flacon qui se souvient,
D'où jaillit toute vive une âme qui revient.

* Dr. E. Régis, *Manuel bratique de Médecine mentale.* 2e édition. Paris, 1892, p. 279.

'Voilà le souvenir enivrant qui voltige
Dans l'air troublé ; les yeux se ferment ; le vertige
Saisit l'âme vaincue et la pousse à deux mains
Vers un gouffre obscurci de miasmes humains ;

'Il la terrasse au bord d'un gouffre séculaire,
Où, Lazare odorant déchirant son suaire,
Se meut dans son réveil le cadavre spectral
D'un vieil amour ranci, charmant et sepulcral.

'Ainsi, quand je serai perdu dans la memoire
Des hommes, dans le coin d'une sinistre armoire
Quand on m'aura jeté, vieux flacon désolé,
Décrépit, poudreux, sale, abject, visqueux, fêlé,

'Je serai ton cercueil, aimable pestilence !
Le témoin de ta force et de ta virulence,
Cher poison préparé par les anges ! . . .'

We now know all the features which compose Baudelaire's character. He has the 'cult of self';* he abhors nature, movement and life ; he dreams of an ideal of immobility, of eternal silence, of symmetry and artificiality ; he loves disease, ugliness and crime ; all his inclinations, in profound aberration, are opposed to those of sane beings ; what charms his sense of smell is the odour of corruption ; his eye, the sight of carrion, suppurating wounds and the pain of others ; he feels happy in muddy, cloudy, autumn weather ; his senses are excited by unnatural pleasures only. He complains of frightful tedium and of feelings of anguish ; his mind is filled with sombre ideas, the association of his ideas works exclusively with sad or loathsome images ; the only thing which can distract or interest him is badness—murder, blood, lewdness and falsehood. He addresses his prayers to Satan, and aspires to hell.

He has attempted to make his peculiarities pass for a comedy and a studied pose. In a note placed at the head of the first edition (1857) of the *Fleurs du Mal*, he says : 'Among the following pieces, the most characteristic . . . has been considered, at least by men of intellect, only for what it really is : the imitation of the arguments of ignorance and fury. Faithful to his painful programme, the author has had, like a good comedian, to fashion his mind to all sophisms, as to all corruptions. This candid declaration will, doubtless, not prevent honest critics from ranking him among the theologians of the people,' etc. Some of his admirers accept this explanation or appear to accept it. 'His intense disdain of the vulgar,' murmurs Paul Bourget, 'breaks out in extremes of paradox, in laborious mystification . . . Among many readers, even the keenest, the fear of being duped by this grand disdainer hinders full admiration.† The

* *Les Fleurs du Mal*, p. 5—'le culte de soi-même.' This is Théophile Gautier's own term.

† Paul Bourget, *op. cit.*, p. 31.

term has become a commonplace of criticism for Baudelaire; he is a 'mystificateur'; everything for him is only a deception; he himself neither feels nor believes anything he expresses in his poetry. It is twaddle, and nothing else. A rhetorician of the Paul Bourget sort, threshing straw, and curling scraps of paper, may believe that an inwardly free man is capable of preserving artificially, all his life long, the attitude of a galley-slave or a madman, well knowing he is only acting a comedy. The expert knows that the choice of an attitude, such as Baudelaire's, is a proof in itself of deep-seated cerebral disturbance.

Mental therapeutics has declared that persons who simulate insanity with some perseverance, even with a rational object, as, for example, in the case of certain criminals on their trial, in order to escape punishment, are almost without exception really mad,* although not to the degree they try to represent, just as the inclination to accuse one's self, or to boast, of imaginary crimes is a recognised symptom of hysteria. The assertion of Baudelaire himself, that his Satanism is only a studied *rôle*, has no sort of value whatever. As is so frequently the case among the 'higher degenerates,' he feels in his heart that his aberrations are morbid, immoral and anti-social, and that all decent persons would despise him or take pity on him, if they were convinced that he was really what he boasts of being in his poems; he has recourse, consequently, to the childish excuse that malefactors also often have on their lips, viz., 'that it was not meant

* Ch J. J. Sazaret, *Etude sur la Simulation de la Folie.* Nancy, 1888. This pamphlet by a beginner, which contains a useful collection of clinical observations, is particularly amusing, in that all the observations cited by the author demonstrate exactly the reverse of what he proposes to prove. After having himself asserted (p. 22) that 'the victims of hysteria are much given to simulate all sorts of maladies,' he says (p. 29): 'Persons mentally affected now and then simulate madness; the case is rare, but it has nevertheless been verified, and if it has not been oftener recorded, it is, we believe, that observers have limited themselves to a superficial examination, and certain actions have not been analyzed.' The case is so far from rare that it is pointed out in every observation quoted by the author. In the case of Baillarger (2nd observation), the so-called simulatrix had been in a lunatic asylum eight years before, as a fully confirmed mad-woman; in the case of Morel (4th observation), the simulator 'had a nervous attack at the sight of a lancet,' which is clearly aichmophobia and a certain stigma of degeneration; in the 6th observation Morel admits that 'the extravagance of the subject, his fear of poison' (thus a case of pronounced iophobia), 'and the fact of picking up filth, indicate a possible mental disorder'; the case of Foville (10th observation) 'had a certain number of insane in his family'; the case of Legrand du Saulle (18th observation) was 'the son of a hysterical woman and grandson of a madman'; the case of Bonnet and Delacroix (19th observation) 'numbers some insane among his ancestors'; the case of Billod (22nd observation) 'has often manifested disturbance and delirium,' etc. All these supposed simulators were insane quite unmistakably, and the fact that they intentionally exaggerated the symptoms of their delirium was only a further proof of their alienation.

seriously.' Perhaps also Baudelaire's consciousness experienced a sincere horror of the perverse instincts of his unconscious life, and he sought to make himself believe that with his Satanism he was laughing at the Philistines. But such a tardy palliation does not deceive the psychologist, and is of no importance for his judgment.

CHAPTER III.

DECADENTS AND ÆSTHETES.

As on the death of Alexander the Great his generals fell on the conqueror's empire, and each one seized a portion of land, so did the imitators that Baudelaire numbered among his contemporaries and the generation following—many even without waiting for his madness and death—take possession of some one of his peculiarities for literary exploitation. The school of Baudelaire reflects the character of its master, strangely distorted; it has become in some sort like a prism, which diffracts this light into its elementary rays. His delusion of anxiety (anxiomania), and his predilection for disease, death and putrefaction (necrophilia), have fallen, as we have seen in the preceding book, to the lot of M. Maurice Rollinat. M. Catulle Mendès has inherited his sexual aberrations and lasciviousness, and besides all the newer French pornographists rely upon them for proving the 'artistic raison d'être' of their depravity. Jean Richepin, in *La Chanson des Gueux*, has spied in him, and copied, his glorification of crime, and, further, in *Les Blasphèmes*, has swelled Baudelaire's imprecations and prayers to the devil to the size of a fat volume, in a most dreary and wearisome manner. His mysticism suckles the Symbolists, who, after his example, pretend to perceive mysterious relations between colours and the sensations of the other senses, with this difference, that they hear colours while he smelt them; or, if you will, they have an eye in their ear, while he saw with the nose. In Paul Verlaine we meet again his mixture of sensuality and pietism. Swinburne has established an English depot for his Sadism, compounded of lewdness and cruelty, for his mysticism and for his pleasure in crime, and I greatly fear that Giosué Carducci himself, otherwise so richly gifted and original, must have turned his eyes towards the *Litanies de Satan*, when he wrote his celebrated *Ode à Satan*.

The diabolism of Baudelaire has been specially cultivated by Villiers de l'Isle-Adam and Barbey d'Aurevilly. These two men have, in addition to the general family likeness of the degenerate, a series of special features in common. Villiers and Barbey attributed to themselves, as the deranged frequently do, a fabulous genealogy; the former aspired to be a descendant of Count de l'Isle-Adam, the celebrated Marshal and Grand-Master of Malta (who as such could not be married, be it understood!), and he claimed one day, in a letter addressed to the Queen of England, the surrender of Malta in virtue of his right of heritage. Barbey annexed the aristocratic surname of d'Aurevilly, and during the whole of his life spoke of his noble race—which had no existence. Both made a theatrical display of fanatical Catholicism, but revelled at the same time in studied blasphemies against God.* Both delighted in eccentricities of costume and modes of life, and Barbey had the habit of graphomaniacs, which we know already, of writing his letters and his literary works with different coloured inks. Villiers de l'Isle-Adam, and still more Barbey d'Aurevilly, created a class of poetry to the worship of the devil, which recalls the craziest depositions of witches of the Middle Ages when put to the torture. Barbey especially may be said to have gone, in this respect, to the limits of the imaginable. His book *Le Prêtre marié* might be written by a contemporary of witch-burners; but it is surpassed in its turn by *Les Diaboliques*, a collection of crack-brained histories, where men and women wallow in the most hideous license, continually invoking the devil, extolling and serving him. All the invention in these ravings Barbey stole with utter shamelessness from the books of the Marquis de Sade, without a shade of shame; that which belongs properly to him is the colouring of Catholic theology he gives to his profligacies. If I only speak in general terms of the books mentioned here, without entering into details, without summarizing the contents, or quoting characteristic passages, it is because my demonstrations do not require a plunge into this filth, and it is sufficient to point the finger from afar at the sink of vice which testifies to Baudelaire's influence on his contemporaries.

Barbey, the imitator of Baudelaire, has himself found an imitator in M. Joséphin Péladan, whose first novel, *Vice suprême*, occupies an eminent place in the literature of diabolism. M. Péladan, who had not yet promoted himself to the dignity of a first-class Assyrian king, paraphrases in his book what he means by '*vice suprême*': 'Let us deny Satan! Sorcery has always sorcerers . . . superior minds which have no need of conjuring-book, their thought being a page written by hell for hell. Instead of the kid they have killed the good soul within them, and

* Fr. Paulhan, *op. cit.*, p. 92: 'While affecting the faith of a seminarist, he [Villiers] delighted in blasphemy. He considered the right to blaspheme as his peculiar property. . . . This Catholic Breton loved the society of Satan more than that of God.'

are going to the Sabbath of the Word.' [May the reader not stumble over obscurities! What were Péladan if he were not mystical?] 'They assemble to profane and soil the idea. Existing vice does not satisfy them; they invent, they rival each other in seeking for, *new evil*, and if they find it they applaud each other. Which is worst, the Sabbath-orgies of the body or those of the mind, of criminal action or of perverted thought? To reason, justify, to apotheosize evil, to establish its ritual, to show the excellence of it—is this not worse than to commit it? To adore the demon, or love evil, the abstract or the concrete term of one and the same fact. There is blindness in the gratification of instinct, and madness in the perpetration of misdeeds; but to conceive and theorize exacts a calm operation of the mind which is the *vice suprême*.'*

Baudelaire has expressed this much more concisely in one single verse: '*La conscience dans le Mal*' ('consciousness in evil').†

The same Villiers de l'Isle-Adam, who has copied his diabolism from Baudelaire, has appropriated the predilection of the latter for the artificial, and has raised it to a funny pitch in his novel *L'Ève future*. In this half-fantastic half-satirical and wholly mad book, he imagines, as the next development of humanity, a state in which the woman of flesh and blood will be abolished, and be replaced by a machine to which he allows (which is a little contradictory) the shape of a woman's body, and which it will be sufficient with the help of a screw so to dispose, in order to obtain from it at once whatever happens to be desired: love, caprices, infidelity, devotion, every perversion and every vice. This is in sooth even more artificial than Baudelaire's tin and glass landscape!

A later disciple, M. Joris Karl Huysmans, is more instructive than all those imitators of Baudelaire who have only developed the one or the other side of him. He has undertaken the toilsome task of putting together, from all the isolated traits which are found dispersed in Baudelaire's poems and prose writings, a human figure, and of presenting to us Baudelairism incarnate and

* Joséphin Péladan, *Vice suprême*. Paris, 1882, p. 169.

† *Les Fleurs du Mal*, p. 244:

> 'Tête-à-tête sombre et limpide
> Qu'un cœur devenu son miroir!
> Puits de vérité, clair et noir,
> Où tremble une étoile livide,
>
> 'Un phare ironique, infernal,
> Flambeau des grâces sataniques,
> Soulagement et gloire uniques,
> —La conscience dans le Mal!'

living, thinking and acting. The book in which he shows us his model 'Decadent' is entitled *A Rebours* ('Against the Grain').

The word 'décadent' was borrowed by the French critics, in the fifties, from the history of the declining Roman Empire, to characterize the style of Théophile Gautier, and notably of Baudelaire. At the present time the disciples of these two writers, and of their previous imitators, claim it as a title of honour. Otherwise than with the expressions 'pre-Raphaelites' and 'Symbolists,' we possess an exact explanation of the sense which those who speak of 'decadence' and 'decadents' attach to these words.

'The style of decadence,' says Théophile Gautier,* '. . . is nothing else than art arrived at that extreme point of maturity produced by those civilizations which are growing old with their oblique suns [!]—a style that is ingenious, complicated, learned, full of shades of meaning and research, always pushing further the limits of language, borrowing from all the technical vocabularies, taking colours from all palettes, notes from all keyboards, forcing itself to express in thought that which is most ineffable, and in form the vaguest and most fleeting contours; listening, that it may translate them, to the subtle confidences of the neuropath, to the avowals of ageing and depraved passion, and to the singular hallucinations of the fixed idea verging on madness. This style of decadence is the last effort of the Word (*Verbe*), called upon to express everything, and pushed to the utmost extremity. We may remind ourselves, in connection with it, of the language of the Later Roman Empire, already mottled with the greenness of decomposition, and, as it were, gamy (*faisandée*), and of the complicated refinements of the Byzantine school, the last form of Greek art fallen into deliquescence. Such is the inevitable and fatal idiom of peoples and civilizations where factitious life has replaced the natural life, and developed in man unknown wants. Besides, it is no easy matter, this style despised of pedants, for it expresses new ideas with new forms and words that have not yet been heard. In opposition to the classic style, it admits of shading, and these shadows teem and swarm with the larvæ of superstitions, the haggard phantoms of insomnia, nocturnal terrors, remorse which starts and turns back at the slightest noise, monstrous dreams stayed only by impotence, obscure phantasies at which the daylight would stand amazed, and all that the soul conceals of the dark, the unformed, and the vaguely horrible, in its deepest and furthest recesses.'

The same ideas that Gautier approximately expresses in this

* *Les Fleurs du Mal*, pp. 17, 18.

rigmarole, Baudelaire enumerates in these terms: 'Does it not seem to the reader, as it does to me, that the language of the later Latin decadence—the departing sigh of a robust person already transformed and prepared for the spiritual life—is singularly appropriate to express passion as it has been understood and felt by the modern poetic world? Mysticism is the opposite pole of that magnet in which Catullus and his followers, brutal and purely epidermic poets, have only recognised the pole of sensuality. In this marvellous language, solecism and barbarism appear to me to convey the forced negligences of a passion which forgets itself and mocks at rules. Words, received in a new acceptation, display the charming awkwardness of the Northern barbarian kneeling before the Roman beauty. Even a play on words, when it enters into these pedantic stammerings, does it not display the wild and bizarre grace of infancy?'*

The reader, who has the chapter on the psychology of mysticism present to his mind, naturally at once recognises what is hidden behind the word-wash of Gautier and Baudelaire. Their description of the state of mind which the 'decadent' language is supposed to express is simply a description of the disposition of the mystically degenerate mind, with its shifting nebulous ideas, its fleeting formless shadowy thought, its perversions and aberrations, its tribulations and impulsions. To express this state of mind, a new and unheard-of language must in fact be found, since there cannot be in any customary language designations corresponding to presentations which in reality do not exist. It is absolutely arbitrary to seek for an example and a model of 'decadent' expression in the language of the Later Roman Empire. It would be difficult for Gautier to discover in any writer whatever of the fourth or fifth century the 'mottled greenness of decomposition and, as it were, gamy' Latin which so greatly charms him. M. Huysmans, monstrously exaggerating Gautier's and Baudelaire's idea, as is the way with imitators, gives the following description of this supposed Latin of the fifth century: 'The Latin tongue, . . . now hung [!], completely rotten, . . . losing its members, dropping suppurations, scarcely preserving, in the total decay of its body, some firm parts which the Christians detached in order to pickle them in the brine of their new language.'†

This debauch in pathological and nauseous ideas of a deranged mind with gustatory perversion is a delirium, and has no foundation whatever in philological facts. The Latin of the later period of decadence was coarse and full of errors, in consequence of the increasing barbarity in the manners and taste of the readers, the narrow-mindedness and grammatical ignorance

* *Les Fleurs du Mal*, pp. 17, 18.

† J. K. Huysmans, *A Rebours*. 4me mille. Paris, 1892, p. 49.

of the writers, and the intrusion of barbarous elements into its vocabulary. But it was very far from expressing 'new ideas with new forms' and from taking 'colours from all palettes'; it surprises us, on the contrary, by its awkwardness in rendering the most simple thoughts, and by its profound impoverishment. The German language has also had a similar period of decadence. After the Thirty Years' War, even the best writers, a Moscherosch, a Zinkgref, a Schupp, were 'often almost incomprehensible' with 'their long-winded and involved periods,' and 'their deportment as distorted as it was stiff';* the grammar displayed the worst deformities, the vocabulary swarmed with strange intruders, but the German of those desolate decades was surely not 'decadent' in the sense of Gautier's, Baudelaire's and Huysmans' definitions. The truth is, that these degenerate writers have arbitrarily attributed their own state of mind to the authors of the Roman and Byzantine decadence, to a Petronius, but especially to a Commodianus of Gaza, an Ausonius, a Prudentius, a Sidonius Apollinaris, etc., and have created in their own image, or according to their morbid instincts, an 'ideal man of the Roman decadence,' just as Rousseau invented the ideal savage and Chateaubriand the ideal Indian, and have transported him by their own imagination into a fabulous past or into a distant country. M. Paul Bourget is more honest when he refrains from fraudulently quoting the Latin authors of the Latin decline, and thus describes the 'decadence,' independently of his Parnassian masters: 'The word "decadence" denotes a state of society which produces too great a number of individuals unfit for the labours of common life. A society ought to be assimilated to an organism. As an organism, in fact, it resolves itself into a federation of lesser organisms, which again resolve themselves into a federation of cells. The individual is the social cell. In order that the whole organism should function with energy, it is necessary that the component organisms should function with energy, but with a subordinate energy. And in order that these inferior organisms should themselves function with energy, it is necessary that their component cells should function with energy, but with a subordinate energy. If the energy of the cells becomes independent, the organisms composing the total organism cease likewise to subordinate their energy to the total energy, and the anarchy which takes place constitutes the decadence of the whole.'†

Very true. A society in decadence 'produces too great a number of individuals unfit for the labours of common life';

* Henri Kurz, in his introduction to the 'Simplician' writings of Grimmelshausen. Leipzig, 1863, 1st part, p. li. See also his remarks on the German of Grimmelshausen (author of *Simplicissimus*), p. xlv. *et seq.*

† Paul Bourget, *op. cit.*, p. 24.

these individuals are precisely the degenerate; 'they cease to subordinate their energy to the total energy,' because they are ego-maniacs, and their stunted development has not attained to the height at which an individual reaches his moral and intellectual junction with the totality, and their ego-mania makes the degenerate necessarily anarchists, *i.e.*, enemies of all institutions which they do not understand, and to which they cannot adapt themselves. It is very characteristic that M. Bourget, who sees all this, who recognises that 'decadent' is synonymous with inaptitude for regular functions and subordination to social aims, and that the consequence of decadence is anarchy and the ruin of the community, does not the less justify and admire the decadents, especially Baudelaire. This is 'la conscience dans le mal' of which his master speaks.

We will now examine the ideal 'decadent' that Huysmans draws so complacently and in such detail for us, in *A Rebours*. First, a word on the author of this instructive book. Huysmans, the classical type of the hysterical mind without originality, who is the predestined victim of every suggestion, began his literary career as a fanatical imitator of Zola, and produced, in this first period of his development, romances and novels in which (as in *Marthe*) he greatly surpassed his model in obscenity. Then he swerved from naturalism, by an abrupt change of disposition, which is no less genuinely hysterical, overwhelmed this tendency and Zola himself with the most violent abuse, and began to ape the Diabolists, particularly Baudelaire. A red thread unites both of his otherwise abruptly contrasted methods, viz., his lubricity. That has remained the same. He is, as a languishing 'Decadent,' quite as vulgarly obscene as when he was a bestial 'Naturalist.'

A Rebours can scarcely be called a novel, and Huysmans, in fact, does not call it so. It does not reveal a history, it has no action, but presents itself as a sort of portrayal or biography of a man whose habits, sympathies and antipathies, and ideas on all possible subjects, specially on art and literature, are related to us in great detail. This man is called Des Esseintes, and is the last scion of an ancient French ducal title.

The Duke Jean des Esseintes is physically an anæmic and nervous man of weak constitution, the inheritor of all the vices and all the degeneracies of an exhausted race. 'For two centuries the Des Esseintes had married their children to each other, consuming their remnant of vigour in consanguineous unions. . . . The predominance of lymph in the blood appeared.' (This employment of technical expressions and empty phrases, scientific in sound, is peculiar to many modern degenerate authors and to their imitators. They sow these words and expressions around them, as the 'learned valet' of a well-known German farce scatters around him his scraps of French, but without being more cognizant of science than the latter was of the French language.) Des Esseintes was educated by the Jesuits, lost his parents early in life, squandered the greater part of his patrimony in foolish carousing which overwhelmed him with ennui, and soon retired from society, which had become insupportable. 'His contempt for humanity increased; he understood at last that the world is composed for the most part of bullies and imbeciles. He had certainly no hope of discovering in others the same aspirations and the same hatreds, no hope of uniting himself with a kindred spirit delighting in a diligent decrepitude [!] as he did. Enervated, moody, exasperated by the inanity of interchanged and accepted ideas, he became like a person aching all over, till at last he was constantly excoriating his epidermis, and suffering from the patriotic and social nonsense which was dealt out each morning in the newspapers. . . . He dreamed of a refined Thebaid, of a comfortable desert, a warm and unmoving ark, where he would take refuge far from the incessant flood of human stupidity.'

He realizes this dream. He sells his possessions, buys Government stock with the ruins of his fortune, draws in this way an annual income of fifty thousand francs, buys himself a house which stands alone on a hill at some distance from a small village near Paris, and arranges it according to his own taste.

'The artificial appeared to Des Esseintes as the distinguishing mark of human genius. As he expressed it, the day of nature is past: by the disgusting uniformity of its landscapes and skies, it has positively exhausted the attentive patience of refined spirits. In sooth, what platitude of a specialist who sees no further than his own line! what pettiness of a tradeswoman keeping this or that article to the exclusion of every other! what a monotonous stock of meadows and trees! what a commonplace agency for mountains and seas!' (p. 31).

He banishes, in consequence, all that is natural from his horizon, and surrounds himself by all that is artificial. He sleeps during the day, and only leaves his bed towards evening, in order to pass the night in reading and musing in his brightly-lit ground-floor. He never crosses the threshold of his house, but remains within his four walls. He will see no one, and even the old couple who wait on him must do their work while he is asleep, so as not to be seen by him. He receives neither letters nor papers, knows nothing of the outer world. He never has an appetite, and when by chance this is aroused, 'he dips his roast meat, covered with some extraordinary butter, into a cup of tea [oh, the devil!], a faultless mixture of Si-a-Fayun, Mo-yu-tan and Khansky, yellow teas brought from China and Russia by special caravans' (p. 61).

His dining-room 'resembled a ship's cabin,' with 'its little French window opening in the wainscot like a port-hole.' It was built within a larger room pierced by two windows, one o which was exactly opposite the port-hole in the wainscot. A large aquarium occupied the whole space between the port-hole and this window. In order, then, to give light to the cabin, the daylight had to pass through the window, the panes of which had been replaced by plate glass, and then through the water 'Sometimes, in the afternoon, when by chance Des Esseintes was awake and up, he set in motion the play of the pipes and conduits which emptied the aquarium and filled it afresh with pure water, introducing into it drops of coloured essences, thus producing for himself at pleasure the green or muddy yellow, opalescent or silver, tones of a real river, according to the colour of the sky, the greater or less heat of the sun, the more or less decided indications of rain; in a word, according to the season and the weather. He would then imagine himself to be between-decks on a brig, and contemplated with curiosity marvellous mechanical fish, constructed with clock-work, which passed before the window of the port-hole, and clung to the sham weeds, or else, while breathing the smell of the tar with which the room had been filled before he entered, he examined the coloured engravings hung on the walls representing steamers sailing for Valparaiso and La Plata, such as are seen at steamship agencies, and at Lloyd's' (p. 27).

These mechanical fish are decidedly more remarkable than Baudelaire's landscapes in tin. But this dream of an ironmonger, retired from business and become an idiot, was not the only pleasure of the Duc des Esseintes, who despised so deeply the 'stupidity and vulgarity of men,' although, of all his acquaintance, probably not one would have stooped to ideas so asinine as these mechanical fish with clock-work movements. When he wishes to do himself a particularly good turn, he composes and plays a gustatory symphony. He has had a cupboard constructed containing a series of little liqueur barrels. The taps of all the barrels could be opened or shut simultaneously by an engine set in motion by pressure on a knob in the wainscot, and under every tap stood an 'imperceptible' goblet, into which, on the turning of the cock, a drop fell. Des Esseintes called this liquor-cupboard his 'mouth organ.' (Notice all these ridiculous complications to mix a variety of liqueurs! As if it required all this deeply thought out mechanism!) 'The organ was then open. The stops labelled "flute, horn, voix céleste," were drawn out ready for action. Des Esseintes drank a drop here and there, played internal symphonies, and succeeded in procuring in the throat sensations analogous to those that music offers to the ear. Each liqueur corresponded in taste, according to him, to the sound of an instrument. Dry curaçoa, for example, to the clarionet, the tone of which is acescent and velvety; kümmel brandy to the oboë, with its sonorous nasal sound; mint and anisette to the flute, which is at the same time sugary and peppery, squeaking and sweet; while, to complete the orchestra, kirsch rages with the blast of a trumpet; gin and whisky scarify the palate with their shrill outbursts of cornets and trombones; liqueur - brandy fulminates with the deafening crash of the tuba; while Chios-raki and mastic roll on to the mucous membrane like the thunder-claps of cymbals and kettledrums struck with the arm!' Thus he plays 'string quartettes under the vault of his palate, representing with the violin old eau-de-vie, smoky and subtle, sharp and delicate; with the tenor simulated by strong rum;' with vespetro as violoncello, and bitters as double bass; green chartreuse was the major, and benedictine the minor key,' etc. (p. 63).

Des Esseintes does not only hear the music of the liqueurs: he sniffs also the colour of perfumes. As he has a mouth organ, he possesses a nasal picture-gallery, *i.e.*, a large collection of flasks containing all possible odorous substances. When his taste-symphonies no longer give him pleasure, he plays an olfactory tune. 'Seated in his dressing-room before his table . . . a little fever disturbed him, he was ready for work. . . . With his vaporizers he injected into the room an essence formed of ambrosia, Mitcham lavender, sweet peas, ess. bouquet, an essence which, when it is distilled by an artist, deserves the name by which it is known, viz., "extract of flowery meadow." Then, in this meadow, he introduced an exact fusion of tuberose, of orange and almond flower, and forthwith artificially-created lilacs sprang up, while limes winnowed each other, pouring down upon the earth their pale emanations. Into this decoration, laid on in broad outlines . . . he blew . . . a light rain of human and quasi-feline essences, savouring of skirts, and indicating the powdered and painted woman, the stephanotis, ayapana, opoponax, cypress, champak, and sarcanthus: on which he juxtaposed a suspicion of syringa, in order to instil into the factitious atmosphere which emanated from them a natural bloom of laughter bathed in sweat (!!), and of joys which riot boisterously in full sunshine' (pp. 154-157).

We have seen how slavishly M. Huysmans, in his drivel about tea, liqueurs and perfumes, follows to the letter the fundamental principle of the Parnassians—of ransacking technical dictionaries. He has evidently been forced to copy the catalogues of commercial travellers dealing in perfumes and soaps, teas and liqueurs, to scrape together his erudition in current prices.

That Des Esseintes should be made ill by this mode of life is not surprising. His stomach rejects all forms of food, and this renders the highest triumph of his love for the artificial possible: he is obliged to be nourished by means of peptonized injections, hence, in a way, diametrically opposed to nature.

Not to be too prolix, I omit many details, *e.g.*, an endless description of tones associated with colours (pp. 17-20); of orchids which he loves, because they have for him the appearance of eruptions, scars, scabs, ulcers and cancers, and seem covered with dressings, plastered with black mercurial axunge, green belladonna unguents (p. 120 *et seq.*); an exposition of the mystical aspect of precious and half-precious stones (pp. 57-60), etc. We will only acquaint ourselves with a few more peculiarities of taste in this decadent type:

'The wild spirit, the rough, careless talent of Goya captivated him; but the universal admiration which Goya's works had gained deterred him somewhat, and for many years he had ceased having them framed. . . . Indeed, if the finest tune in the world becomes vulgar, insupportable, as soon as the public hum it and barrel-organs seize upon it, the work of art to which false artists are not indifferent, which is not disputed by fools, which is not content with stirring up the enthusiasm of some, even it becomes, by this very means, for the initiated polluted, commonplace and almost repulsive' (p. 134).

The reference to barrel-organs is a trick calculated to mislead the inattentive reader. If a beautiful tune becomes insupportable as played on barrel-organs, it is because the organs are false, noisy and expressionless, *i.e.*, they modify the very essence of the tune and drag it down to vulgarity; but the admiration of the greatest fool himself changes absolutely nothing in a work of art, and those who have loved it for its qualities will again find all these qualities complete and intact, even when the looks of millions of impassive Philistines have crawled over it. The truth is, the decadent, bursting with silly vanity, here betrays involuntarily his inmost self. The fellow has not, in fact, the smallest comprehension of art, and is wholly inaccessible to the beautiful as to all external impressions. To know if a work of art pleases him or not, he does not look at the work of art—oh no! he turns his back and anxiously studies the demeanour of the people standing before it. Are they enthusiastic, the decadent despises the work; do they remain indifferent, or even appear displeased, he admires it with full conviction. The ordinary man always seeks to think, to feel, and to do the same as the multitude; the decadent seeks exactly the contrary. Both derive the manner of seeing and feeling, not from their internal convictions, but from what the crowd dictate to them. Both lack all individuality, and they are obliged to have their eyes constantly fixed on the crowd to find their way. The decadent is, therefore, an ordinary man with a *minus* sign, who, equally with the latter, only in a contrary sense, follows in the wake of the crowd, and meanwhile makes things far more difficult for himself than the ordinary man; he is also constantly in a state of irritation, while the latter as constantly enjoys himself. This can be summed up in one proposition—the decadent snob is an anti-social Philistine, suffering from a mania for contradiction, without the smallest feeling for the work of art itself.

Des Esseintes reads occasionally between his gustatory and olfactory *séances*. The only works which please him are naturally those of the most extreme Parnassians and Symbolists. For he finds in them (p. 266) 'the death-struggle of the old language, after it had become ever mouldier from century to century, was ending in dissolution, and in the attainment of that deliquescence of the Latin language which gave up the ghost in the mysterious concepts and enigmatical expressions of St. Boniface and St. Adhelm. Moreover, the decomposition of the French language had set in all at once. In the Latin language there was a long transition, a lapse of 400 years, between the speckled and beautiful speech of Claudian and Rutilius, and the gamy speech of the eighth century. In the French language no lapse of time, no succession in age, had taken place; the speckled (*tacheté*) and superb style of the brothers De Goncourt and the gamy style of Verlaine and Mallarmé rubbed elbows in Paris, existing at the same time and in the same century.'

We now know the taste of a typical decadent in all directions. Let us cast another glance at his character, morals, sentiments and political views.

He has a friend, D'Aigurande, who one day thinks of marrying. 'Arguing from the fact that D'Aigurande possessed no fortune, and that the dowry of his wife was almost nothing, he (Des Esseintes) perceived in this simple desire an infinite perspective of ridiculous misfortunes.' In consequence (!) he encouraged his friend to commit this folly, and what had to happen did happen: the young couple lacked money, everything became a subject for altercations and quarrels; in short, the life of both became insupportable. He amused himself out of doors; she 'sought by the expedients of adultery to forget her rainy and dull life.' By common consent they cancelled their contract and demanded a legal separation. 'My plan of battle was exact, Des Esseintes then said to himself, experiencing the satisfaction of those strategists who see their long-foreseen manœuvres succeeding.'

Another time, in the Rue de Rivoli, he comes upon a boy of about sixteen years old, a 'pale, cunning-looking' child, smoking a bad cigarette, and who asks him for a light. Des Esseintes offers him Turkish aromatic cigarettes, enters into conversation with him, learns that his mother is dead, that his father beats him, and that he works for a cardboard-box maker. 'Des Esseintes listened thoughtfully. "Come and drink," said he, and led him into a café, where he made him drink some very strong punch. The child drank in silence. "Come," said Des Esseintes suddenly, "do you feel inclined for some amusement this evening? I will treat you."' And he leads the unfortunate boy into a disorderly house, where his youth and nervousness astonish the girls. While one of these women draws the boy away, the landlady asks Des Esseintes what was his idea in bringing them such an imp. The decadent answers (p. 95): 'I am simply trying to train an assassin. This boy is innocent, and has reached the age when the blood grows hot; he might run after the girls in his quarter, remain honest while amusing himself. . . . Bringing him here, on the contrary, into the midst of a luxury of which he had no conception, and which will engrave itself forcibly on his memory, in offering him every fortnight such an unexpected treat, he will get accustomed to these pleasures from which his means debar him. Let us admit that it will require three months for them to become absolutely necessary to him. . . . Well, at the end of three months I discontinue the little *rente* which I am going to pay you in advance for this good action, and then he will steal in order to live here. . . . He will kill, I hope, the good gentleman who will appear inopportunely while he is attempting to break open his writing-table. Then my aim will be attained; I shall have contributed, to the extent of my resources, in creating a villain, one more enemy of that hideous society which fleeces us.' And he leaves the poor defiled boy on this first evening with these words: 'Return as quickly as possible to your father. . . . Do unto others what you would not wish them to do to you; with this rule you will go a long way. Good-evening. Above all, don't be ungrateful. Let me hear of you as soon as possible through the police news.'

He sees the village children fighting for a piece of black bread covered with curd cheese; he immediately orders for himself a similar slice of bread, and says to his servant: 'Throw this bread and cheese to those children who are doing for each other in the road. Let the feeblest be crippled, not manage to get a single piece, and, besides, be well whipped by their parents when they return home with torn breeches and black eyes; that will give them an idea of the life that awaits them' (p. 226).

When he thinks of society, this cry bursts from his breast: 'Oh, perish, society! Die, old world!' (p. 293).

Lest the reader should feel curious as to the course of Des Esseintes' history, let us add that a serious nervous illness attacks him in his solitude, and that his doctor imperiously orders him to return to Paris and the common life. Huysmans, in a second novel, '*Là-bas*,' shows us what Des Esseintes eventually does in Paris. He writes a history of Gilles de Rais, the wholesale murderer of the fifteenth century, to whom Moreau de Tours' book (treating of sexual aberrations) has unmistakably called the attention of the Diabolist band, who are in general profoundly ignorant, but erudite on this special subject of erotomania. This furnishes M. Huysmans with the opportunity of burrowing and sniffing with swinish satisfaction into the most horrible filth. Besides this, he exhibits in this book the mystic side of decadentism; he shows us Des Esseintes become devout, but going at the same time to the 'black mass' with a hysterical woman, etc. I have no occasion to trouble myself with this book, as repulsive as it is silly. All I wished was to show the ideal man of decadentism.

We have him now, then, the 'super-man' (*surhomme*) of whom Baudelaire and his disciples dream, and whom they wish to resemble: physically, ill and feeble; morally, an arrant scoundrel; intellectually, an unspeakable idiot who passes his whole time in choosing the colours of stuffs which are to drape his room artistically, in observing the movements of mechanical fishes, in sniffing perfumes and sipping liqueurs. His raciest notion is to keep awake all night and to sleep all day, and to dip his meat into his tea. Love and friendship are unknown to him. His artistic sense consists in watching the attitude of people before some work, in order immediately to assume the opposite position. His complete inadaptability reveals itself in that every contact with the world and men causes him pain. He naturally throws the blame of his discomfort on his fellow-creatures, and rails at them like a fishwife. He classes them all together as villains and blockheads, and he hurls at them horrible anarchical maledictions. The dunderhead considers himself infinitely superior to other people, and his inconceivable stupidity only equals his inflated adoration of himself. He possesses an income of 50,000 francs, and must also have it, for such a pitiable creature would not be in a position to draw one sou from society, or one grain of wheat from nature. A parasite of the lowest grade of atavism, a sort of human sacculus,* he would be condemned, if he were poor, to die miserably of hunger in so far as society, in misdirected charity, did not assure to him the necessaries of life in an idiot asylum.

* The sacculus is a cirripedia which lives in the condition of a parasite in the intestinal canal of certain crustacea. It represents the deepest retrograde transformation of a living being primarily of a higher organization. It has lost all its differentiated organs, and essentially only amounts to a vesicule (hence its name: little bag), which fills itself with juices from its host, absorbed by the parasite with the help of certain vessels, which it plunges into the intestinal walls of the latter. This atrophied creature has retained so few marks of an independent animal that it was looked upon for a long time as a diseased excrescence of its host's intestines.

If M. Huysmans in his Des Esseintes has shown us the Decadent with all his instincts perverted, *i.e.*, the complete Baudelairian with his anti-naturalism, his æsthetic folly and his anti-social Diabolism, another representative of decadent literature, M. Maurice Barrès, is the incarnation of the pure ego-mania of the incapacity of adaptation in the degenerate. He has dedicated up to the present a series of four novels to the *culte du moi*, and has annotated, besides, an edition of the three first in a brochure much more valuable for our inquiry than the novels themselves, inasmuch as all the sophisms by which consciousness forces itself to explain *a posteriori* the impulsions of morbid unconscious life appear here conveniently summed up in a sort of philosophical system.

A few words on M. Maurice Barrès. He first made himself talked of by defending, in the Parisian press, his friend Chambige, the Algerian homicide, a logical cultivator of the 'Ego.' Then he became a Boulangist deputy, and later he canonized Marie Bashkirtseff, a degenerate girl who died of phthisis, a victim to moral madness, with a touch of the megalomania and the mania of persecution, as well as of morbid erotic exaltation. He invoked her as 'Our Lady of the wagon-lit' (*Notre Dame du Sleeping*).*

His novels, *Sous l'Œil des Barbares*, *Un Homme libre*, *Le Jardin de Bérénice*, and *L'Ennemi des Lois*, are constructed after the artistic formula established by M. Huysmans. The description of a human being, with his intellectual life, and his monotonous, scarcely modulated external destinies, gives the author a pretext for expressing his own ideas on all possible subjects; on Leonardo da Vinci and Venice;† on a French provincial museum and the industrial art of the Middle Ages;‡ on Nero,§ Saint Simon, Fourier, Marx, and Lassalle.‖ Formerly it was the custom to utilize these excursions into all possible fields of discussion as articles for newspapers or monthly periodicals, and afterwards to collect them in book form. But experience has taught that the public does not exhibit much interest in these collections of essays, and the Decadents have adopted the clever ruse of connecting them by means of a scarcely perceptible thread of narrative, and presenting them to their readers as a novel. The English novelists of the preceding century, then Stendhal, Jean Paul and Goethe himself, have also made use of these insertions of the author's personal reflections in the course of the story; but with them (with the

* Maurice Barrès, *Trois Stations de Psycho-thérapie*. Paris, 1892. 'Deuxième Station.'

† *Ibid.*, *Un Homme libre*. 3e édition. Paris, 1892.

‡ *Ibid.*, *Le Jardin de Bérénice*. Paris, 1891, p. 37 *et seq.*

§ *Ibid.*, *p.* 245 *et seq.*

‖ *Ibid.*, *L'Ennemi des Lois*. Paris, 1893, pp. 63, 88, 170.

exception, perhaps, of Jean Paul) these interpellations were at least subordinated to the work of art as a whole. It was reserved for M. Huysmans and his school to give them the chief place, and to transform the novel from an epic poem in prose into a hybrid mixture of *Essais* of Montaigne, of *Parerga et Paralipomena* of Schopenhauer, and the effusions in the diary of a girl at a boarding-school.

M. Barrès makes it no secret that he has described his own life in his novels, and that he considers himself a typical representative of a species. 'These monographs . . . are,' he says,* 'a communication of a type of young man already frequently met with, and which, I feel sure, will become still more numerous among the pupils who are now at the Lycée. . . . These books . . . will eventually be consulted as documents.'

What is the nature of this type? Let us answer this question in the author's own words. The hero of the novels is 'somewhat literary, proud, fastidious and *désarmé*' (*Examen*, p. 11); 'a young *bourgeois* grown pale, and starving for all pleasures' (p. 26); 'discouraged by contact with men' (p. 34); he is one of those 'who find themselves in a sad state in the midst of the order of the world . . . who feel themselves weak in facing life' (p. 45). Can one imagine a more complete description of the degenerate incapable of adaptation, badly equipped for the struggle for existence, and for this reason hating and fearing the world and men, but shaken at the same time by morbid desires?

This poor shattered creature, who was necessarily rendered an ego-maniac by the weakness of will in his imperfect brain, and the perpetual turmoil of his unhealthy organs, raises his infirmities to the dignity of a system which he proudly proclaims. 'Let us keep to our only reality, to our "I"' (p. 18). 'There is only one thing which we know and which really exists. . . . This sole tangible reality, it is the "I," and the universe is only a fresco which it makes beautiful or ugly. Let us keep to our "I." Let us protect it against strangers, against Barbarians' (p. 45).

What does he mean by Barbarians? These are the 'beings who possess a dream of life opposed to that which he (the hero of one of his books) forms of it. If they happen to be, moreover, highly cultured, they are strangers and adversaries for him.' A young man 'obliged by circumstances to meet persons who are not of his *patrie psychique*' experiences 'a shock.' 'Ah! what matters to me the quality of a soul which contradicts some sensibility? I hate these strangers who impede, or turn aside the development of such a delicate hesitating and self-searching "I," these Barbarians through whom more than one impressionable young man will both fail in his career and not find his joy of living' (p. 23). 'Soldiers, magistrates,

* Maurice Barrès, *Examen de trois Idéologies*. Paris, 1892, p. 14.

moralists, teachers,' these are the Barbarians who place obstacles in the way of the development of the "I"' (p. 43). In one word, the 'I' who cannot take his bearings in the social order regards all the representatives and defenders of that order as his enemies. What he would like would be 'to give himself up without resistance to the force of his instincts' (p. 25), to distinguish 'where lie his sincere curiosity, the direction of his instinct, and his truth' (p. 47). This idea of setting instinct, passion and the unconscious life free from the superintendence of reason, judgment and consciousness recurs hundreds of times in the author's novels. 'Taste takes the place of morality' (*L'Ennemi des Lois*, p. 3). 'As a man, and a free man, may I accomplish my destiny, respect and favour my interior impulsion, without taking counsel of anything outside me' (p. 22). 'Society enclosed by a line of demarcation! You offer slavery to whoever does not conform to the definitions of the beautiful and the good adopted by the majority. In the name of humanity, as formerly in the name of God and the City, what crimes are devised against the individual!' (p. 200). 'The inclinations of man ought not to be forced, but the social system must be adapted to them' (p. 97). (It would be very much more simple to adapt the inclinations of a single man to the social system which is a law to millions of men, but this does not seem to suggest itself to our philosopher!)

It is absolutely logical that M. Barrès, after having shown us in his three first novels or *idéologies* the development of his 'cultivator of the *moi*,' should make the latter become an anarchist and an *ennemi des lois*. But he feels himself that the objection will be justly raised, that society cannot exist without a law and an order of some sort, and he seeks to forestall this objection by asserting that everyone knows how to behave himself, that instinct is good and infallible: 'Do you not feel,' he says (p. 177), 'that our instinct has profited by the long apprenticeship of our race amid codes and religions?' He admits then that 'codes and religions' have their use and necessity, but only at a primitive period of human history. When the instincts were still wild, bad and unreasonable, they required the discipline of the law. But now they are so perfect that this guide and master is no longer necessary to them. But there are still criminals. What is to be done with them? 'By stifling them with kisses and providing for their wants they would be prevented from doing any harm.' I should like to see M. Barrès obliged to use his method of defence against a night attack of garrotters!

To allow one's self to be carried away by instincts is, in other words, to make unconscious life the master of consciousness, to subordinate the highest nervous centres to the inferior centres. But all progress rests on this, that the highest centres assume more and more authority over the entire organism, that judgment and will control and direct ever more strictly the instincts and passions, that consciousness encroaches ever further on the domain of the unconscious, and continually annexes new portions of the latter. Of course, instinct expresses a directly felt need, the satisfaction of which procures a direct pleasure. But this need is often that of a single organ, and its satisfaction, however agreeable to the organ which demands it, may be pernicious, and even fatal, to the total organism. Then there are anti-social instincts, the gratification of which is not directly injurious to the organism itself, it is true, but makes life in common with the race difficult or impossible, worsening consequently its vital conditions, and preparing its ruin indirectly. Judgment alone is fitted to oppose these instincts by the representation of the needs of the collective organism and of the race, and the will has the task of ensuring the victory over suicidal instinct to the rational representation. Judgment may be deceived, for it is the result of the work of a highly differentiated and delicate instrument, which, like all fine and complicated machinery, gets out of order more easily than a simpler and rougher tool. Instinct, the inherited and organized experience of the race, is as a rule more sure and reliable. This must certainly be admitted. But what harm is done if judgment does make a mistake for once in the opposition which it offers to instinct? The organism is, as a rule, only deprived of a momentary feeling of pleasure; it suffers therefore at most a negative loss; the will, on the other hand, will have made an effort, and acquired strength by the exercise, and this is for the organism a positive gain, which nearly always at least balances those negative losses.

And then all these considerations take for granted the perfect health of the organism, for in such a one only does the unconscious work as normally as consciousness. But we have seen above that the unconscious itself is subject to disease; it may be stupid, obtuse and mad, like consciousness; it then ceases completely to be dependable; then the instincts are as worthless guides as are the blind or drunken; then the organism, if it gives itself up to them, must stagger to ruin and death. The only thing which can sometimes save it in this case is the constant, anxious, tense vigilance of the judgment, and as the latter is never capable, by its own resources, of resisting a strong flood of revolted and riotous instincts, it must demand reinforcements from the judgment of the race, *i.e.*, from some law, from some recognised morality.

Such is the foolish aberration of the 'cultivators of the "I."' They fall into the same errors as the shallow psychologists of the eighteenth century, who only recognised reason; they only see one portion of man's mental life, *i.e.*, his unconscious life; they wish to receive their law only from instinct, but wholly neglect to notice that instinct may become degenerate, diseased, exhausted, and thereby be rendered as useless for legislative purposes as a raving lunatic or an idiot.

Besides, M. Barrès contradicts his own theories at every step. While he pretends to believe that instincts are always good, he depicts many of his heroines, with the most tender expressions of admiration, as veritable moral monsters. The 'little princess' in *L'Ennemi des Lois* is a feminine Des Esseintes: she boasts of having been, as a child, 'the scourge of the house' (p. 146). She looks upon her parents as her 'enemies' (p. 149). She loves children 'less than dogs' (p. 284). Naturally, she gives herself at once to every man that strikes her eye, for, otherwise, where would be the use of being a 'cultivator of the "Ego,"' and an adept at the law of instinct? Such are the good beings of M. Barrès, who no longer need laws, because they have 'profited by the long apprenticeship of our race.'

Yet a few more traits to complete the mental portrait of this Decadent. He makes his 'little princess' relate: 'When I was twelve years old, I loved, as soon as I was alone in the country, to take off my shoes and stockings and plunge my bare feet into warm mud. I passed hours in this way, and that gave me a thrill of pleasure through all my body.' M. Barrès resembles his heroine; he 'experiences a thrill of pleasure through all his body' when he 'plunges himself into warm mud.'

'There is not a detail in the biography of Berenice which is not shocking'—thus begins the third chapter of the *Jardin de Bérénice*. 'I, however, retain of it none but very delicate sensations.' This Berenice was a dancer at the Eden Theatre in Paris, whom her mother and elder sister had sold as a little child to some old criminals, and whom a lover took away later from the prostitution which had already stained her infancy. This lover dies and leaves her a considerable fortune. The hero of the novel, who had known her as a gutter-child, meets her at Arles, where he presents himself as the Boulangist candidate for the Chamber, and he resumes his ancient relations with her. What charms him most in their intercourse, and increases his pleasure in the highest degree, is the idea of the intense love she felt for her dead lover, and the abandonment with which she had reposed in his arms. 'My Berenice, who still bears on her pale lips and against her dazzling teeth the kisses of M. de Transe [the lover in question]. . . . The young man who is no more has left her as much passion as can be contained in a woman's heart' (p. 138). The feeling which M. Barrès seeks to crown with the help of inflated, grandiloquent expressions is simply the well-known excitement that hoary sinners feel at the sight of the erotic exploits of others. All those who are conversant with Parisian life know what is meant in Paris by a *voyeur*, or pryer. M. Barrès reveals himself here as a metaphysical *voyeur*. And yet he would wish to make us believe that his little street-walker, whose dirty adventures he describes with the warmth of love and the enthusiasm of a dilettante, is in reality a symbol; it is only as a Symbolist that he claims to have formed her. 'A young woman is seen about a young man. Is it not rather the history of a soul with its two elements, female and male?' Or is it by the side of the 'I' which guards itself, wishes to know and establish itself, also the imagination in a young and sensitive person, for the taste pleasure and for vagabondage?* One may well ask him, where is the 'symbolism' in the biographical details of Petite Secousse, the name that he gives to his 'symbol.'

Disease and corruption exercise the customary Baudelairian attraction over him. 'When Berenice was a little girl,' he says, in the *Jardin de Bérénice* (p. 72), 'I much regretted that she had not some physical infirmity . . . A blemish is what I prefer above everything . . . flatters the dearest foibles of my mind.' And in one place (p. 282) an engineer is scoffed at 'who wishes to substitute some pond for carp for our marshes full of beautiful fevers.'

The stigmata of degeneracy known as zoöphilia, or excessive love for animals, is strongly shown in him. When he wishes particularly to edify himself he runs 'to contemplate the beautiful eyes of the seal, and to distress himself over the mysterious sufferings of these tender-hearted animals shown in their basin, brothers of the dogs and of us.'† The only educator that M. Barrès admits is—the dog. 'The education which a dog gives is indeed excellent! . . . Our collegians, overloaded with intellectual acquisitions, which remain in them as notions, not as methods of feeling, weighted by opinions which they are unable thoroughly to grasp, would learn beautiful ease from the dog, the gift of listening, the instinct of their "I."'‡ And it must not be imagined that in such passages as these he is quizzing himself or mocking the Philistine who may by inadvertence have become a reader of the book. The part played by two dogs in the novel testifies that the phrases quoted are meant in bitter earnest.

Like all the truly degenerate, M. Barrès reserves for the hysterical and the demented all the admiration and fraternal love which he has not expended on seals and dogs. We have already men-

* *Examen de trois Idéologies*, p. 36.
† *Ibid.*, p. 46.
‡ *L'Ennemi des Lois*, p. 285.

tioned his enthusiastic regard for poor Marie Bashkirtseff. His idea of Louis II. of Bavaria is incomparable. The unfortunate King is, in his eyes, an *insatisfait* (*L'Ennemi des Lois*, p. 201); he speaks of 'his being carried away beyond his native surroundings, his ardent desire to make his dream tangible, the wrecking of his imagination in the clumsiness of execution' (p. 203). Louis II. is 'a most perfect ethical problem' (p. 200). 'How could this brother of Parsifal, so pure, so simple, who set the prompting of his heart in opposition to all human laws—how could he suffer a foreign will to interfere in his life? And it really seems that to have drawn Dr. Gudden under water was his revenge upon a barbarian who had wished to impose his rule of life upon him' (p. 225). It is in such phrases that M. Barrès characterizes a madman, whose mind was completely darkened, and who for years was incapable of a single reasonable idea! This impudent fashion of blinking a fact which boxed his ears on both sides; this incapacity to recognise the irrationality in the mental life of an invalid, fallen to the lowest degree of insanity; this obstinacy in explaining the craziest deeds as deliberate, intentional, philosophically justified and full of deep sense, throw a vivid light on the state of mind in the Decadent. How could a being of this kind discern the pathological disturbance of his own brain, when he does not even perceive that Louis II. was not 'an ethical problem,' but an ordinary mad patient, such as every lunatic asylum of any size contains by dozens?

We now understand the philosophy and moral doctrine of the Barrès type of the 'cultivators of the "I."' Only one word more on their conduct in practical life. The hero of the *Jardin de Bérénice*, Philippe, is the happy guest of Petite Secousse, in the house which her last lover had left to her. After some time he wearies of the latter's 'educational influence'; he leaves her, and strongly advises her to marry his opponent in the election —which she does. 'The enemy of the laws,' an anarchist of the name of André Maltère, condemned to prison for several months for a newspaper article eulogizing a dynamite attempt, has become, by his trial, a celebrity of the day. A very rich orphan offers him her hand, and the 'little princess' her love. He marries the rich girl, whom he does not love, and continues to love the 'little princess,' whom he does not marry. For this is what the 'culture of his "I"' exacts. To satisfy his æsthetic inclinations and to 'act' by word and pen, he must have money, and to relieve the needs of his heart he must have the 'little princess.' After some months of marriage he finds it inconvenient to dissimulate his love for the 'little princess' before his wife. He allows her then to guess at the needs of his heart. His wife understands philosophy. She is 'comprehensive.' She goes herself to the 'little princess,' takes her to the noble anarchist, and from this moment Maltère lives rich, loved, happy, and satisfied between heiress and mistress, as becomes a superior nature. M. Barrès believes he has here created 'a rare and exquisite type.' He deceives himself. The cultivators of the 'I,' like the Boulangist Philippe and the anarchist André, meet by thousands in all large towns, only the police know them under another name. They call them *souteneurs*. The moral law of the brave anarchist has long been that of the gilded Paris prostitutes, who from time immemorial have kept '*l'amant de cœur*,' at the same time as the 'other,' or the 'others.'

Decadentism has not been confined to France alone; it has also established a school in England. We have already mentioned, in the preceding book, one of the earliest and most servile imitators of Baudelaire—Swinburne. I had to class him among the mystics, for the degenerative stigma of mysticism predominates in all his works. He has, it is true, been train-bearer to so many models that he may be ranked among the domestic servants of a great number of masters; but, finally, he will be assigned a place where he has served longest, and that is among the pre-Raphaelites. From Baudelaire he has borrowed principally diabolism and Sadism, unnatural depravity, and a predilection for suffering, disease and crime. The ego-mania of decadentism, its love of the artificial, its aversion to nature, and to all forms of activity and movement, its megalomaniacal contempt for men and its exaggeration of the importance of art, have found their English representative among the 'Æsthetes,' the chief of whom is Oscar Wilde.

Wilde has done more by his personal eccentricities than by his works. Like Barbey d'Aurevilly, whose rose-coloured silk hats and gold lace cravats are well known, and like his disciple Joséphin Péladan, who walks about in lace frills and satin doublet, Wilde dresses in queer costumes which recall partly the fashions of the Middle Ages, partly the rococo modes. He pretends to have abandoned the dress of the present time because it offends his sense of the beautiful; but this is only a pretext in which probably he himself does not believe. What really determines his actions is the hysterical craving to be noticed, to occupy the attention of the world with himself, to get talked about. It is asserted that he has walked down Pall Mall in the afternoon dressed in doublet and breeches, with a picturesque biretta on his head, and a sunflower in his hand, the quasi-heraldic symbol of the Æsthetes. This anecdote has been reproduced in all the biographies of Wilde, and I have nowhere seen it denied. But is a promenade with a sunflower in the hand also inspired by a craving for the beautiful?

Phasemakers are perpetually repeating the twaddle, that it is a proof of honourable independence to follow one's own taste without being bound down to the regulation costume of the Philistine cattle, and to choose for clothes the colours, materials and cut which appear beautiful to one's self, no matter how much they may differ from the fashion of the day. The answer to this cackle should be that it is above all a sign of anti-social ego-mania to irritate the majority unnecessarily, only to gratify vanity, or an æsthetical instinct of small importance and easy to control—such as is always done when, either by word or deed, a man places himself in opposition to this majority. He is obliged to repress many manifestations of opinions and desires out of regard for his fellow-creatures; to make him understand this is the aim of education, and he who has not learnt to impose some restraint upon himself in order not to shock others is called by malicious Philistines, not an Æsthete, but a blackguard.

It may become a duty to combat the vulgar herd in the cause of truth and knowledge; but to a serious man this duty will always be felt as a painful one. He will never fulfil it with a light heart, and he will examine strictly and cautiously if it be really a high and absolutely imperative law which forces him to be disagreeable to the majority of his fellow-creatures. Such an action is, in the eyes of a moral and sane man, a kind of martyrdom for a conviction, to carry out which constitutes a vital necessity; it is a form, and not an easy form, of self-sacrifice, for it means the renunciation of the joy which the consciousness of sympathy with one's fellow-creatures gives, and it exacts the painful overthrow of social instincts, which, in truth, do not exist in deranged ego-maniacs, but are very strong in the normal man.

The predilection for strange costume is a pathological aberration of a racial instinct. The adornment of the exterior has its origin in the strong desire to be admired by others—primarily by the opposite sex—to be recognised by them as especially well-shaped, handsome, youthful, or rich and powerful, or as pre-eminent through rank or merit. It is practised, then, with the object of producing a favourable impression on others, and is a result of thought about others, of preoccupation with the race. If, now, this adornment be, not through mis-judgment but purposely, of a character to cause irritation to others, or lend itself to ridicule—in other words, if it excites disapproval instead of approbation—it then runs exactly counter to the object of the art of dress, and evinces a perversion of the instinct of vanity.

The pretence of a sense of beauty is the excuse of consciousness for a crank of the conscious. The fool who masquerades in Pall Mall does not see himself, and, therefore, does not enjoy the beautiful appearance which is supposed to be an æsthetic necessity for him. There would be some sense in his conduct if it had for its object an endeavour to cause others to dress in accordance with his taste; for them he sees, and they can scandalize him by the ugliness, and charm him by the beauty, of their costume. But to take the initiative in a new artistic style in dress brings the innovator not one hair's breadth nearer his assumed goal of æsthetic satisfaction.

When, therefore, an Oscar Wilde goes about in 'æsthetic costume' among gazing Philistines, exciting either their ridicule or their wrath, it is no indication of independence of character, but rather from a purely anti-socialistic, ego-maniacal recklessness and hysterical longing to make a sensation, justified by no exalted aim; nor is it from a strong desire for beauty, but from a malevolent mania for contradiction.

Be that as it may, Wilde obtained, by his buffoon mummery, a notoriety in the whole Anglo-Saxon world that his poems and dramas would never have acquired for him. I have no reason to trouble myself about these, since they are feeble imitations of Rossetti and Swinburne, and of dreary inanity. His prose essays, on the contrary, deserve attention, because they exhibit all the features which enable us to recognise in the 'Æsthete' the comrade in art of the Decadent.

Like his French masters, Oscar Wilde despises Nature. 'Whatever actually occurs is spoiled for art. All bad poetry springs from genuine feeling. To be natural is to be obvious, and to be obvious is to be inartistic.'*

He is a 'cultivator of the Ego,' and feels deliciously indignant at the fact that Nature dares to be indifferent to his important person. 'Nature is so indifferent, so unappreciative. Whenever I am walking in the park here, I always feel that I am no more to her than the cattle that browse on the slope' (p. 5).

With regard to himself and the human species, he shares the opinion of Des Esseintes. 'Ah! don't say that you agree with me. When people agree with me I always feel that I must be wrong' (p. 202).

His ideal of life is inactivity. 'It is only the Philistine who seeks to estimate a personality by the vulgar test of production. This young dandy sought to be somebody rather than to do something' (p. 65). 'Society often forgives the criminal; it never forgives the dreamer. The beautiful sterile emotions that art excites in us are hateful in its eyes. . . . People . . . are always coming shamelessly up to one . . . and saying in a loud, stentorian voice, "What are you doing?" whereas, "What are you thinking?" is the only question that any civilized being should ever be allowed to whisper to another. . . . Contemplation . . . in the opinion of the highest culture, is the proper occupation of man. . . . It is to do nothing that the elect exist. Action is limited and relative. Unlimited and absolute is the vision of him who sits at ease and watches, who walks in loneliness and dreams' (pp. 166-168). 'The sure way of knowing nothing about

* Oscar Wilde, *Intentions*. London, 1891, p. 197.

life is to try to make one's self useful' (p. 175). 'From time to time the world cries out against some charming artistic poet, because, to use its hackneyed and silly phrase, he has "nothing to say." But if he had something to say, he would probably say it, and the result would be tedious. It is just because he has no new message that he can do beautiful work' (p. 197).

Oscar Wilde apparently admires immorality, sin and crime. In a very affectionate biographical treatise on Thomas Griffith Wainwright, designer, painter, and author, and the murderer of several people, he says: 'He was a forger of no mean or ordinary capabilities, and as a subtle and secret poisoner almost without rival in this or any age. This remarkable man, so powerful with "pen, pencil, and poison,"' etc. (p. 60). 'He sought to find expression by pen or poison' (p. 61). 'When a friend reproached him with the murder of Helen Abercrombie, he shrugged his shoulders and said, "Yes; it was a dreadful thing to do, but she had very thick ankles"' (p. 86). 'His crimes seem to have had an important effect upon his art. They gave a strong personality to his style, a quality that his early work certainly lacked' (p. 88). 'There is no sin except stupidity' (p. 210). 'An idea that is not dangerous is unworthy of being called an idea at all' (p. 179).

He cultivates incidentally a slight mysticism in colours. 'He,' Wainwright, 'had that curious love of green which in individuals is always the sign of a subtle, artistic temperament, and in nations is said to denote a laxity, if not a decadence of morals' (p. 66).

But the central idea of his tortuously disdainful prattling, pursuing as its chief aim the heckling of the Philistine, and laboriously seeking the opposite pole to sound common-sense, is the glorification of art. Wilde sets forth in the following manner the system of the 'Æsthetes': 'Briefly, then, their doctrines are these: Art never expresses anything but itself. It has an independent life, just as Thought has, and develops purely on its own lines. . . . The second doctrine is this: All bad art comes from returning to Life and Nature, and elevating them into ideals. Life and Nature may sometimes be used as part of Art's rough material, but before they are of any real service to Art they must be translated into artistic conventions. The moment Art surrenders its imaginative medium [?] it surrenders everything. As a method Realism is a complete failure, and the two things that every artist should avoid are modernity of form and modernity of subject matter.* To us who live in

* Schiller also says:

'Ewig jung is nur die Phantasie;
Was sich nie und nirgends hat begeben,
Das allein veraltet nie.'—*An die Freunde.*

'Forever young is fantasy alone;
That which nowhere ever has existed,
That alone grows never old.'

the nineteenth century, any century is a suitable subject for art except our own. The only beautiful things are the things that do not concern us. . . . It is exactly because Hecuba is nothing to us that her sorrows are so suitable a motive for a tragedy. . . .'* (pp. 52-54). The third doctrine is that Life imitates Art far more than Art imitates Life. This results not merely from Life's imitative instinct, but from the fact that the self-conscious aim of Life is to find expression, and that Art offers it certain beautiful forms through which it may realize that energy' (p. 65).

On this third point—the influence of art on life—Wilde does not refer to the fact, long ago established by me, that the reciprocal relation between the work of art and the public consists in this, that the former exercises suggestion and the latter submits to it.† What he actually wished to say was that nature—not civilized men—develops itself in the direction of forms given it by the artist. 'Where, if not from the Impressionists, do we get those wonderful brown fogs that come creeping down our streets, blurring the gas-lamps and changing the houses into monstrous shadows? To whom, if not to them and their master, do we owe the lovely silver mists that brood over our river, and turn to faint forms of fading grace curved bridge and swaying barge? The extraordinary change that has taken place in the climate of London during the last ten years is entirely due to this particular school of Art' (p. 40). If he

---

But Schiller did not mean by this that Art should disregard truth and life, but that it must discriminate between what is essential, and consequently lasting, in the phenomenon, and that which is accidental, and therefore ephemeral.

* Compare this with Kant's *Kritik der Urtheilskraft* (*herausgegeben und erläntert von J. H. v. Kirchmann*); Berlin, 1869, p. 65: 'All interest spoils the judgment in matters of taste, and deprives it of its impartiality, especially if it does not, as rational interest does, make the feeling of utility paramount to that of pleasure, but bases it upon the latter, which always happens in an æsthetic judgment in so far as a thing causes pleasure or pain.' Modern psycho-physiology has recognised this notion of Kant's as erroneous, and has demonstrated that 'the feeling of pleasure' in itself is originally a feeling of organic 'utility,' and that 'judgment in matters of taste' does not exist at all without 'interest.' Psycho-physiology makes use of the terms 'organic tendency' or 'proclivity,' instead of 'interest.' Moreover Wilde, who does not mind contradicting his own loose assertions, says (p. 186): 'A critic cannot be fair in the ordinary sense of the word. It is only about things that do not interest one that one can give a really unbiased opinion, which is no doubt the reason why an unbiased opinion is always absolutely valueless. The man who sees both sides of a question is a man who sees absolutely nothing at all.' Hence Hecuba must be something to the critic, that he may be able to criticise at all.

† See in my *Paradoxe* the chapters 'Inhalt der poetischen Literatur' and 'Zur Naturgeschichte der Liebe.'

simply wished to affirm that formerly fog and mist were not felt to be beautiful, and that the artistic rendering of them first drew to them the attention of the multitude, nothing could be said in contradiction; he would have propounded just a hackneyed commonplace with misplaced sententiousness. He asserts, however, that painters have changed the climate, that for the last ten years there have been fogs in London, because the Impressionists have painted fogs—a statement so silly as to require no refutation. It is sufficient to characterize it as artistic mysticism. Lastly, Wilde teaches the following: 'Æsthetics are higher than ethics. They belong to a more spiritual sphere. To discern the beauty of a thing is the finest point to which we can arrive. Even a colour-sense is more important in the development of the individual than a sense of right and wrong' (pp. 210, 211).

Thus the doctrine of the 'Æsthetes' affirms, with the Parnassians, that the work of art is its own aim; with the Diabolists, that it need not be moral—nay, were better to be immoral; with the Decadents, that it is to avoid, and be diametrically opposed to, the natural and the true; and with all these schools of the ego-mania of degeneration, that art is the highest of all human functions.

Here is the place to demonstrate the absurdity of these propositions. This can, of course, be done only in the concisest manner. For to treat fully of the relation of the beautiful to morals and truth to Nature, of the conception of aim in artistic beauty, and of the rank held by art among mental functions, it would be necessary to expound the whole science of æsthetics, on which the somewhat exhaustive text-books amount to a considerable number of volumes; and this cannot be my purpose in this place. Hence I shall of necessity only recapitulate the latest results in a series of the clearest and most obvious deductions possible, which the attentive reader will be able without difficulty to develop by his own reflection.

The 'bonzes' of art, who proclaim the doctrine of 'art for art's sake,' look down with contempt upon those who deny their dogma, affirming that the heretics who ascribe to works of art any aim whatsoever can be only pachydermatous Philistines, whose comprehension is limited to beans and bacon, or stock-jobbers with whom it is only a question of profit, or sanctimonious parsons making a professional pretence of virtue. They believe that they are supported in this by such men as Kant, Lessing, etc., who were likewise of the opinion that the work of art had but one task to perform—that of being beautiful. We need not be overawed by the great names of these guarantors. Their opinion cannot withstand the criticism to which it has been subjected during the last hundred years by a great number of philosophers (I name only Fichte, Hegel and Vischer), and its inadequacy follows from the fact, among others, that it allows absolutely no place for the ugly as an object of artistic representation.

Let us remind ourselves how works of art and art in general originated.

That plastic art originally sprang from the imitation of Nature is a commonplace, open justly to the reproach that it does not enter deeply enough into the question. Imitation is without doubt one of the first and most general reactions of the developed living being upon the impressions it receives from the external world. This is a necessary consequence of the mechanism of the higher activity of the nervous system. Every compound movement must be preceded by the representation of this movement, and, conversely, no representation of movement can be elaborated without at least a faint and hinted accomplishment of the corresponding movement by the muscles. Upon this principle depends, for example, the well-known 'thought-reading.' As often, therefore, as a being (whose nervous system is developed highly enough to raise perceptions to the rank of representations) acquires knowledge, *i.e.*, forms for itself a representation of any phenomenon whatever comprising in itself a more or less molar form of movement (molecular movements, and, *a fortiori*, vibrations of ether are not directly recognised as changes of position in space), it has also a tendency to transform the representation into a movement resembling it, and hence to imitate the phenomenon, in that form, naturally, which, with its means, it is capable of realizing. If every representation be not embodied in perceptible movement, the cause is to be traced to the action of the inhibitive mechanism of the brain, which does not permit every representation at once to set the muscles into activity. In a state of fatigue inhibition is relaxed, and, in fact, all sorts of unintentional imitations make their appearance, as, for example, symmetrical movements, such as the left hand involuntarily and aimlessly makes of those executed by the right hand in writing, etc. There is also a rare disease of the nerves* hitherto observed chiefly in Russia, and especially in Siberia, there called *myriachit,* in which inhibition becomes completely disorganized, so that the diseased persons are forced at once to imitate any action seen by them, even if it be disagreeable or pernicious to them. If, for example, they see someone fall, they are compelled to throw themselves also to the ground, even if they are standing in a muddy road.

* S. A. Tokarski's article on 'Myriachit' in the *Neurologisches Central-Blatt* for November, 1890. Tokarski in this article also informs us that this word should be written *meriatschenja*, and not *myriachit*.

Except in disease and fatigue, the action of inhibition is suspended only when the excitation produced in the nervous system by an impression is strong enough to vanquish it. If this impression is disagreeable, or menacing, the movements set loose by it are those of defence or flight. If, on the contrary, the impression is pleasant, or if it is surprising without being disquieting, then the reaction of the organism against it is a movement without objective aim, most frequently a movement of imitation. Hence, among healthy men possessed of well-working inhibitory mechanism in their nervous system, this movement does not appear with every phenomenon, but only with such as strike it forcibly, fix its attention, engage and stimulate it—in a word, cause an emotion. Activity of imitation (and the plastic arts are at bottom nothing but residuary traces of imitative movements) has consequently an immediate organic aim, viz., the freeing of the nervous system from an excitation set up in it by some visual cause. If the excitation is not caused by the sight of any external phenomenon, but by an internal organic state (*e.g.*, sexual *erethism*), or by a representation of an abstract nature (*e.g.*, the joy of victory, sorrow, or longing), it likewise transforms itself, it is true, into movements; but these are naturally not imitative. They embody no motor representation, but are in part such as have for their sole end the relaxing of the nerve-centres overcharged with motor impulsions, as in the dance, in outcries, song and music, and in part such as disburden the centres of ideation, like declamation, lyric and epic poetry. If artistic activity is frequently exercised and facilitated by habit, it no longer requires emotions of extraordinary strength to provoke it. As often, then, as man is excited by such external or internal impressions as demand no action (conflict, flight, adaptation), but reach his consciousness in the form of a mood, he relieves his nervous system of this excitation through some kind of artistic activity, either by means of the plastic arts or by music and poetry.

Hence imitation is not the source of the arts, but one of the media of art; the real source of art is emotion. Artistic activity is not its own end, but it is of direct utility to the artist; it satisfies the need of his organism to transform its emotions into movement. He creates the work of art, not for its own sake, but to free his nervous system from a tension. The expression, which has become a commonplace, is psycho-physiologically accurate, viz., the artist writes, paints, sings, or dances the burden of some idea or feeling off his mind.

To this primary end of art—the subjective end of the self-deliverance of the artist—a second must be added, viz., the objective end of acting upon others. Like every other animal living in society and partly dependent upon it, man has, in consequence of his racial instinct, the aspiration to impart his own emotions to those of his own species, just as he himself participates in the emotions of those of his own species. This strong desire to know himself in emotional communion with the species is sympathy, that organic base of the social edifice.* In advanced civilization, where the original natural motives of actions are partly obscured and partly replaced by artificial motives, and the actions themselves receive an aim other than the theoretical one proper to them, the artist is, it is true, not limited to sharing his emotions with others, but creates his work of art with the accessory purpose of becoming famous—a wish springing none the less from social instincts, since it is directed towards obtaining the applause of his fellow-creatures, or even of earning money, a motive no longer social, but purely egoistic. This vulgarly egoistic motive is still the only one influencing the countless imitators who practise art, not from original strong desire, and as the natural and necessary mode of expressing their emotions, but whose artistic activity is caused by the envy with which they regard the success of others in art.

Once we have established, as a fact, that art is not practised for its own sake alone, but that it has a double aim, subjective and objective, viz., the satisfaction of an organic want of the artist, and the influencing of his fellow-creatures, then the principles by which every other human activity pursuing the same end is judged are applicable to it, *i.e.*, the principles of law and morality.

We test every organic desire to see whether it be the outcome of a legitimate need or the consequence of an aberration; whether its satisfaction be beneficial or pernicious to the organism. We distinguish the healthy from the diseased impulse, and demand that the latter be combated. If the desire seeks its satisfaction in an activity acting upon others, then we examine to see if this activity is reconcilable with the existence and prosperity of society, or dangerous to it. The activity imperilling society offends against law and custom, which are nothing but an epitome of the temporary notions of society concerning what is beneficial and what is pernicious to it.

Notions healthy and diseased, moral and immoral, social or anti-social, are as valid for art as for every other human activity, and there is not a scintilla of reason for regarding a

* Edmund R. Clay, *L'Alternative. Contribution à la Psychologie. Traduit de l'anglais par A. Burdeau;* Paris, 1886, p. 234: 'Sympathy is an emotion caused in us by that which seems to us to be the emotion or the sensation of others.'

work of art in any other light than that in which we view every other manifestation of an individuality.

It is easily conceivable that the emotion expressed by the artist in his work may proceed from a morbid aberration, may be directed, in an unnatural, sensual, cruel manner, to what is ugly or loathsome. Ought we not in this case to condemn the work and, if possible, to suppress it? How can its right to exist be justified? By claiming that the artist was sincere when he created it, that he gave back what was really existing in him, and for that reason was subjectively justified in his artistic expansion? But there is a candour which is wholly inadmissible. The dipsomaniac and clastomaniac are sincere when they respectively drink or break everything within reach. We do not, however, acknowledge their right to satisfy their desire. We prevent them by force. We put them under guardianship, although their drunkenness and destructiveness may perhaps be injurious to no one but themselves. And still more decidedly does society oppose itself to the satisfaction of those cravings which cannot be appeased without violently acting upon others. The new science of criminal anthropology admits without dispute that homicidal maniacs, certain incendiaries, many thieves and vagabonds, act under an impulsion; that through their crimes they satisfy an organic craving; that they outrage, kill, burn, idle, as others sit down to dinner, simply because they hunger to do so; but in spite of this and because of this, it demands that the appeasing of the sincere longings of these degenerate creatures be prevented by all means, and, if needs be, by their complete suppression. It never occurs to us to permit the criminal by organic disposition to 'expand' his individuality in crime, and just as little can it be expected of us to permit the degenerate artist to expand his individuality in immoral works of art. The artist who complacently represents what is reprehensible, vicious, criminal, approves of it, perhaps glorifies it, differs not in kind, but only in degree, from the criminal who actually commits it. It is a question of the intensity of the impulsion and the resisting power of the judgment, perhaps also of courage and cowardice; nothing else. If the actual law does not treat the criminal by intention so rigorously as the criminal in act, it is because criminal law pursues the deed, and not the purpose; the objective phenomenon, not its subjective roots. The Middle Ages had places of sanctuary where criminals could not be molested for their misdemeanours. Modern law has done away with this institution. Ought art to be at present the last asylum to which criminals may fly to escape punishment? Are they to be able to satisfy, in the so-called 'temple' of art, instincts which the policeman prevents them from appeasing in the street? I do not see how a privilege so inimical to society can be willingly defended.

I am far from sharing Ruskin's opinion that morality alone, and nothing else, can be demanded of a work of art. Morality alone is not sufficient. Otherwise religious tracts would be the finest literature, and the well-known coloured casts of sacred subjects turned out wholesale in Munich factories would be the choicest sculpture. Excellence of form maintains its rights in all the arts, and gives to the finest creation its artistic value. Hence the work need not be moral. More accurately, it need not be designed expressly to preach virtue and the fear of God, and to be destined for the edification of devotees. But between a work without sanctified aim and one of wilful immorality there is a world of difference. A work which is indifferent from a moral point of view will not be equally attractive or satisfying to all minds, but it will offend and repel no one. An explicitly immoral work excites in healthy persons the same feelings of displeasure and disgust as the immoral act itself, and the form of the work can change nothing of this. Most assuredly morality alone does not give beauty to a work of art. But beauty without morality is impossible.

We now come to the second argument with which the Æsthetes wish to defend the right of the artist to immorality. The work of art, they say, need only be beautiful. Beauty lies in the form. Hence the content is a matter of indifference. This may be vice and crime; but it cannot derogate from the excellences of form if these be present.

He alone can venture to advance such principles who is without the least inkling of the psycho-physiology of the æsthetic feelings. Everyone who has studied this subject in the least knows that two kinds of the beautiful are distinguished—the sensuously-beautiful and the intellectually-beautiful. We feel those phenomena to be beautiful, the sense-perception of which is accompanied by a feeling of pleasure—*e.g.*, a particular colour, perhaps a pure red, or a harmony; nay, even a single note with its severally indistinguishable but synchronous overtones. The researches of Helmholtz* and Blaserna† have thrown light on the cause of the feeling of pleasure connected with certain acoustic perceptions, while those of Brücke‡ have led to similar results with regard to the mechanism of the feelings of pleasure following optical impressions. It is a question of discernment by

* Helmholtz, *Die Lehre von den Tonemfindungen.* 4 Aufl. Braunschweig, 1877.

† Pietro Blaserna, *Le Son et la Musique*, followed by *Causes physiologiques de l'Harmonie musicale*, par H. Helmholtz. 4e édition. Paris, 1891.

‡ E. Brücke, *Bruchstücke aus der Theorie der bildenden Künste.* Leipzig, Intern. wissensch. Bibl. (The French edition of Brücke's works contains also Helmholtz's *L'Optique et la Peinture.*)

the sensory nerves of definite simple numerical relations in the vibrations of matter or of ether. We know less concerning the causes of the pleasures connected with smell and touch; yet here also it seems to be a question of more or less strong impressions, hence equally of quantities—*i.e.*, of numbers. The ultimate cause of all these feelings is that certain modes of vibrations are in accord with the structure of the nerves, are easy for them and leave them in order, while other modes disturb the arrangement of the nerve particles, often costing the nerves an effort, often dangerous to their existence or at least their functioning, to restore them to their natural order. The former will be felt as pleasure, the latter as discomfort, and even as pain. With the sensuously-beautiful there can be no question of morality, for it exists as perception only, and does not rise to the rank of representation.

Above the sensuously-beautiful stands the intellectually-beautiful, no longer consisting of mere perceptions, but of representations, of concepts and judgments, with their accompanying emotions elaborated in the unconscious. The intellectually-beautiful must also awaken feelings of pleasure, to be perceived as beautiful; and, as above explained, with feelings of pleasure are united, in healthy, fully-developed human beings equipped with the social instinct (altruism), only those ideas the content whereof is conducive to the existence and prosperity of the individual being, society, or species. Now, that which is favourable to the life and prosperity of the individual and of the species is precisely that which we call moral.

From this it results by an iron necessity that a work which awakens no feelings of pleasure cannot be beautiful, and that it can awaken no feelings of pleasure if it is not moral, and we arrive at the final conclusion, that morality and beauty are in their innermost essence identical. It were not false to assert that beauty is statical repose, and morality beauty in action.

This is only apparently contradicted by the fact that what is incontestably ugly and bad may also be agreeable, and hence awaken feelings of pleasure. The mental process set up by percepts and ideas is not, in this case, so simple and direct as with respect to the beautiful and the good. Associations sometimes of a highly complex nature must first be put into activity, finally. however, to lead to the single great result, viz., the awakening of feelings of pleasure. The well-known Aristotelian catharsis, purging or purification, explains how tragedy, though it offers the spectacle of pain and ruin, finally produces an agreeable effect. The representation of deserved misfortune awakens ideas of justice, a moral, agreeable idea; and even that of unmerited misfortune gives rise to pity, in itself a feeling of pain, though, in its quality of a racial instinct, beneficial and therefore not only moral, but, in its final essence, agreeable. When Valdez, in his famous picture of the *Caridad de Sevilla*, shows us an open coffin in which lies the corpse of an archbishop in full vestments, swarming with worms, this spectacle is in itself undeniably repulsive. Nevertheless it permits us at once to recognise the emotion which the painter wished to express, viz., his feeling of the nothingness of all earthly possessions and honours, the frailty of man in the face of the primeval power of Nature. It is the same emotion embodied by Holbein in his 'Dance of Death,' not so profoundly and passionately as by the Spaniard with his stronger feelings, but with self-mockery and bitterness. The same emotion is heard, somewhat less gloomily and with more of a melancholy resignation, in Mozart's *Requiem*. In the idea of the contrast between the insignificance of individual life and the vastness and eternity of Nature, there mingles itself an element of the sublime, of which the idea, as the choicest form of activity in the highest brain-centres, is united with feelings of pleasure.

Another circumstance in the plastic arts has to be considered. In works of sculpture and painting a broad separation is possible between the form and the content, between the sensuous and the moral. A painting, a group, may represent the most immoral and most criminal incident; nevertheless, the individual constituent parts—the atmosphere, the harmonies of colour, the human figures—may be beautiful in themselves, and the connoisseur may derive enjoyment from them without dwelling on the subject of the work. The engravings in the *Editions des fermiers généraux* of the last century, the works in marble and bronze of the pornographic museum at Naples, are, in a measure, repulsively immoral, because they represent unnatural vice. In themselves, however, they are excellently executed, and are accessible to a mode of contemplation which disregards their idea and keeps in view only the perfection of their form. Here, therefore, the impression of the work of art is a mixture of disgust for the subject treated, and enjoyment of the beauty of the several figures and their attitudes—painted, drawn, or modelled. The feeling of pleasure may preponderate, and the work, in spite of its depravity, produce, not a repellent, but an attractive effect. It is the same in nature. If that which is pernicious and frightful is sometimes felt to be beautiful, it is because it contains certain features and elements which have no cogent reference to the frightful or pernicious character of the whole, and can hence in themselves operate æsthetically. The hammer-headed viper is beautiful on account of its metallic lustre; the tiger for its strength and suppleness; the foxglove (*Digitalis*) for its graceful form and rich rosy hue. The noxiousness of the snake does not lie in its copper-red dorsal bands, nor the terribleness of the beast of prey in its graceful appearance, nor the danger of the poisonous plant in the form and colour of its blossoms. In these cases the sensuously-beautiful outweighs the morally-repulsive, because it is more immediately present, and, in the collective impression, allows the feelings of pleasure to predominate. The spectacle of the display of strength and resolution is equally a beautiful one, on account of the ideas of organic efficiency awakened by it. Would this, however, be thought beautiful if one could see how an assassin overpowers a victim who is resisting violently, hurls him to the ground and butchers him? Certainly not; for before such a picture it is no longer possible to separate the display of strength, beautiful in itself, from its aim, and to enjoy the former regardless of the latter.

In poetry this separation of the form from the content is far less possible than in the plastic arts. The word can hardly in itself produce an effect of sensuous beauty by its auditory or visual image, even if it presents itself rhythmically regulated and strengthened by the more expressive double sound of a rhyme. It operates almost solely by its content, by the representations which it awakens. Hence it is hardly conceivable that one can hear or read a poetical exposition of criminal or vicious facts, without having present at each word a representation of its content, and not of its form—*i.e.*, of its sound. In this case, therefore, the impression can no longer be a composite one, as at the sight of a finely-painted portrayal of a repulsive incident, but must be purely disagreeable. The pictures of Giulio Romano, to which Pietro Aretino dedicated his *Sonetti lussuriosi*, may be found beautiful by the admirers of the effeminate style of that pupil of Raphael; the sonnets are only the more disgusting. Who would experience feelings of pleasure from the perusal of the writings of the Marquis de Sade, Andrea de Nercia or Liseux? Only one species of human beings—that of the degenerate with perverted instincts. Portrayals of crime and vice in art and literature have their public; that we well know. It is the public of the gaols. Besides dismally sentimental books, criminals read nothing so willingly as stories of lust and violence;* and the drawings and inscriptions with which they cover the walls of their cells have, for the most part, their crimes as subjects.† But the healthy man feels himself violently repelled by works of this kind, and it is impossible for him to receive an æsthetic impression from

* Henry Joly, *Les Lectures dans les Prisons de la Seine.* Lyon, 1891. See also Lombroso, *L'Uomo delinquente.* Turin, 1884, p. 366 *et seq.*, and p. 387 *et seq.*

† Pitrè, *Sui Canti popolari italiani in Carcere.* Firenze, 1876. See also the portrait-group of the three brigands of Ravenna in Lombroso, *op. cit.*, Plate XV., facing p. 396.

them, be their form never so conformable to the most approved rules of art.

In yet another case it is possible for that which is most ugly and vicious in artistic portrayal to operate in the direction of the morally beautiful. This is when it allows us to recognise the moral purpose of the author and betrays his sympathetic emotion. For that which we, consciously or unconsciously, perceive behind every artistic creation is the nature of its creator and the emotion from which it sprang, and our sympathy with, or antipathy for, the emotion of the author has the lion's share in our appreciation of the work. When Raffaelli paints shockingly degraded absinthe-drinkers in the low drinking dens of the purlieus of Paris, we clearly feel his profound pity at the sight of these fallen human beings, and this emotion we experience as a morally beautiful one. In like manner we have not a momentary doubt of the morality of the artist's emotions when we behold Callot's pictures of the horrors of war, or the bleeding, purulent saints of Zurbaran, or the monsters of Breughel van der Hölle, or when we read the murder scene in Dostojevsky's *Raskolnikow*.* These emotions are beautiful. Sympathy with them gives us a feeling of pleasure. Against this feeling the displeasure caused by the repulsiveness of the work cannot prevail. When, however, the work betrays the indifference of the author to the evil or ugliness he depicts, nay, his predilection for it, then the abhorrence provoked by the work is intensified by all the disgust which the author's aberration of instinct inspires in us, and the aggregate impression is one of keenest displeasure. Those who share the emotions of the author, and hence are with him attracted and pleasurably excited by what is repugnant, diseased and evil, are the degenerate.

The Æsthetes affirm that artistic activity is the highest of which the human mind is capable, and must occupy the first place in the estimation of men. How do they manage to establish this assertion from their own standpoint? Why should I place a high value on the activity of a fellow who with rapture describes the colours and odours of putrid carrion; and why should I bestow my especial esteem on a painter who shows me the libidinousness of a harlot? Because the amount of artistic technique involved is difficult? If that is to be the decisive point, then, to be logical, the Æsthetes must place the acrobat higher than the artist of their species, since it is much more difficult to learn the art of the trapezist than the rhyming and daubing which constitutes the 'art' of the Æsthetes. Is it

* *Raskolnikow*, Roman von F. M. Dostojewskij, Nach der vierten Auflage des russichen Originals; *Prestuplenie i Nakazanie*, übersetzt von Wilhelm Henckel. Leipzig, 1882, Band I., pp. 122-128.

to be on account of sensations of pleasure given by artists? First of all, those artists over whom the Æsthetes grow so enthusiastic create in the healthy man no pleasure, but loathing or boredom. But granted that they do provide sensations, the first inquiry must then be of what sort these sensations are. Every sensation, even if we for the moment find it agreeable, does not inspire us with esteem for the person to whom we are indebted for it. At the card-table, in the public-house and the brothel, a base nature may procure sensations the intensity of which those offered by any work of the Æsthetes is far from being able to rival. But even the most dissolute drunkard does not in consequence hold the keepers of these places of his pleasures in specially high esteem.

The truth is that the claim of the highest rank for art advanced by the Æsthetes involves the complete refutation of their other dogmas. The race estimates individual activities according to their utility for the whole. The higher this develops itself, the more exact and profound is the understanding it acquires of that which is really necessary and beneficial to it. The warrior, who in a low grade of civilization rightly plays the most prominent part, because society must live, and to this end must defend itself against its enemies, recedes to a more humble position as manners become more gentle, and the relations between peoples cease to resemble those between beasts of prey, and assume a human character. Once the race has attained in some degree to a clear comprehension of its relation to nature, it knows that knowledge is its most important task, and its profoundest respect is for those who cultivate and enlarge knowledge—*i.e.*, for thinkers and investigators. Even in the monarchical state, which, conformably with its own atavistic nature, gauges the importance of the warrior by the standard of primitive men (and in the present condition of Europe, in the presence of the scarcely restrained fury for war, among a whole series of nations, the *raison d'être* for this atavism cannot, alas! be contested), the scholar, as professor, academician, counsellor, is a constituent part of the governmental machine, and honours and dignities fall far more to his lot than to the poet and artist. The enthusiasts of the latter are youths and women—*i.e.*, those components of the race in whom the unconscious outweighs consciousness; for artist and poet address themselves first of all to emotion, and this is more easily excited in the woman and the adolescent than in the mature man; their accomplishments are, moreover, more accessible to the multitude than those of the scholar whom almost the best alone of his time can follow, and whose importance is in general fully appreciated only by a few specialists, even in our days of the popularization of science by the press. State and society, however, seek to compensate him for the evasion of this reward, by surrounding him with official forms of high esteem.

It is true that very great artists and poets, admitted pioneers, whose influence is recognised as lasting, likewise receive their share of the official honours disposed of by the organized commonwealth as such, and these exceptional men obtain a more brilliant reward than any investigator or discoverer; for together with the common distinctions shared by them with the latter, they possess the wide popularity which the investigator and discoverer must dispense withal. And why is the artist sometimes placed, even by persons of good and serious minds, on a level with, or even above, the man of science? Because these persons value the beautiful more than the true, emotion more than knowledge? No; but because they have the right feeling that art is equally a source of knowledge.

It is so in three ways. Firstly, the emotion evoked by the work of art is itself a means of obtaining knowledge, as Edmund R. Clay, James Sully, and other psychologists have seen, without, however, dwelling on the important fact. It constrains the higher centres to attend to the causes of their excitations, and in this way necessarily induces a sharper observation and comprehension of the whole series of phenomena related to the emotion. Next, the work of art grants an insight into the laws of which the phenomenon is the expression; for the artist, in his creation, separates the essential from the accidental, neglects the latter, which in nature is wont to divert and confuse the less gifted observer, and involuntarily gives prominence to the former as that which chiefly or solely occupies his attention, and is therefore perceived and reproduced by him with especial distinctness. The artist himself divines the idea behind the structure, and its inner principle and connection, intelligible but not perceivable, in the form, and discloses it in his work to the spectator. That is what Hegel means when he calls the beautiful 'the presence of the idea in limited phenomenon.' By means of his own deep comprehension of natural law, the artist powerfully furthers the comprehension of it by other men.* Finally, art is the only glimmer of light, weak and dubious though it be, which projects itself into the future, and gives us at

* The knowledge of this fact is as old as æsthetic science itself. It is well expressed, as by others, so by Dr. Wilh. Alex. Freund, in his *Blicken ins Culturleben;* Breslau, 1879, p. 9: 'Idealization consists . . . in the removal of accidental accessories disturbing the true expression of the essential;' p. 11: 'All [eminent artists] raise that which they see to a purified image, purged of all that is unessential, accidental, disturbing; from that image springs up in all of them the idea lying at the base of the vision;' p. 13: 'He [the artist] comprehends the essential . . . from which the accidental disturbing accessories of the external phenomenon fall off like withered leaves, so that to his inner eye the truth appears as a living idea,' etc.

least a dream-like idea of the outlines and direction of our further organic developments. This is not mysticism, but a very clear and comprehensible fact. We have seen above* that every adaptation—*i.e.*, every change of form and function of the organs—is preceded by a representation of this change. The change must first be felt and desired as necessary; then a representation of it becomes elaborated in the higher or highest nerve-centres, and finally the organism endeavours to realize this representation. This process repeats itself in the same way in the race. Some state is disturbing to it. It experiences feelings of discomfort from this state. It suffers from it. From this results its desire to change the state. It elaborates for itself an image of the nature, direction and extent of this change. According to the older, mystic phrase, 'it creates for itself an ideal.' The ideal is really the formative idea of future organic development with a view to better adaptation. In the most perfect individuals of the species it exists earlier and more distinct than in the average multitude, and the artist ventures with uncertain hand to make it accessible to sense through the medium of his work of art long before it can be organically realized by the race. Thus art vouchsafes the most refined and highest knowledge, bordering on the marvellous, viz., the knowledge of the future. Not so definitely, of course, nor so unequivocally, does art express the secret natural law of being and becoming as science. Science shows the present, the positive; Art prophesies the future, the possible, though stammeringly and obscurely. To the former Nature unveils her fixed forms; to the latter she grants, amidst shudderings, a rapid, bewildered glimpse of the depths where what is yet formless is struggling to appear. The emotion from which the divining work of art springs is the birth throe of the quick and vigorous organism pregnant with the future.†

This art of presentiment is certainly the highest mental activity of the human being. But it is not the art of the Æsthetes. It is the most moral art, for it is the most ideal, a word only meaning that it is parallel with the paths along which the race is perfecting itself—nay, coincides with these.

By the most diverse methods we have always attained the same result, viz., it is not true that art has nothing in common

* See footnote to p. 38.

† Wilhelm Loewenthal makes the feeling and need of religion spring from the same presentient emotion. For the author of *Grundzüge einer Hygiene des Unterrichts*, religion is the form assumed in man's consciousness by the ideal, *i.e.*, the presentient knowledge of the aim of evolution. 'The instinct of development—the indispensable base of all life and all knowledge—is identical with the religious need.' Thus he writes in a memoir, unfortunately only 'printed as a manuscript,' but most worthy of being made accessible to all the world.

with morality. The work of art must be moral, for its aim is to express and excite emotions. In virtue of this aim it falls within the competence of criticism, which tests all emotions by their utility or perniciousness to the individual or the race; and if it is immoral, it must be condemned like every other organic activity opposed to this aim. The work of art must be moral, for it is intended to operate æsthetically. It can only do this if it awakens feelings of pleasure, at least ultimately; it provides such, only if it includes beauty in itself; but beauty is in its essence synonymous with morality. Finally, the highest work of art can, from its inmost nature, be none other than moral, since it is a manifestation of vital force and health, a revelation of the capacity for evolution of the race; and humanity values it so highly because it divines this circumstance.

Concerning the last doctrine of the Æsthetes, viz., that art must shun the true and the natural, this is a commonplace pushed to an absurdity, and converted into its contrary. Perfect, actual truth and naturalness need not be denied to art; they are impossible to it. For whereas the work of art makes the artist's idea tangible, an idea is never an exact copy of a phenomenon of the external world. Before it can become an idea in a human consciousness every phenomenon experiences two very essential modifications—one in the afferent and receptive organs of sense, the other in the centres elaborating sense-perceptions into representations. These sensory nerves and centres of perception change the modes of the external stimuli conformably with their own nature; they give to these their particular colouring, as different wind-instruments played by the same person give forth different shades of sound with the same force of breath. The centres forming representations modify in their turn the actual relation of the phenomena to each other, in that they bring some into stronger relief, and neglect others of really equal value. Consciousness does not take cognizance of all the countless perceptions uninterruptedly excited in the brain, but of those only to which it is attentive. But by the simple fact of attention, consciousness selects individual phenomena, and gives them an importance they do not possess in the unceasing uniformity of universal movement.

But if the work of art never renders reality in its exact relations, it can, on the other hand (and this is both a psychological and æsthetical commonplace), never be constructed from constituents other than those supplied by reality. The mode in which these constituents are blended and united by the artist's imagination permits the recognition of another fact, as true and natural as any that is habitually designated by us as real, to wit, the character, mode of thought, and emotion of the artist. For what is imagination? A special case of the general psychological law of association. In scientific observation and judgment the play of association is most rigorously supervised by attention; the will violently inhibits the propagation of stimuli along the most convenient paths, and prevents the penetration of mere similarities, contrasts, and contiguities in space or time into consciousness, which is reserved for the images of immediate reality transmitted by the senses. In artistic creation imagination rules—that is to say, the inhibition exercised by the will is relaxed; in accordance with the laws of association a presentation is allowed to summon into consciousness representations which are similar, contrasted, or contiguous in space or time. But inhibition is not wholly inactive, and the will does not permit the union of reciprocally exclusive representations into a concept; thus it prohibits the elaboration of an intellectual absurdity, such as is yielded by purely automatic association or fugitive ideation. The emotion of the artist reveals itself in accordance with the way in which representations supplied by association are grouped into concepts, for it causes representations agreeing with it to be retained, and the indifferent or contradictory to be suppressed. Even fantastic images, as extravagant as a winged horse or a woman with lion's paws, reveal a true emotion: the former an aspiration proceeding from the spectacle of the bird soaring light and free; the latter a horror of the power of sexuality subjugating reason and conjuring up devouring passion. It would be a grateful task for workers in the histology of psychology to trace the emotions whence the best known fantastic figures of art and the metaphors of poets have proceeded. Hence it may be said that every work of art always comprises in itself truth and reality in so far as, if it does not reflect the external world, it surely reflects the mental life of the artist.

Hence, as we have seen, not one of the sophisms of the Æsthetes withstands criticism. The work of art is not its own aim, but it has a specially organic, and a social task. It is subject to the moral law; it must obey this; it has claim to esteem only if it is morally beautiful and ideal. And it cannot be other than natural and true, in so far, at least, as it is the offprint of a personality, which is also a part of nature and reality. The entire system takes as its point of departure a few erroneous or imprudent assertions of thinkers and poets commanding respect, but developed by the Parnassians and Decadents in a way of which Lessing, Kant and Schiller never allowed themselves to dream. This is no other than the well-known attempt to explain and justify impulsions by motives more or less obvious and invented *post facto*. The degenerate who, in consequence of their organic aberrations, make the repulsive and ugly, vice and crime, the subject-matter of plastic and literary works of art, naturally have recourse to the theory that art has nothing in common with morality, truth and beauty, since this theory has for them the value of an excuse. And must not the excessive value set upon artistic activity as such, without regard to the worth of its results, be highly welcome to the limitless crowd of imitators who practise art, not from an inner prompting, but from a foolhardy craving for the respect surrounding real artists—imitators who have nothing of their own to say, no emotion, not an idea, but who, with a superficial professional dexterity easily acquired, falsify the views and feelings of masters in all branches of art? This rabble, which claims for itself a top place in the scale of intellectual rank, and freedom from the constraint of all moral laws as its most noble privilege, is certainly baser than the lowest scavenger. These creatures are of absolutely no use to the commonwealth, and injure true art by their productions, whose multitude and importunateness shut out from most men the sight of the genuine works of art—never very numerous—of the epoch. They are weaklings in will, unfitted for any activity requiring regular uniform efforts, or else victims to vanity, wishing to be more famous than is possible to a stone-breaker or a tailor. The uncertainty of comprehension and taste among the majority of mankind, and the incompetency of most professional critics, allow these intruders to make their nest among the arts, and to dwell there as parasites their life long. The buyer soon distinguishes a good boot from a bad one, and the journeyman cobbler who cannot properly sew on a sole finds no employment. But that a book or painting void of all originality is indifferent in quality, and for that reason superfluous, is by no means so easily recognised by the Philistine, or even by the man armed with the critical pen, and the producer of such chaff can apply himself undisturbed to his assiduous waste of time. These bunglers with pen, brush and modelling spattle, strutting about in cap and doublet, naturally swear by the doctrine of the Æsthetes, carry themselves as if they were the salt of humanity, and make a parade of their contempt for the Philistine. They belong, however, to the elements of the race which are most inimical to society. Insensible to its tasks and interests, without the capacity to comprehend a serious thought or a fruitful deed, they dream only of the satisfaction of their basest instincts, and are pernicious—through the example they set as drones, as well as through the confusion they cause in minds insufficiently forewarned, by their abuse of the word 'art' to mean demoralization and childishness. Ego-maniacs, Decadents and Æsthetes have completely gathered under their banner this refuse of civilized peoples, and march at its head.

CHAPTER IV.

IBSENISM.

IN the course of the last two centuries the whole civilized world has, with greater or less unanimity, repeatedly recognised a sort of intellectual royalty in some contemporary, to whom it has rendered homage as the first and greatest among living authors. For a great part of the eighteenth century Voltaire, '*le roi Voltaire*,' was the 'poet laureate' of all civilized nations. During the first third of the present century this position was held by Goethe. After his death the throne remained vacant for a score of years, when Victor Hugo ascended it amidst the enthusiastic acclamations of the Latin and Slavonic races, and with a feeble opposition from those of Teutonic origin, to hold it until the end of his life.

At the present time voices have for some years been heard in all countries claiming for Henrik Ibsen the highest intellectual honours at the disposal of mankind. It is wished that the Norwegian dramatist should, in his old age, be recognised as the world-poet of the closing century. It is true that only a part of the multitude and of the critical representatives of its taste acclaims him; but the fact that it has entered anyone's mind at all to see in him a claimant for the throne of poetry makes a minute examination of his titles to the position necessary.

That Henrik Ibsen is a poet of great verve and power is not for a moment to be denied. He is extraordinarily emotive, and has the gift of depicting in an exceptionally lifelike and impressive manner that which has excited his feelings. (We shall see that these are almost always feelings of hatred and rage, *i.e.*, of displeasure.) A natural capacity drew him towards the stage—a capacity for imagining situations in which the characters are forced to turn inside out their inmost nature; in which abstract ideas transform themselves into deeds, and modes of opinion and of feeling, imperceptible to the senses, but potent as causes, are made patent to sight and hearing in attitudes and gestures, in the play of feature and in words. Like Richard Wagner, he knows how to group events into living frescoes possessing the charm of significant pictures; with this difference, however, that Ibsen works, not like Wagner, with strange costumes and properties, architectural splendour, mechanical magic, gods and fabulous beasts, but with penetrating vision into the backgrounds of souls and the conditions of humanity. Fairy-lore is not lacking in Ibsen either, but he does not allow the imagination of the spectators to run riot in mere spectacles; he forces them into moods, and binds them by his spell in circles of ideas, through the pictures which he unrolls before them.

His strong desire to embody the thought occupying his mind in a single picture, which can be surveyed at one view, also dictated to him the set form of his drama—a form not invented, but largely perfected, by him. His pieces are, as it were, final words terminating long anterior developments. They are the sudden breaking into flame of combustible materials accumulating during years, it may be during whole human lives, or even generations, and of which the sudden flare brilliantly illumines a wide extent of time and space. The incidents of the Ibsen drama more frequently take place in a day, or at most in twice twenty-four hours, and in this short space of time there are concentred all the effects of the course of the world and of social institutions on certain characters, in such a conspectus that the destinies of the dramatis personæ become clear to us from the moment of their first appearance. *The Doll's House*, *Ghosts*, *Rosmersholm*, *The Pillars of Society*, and *Hedda Gabler* comprise about twenty-four hours; *An Enemy of Society*, *The Wild Duck*, *The Lady from the Sea*, about thirty-six hours. It is the return to the Aristotelian doctrine of the unities of time and space with an orthodoxy compared with which the French classicists of the age of Louis XIV. are heretics. I might well term the Ibsenite technique a technique of fireworks, for it consists in preparing long in advance a staging on which the suns, Roman candles, squibs, fireballs and concluding fire-sheaves are carefully placed in proper position. When all is ready the curtain rises, and the artistically-constructed work begins to crackle, explosion following explosion uninterruptedly with thunder and lightning. This technique is certainly very effective, but hardly true. In reality events rarely lead up to a catastrophe so brilliant and succinct. In Nature all is slowly prepared, and unrolls itself gradually, and the results of human deeds covering years of time do not compress themselves into a few hours. Nature does not work epigrammatically. She cannot trouble herself about Aristotelian unities, for she has always an infinity of affairs of her own in progress at one and the same time. As a matter of handicraft, one is certainly often forced to admire the cleverness with which Ibsen guides and knots the threads of his plot. Sometimes the labour is more successful than at other times, but it always implies a great expenditure of textile skill. Whoever sets most store on truth in a poem—that is, on the natural action of the laws of life—will often enough bring away from Ibsen's dramas an impression of improbability, and of toilsome and subtle lucubrations.

The power with which Ibsen, in a few rapid strokes, sketches a situation, an emotion, a dim-lit depth of the soul, is very much higher than his skill, so much extolled, of foreshortening in time, which may be said to be the poetic counterpart of the painter's artifice (difficult, but for the most part barren) of foreshortening in space. Each of the terse words which suffice him has something of the nature of a peephole, through which limitless vistas are obtained. The plays of all peoples and all ages have few situations at once so perfectly simple and so irresistibly affecting as the scenes—to cite only a few—where Nora is playing with her children,* where Dr. Rank relates that he is doomed to imminent death by his inexorable disease,† where

* NORA (*the children talk all at once to her during the following*). And so you have been having great fun? That is splendid. Oh, really! you have been giving Emmy and Bob a slide, both at once! Dear me! you are quite a man, Ivar. Oh, give her to me a little, Mary Ann. My sweetheart! (*Takes the smallest from the nurse, and dances it up and down.*) Yes, yes; mother will dance with Bob, too. What! did you have a game of snowballs as well? Oh, I ought to have been there. No, leave them, Mary Ann; I will take their things off. No, no, let me do it; it is so amusing. Go to the nursery for awhile, you look so frozen. You'll find some hot coffee on the stove. (*The nurse goes to the room on the left.* NORA *takes off the children's things and throws them down anywhere, while she lets the children talk to each other and to her.*) Really! Then there was a big dog there who ran after you all the way home? But I'm sure he didn't bite you. No; dogs don't bite dear dolly little children. Don't peep into those parcels, Ivar. You want to know what there is? Yes, you are the only people who shall know. Oh, no, no, that is not pretty. What! must we have a game? What shall it be, then? Hide and seek? Yes, let us play hide and seek. Bob shall hide first. Am I to? Very well, I will hide first.—*A Doll's House*, Griffith and Farran, p. 30.

† RANK (*in* NORA'S *and* HELMER'S *room*). [He has that day discovered a symptom in himself which he knows is an infallible sign of approaching death.] Yes, here is the dear place I know so well. It is so quiet and comfortable here with you two.

HELMER. You seemed to enjoy yourself exceedingly upstairs, too.

RANK. Exceedingly. Why should I not? Why shouldn't one get enjoyment out of everything in this world? At any rate, as much and as long as one can. The wine was splendid.

HELMER. Especially the champagne.

RANK. Did you notice it, too? It was perfectly incredible the quantity I contrived to drink. . . . Well, why should one not have a merry evening after a well-spent day?

HELMER. Well spent? As to that, I have not much to boast of.

RANK (*tapping him on the shoulder*). But I have, don't you see.

NORA. Then, you have certainly been engaged in some scientific investigation, Dr. Rank.

RANK. Quite right. . . .

NORA. And am I to congratulate you on the result?

RANK. By all means you must.

NORA. Then the result was a good one?

Frau Alving with horror discerns his dissolute father* in her only son, where the housekeeper, Frau Helseth, sees Rosmer and Rebecca die in each other's arms,† etc.

Similarly, it must be acknowledged that Ibsen has created some characters possessing a truth to life and a completeness such as are not to be met with in any poet since Shakespeare. Gina (in *The Wild Duck*) is one of the most profound creations of world-literature—almost as great as Sancho Panza, who inspired

---

RANK. The best possible, alike for the physician and patient—namely, certainty.

NORA (*quickly and searchingly*). Certainty?

RANK. Complete certainty. Ought not I, upon the strength of it, to be very merry this evening?

NORA. Yes, you were quite right to be, Dr. Rank. . . . I am sure you are very fond of masquerade balls.

RANK. When there are plenty of interesting masks present, I certainly am. . . .

HELMER. . . . But what character will you take [at our next masquerade]?

RANK. I am perfectly clear as to that, my dear friend.

HELMER. Well?

RANK. At the next masquerade I shall appear invisible.

HELMER. What a comical idea!

RANK. Don't you know there is a big black hat—haven't you heard stories of the hat that made people invisible? You pull it all over you, and then nobody sees you. . . . But I am quite forgetting why I came in here. Helmer, just give me a cigar—one of the dark Havanas. . . . Thanks. (*He lights his cigar.*) And now good-bye . . . and thank you for the light.

[*He nods to them both and goes.—A Doll's House*, pp. 96-100.

* Frau Alving is speaking with Pastor Manders, and is just relating that she was one day witness to a scene in the adjoining room which proved to her that her departed husband was carrying on an intrigue with her maid-servant. In the next room are Oswald, her son, and Regina, the offspring of the intercourse of her husband with the maid-servant.

[*From within the dining-room comes the noise of a chair overturned, and at the same moment is heard:*

REGINA (*sharply, but whispering*). Oswald, take care! Are you mad? Let me go!

MRS. ALVING (*starts in terror*). Ah! (*She stares wildly towards the half-opened door;* OSWALD *is heard coughing and humming inside. A bottle is uncorked.*)

MANDERS (*excited*). What in the world is the matter? What is it, Mrs Alving?

MRS. ALVING (*hoarsely*). Ghosts! The couple from the conservatory have risen again!—*Ghosts, The Pillars of Society, and other Plays.* By Henrik Ibsen, Camelot Series, p. 150.

† Frau Helseth has in vain sought for Rosmer and Rebecca in the house.

MADAME HELSETH (*goes to the window and looks out*). Oh, good God! that white thing *there!*—My soul! They're both of them out on the bridge! God forgive the sinful creatures—if they're not in each other's arms! (*Shrieks aloud.*) Oh—down—both of them! Out into the mill-race! Help! help! (*Her knees tremble, she holds on to the chair-back, shaking all over; she can scarcely get the words out.*) No. No help here. The dead wife has taken them.—*Rosmerholm.* London, Walter Scott, p. 144. The last sentence is not a happy one. It is commonplace, upsetting the mood of the hearer or reader.

it. Ibsen has had the daring to create a female Sancho, and in his temerity has come very near to Cervantes, whom no one has equalled. If Gina is not quite so overpowering as Sancho, it is because there is wanting in her his contrast to Don Quixote. Her Don Quixote, Hjalmar, is no genuine, convinced idealist, but merely a miserable self-deluding burlesquer of the ideal. None the less, no poet since the illustrious Spanish master has succeeded in creating such an embodiment of plain, jolly, healthy common-sense, of practical tact without anxiety as to things eternal, and of honest fulfilment of all proximate, obvious duties, without a suspicion of higher moral obligations, as this Gina, *e.g.*, in the scene where Hjalmar returns home after having spent the night out.* Hjalmar also is a perfect creation, in which Ibsen has not once succumbed to the cogent temptation to exaggerate, but has exercised most entrancingly that 'self-restraint' in every word which, as Goethe said, 'reveals the master.' Little Hedwig (again in *The Wild Duck*), the aunt Juliane Tesman (in *Hedda Gabler*), perhaps also the childishly egoistical consumptive Lyngstrand (in *The Lady frcm the Sea*), are not inferior to these characters. It should, however, be noticed that, with the exception of Gina, Hjalmar and Hedwig, the lifelike and artistically delightful persons in Ibsen's dramas never play the chief parts, but move in subordinate tasks around the central figures. The latter are not human beings of flesh and blood, but abstractions such as are evoked by a morbidly-excited brain. They are attempts at the embodiment of Ibsenite doctrines, *homunculi*, originating not from natural procreation, but through the black art of the poet.

* Hjalmar has passed the night away from home, having learned that his wife before her marriage with him had had a *liaison* with another. He returns in the morning, crapulous and hipped. He is bombastic and melodramatic, while his wife is calm and practical :—

GINA (*standing with the brush in her hand, and looking at him*). Oh, there now, Ekdal ; so you've come after all ?

HJALMAR (*comes in and answers in a toneless voice*). I come—only to depart again immediately.

GINA. Yes, yes ; I suppose so. But, Lord help us, what a sight you are !

HJALMAR. A sight ?

GINA. And your nice winter coat, too ! Well, that's done for. . . . Then, you are still bent on leaving us, Ekdal ?

HJALMAR. Yes ; that's a matter of course, I should think.

GINA. Well, well . . . (*Sets a tray with coffee, etc., on the table.*) Here's a drop of something warm, if you'd like it. And there's some bread and butter and a snack of salt meat.

HJALMAR (*glancing at the tray*). Salt meat ! Never under this roof ! It's true I haven't had a mouthful of solid food for nearly twenty-four hours, but no matter. . . . Oh no, I must go out into the storm and the snow-blast—go from house to house and seek shelter for my father and myself.

GINA. But you've got no hat, Ekdal. You've lost your hat, you know, etc. —*The Wild Duck*, Act V.

This is even admitted, although reluctantly and with reservation, by one of his most raving panegyrists, the French professor, Auguste Ehrhard.* Doubtless Ibsen takes immense pains to rouge and powder into a semblance of life the talking puppets who are to represent his notions. He appends to them all sorts of little peculiarities for the purpose of giving them an individual physiognomy. But this perpetually recurring imbecile 'Eh?' of Tesman† (in *Hedda Gabler*), this 'dash it all!' and stealthy nibbling of sweetmeats by Nora‡ (in *A Doll's House*), this 'smoking a large meerschaum' and champagne-drinking of Oswald (in *Ghosts*), do not delude the attentive observer as to their being anything but automata. In spite of the poet's artifices, one sees, behind the thin varnish of flesh-colour, the hinges and joints of the mechanism, and hears, above the tones of the phonographs concealed in them, the creaking and grating of the machinery.

I have endeavoured to do justice to the high poetical endowment of Ibsen, and shall sometimes be able in the course of this inquiry to recognise this gift again. Is it this, however, which alone or chiefly has gained for him his admirers in all lands? Do his retinue of fifers and bagpipers prize him for his homely emotional scenes, and for his truly lifelike accessory figures? No. They glorify something else in him. They discover in his pieces world-pictures of the greatest truth, the happiest poetic use of scientific methods, clearness and incisiveness of ideas, a fiercely revolutionary desire for freedom, and a modernity pregnant with the future. Now we will test and examine these affirmations *seriatim*, and see if they can be supported by

* Auguste Ehrhard, Professor à la Faculté des Lettres de Clermont-Ferrand, *Henrik Ibsen et le Théâtre contemporain*, Paris, 1892, p. 233: 'Ibsen's characters may in general be divided into two categories—those in which the moral element, the life of the soul, dominates, and those in which the animal prevails. The first are, for the most part, mouthpieces of the theories dear to the poet. . . . They have their primary origin in the brain of the poet. . . . It is he who gives them life.'

† Right out here so early—eh? . . . Well, did you get safe home from the quay—eh? Look here. Let me untie the bow—eh? etc.—*Hedda Gabler*. London, W. Heinemann, pp. 7-9.

‡ NORA. Yes, I really am now in a state of extraordinary happiness. There is only one thing in the world that I should really like.

RANK. Well, and what's that?

NORA. There's something that I should so like to say—but for Torvald to hear it.

RANK. Then, why don't you say it to him?

NORA. Because I daren't, for it sounds so ugly. . . .

RANK. In that case I would advise you not to say it. But you might say it to us, at any rate. . . . What is it that you would like to say in Helmer's presence?

NORA. I should like to shout with all my heart—Oh dash it all —*A Doll's House*, *op. cit.*, pp. 26, 27.

Ibsen's works, or are merely the arbitrary and undemonstrable expressions of æsthetic wind-bags.

It is pretended that Ibsen is before all things exemplary in truthfulness. He has even become the model of 'realism.' As a matter of fact, since Alexandre Dumas père, author of *The Three Musketeers* and *Monte Cristo*, no writer has heaped up in his works so many startling improbabilities as Ibsen. (I say improbabilities, because I dare not say impossibilities; for, after all, everything is possible as the unheard-of exploit of some fool, or as the extraordinary effect of a unique accident.) Is it conceivable that (in *Ghosts*) the joiner Engstrand, wishing to open a tavern for sailors, should call upon his own daughter to be the odalisque of his 'establishment'—this daughter who reminds him that she has been 'brought up in the house of Madam Alving, widow of a lord-in-waiting,' that she has been treated 'almost as a child of the house'? Not that I imagine Engstrand to be possessed of any moral scruples. But a man of this stamp knows that one woman does not suffice for his house; and since he must engage others, he would certainly not turn to his daughter, bred as she was in the midst of higher habits of life, and knowing that, if she wishes to lead a life of pleasure, it would not be necessary to become straightway a prostitute for sailors. Is it conceivable that Pastor Manders (*Ghosts*), a liberally educated clergyman in the Norway of to-day, a country of flourishing insurance companies, banks, railways, prosperous newspapers, etc., should dissuade Madam Alving from insuring against fire the asylum she had just founded? 'For my own part,' he says, 'I should not see the smallest impropriety in guarding against all contingencies. . . . I mean [by really responsible people] men in such independent and influential positions that one cannot help allowing some weight to their opinions. . . . People would be only too ready to interpret our action as a sign that neither you nor I had the right faith in a Higher Providence.' Does Ibsen really wish to make anyone believe that in Norway there are persons who have religious scruples concerning insurance against fire? Has not this nonsensical idea come into his head simply because he wishes to have the asylum burned down and finally destroyed? For this purpose Madam Alving must have no money to rebuild the asylum, it must not be insured, and hence Ibsen thought it necessary to assign a motive for the omission of the insurance. A poet who introduces a fire into his work, as a symbol and also as an active agent—for it has the dramatic purpose of destroying the lying reputation for charity of the defunct sinner Alving—should also have the courage to leave unexplained the omission of the insurance, strange as it may seem. Oswald Alving relates to his mother (*Ghosts*) that a Paris doctor on examining him had told him he had a 'kind of softening of the brain.' Now, I appeal to all the doctors of the world if they have ever said plainly to a patient, 'You have softening of the brain.' To the family it perhaps may be revealed, to the patient never. Chiefly because, if the diagnosis be correct, the invalid would not understand the remark, and would certainly no longer be in a fit state to go alone to the doctor. But for yet another reason these words are impossible. In any case, Oswald's disease could not have been a softening, but a hardening, a callous, sclerotic condition of the brain.

In *A Doll's House* Helmer, who is depicted as somewhat sensual, although prosaic, homely, practical, and commonplace, says to his Nora: 'Is that my lark who is twittering outside there? . . . Is the little squirrel running about? . . . Has my little spendthrift bird been wasting more money? . . . Come, come; my lark must not let her wings droop immediately. . . . What do people call the bird who always spends everything? . . . My lark is the dearest little thing in the world; but she needs a very great deal of money. . . . And I couldn't wish you to be anything but exactly what you are—my own true little lark. . . .' And it is thus that a husband, a bank director and barrister, after eight years of married life, speaks to his wife, the mother of his three children; and not in a momentary outburst of playful affection, but in the full light of an ordinary day, and in an interminable scene of seven pages (pp. 2-8), with a view to giving us an idea of the habitually prevalent tone in this 'doll's home!' I should much like to know what my readers of both sexes who have been married at least eight years think of this specimen of Ibsen's 'realism.'

In *The Pillars of Society* all the characters talk about 'society.' 'You are to rise and support society, brother-in-law,' says Miss Hessel, 'earnestly and with emphasis.' 'If you strike this blow, you ruin me utterly, and not only me, but also a great and blessed future for the community which was the home of your childhood.' And a little further on: 'See, this I have dared for the good of the community! . . . Don't you see that it is society itself that forces us into these subterfuges?' The persons thus holding forth are a wholesale merchant and consul, and a school-mistress who has long resided in America, and has broad views. Can the word 'society' in the mouth of cultivated people, when so used, have any other meaning than 'social edifice?' Well, but the characters in the piece, as it is again and again repeated, employ the word 'society' in reference to the well-to-do classes in a small seaside place in Norway—that is, to a clique of six or eight families! Ibsen makes the readers of his piece believe that it is a question of upholding the social edifice, and they learn with astonishment that this only concerns the protection of a diminutive coterie of Philistines in a northern Gotham.

The American ship *Indian Girl* is undergoing repairs in Consul Bernick's dock. Her hull is quite rotten. If she is sent to sea she will assuredly founder. Bernick, however, insists that she shall sail in two days. His foreman Aune pronounces this impossible. Then Bernick threatens Aune with dismissal, at which the latter yields, and promises that 'in two days the *Indian Girl* will be ready to sail.' Bernick knows that he is sending the *Indian Girl's* crew of eighteen men to certain death. And why does he commit this wholesale murder? He gives the following explanation: 'I have my reasons for hurrying on the affair. Have you read this morning's paper? Ah! then you know that the Americans have been making disturbances again. The shameless pack put the whole town topsy-turvy. Not a night passes without fights in the taverns or on the street, not to speak of other abominations. . . . And who gets the blame for all this disturbance? It is I—yes, I—that suffer for it. These newspaper scribblers are always covertly carping at us for giving our whole attention to the *Palm Tree*. And I, whose mission it is to be an example to my fellow-citizens, must have such things thrown in my teeth! I cannot bear it. It won't do for me to have my name bespattered in this way. . . . Not just now; precisely at this moment I need all the respect and good-will of my fellow-citizens. I have a great undertaking on hand, as you have probably heard; but if evil-disposed persons succeed in shaking people's unqualified confidence in me, it may involve me in the greatest difficulties. So I must silence these carping and spiteful scribblers at any price, and that is why I give you till the day after to-morrow.' This paltry motive for the coldly-planned murder of eighteen men is so ridiculous that even Ehrhard, who admires everything in Ibsen, dares not defend it, and timidly remarks that 'the author does not very well explain why the anxiety for his reputation should require the sending to sea of a vessel which he has not had time thoroughly to repair.'*

At the head of a delegation of his fellow-citizens, sent to thank him for the establishment of a railway, Pastor Rörlund delivers an address to Bernick in which the following passages occur: 'We have often expressed to you our gratitude for the broad moral foundation upon which you have, so to speak, built up our society. This time we chiefly hail in you the . . . citizen, who has taken the initiative in an undertaking which, we are credibly assured, will give a powerful impetus to the temporal prosperity and well-being of the community. . . . You are in an eminent sense the pillar and corner-stone of this com-

* Auguste Ehrhard, *op. cit.*, p. 270.

munity. . . . And it is just this light of disinterestedness shining over all your actions that is so unspeakably beneficent, especially in these times. You are now on the point of procuring for us—I do not hesitate to say the word plainly and prosaically—a railway. . . . But you cannot reject a slight token of your grateful fellow-citizens' appreciation, least of all on this momentous occasion, when, according to the assurances of practical men, we are standing on the threshold of a new era.' I have not interrupted by a single remark or note of exclamation this unheard-of balderdash. It shall produce its own unaided effect upon the reader. If this nonsense appeared in a burlesque farce, it would be hardly funny enough, but otherwise acceptable. Now, this claims to be 'realistic'! We are to take Ibsen's word for it that Pastor Rörlund was sober when he made this speech! A more insulting demand has never been made by an author on his readers.

In *An Enemy of Society* the subject treats of a rather incomprehensible bathing establishment, comprising at once mineral waters, medicinal baths and sea-bathing. The doctor of the establishment has discovered that the springs are contaminated with typhoid bacilli, and insists that the water shall be taken from a place higher up in the mountains, where it would not be polluted by sewage. He is the more urgent in his demands, as without this precaution a fatal epidemic will break out among the visitors. And to this the burgomaster of the town is supposed to reply: 'The existing supply of water for the baths is once for all a fact, and must naturally be treated as such. But probably the directors, at some future time, will not be indisposed to take into their consideration whether, by making certain pecuniary sacrifices, it may not be possible to introduce some improvements.' This is a question of a place which, as Ibsen insists, has staked its future on the development of its youthful bathing establishment; the place is situated in Norway, in a small district where all the inhabitants are mutually acquainted, and where every case of illness and death is noticed by all. And the burgomaster will run the risk of having a number of the visitors at the establishment attacked with typhoid, when he is forewarned that this will certainly happen if the conduit pipes of the spring are not transferred. Without having an exaggeratedly high opinion of the burgomaster mind in general, I deny that any idiot such as Ibsen depicts is at the head of the local administration of any town whatsoever in Europe.

Tesman, in *Hedda Gabler*, expects that his publication, *Domestic Industries of Brabant during the Middle Ages*, will secure him a professorship in a college. But he has a dangerous competitor in Ejlert Lövborg, who has published a book on *The General*

March of Civilization. This work has already made a 'great sensation,' but the sequel is far to surpass this, and 'treats of the future.' 'But, good gracious! we don't know anything about that!' someone objects. 'No; but there are several things though can be said about it, all the same. . . . It is divided into two sections. The first is about the civilizing forces of the future, and the other is about the civilizing progress of the future.' Special stress is laid upon the fact that it lies wholly outside the domain of science, and consists in mere prophecy. 'Do you believe it impossible to reproduce such a work—that it cannot be written a second time? No. . . . For the inspiration, you know. . . .' We are acquainted, were it only through popular histories of morals such as the *Democritus* of Karl Julius Weber, with the strange questions with which the casuists of the Middle Ages used to occupy themselves. But that, in our century, such works as those of Tesman and Lövborg could gain for their authors a professorship of any kind in either hemisphere, or even the position of *privat docent*, is an infantile invention, fit to raise a laugh in all academical circles.

In *The Lady from the Sea* the mysterious sailor returns to find that his old sweetheart has been for some years the wife of Dr. Wangel. He urges her to follow him, saying she really belongs to him. The husband is present at the interview. He shows the stranger that he is wrong in wishing to carry off Ellida. He represents to the sailor that it would be preferable if he addressed himself to him (the husband), and not to the wife. He mildly remonstrates with the stranger for addressing Ellida with the familiar 'thou,' and calling her by her Christian name. 'Such a familiarity is not customary with us, sir.' The scene is unspeakably comic, and would be worthy of reproduction in its entirety. We will limit ourselves to quoting the conclusion :—

STRANGER. To-morrow night I will come again, and then I shall look for you here. You must wait for me here in the garden, for I prefer settling the matter with you alone. You understand?

ELLIDA (*in low, trembling tone*). Do you hear that, Wangel?

WANGEL. Only keep calm. We shall know how to prevent this visit.

STRANGER. Good-bye for the present, Ellida. So to-morrow night——

ELLIDA (*imploringly*). Oh, no, no! Do not come to-morrow night! Never come here again!

STRANGER. And should you, then, have a mind to follow me over seas?

ELLIDA. Oh, don't look at me like that!

STRANGER. I only mean that you must then be ready to set out.

WANGEL. Go up to the house, Ellida, etc.

And Ibsen depicts Wangel, not as a senile, debile old man, but in the prime of life and in full possession of all his faculties!

All these crack-brained episodes are, however, far surpassed by the scene in *Rosmersholm*, where Rebecca confesses to the doughty Rosmer that she is consumed by ardent passion for him :—

ROSMER. What have you felt? Speak so that I can understand you.
REBECCA. It came over me—this wild, uncontrollable desire—oh, Rosmer!
ROSMER. Desire? You! For what?
REBECCA. For you.
ROSMER (*tries to spring up*). What is this? [Idiot!]
REBECCA (*stops him*). Sit still, dear; there is more to tell.
ROSMER. And you mean to say—that you love me—in that way?
REBECCA. I thought that it should be called love. Yes, I thought it was love; but it was not. It was what I said. It was a wild, uncontrollable desire. . . . It came upon me like a storm on the sea. It was like one of the storms we sometimes have in the North in the winter-time. It seizes you—and sweeps you along with it—whither it will. Resistance is out of the question.'

Rosmer, the object of this burning passion, is forty-three years old, and has been a clergyman. This makes it somewhat droll, but not impossible, for erotomaniacs can love all sorts of creatures, even boots.* What, however, is inconceivable is the way in which the nymphomaniac sets about satisfying her 'wild, uncontrollable desire,' this 'storm upon the sea' which 'seizes you, and sweeps you along with it.' She had become the friend of Rosmer's sickly wife, and had for eighteen months tormented her by hinting that Rosmer is unhappy because she has no children, that he loves her, the nymphomaniac, but has controlled his passion as long as his wife is living. By means of this poison, patiently and unceasingly dropped into her soul, she had happily driven her to suicide. After a year and a half! To appease her 'wild, uncontrollable passion'! This is exactly as if a man driven wild by hunger should, with a view to satisfying his craving, devise a deep plan for obtaining a field by fraud, so that he might grow wheat, have it ground, and afterwards bake himself a splendid loaf, which would then be Oh, so delicious! The reader may judge for himself if this is the usual way in which famished persons, or nymphomaniacs over whom passion 'sweeps like a storm upon the sea,' satisfy their impulses.

Such are the presentations of the world's realities as figured to himself by this 'realist'! Many of his infantile or silly lucubrations are petty, superficial details, and a benevolent friend, with some experience of life and some common-sense, could easily have preserved him in advance from making himself ridiculous. Others of his inventions, however, touch the very essence of his poems and convert these into out and out grotesque moonshine. In *The Pillars of Society*, Bernick, the man who calmly plans the

* Dr. R. von Krafft-Ebing, *Psychopathia sexualis mit besonderer Berücksichtigung der conträren Sexualempfindung. Eine klinisch-forensische Studie.* Dritte vermehrte und verbesserte Auflage. Stuttgart, 1888. See (p. 120) the observation relative to the young nobleman who was erotically excited by his 'boot-thoughts.' I cite this single case only, but it would be possible to instance dozens of cases where nightcaps, shoe-nails, white aprons, the wrinkled head of an old woman, etc., have excited sensuality in the highest degree.

murder of eighteen men to maintain his reputation as a capable dock-owner (we may remark, in passing, the absurdity of this means for attaining such an end), all at once confesses to his fellow-citizens, without any compulsion, and solely on the advice of Miss Hessel, that he has been a villain and a criminal. In *A Doll's House*, the wife, who was only a moment before playing so tenderly with her children, suddenly abandons these children without a thought for them.* In *Rosmersholm* we are to believe that the nymphomaniac Rebecca, while in constant intercourse with the object of her flame, has become chaste and virtuous, etc. Many of Ibsen's principal characters present this spectacle of impossible and incomprehensible metamorphoses, so that they look like figures composed of odd halves, which some bungling artisan has stuck together.

After the life-like truthfulness of Ibsen, let us inquire into the scientific character of his work. This reminds us of the civilization of Liberian negroes. The constitution and laws of that West African republic read very much like those of the United States of North America, and on paper command our respect. But anyone living in Liberia very soon recognises the fact that these black republicans are savages, having no idea of the political institutions nominally existing among them, of their code of laws, etc. Ibsen likes to give himself the appearance of standing in the domain of natural science and of profiting by its latest results. In his plays Darwin is quoted. He has evidently dipped, though with a careless hand, into books on heredity, and has picked up something about medical science. But the scanty, ludicrously misunderstood stock phrases which have remained in his memory are made use of by him much as my illustrative Liberian negro uses the respectable paper collars and top-hats of Europe. The expert can never preserve his gravity when Ibsen displays his scientific and medical knowledge.

Heredity is his hobby-horse, which he mounts in every one of his pieces. There is not a single trait in his personages, a single peculiarity of character, a single disease, that he does not trace to heredity. In *A Doll's House*, Dr. Rank's 'poor innocent spine must do penance for "his" father's notions of amusement when he was a lieutenant in the army.' Helmer explains to Nora that 'a misty atmosphere of lying brings contagion into the whole family. Every breath the children draw contains

* *A Doll's House*, p. 112:

HELMER. To forsake your home, your husband, and your children! And only think what people will say about it.

NORA. I cannot take that into consideration. I only know that to go is necessary for me. . . .

HELMER. . . . Your duties to . . . your children?

NORA. I have other duties equally sacred . . . duties towards myself, etc.

some germ of evil. . . . Nearly all men who go to ruin early have had untruthful mothers. . . . In most cases it comes from the mother; but the father naturally works in the same direction.' And again: 'Your father's low principles you have inherited, every one of them. No religion, no morality, no sense of duty.' In *Ghosts* Oswald has learned from the extraordinary doctor in Paris who told him he had softening of the brain, that he had inherited his malady from his father.* Regina, the natural daughter of the late Alving, exactly resembles her mother.

REGINA (*to herself*). So mother was that kind of woman, after all.

MRS. ALVING. Your mother had many good qualities, Regina.

REGINA. Yes; but she was one of that sort, all the same. Oh! I've often suspected it. . . A poor girl must make the best of her young days. . . . And I, too, want to enjoy my life, Mrs. Alving.

MRS. ALVING. Yes, I see you do. But don't throw yourself away, Regina.

REGINA. Oh! what must be, must be. If Oswald takes after his father, I take after my mother, I dare say.

In *Rosmersholm* Rebecca's nymphomania is explained by the fact that she is the natural daughter of a Lapland woman of doubtful morals. 'I believe your whole conduct is determined by your origin,' Rector Kroll says to her (p. 82). Rosmer never laughs, because 'it is a trait of his family.' He is 'the descendant of the men that look down on us from these walls' (p. 80). His 'spirit is deeply rooted in his ancestry' (p. 80). Hilda, the stepdaughter of the 'Lady from the Sea,' says: 'I should not wonder if some fine day she went mad. . . . Her mother went mad, too. She died mad. I know that.' In *The Wild Duck* nearly everyone has a hereditary mark. Gregers Werle, the malignant imbecile, who holds and proclaims his passion for gossip as an ardent desire for truth, inherits this craze from his mother.† Little Hedwig becomes blind, like her father, old Werle.‡

* *Ghosts*, p. 170: OSWALD. At last he said, 'You have been worm-eaten from your birth.' . . . I didn't understand either, and begged of him to give me a clearer explanation. And then the old cynic said, 'The father's sins are visited upon the children.' And p. 194: OSWALD. The disease I have as my birthright (*he points to his forehead, and adds very softly*) is seated here.

† *The Wild Duck*, Act III.:

GREGERS. Besides, if I'm to go on living, I must try and find some cure for my sick conscience.

WERLE. It will never be well. Your conscience has been sickly from childhood. That's an inheritance from your mother, Gregers—it is the only inheritance she left you. . . .

RELLING. But, deuce take it, don't you see the fellow's mad, cracked, demented!

GINA. There, you hear! His mother before him had mad fits like that sometimes.

‡ *The Wild Duck*, Act II.:

HJALMAR. She is in danger of losing her eyesight.

GREGERS. Becoming blind?

In the earlier philosophical dramas the same idea is constantly repeated. Brand gets his obstinacy, and Peer Gynt his lively, extravagant imagination, from the mother. Ibsen has evidently read Lucas's book on the first principles of heredity, and has borrowed from it uncritically. It is true that Lucas believes in the inheritance even of notions and feelings as complex and as nearly related to specific facts as, *e.g.*, the horror of doctors,* and that he does not doubt the transmission of diseased deviations from the norm, *e.g.*, the appearance of blindness at a definite age.† Lucas, however, whose merits are not to be denied, did not sufficiently distinguish between that which the individual receives in its material genesis from its parents, and that which is subsequently suggested by family life and example, by continuous existence in the same conditions as its parents, etc. Ibsen is the true 'man of one book.' He abides by his Lucas. If he had read Weismann,‡ and, above all, Galton,§ he would have known that nothing is more obscure and apparently more capricious, than the course of heredity. For the individual is, says Galton, the result—the arithmetic mean—of three different quantities: its father, its mother and the whole species, represented by the double series, going back to the beginnings of all terrestrial life, of its paternal and maternal progenitors. This third datum is the unknown quantity—the *x*—in the problem. Reversions to distant ancestors may make the individual wholly unlike its parents, and the influence of the species so far exceed, as a general rule, those of the immediate progenitors, that children who are the exact cast of their father or mother, especially with respect to the most complex manifestations of personality, of character, capacities and inclinations, are the greatest rarities. But Ibsen is not at all concerned about seriously justifying his ideas on heredity in a scientific manner. As we shall see later on, these ideas have their root in his mysticism; Lucas's work was for him only a lucky treasure-trove,

---

HJALMAR. . . . But the doctor has warned us. It's coming, inexorably.
GREGERS. What an awful misfortune! How do you account for it?
HJALMAR (*sighs*). Hereditary, no doubt.
Again, Act IV.:
MRS. SÖRBY. . . . He (Werle) is going blind.
HJALMAR (*with a start*). Going blind? That's strange—Werle, too, becoming blind!

* Dr Prosper Lucas, *Traité philosophique et physiologique de l'Hérédité naturelle dans les États de Santé et de Maladie du Système nerveux*, etc. (The title occupies seven lines more!) Paris, 1847, 2 volumes, t. i., p. 250. (It appears that Montaigne had this inherited horror of doctors.)

† Lucas, *op. cit.*, t. i., pp. 391-420: *De l'hérédité des modes sensitifs de la vue.* On page 400 he tells of a family in which the mother became blind at the age of twenty-one years, and the children at sixteen and seventeen respectively, etc.

‡ August Weismann, *Ueber die Vererbung.* Jena, 1883.

§ F. Galton, *Natural Inheritance.* London, 1888.

which he seized on with joy, because it offered him the possibility of scientifically cloaking his mystic obsession.

Ibsen's excursions in the domain of medical science, which he hardly ever denies himself, are most delightful. In *The Pillars of Society* Rector Rörlund glorifies the women of his côterie as a kind of 'sisters of mercy who pick lint.' Pick lint! In an age of antiseptics and aseptics! Let Ibsen only take into his head to enter any surgical ward with his 'picked lint'! He would be astonished at the reception given to him and his lint. In *An Enemy of Society* Dr. Stockmann declares that the water of the baths with its 'millions of bacilli is absolutely injurious to health, whether used internally or externally.' The only bacilli which can be referred to in this scene, as throughout the whole piece, are the typhoid bacilli of Eberth. Now, it may be true that bathing in contaminated water may produce Biskra boils, and perhaps béri-béri; but it would be difficult for Dr. Stockmann and Ibsen to instance a single case of typhoid fever contracted through bathing in water containing bacilli. In *A Doll's House* Helmer's life 'depended on a journey abroad.' That might be true for a European in the tropics, or for anyone living in a fever-district. But in Norway there is no such thing as an acute illness in which the life of the invalid depends on 'a journey abroad.' Further on Dr. Rank says (p. 60): 'In the last few days I have had a general stock-taking of my inner man. Bankruptcy! Before a month is over I shall be food for worms in the churchyard. . . . There is only one more investigation to be made, and when I have made it I shall know exactly at what time dissolution will take place.' According to his own declaration, Dr. Rank suffers from disease of the dorsal marrow (it is true that he speaks of the dorsal column, but the mistaken expression need not be taken too rigidly). Ibsen is evidently thinking of consumption of the spinal marrow. Now, there is in this disease absolutely no symptom which could with certainty authorize the prediction of death three weeks beforehand; there is no 'general stock-taking of the inner man' which the invalid, if he were a doctor, could carry out on himself to gain a clear knowledge of 'when the dissolution' was to take place; and there is no form of consumption of the spinal marrow which would allow the invalid four weeks before his death (not an accidental death, but one necessitated by his disease) to go to a ball, drink immoderately of champagne, and afterwards to take an affecting leave of his friends. Oswald Alving's illness in *Ghosts* is, from a clinical standpoint, quite as childishly depicted as that of Rank. From all that is said in the piece the disease inherited by Oswald from his father can only be diagnosed either as *syphilis hereditaria tarda*, or *dementia paralytica*. The first of these diseases is out of the question, for Oswald is depicted as a model of manly strength and health.* And even if, in exceptional and extremely rare cases, the malady does not show itself till after the victim is well on in his twenties, it yet betrays itself from the earliest childhood by certain phenomena of degeneracy which would prevent even a mother, blinded by love and pride, from glorifying her son's 'outer self' in the style of Mrs. Alving. Certain minor features might perhaps indicate *dementia paralytica*, as, for example, Oswald's sensual excitability, the artless freedom with which he speaks before his mother of the amours of his friends in Paris, or gives expression to his pleasure at the sight of the 'glorious' Regina, the levity with which, at the first sight of this girl, he makes plans for his marriage, etc.† But together with these exact, though subordinate, features there appear others infinitely more important, which wholly preclude the diagnosis of *dementia paralytica.* There is in Oswald no trace of the megalomania which is never absent in the first stage of this malady; he is anxious and depressed, while the sufferer from general paralysis feels extremely happy, and sees life through rose-coloured spectacles. Oswald forebodes and dreads an outburst of madness—a fact which I, for my part, have never observed in a paralytic, nor found indicated by any clinicist whatever. Finally, Oswald's dementia declares itself with a suddenness and completeness found in acute mania only; but the description given of Oswald in the last scene—his immobility, his 'dull and toneless' voice, and his idiotic murmuring of the words 'the sun, the sun,' repeated half a dozen times—does not in the remotest degree correspond with the picture of acute mania.

The poet has naturally no need to understand anything of pathology. But when he pretends to describe real life, he ought to be honest. He should not get out of his depth in scientific observation and precision simply because these are demanded or preferred by the age. The more ignorant the poet is in pathology, the greater is the test of his veracity given by his clinical pictures. As he cannot, in his lay capacity, draw on his imagination for them by combining clinical experiences and reminiscences of books, it is necessary that he shall have seen with his own eyes each case represented to depict it accurately. Shakespeare was likewise no physician; and, besides, what did the physicians of his time know? Yet we can to this day still

* Page 136:

MRS. ALVING. I know one who has kept both his inner and his outer self unharmed. Only look at him, Mr. Manders.

† Krafft-Ebing, *Psychopathia sexualis*, p. 139. The author here cites all the features in question as characteristic of the first stage of general paralysis: 'Libidinous talk, unconstraint in intercourse with the opposite sex, plans of marriage.'

diagnose without hesitation the *dementia senilis* of Lear, Hamlet's weakness of will through nervous exhaustion (*neurasthenic* '*aboalie*'), the melancholia, accompanied with optical hallucination, of Lady Macbeth. Why? Because Shakespeare introduced into his creations things really seen. Ibsen, on the contrary, has freely invented his invalids, and that this method could, in the hands of a layman, only lead to laughable results, needs no proof. A moving or affecting situation offers itself to his imagination—that of a man who clearly foresees his near and inevitable death, and with violent self-conquest lifts himself to the stoic philosophy of renunciation; or that of a young man who adjures his mother to kill him when the madness he awaits with horror shall break out. The situation is very improbable. Perhaps it has never occurred. In any event, Ibsen has never witnessed it. But if it occurred it would possess great poetic beauty, and produce a great effect on the stage. Consequently Ibsen calmly turns out the novel and unknown maladies of a Dr. Rank or an Oswald Alving, the progress of which might make these situations possible. Such is the procedure of the poet whose realism and accurate observation are so much vaunted by his admirers.

His clearness of mind, his love of liberty, his modernity! Careful readers of Ibsen's works will not trust their eyes when they see these words applied to him. We will at once put immediate and exhaustive tests to the clearness of his thought. His love of liberty will be revealed by analysis as anarchism; and his modernity amounts essentially to this, that in his pieces railways are constructed (*The Pillars of Society*), that there is a cackle about bacilli (*An Enemy of the People*), that the struggles of political parties play a part in them (*The League of the Young, Rosmersholm*)—all put on superficially with a brush, without inner dependence upon the true active forces in the poem. This 'modern,' this 'apostle of liberty,' has an idea of the press and its functions fit for a clerk in a police-station, and he pursues journalists with the hatred, droll in these days, of a tracker of demagogues in the third decade of this century. All the journalists whom he sets before us—and they are numerous in his pieces, Peter Mortensgaard in *Rosmersholm*, Haustad and Billing in *An Enemy of the People*, Bahlmann in *The League of the Young*—are either drunken ragamuffins or poor knock-kneed starvelings, constantly trembling at the prospect of being thrashed or kicked out, or unprincipled rascals who write for anyone who pays. He has so clear a grasp of the social question that he makes a foreman mix with the workmen and threaten a strike because machines are about to be used on the wharves (*The Pillars of*

Society)! He looks upon the masses with the fine contempt of the great feudal landlords. When he mentions them it is either with biting derision or a most aristocratic and arrogant disdain.*

The greater part of his notions, moreover, belong to no time, but are emanations from his personal perversity, and can, therefore, be neither modern or not modern; the least uncouth of them, however, having their root in a definite period, spring from the circle of ideas of a Gothamist of the first third of the present century. The label 'modern' was arbitrarily attached to Ibsen by George Brandes (*Moderne Geister*, Frankfurt, 1886), one of the most repulsive literary phenomena of the century. George Brandes, a sponger on the fame or name of others, has throughout his life followed the calling of a 'human orchestra,' who with head, mouth, hands, elbows, knees, and feet, plays ten noisy instruments at once, dancing before poets and authors, and, after the hubbub, passes his hat round among the deafened public. For a quarter of a century he has assiduously courted the favour of all who for any reason had a following, and written rhetorical and sophistical phrases about them, as long as he could find a market. Adorned with a few feathers plucked from the stately pinions of Taine's genius, and prating of John Stuart Mill, whose treatise *On Liberty* he has glanced at, but hardly read, and certainly not understood, he introduced himself among the youth of Scandinavia, and, abusing their confidence, obtained by this means, has made their systematic moral poisoning the task of his life. He preached to them the gospel of passion, and, with truly diabolical zeal and obstinacy, confused all their notions, giving to whatever he extolled that was mean and reprehensible the most attractive and honourable names. It has always been thought weak and cowardly to yield to base impulses condemned by judgment, instead of combating and stifling them. If Brandes had said to the young, 'Renounce your judgment! Sacrifice duty to your passions! Be ruled by your senses! Let your will and consciousness be as feathers before the storm of your appetites!'—the better among his hearers would have spit at him. But he said to them: 'To obey one's senses is to have character. He who allows himself to be guided by his passions has individuality. The man of strong will despises discipline and duty, and follows every caprice, every temptation, every movement of his stomach or his other organs'; and these

* *Rosmersholm*, p. 23:
REBECCA (*to Brendel*). You should apply to Peter Mortensgaard.
BRENDEL. *Pardon, Madame*—what sort of an idiot is he?
See the flat travesty in *An Enemy of the People* (Act IV.) of the forum scene in Shakespeare's *Julius Cæsar*, and the characterization of the 'crowd,' in *Brand* (Act V.).

vulgarities, thus presented, no longer had the repulsive character which awakens distrust and serves as a warning. Proclaimed under the names of 'liberty' and 'moral autonomy,' debauchery and dissoluteness gain easy admission into the best circles, and depravity, from which all would turn if it appeared as such, seems to insufficiently informed minds attractive and desirable when disguised as 'modernity.' It is comprehensible that an educator who turns the schoolroom into a tavern and a brothel should have success and a crowd of followers. He certainly runs the risk of being slain by the parents, if they come to know what he is teaching their children; but the pupils will hardly complain, and will be eager to attend the lessons of so agreeable a teacher. By a similar method Brandes acquitted himself of his educational functions. This is the explanation of the influence he gained over the youth of his country, such as his writings, with their emptiness of thought and unending tattle, would certainly never have procured for him.

Brandes discovered in Ibsen a revolt against the prevailing moral law, together with a glorification of bestial instincts, and accordingly trumpeted his praises in spite of his astounding reactionary views, as a 'modern spirit,' recommending Ibsen's works, with a wink of the eye, to the knowledge-craving youth, whom he served as *maître de plaisir*. But this 'modern,' this 'realist,' with his exact 'scientific' observation, is in reality a mystic and an egomaniacal anarchist. An analysis of his intellectual peculiarities will enable us to discern a resemblance to those of Richard Wagner, which is not surprising, since a similarity in features is precisely a stigma of degeneracy, and for this reason is common to many, or to all, higher degenerates.

Ibsen is the child of a rigorously religious race, and grew up in a family of believers. The impressions of childhood have determined the course of his life. His mind has never been able to iron out the theological crease it got through nurture. The Bible and Catechism became for him the bounds beyond which he has never passed. His free-thinking diatribes against established Christianity (*Brand*, *Rosmersholm*, etc.), his derision of the shackled pietism of divines (Manders in *Ghosts*, Rörlund in *The Pillars of Society*, the dean in *Brand*), are an echo of his teacher, the theosophist, Sœren Kierkegaard (1815-55), a zealot certainly for quite another Christianity than that ordained by the state, and provided with powers of nomination and fixed salaries, but nevertheless an austere and exclusive Christianity, demanding the whole being of man. Perhaps even Ibsen looks upon himself as a freethinker. Wagner did the same. But what does that prove? He is not clear with regard to his own thought.

'It is curious,' writes Herbert Spencer,* 'how commonly men continue to hold, in fact, doctrines which they have rejected in name, retaining the substance after they have abandoned the form. In theology an illustration is supplied by Carlyle, who, in his student days, giving up, as he thought, the creed of his fathers, rejected its shell only, keeping the contents, and was proved by his conceptions of the world, and man and conduct, to be still among the sternest of Scotch Calvinists.' If Spencer, when he wrote this, had known Ibsen, he would perhaps have cited him as a second example. As Carlyle was always a Scotch Calvinist, so Ibsen has always remained a Norwegian Protestant of the school of Kierkegaard—that is to say, a Protestant with the earnest mysticism of a Jacob Boehme, a Swedenborg, or a Pusey, which easily passes over into the Catholicism of a St. Theresa or a Ruysbroek.

Three fundamental ideas of Christianity are ever present in his mind, and about these as round so many axes revolves the entire activity of his poetical imagination. These three unalterable central ideas, constituting genuine obsessions, reaching up from the unconscious into his intellectual life, are original sin, confession and self-sacrifice or redemption.

Æsthetic chatterers have spoken of the idea of heredity influencing all Ibsen's works, an idea which cannot escape even the feeblest attention, as something appertaining to modern science and Darwinism. As a matter of fact, it is the ever-recurring original sin of St. Augustine, and it betrays its theological nature, firstly by the circumstance that it makes its appearance in conjunction with the two other theological ideas of confession and redemption, and secondly, by the distinguishing characteristic of hereditary transmission. As we have above seen, Ibsen's personages always inherit a disease (blindness, consumption of the spinal marrow, madness), a vice (mendaciousness, levity, lewdness, obduracy), or some defect (incapacity for enjoyment), but never an agreeable or useful quality. Now what is good and wholesome is just as frequently inherited as what is evil and diseased—even more frequently, according to many investigators. Hence if Ibsen had really wished to exhibit the operation of the law of heredity as understood by Darwin, he would have offered us at least one example, if only one, of the inheritance of good qualities. But not a single instance is to be met with in all his dramas. What his beings possess of good, comes one knows not whence. They have always inherited nothing but evil. The gentle Hedvig in *The Wild Duck* becomes blind like her father, Werle. But from whom does she get her dreamy wealth of imagination, her devoted loving heart? Her father is a cold egoist, and her

* Herbert Spencer, *The Man* versus *the State*, 1884, p. 78.

mother a clever, practical, prosaic housewife. Thus she can never have inherited her fine qualities from either of her parents. From them she receives only her eye-disease. With Ibsen heredity is only a visitation, a punishment for the sins of the fathers; science knows of no such exclusive heredity; theology alone knows it, and it is simply original sin.

Ibsen's second theological *motif* is confession; in nearly all his pieces such is the goal to which all the action tends; not, perchance, forced by circumstances upon a dissimulating offender, not the inevitable revelation of a hidden misdeed, but the voluntary outpouring of a pent-up soul, the voluptuous, self-tormenting disclosure of an ugly inner wound, the remorseful 'My guilt, my deepest guilt!' of the sinner breaking down under the weight of his burdened conscience, humbling himself to an avowal that he may find inward peace; in short, genuine confession as required by the Church. In *A Doll's House*, Helmer informs his wife (p. 44): 'Many a man can lift himself up again morally if he openly recognises his offence and undergoes its punishment. . . . Only just think how a man so conscious of guilt as that must go about everywhere lying, and a hypocrite, and an actor; how he must wear a mask towards his neighbour, and even his wife and children.' For him not the guilt, but the dissimulation, is the great evil, and its true expiation consists in 'public avowal'—*i.e.*, in confession. In the same piece Mrs. Linden, without any external necessity, and simply in obedience to an inner impulse, makes the following confession (p. 87): 'I, too, have suffered shipwreck. . . . I had no choice at the time'; while later on she develops the theory of confession once more (p. 90): 'Helmer must know everything; between those two there must be the completest possible understanding, and that can never come to pass while all these excuses and concealments are going on.'

In *The Pillars of Society* Miss Hessel exacts a confession in these terms (p. 70):

Here you are, the first man in the town, living in wealth and pride, in power and honour—you who have set the brand of crime upon an innocent man.

BERNICK. Do you think I do not feel deeply how I have wronged him: Do you think I am not prepared to make atonement?

LONA. How? By speaking out?

BERNICK. Can you ask such a thing?

LONA. What else can atone for such a wrong?

And Johan also says (p. 75):

In two months I shall be back again.

BERNICK. And then you will tell all?

JOHAN. Then the guilty one must take the guilt upon himself.

Bernick actually makes the confession demanded of him from pure contrition, for at the time he makes it all proofs of his crime are destroyed, and he has nothing more to fear from other persons. His confession is couched in most edifying terms (p. 108):

I must begin by rejecting the panegyric with which you . . . have overwhelmed me. I do not deserve it; for until to-day I have not been disinterested in my dealings . . . I have no right to this homage; for . . . my intention was to retain the whole myself. . . . My fellow-citizens must know me to the core . . . that from this evening we begin a new time. The old, with its tinsel, its hypocrisy, its hollowness, its lying propriety, and its pitiful cowardice, shall lie behind us like a museum open for instruction. . . . My fellow-citizens, I will come out of the lie; it had almost poisoned every fibre of my being. You shall know all. Fifteen years ago *I* was the guilty one, etc.

In *Rosmersholm* there is hardly any other subject treated of than the confession of all before all. In the very first visit of Kroll (p. 15) Rebecca urges Rosmer to confess:

REBECCA (*comes up close to Rosmer, and says rapidly and in a low voice, so that the Rector does not hear her*). Do it now!
ROSMER (*also in a low voice*). Not this evening.
REBECCA (*as before*). Yes, this very evening.

As he does not at once obey she will speak for him (p. 19):

REBECCA. You must let me tell you frankly.
ROSMER (*quickly*). No, no; be quiet. Not just now!

Rosmer soon does it himself (p. 28):

KROLL. We two are in practical agreement—at any rate, on the great essential questions.
ROSMER (*in a low voice*). No; not now.
KROLL (*tries to jump up*). What is this?
ROSMER (*holding him*). No; you must sit still. I entreat you, Kroll.
KROLL. What can this mean? I don't understand you. Speak plainly.
ROSMER. A new summer has blossomed in my soul. I see with eyes grown young again; and so now I stand——
KROLL. Where? where, Rosmer?
ROSMER. Where your children stand.
KROLL. You? you? Impossible! Where do you say you stand?
ROSMER. On the same side as Laurits and Hilda.
KROLL (*bows his head*). An apostate! Johannes Rosmer an apostate! . . . Is this becoming language for a priest?
ROSMER. I am no longer a priest.
KROLL. Well, but—the faith of your childhood——?
ROSMER. Is mine no longer. . . . I have given it up. I *had* to give it up. . . . Peace, and joy, and mutual forbearance must once more enter our souls. That is why I am stepping forward and openly avowing myself for what I am. . . .
REBECCA. There now; he's on his way to his great sacrifice.

(We may here note the purely theological designation given to Rosmer's act.)

ROSMER. I feel so relieved now it is over. You see, I am quite calm Rebecca. . . .

Like Rosmer, Rebecca also confesses to Rector Kroll (p. 86):

REBECCA. Yes, Herr Rector, Rosmer and I—we say *thou* to each other. The relation between us has led to that. . . . Come, let us sit down, dear—all three of us—and then I will tell the whole story.

ROSMER (*seats himself mechanically*). What has come over you, Rebecca? This unnatural calmness—what is it?

REBECCA. I have only to tell you something. . . . Now it must out. It was not you, Rosmer. You are innocent; it was *I* who lured Beata out into the paths of delusion . . . that led to the mill-race. Now you know it, both of you. . . .

ROSMER (*after a pause*). Have you confessed all now, Rebecca?

No, not yet all. But she hastens to complete to Rosmer the confession begun to Kroll (p. 98):

ROSMER. Have you more confessions to make?

REBECCA. The greatest of all is to come.

ROSMER. The greatest?

REBECCA. What you have never suspected. What gives light and shade to all the rest, etc.

In *The Lady from the Sea*, Ellida (p. 19) confesses to Arnholm the story of her insensate betrothal with the foreign sailor. Arnholm so little comprehends the need of this confession, made without rhyme or reason, that he asks with astonishment: 'What is your object, then, in telling me that you were bound?' 'Because I must have someone in whom to confide,' is Ellida's sole—and, moreover, sufficient—answer.

In *Hedda Gabler* the inevitable confessions take place before the commencement of the piece. 'Yes, Hedda,' Lövborg says (p. 123). 'And when I used to confess to you! Told you about myself—things that nobody else knew in those days. Sat there and admitted that I had been out on the loose for whole days and nights. . . . Ah, Hedda, what power was it in you that forced me to acknowledge things like that? . . . Had not you an idea that you could wash me clean if only I came to you in confession?' He confesses in order to receive absolution.

In *The Wild Duck* confession is equally prominent, but it is deliciously ridiculed. The scene in which Gina confesses to her husband her early liaison with Werle is one of the most exquisite things in contemporary drama (Act IV.).

HJALMAR. Is it true—can it be true that—that there was an—an understanding between you and Mr. Werle, while you were in service there?

GINA. That's not true. Not at that time. Mr. Werle did come after me, I own it; and his wife thought there was something in it . . . so that I left her service.

HJALMAR. But afterwards, then!

GINA. Well, then I went home. And mother—well, she wasn't the woman you took her for, Ekdal; she kept on worrying and worrying at me about one thing and another. For Mr. Werle was a widower by that time.

HJALMAR. Well, and then?

GINA. I suppose you must know it. He didn't give it up until he'd had his way.

HJALMAR (*striking his hands together*). And this is the mother of my child! How could you hide this from me?

GINA. It was wrong of me; I ought certainly to have told you long ago.

HJALMAR. You should have told me at the very first; then I should have known what you were.

GINA. But would you have married me all the same?

HJALMAR. How can you suppose so?

GINA. That's just why I didn't dare to tell you anything then. I'd come to care for you so much, you know; and I couldn't go and make myself utterly miserable. . . .

HJALMAR. Haven't you every day, every hour, repented of the spider's web of deceit you had spun around me? Answer me that! How could you help writhing with penitence and remorse?

GINA. My dear Ekdal, I've plenty to do looking after the house, and all the daily business——

Further on the idea of self-deliverance and purification through confession is pitilessly travestied.

GREGERS. Haven't you done it yet?

HJALMAR (*aloud*). It *is* done.

GREGERS. It *is?* . . . After so great a crisis—a crisis that's to be the starting-point of an entirely new life—of a communion founded on truth, and free from falsehood of any kind. . . . Surely you feel a new consecration after the great crisis.

HJALMAR. Yes, of course I do—that is, in a sort of way.

GREGERS. For I'm sure there's nothing in the world to compare with the joy of forgiving one who has erred, and raising her up to one's self in love, etc.

On his way to the guillotine, Avinain, the French assassin, condensed the experience of his life in the pithy saying, 'Never confess.' But this is advice which only those of strong will and healthy minds can follow. A lively idea vehemently demands to be transformed into movement. The movement exacting the least effort is that of the small muscles of the larynx, tongue, and lips, *i.e.*, the organs of speech. Anyone, therefore, having a specially lively idea experiences a strong desire to relax those cell-groups of his brain in which this idea is elaborated by allowing the transmission of their stimulus to the organs of speech. In a word, he desires to speak out. And if he is weak, if the inhibitive power of the will is not greater than the motor impulse proceeding from the ideational centre, he will burst out into speech, be the consequences what they may. That this psychological law has always been known is proved by all literature, from the fable of King Midas to Dostojewski's *Raskolnikow;* and the Catholic Church furnished one more proof of her profound knowledge of human nature which she transformed the primitive Christian custom of confession before the assembled congregation, which was to be a self-humiliation and expiation, into auricular confession, which serves the purpose of a safe and blissful alleviation and relaxation, and constitutes for ordinary men a primary psychic need of the first order. It was this sort of confession which Ibsen, probably unconsciously, had in view. ('Because I must have someone in whom I can confide,' as Ellida says.) Himself a degenerate, Ibsen can picture to himself only the intellectual life of degenerates, in whom the mechanism of inhibition is always disordered, and who, therefore, cannot escape from the impulse to confess, when anything of an absorbing or exciting character exists in their consciousness.

The third and most important theological obsession of Ibsen is the saving act of Christ, the redemption of the guilty by a voluntary acceptance of their guilt. This devolution of sin upon a lamb of sacrifice occupies the same position in Ibsen's drama as in Richard Wagner's. The *motif* of the sacrificial lamb and of redemption is constantly present in his mind, certainly not always clear and comprehensible, but, conformably with the confusion of his thought, diversely distorted, obscured, and, so to speak, in *contrapuntal* inversion. Now Ibsen's personages voluntarily and joyfully bear the cross, in keeping with the Christ-idea; now it is put upon their shoulders by force or artifice, which is, as theologians would say, a diabolical mockery of this idea; now the sacrifice for another is sincere, now mere hypocrisy; the effects Ibsen draws from the incessantly recurring *motif* are, agreeably with its form, now moral and affecting, now comically base and repulsive.

In *The Pillars of Society* there is a talk of some 'scandal' which occurred years before the commencement of the piece. The husband of the actress Dorf, on returning home one evening, found her with a stranger, who, on his entrance, sprang out of the window. The affair caused great excitement and indignation in the Norwegian Gotham. Immediately afterwards Johan Tönnesen fled to America. Everyone looked upon him as the 'culprit.' In reality, however, it was his brother-in-law, Bernick. Johan had voluntarily incurred the blame of Bernick's fault. On his return from America the sinner and the sacrificial lamb discuss the circumstance (p. 45):

BERNICK. Johan, now we are alone, you must give me leave to thank you.

JOHAN. Oh, nonsense!

BERNICK. My house and home, my domestic happiness, my whole position as a citizen in society—all these I owe to you.

JOHAN. Well, I am glad of it. . . .

BERNICK. Thanks, thanks all the same. Not one in ten thousand would have done what you then did for me.

JOHAN. Oh, nonsense! . . . One of us had to take the blame upon him.

BERNICK. But to whom did it lie nearer than to the guilty one?

JOHAN. Stop! *Then* it lay nearer to the innocent one. I was alone, free, an orphan. . . . You, on the other hand, had your old mother in life; and, besides, you had just become secretly engaged to Betty, and she was very fond of you. What would have become of her if she had come to know——?

BERNICK. True, true, true; but . . . but yet, that you should turn appearances against yourself, and go away——

JOHAN. Have no scruples, my dear Karsten . . . you had to be saved, and you were my friend.

Here the idea of the sacrificial lamb is normal and rational. But it is soon afterwards introduced into the same piece in a distorted shape. Bernick sends the rotten-keeled *Indian Girl* to sea, to her certain destruction, in spite of his foreman Aune's opposition. While, however, planning this wholesale murder, he also schemes for laying the burden of his crime on the innocent Aune (p. 65):

KRAP. . . . There is rascality at work, Consul.

BERNICK. I cannot believe it, Krap. I cannot, and will not believe such a thing of Aune.

KRAP. I am sorry for it, but it is the plain truth. . . . All bogus! The *Indian Girl* will never get to New York. . . .

BERNICK. But this is horrible! What do you think can be his motive?

KRAP. He probably wants to bring the machines into discredit. . . .

BERNICK. And for that he would sacrifice all these lives? . . . But such a piece of villainy as this! Listen, Krap; this affair must be examined into again. Not a word of it to anyone. . . . During the dinner-hour you must go down there again; I must have perfect certainty. . . . We cannot make ourselves accomplices in a crime. I must keep my conscience unspotted, etc.

In *Ghosts* the idea of the lamb of sacrifice is equally travestied. The asylum founded by Mrs. Alving has been burnt. The joiner, Engstrand, that theatrical villain, succeeds in persuading the idiotic pastor, Manders, that he—Manders—was the cause of the fire. And as the pastor is made desperate by the possible legal consequences, Engstrand goes to him and says (p. 184):

Jacob Engstrand isn't the man to desert a noble benefactor in the hour of need, as the saying is [!].

MANDERS. Yes; but, my good fellow, how——?

ENGSTRAND. Jacob Engstrand may be likened to a guardian angel—he may, your reverence.

MANDERS. No, no; I can't accept that.

ENGSTRAND. Oh, you will though, all the same. I know a man that's taken others' sins upon himself before now, I do.

MANDERS. Jacob (*wrings his hand*). You are a rare character.

In *A Doll's House* the idea develops itself with great beauty. Nora confidently expects that her husband, on hearing of her forgery, will assume the blame, and she is resolved not to accept his sacrifice (p. 76):

NORA. I only wanted to tell you that, Christina; you shall be my witness. . . . In case there were to be anybody who wanted to take the . . . the whole blame, I mean . . . then you will be able to bear witness that it is not true, Christina. I know very well what I am saying; I am in full possession of my senses, and I say to you, Nobody else knew anything about it; I alone have done everything. . . . But a miracle will come to pass even yet . . . but it is so terrible, Christina! It must not happen for anything in the world!

In the deepest excitement she looks for the expected miracle, the renewal of Christ's act of salvation in the narrow circumstances of a small village—'I am the Lamb of God, who taketh away the sins of the world.' And, since the miracle does not come to pass, there takes place the immense transformation in her nature which forms the real subject of the piece. Nora explains this to her husband with the greatest clearness (p. 116):

. . . The thought never once occurred to me that you could allow yourself to submit to the conditions of such a man. I was so firmly convinced that you would say to him, 'Pray make the affair known to all the world'; and when that had been done . . . then you would, as I firmly believed, stand before the world, take everything upon yourself, and say, 'I am the guilty person.' . . . That was the miracle that I hoped and feared. And it was to hinder that that I wanted to put an end to my life.

In *The Wild Duck* the idea of the sacrificial lamb recurs no less than three times, and is the moving force of the whole piece. The infringement of the forest laws, of which the elder Ekdal was convicted, was not committed by him, but by Werle:

WERLE . . . I was quite in the dark as to what Lieutenant Ekdal was doing.

GREGERS. Lieutenant Ekdal seems to have been in the dark as to what he was doing.

WERLE. That may be. But the fact remains that he was found guilty, and I acquitted.

GREGERS. Yes, of course I know that nothing was proved against you.

WERLE. Acquittal is acquittal. Why do you rake up old troubles? . . . I've done all I could without positively exposing myself, and giving rise to all sorts of suspicion and gossip. . . . I've given Ekdal copying to do from the office, and I pay him far, far more for it than his work is worth.

Werle thus shuffles his fault on Ekdal, and the latter breaks down under the weight of the cross. Afterwards, when Hjalmar learns that little Hedwig is not his child, and disowns her, the idiot Gregers Werle goes to the despairing maiden, and says:

But suppose you were to sacrifice the wild duck, of your own free will, for his sake?

HEDWIG (*rising*). The wild duck!

GREGERS. Suppose you were to sacrifice, for his sake, the dearest treasure you have in the world?

HEDWIG. Do you think that would do any good?

GREGERS. Try it, Hedwig.

HEDWIG (*softly, with flashing eyes*). Yes, I will try it.

Here, then, Hedwig is not to offer herself in sacrifice, but a pet animal, thus abasing the idea from Christianity to paganism. Finally, it crops up a third time. At the last moment Hedwig cannot make up her mind to kill the duck, and prefers turning the pistol against her own breast, thus purchasing with her own life that of the bird. This dismal dénouement is worrying and foolish, because useless; the poetical effect would have been fully attained if Hedwig, instead of dying, had only slightly wounded herself; for in this way she would have furnished equally strong proof that she was seriously determined to bear witness to her love for her father by the sacrifice of her young life, and to restore peace between him and her mother. But æsthetic criticism is not my function; I willingly yield that to phrase-makers. All that I have to indicate is the triple recurrence in *The Wild Duck* of the idea of the sacrificial lamb.

At its third appearance this idea suffers a significant transformation. Hedwig sacrifices herself, not in expiation of an offence—for she is ignorant of her mother's guilt—but to accomplish a work of love. Here the mystico-theological element of redemption recedes into the background so far as to be almost imperceptible, and there remains hardly more than the purely human element of the joy felt in self-sacrifice for others—an impulse not rare among good women, and which is a manifestation of the unsatisfied yearning for maternity (often unknown to themselves), and at the same time one of the noblest and holiest forms of altruism. Ibsen shows this impulse in many of his female characters, the source of which in the religious mysticism of the poet would not be at once noticed, if from the numerous other conjugations of the root-idea of the sacrificial lamb we had not already acquired the sure habit of recognising it even in its obscurations. Hedwig constitutes a transition from the theological to the purely human form of voluntary self-sacrifice. The over-strung child carries renunciation to the orthodox extreme of yielding up her life; Ibsen's other women, to whose character Hedwig supplies the key, go only to the point of lovingly active self-denial. They do not die for others, but they live for others. In *A Doll's House* Mrs. Linden has this hunger for self-sacrifice.

I must work in order to endure life [she says to Krogstad—p. 87]. I have worked from my youth up, and work has been my one best friend. But now I am quite alone in the world—so terribly empty and forsaken. There is no happiness in working for one's self. Nils, give me somebody and something to work for. . . .

KROGSTAD. What! you really could? Tell me, do you know my past?

MRS. LINDEN. Yes.

KROGSTAD. And do you know my reputation?

MRS. LINDEN. Did you not hint it just now, when you said that with me you could have been another man?

KROGSTAD. I am perfectly certain of it.

MRS. LINDEN. Could it not yet be so?

KROGSTAD. Christina, do you say this after full deliberation? . . .

MRS. LINDEN. I need somebody to mother, and your children need a mother.

Here the idea is not so disguised as to be unrecognisable. Krogstad is a culprit and an outlaw. If Mrs. Linden offers to live for him, it is certainly chiefly from the instinct of maternity. But in this natural feeling there is also a tinge of the mystic idea of the sinner's redemption through disinterested love. In *The Lady from the Sea*, Ellida wishes to return to her birthplace on the sea, Skjoldvik, because she believes there is nothing for her to do in Wangel's house. At the announcement of her resolution her step-daughter, Hilda, evinces a profound despair. Then for the first time Ellida learns that Hilda loves her; there is then born in her the thought that she has someone to live for, and she says dreamily: 'Oh, if there should be something for me to do here!' In *Rosmersholm* Rebecca says to Kroll (p. 8):

So long as Mr. Rosmer thinks I am of any use or comfort to him, why, so long, I suppose, I shall stay here.

KROLL (*looks at her with emotion*). Do you know, it's really fine for a woman to sacrifice her whole youth to others, as you have done.

REBECCA. Oh, what else should I have had to live for?

In *The Pillars of Society* there are two of these touching self-sacrificing souls — Miss Martha Bernick and Miss Hessel. Miss Bernick has reared the illegitimate child Dina, and has consecrated her own life to her (p. 52):

MARTHA. I have been a mother to that much-wronged child — have brought her up as well as I could.

JOHAN. And sacrificed your whole life in so doing.

MARTHA. It has not been thrown away.

She loves Johan, but as she sees that he is attracted by Dina she unites the two. She explains herself in regard to the incident in an exceedingly affecting scene with Johan's half-sister (p. 95):

LONA. Now we are alone, Martha. You have lost her, and I him.

MARTHA. You him?

LONA. Oh, I had half lost him already over there. The boy longed to stand on his own feet, so I made him think *I* was longing for home.

MARTHA. That was it? Now I understand why you came. But he will want you back again, Lona.

LONA. An old stepsister—what can he want with her now? Men snap many bonds to arrive at happiness.

MARTHA. It is so, sometimes.

LONA. But now we two must hold together, Martha.

MARTHA. Can I be anything to you?

LONA. Who more? We two foster-mothers—have we not both lost our children? Now we are alone.

MARTHA. Yes, alone. And therefore I will tell you—I have loved him more than all the world.

LONA. Martha! (*seizes her arm*). Is this the truth?

MARTHA. My whole life lies in the words. I have loved him, and waited for him. From summer to summer I have looked for his coming. And then he came, but he did not see me.

LONA. Loved him! and it was you that gave his happiness into his hands

MARTHA. Should I not have given him his happiness, since I loved him?

Yes, I have loved him. My whole life has been for him . . . He did not see me.

LONA. It was Dina that overshadowed you, Martha.

MARTHA. It is well that she did! When he went away we were of the same age. When I saw him again—oh, that horrible moment!—it seemed to me that I was ten years older than he. He had lived in the bright, quivering sunshine, and drunk in youth and health at every breath; and here sat I, the while, spinning and spinning——

LONA. The thread of his happiness, Martha.

MARTHA. Yes, it was gold I spun. No bitterness! Is it not true, Lona, we have been two good sisters to him?

In *Hedda Gabler* it is Miss Tesman, aunt of the imbecile Tesman, who plays the pathetic part of the sacrificial mother. She has brought him up, and when he marries gives him the largest part of her modest income. 'Oh, aunt,' bleats the poor idiot (p. 18), 'you will never be tired of sacrificing yourself for me!' 'Do you think,' replies the good creature, 'I have any other joy in this world than to smooth the way for you, my dear boy—you who have never had a father or a mother to look after you?' And when subsequently the paralytic sister of Miss Tesman is dead, Hedda and she hold this conversation (p. 196):

HEDDA. It will be lonesome for you now, Miss Tesman.

MISS TESMAN. The first few days, yes. But that won't last very long. Dear Rina's little room will not always be empty, that I know.

HEDDA. Indeed! Who is going to move into it, eh?

MISS TESMAN. Oh, there is always some poor invalid or other who needs to be looked after and tended, unfortunately.

HEDDA. Will you really take such a burden upon you again?

MISS TESMAN. Burden! God forgive you, child! that has never been a burden to me.

HEDDA. But now, if a stranger should come, then surely——

MISS TESMAN. Oh, one soon becomes friends with sick people. And I must positively have someone to live for, too.

The three Christo-dogmatic obsessions of original sin, confession, and self-sacrifice, filling Ibsen's dramas, as we have seen, from the first line to the last, are not the only tokens of his mysticism. This betrays itself by a whole series of other peculiarities, which shall be briefly indicated.

At the head of these stands the astoundingly chaotic nature of his thought. One cannot believe one's eyes while reading how his fulsome flatterers have had the audacity to extol him for the 'clearness' and 'precision' of his thought. Do these individuals, then, imagine that no one capable of forming a judgment will ever read a line of Ibsen? A clearly-defined thought is an extraordinary rarity in this Norwegian dramatist. Everything floats and undulates, nebulous and amorphous, such as we are accustomed to see in weak-brained degenerates. And if he once succeeds, with toil and stress, in grasping anything and expressing it in a moderately intelligible manner, he unfailingly hastens, a few pages later, or in a subsequent piece, to say the exact opposite. A talk is made of Ibsen's 'ideas on morality' and of his 'philosophy.' He has not formulated a single proposition on morality, a single conception of the world and life, that he has not himself either refuted or fittingly ridiculed.

He seems to preach free love, and his eulogy of a licentiousness unchecked by any self-control, regardless of contracts, laws, and morality, has made of him a 'modern spirit' in the eyes of Georg Brandes and similar protectors of those 'youths who wish to amuse themselves a little.' Mrs. Alving (*Ghosts*, p. 158), calls a 'crime' the act of Pastor Manders in repulsing her, after she has quitted her husband and thrown herself on the pastor's neck. This highly-strung dame pushes Regina into the arms of Oswald, her son, when in shameless speech he informs her that it would give him pleasure to possess the girl. And this very same Mrs. Alving speaks in terms of the deepest indignation of her dead husband as 'profligate' (p. 146), and again designates him in the presence of her son as a 'broken-down man' (in the original it is 'et forfaldent Menneske,' an epithet usually bestowed on fallen women), and why? Because he had had wanton relations with women! Well, but is it in Ibsen's opinion permissible, or not permissible, to gratify carnal lust as often as it is awakened? If it is permissible, how does Mrs. Alving come to speak with scorn of her husband? If it is not permissible, how dared she offer herself to Pastor Manders, and be the procuress between Regina and her own half-brother? Or does the moral law hold good for man only, and not for woman? An English proverb says, 'What's sauce for the goose is sauce for the gander.' Ibsen evidently does not share the opinion of popular lore. A woman who runs away from her legal husband and pursues a lover (Mrs. Elvsted and Ejlert Lövborg, in *Hedda Gabler*), or who offers to form an illicit connection with a man, although nothing prevents their marrying without further ado like other rational ratepayers (Mrs. Linden and Krogstad in *A Doll's House*)—such women have Ibsen's entire approbation and sympathy. But if a man seduces a maiden and liberally provides for her subsequent maintenance (Werle and Gina in *The Wild Duck*), or, again, if he has illicit relations with a married woman (Consul Bernick and the actress Dorf in *The Pillars of Society*), then it is so heinous a crime that the culprit remains branded his whole life, and is nailed by the poet to the pillory with the cruelty of a mediæval executioner.

The same contradiction finds its expression in another and more general form. At one time Ibsen contends with ferocious impetuosity that everyone is 'a law unto himself' alone, *i.e.*, that

24

he should obey every one of his caprices, nay, even of his diseased impulsions; that, as his commentators idiotically put it, he should (*sich auslebe*) 'live out his life.' In *The Pillars of Society* Miss Bernick says to Dina (p. 94):

> Promise me to make him [her betrothed] happy.
>
> DINA. I will not promise anything. I hate this promising; things must come as they can [*i.e.*, as the circumstances of the moment may suggest to the wayward brain].
>
> MARTHA. Yes, yes; so they must. You need only remain as you are, true and faithful to yourself.
>
> DINA. That I will, Aunt Martha.

In *Rosmersholm*, Rosmer says admiringly of the scoundrel Brendel (p. 28): 'At least he has had the courage to live his life his own way. I don't think that's such a small matter after all.' In the same piece Rebecca complains (p. 97): 'Rosmersholm has broken me. . . . Broken me utterly and hopelessly. I had a fresh, undaunted will when I came here. Now I have bent my neck under a strange law.' And further on (p. 102): 'It is the Rosmer view of life . . . that has infected my will. . . . and made it sick, enslaved it to laws that had no power over me before.' Ejlert Lövborg laments in like fashion in *Hedda Gabler*. 'But it is *this*—that I don't want to live that kind of life either. Not now, over again. It is the courage of life and the defiance of life that she' (Thea Elvested, with her sweet, loving constraint) 'has snapped in me.' Quite in opposition to these views, Ibsen, in his *Ghosts*, makes Regina proclaim her 'right to live out her life' in these words (p. 189): 'Oh! I really can't stop out here in the country and wear myself out nursing sick people . . . a poor girl must make the best of her young days. . . . I, too, want to enjoy my life, Mrs. Alving.' Mrs. Alving replies: 'Alas! yes.' This 'alas' is bewildering. Alas? Why 'alas'? Does she not obey her 'law' if she satisfies her 'joy in living,' and, as she forthwith explains, enters the house of ill-fame for sailors set up by the joiner Engstrand? How can Mrs. Alving utter this 'alas,' when she also was 'obeying her law' in offering herself as the mistress of Pastor Manders, and since she wished to aid her son in 'obeying his law,' when he had set his eyes on Regina? It is because Ibsen, in his lucid moments, feels that there may be something of danger in 'obeying one's law,' and this 'alas' of Mrs. Alving escapes him as a confession. In *The Wild Duck* he ridicules his own dogma in the most liberal style. In that piece there is one Molvig, a candidate for a University degree, who also 'obeys his law.' This law prescribes that he shall learn nothing, evade his examinations, and pass his nights in taverns. The scoffer, Relling, asserts (p. 317) that it 'comes over him like a sort of possession; and then I have to go out on the loose with him. Molvig is a demoniac, you see, . . . and demoniac natures are not made to walk straight through the world; they must meander now and then. And in order that there shall be no doubt as to what Relling means by this, he subsequently explains (p. 361): '"What the devil do you mean by demoniac?" "It's only a piece of hocus-pocus I've invented to keep up a spark of life in him. But for that the poor harmless creature would have succumbed to self-contempt and despair many a long year ago."'

That is true. Molvig is a pitiable weakling, unable to conquer his indolence and passion for drink; abandoned to his own devices, he would recognise himself for the miserable creature he is, and despise himself as profoundly as he deserves; but Relling arrives on the scene, and gives his lack of character the title 'demoniac,' and now 'the child has a fine name,' which Molvig can make a parade of to himself and others. Ibsen does exactly the same thing as his Relling. The weakness of will, incapable of resisting base and pitiable instincts, he praises as the 'will to live out one's life,' as the 'freedom of a spirit who obeys his own law only,' and recommends it as the sole rule of life. But, unlike Relling, he is for the most part ignorant of the fact that he is practising a deception (which I by no means regard in Relling's light as pious and charitable), and believes in his own humbug. That is, for the most part; not always. Here and there, as in *The Wild Duck*, he recognises his error and scourges it severely; and his inmost feeling is so little influenced by his self-deceptive phrase, fit for a weak-willed degenerate, that he involuntarily and unconsciously betrays, in all his productions, his deep abhorrence of men who 'obey their own law in order to live out their life.' He punishes Chamberlain Alving in his son, and makes him cursed by his widow because he has 'lived out his life.' He imputes it as a crime to Consul Bernick and the merchant Werle that they have 'lived out their life,' the former in sacrificing his brother-in-law Johan to protect himself, and for his intrigue with Mrs. Dorf, the actress; and the latter for allowing Ekdal to bear the blame of his fault, and for seducing Gina. He surrounds with an aureole the glorified heads of Rosmer and Rebecca, because they did not 'live out their life,' but, on the contrary, 'died their death,' if I may put it so; because they obeyed, not 'their own law,' but that of others, the universal moral law that annihilated them. Whenever one of his characters acts in accordance with Ibsen's doctrine, and does what is agreeable to himself regardless of morals and law, he experiences such contrition and self-torment that he is unable to find calm and joy until he has disburdened his conscience by confession and expiation.

'This living out one's life' makes its appearance in Ibsen in the form also of a rigid individualism. The 'self' is the only real thing; the 'I' must be cherished and developed, as, indeed, Barrès preaches independently of Ibsen. The first duty of every human being is to be just to his 'I,' to satisfy its demands, to sacrifice to it every consideration for others. When Nora wishes to abandon her husband, he cries (p. 112):

Only think what people will say about it!

NORA. I cannot take that into consideration. I only know that to go is necessary for me.

HELMER. Oh, it drives one wild! Is this the way you can evade your holiest duties?

NORA. What do you consider my holiest duties?

HELMER . . . . Are they not your duties to your husband and your children?

NORA. I have other duties equally sacred.

HELMER. . . . What duties do you mean?

NORA. Duties towards myself.

HELMER. Before all else you are a wife and a mother.

NORA. I no longer think so. I think that before all else I am a human being just as you are, or, at least, I will try to become one.

In *Ghosts* Oswald says to his mother with triumphant brutality (p. 192): 'I can't be much taken up with other people. I have enough to do thinking about myself.' How in the same piece Regina emphasizes her 'I' and its rights, we have already seen. In *An Enemy of the People*, Stockmann proclaims the right of the 'I' in face of the majority, and even the race, in these words (p. 283): 'It is a hideous lie: the doctrine that the multitude, the vulgar herd, the masses, are the pith of the people—that, indeed, they are the people—that the common man, that this ignorant, undeveloped member of society, has the same right to condemn or to sanction, to govern and to rule, as the few people of intellectual power.' And (p. 312): 'I only want to drive into the heads of these curs that the Liberals are the worst foes of free men . . . that the considerations of expediency turn morality and righteousness upside down until life is simply hideous. . . . Now I am one of the strongest men upon earth. . . . You see the fact is that the strongest man upon earth is he who stands most alone.' But this very Stockmann, who will hear nothing of 'the multitude, the vulgar herd, the masses,' as he reiterates with insufferable tautology, who feels his 'I' powerful only in a majestic solitude, calls his fellow-citizens 'old women who think only of their families,* and not of the general good.' And in the very same piece (*A Doll's House*), in which Ibsen evidently bestows loud applause on Nora for declaring that 'her only duties were to herself,' and that she 'could have no consideration for anyone else,' he stigmatizes her husband as a pitiable, low-spirited weakling, because on his

* In the German text, 'only of themselves and their families.'—TRANSLATOR.

wife's confession of forgery he first of all thinks of his own reputation only, and hence of his 'duty to himself,' his only consideration being for himself, and not for his wife. Here there recurs the same phenomenon as in Ibsen's notions concerning sexual morality. Unchastity in a man is a crime, but in a woman is permissible. In the same way the rude emphasizing of the 'I' is a merit only in the woman. The man has no right to be an egoist. How, for example, Ibsen rails at egoism through Bernick (in *The Pillars of Society*), whom he makes say naïvely, in reference to his sister Martha, that she 'is quite insignificant' (p. 49), and that he does not wish to have her otherwise!

You know, in a large house like ours, it is always well to have some steady-going person like her, whom one can put to anything that may turn up.

JOHAN. Yes, but she herself?

BERNICK. She herself? Why, of course she has enough to interest herself in—Betty and Olaf, and me, you know. People should not think of themselves first, and women least of all.

And how severely Ibsen condemns the egoism of Mrs. Elvsted's husband (*Hedda Gabler*), when he puts these bitter words into her mouth (p. 52): 'He is not really fond of anybody but himself. Perhaps of the children a little!'

But the most remarkable thing about this philosopher of individualism is that he not only expressly condemns egoism in the man as a low vice, but unconsciously also admires disinterestedness in the woman as an angelic perfection. In *A Doll's House* (p. 113) he brags that 'my most sacred duties are towards myself.' And yet the only touching and charming characters in his pieces with whom this inflexible individualist is successful are the saintly women who live and die for others only—these Hedwigs, Miss Bernicks, Miss Hessels, Aunt Tesmans, etc., who never think of their 'I,' but make the sacrifice of all their impulses and wishes to the welfare of others their sole task on earth. This contradiction, violent to the point of absurdity, is very well explained by the nature of Ibsen's mind. His mystico-religious obsession of voluntary self-sacrifice for others is necessarily stronger than his pseudo-philosophic lucubration on individualism.

Among the 'moral ideas' of Ibsen are counted his professed thirst for truth. At least enough has been said and written on this subject. 'Only just think,' Helmer says to Nora (*A Doll's House*, pp. 44, 45), 'how a man so conscious of guilt as that must go about everywhere lying, and a hypocrite, and an actor; how he must wear a mask towards his neighbour, and even his wife and children, his own children. That's the worst, Nora. . . . Because such a misty atmosphere of lying brings contagion into the whole family.' 'Is there no voice in your mother's heart that forbids you to destroy your son's ideals?' asks Pastor Manders in *Ghosts* (p. 155), when Mrs. Alving has revealed to her son her defunct husband's 'immorality.' To which Mrs. Alving magniloquently replies, 'But what about the truth?' In *The Pillars of Society*, Lona Hessel thus preaches to Consul Bernick (p. 57):

Is it for the sake of the community, then, that for these fifteen years you have stood upon a lie?

BERNICK. A lie? . . . You call that——

LONA. I call it the lie—the threefold lie. First the lie towards me; then the lie towards Betty; then the lie towards Johan. . . . Is there not something within you that asks you to get clear of the lie?

BERNICK. You would have me voluntarily sacrifice my domestic happiness, and my position in society?

LONA. What right have you to stand where you are standing?

And subsequently (p. 70):

LONA. A lie, then, has made you the man you now are?

BERNICK. Whom did it hurt, then? . . .

LONA. You ask whom it hurt? Look into yourself, and see if it has not hurt you.

Bernick then examines himself, and shortly before his confession there takes place a highly edifying dialogue between him and the severe guardian of his conscience (p. 98):

BERNICK. Yes, yes, yes; it all comes of the lie. . . .

LONA. Then, why do you not break with all this lying? . . . What satisfaction does this show and deception give you?

BERNICK . . . . It is my son I am working for. . . . There will come a time when truth shall spread through the life of our society, and upon it he shall found a happier life than his father's.

LONA. With a lie for its groundwork? Reflect what it is you are giving your son for an inheritance.

In *An Enemy of the People*, words of truth are ever coming from the mouths of the Stockmann family: 'There's so much falseness both at home and at school,' declaims their daughter, Petra. 'At home you mustn't speak, and at school you have to stand there and lie to the children. . . . We have to teach many and many a thing we don't believe ourselves. . . . If only I could afford it I'd start a school myself, and things should be very different there.' The courageous maiden quarrels with an editor who wished to marry her about his want of veracity (p. 255): 'What I am angry with you for is that you have not acted honestly towards my father. You told him it was only the truth and the good of the community you cared about. . . . You are not the man you pretend to be. And I shall never forgive you—never!' 'The whole of our developing social life,' cries the father Stockmann in his turn (p. 242), 'is rooted in a lie.' And later on (p. 287): 'Yes, I love my native town so well I would rather ruin it than see it flourishing upon a lie. . . . All men who live upon lies must be exterminated like vermin. You'll poison the whole country in time; you'll bring it to such a pass that the whole country will deserve to perish.' Now, all this would certainly be very fine, if we did not know that this fervent worship of truth is only one of the forms under which there appears in Ibsen's consciousness the mystico-religious obsession of the sacrament of confession, and also, if he were not careful, conformably with his habit, to destroy any too hasty belief in the sincerity of his phraseology by himself ridiculing it. In Gregers Werle he has created the best caricature of his men of truth. Gregers speaks in exactly the same terms as Lona Hessel, Petra Stockmann, and her father, but in his mouth the words are intended to excite laughter: 'And look at this confiding nature, this great child,' he says of his friend Hjalmar (p. 41). 'See him enveloped in a net of perfidy, living under the same roof as a woman of that kind, not suspecting that his home, as he calls it, rests upon a lie. . . . At length I see an object in life.' This object consists in operating on Hjalmar's moral cataract. And he does it, too. 'You are sunk in a poisoned quagmire, Hjalmar,' Gregers says to him (p. 101). 'You have an insidious disease within you, and you've sunk down to die in the dark. . . . Don't be afraid; I will try to help you up again. I, too, have a mission in life now.' And shortly afterwards he says to the father: 'But Hjalmar I can rescue from all the falsehood and deception that are bringing him to ruin.' The scoffer Relling treats no worse than he deserves the idiot who, in fulfilling his 'mission in life' disturbs the peace between Hjalmar and his wife, destroys their comfortable home, and drives Hedwig to her death.

Yours is a complicated case . . . that troublesome integrity-fever [he says to him—p. 360] . . .

I'm fostering the life-illusion [literally 'the life-lie'] in him.

GREGERS. Life-illusion? Is that what you said?

RELLING. Yes, I said illusion. For illusion, you know, is the stimulating principle. . . . Rob the average man of his life-illusion, and you rob him of his happiness at the same time.

Now, what is Ibsen's real opinion? Is a man to strive for truth, or to swelter in deceit? Is Ibsen with Stockmann or with Relling? Ibsen owes us an answer to these questions, or, rather, he replies to them affirmatively and negatively with equal ardour and equal poetic power.

Another 'moral idea' of Ibsen, about which his choristers chatter most loudly, is that of 'true marriage.' It is certainly not easy to discover what his mystic brain conceives by these mysterious words, but it is nevertheless possible to guess it from the hundred obscure notions in his plays. He does not seem to approve of the idea that the woman should regard marriage as merely a means of maintenance. In nearly all his pieces he comes to this conclusion with the monotony peculiar to him. In *Ghosts*, Mrs. Alving ascribes her whole life's unhappiness to the fact that she married the chamberlain for his money—that she sold herself. 'The sums which I have spent upon the orphanage year by year make up the amount—I have reckoned it up precisely—the amount which made Lieutenant Alving a good match in his day. . . . It was the purchase-money. I do not choose that money should pass into Oswald's hands' (p. 149). In *The Lady from the Sea*, Ellida sings the same song (p. 139): 'It could bring nothing but unhappiness, after the way in which we came together. . . . Yes, we are (doing so), or, at least, we suppress the truth. For the truth . . . is, that you came out there and bought me. . . . I was not a bit better than you. I accepted the bargain—sold myself to you. I was so helpless and bewildered, and so absolutely alone. Oh, it was so natural I should accept the bargain when you came and proposed to provide for me all my life.' In almost the same words Hedda says (*Hedda Gabler*, p. 86): 'And then he would go and make such a tremendous fuss about being allowed to provide for me. I did not know why I should not accept it.' She did not know why; but her inner feverishness and restlessness, her final suicide, are the consequence of her having allowed herself to be 'provided for.' The regard paid to the 'being provided for' became also the lifelong misery of another woman in the same piece—Mrs. Elvsted. She went originally as 'governess in the house of her future husband.' She subsequently undertook the management of the household. Then she allowed herself to be married, although 'everything around him is distasteful to me,' and 'we do not possess a thought in common.' Ibsen condemns the man who marries for money not less than the woman who allows herself to be 'provided for.' The cause of Bernick's moral downfall (*The Pillars of Society*, p. 56), is chiefly that he did not marry Lona Hessel, whom he loved, but another. 'It was for no new fancy that I broke with you; it was entirely for the sake of the money.'

Hence one should not marry for gain. That is a principle to which every rational and moral man will subscribe. But why should one marry? The most reasonable answer can only be, 'From inclination.' But Ibsen will have none of this either. The marriage of Nora and Helmer is purely a love-match. It leads to a sudden rupture. Wangel (*The Lady from the Sea*) has married Ellida from inclination. She expressly affirms it (p. 108): 'You had only seen me and spoken to me a few times. Then you wanted me, and so . . .' And then she feels herself a stranger to him, and wishes to leave him. So Mrs. Alving, Ellida, Wangel, Hedda Gabler, Mrs. Elvsted, marry from self-interest, and atone for it by the happiness of their life. Nora marries for love, and becomes profoundly unhappy. Consul Bernick marries a girl because she is rich, and pays for this fault with his moral downfall. Dr. Wangel marries a girl because she pleases him, and as a reward she wishes to quit him and her home. What conclusion is to be drawn from all this? That marriage from prudence is bad, and marriage from love no better? That marriage in general is worth nothing, and should be abolished? That would be at least an inference and a solution. It is not there that Ibsen arrives. Inclination does not suffice, even if, as in the case of Nora, it is reciprocal. Something else is still necessary—the man must become the educator of his wife. He must help her intellectually. He must let her participate in all his concerns, make of her a companion possessing equal rights, and have unlimited confidence in her. Otherwise she always remains a stranger in her house. Otherwise the marriage is no 'true marriage.' 'I have no right to claim my husband wholly and solely for myself,' Ellida confesses (*The Lady from the Sea*, p. 57). 'Why, I, too, live in something from which others are shut out.' In the same piece Wangel blames himself in this way (p. 130): 'I ought to have been at once a father to her and a guide; I ought to have done my best to develop and enlighten her mind. Unfortunately, nothing ever came of that. . . . I preferred her just as she was.' In *The Pillars of Society* Mrs. Bernick bemoans (p. 141): 'For many years I believed that I had at one time possessed you and lost you again. Now I know that I have never possessed you.' And Lona Hessel draws the moral from this story (p. 97):

And do you never think what she might have been to you—she, whom you chose in my stead?

BERNICK. I know, at any rate, that she has been to me nothing of what I required.

LONA. Because you have never shared your life-work with her; because you have never placed her in a free and true relation to you.

In *Rosmersholm* Rector Kroll has treated his wife in the same way; he has intellectually suppressed her, and is painfully surprised when she finally revolts against the domestic tyrant who has extinguished her mental light (p. 14). 'My wife, who all her life long has shared my opinions and concurred in my views both in great things and small, is actually inclined to side with the children on many points. And she blames me for what has happened. She says I tyrannize over the children. As if it weren't necessary to. Well, you see how my house is divided against itself. But, of course, I say as little about it as possible. It's best to keep such things quiet.'

Upon this point also there may be complete agreement. Most assuredly should marriage be not merely a union of bodies, but also a community of minds; most assuredly should the man help and educate the wife intellectually, although it is to be remarked that this *rôle* of teacher and guardian assigned with justice by Ibsen to the man, decisively excludes the full intellectual equality of the two married parties equally claimed by him. But how can one reconcile with these notions about the true relation between the man and his wife Nora's words to her husband (*A Doll's House*, p. 111): 'I must first try to educate myself. In that you are not the man to help me. I must set to work alone. And that is why I am going away from you now. . . . I must be thrown entirely upon myself'? We rub our eyes and ask ourselves if we have read aright. What, then, is the duty of the husband in 'true marriage'? Shall he help his wife intellectually? Wangel, Mrs. Bernick, Lona, Mrs. Kroll, say so. But Nora furiously denies it, and repels all assistance. *Farà da se!* She will educate and form herself. As though this contradiction were not already sufficiently bewildering, Ibsen still further mocks those pitiable souls, who would fain obtain rules of morality from him, when, in *The Wild Duck*, he derides, as he is wont, all that he has preached on the subject of 'true marriage' in all the rest of his pieces. In that production a delicious dialogue is brought about between the malevolent idiot Gregers and the scoffer Relling (p. 337):

GREGERS. [I want] to lay the foundations of a true marriage.

RELLING. So you don't find Ekdal's marriage good enough as it is?

GREGERS. No doubt it's as good a marriage as most others, worse luck. But a *true* marriage it has never been.

HJALMAR. You have never had eyes for the claims of the ideal, Relling.

RELLING. All rubbish, my boy! But, excuse me, Mr. Werle, how many . . . true marriages have you seen in the course of your life?

GREGERS. Scarcely a single one.

RELLING. Nor I, either.

And still more incisive is the mockery contained in Hjalmar's words (p. 345): 'Well, then, isn't it exasperating to think that it's not I, but he (Werle, senior), who will realize the true marriage? . . . Isn't the marriage between your father and Mrs. Sœrby founded upon complete confidence, upon entire and unreserved candour on both sides? They hide nothing from each other. Their relation is based, if I may put it so' (!) 'on mutual confession and absolution.' Hence no one has yet seen a 'true marriage'; and when by chance this miracle does happen it is fulfilled in the case of Mr. Werle and Mrs. Sœrby—Mr. Werle, who confesses to his wife that he has seduced young girls and sent old friends to prison in his place—Mrs. Sœrby, who confides to her husband that she has had illicit relations with every imaginable sort of man. It is a tame imitation of the scene in *Ruskolnikow* by Dostojewski, where the assassin and the prostitute, after a contrite confession, unite their soiled and broken lives; except that in Ibsen the scene is stripped of its sombre grandeur and lowered to the ridiculous and vulgar.

With Ibsen, when women discover that they are not living in 'true marriage,' their husband suddenly becomes 'a strange man,' and, without further ceremony, they abandon their home and their children, some, like Nora, 'to return to their birthplace,' where 'it will be easier for me to get something to do of one sort or another'; others, like Ellida, without giving a thought to what will become of them; others, again, like Mrs. Alving and Hedda Gabler, to rush full speed to a lover and throw themselves on his neck. Ibsen has even deliciously parodied this last departure, and in a doubly grotesque fashion, for he assigns the laughable *rôle* of the tragic runaway to a man. 'I must out into the snow and tempest,' declaims Hjalmar (*The Wild Duck*, p. 166), 'and seek from house to house a shelter for my old father and myself.' And he really goes, but naturally only to return home the next day, crestfallen, but stout-hearted, to breakfast. Truly nothing more need be said against the idiocy of Nora's high-flown leave-taking, which has become the gospel for the hysterical of both sexes, since Ibsen spared us this trouble in creating his Hjalmar.

We have not yet done with Ibsen's drivel on the subject of marriage. He seems to exact that no girl should marry before she is fully matured, and possesses an experience of life and a knowledge of the world and of men (*A Doll's House*, p. 111):

NORA. And I—how have I been prepared to educate the children? . . . For that task I am not ready. . . . I must first try to educate myself. . . . I cannot be satisfied any longer with what most people say, and with what is in books.

HELMER. You don't understand the society in which you live.

NORA. No, no more I do. But now I will set to work and learn it.

This necessary maturity the young girl best acquires by going in quest of adventures, by becoming closely acquainted with the largest possible number of persons, to make a trial, if possible, of a few men before binding herself definitely. A young girl is thoroughly prepared for marriage when she has attained to a respectable age, managed a few households, perhaps also given birth to sundry children, and in this way proved to herself and others that she understands the duties of a housewife and a mother. Ibsen does not expressly say this, but it is the only reasonable conclusion which can be deduced from the whole series of his plays. The great reformer has no suspicion that he is here preaching something long ago tried by mankind and rejected as unsuitable, or not more suitable. Experimental marriage for a longer or shorter period, the preference for brides endowed with a rich experience in love-affairs and sundry children, all this has already existed. Ibsen may learn all that he needs on this subject from his half-compatriot, Professor Westermarck.* But he would be no degenerate if he did not regard as progress the return to conditions of the most primitive character long since gone by, and if he did not mistake the far-away past for the future.

Let us recapitulate his marriage-canon as gained from his dramas. There should be no marriage from interest (Hedda, Mrs. Alving, Bernick, etc.). There should be no marriage from love (Nora, Wangel). A marriage of prudence is not a true marriage. But to marry because each pleases the other is equally good for nothing. To enter into matrimony with the full approbation of reason, there should be first of all a thorough knowledge of each other by the contracting parties (Ellida). The man should be the woman's instructor and educator (Wangel, Bernick). The wife should not allow herself to be instructed and educated by the husband, but acquire the necessary knowledge quite alone (Nora). If the wife discovers that her marriage is not a 'true marriage,' she leaves the husband, for he is a stranger (Nora, Ellida). She also abandons her children, for children which she has had by a stranger are naturally strangers also. She must, however, at the same time remain with the husband, and endeavour to transform him from a stranger into her own husband (Mrs. Bernick). Marriage is not intended permanently to unite two beings. When anything in the one is not agreeable to the other, they return the ring and go their respective ways (Nora, Mr. Alving, Ellida, Mrs. Elvsted). If a man abandons his wife he commits a heinous crime (Bernick, Werle). And, to sum up, there is no true marriage (Relling). This is Ibsen's doctrine concerning marriage. It leaves nothing to be desired in the matter of clearness. It amply suffices for the diagnosis of the state of the Norwegian poet's intellect.

Independently of his religious obsessions and his bewildering contradictions, Ibsen's mysticism reveals itself, step by step, in absurdities of which a healthy intellect would be incapable. We have seen in *The Lady from the Sea* that Ellida wishes to abandon her husband, because her marriage is not a true one, and because her husband has become a stranger to her. Why is he a stranger to her? Because he has married her without mutual close acquaintance. 'You had only seen me and spoken a few words to me.' She ought not to have let herself be provided for. 'Rather the meanest labour, rather the most wretched surroundings, so long as they were the result of free will, of free choice.' From this one can only reasonably conclude that Ellida is of the opinion no true marriage is possible, unless the

* Edward Westermarck, *The History of Human Marriage*. London: Macmillan, 1892. See especially the two chapters on 'The Forms of Human Marriage,' and 'The Duration of Marriage.'

woman possesses a thorough knowledge of her suitor and has had full freedom in her choice. She is convinced that these conditions existed in the case of the first claimant for her hand. 'The first—that might have been a complete and real marriage.' Now, the same Ellida, a few pages before (78), says that she knew absolutely nothing concerning her lover; she did not even know his name, and, as a matter of fact, he is spoken of throughout the piece only as 'the stranger.'

WANGEL. What else do you know about him?
ELLIDA. Only that he went to sea very young; and that he had been on long voyages.
WANGEL. Is there nothing more?
ELLIDA. No; we never spoke of such things.
WANGEL. Of what did you speak, then?
ELLIDA. About the sea!

And she betrothed herself to him

Because he said I must.
WANGEL. You must? Had you no will of your own, then?
ELLIDA. Not when he was near.

So, then, Ellida is forced to abandon Wangel for the reason that, previously to her marriage with him, she did not thoroughly know him, and she must go to 'the stranger,' of whom she knows nothing. Her marriage with Wangel is no marriage, because she did not enter into it with perfect freedom of will, but the marriage with 'the stranger' will be 'perfect and pure,' although when she betrothed herself to him she had 'no will of her own.' After this example of his mental maze, it is truly humiliating to be obliged to waste more words concerning the intellectual state of such a man. But since this man is foisted by fools and fanatics to the rank of a great moralist and poet of the future, the psychiatrical observer must not spare himself the labour of referring to his other absurdities.

In this same *Lady from the Sea*, Ellida renounces her project of leaving her husband Wangel, and going away with the 'stranger,' as soon as Wangel says 'with aching heart': 'Now you can choose your own path in perfect freedom.' She remains with Wangel. She chooses him. 'Whence came the change?' asks Wangel and the reader with him. 'Ah, don't you understand,' Ellida gushingly replies, 'that the change came—was bound to come—when I could choose in freedom!' (p. 141). This second choice, then, is intended to form a complete contrast to the first, in which Ellida plighted her troth to Wangel. But all the conditions, without a single exception, have remained the same. Ellida is now free because Wangel expressly gives her her freedom; but she was still freer on the first occasion, because Wangel had as yet no rights over her, and did not need to begin by setting her free. As little was external coercion exercised on her at the betrothal as subsequently after marriage. Her resolution depended then, as now, entirely on herself. If at the betrothal she felt herself fettered, it was, as she herself explains, because she was at that time poor, and allowed herself to be enticed by the alluring prospect of being provided for. But in this respect nothing has changed. She has come into no property since her marriage, so far as we know from Ibsen. She is just as poor as she ever was. If she quits Wangel, she will sink once more into the penury she found insupportable when a young girl. If she remains with him, she is quite as much provided for as she hoped to be when she betrothed herself to him. Wherein, then, lies the contrast between her former want of liberty and her present freedom to explain the change? There is none. It exists in the confused thought of Ibsen alone. If the whole of this piratical story about Ellida, Wangel, and the stranger is intended to mean, or to prove, anything, it can only be that a woman must first live a few years with her husband on trial before she can bind herself definitively; and that her decision may be valid, she is to be free at the end of the period of probation to go or to stay. The only meaning of the piece is, therefore, pure idiocy—experimental marriage.

We find the same absurdity repeated, in the fundamental idea, in the premises and deductions of nearly all his plays. In *Ghosts* Oswald Alving's disease is represented as a chastisement for the sins of his father, and for the moral weakness of his mother in marrying for self-interest a man she did not love. Now, Oswald's state is the consequence of a complaint which may be contracted without any depravity whatsoever. It is a silly antiquated idea of the bigoted members of societies for the suppression of immorality that a contagious disease is the consequence and punishment of licentiousness. Doctors know better than that. They know hundreds—nay, thousands—of cases where a young man is infected for his whole life, for no other act than one which, with the views now prevailing, is looked upon as venial. Even holy matrimony is no protection against such a misfortune, to say nothing of the cases where doctors, nurses, etc., have contracted the malady in the discharge of their duties, and without carnal transgression. Ibsen's drivel proves nothing of that which, according to him, it should prove. Chamberlain Alving might be a monster of immorality without for that reason falling ill, or having an insane son; and his son could be insane without more culpability on the part of the father than is the case with all men who have been unchaste before marriage. Ibsen, however, gives obtrusive evidence of having had no wish to write a tract in praise of continence, by making Mrs. Alving throw herself into the arms of Pastor Manders, and by making the mother the intermediary of an illicit union out of wedlock between the son and his own sister, putting, moreover, into the mouth of Oswald a panegyric on concubinage—one of the most incredible things met with in the incredible Ibsen. 'What are they to do?' replies Oswald Alving to the horrified pastor. 'A poor young artist—a poor young girl. It costs a lot of money to get married.' I can only suppose that the innocent Norwegian villager has never with his own bodily eyes seen a 'free union,' and that he has drawn his idea of one from the depths of a nature filled with anarchistic rage against the existing order of things. An inhabitant of any large town, having daily opportunities for getting insight into dozens and hundreds of free unions, will burst into hearty laughter over Ibsen's infantine fantasies, worthy of a lascivious schoolboy. In no country in the world does civil marriage cost more than a trifling sum, very much less than the first repast offered by a young fellow to the girl he has persuaded to live with him; and religious marriage, far from costing anything, brings to the bridal couple a donation in money, clothes, and household articles, if they are indelicate enough to accept them. Pious societies, which expend large sums of money in legalizing free unions, exist everywhere. When persons form unions without the aid of the civil law or of priests, it is probably never for the purpose of saving the expense of marriage, but either from culpable levity, or because either one or other of them makes a mental reservation not to bind him or herself, but to enjoy something agreeable without undertaking any serious duties; or, finally, in the few cases which a moral man may approve, or, at least, excuse, because on one side or the other there exists some legal obstacle above which they raise themselves, strong in love, and justified in their own eyes by the earnestness of their intention to be faithful to each other unto death.

But to return from this subordinate absurdity to the capital absurdity of the piece. Chamberlain Alving is punished for his illicit indulgence in carnal pleasure, in his own body, and in his children Oswald and Regina. That is very edifying, and would, doubtless, meet with approbation at a conference of clergymen, although nonsensical and inaccurate to the highest degree. We will only mention in passing that Ibsen constantly recommends and glorifies unchastity, the 'living out one's life.' But what inference does Mrs. Alving draw from the case of her husband? That all should remain chaste and pure, an idea worked out by Bjornson in his *Glove?* No. She is led by it to the conclusion that the existing order of morals and the law are bad. 'Oh, that perpetual law and order!' she exclaims (p. 154); 'I often think it is that which does all the mischief here in the world. . . . I can endure all this constraint and cowardice no longer. It is too much for me. I must work my way out to freedom.' What in the world has Alving's story to do with 'law and order?' and how does 'freedom' enter into this *Credo?* What connection with the piece have the silly speeches of this woman, unless it be that they are lugged in to tickle the radical patrons of the gallery into applause. In Tahiti neither 'order' nor 'morals' reign in the sense given them by Mrs. Alving. There the brown beauties have all the 'freedom' to which Mrs. Alving wishes to 'work her way out,' and the men so 'live out their lives' that ships' officers, not otherwise modest, avert their eyes with shame. And in that very region Chamberlain Alving's disease is so widespread that, according to Ibsen's medical theory, all the young Tahitians must be Oswalds.

But this is a constant habit of Ibsen's, evidenced in all his pieces. He puts into the mouth of his characters phrases used for effect by orators in popular meetings of the lowest class, having nothing in the least to do with the piece. 'I don't know what religion is,' Nora says in the well-known scene where she leaves her husband (p. 114). '. . . I know nothing but what our clergyman told me when I was confirmed. He explained that religion was this and that. When I have got quite away from here and am all by myself, then I will examine that matter too. I will see whether what our clergyman taught is true. . . . I have now learnt, too, that the laws are different from what I thought they were; but I can't convince myself that they are right.' Now her case has no relation to the religious doctrine of Pastor Hansen and the excellence or badness of the laws. No law in the world concedes the right to a child to sign her father's name to a cheque without his knowledge, and all the laws of the world not only permit but compel a judge to inquire into the motives of every misdemeanour, although Ibsen makes Krogstad the mouthpiece of this idiocy (p. 39): 'The laws inquire little into motives.' The whole of this scene, in view of which, however, the piece was written, is foreign to the play, and does not originally spring from it. If Nora wishes to abandon her husband, it can only be on the supposition that she has discovered he does not love her so devotedly as she had wished and hoped. The hysterical fool, however, utters an inflammatory diatribe against religion, law, and society (which are profoundly innocent of the weakness of character and absence of love in her husband), and departs like a feminine Coriolanus shaking her fist at her fatherland. In *The Pillars of Society* Bernick, wishing to confess his own baseness, introduces his avowal with the words (p. 110): 'Let everyone examine himself, and let us realize the prediction that from this evening we begin a new time. The old, with its tinsel, its hypocrisy, its hollowness, its lying propriety, and its pitiful cowardice, shall lie behind us like a museum,' etc. 'Speak for yourself, Bernick, speak for yourself,' one might well call out to the old wind-bag, who in this sermonizing tone thus generalizes his own individual case. 'I wish to speak of the great discovery that I have made within the last few days,' exclaims Stockmann in *An Enemy of the People*, 'the discovery that all our spiritual sources of life are poisoned, and that our whole bourgeois society rests upon a soil teeming with the pestilence of lies.' That may in itself be true; but nothing in the piece gives Stockmann the right to arrive reasonably at this conclusion. Even in Plato's republic it might happen that a ragamuffin, more foolish for that matter than wicked, should refuse to cleanse an infected spring, and only a fool could deduce from this single fact, and from the conduct of a clique of Philistines in an impossible Norwegian village, the general proposition that 'our whole bourgeois society rests upon a soil teeming with the pestilence of lies.' In *Rosmersholm*, Brendel says in an obscurely profound prophetic tone, which shudders with foreboding (p. 23): 'We live in a tempestuous, an equinoctial age.' This expression also, true enough in itself, strikes one like a blow in the eye in the place where it occurs, for *Rosmersholm* has no connection with any definite period of time; and it is not necessary to change a single essential word in the piece, in order to transport it at pleasure to the Middle Ages, or the age of the Roman emperors, to China, or the land of the Incas—to any age or any land where there are hysterical women and idiotic men.

We are familiar with the method pursued by brawlers who wish to pick a quarrel: 'Sir, why did you look at me in that way?' 'Pardon me, I did not look at you.' 'What! you say, then, that I lie?' 'I said nothing of the sort.' 'You give me the lie a second time. You must give me satisfaction.' This is Ibsen's method. What he wishes is to denounce society, the state, religion, law, and morals in anarchistic phrases. Instead, however, of publishing them like Nietzsche, in brochures, he sticks them into his pieces at haphazard, where they appear as unexpectedly as the couplets sung in the naïve farces of our fathers. Cleanse Ibsen's dramas of these pasted-on phrases, and even a Brandes will no longer be able to trumpet them as 'modern' productions; there will remain only a tissue of absurdities, belonging to no time or place, in which here and there emerge single poetically fine scenes and accessory figures, not changing in the least the atrociousness of the whole. In fact, Ibsen always begins by finding some thesis—*i.e.*, some anarchist phrase. Then he tries to find out beings and events which embody and prove his thesis, for which task, however, his poetical power, and, above all, his knowledge of life and men, are insufficient. For he goes through the world without seeing it, and his glance is always turned inward on himself. In contradiction to the saying of the poet, 'All that is human is alien to him,' and his own 'I' alone occupies him and absorbs his attention. He himself proclaims this in a well-known poem wherein he says, 'Life is a battle with the ghost in the vaults of the heart and brain. To be a poet is to hold judgment day over one's own self.'*

The 'ghost in the heart and brain' is the obsessions and impulses in conflict with which the life of the higher degenerate is certainly spent. It is as clear as day that a poem, which is nothing but a 'judgment day' of the poet over himself, cannot be a mirror of universal human life, freely and broadly flowing, but simply the intricate arabesques adorning the walls of a distorted, isolated existence. He sees the image of the world with the eye of an insect; a diminutive single feature which shows itself to one of the polished facets of such a discoidal eye, and which he perchance perceives, he firmly seizes, and renders with distinctness. But he does not comprehend its connection with the whole phenomenon, and his organ of vision is not able to span a large comprehensive picture. This explains the fidelity to nature in petty details and quite accessory figures, while the chief events and central characters are always astonishingly absurd and alien to all the realities of the world.

It is in *Brand* that Ibsen's absurdity apparently achieves its greatest triumph. Northern critics have reiterated *ad nauseam* that this silly piece is a dramatic translation of Kierkegaard's crazy 'Either-Or.' Ibsen shows a fool who wishes to be 'all or nothing,' and who preaches the same to his fellow-citizens. What he especially understands by these high-sounding words the piece nowhere reveals by a single syllable. Brand, however, succeeds in infecting his fellow-citizens with his madness, and one fine day they sally forth from the village and are led by him into impassable mountain solitudes. What his purpose is no one knows or suspects. The sexton, who seems to be somewhat less crazy than the others, finally becomes uneasy concerning this wholly senseless mountain climbing, and asks whither Brand is really leading them, and what may be the object of this scramble. Whereupon Brand gives him the following wonderful information (p. 151): 'How long will the struggle last?' (viz., the climbing, for there is no other struggle in this Act). 'It lasts until life's end. Until you have sacrificed all; until you are freed from your compact; until that which you may wish for you shall wish for unswervingly.' (What

* 'At leve—er Kamp med Trolde
J Hjertet og Hjernens Hvaelv;
At digte—det er at holde
Dommedag over sig selv.'

this is which is to be wished for is not explained.) 'Until every doubt shall have vanished and nothing separates you from the All or Nothing. And your sacrifices? All the gods which with you take the place of the eternal God; the shining golden chains of slavery, together with the beds of your languid slothfulness. The reward of victory? Unity of will, activity of faith, pureness of soul.' Naturally on listening to this ranting the good people 'come to their senses and go home,' but the lunatic Brand is offended because his fellow-citizens do not want to pant uphill in order to 'wish for something unswervingly,' to attain to 'all or nothing,' and to arrive at 'unity of will.' For it is 'the all' which seems to inhabit mountains; not merely freedom, which an early poet sought for there. ('Liberty dwells in the mountains,' Schiller has said.)

And yet Brand is a remarkable figure. In him Ibsen has unconsciously created a very instructive type of those deranged beings who run, speak, and act at the bidding of a ruling impulse,* who with furious passion are continually and reiteratingly talking of 'the goal' which they wish to attain, but who neither themselves have a suspicion of what this goal really is, nor are in a position to indicate it to others in an intelligible way. Brand thinks the power which impels him is his inflexible iron will. It is in reality his inflexible iron impulsion which his consciousness in vain seeks to grasp and to interpret by the aid of a flood of unintelligible words.

Ibsen's absurdity is not always so clearly apparent as in the examples cited. It frequently manifests itself in a blurred and indefinite phrase, plainly expressing the state of a mind which endeavours to formulate in words a nebulous representation springing up in it, but which lacks the necessary power and loses itself in mechanical mutterings void of sense. There are three sorts of phrases of this kind to be distinguished in Ibsen. One kind say absolutely nothing, and contain no more of an idea than the 'tra-la-la' sung to a song of which one has forgotten the words. They are a symptom of a temporary arrest of function† in the cerebral centres of ideation, and appear in healthy persons also in a state of extreme fatigue, under the form of incidental embarrassment, causing hesitation in speech. In persons suffering from hereditary exhaustion they are continuously present. Another kind affect an appearance of profundity and significant allusions, but exact observation recog-

* Dr. Wilhelm Griesinger, *Pathologie und Therapie der psychischen Krankheiten für Aerzte und Studirende*. 5te Auflage. Gänzlich umgearbeitet und erweitert. Von Dr. Willibald Levinstein-Schleger; Berlin, 1892. (See p. 143, on 'Diseased Impulses'; and p. 147, on 'Excessive Energy of Will.')

† Griesinger, *op. cit.*, p. 77: 'Retardation of thought may be produced . . . by the state of constriction following a mental depression, by complete inertia extending to the arrest of thought.'

nises them as an empty jingle of words devoid of all import. Finally, the third kind are such evident and unequivocal idiocy that even unprofessional listeners regard each other in consternation, and would feel it to be their duty to give his family a gentle hint if they heard anything of the kind from one of their table companions at the habitual café. I will give some illustrations of each of these three kinds of phraseology.

Firstly, phrases saying absolutely nothing, interpolated between intelligible words, and indicating a temporary paralysis of the centres of ideation.

In *The Lady from the Sea* (p. 25) Lyngstrand says: 'I am to a certain extent a little infirm.'* This 'to a certain extent' is admirable! Lyngstrand, a sculptor, is speaking of his artistic projects (p. 51):

As soon as I can set about it, I am going to try if I can produce a great work—a group, *as they call it.*

ARNHOLM. Is there anything else?

LYNGSTRAND. Yes, there is to be another figure—*a sort of apparition, as they say.*

As Ibsen makes Lyngstrand a fool, it might be believed that he intentionally put these idiotic turns of expression into the sculptor's mouth. But in *Hedda Gabler*, Brack, a sharp and clever *bon vivant*, says (p. 87): 'But as far as regards myself, you know very well that I have always entertained a—a certain respect for the marriage tie, *generally speaking*, Mrs. Hedda.' In *Rosmersholm* Brendel says (p. 24): 'So you see when golden dreams descended and enwrapped me . . . I fashioned them into poems, into visions, into pictures—*in the rough,* as it were, you understand. Oh, what pleasures, what intoxications I have enjoyed in my time! The mysterious bliss of creation—*in the rough,* as I said.' Rector Kroll says (p. 18): 'A family that now soon for some centuries has held its place as the first in the land.'† 'Now soon for some centuries'! That means that it is not yet 'some centuries,' but 'soon' will be 'some centuries.' Hence 'soon' must include in itself 'some centuries.' By what miracle? In *The Wild Duck* we have the intentionally, but, in their exaggeration impossibly, idiotic conversations of the 'fat,' 'bald,' and 'short-sighted' gentlemen in the first act, but also this remark by Gina, who is in no way depicted as an idiot (p. 270):

Are you glad when you have some good news to tell father when he comes home in the evening?

HEDWIG. Yes, for then we have a pleasanter time.

GINA. Yes, *there is something* [*true*]‡ *in that!!*

---

* Rationalized in the English version cited, as follows (p. 25): 'Yes, perhaps I am a little delicate.'—TRANSLATOR.

† Rationalized in the English version by 'now soon,' being rendered as 'nearly.'—TRANSLATOR.

‡ 'True' is omitted in the English version quoted.—TRANSLATOR.

In the conversation about the wild duck between Ekdal, Gregers and Hjalmar we read (p. 289):

EKDAL. He was out in a boat, *you see*, and he shot her. But father's sight is pretty bad now. H'm ; he only wounded her.
GREGERS. Ah! she got a couple of shot in her body, I suppose.
HJALMAR. Yes, *two or three. . . .*
GREGERS. And she thrives all right in the garret there?
HJALMAR. Yes, wonderfully well. She's got fat. She's been in there so long now that she's forgotten her natural wild life, and it all depends on that.
GREGERS. *You're right there*, Hjalmar.

And in a dialogue between Hedwig and Gregers Werle (p. 305):

HEDWIG. . . . If I had learnt basket-making, I could have made the new basket for the wild duck.
GREGERS. So you could; and it was, strictly speaking, your business, wasn't it?
HEDWIG. Yes, for she's *my* wild duck.
GREGERS. *Of course she is!*

Now for some examples of phrases which sound excessively profound, but in reality express nothing, or mere foolishness.

In *A Doll's House* (p. 25) Mrs. Linden expresses the opinion: 'Well, after all, it is better to open the door to the sick, and get them safe in;' to which Rank significantly replies: 'Yes, so people say. And it is that very consideration which turns society into a hospital.' What does this meditative and oracular speech mean? Is it Rank's opinion that society is a hospital because it cares for its sick, and that it would be healthy if its sick were not cared for? Would the untended sick be any less sick? If he believes that he believes an idiocy. Or are the sick to be left to die uncared for, and in this manner got rid of? If he preaches that, he preaches a barbarism and a crime, and that is not in accordance with Rank's character as Ibsen depicts him. We may turn and twist the vague, mysterious words as we will, we shall always find either stupidity or want of meaning.

In *Rosmersholm*, Rosmer (p. 30) wishes to 'devote all his life and all his energies to this one thing—the creation of a true democracy in this country.' And, wonderful to relate, the persons to whom Rosmer says these words all seem to comprehend what the 'true democracy' is. Without being asked, Rosmer offers, besides, some explanation of his Pythian utterance: 'I want to awaken the democracy to its true task—that of making all the people of this country noblemen . . . by setting free their minds and purifying their wills. . . . I will only try to arouse them to their task. They themselves must accomplish it . . . by their own strength. There is no other. . . . Peace and joy and mutual forbearance must once more enter into their souls.' Rebecca repeats to him his programme (p. 62):

> You were to set resolutely to work in the world—the living world of to-day, as you said. You were to go as a messenger of emancipation from home to home; to win over minds and wills; to create noble men around you in wider and wider circles. Noblemen.
>
> ROSMER. Joyful noblemen.
>
> REBECCA. Yes, joyful.
>
> ROSMER. For it is joy that ennobles the mind.

It is impossible to avoid calling up a comic picture of Rosmer going 'from home to home' 'in wider and wider circles,' and making the persons before whom he talks into 'joyful noblemen,' while he 'awakens' them and 'purifies their wills,' and thus 'creates a true democracy.' This rigmarole is, it is true, incomprehensible; but, at all events, it must be something agreeable, for Rosmer expressly says that he needs 'joy' to create 'noblemen.' And in spite of this Rebecca suddenly discovers (p. 102): 'The Rosmer view of life ennobles, but it kills happiness.' What! Rosmer kill happiness when he 'goes from home to home,' awakening, winning, making people free, etc., and creating joyful noblemen? The word 'joyful' includes, at least, something of happiness, and yet the education of men to 'joyful noblemen' is to kill happiness? Rosmer finds (p. 97) 'the work of ennobling men's minds is not for him. And, besides, it is so hopeless in itself.' This is in a measure intelligible, though it is not stated from what experience Rosmer has been led to such a change in his views. But quite beyond comprehension is Rebecca's speech about the fatal influence of 'the Rosmer view of life.' In *Ghosts*, Mrs. Alving endeavours to explain her defunct husband's vagaries in this balderdash (p. 187): 'When he was a young lieutenant, he was brimming over with the joy of life. It was like a breezy day only to look at him. And what exuberant strength and vitality there was in him! And then, child of joy as he was—for he *was* like a child at the time—he had to live here at home in a half-grown town, which had no joys to offer him, but only amusements. He had no object in life, but only an office. He had no work into which he could throw himself heart and soul; he had only business. He had not a single comrade that knew what the joy of life meant, only loungers and boon companions.' These antitheses seem to have something in them; but if we seriously set about hunting for a definite idea in them, they vanish in smoke. 'Object in life—office'—'work—business'—'comrades—boon companions,' are not in themselves oppositions, but become such through the individual. With a decent man they are perfectly coincident; with a base man they fall into opposition. A large or a small town has nothing to do with it. 'For Kant in the small town of Kœnigsberg, in the last century, the 'office' was 'the object in life,' 'work' was 'business,' and he so chose his 'boon companions' that they were at the same time his 'comrades,' as far, indeed, as he could have such. And, on the other hand, there is, in the largest metropolis, no occupation and no circle of men in which a degenerate, burdened with his disorder, could feel at ease and in inward harmony.

In *Hedda Gabler* we find quite a multitude of such words, apparently saying much, but in reality saying nothing. 'It was the passion for life in you!' exclaims Lövborg to Hedda (p. 128), with the seeming conviction that he has, in this utterance, explained something to her. And Hedda says (p. 142): '*I* see him before me. With vine-leaves in his hair. Hot and bold' (p. 151). 'And Ejlert Lövborg, he is sitting with vine-leaves in his hair, and reading aloud' (p. 157). 'Had he vine-leaves in his hair?' (p. 171). 'So that is how it all happened. Then he did not have vine-leaves in his hair' (p. 188).

HEDDA. Could you not contrive that it should be done gracefully?
LÖVBORG. Gracefully? With vine-leaves in my hair?

'With vine-leaves in his hair;' 'the passion for life'—these are words meaning, in the connection assigned to them, absolutely nothing, but giving scope for dreaming. In a few instances Ibsen employs these dreamily-nebulous, shadowy expressions with poetic licence, *e.g.*, when we read in *The Pillars of Society* (p. 19):

RÖRLUND. Tell me, Dina, why you do like so much to be with me?
DINA. Because you teach me so much that is beautiful.
RÖRLUND. Beautiful? Do you call what I can teach you beautiful?
DINA. Yes; or, rather, you teach me nothing; but when I hear you speak, it makes me think of so much that is beautiful.
RÖRLUND. What do you understand, then, by a beautiful thing?
DINA. I have never thought of that.
RÖRLUND. Then think of it now. What do you understand by a beautiful thing?
DINA. A beautiful thing is something great and far away.

Dina is a young girl living under sad and painful conditions. It is psychologically accurate that she should condense all her longing for a new and happy existence in a word of emotional colouring, such as 'beautiful.' It is the same with the dialogue between Gregers and Hedwig in *The Wild Duck* (p. 53):

GREGERS. And she [the wild duck] has been down in the depths of the sea.
HEDWIG. Why do you say 'in the depths of the sea'?
GREGERS. What else could I say?
HEDWIG. You could say 'the bottom of the sea' [or 'at the bottom of he water'].*
GREGERS. Oh, mayn't I just as well say the depths of the sea?

* Bracketed clause not in English version.—TRANSLATOR.

HEDWIG. Yes ; but it sounds so strange to me when other people speak of the depths of the sea.

GREGERS. Why so? . . .

HEDWIG. . . . It always seems to me that the whole room and everything in it should be called the depths of the sea. But that's so stupid. . . . Because it's only a garret [the place where the wild duck lives, the old Christmas-trees are put, where old Ekdal chases the rabbit, etc.].

Hedwig is a highly excitable child at the age of puberty (Ibsen thinks it necessary expressly to affirm that her voice is changing, and that she willingly plays with fire) ; hence it is natural that she should be thrilled with presentiments, dreams, and obscure instincts, and invest poetical expressions denoting something far away and wild, such as 'in the depths of the sea,' with the secret significance of all the mysterious and marvellous surging in her. But when expressions of this sort are used, not by little growing girls, but by full-grown persons depicted as rational beings, it is no longer a question of dreaming explicable on pathological grounds, but of diseased cerebral centres.

These words often assume the nature of an obsession. Ibsen obstinately repeats them, at the same time imparting to them a mysterious significance. It is thus, for example, that the words 'joy of life' appear in *Ghosts* (p. 176) :

OSWALD. . . . She was full of the joy of life (p. 177).

MRS. ALVING. What were you saying about the joy of life?

OSWALD. Have you noticed that everything I have painted has turned upon the joy of life?—always, always upon the joy of life? (p. 187).

MRS. ALVING. You spoke of the joy of life ; and at that word a new light burst for me over my life and all it has contained. . . . You ought to have known your father. . . . He was brimming over with the joy of life.

In *Hedda Gabler* the word 'beauty' plays a similar part (p. 190):

HEDDA (*to* Lövborg). *You* use it [the pistol] now. . . . And do it beautifully (p. 214).

HEDDA. I say that there is something beautiful in this [Lövborg's suicide] (p. 219).

HEDDA. A relief to know that it is still possible for an act of voluntary courage to take place in the world. Something over which there falls a veil of unintentional beauty. . . . And then now—the great act! That over which the sense of beauty falls!

The 'vine leaves in the hair,' in the same piece, belongs with equal exactness to this category of words, amounting to an obsession. The use of expressions full of mystery, incomprehensible to the hearer, and either freely coined by the speaker, or endowed by him with a peculiar sense, deviating from that usually assigned them in speech, is one of the most frequent phenomena among the mentally deranged. Griesinger* often

* Griesinger, *op. cit.*, p. 176. He names the coining of words 'phraseomania.' Kussmaul gives the name *Paraphrasia vesana* to the coining of incomprehensible words, or the using of known words in a sense wholly foreign to them.

lays stress on this, and A. Marie* adduces some characteristic examples of words and phrases, either newly invented or employed in a sense differing from the customary one, which have been repeated by the insane.

Ibsen is certainly not wholly diseased in mind, but only a dweller on the borderland—a 'mattoid.' His use of formalized expressions does not therefore go so far as the invention of new words, as cited by Dr. Marie. But that he ascribes a mysterious meaning to the expressions 'beauty,' 'joy of life,' 'courage of life,' etc., and one which they do not possess when rationally used, follows clearly enough from the examples quoted.

Finally let us adduce a few specimens of sheer nonsense, corresponding to conversations held in dreams, and the silly rambling speech of persons suffering from fever or acute mania. In *The Lady from the Sea*, Ellida says (p. 39): 'The water in the fjord here is sick, . . . yes, sick. And I believe it makes one sick, too' (p. 79). 'We' (Ellida and the 'stranger') 'spoke of the gulls and the eagles, and all the other sea-birds. I think —isn't it wonderful?—when we talked of such things it seemed to me as if both the sea-beasts and sea-birds were one with him. . . . I almost thought I belonged to them all, too' (p. 100).

I don't think the dry land is really our home. . . . I think that if only men had from the beginning accustomed themselves to live on the sea, or *in* the sea, perhaps, we should be more perfect than we are—with better and happier . . .

ARNHOLM (*jestingly*). Well, perhaps! But it can't be helped. We've once for all entered upon the wrong path, and have become land-beasts instead of sea-beasts. Anyhow, I suppose it's too late to make good the mistake now.

ELLIDA. Yes, you've spoken a sad truth. And I think men instinctively feel something of this themselves. And they bear it about with them as a secret regret and sorrow. Believe me, herein lies the deepest cause for the sadness of men.

And Dr. Wangel, who is depicted as a rational man, says (p. 129):

And then she is so changeable, so capricious—she varies so suddenly.

ARNHOLM. No doubt that is the result of her morbid state of mind.

WANGEL. Not altogether. Ellida belongs to the sea-folk. That is the matter (! !).

---

* Dr. A. Marie, *Études sur quelques Symptômes des Délires systématisés et sur leur Valeur;* Paris, 1892, chap. ii.: 'Eccentricities of language. Neologisms and conjuring incantations.' Tanzi cites, among others, the following examples: A patient used continuously to repeat, 'That is true, and not false'; another began every phrase with, 'God's Word'; a third said, 'Out with the vile beast!' making at the same time a sign of benediction with the right hand; a fourth said unceasingly, 'Turn over the page'; a fifth cried, in a tone of command, 'Lips acs livi cux lips sux!' etc. One of Krafft-Ebing's patients (*op. cit.*, p. 130) constructed, among others, the following words: 'Magnetismusambosarbeitswellen, Augengedanken Austrahlung, Glückseligkeitsbetten, Ohrenschussmaschine,' etc. Krafft-Ebing, *op. cit.*, pp. 130, 131.

We must insist that precisely the absurdities, the nugatory, blurred, deep-sounding phrases, the formalized words, and the dream-like drivel, have essentially conduced to obtain for Ibsen his particular admirers. Over them hysterical mystics can dream, like Dina and Hedwig, over the words 'beautiful' and 'in the depths of the sea.' As they mean absolutely nothing, an inattentive and vagrant mind can impart to them whatever significance may be suggested by the play of association under the influence of momentary emotion. They are, moreover, exceedingly grateful material for the (so-called) 'comprehensives,' for whom nothing is ever obscure. 'Comprehensives' always explain everything. The greater the idiocy, the more involved, the richer in import, the more exhaustive is its interpretation, and the greater the arrogance with which these beings of 'perfect comprehension' look down upon the barbarian, who stoutly refuses to see in fustian anything but fustian.

In an exceedingly amusing French farce, *Le Homard*, a husband suddenly returning home one evening surprises a stranger with his wife. The latter does not lose her presence of mind, and says to the husband that, having suddenly been seized with illness, she had sent her maid for the first available doctor, and that this gentleman was the doctor. The husband thanks the gallant for his speedy appearance, and asks if he has already prescribed anything. The gallant, who, of course, is not a doctor, tries to make himself scarce; but the anxious husband insists on having a prescription, so that the Galen, bathed in cold perspiration, is compelled to give one. The husband casts a glance at it; it consists of wholly illegible marks. 'And will the chemist be able to read that?' asks the husband, shaking his head. 'As if it were print,' asseverates the false physician, again trying to make his escape. The husband, however, adjures him to remain, and holds him fast until the maid returns from the chemist. In a few minutes she makes her appearance. The Galen prepares himself for a catastrophe. No. The maid brings a phial of medicine, a box of pills, and some powders. 'Did the chemist give you those?' demands the Galen in bewilderment. 'Certainly.' 'On my prescription?' 'Of course it was on your prescription,' replies the astonished maid. 'Has the chemist made some mistake?' interposes the troubled husband. 'No, no,' our Galen hastens to reply; but he contemplates the medicines for a long time, and becomes lost in reverie.

These 'comprehensives' are like the chemist in *Le Homard*. They read with fluency all Ibsen's prescriptions, and especially those containing absolutely no written characters, but simply crow's feet devoid of all meaning. It is also their trade to supply critical pills and electuaries when a piece of paper is brought to them bearing the signature of a self-styled doctor, and they dispense them without wincing, be there anything of any sort, or even nothing, on the slip of paper. Is it not significant that the sole thing in Ibsen which the French mystic De Vogué, one of these 'comprehensives,' finds to praise is one of the meaningless phrases above cited?*

A final stigma of Ibsen's mysticism must be considered—his symbolism. In *The Wild Duck*, this bird is the symbol of Hjalmar's destiny, and the garret next the photographic studio a symbol of the 'living lie,' of which, according to Relling, everyone stands in need. In *The Lady from the Sea*, Lyngstrand wishes to make a group which shall be the symbol of Ellida, as the 'stranger' with the changing eyes of a fish is of the sea and the latter again of freedom, so that the 'stranger' is really the symbol of a symbol. In *Ghosts*, the burning of the asylum is the symbol of the annihilation of Alving's 'living lie,' and the rainy weather prevailing throughout the whole piece the symbol of the depressed and sullen frame of mind of the personages in action. Ibsen's earlier pieces, *Emperor and Galilean*, *Brand*, *Peer Gynt*, literally swarm with symbols. A mysterious collateral significance is given to every figure and every stage accessory, and every word includes a double meaning. From the 'Psychology of Mysticism' we already know this peculiarity of the mystic mind to divine obscure relations between phenomena. It seeks so to explain the nexus of the wholly unconnected representations springing up in consciousness through the play of automatic association, that it attributes hidden but essential reference to each other in these representations. The 'comprehensives' believe they have said all when, with an extremely consequential and self-satisfied air, they demonstrate that the 'stranger' in *The Lady from the Sea* signifies the sea, and the sea freedom. They quite overlook the fact that the thing to be explained is not what the poet intended by his symbol, but, firstly, and in particular, why he hit upon the idea of making use of a symbol at all. In the well-known words of the French satirist, a clear-headed poet calls 'a cat a cat.' That to express so sober an idea as that persons of fine feelings, living in narrow conditions, have a deep longing for a free, expanded, unrestrained existence, one should have the whim to invent a 'stranger with fish-like eyes,' pre-

* Vicomte E. M. de Vogué, 'Les Cigognes,' *Revue des deux Mondes*, February 15, 1892, p. 922: 'Ibsen would have won our trust, were it only by certain axioms [?] which appeal to our actual distrusts, such as this . . . in *Rosmersholm:* "The Rosmer view of life ennobles, but it kills happiness."' I am convinced that, unless previously told that they emanated from confined lunatics, these 'comprehensives' would, without difficulty, understand and interpret the expression 'little-cupboards-of-appetite-of-representation' (*Vorstellungs-Appetitschränkchen*), freely used by one of Meynert's lunatic patients, or the words of a patient under Griesinger's care (*op. cit.*, p. 176) that 'the lady superior was establishing herself in the military side-tone and in the retardation of her teeth.'

supposes a diseased mental activity. In imbeciles, the tendency to allegory and symbolism is very common. 'Intricate arabesques, symbolical figures, cabalistic gestures and attitudes, strange interpretations of natural events, punning, word-coining, and peculiar modes of expression, frequently occurring in paranoia, give the delirium a lively and grotesque colouring.' Thus writes Tanzi,* and in the symbolism of the insane he saw, as Meynert had previously seen, a form of atavism. Among men low in the grade of civilization symbolism is, in fact, the habitual form of thought. We know the reason—their brain is not yet trained to attention; it is too weak to suppress irrational associations, and refers all that shoots through its consciousness to some chance phenomenon either just perceived, or else remembered.

After all the mental stigmata of Ibsen with which we have become acquainted—his theological obsessions of original sin, of confession and redemption, the absurdities of his invention, the constant contradiction in his uncertain opinions, his vague or senseless modes of expression, his onomatomania and his symbolism—he might be numbered among the mystic degenerates with which I have concerned myself in the previous chapters. We are, however, justified in assigning him his place among the ego-maniacs, because the diseased intensification of his ego-consciousness is even more striking and characteristic than his mysticism. His ego-mania assumes the form of anarchism. He is in a state of constant revolt against all that exists. He never exercises rational criticism with regard to this; he never shows what is bad, why it is bad, and how it could be made better. No; he only reproaches it with its existence, and has only one longing—to destroy it. 'The ruin of everything' was the programme of certain destructives in 1848, and has remained that of Ibsen. He condenses it with a clearness which leaves nothing to be desired in his well-known poem, *To my Friend the Destructive Orator*. In this he glorifies the deluge as the 'sole revolution not made by a half-and-half dabbler' (*Halohedsfusker*); but even it was not radically ruinous enough. 'We want to make it still more radical, but for that end we need men and orators. You charge yourselves with flooding the terrestrial garden. I place blissfully a torpedo under the ark.'† In a series of letters offered by elephant-driver Brandes

* Tanzi, *I Neologismi in rapporta col Delirio cronico.* Turin, 1890.

† 'Vi vil gjöre det om igjen raditalere,
Men dertil sordres baade Maend og Talere.
J sörger sor Vandflom til Verdensparken,
Jeg laegger med Lyst Torpedo under Arken.'

Observe the purely mystic vapours of this thought. The poet wishes to destroy everything, even the ark which shelters the saved remnants of terrestrial life, but sees himself placed beyond the reach of the destruction, and hence will survive the annihilation of everything else on earth.

for the edification of the adorers of Ibsen, the poet gives conspicuous specimens of his theories.* The state must be destroyed. Unfortunately the Paris Communists bungled this beautiful and fertile idea by clumsy execution. The fight for freedom has not for its end the conquest of liberty, but is its own end. As soon as we believe liberty to be attained, and cease to fight for it, we prove it to be lost to us. The meritorious thing in the fight for liberty is the state of permanent revolt against all existing things which it presupposes. There is nothing fixed and permanent. 'Who warrants me that in the planet Jupiter twice two are not five?' (This remark is an unmistakable manifestation of the insanity of doubt,† which in recent years has been deeply studied.) There is no true marriage. Friends are a costly luxury. 'They have long hindered me from being myself.' The care of the 'I' is the sole task of man. He ought not to allow himself to be diverted from it by any law or any consideration.

These thoughts, expressed by himself in his letters, he also puts into the mouth of his dramatic characters. I have already cited some of Mrs. Alving's and Nora's ego-maniacal and anarchical phrases. In *The Pillars of Society*, Dina says (p. 19): 'If only the people I lived amongst weren't so proper and moral. Every day Hilda and Netta come here that I may take example by them. I can never be as well behaved as they are, and I *won't be*' (p. 44).

But I wanted to know, too, if people over there [in America] are very—very moral . . . if they are so—so proper and well-behaved as here.

JOHAN. Well, at any rate, they're not so bad as people here think.

DINA. You don't understand me. What I want is just that they should not be so very proper and moral (p. 92). I am sick of all this goodness.

MARTHA BERNICK. Oh, how we writhe under this tyranny of custom and convention! Rebel against it, Dina. Do something to defy all this use-and-wont!

In *An Enemy of the People* (p. 278) Stockmann declares: 'I detest leading men . . . they stand in the path of a free man wherever he turns—and I should be glad if we could exterminate them like other noxious animals.' (P. 280) 'The most dangerous enemies of truth and freedom in our midst are the

---

* Georges Brandes, *op. cit.*, pp. 431, 435, 438, etc.

† J. Cotard, *Études sur les Maladies cérébrales et mentales*; Paris, 1891. In this book the *délire des négations* is for the first time recognised and described as a form of melancholia. The Third Congress of French Alienists, which sat at Blois from the 1st to the 6th of August, 1892, devoted almost the whole of its conferences to the insanity of doubt. In a work by F. Raymond and F. L. Arnaud, 'Sur certains cas d'aboulie avec obsession interrogative et trouble des mouvements' (*Annales médico-psychologiques*, 7e séries, t. xvi.), we read, p. 202: 'The invalids occupy themselves with questions intrinsically insoluble, such as the creation, nature, life, etc. Why the trees are green? Why the rainbow has seven colours? Why men are not as tall as houses?' etc.

compact majority. Yes, this execrable compact, Liberal majority—they it is. . . . The majority is never right. . . . The minority is always right.' Where Ibsen does not seriously attack the majority he derides it—*e.g.*, when he entrusts the maintenance of society to grotesque Philistines, or makes self-styled Radicals betray the hypocrisy of their Liberal views. In *An Enemy of the People* (p. 238):

BURGOMASTER. You want to fly in the face of your superiors; and that's an old habit of yours. You can't endure any authority over you.'

In *Rosmersholm* (p. 53):

MORTENSGAARD [the journalist who poses as a Freethinker]. We have plenty of Freethinkers already, Pastor Rosmer—I almost might say too many. What the party requires is a Christian element—something that everyone must respect. That's what we're sadly in need of.

With the same purpose of anarchistic ridicule he always personifies the sense of duty in idiots or contemptible Pharisees only. In *Ghosts* the blockhead, Pastor Manders, thus preaches (p. 142): 'What right have we human beings to happiness? No, we have to do our duty! And your duty was to hold firmly to the man you had once chosen, and to whom you are bound by a holy tie.' In *The Pillars of Society* it is the rogue Bernick who is made to proclaim the necessity of the subordination of the individual to the community (p. 58): 'People must learn to moderate their personal claims if they are to fulfil their duties in the community in which they are placed.' In *An Enemy of the People* the not less pitiable burgomaster sermonizes his brother Stockmann in this fashion (p. 209): 'Anyhow, you've an ingrained propensity for going your own way. And that in a well-ordered community is almost always dangerous. The individual must submit himself to the whole community.'

The trick is evident: to make the conception of the necessary subordination of the individual ridiculous and contemptible, Ibsen appoints as its mouthpieces ridiculous and contemptible beings. On the other hand, it is the characters on whom he lavishes all the wealth of his affection to whom he entrusts the duty of defending rebellion against duty, the aspersion or derision of laws, morals, institutions, self-discipline, and the proclaiming of unscrupulous ego-mania as the sole guide of life.

The psychological roots of Ibsen's anti-social impulses are well known. They are the degenerate's incapacity for self-adaptation, and the resulting discomfort in the midst of circumstances to which, in consequence of his organic deficiencies, he cannot accommodate himself. 'The criminal,' Lombroso*

* Lombroso and B. Laschi, *Le Crime politique et les Révolutions par rapport au Droit, à l'Anthropologie criminelle et à la Science du Gouvernement. Traduit de l'Italien par H. Bouchard.* Paris, 1892, t. i., p. 195.

says, 'in consequence of his neurotic and impulsive nature, and his hatred of the institutions which have punished or imprisoned him, is a perpetual latent political rebel, who finds in insurrection the means not only of satisfying his passions, but of even having them countenanced for the first time by a numerous public.' This utterance is exactly applicable to Ibsen, with the slight change, that he is merely a theoretic criminal, his motor centres not being powerful enough to transmute his anarchically criminal ideas into deeds, and that he finds the satisfaction of his destructive impulses not in the insurrection, but in the activity of dramatic composition.

His incapacity for self-adaptation makes him not only an anarchist, but also a misanthrope, and fills him with a profound weariness of life. The doctrine of *An Enemy of the People* is contained in Stockmann's exclamation (p. 315): 'The strongest man on earth is he who stands most alone'; and in *Rosmersholm* (p. 24), Brendel says: 'I like to take my pleasures in solitude, for then I enjoy them doubly.' The same Brendel subsequently laments (p. 105): 'I am going homewards; I am home-sick for the mighty Void. . . . Peter Mortensgaard never wills more than he can do. Peter Mortensgaard is capable of living his life without ideals. And that, do you see, that is just the mighty secret of action and of victory. It is the sum of the whole world's wisdom. . . . The dark night is best. Peace be with you!' Brendel's words have a peculiar significance, for, on the evidence of Ehrhard,* Ibsen wished to portray himself in that personage. That which is expressed in these passages is the *dégoût des gens* and the *tedium vitæ* of alienists, phenomena never absent in depressed forms of mental alienation.

In addition to his mysticism and ego-mania, Ibsen's extraordinary poverty of ideas indicates another stigma of degeneracy. Superficial or ignorant judges, who appraise an artist's intellectual wealth by the number of volumes he has produced, believe that when they point at the high pile of a degenerate's works they have victoriously refuted the accusation of his infecundity. The well-informed are of course not entrapped by this paltry method of proof. The history of insane literature knows of a large number of cases in which fools have written and published dozens of thick volumes. For tens of years and in feverish haste they must have driven the pen, almost continuously, night and day; but since all

* Auguste Ehrhard, *op. cit.*, p. 412: 'He [Ibsen] assigns himself a *rôle* to acquaint us in a direct manner with his own disillusionings. . . . He presents himself in the fantastic and tormented character of Ulric Brendel. Let us not be deceived by the disguise in which he veils himself. Ulric Brendel, the fool, is no other than Henrik Ibsen, the idealist' (?).

these bulky tomes contain not a single idea of any utility, this restless activity is not to be termed fruitful, in spite of the abundant typographical results. We have seen that Richard Wagner never invented a tale, a figure, a situation; but that he sponged on ancient poems or the Bible. Ibsen has almost as little genuine original creative power as his intellectual relative, and as he, in his beggar's pride, disdains for the most part to borrow from other poets of procreative capacity, or from popular traditions exuberant with life, his poems reveal, when closely and keenly examined, an even greater poverty than those of Wagner. If we do not allow ourselves to be dazzled by the art of variation in a contrapuntist extraordinarily clever in dramatic technique, and follow the themes he so adroitly elaborates, we at once recognise their dreary monotony.

At the central point of all his pieces (with the exception of those of a romantic character, written by him in his first period of pure imitation) stand two figures, always the same and fundamentally one, but having now a negative and now a positive sign, a thesis and antithesis in the Hegelian sense. They are, on the one hand, the human being who obeys his inner law only (that is, his ego-mania), and dauntlessly and defiantly makes a parade of it; and, on the other, the individual who, it is true, really acts in obedience to his ego-mania only, but has not the courage to display it, feigning respect for the law of others and for the notions of the majority—in other words, the avowed and violent anarchist, and his opposite, the crafty and timorously deceitful anarchist.

The avowed ego-maniac is, with one single exception, always embodied in a woman. The exception is Brand. On the contrary, the hypocrite is always a man—again with a single exception, viz., that of Hedda Gabler, who does not personify the idea in its purity, frank anarchism in her nature being mingled with something of hypocrisy. Nora (*A Doll's House*), Mrs. Alving (*Ghosts*), Selma Malsberg (*The League of the Young*), Dina, Martha Hessel, Mrs. Bernick (*The Pillars of Society*), Hedda Gabler, Ellida Wangel (*The Lady from the Sea*), Rebecca (*Rosmersholm*), are one and the same figure, but seen, as it were, at different hours of the day, and consequently in different lights. Some are in the major, others in the minor, key; some are more, others less hysterically deranged; but essentially they are not only similar, but identical. Selma Malsberg (p. 60) cries: 'Bear our unhappiness in common? Am I yet good enough? No. I can no longer keep silent, be a hypocrite and a liar. Now you shall know. . . . O, how you have wronged me! Infamously, all of you! . . . How I have thirsted for a drop of your care! But when I begged for it you repulsed me with a polite joke. You dressed me like a doll. You played with me as with a child. . . . I want to go away from you. . . . Let me, let me.' And Nora (p. 110): 'I lived by performing tricks for you, Torvald. . . . You and your father have sinned greatly against me. It is the fault of you two that nothing has been made of me. I was never happy, only merry. . . . Our house has been nothing but a nursery. Here I have been your doll-wife, just as at home I used to be papa's doll-child. . . . That is why I am going away from you now. . . . I shall now leave your house at once.' Ellida (*The Lady from the Sea*): 'What I want is that we should, of our own free will, release each other. . . . I am not what you took me for. Now you see it yourself. Now we can separate as friends, and freely. . . . Here there is no single thing that attracts me and binds me. I am so absolutely rootless in your house, Wangel.' Selma threatens to leave, Ellida resolves to leave, Nora does leave, Mrs. Alving did leave. (*Ghosts*, p. 144) Pastor Manders: 'All your efforts have been bent towards emancipation and lawlessness. You have never been willing to endure any bond. Everything that has weighed upon you in life you have cast away without care or conscience, like a burden you could throw off at will. It did not please you to be a wife any longer, and you left your husband. You found it troublesome to be a mother, and you sent your child forth among strangers.' Mrs. Bernick was, equally with her double, Mrs. Alving, a stranger in her own house. She, however, does not wish to leave, but to remain and endeavour to win over her husband (p. 112): 'For many years I believed that you had once been mine, and I had lost you again. Now I know that you never were mine; but I shall win you.' Dina (*The Pillars of Society*) cannot leave because she is not yet married, but as becomes her state of maidenhood, she gives her rebellious thoughts this form (p. 93): 'I will be your wife; but first I will work, and become something for myself, just as you are. I will give myself; I will not be taken.' Rebecca (*Rosmersholm*) is also unmarried, yet she runs away (p. 96):

I am going.
ROSMER. Where are you going, Rebecca?
REBECCA. North, by the steamer. It was there I came from.
ROSMER. But you have no ties there now.
REBECCA. I have none here either.
ROSMER. What do you think of doing?
REBECCA. I don't know. I only want to have done with it all.

Now for the antithesis, the hypocritical egoist who satisfies his ego-mania without giving offence to society. This personage presents himself under the names successively of

Torvald Helmer, Consul Bernick, Curate Rörlund, Rector Kroll, Pastor Manders, Burgomaster Stockmann, Werle, and once, to a certain extent, Hedda Gabler, always with the same ideas and the same words. In *A Doll's House* (p. 104, *et seq.*), after his wife's confession, Helmer cries: 'Oh, what an awful awakening! . . . No religion, no morality, no sense of duty. . . . He can publish the whole story; and if he does publish it, perhaps I should be suspected of having been a party to your criminal transactions. . . . I must try to pacify him in one way or the other. The story must be kept secret, cost what it may.' In *Ghosts* Pastor Manders on different occasions expresses himself thus: 'One is certainly not bound to account to everybody for what one reads and thinks within one's own four walls. . . . We must not expose ourselves to false interpretations, and we have no right whatever to give offence to our neighbours. . . . You go and risk your good name and reputation, and nearly succeed in ruining other people's reputation into the bargain. It was unspeakably reckless of you to seek refuge with me. . . . Yes, that is the only thing possible' (to 'hush the matter up') ' . . . yes, family life is certainly not always so pure as it ought to be. But in such a case as you point to' (an incestuous union), 'one can never know.' Rörlund (*The Pillars of Society*): 'See how the family is undermined over there! how a brazen spirit of destruction is attacking the most vital truths! . . . Of course, a tare now and then springs up among the wheat, alas! but we honestly do our best to weed it out. . . . Oh, Dina, you can form no conception of the thousand considerations! When a man is placed as a moral pillar of the society he lives in, why—he cannot be too careful. . . . Oh, Dina, you are so dear to me! Hush! someone is coming. Dina, for my sake, go out to the others. . . . A good book forms a refreshing contrast to what we unhappily see every day in newspapers and magazines.' Consul Bernick, in the same piece: 'Just at this time, when I depend so much on unmixed good feeling, both in the press and in the town. There will be paragraphs in the papers all over the country-side. . . . These newspaper scribblers are always covertly carping at us. . . . I whose mission it is to be an example to my fellow-citizens, must have such things thrown in my teeth! I cannot bear it. It won't do for me to have my name bespattered in this way. . . . I must keep my conscience unspotted. Besides, it will make a good impression on both the press and the public at large when they see that I set aside all personal considerations, and let justice take its course.' Kroll, in *Rosmersholm*: 'Do you ever see the Radical papers? . . . But you've seen, then, I suppose, how these gentlemen of "the people" have been pleased to treat me?

what infamous abuse they've dared to heap upon me?' Werle, in *The Wild Duck*: 'Even if, out of attachment to me, she were to disregard gossip and scandal and all that——?' The Burgomaster, in *An Enemy of the People*: 'If, perhaps, I do watch over my reputation with some anxiety, I do it for the good of the town. . . . Your statement . . . must be kept back for the good of all . . . we will do the best we can quietly; but nothing whatever, not a single word, of this unfortunate business must be made public. . . . And then you have an unhappy propensity for rushing into print upon every possible and impossible matter. You no sooner hit upon an idea than you must write at once some newspaper article or a whole pamphlet about it.' Finally, Hedda Gabler: 'And so you went off perfectly openly? . . . But what do you suppose that people will say about you, then? . . . I so dread a scandal! You should accept for your own sake, or, better still, for the world's sake.'

If all the Nora-like and all the Helmer-like utterances are read successively, an impression must be formed that they are part of the same *rôle;* and this impression is correct, for under all the different names there is only one *rôle*. The same is true of the women who, in contrast to the ego-maniac Nora, unselfishly sacrifice themselves. Martha Bernick, Miss Hessel, Hedwig, Miss Tesman, etc., are always the same figure in different guises. The monotony, moreover, extends to minutest details. Rank's inherited disease is in Oswald's case only carried further. Nora's flight is repeated in almost every piece, and in *The Wild Duck* is travestied in Hjalmar's departure from his house. One feature of this scene appears word for word in all the *réchauffés* of it:

NORA. Here I lay the keys down. The maids know how to manage everything in the house far better than I do.

ELLIDA. If I do go . . . I haven't a key to give up, an order to give. . . . I am absolutely rootless in your house, etc.

In *A Doll's House*, the heroine, who has settled her account with life and is filled with dread of the impending catastrophe, makes Rank play a wild tarantella on the piano, while she dances to it. In *Hedda Gabler*, the heroine is heard 'suddenly playing a wild dance' before she shoots herself. Rosmer says to Rebecca, when the latter makes known her wish to die: 'No; you recoil. You have not the heart to do what *she* dared.' The extortioner Krogstad says to Nora, who threatens to commit suicide: 'Oh, you don't frighten me! An elegant spoilt lady like you. . . . People don't do things of that sort.' Brack says, in response to Hedda Gabler's outburst: 'Rather die! That's what people *say*, but nobody does it!' In much the same words Helmer reproaches his wife Nora with having sacrificed her honour by the forgery, and Pastor Manders upbraids Mrs. Alving for wishing to sacrifice her honour to him. Lona Hessel demands confession from Consul Bernick, and Rebecca from Rosmer, in the same terms. Werle's crime was the seduction of the maidservant Gina. Alving's crime was the seduction of his own maidservant. This pitiable and imbecile self-repetition in Ibsen, this impotence of his indolent brain to wash out the imprint of an idea once painfully elaborated, goes so far that, even in the invention of names for his characters, he is, consciously or unconsciously, under the influence of a reminiscence. In *A Doll's House* we have Helmer; in *The Wild Duck,* Hjalmar; in *The Pillars of Society,* Hilmar, Mrs. Bernick's brother.

Thus Ibsen's drama is like a kaleidoscope in a sixpenny bazaar. When one looks through the peep-hole, one sees, at each shaking of the cardboard tube, new and parti-coloured combinations. Children are amused at this toy. But adults know that it contains only splinters of coloured glass, always the same, inserted haphazard, and united into symmetrical figures by three bits of looking-glass, and they soon tire of the expressionless arabesques. My simile applies not only to Ibsen's plays, but to the author himself. In reality, he is the kaleidoscope. The few paltry bits of glass which for thirty years he has rattled and thrown into cheap mosaic patterns, these are his obsessions. These have existed in his own diseased mind, and have not sprung from observation of the world's drama. The pretended 'realist' knows nothing of real life. He does not comprehend it; he does not even see it, and cannot, therefore, renew from it his store of impressions, ideas, and judgments. The well-known method of manufacturing cannon is to take a tube and pour molten metal round it. Ibsen proceeds in a similar way with his poems. He has a thesis — more accurately, some anarchistic folly; this is the tube. It is now only a question of enveloping this tube with the metal of life's realities. But that lies beyond Ibsen's power. At best he occasionally finds some bits of worn-down horseshoe-nails, or castaway sardine-box, by rummaging among dust-heaps; but this small quantity of metal does not suffice for a cannon. Where Ibsen makes strenuous efforts to produce a picture of actual contemporaneous events, he astounds us with the niggardliness in incidents and human beings evinced by the range of his experience.

Philistine, ultra-provincial, these are no fit words for this. It sinks below the level of the human. The naturalist Huber and Sir John Lubbock have recorded incidents of this sort in their observations of colonies of ants. The small features pinned by Ibsen to his two-legged theses, to give them, at least, as much resemblance to humanity as is possessed by a scarecrow, are borrowed from the society of a hideous hole on the Norwegian coast, composed of drunkards and silly louts, of idiots and crazed hysterical geese, who in their whole life have never formed a clearer thought than: 'How can I get hold of a bottle of brandy?' or 'How can I make myself interesting to men?' The sole characteristic distinguishing these Lövborgs, Ekdals, Oswald Alvings, etc., from beasts is that they are given to drink. The Noras, Heddas, Ellidas, do not tipple, but make up for that by raving so wildly as to require strait-jackets. The great events of their lives are the obtaining of a position in a bank (*A Doll's House*); their catastrophes, that one no longer believes in the articles of their creed (*Rosmersholm*); the loss of an appointment as physician at a watering-place (*An Enemy of the People*); the raked-up rumours of an amorous nocturnal *péché de jeunesse* (*The Pillars of Society*); the frightful crimes darkening, like a thunder-cloud, the lives of these beings and their social circle are an intrigue with a maidservant (*Ghosts, The Wild Duck*); a *liaison* with an itinerant music-hall singer (*An Enemy of the People*); the felling, by mistake, of wood in a state-forest (*The Wild Duck*); the visit to a house of ill-fame after a good dinner (*Hedda Gabler*). It sometimes happens to me to pass a half-hour in the nursery, amusing myself with the chatter and play of the little ones. One day the children by accident saw the arrest of someone in the street. Although their attendant hurried them away from the unpleasant spectacle, they had seen enough of the tumult to be violently excited by it. Some days afterwards on entering the nursery I found them full of the great event, and I became the auditor of the following dialogue:

MATILDA (*aged three years*). Why did they put the gentleman in prison?

RICHARD (*five years old, very dignified and sententious*). It wasn't a gentleman; it was a bad man. They put him in prison because he was wicked.

MATILDA. What had he done then?

RICHARD (*after reflecting a little*). His mamma had said he wasn't to take chocolate; but he did take chocolate. That's why his mamma had him put in prison.

This childish conversation always came into my mind when I lighted, in Ibsen's plays, upon one of his crimes treated with such overawing importance.

We have now made the complete tour of Ibsen. At the risk of being prolix and tedious, I have made copious quotations from his writings, in order that the reader might himself see the matter from which I have formed my judgments.

Ibsen stands before us as a mystic and an ego-maniac, who would willingly prove the world and mankind not worth powder and shot, but who only proves that he has not the faintest inkling of one or the other. Incapable of adapting himself to any state of things whatsoever, he first abuses the state of things in Norway, then that of Europe generally. In no one of his productions is a single thought to be met with belonging to, or having an active influence on, the present age, unless we bestow this honour on his anarchism, which is explained by the diseased constitution of his mind, and his travesties of the least certain results of investigations in hypnotism and telepathy. He is a skilful dramatic technician, and knows how to represent with great poetic power personages in the background, and situations out of the chief current of the piece. This, however, is all that a conscientious and lucid analysis can really find in him. He has dared to speak of his 'moral ideas,' and his admirers glibly repeat the expression. Ibsen's moral ideas! Any reader of the Ibsen drama, who finds in *them* no food for laughter, has truly no sense of humour. He seems to preach apostacy, yet cannot free himself from the religious ideas of confession, original sin, and the Saviour's act of redemption. He sets up egoism and the freedom of the individual from all scruples as an ideal, yet hardly has anyone acted somewhat unscrupulously, but he begins to whimper contritely, and continues until his heart, full to suffocation, has poured itself out in confession; while the only persons with whom he succeeds are women, who sacrifice their individuality to the point of annihilation for the sake of others. He extols every offence against morality as heroism, while he punishes, with nothing less than death, the smallest and stupidest love affair. He uses the words freedom, progress, etc., as a gargle, and in his best works honours lying and stagnation. And all these contradictions appear forsooth not successively as stations on the road of his development, but at one and the same time, and side by side. His French admirer, Ehrhard,* sees this disconcerting fact, and endeavours as best he can to excuse it. His Norwegian interpreter, Henrik Jaeger, on the contrary, asserts with the utmost placidity† that the most prominent characteristic of Ibsen's works is their unity

* Auguste Ehrhard, *op. cit.*, p. 120: 'With admirable frankness Ibsen, in his latest works, points out the abuse which may be made of his ideas [!]. He counsels reformers to extreme prudence, if not to silence. As for himself, he ceases to excite the multitude to the pursuit of moral and social progress [!]; he entrenches himself in his disdainful pessimism, and in aristocratic solitude enjoys the serene vision of future ages.'

† Henrik Jaeger, *Henrik Ibsen og haus Vaerker. En Fremstilling i Grundrids.* Christiania, 1892, *passim.*

(*Enhed*). The Frenchman and the Norwegian were most incautious in not preconcerting, prior to praising their great man in manners so divergent. The single discoverable unity in Ibsen is his faculty of distortion. The point in which he always resembles himself is his entire incapacity to elaborate a single clear thought, to comprehend a single one of the watchwords daubed here and there on to his works, or to deduce the true conclusions from a single one of his premises.

And this malignant, anti-social simpleton, highly gifted, it must be admitted, in the technique of the stage, they have had the audacity to try to raise upon the shield as the great world-poet of the closing century. His partizans have continued to shout, 'Ibsen is a great poet!' until all stronger judgments have become at least hesitating, and feebler ones wholly subjugated. In a recent book on Simon Magus,* there occurs this pretty story: 'Apsethus, the Libyan, wished to become a god. In spite, however, of his most strenuous efforts he could not succeed in satisfying his longing. But, at any rate, he would make the people believe that he had become a god. He therefore collected a large number of parrots, in which Libya abounds, and shut them all in a cage. He kept them so for some time, and taught them to say, "Apsethus is a god." When the birds had learnt this, he opened the cage and set them free. And the birds spread themselves throughout Libya, so that the words penetrated to the Greek settlements. And the Libyans, astonished at the voice of the birds, and not suspecting the trick Apsethus had played, looked upon him as a god.' In imitation of the ingenious Apsethus, Ibsen has taught a few 'comprehensives'—the Brandes, Ehrhards, Jaegers, etc.—the words: 'Ibsen is a modern! Ibsen is a poet of the future!' and the parrots have spread over all the lands, and are chattering with deafening din in books and papers, 'Ibsen is great! Ibsen is a modern spirit!' and imbeciles among the public murmur the cry after them, because they hear it frequently repeated, and because, on such as they, every word uttered with emphasis and assurance makes an impression.

It would certainly be a proof of superficiality to believe that the audacity of his Corybantes alone explains the high place to which Ibsen has been fraudulently elevated. Without question he possesses characteristics by which he could not but act upon his contemporaries.

Firstly, we have his vague phrases and indefinite incidental hints concerning 'the great epoch in which we live,' 'the new era about to dawn,' 'freedom,' 'progress,' etc. These phrases were bound to please all dreamers and drivellers, for they

* G. R. S. Mead, *Simon Magus*. London, 1892.

give free scope to any interpretation, and, in particular, allow the presumption that their author is possessed of modernity and a bold spirit of progress. They are not discouraged by the fact that Ibsen himself makes cruel sport of these 'comprehensives,' when, in *The Wild Duck*, he makes Relling (p. 361) use the word 'demoniac,' while admitting it to be wholly meaningless, just as the poet himself employs his own bunkum about progress and freedom. They are 'comprehensives' precisely because they interpret every passage according to their own sweet will.

Then there is Ibsen's doctrine of the right of the individual to live in accordance with his own law. Is this really his doctrine? This must be denied when, after struggling through his countless contradictions and self-refutations, we see that he treats with peculiar affection the sacrificial lambs, who are all negation of their own 'I,' all suppression of their most natural impulses, all neighbourly love and consideration for others. In any case, his apostles have brought forward anarchistic individualism as the central doctrine of his drama. Ehrhard* sums up this doctrine in these words: 'The revolt of the individual against society. In other words, Ibsen is the apostle of moral autonomy (*autonomie morale*).' Now such a doctrine is surely well fitted to cause ravages among the intellectually indolent or intellectually incapable.

Ehrhard dares to use the expression 'moral autonomy.' In the name of this fine principle Ibsen's critical heralds persuade the youth who gather round him that they have the right to 'live out their lives,' and they smile approvingly when their auditors understand by this term the right to yield to their basest instincts and to free themselves from all discipline. As the scoundrels in Mediterranean ports do with well-dressed travellers, they whisper in the ear of their public, 'Amuse yourselves! Enjoy yourselves! Come with me; I will show you the way!' But to confound 'moral autonomy' with absence of restraint is, on the part of their faith, a monstrous error, and in the corrupters of youth, hoping for the pay of procuration, an infamous deception.

These two notions are not only not synonymous, they are diametrically opposed and mutually exclusive. Liberty of the individual! The right to autonomy! The Ego its own legislator! Who is this 'I' that is to make laws for itself? Who is this 'Self' for whom Ibsen demands the right of autonomy? Who is this free individual? That the entire notion of a Self opposed to the rest of the world as something alien and exclusive is an illusion of consciousness, we have already seen in the chapter on the 'Psychology of Ego-mania,' and I need

* Ehrhard, *op. cit.*, p. 94.

not, therefore, dwell again on the subject in this place. We know that man, like every other complex and highly-developed living being, is a society or state, of simpler, and of simplest, living beings, of cells and cell-systems, or organs, all having their own functions and wants. In the course of the development of life on earth they have become associated, and have undergone changes, in order to be able to perform higher functions than are possible to the simple cell and primitive agglomeration of cells. The highest function of life yet known to us is clear consciousness; the most elevated content of consciousness is knowledge; and the most obvious and immediate aim of knowledge is constantly to procure better conditions of life for the organism, hence to preserve its existence as long as possible, and to fill it with the greatest possible number of pleasurable sensations. In order that the collective organism may be able to perform its task, its constituent parts are bound to submit to a severe hierarchical order. Anarchy in its interior is disease, and leads rapidly to death. The single cell executes its chemical work of decomposition and of integration without troubling itself about aught else. It labours almost for itself alone. Its consciousness is the most limited conceivable; it has hardly any prevision; its own power of adaptation is so minute that if a cell is in the smallest degree less well nourished than its neighbour, it cannot hold its ground against the latter, and is immediately devoured by it.* The differentiated cell-group, or organ, already possesses a wider consciousness, whose seat is its own nerve-ganglia; its function is more complex, and no longer operates wholly, or even chiefly, for its own benefit, but for that of the collective organism; it also has already, I might say, a constitutional influence on the direction of the affairs of the whole organism, asserting itself in the power of the organ to suggest to consciousness presentations prompting the will to acts. The most exalted organ, however, the condensation of all the other organs, is the gray cerebral cortex. It is the seat of clear consciousness. It works least of all for itself, most of all for the commonwealth—*i.e.*, for the whole organism. It is the government of the State. To it come all reports from the interior as well as the exterior; it has to find its way in the midst of all complications; it has to exercise foresight, and to take into consideration not only the immediate effect of an act,

* W. Roux, *Ueber den Kampf der Theile des Organismus.* Leipzig, 1881. Since the appearance of Roux's work, the theory of phagocytose, or the digestion of weaker cells by the stronger, has been considerably extended. This, however, is not the place to cite the numerous communications bearing on this subject which have appeared in the *Zeitschrift für wissenschaftliche Zoologie*, in Virchow's *Archivs*, in the *Biologische Centralblatt*, in the *Zoologische Jahrbücher*, etc.

but also the more remote consequences for the commonwealth. When, therefore, it is a question of the 'I,' the 'Self,' the 'Individual,' it cannot be any subordinate part of the organism which is meant, such as the little toe or the rectum, but only the gray cerebral cortex. To it certainly belongs the right and duty of directing the individual and of prescribing its law. It is consciousness itself. But how does consciousness form its judgments and its decisions? It forms them from representations awakened in it by excitations proceeding from the internal organs and from the senses. If consciousness allows itself to be directed solely by the organic excitations, it seeks to gratify its momentary appetites, on the spot, at the cost of well-being, it injures an organ by favouring the need of another, and it neglects to take into consideration circumstances of the external world which must be dealt with in the interest of the whole organism. Let me give some quite simple illustrations. A man is swimming under water. His cells know nothing of it, and do not trouble themselves about it. They quietly absorb from the blood the oxygen which they need at the moment, and set free, in exchange, carbonic dioxide. The decomposed blood excites the medulla oblongata, and the latter impetuously demands a movement of inspiration. Were the gray cerebral cortex to yield to the perfectly justifiable demand of one organ, and allow an impulse to inspire to proceed to the muscles concerned, the consequence would be the filling of the lungs with water, and death of the entire organism in consequence. Hence consciousness does not obey the demand of the medulla oblongata, and, instead of sending motor impulses to the intercostal muscles and those of the diaphragm, communicates them to the muscles of the arms and legs; instead of breathing under water, the swimmer emerges at the surface. Another instance. A typhoid convalescent feels ragingly hungry. Were he to yield to this desire, he might give himself a momentary satisfaction, but twenty-four hours later he would probably die from perforation of the intestines. Hence his consciousness resists the desire of his organs for the benefit of the whole organism. The cases are, of course, generally much more complex. But it is always the task of consciousness to test the stimuli which it receives from the depths of the organs, to comprise in the motor images which they excite all its earlier experiences, its knowledge, the directions given by the external world, and to disregard the stimuli if the judgments opposed to them are more powerful than they.

Even a perfectly healthy organism quickly goes to rack and ruin if the inhibitive activity of consciousness is not exercised, and if, through this want of exercise, its inhibitive strength becomes atrophied. Cæsarian madness* is nothing but the consequence of the systematic indulgence by consciousness of every demand of the organs. If, however, the organism is not perfectly healthy; if it is degenerate, its ruin is much more speedy and certain when it obeys the urging of its organs, for in such a case these organs are suffering from perversions; they exact satisfactions, not only pernicious in their remote consequences to the whole organism, but immediately so to the organs themselves.

When, therefore, the 'I' is spoken of, which is to have the right to dispose of itself, only the conscious 'Ego' can be meant, the pondering, remembering, observing, comparing intellect, not, however, the sub-'Egos'—unconnected, and for the most part at strife with each other—which are included in sub-consciousness.† The individual is the judging, not the instinctive, human being. Liberty is the capacity of consciousness to derive excitations, not only from the stimuli of the organs, but from those of the senses, and from original memory-images. Ibsen's liberty is the most abject, and always suicidal,‡ slavery. It is the subjugation of judgment to instinct, and the revolt of some single organ against the domination of that power, which has to watch over the well-being of the whole organism. Even so individualistic a philosopher as Herbert Spencer§ says: 'To become fitted for the social state, it is necessary that the man . . . should possess the energy capable of renouncing a small enjoyment of the moment, in order to obtain a greater one in the future.' A healthy man in the full vigour of intellect cannot sacrifice his judgment. The *sacrifizio dell' intelletto* is the only one he cannot afford. If law and custom impose upon him acts which he recognises as absurd because they defeat their end, not only will he have the right, but it will be his duty, to defend reason against nonsense, and knowledge against error.

* Jacoby, *La Folie de Césars.* Paris, 1880.

† Alfred Binet, *Les Altérations de la Personnalité*, Paris, 1892, p. 23, communicates the case (observed by Bourru and Burot, and often cited) of Louis B., who united in himself six different personalities—six 'I's' having not the slightest knowledge of each other, each possessing another character, another memory, other peculiarities of feeling and movement, etc.

‡ 'Suicidal' is here not a mere rhetorical expression. If the tyrannical power of instinct always ends by leading the individual in the long-run to his destruction, it sometimes does this directly. Instinct, namely, may have for its direct object suicide or self-mutilation; and the 'free' man obeying his instinct has then the 'liberty' of mutilating or killing himself, although that so little tallies with his real wish that he seeks in others a protection from himself. See Dr. R. von Krafft-Ebing, *Lehrbuch der gerichtlichen Psychopathologie.* Dritte umgearbeitete Auflage. Stuttgart, 1892, p. 311.

§ Herbert Spencer, *The Individual versus the State.* London, 1884.

But his revolt will always be in the name of judgment, not in the name of instinct.

All this philosophy of self-restraint can, it is true, be preached to healthy human beings only. It has no application to degenerates. Their defective brain and nervous system are not in a state to respond to its demands. The processes within their organs are morbidly intensified. Hence the latter send particularly powerful stimuli to consciousness. The sensory nerves conduct badly. The memory-images in the brain are faint. Perceptions of the external world, representations of anterior experiences, are, therefore, non-existent or too feeble to subdue the stimulus originating in the organs. Such persons can do nought else but follow their desires and impulsions. They are the 'instinctivists' and 'impulsivists' of mental therapeutics. To this species belong the Noras, Ellidas, Rebeccas, Stockmanns, Brands, etc. This company, being dangerous to themselves and to others, require to be put under the guardianship of rational men, or, better still, in lunatic asylums. Such must be the answer to those fools or charlatans who vaunt Ibsen's figures as 'free men' and 'strong personalities,' and with the sweet-sounding tones of a Pied Piper's air on 'self-disposal,' 'moral independence,' and 'living life out,' attract children devoid of judgment heaven knows whither, but in any case to their ruin.

The third feature of Ibsen's drama accounting for his success is the light in which he shows woman. 'Women are the pillars of society,' he makes Bernick say (in *The Pillars of Society*, p. 114). With Ibsen woman has no duties and all rights. The tie of marriage does not bind her. She runs away when she longs for liberty, or when she believes she has cause of complaint against her husband, or when he pleases her a little less than another man. The man who plays the Joseph, and does not comply with the will of Madame Potiphar, does not draw on himself the customary ridicule; he is roundly pronounced a criminal (*Ghosts*, p. 158):

PASTOR MANDERS. It was my greatest victory, Helen—the victory over myself.

MRS. ALVING. It was a crime against us both.

Woman is always the clever, strong, courageous being; man always the simpleton and coward. In every encounter the wife is victorious, and the man flattened out like a pancake. Woman need live for herself alone. With Ibsen she has even overcome her most primitive instinct—that of motherhood—and abandons her brood without twitching an eyelid when the caprice seizes her to seek satisfactions elsewhere. Such abject adoration of woman—a pendant to Wagner's woman-idolatry—such unqualified approval of all feminine depravities, was bound to secure the applause of those women who in the viragoes of Ibsen's drama—hysterical, nymphomaniacal, perverted in maternal instinct*—recognise either their own portrait or the ideal of development of their degenerate imagination. Women of this species find, as a matter of fact, all discipline intolerable. They are by birth *les femmes de ruisseau* of Dumas fils. They are not fit for marriage—for European marriage with one man only. Promiscuous sexual intercourse and prostitution are their most deeply-seated instincts, according to Ferrero† the atavistic form of degeneration in women, and they are grateful to Ibsen for having catalogued, under the fine designations of 'The struggle of woman for moral independence' and 'The right of woman to assert her own personality,' those propensities to which opprobrious names are usually given.

In his fiercely travestied exaggerations of Ibsen's doctrines, entitled *Der Vater*, *Gräfin Julie*, *Gläubiger*, etc., poor Grindberg, whose brain is equally deranged, but who possesses great creative power, goes to the greatest pains to show the absurdity of Ibsen's notions on the nature of woman, her rights, her relations to man. His method, however, is a false one. He will never convince Ibsen by rational arguments that his doctrines are foolish, for they do not spring from his reason, but from his unconscious instincts. His figures of women and their destinies are the poetical expression of that sexual perversion of degenerates called by Krafft-Ebing 'masochism.'‡

* Dr. Ph. Boileau de Castelnau, 'Misopédie ou Lésion de l'Amour de la Progeniture' (*Annales médico-psychologiques*, 3e série, 7e volume, p. 553). In this work the author communicates twelve observations, in which the natural feeling of the mother for her children was transformed by disease into hatred.

† G. Ferrero, 'L'Atavisme de la Prostitution,' *Revue scientifique*, 50e volume, p. 136.

‡ R. von Krafft Ebing, *Psychopathia sexualis*, etc., 7te Auflage, p. 89 (the third edition of this book, from which I have made my previous citations, contains nothing on masochism), and *Neue Forschungen auf dem Gebiete der Psychopathia sexualis eine medicinisch-psychologische Studie*, Zweite umgearbeitete und vermehrte Auflage, Stuttgart, 1891, p. 1 *ff.* Krafft-Ebing gives this explanation of his word (p. 1 *et seq.*): 'By masochism I understand a peculiar perversion of the psychic *vita sexualis*, consisting in this, that the individual seized with it is dominated in his sexual feeling and thought by the idea that he is wholly and unconditionally subjected to the will of a person of the opposite sex, who treats him imperiously, humiliates and maltreats him.' The word is formed from the name Sacher-Masoch, because 'his writings delineate exactly typical pictures of the perverted psychic life of men of this kind' (*Neue Forschungen*, etc., p. 37). I do not look upon this designation as a happy one. Krafft-Ebing himself shows that Zola and, long before him, Rousseau (he might have added Balzac in Baron Hulot in *Parents pauvres*, part i.: *La cousine Bette*) have embodied this condition quite as clearly as Sacher-Masoch. Hence I prefer the designation 'passivism,' proposed by Dimitry Stefanowsky. See *Archives de l'Anthropologie criminelle*, 1892, p. 294.

Masochism is a sub-species of 'contrary sexual sensation.' The man affected by this perversion feels himself, as regards woman, to be the weaker party; as the one standing in need of protection; as the slave who rolls on the ground, compelled to obey the behests of his mistress, and finding his happiness in obedience. It is the inversion of the healthy and natural relation between the sexes. In Sacher-Masoch imperious and triumphant woman wields the knout; in Ibsen she exacts confessions, inflicts inflammatory reprimands, and leaves in a flare of Bengal lights. In essence, Ibsen's heroines are the same as Sacher-Masoch's, though the expression of feminine superiority is a little less brutal. It is remarkable that the women who exult over Ibsen's Nora-types are not shocked by the Hedwigs, Miss Tesmans, and other womanly embodiments of sacrifice, in whom the highly contradictory thoughts and feelings of the confused mystic come to light. But it has been psychologically established that human beings overlook what is in dissonance with their own propinquities, and dwell on that only which is in harmony with them.

Ibsen's feminine clientèle is, moreover, not composed merely of hysterical and degenerate characters, but includes also those women who are leading an unhappy married life, or believe themselves misunderstood, or suffer from the discontent and inner void resulting from insufficient occupation. Clear thinking is not the most prominent quality of this species of woman. Otherwise they would not have found their advocate in Ibsen. Ibsen is not their friend. No one is who, as long as the present order of society exists, attacks the institution of marriage.

A serious and healthy reformer will contend for the principle that marriage should acquire a moral and emotional import, and not remain a lying form. He will condemn the marriage for interest, a dowry or business marriage; he will brand as a crime the action of married couples who feel for some other human being a strong, true love, tested by time and struggle, and yet remain together in a cowardly pseudo-union, deceiving and contaminating each other, instead of honourably separating and contracting genuine connections elsewhere; he will demand that marriage be based on reciprocal inclination, maintained by confidence, respect, and gratitude, consolidated by consideration for the offspring; but he will guard himself from saying anything against marriage itself, this bulwark of the relations between the sexes afforded by definite, permanent duty. Marriage is a high advance from the free copulation of savages. To abandon it and return to primitive promiscuity would be the most profound atavism of degeneracy. Marriage, moreover, was not instituted for the man, but for the woman and the child. It is a protective social institution for the benefit of the weaker part. Man has not yet conquered and humanized his polygamous animal instincts to the same extent as woman. It would for the most part be quite agreeable to him to exchange the woman he possesses for a new one. Departures à la Nora are as a rule not of a nature to frighten him. He could open the door very wide for Nora, and bestow on her his parting benediction with much pleasure. Were it once the law and custom in a society where each was forced to care for himself alone (and needed only to trouble himself about the offspring of others, when it was a question of orphan, abandoned, or begging children) that man and wife should separate as soon as they ceased to be agreeable to each other, it would be the men and not the women who would first make use of the new liberty. Departures à la Nora are perhaps without danger for rich wives, or those eminently capable of acquiring means of support, and hence pecuniarily independent. Such, however, in present society constitute a minute minority. Under Ibsen's code of morals the vast majority of wives would have everything to lose. The severe discipline of matrimony is their bulwark. It obliges the man to take care of the children and of the wife as she declines in years. Hence it should be the true duty of rational wives to declare Ibsen infamous, and to revolt against Ibsenism, which criminally threatens them and their rights. Only through error can women of spirit and indisputable morality join the ranks of Ibsen's followers. It is necessary to enlighten them concerning the range of his doctrines, and in particular concerning their effect on the position of woman, so that they may abandon a company which can never be their own. May he remain surrounded by those only who are spirit of his spirit, that is to say, by hysterical women and masculine masochists, who, with Ehrhard,* believe that 'sound common-sense and optimism are the two destructive principles of all poetry'!

CHAPTER V.

FRIEDRICH NIETZSCHE.

As in Ibsen ego-mania has found its poet, so in Nietzsche it has found its philosopher. The deification of filth by the Parnassians with ink, paint, and clay; the censing among the Diabolists and Decadents of licentiousness, disease, and corruption; the glorification, by Ibsen, of the person who

* Ehrhard, *op. cit.*, p. 88

'wills,' is 'free' and 'wholly himself'—of all this Neitzsche supplies the theory, or something which proclaims itself as such. We may remark, in passing, that this has ever been the task of philosophy. It plays in the race the same *rôle* as consciousness in the individual. Consciousness has the thankless task of discovering rational and elucidatory grounds for the explanation of the impulses and acts springing up in subconsciousness. In the same way philosophy endeavours to find formulæ of apparent profundity for the peculiarities of feeling, thought and deed, having their roots in the history of politics and civilization—in climatic and economic conditions—and to fit them with a sort of uniform of logic. The race lives on, conformably with the historical necessity of its evolution, not troubling itself about a theory of its peculiarities; and philosophy hobbles busily after it, gathers with more or less regularity into its album the scattered features of racial character, and the manifestations of its health and disease; methodically provides this album with a title, paging, and full stop, then places it with a contented air in the library, among the systems of the same regulation size. Genuine truths, real, apposite explanations—these are not contained in philosophical systems. But they furnish instructive evidence of the efforts of the racial consciousness to supply reason, skilfully or clumsily, with the excuses it demands for the unconscious impulses of the race during a given period of time.

From the first to the last page of Nietzsche's writings the careful reader seems to hear a madman, with flashing eyes, wild gestures, and foaming mouth, spouting forth deafening bombast; and through it all, now breaking out into frenzied laughter, now sputtering expressions of filthy abuse and invective, now skipping about in a giddily agile dance, and now bursting upon the auditors with threatening mien and clenched fists. So far as any meaning at all can be extracted from the endless stream of phrases, it shows, as its fundamental elements, a series of constantly reiterated delirious ideas, having their source in illusions of sense and diseased organic processes, which will be pointed out in the course of this chapter. Here and there emerges a distinct idea, which, as is always the case with the insane, assumes the form of an imperious assertion, a sort of despotic command. Nietzsche never tries to argue. If the thought of the possibility of an objection arises in his mind, he treats it lightly, or sneers at it, or curtly and rudely decrees, 'That is false!' (' How much more rational is that . . . theory, for example, represented by Herbert Spencer! . . . According to this theory, good is that which has hitherto always proved itself to be useful, so that it may be estimated as valuable in the highest degree, as valuable in itself. Although this mode of explanation is also false, the explanation itself is at least rational and psychologically tenable.'—*Zur Genealogie der Moral*, 2 Aufl., p. 5. 'This mode of explanation is also false.' Full-stop! Why is it false? Wherein is it false? Because Nietzsche so orders it. The reader has no right to inquire further.) For that matter, he himself contradicts almost every one of his violently dictatorial dogmas. He first asserts something and then its opposite, and both with equal vehemence, most frequently in the same book, often on the same page. Now and then he becomes conscious of the self-contradiction, and then he pretends to have been amusing himself and making sport of the reader. ('It is difficult to be understood, especially when one thinks and lives gangasrotogati, among plain men who think and live otherwise—in other words, kromagati, or under the most favourable circumstances, among mandeigati, who "have the frog's mode of progression"—I just do all I can to make myself hard to understand. . . . But with regard to the "good friends" . . . it is well to accord them in advance room for the play and exercise of misconception; in this way one has still something to laugh at—or wholly to abolish these good friends—and still laugh!'—*Jenseits von Gut und Böse*, 2 Aufl., p. 38. Similarly on p. 51: 'All that is profound loves the mask; the most profound things even hate imagery and parable. Should not *contrast* rather be the right disguise in which the shamefacedness of a god might walk abroad?')

The nature of the individual dogmatic assertions is very characteristic. First of all it is essential to become habituated to Nietzsche's style. This is, I admit, unnecessary for the alienist. To him this sort of style is well known and familiar. He frequently reads writings (it is true, as a rule, unprinted) of a similar order of thought and diction, and he reads them, not for his pleasure, but that he may prescribe the confinement of the author in an asylum. The unprofessional reader, on the contrary, is easily confused by the tumult of phrases. Once, however, he has found his way, once he has acquired some practice in discerning the actual theme among the drums-and-fifes of this ear-splitting, merry-go-round music, and, in the hailstorm of rattling words, that render clear vision almost impossible, has learned to perceive the fundamental thought, he at once observes that Nietzsche's assertions are either commonplaces, tricked out like Indian caciques with feather-crown, nose-ring, and tattooing (and of so mean a kind that a high-school girl would be ashamed to make use of them in a composition-exercise); or bellowing insanity, rambling far beyond the range of rational examination and refutation. I will give only one or two examples of each kind among the thousands that exist:

*Also sprach Zarathustra** ('Thus spake Zoroaster'), 3 Theil, p. 9: 'We halted just by a gateway. "See this gateway, dwarf"—I said again—"it has two faces. Two roads meet here; no one has yet travelled to their end. This long road behind—it lasts an eternity. And that long road in front—that is another eternity. They contradict each other, these roads; they offend each other; and it is here at this gateway that they meet. The name of the gateway is inscribed above, "Now." But if one continues to follow one of them further, and ever further, and ever further, believest thou, dwarf, that these roads eternally contradict each other?"'

Blow away the lather from these phrases. What do they really say? The fleeting instant of the present is the point of contact of the past and the future. Can one call this self-evident fact a thought?

Also sprach Zarathustra, 4 Theil, p. 124 *ff.*: 'The world is deep, and deeper than the day thinks it. Forbear! forbear! I am too pure for thee. Disturb me not! Has my world not become exactly perfect? My flesh is too pure for thy hands. Forbear, thou dull doltish and obtuse day! Is not the midnight clearer? The purest are to be lords of earth, the most unknown, the strongest, the souls of midnight, who are clearer and deeper than each day. . . . My sorrow, my happiness, are deep, thou strange day; but yet am I no God, no Hell of God: deep is their woe. God's woe is deeper, thou strange World! Grasp at God's woe, not at me! What am I! A drunken sweet lyre—a lyre of midnight, a singing frog, understood by none, but who *must* speak before the deaf, O higher men! For ye understand me not! Hence! hence! O youth! O mid-day! O midnight! Now came evening and night and midnight. . . . Ah! ah! how it sighs! how it laughs, how it rattles and gasps, the midnight! How soberly even she speaks, this poetess! Without doubt she has overdrunk her drunkenness! She became too wide awake! She chews the cud! She chews the cud of her woe in dream, the old deep midnight, and still more her joy. For joy, if woe be already deep: joy is deeper still than heart-pain. . . . Woe says, "Away! get thee gone, woe! . . . But joy wishes for a second coming, wishes all to be eternally like itself. Woe says, "Break, bleed, O heart! Wander, limb! Wing, fly! Onward! Upward! Pain!" Well, then! Cheer up! Oh, my old heart! Woe says, "Away!" Ye higher men . . . should ye ever wish for one time twice, should ye ever say, "Thou pleasest me, happiness! Quick! instant! then would

* Persian for Zoroaster.

ye wish *all* back again! All anew, all eternally, all enchained, bound, amorous. Oh! then *loved* ye the world; ye eternities love it eternally and always; and to woe also speak ye: hence, but return! For all pleasure wishes—eternity. All pleasure wishes for the eternity of all things, wishes for honey, for the lees, wishes for drunken midnight, tombs, the consolation of the tears of tombs, gilded twilight—what does pleasure not wish for! She is thirstier, heartier, hungrier, more terrible, more secret than all woe; she wishes for *herself*, she gnaws into herself, the will of the ring struggles in her. . . . Pleasure wishes for the eternity of all things, wishes for deep, deep eternity!'

And the sense of this crazy shower of whirling words? It is that men wish pain to cease and joy to endure! This the astounding discovery expounded by Nietzsche in this demented raving.

The following are obviously insane assertions or expressions:

Die fröhliche Wissenschaft, p. 59: 'What is life? Life—it is the ceaseless rejection from itself of something wishing to die. Life—it is the being cruel and pitiless towards all in us that is weak and old, and not in us alone.'

Persons capable of thought have hitherto always believed that life is the unceasing reception into itself of something agreeable; the rejection of what is used up is only an accompanying phenomenon of the reception of new material. Nietzsche's phrase expresses in a highly mysterious Pythian form the idea of the matutinal visit to a certain place. Healthy men connect with the conception of life the idea rather of the dining-room than that of the privy.

Jenseits von Gut und Böse, p. 92: 'It is a delicacy that God learned Greek when He wished to become an author—and that He did not learn it better.' P. 95: 'Advice in the form of an enigma. If the cord is not to snap . . . thou must first bite on it.'

I have no explanation or interpretation of this profundity to offer.

The passages quoted will have given the reader an idea of Nietzsche's literary style. In the dozen volumes, thick or thin, which he has published it is always the same. His books bear various titles, for the most part characteristically crack-brained, but they all amount to one single book. They can be changed by mistake in reading, and the fact will not be noticed. They are a succession of disconnected sallies, prose and doggerel mixed, without beginning or ending. Rarely is a thought developed to any extent; rarely are a few consecutive pages connected by any unity of purpose or logical argument.

Nietzsche evidently had the habit of throwing on paper with feverish haste all that passed through his head, and when he had collected a heap of snippings he sent them to the printer, and there was a book. These sweepings of ideas he himself proudly terms 'aphorisms,' and the very incoherence of his language is regarded by his admirers as a special merit.* When Nietzsche's moral system is spoken of, it must not be imagined that he has anywhere developed one. Through all his books, from the first to the last, there are scattered only views on moral problems, and on the relation of man to the species and to the universe, from which, taken together, there may be discerned something like a fundamental conception. This is what has been called Nietzsche's philosophy. His disciples, *e.g.*, Kaatz, already cited, and, in addition, Zerbst,† Schellwien,‡ and others, have attempted to give this pretended philosophy a certain form and unity by fishing out from Nietzsche's books a number of passages in some measure agreeing with each other, and placing them in juxtaposition. It is true that it would be possible in this way to set up a philosophy of Nietzsche exactly opposed to the one accepted by his disciples. For, as has been said, each one of Nietzsche's assertions is contradicted by himself in some place or other, and if it be resolved, with barefaced dishonesty, to pay regard to dicta of a definite kind only, and to pass over those in opposition to them, it would be possible at pleasure to extract from Nietzsche a philosophical view or its sheer opposite.

Nietzsche's doctrine, promulgated as orthodox by his disciples, criticises the foundations of ethics, investigates the

* Dr. Hugo Kaatz, *Die Weltanschauung Friedrich Nietzsche:* Erster Theil, 'Cultur und Moral'; Zweiter Theil, 'Kunst und Leben.' Dresden und Leipzig, 1892, 1 Th., p. vi.: 'We are accustomed, especially in matters concerning the deepest problems of thought, to a finished, systematic exposition. . . . There is none of all this in Nietzsche. No single work of his forms a finished whole, or is wholly intelligible without the others. Each book, moreover, is totally wanting in organic structure. Nietzsche writes almost exclusively in aphorisms, which, filling sometimes two lines, sometimes several pages, are complete in themselves, and seldom manifest any direct connection with each other. . . . With proud indifference to the reader, the author has avoided cutting even *one* gap in the hedge with which he has closely surrounded his intellectual creations. Access to him must be gained by fighting,' etc. In spite of its seeming obscurity, Nietzsche has himself given such pointed information concerning his method of work as amounts to an avowal. 'All writing makes me angry or ashamed; for me, writing is a necessity.' 'But why, then, do you write?' 'Yes, my dear friend, let me say it in confidence: I have hitherto found no other means of *ridding* myself of my thoughts.' (The italics are Nietzsche's.) 'And why do you wish to rid yourself of them?' 'Why I wish? Do I so wish? I must.' *Die fröhliche Wissenschaft.* Neue Ausgabe, p. 114.

† Dr. Max Zerbst, *Nein und Ja!* Leipzig, 1892.

‡ Robert Schellwien, *Max Stirner und Friedrich Nietzsche, Erscheinungen des modernen Geister und das Wesen des Menschen.* Leipzig, 1892.

genesis of the concept of good and evil, examines the value of that which is called virtue and vice, both for the individual and for society, explains the origin of conscience, and seeks to give an idea of the end of the evolution of the race, and, consequently, of man's ideal—the 'over man' (*Uebermensch*). I desire to condense these doctrines as closely as possible, and, for the most part, in Nietzsche's own words, but without the cackle of his mazy digressions or useless phrases.

The morality now prevailing 'gilds, deifies, transports beyond the tomb, the non-egoistical instincts of compassion, self-denial, and self-sacrifice.' But this morality of compassion 'is humanity's great danger, the beginning of the end, the halting, the backward-glancing fatigue of the will, turning against life.' 'We need a criticism of moral values. The value of these values is first of all itself to be put in question. There has hitherto been no hesitation in setting up good as of higher value than evil, of higher value in the sense of advancement, utility, prosperity, as regards man in general, including the future of man. What if truth lay in the contrary? What if good were a symptom of retrogression, a danger, a seduction, a poison, a narcotic, by means of which the present should live at the cost of the future? Perhaps more comfortably, less dangerously, but also on a smaller scale, more basely? So that precisely morality would be to blame for the fact that the highest might and splendour possible to the human type should never be attained? So that morality should be precisely the danger of dangers?'

Nietzsche replies to these questions thrown out by him in the preface to the book *Zur Genealogie der Moral*, in developing his idea of the genesis of present morality.

He sees at the beginnings of civilization 'a beast of prey, a magnificent blond brute, ranging about and lusting for booty and victory.' These 'unchained beasts of prey were free from every social restraint; in the innocence of their wild-beast conscience they returned as exultant monsters from a horrible train of murder, incendiarism, rapine, torture, with an arrogance and composure as if nothing but a student's freak had been perpetrated.' The blond beasts constituted the noble races. They fell upon the less noble races, conquered them, and made slaves of them. 'A herd of blond beasts of prey, a race of conquerors and masters, with military organization' (this word 'organization' should be noticed; we shall have to revert to it), 'with the power to organize, unscrupulously placing their fearful paws upon a population perhaps vastly superior in numbers, but still amorphous and wandering—this herd founded the State. The dream is dispelled which made the State begin with a contract. What has he to do with contracts, who can command, who is master by nature, who comes on the scene with violence in deed and demeanour?'

In the State, then, thus established there were a race of masters and a race of slaves. The master-race first created moral ideas. It distinguished between good and evil. Good was with it synonymous with noble; evil with vulgar. All their own qualities they felt as good; those of the subject race as evil. Good meant severity, cruelty, pride, courage, contempt of danger, joy in risk, extreme unscrupulousness. Bad meant 'the coward, the nervous, the mean, the narrow utilitarian, and also the distrustful with his disingenuous glance, the self-abasing, the human hound who allows himself to be abused, the begging flatterer—above all, the liar.' Such is the morality of the masters. The radical meaning of the words now expressing the concept 'good' reveals what men represented to themselves as 'good' when the moral of the masters still held sway. 'The Latin *bonus* I believe I may venture to interpret as "the warrior." Provided I rightly trace *bonus* to a more ancient *duonus* (compare *bellum*, *duellum*, *duenlum*, in which it seems to me that *duonus* is contained). *Bonus*, then, as a man of discord, of disunion (*duo*), as warrior: whereby it is seen what in ancient Rome constituted the "goodness" of a man.'

The subjugated race had naturally an opposing morality—the morality of the slaves. 'The slave looks with envy on the virtues of the powerful; he is sceptical and distrustful; he has the cunning of distrust towards everything honoured by them as "good." Conversely, those qualities were distinguished and glorified which served to ameliorate the existence of sufferers. Here the place of honour is given to compassion, to the complaisant hand ready to help, to the warm heart, to patience, diligence, humility, friendliness, for those are here the most useful qualities, and almost the only means by which the burden of existence can be borne. Slave-morality is essentially utilitarian morality.'

For a certain period the morality of masters and slaves subsisted side by side, or, more accurately, the one above the other. Then an extraordinary event occurred—slave-morality rebelled against master-morality, conquered and dethroned it, and set itself in the place thereof. Then ensued a new valuation of all moral concepts. (In his insane gibberish Nietzsche names this 'transvaluation of values'—*Umwerthung der Werthe*.) That which, under the master-morals, had passed for good was now esteemed bad, and *vice versâ*. Weakness was meritorious, cruelty a crime; self-sacrifice, pity for the pain of others, unselfishness, were virtues. That is what Nietzsche terms 'the slave revolt in morality.' 'The Jews have brought about that marvel of inversion in values. Their prophets have melted into one substance "rich," "godless," "wicked," "violent," "sensual," and for the first time minted the word "world" as one of opprobrium. In this inversion of values (to which belongs the use of the word "poor" as a synonym of "holy" and "friend") lies the importance of the Jewish race.'

The Jewish 'slave-revolt in morality' was an act of vengeance on the master-race which had long oppressed the Jews, and the instrument of this vast vengeance was the Saviour. 'Has not Israel, by the very subterfuge of this "Redeemer," this seeming adversary and destroyer of Israel, attained the final goal of its sublime rage for vengeance? Does it not belong to the secret black art of a truly *grand* policy of vengeance, of a far-seeing, underground, slowly-gripping, fore-planning vengeance, that Israel itself should deny the proper instrument of its vengeance before the whole world, as something deadly inimical, and nail him to the cross, in order that the "entire universe," viz., the enemies of Israel, might unhesitatingly bite at this very bait? And on the other hand, would it be possible, by all the refinement of intellect, to imagine a more dangerous bait? Something that should resemble in enticing, intoxicating, bewildering, corrupting power that symbol of the "holy cross," that awful paradox of a "God on the cross," that mystery of an ineffable final and utmost cruelty, and self-crucifixion of God for the salvation of man? It is at least certain that *sub hoc signo* Israel, with its vengeance and transvaluation of all values, has hitherto triumphed again and again over all other ideals, over all nobler ideals.'

To this passage I would most specially direct the reader's attention, and beg him to transform into mental images all that jingle and clatter of words. Well, then, Israel wished to revenge itself on all the world, and therefore decided to nail the Saviour to the cross, and thereby create a new morality. Who was this Israel which conceived and executed the plan? Was it a parliament, a ministry, a ruler, a popular assembly? Was the plan, before 'Israel' set about realizing it, submitted for general deliberation and resolution? Before the total insanity of this string of words can be distinctly seen, an effort must be made to bring clearly to the mind, in all its actual details, the event described by Nietzsche as premeditated, intended, and of conscious purpose.

Since the Jewish slave-revolt in morality, life, till then a delight, at least for the powerful and bold, or the nobles and masters, has become a torment. Since that revolt the unnatural holds sway, under which man is becoming dwarfed, enfeebled, vulgarized, and gradually degenerate. For the fundamental instinct of the healthy man is not unselfishness and pity, but selfishness and cruelty. 'No injury, violence, exploitation, annihilation, can in itself be a "wrong," inasmuch as life operates *essentially—i.e.*, in its fundamental functions—by injuring, violating, exploiting, annihilating, and is absolutely inconceivable without this character. A legal regulation . . . would be a principle hostile to existence, a destroyer and dissolver of man, a mark of lassitude, a crime against the future of man, a secret way to nothingness.' 'There is at present universal enthusiasm, even in scientific disguises, concerning coming conditions of society in which the exploiting character is to disappear. That sounds in my ears as if someone should promise to invent a life which should abstain from all organic functions. Exploitation does not belong to a decayed, imperfect, or primitive society: it belongs to the *essence* of living things, as organic function.'*

Thus the fundamental instinct of man is cruelty. For this, in the new slave-morality, there is no place. A fundamental instinct, however, is not to be uprooted. It still lives and demands its rights. Hence a series of diversions have been sought for it. 'All instincts, not discharged outwardly, turn inwards. Those terrible bulwarks with which political organization protected itself against the ancient instincts of freedom —and punishments belong to the front line of these bulwarks —had for their result, that all those instincts of the savage roaming at large were turned backwards and against man. Animosity, cruelty, the joy of pursuit, of sudden assault, of change, of destruction—all that turns itself against the possessors of such instincts is the origin of a "bad conscience." The man who, from the absence of external foes and opposition, forced into the oppressive constriction and regularity of custom,

* I refuted this silly sophism before Nietzsche propounded it in the passages above quoted from *Zur Genealogie der Moral*, p. 66, and *Jenseits von Gut und Böse*, p. 228. See *Die conventionellen Lügen der Kulturmenschheit*, 14 Aufl., pp. 211, 212: 'This expression [of Proudhon's, that property is theft] can be regarded as true only from the sophistical standpoint that everything existing exists for itself, and from the fact of its existence derives its right to belong to itself. According to this view, forsooth, a man steals the blade of grass he plucks, the air he breathes, the fish he catches; but, then, the martin, too, is stealing when it swallows a fly, and the grub when it eats its way into the root of a tree; then Nature is altogether peopled by arch-thieves, and, in general, everything steals that lives, *i.e.*, absorbs from without materials not belonging to it, and organically elaborates them, and a block of platinum, which does not even pilfer from the air a little oxygen with which to oxidize itself, would be the sole example of honesty on our globe. No; property resulting from earning, that is, from the exchange of a determined amount of labour for a corresponding amount of goods, is not theft.' If, throughout this passage, 'theft' be substituted for the word 'exploitation,' used by Nietzsche, his sophism is answered.

impatiently tore himself, persecuted, gnawed, hunted, maltreated himself—this animal which it is sought to "tame," wounding himself against the bars of his cage; this destitute creature, consumed with homesickness for the desert, who had to create his adventures, his places of torture, his insecure and dangerous wildernesses, out of his own self—this fool, this yearning, despairing prisoner, became the inventor of the evil conscience.' 'That inclination to self-torture, that retreating cruelty, of the human brute, forced into inner life, scared back into himself, he who had invented evil conscience that he might torture himself, after the natural outlet of this wish to inflict pain was stopped up,' formed also the concept of guilt and sin. 'We are the inheritors of the vivisection of conscience and of animal self-torture of thousands of years.' But all administration of justice, the punishment of 'so-called' criminals, the greater part of art, especially tragedy, are also disguises in which primitive cruelty can still manifest itself.

Slave-morality, with its 'ascetic ideal' of self-suppression and contempt of life, and its tormenting invention of conscience, allowed the slaves, it is true, to take vengeance on their masters; it also subjugated the mighty man-beasts of prey and created better conditions of existence for the small and weak, for the rabble, the gregarious animals; but it has been pernicious to humanity as a whole, because it has prevented the free evolution of precisely the highest human type. 'The collective degeneration of man to that which, in the eyes of socialistic ninnies and blockheads of the present day, seems their "man of the future"—their ideal!—this degeneration and dwarfing of man to the perfect herd animal (or, as they say, to the man of "free society"), this brutalizing of man to the animal pigmy of equal rights and pretensions,' is the destructive work of slave-morality. In order to discipline humanity to supreme splendour we must revert to nature, to the morality of the masters, to the unchaining of cruelty. 'The well-being of the most and the well-being of the fewest are contrary standpoints of valuation; we will leave it to the simplicity of English biologists to hold that the first as such is undoubtedly of the higher value.' 'In opposition to the lying watchword of the privilege of the majority, in opposition to the desire for abasement, humiliation, levelling, for the downward and duskward of man,' we must sound forth 'the watchword of the privilege of the minority.' 'As a last indicator of the other way appeared Napoleon, man most unique, and latest born of all time, and in him the incarnate problem of the aristocratic ideal as such,—Napoleon, that synthesis of the inhuman and the superhuman (*Unmensch und Uebermensch*).'

The intellectually free man must stand 'beyond good and

evil'; these concepts do not exist for him; he tests his impulses and deeds by their value for himself, not by that which they have for others, for the herd; he does that which causes him pleasure, even when, and especially when, it torments and injures—nay, annihilates others; for him holds good the secret rule of life of the ancient Assassins of the Lebanon: 'Nothing is true, all is permissible.' With this new morality, humanity will finally be able to produce the 'over-man.' 'Thus we find, as the ripest fruit on its tree, the sovereign individual, resembling himself alone, freed again from the morality of custom, the autonomous super-moral individual (for "autonomous" and "moral" are mutually exclusive)—in short, the man of his own, independent, long will.' In *Zarathustra* the same thought is expressed dithyrambically: '"Man is wicked," so spake to me in consolation all the wisest. Ah, if only it is yet true to-day! For wickedness is man's best strength. Man must become better and more wicked, so I teach. The greatest wickedness is necessary to the best of the over-man. It might be good for that preacher of little people that he suffered and bore the sins of man. But I rejoice in great sins as my great consolation.'

This is Nietzsche's moral philosophy which (disregarding contradictions) is deduced from separate concordant passages in his various books (in particular *Menschliches Allzumenschliches*, *Jenseits von Gut und Böse*, and *Zur Genealogie der Moral*). I will take it for a moment and subject it to criticism, before confronting it with Nietzsche's own assertions diametrically opposed to it.

Firstly, the anthropological assertion. Man is supposed to have been a freely roaming solitary beast of prey, whose primordial instinct was egoism and the absence of any consideration for his congeners. This assertion contradicts all that we know concerning the beginnings of humanity. The *Kjökkenmöddinge*, or kitchen-middens, of quaternary man, discovered and investigated by Steenstrup, have in some places a thickness of three metres, and must have been formed by a very numerous horde. The piles of horses' bones at Solutré are so enormous as quite to preclude the idea that a single hunter, or even any but a very large body of allied hunters, could have collected and killed such a large number of horses in one place. As far as our view penetrates into prehistoric time, every discovery shows us primitive man as a gregarious animal, who could not possibly have maintained himself if he had not possessed the instincts which are presupposed in life in a community, viz., sympathy, the feeling of solidarity and a certain degree of unselfishness. We find these instincts already existent in apes; and if, in those most like human beings, the ourang-outang and gibbon, these instincts fail to appear, it is to many investigators a sufficient proof that these animals are degenerating and dying out. Hence it is not true that at any time man was a 'solitary, roving brute.'

Now with regard to the historical assertion. At first the morality of masters is supposed to have prevailed, in which every selfish act of violence seemed good, every sort of unselfishness bad. The inverted valuation of deeds and feelings is said to have been the work of a slave-revolt. The Jews are said to have discovered 'ascetic morality,' *i.e.*, the ideal of combating all desires, contempt of all pleasures of the flesh, pity, and brotherly love, in order to avenge themselves on their oppressors, the masters—the 'blond beasts of prey.' I have shown above, the insanity of this idea of a conscious and purposed act of vengeance on the part of the Jewish people. But is it, then, true that our present morality, with its conceptions of good and evil, is an invention of the Jews, directed against 'blond beasts,' an enterprise of slaves against a master-people? The leading doctrines of the present morality, falsely termed Christian, were expressed in Buddhism six hundred years prior to the rise of Christianity. Buddha preached them, himself no slave, but a king's son, and they were the moral doctrines, not of slaves, not of the oppressed, but of the very masterfolk themselves, of the Brahmans, of the proper Aryans. The following are some of the Buddhist moral doctrines, extracted from the Hindu *Dhammapada** and from the Chinese *Fo-sho-hing-tsan-king*:† 'Do not speak harshly to anybody' (*Dhammapada*, verse 133). 'Let us live happily then, not hating those who hate us! Among men who hate us let us dwell free from hatred' (verse 197). 'Because he has pity on all living creatures, therefore is a man called Ariya' (elect) (verse 270). 'Be not thoughtless, watch your thoughts!' (verse 327). 'Good is restraint in all things' (verse 361). 'Him I call indeed a Brâhmaṇa who, though he has committed no offence, endures reproach, bonds, and stripes' (verse 399). 'Be kind to all that lives' (*Fo-sho-hing-tsan-king*, verse 2,024). 'Conquer your foe by force, you increase his enmity; conquer by love, and you will reap no after-sorrow' (verse 2,241). Is that a morality of slaves or of masters? Is it a notion of roving beasts of prey, or that of compassionate, unselfish,

* *The Sacred Books of the East*. Translated by various Oriental scholars, and edited by F. Max Müller. The Clarendon Press, Oxford, 1st series, vol. x.: *Dhammapada*, by F. Max Müller; and *Sutta-Nipâta*, by V. Fausböll.

† *The Sacred Books of the East*, etc., vol. xix.: *Fo-sho-hing-tsan-king*, by Rev. S. Beal.

social human beings? And this notion did not spring up in Palestine, but in India, among the very people of the conquering Aryans, who were ruling a subordinate race; and in China, where at that time no conquering race held another in subjection. Self-sacrifice for others, pity and sympathy, are supposed to be the morality of Jewish slaves. Was the heroic baboon mentioned by Darwin,* after Brehm, a Jewish slave in revolt against the master-folk of blond beasts?

In the 'blond beast' Nietzsche evidently is thinking of the ancient Germans of the migratory ages. They have inspired in him the idea of the roving beast of prey, falling upon weaker men for the voluptuous assuaging of their instincts of bloodthirstiness and destruction. This beast of prey never entered into contracts. 'He who comes on the scene violent in deed and demeanour . . . what has he to do with contracts?' † Very well; history teaches that the 'blond beast,' *i.e.*, the ancient German of the migratory ages, not yet affected by the 'slave-revolt in morals,' was a vigorous but peace-loving peasant, who made war not to riot in murder, but to obtain arable land, and who always first sought to conclude peaceful treaties before necessity forced him to have recourse to the sword.‡ And long before intelligence of the 'ascetic ideal' of Jewish Christianity reached it, the same 'blond beast' developed the conception of feudal fidelity, *i.e.*, the notion that it is most glorious for a man to divest himself of his own 'I'; to know honour only as the resplendence of another's honour, of whom one has become the 'man'; and to sacrifice his life for the chief!

* Charles Darwin, *The Descent of Man, and Selection in Relation to Sex;* London, J. Murray, 1885, p. 101: 'All the baboons had reascended the heights, excepting a young one, about six months old, who, loudly calling for aid, climbed on a block of rock, and was surrounded. Now one of the largest males, a true hero, came down again from the mountain, slowly went to the young one, coaxed him, and triumphantly led him away, the dogs being too much astonished to make an attack.'

† Friedrich Nietsche, *Zur Genealogie der Moral. Eine Streitschrift.* Zweite Auflage. Leipzig, 1892, § 80.

‡ Gustav Freytag, *Bilder aus der deutschen Vergangenheit.* Erster Band, aus dem Mittelalter. Leipzig, 1872, p. 42 *ff.*: 'The Roman Consul, Papirius Carbo . . . denies the strangers [the Cimbrians and Teutons!] the right of sojourn because the inhabitants are enjoying the rights of hospitality of the Romans. The strangers excuse themselves by saying they did not know that the natives were under Roman protection, and they are ready to leave the country. . . . The Cimbrians do not seek a quarrel; they send to Consul Silanus, and urgently entreat him to assign them lands; they are willing in return for it to serve the Romans in time of war. . . . Once more the strangers do not invade Roman territory, but send an embassy to the Senate and repeat the request for an assignment of land. . . . The victorious Germans now sent a fresh embassy to the leader of the other army, for the third time, to sue for peace and ask for land and seed-corn.'

Conscience is supposed to be 'cruelty introverted.' As the man to whom it is an irrepressible want to inflict pain, to torture, and to rend, cannot assuage this want on others, he satisfies it on himself.*

If this were true, then the respectable, the virtuous man, who had never satisfied the pretended primeval instinct of causing pain by means of a crime against others, would be forced to rage the most violently against himself, and would therefore of necessity have the worst conscience. Conversely, the criminal directing his fundamental instinct outwardly, and hence having no need to seek satisfaction in self-rending, would necessarily live in the most delightful peace with his conscience. Does this agree with observation? Has a righteous man who has not given way to the instinct of cruelty ever been seen to suffer from the stings of conscience? Are these not, on the contrary, to be observed in the very persons who have yielded to their instinct, who have been cruel to others, and hence have attained to that satisfaction of their craving, vouchsafed them, according to Nietzsche, by the evil conscience? Nietzsche says,† 'It is precisely among criminals and offenders that remorse is extremely rare; prisons and reformatories are not the brooding places in which this species of worm loves to thrive,' and believes that in this remark he has given a proof of his assertion. But by the commission of crime prisoners have shown that in them the instinct of evil is developed in special strength; in the prison they are forcibly prevented from giving way to their instinct; it is, therefore, precisely in them that self-rending through remorse ought to be extraordinarily violent, and yet among them 'the prick of conscience is extremely rare.' It is evident that Nietzsche's idea is nothing but a delirious sally, and not worthy for a moment to be weighed seriously against the explanation of conscience proposed by Darwin, and accepted by all moral philosophers.‡

Now for the philological argument. Originally, *bonus* is supposed to have read *duonus*, and hence signified 'man of

* *Zur Genealogie der Moral*, p. 79.

† *Ibid.*, p. 73.

‡ Charles Darwin, *op. cit.*, p. 98: 'As soon as the mental faculties had become highly developed, images of all past actions and motives would be incessantly passing through the brain of each individual; and that feeling of dissatisfaction, or even misery, which invariably results . . . from any unsatisfied instinct, would arise as often as it was perceived that the enduring and always present social instinct had yielded to some other instinct, at the time stronger, but neither enduring in its nature nor leaving behind it a very vivid impression. It is clear that many instinctive desires, such as that of hunger, are, in their nature, of short duration, and, after being satisfied, are not readily or vividly recalled,' etc.

discord, disunion (*duo*), warrior.'* The proof of the ancient form *duonus* is offered by '*bellum* = *duellum* = *duen-lum*.' Now *duen-lum* is never met with, but is a free invention of Nietzsche, as is equally *duonus*. How admirable is this method! He invents a word *duonus* which does not exist, and bases it on the word *duen-lum*, which is just as non-existent and equally drawn from imagination. The philology here displayed by Nietzsche is on a level with that which has created the beautiful and convincing series of derivations *alopex* = *lopex* = *pexpix* = *pux* = *fechs* = *fichs* = *Fuchs* (fox). Nietzsche is uncommonly proud of his discovery, that the conception of *Schuld* (guilt) is derived from the very narrow and material conception of *Schulden* (debts).† Even if we admit the accuracy of this derivation, what has his theory gained by it? This would only prove that, in the course of time, the crudely material and limited conception had become enlarged, deepened, and spiritualized. To whom has it ever occurred to contest this fact? What dabbler in the history of civilization does not know that conceptions develop themselves? Did love and friendship, as primitively understood, ever convey the idea of the delicate and manifold states of mind now expressed by these words? It is possible that the first guilt of which men were conscious was the duty of restoring a loan. But neither can guilt, in the sense of a material obligation, arise amongst 'blond brutes,' or 'cruel beasts of prey.' It already presupposes a relation of contract, the recognition of a right of possession, respect for other individuals. It is not possible if there does not exist, on the part of the lender, the disposition to be agreeable to a fellow-creature, and a trust in the readiness of the latter to requite the benefit; and, on the part of the borrower, a voluntary submission to the disagreeable necessity of repayment. And all these feelings are really already morality—a simple, but true, morality—the real 'slave-morality' of duty, consideration, sympathy, self-constraint; not the 'master-morality' of selfishness, cruel violence, unbounded desires! Even if single words like the German *schlecht* (*schlicht*) (bad, plain, or straight) have to-day a meaning the opposite of their original one, this is not to be explained by a fabulous 'transvaluation of values,' but, naturally and obviously, by Abel's theory of the 'contrary double-meaning of primitive words.' The same sound originally served to designate the two opposites of the same concept, appearing, in agreement with the law of association, simultaneously in consciousness, and it was only in the later life of language that the word became the exclusive vehicle of one or other of the contrary concepts. This phenomenon

* *Zur Genealogie der Moral*, p. 9.

† *Ibid.*, p. 48.

has not the remotest connection with a change in the moral valuation of feelings and acts.

Now the biological argument. The prevailing morality is supposed to be admittedly of a character tending to improve the chances of life in gregarious animals, but to be an obstacle to the cultivation of the highest human type, and hence pernicious to humanity as a whole, as it prevents the race from rising to the most perfect culture, and the attainment of its possible ideal. Hence the most perfect human type would, according to Nietzsche, be the 'magnificent beast of prey,' the 'laughing lion,' able to satisfy all his desires without consideration for good or evil. Observation teaches that this doctrine is rank idiocy. All 'over-men' known to history, who gave the reins to their instincts, were either diseased from the outset, or became diseased. Famous criminals—and Nietzsche expressly ranks these among the 'over-men'* — have displayed, almost without exception, the bodily and mental stigmata characterizing them as degenerates, and hence as cripples or atavistic phenomena, not as specimens of the highest evolution and florescence. The Cæsars, whose monstrous selfishness could batten on all humanity, succumbed to madness, which it will hardly be wished to designate as an ideal condition. Nietzsche readily admits that the 'splendid beast of prey' is pernicious to the species, that he destroys and ravages; but of what consequence is the species? It exists for the sole purpose of making possible the perfect development of individual 'over-men,' and of satisfying their most extravagant needs.† But the 'splendid beast of prey' is pernicious to itself; it rages against itself, it even annihilates itself, and yet that cannot possibly be a useful result of highly-trained qualities. The biological truth is, that constant self-restraint is a necessity of existence as much for the strongest as for the weakest. It is the activity of the highest human cerebral centres. If these are not exercised they waste away, *i.e.*, man ceases to be man, the pretended 'over-man' becomes sub-human—in other words, a beast. By the relaxation or breaking up of the mechanism of inhibition in the brain the organism sinks into irrecoverable anarchy in its constituent

* *Jenseits von Gut und Böse*, p. 91: 'The criminal is, often enough, not grown to the level of his deed: he dwarfs and traduces it. The legal defenders of the criminal are rarely artists enough to turn the beautiful terribleness of the deed to the profit of the doer.'

† 'A people is the detour of nature, in order to arrive at six or seven great men.' See also: 'The essential thing in a good and healthy aristocracy is, that it should feel itself to be *not* the function, but the *end* and justification, be it of royalty or of the commonwealth—that it should, therefore, with a good conscience, suffer the sacrifice of a countless number of men who, *for its sake*, must be humbled and reduced to imperfect beings, to slaves, to instruments.'—*Jenseits von Gut und Böse*, p. 226.

parts, and this leads, with absolute certainty, to ruin, to disease, madness and death, even if no resistance results from the external world against the frenzied egoism of the unbridled individual.

What now remains standing of Nietzsche's entire system? We have recognised it as a collection of crazy and inflated phrases, which it is really impossible seriously to seize, since they possess hardly the solidity of the smoke-rings from a cigar. Nietzsche's disciples are for ever murmuring about the 'depth' of his moral philosophy, and with himself the words 'deep' and 'depth' are a mental trick repeated so constantly as to be insufferable.* If we draw near to this 'depth' for the purpose of fathoming it, we can hardly trust our eyes. Nietzsche has not thought out one of his so-called ideas. Not one of his wild assertions is carried a finger's-breadth beneath the uppermost surface, so that, at least, it might withstand the faintest puff of breath. It is probable that the entire history of philosophy does not record a second instance of a man having the impudence to give out as philosophy, and even as profound philosophy, such railway-bookstall humour and such tea-table wit. Nietzsche sees absolutely nothing of the moral problem, around which, nevertheless, he has poured out ten volumes of talk. Rationally treated, this problem can only run thus: Can human actions be divided into good and evil? Why should some be good, the others evil? What is to constrain men to perform the good and refrain from the evil?

Nietzsche would seem to deny the legitimacy of a classification of actions from moral standpoints. 'Nothing is true, all is permissible.'† There is no good and no evil. It is a super-

* The following are a few examples, which could easily be centupled (literally, not hyperbolically)—*Jenseits von Gut und Böse*, p. 63: 'It is the Orient, the deep Orient.' P. 239: 'Such books of depth and of the first importance.' P. 248: 'Deep suffering ennobles.' 'A bravery of taste, resisting all that is sorrowful and deep.' P. 249: 'Any fervour and thirstiness which constantly drives the soul . . . into the bright, the brilliant, the deep, the delicate.' P. 256: 'An odour quite as much of depth [!] as of decay.' P. 260: 'To lie tranquilly like a mirror, so that the deep heaven might reflect itself in them.' P. 262: 'I often think how I may make him [man] stronger, wickeder, and deeper.' *Also sprach Zarathustra*, pt. i., p. 71: 'But thou Deep One, thou sufferest too deeply even from little wounds.' Pt. ii., p. 52: 'Immovable is my depth; but it sparkles with floating enigmas and laughters' (!!). P. 64: 'And this for me is knowledge: all depth should rise—to my height.' P. 70: 'They did not think enough into the depth.' Pt. iii., p. 22: 'The world is deep, and deeper than the day has ever thought it.' Pt. iv., p. 129: 'What says the deep midnight? . . . From a deep dream am I awakened. The world is deep, and deeper than the day thought. Deep in its woe. Joy—deeper still than sorrow of heart. All joy . . . wishes for deep, deep eternity,' etc.

† *Zur Genealogie der Moral*, p. 167.

stition and hereditary prejudice to cling to these artificial notions. He himself stands 'beyond good and evil,' and he invites the 'free spirits' and 'good Europeans' to follow him to this standpoint. And thereupon this 'free spirit,' standing 'beyond good and evil,' speaks with the greatest candour of the 'aristocratic virtues,'* and of the 'morality of the masters.' Are there, then, virtues? Is there, then, a morality, even if it be opposed to the prevailing one? How is that compatible with the negation of all morality? Are men's actions, therefore, not of equal value? Is it possible in these to distinguish good and evil? Does Nietzsche, therefore, undertake to classify them, designating some as virtues—'aristocratic virtues'—others as 'slave actions,' bad for the 'masters, the commanders,' and hence wicked; how, then, can he still affirm that he stands 'beyond good and evil'? He stands, in fact, mid-way between good and evil, only he indulges in the foolish jest of calling that evil which we call good, and *vice-versâ*—an intellectual performance of which every naughty and mischievous child of four is certainly capable.

This first and astounding non-comprehension of his own standpoint is already a good example of his 'depth.' But further. As the chief proof of the non-existence of morality, he adduces what he calls the 'transvaluation of values.' At one time good is said to have been that which is now esteemed evil, and conversely. We have seen that this idea is delirious, and expressed in a delirious way.† But let it be granted that Nietzsche is right; we will for once enter into the folly and accept the 'revolt of slaves in morality' as a fact. What has his fundamental idea gained by this? A 'transvaluation of values' would prove nothing against the existence of a morality, for it leaves the concept of value itself absolutely intact. These, then, are values; but now this, now that, species of action acquires the rank of value. No historian of civilization denies the fact that the notions concerning what is moral or immoral have changed in the course of history, that they con-

* *Jenseits von Gut und Böse*, p. 159: 'Our virtues? It is probable that we, too, still have our virtues, albeit they are no longer the true-hearted and robust virtues for which we hold our grandfathers in honour—though at a little distance.' P. 154: 'The man beyond good and evil, the master of his virtues . . . he ought to be the greatest.' So then, 'beyond good and evil,' and yet having 'virtues'!

† *Zur Genealogie der Moral*, p. 79: 'As a premise to this hypothesis concerning the origin of the evil conscience [through the 'transvaluation of values' and the 'revolt of slaves in morality'] belongs the fact . . . that this transformation was in no way gradual, or voluntary, and did not manifest itself as an organic growing into new conditions, but as a rapture, a leap, a compulsion.' Hence, not only was that good which had previously been evil, but this 'transvaluation' even occurred suddenly, ordered one fine day by authority!

tinually change, that they will change in the future. The recognition of this has become a commonplace. If Nietzsche assumes this to be a discovery of his own, he deserves to be decked with a fool's cap by the assistant teacher of a village school. But how can the evolution, the transformation, of moral concepts in any way contradict the fundamental fact of the existence of moral concepts? Not only does this transformation not contradict these, but it confirms them! They are the necessary premise of this transformation! A modification of moral concepts is evidently possible only if there are moral concepts; but this is exactly the problem—'are there moral concepts?' In spite of all his spouting about the 'transvaluation of values' and the 'revolt of slaves in morality,' Nietzsche never approaches this primary and all-important question.

He contemptuously reproaches slave-morality as being a utilitarian morality,* and he ignores the fact that he extols his 'noble virtues,' constituting the 'morality of masters,' only because they are advantageous for the individual, for the 'over-man.'† Are, then, 'advantageous' and 'useful' not exactly synonymous? Is, therefore, master-morality not every whit as utilitarian as slave-morality? And the 'deep' Nietzsche does not see this! And he ridicules English moralists because they have invented the 'morality of utilitarianism.'‡

He believes he has unearthed something deeply hidden, not yet descried by human eye, when he announces,§ 'What is there that is not called love? Covetousness and love—what different feelings do we experience at each of these words! And yet it might be the same instinct. . . . Our love for our neighbours—is it not an ardent desire for a possession? . . . When we see anyone suffering, we willingly utilize the oppor-

* *Jenseits von Gut und Böse*, p. 232: 'Slave-morality is essentially a utilitarian morality.'

† *Die fröhliche Wissenschaft*, p. 32: 'In reality, however, evil instincts are just as purposive, as conservative of the species, and as indispensable as the good, only they have a different function.' *Zur Genealogie der Moral*, p. 21: 'At the root of all . . . noble races lies the beast of prey . . . this foundation needs from time to time to disburden itself; the animal must out, must hie him back to the desert.' This means that it is essential to his health, and, consequently, of utility to him.

‡ *Zur Genealogie der Moral*, p. 6: 'To what disorders, however, this [democratic] prejudice can give rise, is shown by the infamous [!] case of Buckle. The plebeianism of the modern spirit, which is of English origin, once more breaks forth . . . there.' *Jenseits von Gut und Böse*, p. 212: 'There are truths that are best recognised by mediocre heads. . . . We are driven to this proposition since the intellect of mediocre Englishmen—I may mention Darwin, John Stuart Mill, and Herbert Spencer—acquired preponderance in the mean region of European taste.'

§ *Die fröhliche Wissenschaft*, p. 43.

tunity proferred us to take possession of him; the pitying and charitable man, for example, does this; he also calls by the name "love" the desire for a new possession awakened in him, and takes pleasure in it, as he would in a fresh conquest which beckons him on.' Is it any longer necessary to criticise these silly superficialities? Every act, even seemingly the most disinterested, is admittedly egoistic in a certain sense, *viz.*, that the doer promises himself a benefit from it, and experiences a feeling of pleasure from the anticipation of the expected benefit. Who has ever denied this? Is it not expressly emphasized by all modern moralists?* Is it not implied in the accepted definition of morality, as a knowledge of what is useful? But Nietzsche has not even an inkling of the essence of the subject. To him egoism is a feeling having for its content that which is useful to a being, whom he pictures to himself as isolated in the world, separated from the species, even hostile to it. To the moralist, the egoism which Nietzsche believes himself to have discovered at the base of all unselfishness, is the knowledge of what is useful not alone to the individual, but to the species as well; to the moralist, the creator of the knowledge of the useful is not the individual, but the whole species; to the moralist also egoism is morality, but it is a collective egoism of the species, an egoism of humanity in face of the non-human co-habitants of the earth, and in the face of Nature. The man whom the healthy-minded moralist has before his eyes is one who has attained a sufficiently high development to extricate himself from the illusion of his individual isolation, and to participate in the existence of the species, to feel himself one of its members, to picture to himself the states of his fellow-creatures—*i.e.*, to be able to sympathize with them. This man Nietzsche calls a herd animal —a term which he has found used by all Darwinist writers, but which he seems to regard as his own invention. He endows the word with a meaning of contempt. The truth is that this herding animal—*i.e.*, man, whose 'I' consciousness has expanded itself to the capacity of receiving the consciousness of the species—represents the higher development, to which mental cripples and degenerates, for ever enclosed in their diseased isolation, cannot ascend.

* See, in my novel, *Die Krankheit des Jahrhunderts*, Leipzig, 1889, Band I., p. 140, Schrötter's remarks: 'Egoism is a word. All depends upon the interpretation. Every living being strives for happiness, *i.e.*, for contentment. . . . He [the healthy man] cannot be happy when he sees others suffer. The higher the man's development, the livelier is this feeling. . . . The egoism of these men consists in their seeking out the pain of others and striving to alleviate it, in which, while combating the sufferings of others, they are simply struggling to attain to their own happiness. A Catholic would say of St. Vincent de Paul or of Carlo Borromeo, He was a great saint; I should say of him, He was a great egoist.'

Quite as 'deep' as his discovery of the egoism of all unselfishness is Nietzsche's harangue 'to the teachers of unselfishness.'* The virtues of a man are called good, not in respect of their effects upon himself, but in respect of the effects which we suppose them to have upon ourselves and society. 'The virtues (such as diligence, obedience, chastity, piety, justice), are for the most part pernicious to their possessors.' 'Praise of the virtues is praise of something pernicious to the individual—the praise of instincts which deprive a man of his noblest egoism, and of the power of the highest self-protection.' 'Education . . . seeks to determine the individual to modes of thought and conduct which, if they have become habit, instinct, and passion, rule in him and over him, against his ultimate advantage, but "for the general good."' This is the old silly objection against altruism which we have seen floating in every gutter for the last sixty years. 'If everyone were to act unselfishly, to sacrifice himself for his neighbour, the result would be that everyone would injure himself, and hence humanity, as a whole, would suffer great prejudice.' Assuredly it would, if humanity were composed of isolated individuals in no communication with each other. Whereas it is an organism; each individual always gives to the higher organism only the surplus of his effective force, and in his personal share of the collective wealth profits by the prosperity of the whole organism, which he has increased through his altruistic sacrifice. What would probably be said to the canny householder who should argue in this way against fire insurance: 'Most houses do not burn down. The house-owner who insures himself against fire pays premiums his life long, and as his house will probably never burn down, he has thrown away his money to no purpose. Fire insurance is consequently injurious.' The objection against altruism, that it injures each individual by imposing on him sacrifices for others, is of exactly the same force.

We have had quite enough tests of the 'depth' of Nietzsche and his system. I now wish to point out some of his most diverting contradictions. His disciples do not deny these, but seek to palliate them. Thus Kaatz says: 'He had experienced a change in his own views concerning so many things, that he warned men against the rigid principle which would pass off dishonesty to self as "character." In view of the shifting of opinions as evidenced in Nietzsche's works, it is, of course, only that theory of life to which Nietzsche ultimately wrestled his way that can be taken

* *Die fröhliche Wissenschaft*, p. 48.

into consideration for the purposes of this book.'* This is, however, a conscious and intended falsification of the facts, and the hand of the falsifier ought, like that of the cheater at cards, to be forthwith nailed to the table. The fact is that the contradictions are to be found, not in works of different periods, but in the same book, often on the same page. They are not degrees of knowledge, of which the higher naturally surpass the lower, but opposing, mutually incompatible opinions co-existing in Nietzsche's consciousness, which his judgment is neither capable of reconciling, nor among which it can suppress either term.

In *Also sprach Zarathustra*, pt. iii., p. 29, we read: 'Always love your neighbour as yourself, but first be of those who love themselves.' P. 56: 'And at that time it happened also . . . that his word praised selfishness as blessed, hale, healthy selfishness, which wells forth from the mighty soul.' And p. 60: 'One must learn to love one's self—thus I teach—with a hale and healthy love, so that one bear with one's self, and not rove about.' In opposition to this, in the same book, pt. i., p. 108: 'The degenerating sense which says, "All for me," is to us a horror.' Is this contradiction explained by an 'effort to wrestle his way to an ultimate theory of life'? The contrary assertions are in the same book a few pages apart.

Another example. *Die fröhliche Wissenschaft*, p. 264: 'The absence of personality avenges itself everywhere; an enfeebled, thin, effaced personality, denying and calumniating itself, is worthless for any further good thing, most of all for philosophy.' And only four pages further in the same book, p. 268: 'Have we not been seized with . . . the suspicion of a contrast — a contrast between the world — in which, hitherto, we were at home with our venerations . . . and of another world, which is ourselves . . . a suspicion which might place us Europeans . . . before the frightful alternative, Either—Or: "either do away with your venerations or yourselves."' Here, therefore, he denies, or, at least, doubts, his personality, even if in an interrogative form; on which the reader need not dwell, since Nietzsche 'loves to mask his thoughts, or to express them hypothetically; and to conclude the problems he raises by an interrupted phrase or a mark of interrogation.'†

But he denies his personality, his 'I,' still more decidedly. In the preface to *Jenseits von Gut und Böse*, p. 6, he explains that the foundation of all philosophies up to the present time has been 'some popular superstition,' such as 'the super-

* Dr. Hugo Kaatz, *op. cit.*, Thiel I., Vorrede, p. viii.

† Robert Schellwien, *Max Stierner und Friedrich Nietzsche.* Leipzig 1892, p. 23.

stition of the soul, which, as a superstition of the subjective and the "I," has not ceased, even in our days, to cause mischief.' And in the same book, p. 139, he exclaims: 'Who has not already been sated to the point of death with all subjectivity and his own accursed ipsissimosity!' Hence the 'I' is a superstition! Sated to the point of death with 'subjectivity'! And yet the 'I' should be 'proclaimed as holy.'* And yet the 'ripest fruit of society and morality is the sovereign individual, who resembles himself alone.'† And yet 'a personality which denies itself is no longer good for anything'!

The negation of the 'I,' the designation of it as a superstition, is the more extraordinary, as Nietzsche's whole philosophy—if one may call his effusions by that name—is based only on the 'Ego,' recognising it as alone justifiable, or even as alone existing.

In all Nietzsche's works we shall, it is true, find no more subversive contradiction than this; but a few other examples will show to what extent he holds mutually-destructive opposites in his mind in uncompromising juxtaposition.

We have seen that his last piece of wisdom is: 'Nothing is true; all is permissible.' At bottom all those ethics are repugnant to me which say: 'Do not do this! Renounce! Overcome self!' 'Self-command!' Those ethical teachers who . . . enjoin man to place himself in his own power induce thereby in him a peculiar disease.‡ And now let the following sentences be weighed: 'Through auspicious marriage customs there is a continual increase in the power and pleasure of willing, in the will to command self.' 'Asceticism and puritanism are almost indispensable means of education and ennoblement, if a race desires to triumph over its plebeian origin, and raise itself at some time to sovereignty.' 'The essential and priceless feature of every morality is that it is a long constraint.'§

The characteristic of the over-human is his wish to stand alone, to seek solitude, to flee from the society of the gregarious. 'He should be the greatest who can be the most solitary.' 'The lofty independent spirituality—the will to stand alone. . . .' (*Jenseits von Gut und Böse*, pp. 154, 123.) 'The strong are constrained by their nature to segregate, as much as the feeble are by theirs to aggregate' (*Zur Genealogie der Moral*, p. 149). In opposition to this he teaches

* *Also sprach Zarathustra*, pt. i., p. 84: 'The "thou" is proclaimed holy, but not yet the "I."'

† *Zur Genealogie der Moral*, p. 43.

‡ *Die fröhliche Wissenschaft*, p. 222.

§ *Jenseits von Gut und Böse*, pp. 78, 106.

in other places: 'During the longest interval in the life of humanity there was nothing more terrible than to feel one's self alone' (*Die fröhliche Wissenschaft*, p. 147). Again: 'We at present sometimes undervalue the advantages of life in a community' (*Zur Genealogie der Moral*, p. 59). We? That is a calumny. We value these advantages at their full worth. He alone does not value them who, in expressions of admiration, vaunts 'segregation,' *i.e.*, hostility to the community and contempt of its advantages, as characterizing the strong.

At one time the primitive aristocratic man is the freely-roving, splendid beast of prey, the blond beast; at another: 'these men are rigorously kept within bounds by morality, veneration, custom, gratitude, still more by reciprocal surveillance, by jealousy *inter pares;* and, on the other hand, in their attitude towards each other, inventive in consideration, self-command, delicacy, fidelity, pride, and friendship.' Ay, if these be the attributes of 'blond beasts,' may someone speedily give us a society of 'blond beasts'! But how does 'morality, veneration, self-command,' etc., accord with the 'free-roving' of the splendid beast of prey? That remains an unsolved enigma. It is true that Nietzsche, while making our mouths water by his description, adds to it this limitation: 'Towards what lies beyond, where the stranger, and what is strange, begins, they are not much better than beasts of prey set free' (*Zur Genealogie der Moral*, p. 21). But this is in reality no limitation. Every organized community regards itself, in respect of the rest of the world, as a conjoint unity, and does not accord to the foreigner, the man from without, the same rights as to a member of its own body. Rights, custom, consideration, are not extended to the stranger, unless he knows how to inspire fear and to compel a recognition of his rights. The progress in civilization, however, consists in the very fact that the boundaries of the community are continually enlarged, that which is strange and without rights or claim to consideration being constantly made to recede further and ever further. At first there existed in the horde reciprocal forbearance and right alone; then the feeling of solidarity extended itself to the tribe, the country, state, and race. At the present day there is an international law even in war; the best among contemporaries feel themselves one with all men, nay, no longer hold even the animal to be without rights; and the time will come when the forces of Nature will be the sole strange and external things which may be treated according to man's need and pleasure, and in regard to which he may be the 'freed beast of prey.' The 'deep' Nietzsche is not capable, it is true, of comprehending a state of the case so simple and clear.

At one moment he makes merry over the 'naiveté' of those

who believe in an original social contract (*Zur Genealogie der Moral*, p. 80), and then says (in the same book, p. 149): 'If they' (the strong, the born masters, the 'species of solitary beasts of prey') 'unite, it is only with a view to a collective act of aggression, a collective satisfaction of their volition to exert their power, with much resistance from the individual conscience.' With resistance or without, does not a 'union for the purpose of a collective satisfaction' amount to a relation of contract, the acceptation of which Nietzsche with justice terms 'a naïveté'?

At one time 'agony is something which inspires pity' (*Jenseits von Gut und Böse*, p. 136), and a 'succession of crimes is horrible' (*Zur Genealogie der Moral*, p. 21); and then, again, the 'beauty' of crime is spoken of (*Jenseits von Gut und Böse*, p. 91), and complaint is made that 'crime is calumniated' (the same book, p. 123).

Examples enough have been given. I do not wish to lose myself in minutiæ and details, but I believe that I have demonstrated Nietzsche's own contradiction of every single one of his fundamental assertions, most emphatically of the foremost and most important, viz., that the 'I' is the one real thing, that egoism alone is necessitated and justifiable.

If the conceits which he wildly ejaculates—as it were, shrieks forth—are examined somewhat more closely, we cannot but marvel at the profusion of fabulous stupidity and abecedarian ignorance they contain. It is thus he terms the system of Copernicus (*Jenseits von Gut und Böse*), 'which has persuaded us, against all the senses, that the earth is not immovable,' 'the greatest triumph over the senses hitherto achieved on earth.' Hence he does not suspect that the system of Copernicus has for its basis exact observation of the starry heavens, the movements of the moon and planets, and the position of the sun in the zodiac; that this system was, therefore, the triumph of exact sense-perceptions over sense-illusions—in other words, of attentiveness over fugacity and distraction. He believes that 'consciousness developed itself under the pressure of the need of communication,' for 'conscious thought eventuates in words, *i.e.*, in signs of communication, by which fact the origin of consciousness itself is revealed' (*Die fröhliche Wissenschaft*, p. 280). He does not know, then, that animals without the power of speech also have a consciousness; that it is possible also to think in images, in representations of movement, without the help of a word, and that speech is not added to consciousness until very late in the course of development. The drollest thing is that Nietzsche very much fancies himself as a psychologist, and wishes most particularly to be esteemed as such! According to this profound man, socialism has its roots in the fact that 'hitherto manufacturers and entrepreneurs lack those forms and signs of distinction of the higher races which alone make persons interesting; if they had in look and gesture the distinction of those born noble, there would, perhaps, be no socialism of the masses [! !]. For the latter are at bottom ready for slavery of every kind, on the condition that the higher class constantly legitimizes itself as higher, as born to command, by outward distinction' [! !] (*Die fröhliche Wissenschaft*, p. 68). The concept 'thou oughtest,' the idea of duty, of the necessity of a definite measure of self-command, is a consequence of the fact that 'at all times since men have existed, human herds have also existed, and always a very large number of those who obey relatively to the small number of those who command (*Jenseits von Gut und Böse*, p. 118). Anyone less incapable of thought than Nietzsche will understand that, on the contrary, human herds, those obeying and those commanding, were possible at all, only after and because the brain had acquired the power and capacity to elaborate the idea, 'thou oughtest,' *i.e.*, to inhibit an impulse by a thought or a judgment. The descendant of mixed races 'will on the average be a weaker being' (*Jenseits von Gut und Böse*, p. 120); indeed, the 'European *Weltschmerz*, the pessimism of the nineteenth century, is essentially the consequence of a sudden and irrational mixture of classes'; social classes, however, always 'express differences of origin and of race as well' (*Zur Genealogie der Moral*, p. 142). The most competent investigators are convinced, as we well know, that the crossing of one race with another is conducive to the progress of both, and is 'the first cause of development.'* 'Darwinism, with its incomprehensibly one-sided theory of the struggle for existence,' is explained by Dàrwin's origin. His ancestors were 'poor and humble persons who were only too familiar with the difficulty of making both ends meet. Around the whole of English Darwinism there floats, as it were, the mephitic vapour of English over-population, the odour of humble life, of pinched and straitened circumstances' (*Die fröhliche Wissenschaft*, p. 273). It is presumably known to all my readers that Darwin was a rich man, and was never compelled to follow any profession, and that, for at least three or four generations, his ancestors had lived in comfort.

Nietzsche lays special claim to extraordinary originality. He places this epigraph at the beginning of his *Fröliche Wissenschaft*:

'I live in a house that's my own,
I've never in nought copied no one,
And at every Master I've had my laugh,
Who had not first laughed at himself.'

* C. Lombroso and R. Laschi, *Le Crime politique et les Révolutions*. Paris, 1892, t. i., p. 142.

His disciples believe in this brag, and, with upturned eyes, bleat it after him in sheep-like chorus. The profound ignorance of this flock of ruminants permits them, forsooth, to believe in Nietzsche's originality. As they have never learnt, read, or thought about, anything, all that they pick up in bars, or in their loafings, is naturally new and hitherto non-existent. Anyone, however, who regards Nietzsche relatively to analogous phenomena of the age, will recognise that his pretended originalities and temerities are the greasiest commonplaces, such as a decent self-respecting thinker would not touch with a pair of tongs.

Whenever he rants, Nietzsche is no doubt really original. On such occasions his expressions contain no sense at all, not even nonsense; hence it is impossible to unite them with anything previously thought or said. When, on the contrary, there is a shimmer of reason in his words, we at once recognise them as having their origin in the paradoxes or platitudes of others. Nietzsche's 'individualism' is an exact reproduction of Max Stirner, a crazy Hegelian, who fifty years ago exaggerated and involuntarily turned into ridicule the critical idealism of his master to the extent of monstrously inflating the importance—even the grossly empirical importance—of the 'I'; whom, even in his own day, no one took seriously, and who since then had fallen into well-merited profound oblivion, from which at the present time a few anarchists and philosophical 'fops'—for the hysteria of the time has created such beings—seek to disinter him.* Where Nietzsche extols the 'I,' its rights, its claims, the necessity of cultivating and developing it, the reader who has in mind the preceding chapters of this book will recognise the phrases of Barrès, Wilde, and Ibsen. His philosophy of will is appropriated from Schopenhauer, who throughout has directed his thought and given colour to his language. The complete similarity of his phrases concerning will with Schopenhauer's theory has evidently penetrated to his own consciousness and made him uncomfortable; for, in order to obliterate it, he has placed a false nose of his own invention on the cast he has made, viz., he contests the fact that the motive force in every being is the desire for self-preservation; in his view it is rather the desire for power. This addition is pure child's play. In the lower orders of living beings it is never a 'desire for power,' but always only a desire for self-preservation, that is perceptible; and among men this seeming 'desire for power' can, by anyone

* R. Schellwien, *op. cit.*, p. 7: 'The literary activity of the two thinkers [!] is separated by more than fifty years; but great as may be the difference between them, the agreement is not less, and thus the essential characters of systematic individualism are presented with all the more distinctness.'

but the 'deep' Nietzsche, be traced to two well-known roots—either to the effort to make all organs act to the limit of their functional capacity, which is connected with feelings of pleasure, or to procure for themselves advantages ameliorative of the conditions of existence. But the effort towards feelings of pleasure and better conditions of existence is nothing but a form of the phenomenon of the desire for existence, and he who regards the 'desire for power' as anything different from, and even opposed to, the desire for existence, simply gives evidence of his incapacity to pursue this idea of the desire for existence any distance beyond the length of his nose. Nietzsche's chief proof of the difference between the desire for power and the desire for existence is that the former often drives the desirer to the contemning and endangering, even to the destruction, of his own life. But in that case the whole struggle for existence, in which dangers are continually incurred, and for that matter are often enough sought, would also be a proof that the struggler did not desire his existence! Nietzsche would, indeed, be quite capable of asserting this also.

The degenerates with whom we have become acquainted affirm that they do not trouble themselves concerning Nature and its laws. Nietzsche is not so far advanced in self-sufficiency as Rossetti, to whom it was a matter of indifference whether the earth revolved around the sun or the sun around the earth. He openly avows that this is not a matter of indifference to him; he regrets it; it troubles him, that the earth is no longer the central point of the universe, and he the chief thing on the earth. 'Since Copernicus, man seems to have fallen upon an inclined plane; he is now rolling ever faster away from the central point—whither?—into the nothing? into the piercing feeling of his nothingness?' He is very angry with Copernicus concerning this. Not only with Copernicus, but with science in general. 'All science is at present busied in talking man out of the self-respect he has hitherto possessed, just as if this had been nothing but a bizarre self-conceit' (*Zur Genealogie der Moral*, p. 173). Is this not an echo of the words of Oscar Wilde, who complains that Nature 'is so indifferent' to him, 'so unappreciative,' and that he 'is no more to Nature than the cattle that browse on the slope'?

In other places, again, we find the current of thought and almost the very words of Oscar Wilde, Huysmans, and other Diabolists and Decadents. The passage in *Zur Genealogie der Moral* (p. 171) in which he glorifies art, because 'in it the lie sanctifies itself, and the will to deceive has a quiet conscience on its side,' might be in the chapter in Wilde's *Intentions* on 'The Decay of Lying,' as, conversely, Wilde's aphorisms:

'There is no sin except stupidity.' 'An idea that is not dangerous is unworthy of being called an idea at all.' And his praises of Wainwright, the poisoner, are in exact agreement with Nietzsche's 'morality of assassins,' and the latter's remarks that crime is calumniated, and that the defender of the criminal is 'oftenest not artist enough to turn the beautiful terribleness of the crime to the advantage of the doer.' Again, by way of joke, compare these passages: 'It is necessary to get rid of the bad taste of wishing to agree with many. Good is no longer good when a neighbour says it's good' (Nietzsche, *Jenseits von Gut und Böse*, p. 54), and 'Ah! don't say that you agree with me. When people agree with me, I always feel that I must be wrong' (Oscar Wilde, *Intentions*, p. 202). This is more than a resemblance, is it not? To avoid being too diffuse, I abstain from citing passages exactly resembling these from Huysmans' *A Rebours*, and from Ibsen. At the same time it is unquestionable that Nietzsche could not have known the French Decadents and English Æsthetes whom he so frequently approaches, because his books are in part antecedent to those of the latter; and neither could they have drawn from him, because, perhaps with the exception of Ibsen, it is only about two years since they could have heard as much as Nietzsche's name. The similarity, or rather identity, is not explained by plagiarism; it is explained by the identity of mental qualities in Nietzsche and the other egomaniacal degenerates.

Nietzsche presents a specially droll aspect when he confronts truth, in order to declare it unnecessary, or even to deny its existence. 'Why not rather untruth? And uncertainty? Or even ignorance?' (*Jenseits von Gut und Böse*, p. 3). 'What, after all, are the truths of man? They are the irrefutable errors of man' (*Die fröhliche Wissenschaft*, p. 193). 'The will for truth—that might be a hidden will for death' (*Ibid.*, p. 263). The section of this book in which he deals with the question of truth is entitled by him, 'We the Fearless,' and he prefixes to it, as a motto, Turenne's utterance: 'Thou tremblest, carcass? Thou wouldst tremble much more if thou knewest whither I shall soon lead thee!' And what is this terrible danger into which the fearless one runs with such heroic mien? The investigation of the essence and value of truth. But this investigation is really the A B C of all serious philosophy! The question as to whether objective truth exists at all has been also drawn up by him,* it is true with less blowing of trumpets, beating of drums, and shaking of locks, as its prologue, accompaniment, and conclusion. It is, moreover, highly characteristic that the same dragon-slayer who, with

* See, in my *Paradoxe*, the chapter 'Wo ist die Wahrheit?'

such swaggering and snorting takes up the challenge against 'truth,' finds submissive words of most humble apology when he ventures very gently to doubt the perfection of Goethe in all his pieces. Speaking of the 'viscosity' and 'tediousness' of the German style, he says (*Jenseits von Gut und Böse*, p. 39): 'I may be pardoned for affirming that even Goethe's prose, with its mixture of stiffness and grace, is no exception.' When he timidly criticises Goethe, he begs pardon; his heroic attitude of contempt for death is assumed only when he challenges morality and truth to combat. That is to say, this 'fearless one' possesses the cunning often observed among the insane, and comprehends that there is absolutely no danger in his babbling before the imbeciles composing his congregation, that fabulous philosophical nonsense, at which, on the contrary, they would be much enraged the instant it shocked their æsthetic convictions or prejudices.

Even in the minutest details it is surprising how Nietzsche agrees, word for word, with the other ego-maniacs with whom we have become acquainted. Compare, for example, the phrase in *Jenseits von Gut und Böse*, p. 168, where he vaunts, 'What is really noble in works and in men, their moment of smooth sea and halcyon self-sufficiency, the *golden* and the *cool*,' with Baudelaire's praise of immobility and his enraptured description of a metallic landscape; or the remarks of Des Esseintes, and the side-thrusts at the press put by Ibsen into the mouths of his characters, with the insults continually heaped on newspapers by Nietzsche. 'Great ascetic spirits have an abhorrence of bustle, veneration, newspaper' (*Zur Genealogie der Moral*, p. 113). The cause of 'the undeniably gradual and already tangible desolation of the German mind' lies in being 'all too exclusively nourished on newspapers, politics, beer, and Wagnerian music' (*Ibid.*, p. 177). 'Behold these superfluities! . . . They vomit their bile, and name it a newspaper' (*Also sprach Zarathustra*, pt. i., p. 67). 'Dost thou not see the souls hanging like limp dirty rags? And they make newspapers out of those rags! Hearest thou not how the spirit has here become a play on words? He vomits a loathsome swill of words. And of this swill of words they make newspapers!' (*Ibid.*, pt. iii., p. 37). It would be possible to multiply these examples tenfold, for Nietzsche harks back to every idea with an obstinacy enough to make the most patient reader of sound taste go wild.

Such is the appearance presented by Nietzsche's originality. This 'original' and 'audacious' thinker, imitating the familiar practices of tradesmen at 'sales,' endeavours to palm off as brand new goods the most shop-worn rubbish of great philosophers. His most powerful assaults are directed against doors that stand open. This 'solitary one,' this 'dweller on the highest mountain peaks,' exhibits by the dozen the physiognomy of all decadents. He who is continually talking with the utmost contempt of the 'herd' and the 'herd-animal' is himself the most ordinary herd-animal of all. Only the herd to which he belongs, body and soul, is a special one; it is the flock of the mangy sheep.

Upon one occasion the habitual cunning of the insane has deserted him, and he has himself revealed to us the source of his 'original' philosophy. The passage is so characteristic that I must quote it at length:

'The first impetus, to make known something of my hypotheses concerning the origin of morality, was given me by a clear, tidy, and clever—ay, precocious [!]—little book, in which there was for the first time presented to me an inverted and perverted kind of genealogical hypotheses, the truly *English* kind, and which attracted me with that attractive force possessed by everything contrary, everything antipodal. The title of this little book was *Der Ursprung der moralischen Empfindunger* ["The Origin of Moral Sensations"]; its author, Dr. Paul Rée; the year of its publication, 1877. I have, perhaps, never read anything to which I have in the same measure mentally said "No" as I did to every proposition and every conclusion in this book, yet without anger or impatience. In the previously-mentioned work on which I was at that time engaged [*Menschliches Allzumenschliches*—["Things Human, Things all too Human"], I referred, in season and out of season, to the propositions of that book, not refuting them—what have I to do with refutations?—but, as befits a positive spirit, to substitute the more probable for the improbable, and at times one error for another' (*Zur Genealogie der Moral*, p. 7).

This gives the reader the key to Nietzsche's 'originality.' It consists in simple infantile inversion of a rational train of thought. If Nietzsche imagines that his insane negations and contradictions grew spontaneously in his head, he is really the victim of a self-delusion. His rant may have existed in his mind before he had read Dr. Rée's book. But in that case it had sprung up as a contradiction to other books without his having been so clearly conscious of its origin as after the perusal of Dr. Rée's work. But he pushes the self-delusion to an incredible height, in terming himself a 'positive spirit,' after he has just frankly confessed his method of procedure, viz., that he does not 'refute'—he would not have found that so easy, either—but that 'to every proposition and every conclusion he says 'No!'

This explanation of the source of his 'original' moral

philosophy comprehends in itself a diagnosis, which at once obtrudes on the most short-sighted eye. Nietzsche's system is the product of the mania of contradiction, the delirious form of that mental derangement, of which the melancholic form is the mania of doubt and negation, treated of in the earlier chapters of this work. His *folie des négations* betrays itself also in his peculiarities of language. There is ever in his consciousness a questioning impulse like a mark of interrogation. Of no word is he so fond as of the interrogative 'What?' constantly used by him in the most marvellous connection,* and he makes use *ad nauseam* of the turn of expression, that one should 'say No' to this and that, that this one and that one is a 'No-sayer'—an expression which suggests to him by association the same immeasurably frequent use of the contrary expression, 'say Yes' and 'Yes-sayer.' This 'saying-No' and 'saying-Yes' is in his case a veritable *Paraphasia vesana*, or insane language opposed to usage, as the reader is shown by the examples cited in foot-note.†

* 'With what magic she lays hold of me! What? Has all the world's repose embarked here?' 'What use has the inspired one for wine? What? Give the mole wings and proud imaginings?' 'In so far as he says Yes to this other world, what? must he not then say No to its counterpart, this world?' 'Round about God all becomes—what? perhaps world?' 'A pessimist . . . who says Yes to morality . . . to *læde-neminem*-morality; what? is that really—a pessimist?' 'Fear and pity: with these feelings has man hitherto stood in the presence of woman. What? Is there now to be an end of this?' I will content myself with these examples, but let it be remarked once for all, that all the specimens I adduce here for the purpose of examining Nietzsche's mental state could easily be multiplied a hundredfold, as the characteristic peculiarities recur in him hundreds of times. On one occasion he plainly becomes conscious of this living note of interrogation, always present in his mind as an obsession. In *Also sprach Zarathustra*, pt. iii., p. 55, he calls the passion for rule, 'the flashing note of interrogation by the side of premature answers.' In this connection, this expression has absolutely no sense; but it at once becomes intelligible when it is remembered that the insane are in the habit of suddenly giving utterance to the ideas springing up in their consciousness. Nietzsche plainly *saw* in his mind 'the flashing note of interrogation,' and suddenly, and without transition, spoke of it.

† 'A Greek life, to which he said, No.' 'A pessimist who not merely says, No, wishes No [!] but who . . . does No' [!!]. 'An inward saying No to this or that thing.' 'Free for death, and free in death, a holy No-sayer.' Then as a complementary counterpart: 'Pregnant with lightnings, who say, Yes! laugh Yes!' 'While all noble morality grows to itself out of a triumphant saying Yea.' (He feels himself to be something) 'at least saying Yea to life.' 'To be able to say Yea to yourself, that is . . . a ripe fruit.' (Disinterested wickedness is felt by primitive humanity to be something) 'to which conscience valiantly says Yea.' We see what use Nietzsche makes of his saying 'Nay' and 'Yea.' It stands in the place of nearly all verbs joining subject with predicate. The thought 'I am thirsty' would, by Nietzsche, be thus expressed, 'I say Yes to water.' Instead of 'I am sleepy,' he would say, 'I say Nay to wakefulness,' or, 'I say Yes to bed,' etc. This is the way in which invalids in incomplete aphasia are in the habit of paraphrasing their thoughts.

Nietzsche's assurance that 'without anger or impatience' he 'said No' to all Rée's assertions may be believed. Persons afflicted with the mania of doubt and of denial do not get angry when they question or contradict; they do this under the coercion of their mental derangement. But those among them who are delirious have the conscious intention of making others angry, even if they themselves are not so. On this point Nietzsche allows an avowal to escape him: 'My mode of thought demands a warlike soul, a wish to give pain, a pleasure in saying, No' (*Die fröhliche Wissenschaft*, p. 63) This confession may be compared with the passages from Ibsen: 'You were becoming reckless! In reality that you might anger these affected beings of both sexes here in the town'; and, 'Something shall happen which will be a slap in the face to all this decorum' (*The Pillars of Society*).

The origin of one of the most 'original' of Nietzsche's doctrines, viz., the explanation of conscience as a satisfaction of the instinct of cruelty through inner self-rending, has already been gone into by Dr. Türck, in an excellent little work. He very justly recognises the diseased state of moral aberration at the base of this insane idea,* and continues thus:

'Let us now picture to ourselves a man of this kind, with innate instincts of murder, or in general with 'Anomalies or perversion of the moral feelings' (Mendel); at the same time highly gifted, with the best instruction and an excellent education, reared in the midst of agreeable circumstances, and under the careful . . . nurture of women . . . and occupying at an early age a prominent position in society. It is clear that the better moral instincts must gain such strength as to be able to drive back to the deepest inner depths the bestial instinct of destruction and completely to curb it, yet without wholly annihilating it. It may not, indeed, be able to manifest itself in deeds, but, because it is inborn, the instinct remains in existence as an unfulfilled wish, cherished in the inmost heart . . . as an ardent desire . . . to yield itself up to its cruel lust. But every non-satisfaction of a . . . deeply imprinted instinct has as its consequence pain and inner torment. Now, we men are very much inclined to regard as naturally good and justifiable that which gives us decided pleasure, and conversely to reprobate, as bad and contrary to nature, that which produces pain. Thus, it may happen that an intellectual and highly gifted man, born with perverted instincts, and feeling as torment . . . the non-satisfaction of the instinct, will hit upon the idea of justifying the passion for murder, the extremest egoism . . . as something good, beautiful, and according to Nature, and to char-

* Dr. Hermann Türck, *Fr. Nietzsche und seine philosophischen Irrwege*, Zweite Auflage. Dresden, 1891, p. 7.

acterize as morbid aberration the better opposing moral instincts, manifesting themselves in us as that which we call conscience.

Dr. Türck is right in admitting Nietzsche's innate moral aberration and the inversion in him of healthy instincts. Nevertheless, in the interpretation of the particular phenomena in which the aberration manifests itself, he commits an error, which is explained by the fact that Dr. Türck is seemingly not deeply conversant with mental therapeutics. He assumes that in Nietzsche's mind the evil instincts are in severe conflict with those better notions instilled in him by education, and that he experiences as pain the suppression of his instincts by judgment. That is hardly the true state of the case. It is not necessary that Nietzsche should have the wish to commit murder and other crimes. Not every aberrant person (*pervers*) is subject to impulsions. The perversion may be limited exclusively to the sphere of ideation, and get its satisfaction wholly in ideas. A subject thus affected never gets the notion of transforming his ideas into deeds. His derangement does not encroach upon the centres of will and movement, but carries on its fell work within the centres of ideation. We know forms of sexual perversion in which the sufferers never experience the impulse to seek satisfaction in acts, and who revel only in thought.* This astonishing rupture of the natural connection between idea and movement, between thought and act, this detachment of the organs of will and movement from the organs of conception and judgment which they normally obey, is in itself a proof of deepest disorder throughout the machinery of thought. Incompetent critics eagerly point to the fact that many authors and artists live unexceptionable lives in complete contrast to their works, which may be immoral or contrary to nature, and deduce from this fact that it is unjustifiable to draw from his works conclusions as to the mental and moral Nature of their author. Those who talk in this manner do not even suspect that there are purely mental perversions which are quite as much a mental disease as the impulsions of the 'impulsivists.'

This is obviously the case with Nietzsche. His perversion is of a purely intellectual character, and has hardly ever impelled him to acts. Hence, in his mind there has been no conflict between instincts and the morality acquired by

* B. Ball, *La Folie érotique*, Paris, 1888, p. 50: 'I have sketched for you the picture of chaste love (amorous lunacy, or the erotomania of Esquirol), where the greatest excesses remain enclosed within the limits of feeling, and are never polluted by the intervention of the senses. I have shown you some examples of this delirium pushed to the extreme bounds of insanity, without the intermixture of a single idea foreign to the domain of platonic affection.'

education. His explanation of conscience has quite another source than that assumed by Dr. Türck. It is one of those perverted interpretations of a sensation by the consciousness perceiving it which are so frequently observed. Nietzsche remarks that with him ideas of a cruel kind are accompanied by feelings of pleasure—that they are, as mental therapeutics expresses it, 'voluptuously accentuated.' In consequence of this accompaniment of pleasure he has the inclination to conjure up sensually sensuous representations of that kind, and to dwell on them with enjoyment.* Consciousness then seeks to give some sort of rational explanation of these experiences by assuming cruelty to be a powerful primordial instinct of man, that, since he may not actually commit cruel deeds, he may, at least, take pleasure in the representation of them, and that the rapturous lingering over representations of this kind, man calls his conscience. As I have shown above, it is Nietzsche's opinion that stings of conscience are not the consequence of evil deeds, but appear in men who have never committed any evil. Hence he obviously makes use of the word in a sense quite different from that of current usage, a sense peculiar to himself; he designates by it, simply his revelling in voluptuously accentuated representations of cruelty.

The alienist, however, is familiar with the perversion in which the invalid experiences voluptuous stimulation from acts or representations of a cruel nature. Science has a name for it. It is called Sadism. Sadism is the opposite form of sexual perversion to masochism.† Nietzsche is a sufferer from Sadism in its most pronounced form, only with him it is

* In one passage of *Zur Genealogie der Moral*, p. 132, Nietzsche speaks of the 'species of moral onanists and self-indulgers.' He does not apply the expression to himself; but it was unquestionably suggested by an obscure suspicion of his own state of mind.

† Dr. R. von Krafft-Ebing, *Neue Forschungen*, u. s. w., p. 45 *ff.*: 'The complete contrary of masochism is Sadism. While in the former the subject desires to suffer sorrows, and to feel himself in subjection to violence, in the latter his aim is to cause sorrows, and to exercise violence. . . . All the acts and situations carried out in the active part played by Sadism constitute, for masochism, the object of longing, to be attained passively. In both perversions these acts form a progression from purely symbolic events to grievous misdeeds. . . . Both are to be considered as original psychopathies of mentally abnormal individuals, afflicted in particular with psychic *Hyperæsthesia sexualis*, but also, as a rule, with other anomalies. . . . The pleasure of causing sorrow and the pleasure of experiencing sorrow appear only as two different sides of the same psychic event, the primary and essential principle in which is the consciousness of active and passive subjection respectively.' See Nietzsche, *Also sprach Zarathustra*, pt. i., p. 95: 'Thou art going to women? Forget not the whip!' *Jenseits von Gut und Böse*, p. 186: 'Woman unlearns the fear of man,' and thus 'exposes her most womanly instincts.'

confined to the intellectual sphere alone, and is satisfied by ideal debauchery. I do not wish to dwell too long on this repulsive subject, and will, therefore, quote only a few passages, showing that, in Nietzsche's thought, images of cruelty are without exception accompanied by ideas of a sensual character, and are italicized by him: 'The splendid beast ranging *in its lust* after prey and victory' (*Zur Genealogie der Moral*, p. 21). 'The *feeling of content* at being able, without scruple, to wreak his power on a powerless being, the *voluptuousness de faire le mal pour le plaisir de le faire*, the *enjoyment* of vanquishing' (*Ibid.*, p. 51). 'Do your pleasure, ye wantons; roar for very *lust* and wickedness' (*Die fröhliche Wissenschaft*, p. 226). 'The path to one's own heaven ever leads through the *voluptuousness* of one's own hell' (*Ibid.*, p. 249). 'How comes it that I have yet met no one . . . who knew morality as a problem, and this problem as his personal distress, torment, *voluptuousness*, passion?' (*Ibid.*, p. 264). 'Hitherto he has felt most at ease on earth at the sight of tragedies, bull-fights, and crucifixions; and when he invented hell, behold, that was his heaven on earth. When the great man cries aloud, the little man runs swiftly thither, and his tongue hangs out from his throat for very *lusting*' (*Also sprach Zarathustra*, pt. iii., p. 96), etc. I beg the unprofessional reader particularly to observe the association of the words italicized with those expressing something evil. This association is neither accidental nor arbitrary. It is a psychical necessity, for in Nietzsche's consciousness no image of wickedness and crime can arise without exciting him sexually, and he is unable to experience any sexual stimulation without the immediate appearance in his consciousness of an image of some deed of violence and blood.

Hence the real source of Nietzsche's doctrine is his Sadism. And I will here make a general remark on which I do not desire to linger, but which I should like to recommend to the particular attention of the reader. In the success of unhealthy tendencies in art and literature, no quality of their authors has so large and determining a share as their sexual psychopathy. All persons of unbalanced minds—the neurasthenic, the hysteric, the degenerate, the insane—have the keenest scent for perversions of a sexual kind, and perceive them under all disguises. As a rule, indeed, they are ignorant of what it is in certain works and artists which pleases them, but investigation always reveals in the object of their predilection a veiled manifestation of some *Psychopathia sexualis*. The masochism of Wagner and Ibsen, the Skoptzism of Tolstoi, the erotomania (*folie amoureuse chaste*) of the Diabolists, the Decadents, and of Nietzsche, unquestionably obtain for these authors and tendencies a large, and, at all events, the most sincere and fanatical fraction of their partisans. Works of a sexually psychopathic nature excite in abnormal subjects the corresponding perversion (till then slumbering and unconscious, perhaps also undeveloped, although present in the germ), and give them lively feelings of pleasure, which they, usually in good faith, regard as purely æsthetic or intellectual, whereas they are actually sexual. Only in the light of this explanation do the characteristic artistic tendencies of the abnormals, of which we have proof,* become wholly intelligible. This confounding of æsthetic with sexual feelings is not surprising, for the spheres of these two feelings are not only contiguous, but, as has been proved elsewhere, are for the most part even coincident.† At the base of all oddities of costume, especially that of women, there is hidden an unconscious speculation in something of a sexual-psychopathy, which finds incitation and attraction in the temporary fashion in dress. No professional person has yet viewed fashions from this standpoint. I may not here allow myself so broad a departure from my principal theme. The subject may, however, be most emphatically recommended to the consideration of experts. In the domain of fashions they will make the most remarkable psychiatrical discoveries.

I have devoted very much more space to the demonstration of the senselessness of Nietzsche's so-called philosophical system than the man and his system deserve. It would have been enough simply to refer to the all-sufficient and expressive fact that, after having been repeatedly confined in lunatic asylums, he has for some years past been living as incurably mad in the establishment of Professor Binswanger at Jena—'the right man in the right place.' It is true that a critic is of the opinion that 'it is possible for mental darkness to extinguish the clearest mental light; for this reason its appearance cannot with certitude be urged against the value and accuracy of what anyone has taught before the appearance of his affliction.' The answer to this is that Nietzsche wrote his most important

* Krafft-Ebing, *Neue Forschungen*, u. s. w., p. 108. (A sexual-psychopath thus writes): 'I take great interest in art and literature. Among poets and authors, those attract me most who describe refined feelings, peculiar passions, choice impressions: an artificial (or ultra-artificial) style pleases me. In music, again, the nervous, stimulating music of a Chopin, a Schumann, a Schubert [!], a Wagner, etc., appeal to me most. In art, all that is not only original, but bizarre, attracts me.' P. 128 (another patient): 'I am passionately fond of music, and am an enthusiastic partisan of Richard Wagner, for whom I have remarked a predilection in most of us [sufferers from contrary-sexual-feeling]; I find that this music accords so very much with our nature,' etc.

† See, in *Paradoxe*, the chapter on 'Evolutionistische Æsthetik.'

works between two detentions in a lunatic asylum, and hence not 'before,' but 'after, the appearance of his affliction,' and that the whole question hinges on the kind of mental disease appealed to as proof of the senselessness of any doctrine. It is clear that insanity caused by an accidental lesion of the brain, by a fall, blow, etc., can prove nothing against the accuracy of that which the patient may have taught previous to his accident. But the case is different when the malady is one which has undoubtedly existed in a latent condition from birth, and can with certainty be proved from the works themselves. Then it amply suffices to establish the fact that the author is a Bedlamite, and his work the daubing of a lunatic, and all further criticism, all efforts at rational refutation of individual inanities, become superfluous, and even —at least, in the eyes of those who are competent—a little ridiculous. And this is the case with Nietzsche. He is obviously insane from birth, and his books bear on every page the imprint of insanity. It may be cruel to insist on this fact.* It is, however, a painful, yet unavoidable, duty to refer to it anew, because Nietzsche has become the means of raising a mental pestilence, and the only hope of checking its propagation lies in placing Nietzsche's insanity in the clearest light, and in branding his disciples also with the marks most suited to them, viz., as hysterical and imbecile.

Kaatz† affirms that Nietzsche's 'intellectual seed' is everywhere 'beginning to germinate. Now it is one of Nietzsche's most incisive points which is chosen as the epigraph of a modern tragedy, now one of his pregnant turns of expression incorporated in the established usage of language. . . . At the present time one can . . . read hardly any essay touching even lightly on the province of philosophy, without meeting with the name of Nietzsche.' Now, that is certainly a calumnious

* Dr. Max Zerbst, *Nein und Ja!* Leipzig, 1892, p. vii. : 'It is not impossible that this little book may fall into the hands of some who are nearly connected with the invalid . . . whom every indelicate treatment of his affliction must wound most deeply.' The very last person having the right to complain of indelicate treatment, and to demand consideration, is surely a partisan of Nietzsche's, who claims for himself the 'joy in wishing to cause woe,' and 'grand unscrupulousness' as the 'privilege of the over-man'! Zerbst calls his book a reply to that by Dr. Hermann Türck; but it is nothing but a childishly obstinate and insolent repetition of all Nietzsche's assertions, the insanity of which has been proved by Dr. Türck. It is exceedingly droll that Zerbst, appealing to a feeble compilation by Ziehen, wishes to demonstrate to Türck that there are no such things as psychoses of the will. Now, Türck has not said a single word about a psychosis of the will in Nietzsche; but Nietzsche, indeed, in *Fröhliche Wissenschaft*, p. 270, does speak of 'monstrous disease of the will,' and of a 'will-disease.' Zerbst's objection, therefore, applies, not to Türck, but to his own master—Nietzsche.

† Dr. Hugo Kaatz, *op. cit.*, pt. i., p. 6.

exaggeration. Things are not quite so bad as that. The only 'philosophers' who have hitherto taken Nietzsche's insane drivel seriously are those whom I have above named the 'fops' of philosophy. But the number of these 'fops' is, as a matter of fact, increasing in a disquieting way, and their effrontery surpasses anything ever witnessed.

It is, of course, unnecessary to say that Georges Brandès has numbered himself among Nietzsche's apostles. We know, indeed, that this ingenious person winds himself around every human phenomenon in whom he scents a possible prima-donna, in order to draw from her profit for himself as the impresario of her fame. He gave lectures in Copenhagen on Nietzsche, 'and declaimed in words of enthusiasm about this German prophet, for whom Mill's morality is nothing but a diseased symptom of a degenerate age; this radical "aristocrat," who degrades to the rank of slave-revolts all the great popular movements in history for freedom—the Reformation, the French Revolution, modern socialism—and dares to assert that the millions on millions of individuals composing the nations exist only for the purpose of producing, a few times in each century, a great personality.'*

A series of imitators are eagerly busying themselves to make Nietzsche their model, whether in clearing the throat or in expectorating. His treatise *Schopenhauer als Erzieher* (*Unzeitgemässe Betrachtungen*, 3 *Stück*) has found a monstrous travesty in *Rembrandt als Erzieher*. True, the imbecile author of the latter parody could not imitate Nietzsche's gushing redundancy of verbiage and the mad leaps of the maniac's thought. This symptom of disease it were indeed hardly possible to simulate; but he has appropriated as his own the word-quibbling, the senseless echolalia of his model, and endeavours also stammeringly to imitate, as well as his small means allow, Nietzsche's megalomaniacal and criminal individualism. Albert Kniepf,† another imbecile, has been smitten chiefly by Nietzsche's affected superiority, and with princely mien and gestures struts about in the most diverting manner. He calls himself 'a man of superior taste and more refined feeling'; he speaks contemptuously of the 'profane daily bustle of the masses'; sees 'the world beneath him' and himself 'exalted above the world of the multitude'; he does not wish to 'go into the streets, and squander his wisdom on everyone,' etc., quite in the style of Zarathustra, the dweller

* Ola Hansson, *Das junge Skandinavien. Vier Essays.* Dresden und Leipzig, 1891, p. 12.

† Albert Kniepf, *Theorie der Geisteswerthe.* Leipzig, 1892.

on the highest peaks. The already mentioned Dr. Max Zerbst affects, like Nietzsche, to regard himself as terrible, and to believe that his opponents tremble before him. When he makes them speak he puts whimpering tones into their mouths,* and he enjoys with cruelly superior scorn the mortal fear with which he inspires them. In a maniac this attitude is natural and excites pity. But when a fellow like this Dr. Max Zerbst assumes it, it produces an irresistibly comic effect, and calls to remembrance the young man with the weak legs in *Pickwick,* who 'believes in blood alone,' 'will have blood.' Zerbst dares to utter the words 'natural science' and 'psycho-physiology.' That is an agreement among Nietzsche's disciples: they pass off the insane word-spouter whom they worship for a psycho-physiologist and a physicist! Ola Hansson speaks of Nietzsche's 'psycho-physiological intuition'! and in another place says: 'With Nietzsche, that modern subtle psychologist, who possesses in the highest degree psycho-physical intuition [again], that peculiar power of the end of the nineteenth century, of listening to and spying out all the secret processes and hidden corners in itself,' etc. 'Psycho-physical intuition!' 'Listening to and spying out itself!' Our very eyes deceive us. These men, therefore, have no suspicion of what constitutes 'psycho-physics,' they do not suspect that it is the exact contrary of ancient psychology, which dealt with 'intuition' and introspection, *i.e.*, 'listening to one's self' and 'spying out one's self'; that it patiently counts and mixes with the apparatus in laboratories, and 'spies and listens to,' not itself, but its experimentists and instruments! And such babble of brainless parrots, who chatter in repetition the words they accidentally hear, without comprehending them, is able to make its way in Germany, the creator of the new science of psycho-physiology, the fatherland of Fechner, Weber, Wundt! And no professional has rapped with a ruler the knuckles of these youths, whose fabulous ignorance is surpassed only by their impudence!

But worse still has befallen—something at which all jesting really ceases. Kurt Eisner, who it is true does not agree with Nietzsche's 'philosophy,' is, nevertheless, of the opinion that

* Dr. Max Zerbst, *op. cit.*, p. 1: 'O, this modern natural science! these modern psychologists! Nothing is sacred to them!' 'When a man, grown up in the school of sickly "idealism," confronts a cruel savant of this kind . . . this godless man takes a small piece of chalk in his hand,' etc. He 'turns to the nonplussed idealist,' and the latter somewhat timidly answers, and 'adds something sorrowfully,' whereupon 'the young psychologist replies, with a gentle shrug of his shoulders.' Quite so! the 'cruel,' the 'godless,' the 'shoulder-shrugging' young psychologist is himself, Zerbst; the whimpering idealist, the 'timid' and 'sorrowful' speaker and questioner is his opponent, Dr. Türck!

he has 'bequeathed us some powerful poems,'* and goes so far as to make use of this unheard-of expression: 'Nietzsche's *Zarathustra* is a work of art like *Faust*.' The question first of all obtruding itself is: Has Kurt Eisner at any time read a line of *Faust?* This, I take it, must be answered in the affirmative, for it is hardly conceivable that at this time of day there is in Germany any adult, seemingly able to read and write, into whose hands *Faust* has not fallen at some time or other. Then there remains only one other question: What may Kurt Eisner have understood of *Faust?* To name in the same breath the senseless spirting jet of words of a *Zarathustra* with *Faust* is such a defilement of our most precious poetical treasure that verily if a man of any greater importance than Kurt Eisner had perpetrated it there had been need of an expiatory festival to atone for the insult to Goethe, even as the Church newly consecrates a place of worship when it has been profaned by a sacrilegious act.

Not only in Germany is the Nietzsche gang working mischief; it is also infesting other lands. Ola Hansson,† already mentioned, entertains his Swedish fellow-countrymen most enthusiastically with 'Nietzsche's Poetry' and 'Nietzsche's Midnight Hymn'; T. de Wysewa‡ assures the French, who are not in the position to prove the accuracy of his assertions, that 'Nietzsche is the greatest thinker and most brilliant author produced by Germany in the last generation,' etc.

It has, nevertheless, been reserved to a lady to beat the male disciples of Nietzsche, in the audacious denial of the most openly manifest truth. This feminine partisan of Nietzsche, Lou Salomé, with a cool imperturbability fit to take away the breath of the most callous spectator, turns her back on the fact that Nietzsche has for years been confined in a lunatic asylum, and proclaims with brazen brow that Nietzsche, from the aristocratic contempt of the world belonging to the 'over-human,' has voluntarily ceased to write, and withdrawn himself into solitude. Nietzsche is a man of science and a psycho-physiologist, and Nietzsche keeps silence, because he no longer finds it worth the trouble to speak to the men of the herd; these are the catch-words cried aloud throughout the world by the Nietzsche band. In the face of such a conspiracy against truth, honesty, sound reason, it is not enough to have proved the senselessness of Nietzsche's system, it must

* Kurt Eisner, *Psychopathia spiritualis. Friedrich Nietzsche und die Apostel der Zukunft.* Leipzig, 1892.

† Ola Hansson, *Materialisimen i Skönlitteraturen, Populär-vetenskapliga* [scientific!] *Afhandlingar.* Stockholm, undated, pp. 28, 50. In this brochure Hansson also designates the author of *Rembrandt als Erzieher* as a 'genius'!!

‡ *Revue politique et littéraire*, année 1891.

also be shown that Nietzsche has always been insane, and that his writings are the abortions of frenzy (more exactly, of 'maniacal exaltation').

A few followers of Nietzsche, undoubtedly not fit to hold a candle to Lou Salomé, do not contest the fact of Nietzsche's insanity, but say that he became insane because he withdrew himself too much from men, because he lived too long in the deepest solitude, because his speed of thought was so ruinously, unnaturally rapid. This unheard-of idiocy could circulate throughout the entire German press, and yet not a single newspaper had the gumption to remark that insanity can never be the consequence of solitude and too speedy thought, but that, on the contrary, a propensity for solitude and vertiginously rapid thought are the primary and best known signs of existing insanity, and that this prattle of Nietzsche's partisans is, perhaps, of equal force with the assertion that someone had contracted lung disease through coughing and hæmorrhage!

For Nietzsche's 'anthropophobia' we have the evidence of his biographers, who cite curious examples of it.* His rapid thought, however, is a phenomenon never absent in frenzied madness. That the unprofessional reader may know what he is to understand by this, we will present him with the clinical picture of this form of insanity traced by the hand of the most authoritative masters.

'The acceleration of the course of thought in mania,' says Griesinger, 'is a consequence of the facilitation of the connection between representations, where the patient humbugs, romances, declaims, sings, calls into service all the modes of exteriorizing ideas, rambles incoherently from one topic to another, the ideas hurtling against and overthrowing each other. The same acceleration of ideation is found in certain forms of dementia and in secondary psychical enfeeblement, "with activity produced by hallucinations." The logical concatenations are not in this case intact, as in argumentation and hypochondriacal dementia; or the precipitate sequence of representations no longer follows any law; or, again, only words and sounds devoid of meaning succeed each other with impetuous haste. . . . Thus there arises . . . a ceaseless chase

* 'During his sojourn of several years in the solitary mountainous district of Sils Maria . . . he was in the habit . . . of lying on a verdant neck of land stretching into the lake. One spring he returned, to find, on the consecrated [!] spot, a seat, on which trivial folk might rest, in the place hitherto peopled only by his most secret thoughts and visions. And the sight of this all too human [!] structure was enough to render the beloved place of sojourn insupportable to him. He never set foot there again.'—Ola Hansson, quoted from Dr. Hermann Türck, *op. cit.*, p. 10.

of ideas, in the torrent of which all is borne away in pell-mell flight. The latter conditions appear chiefly in raving madness; at its inception especially, a greater mental vivacity often manifests itself, and cases have been observed where the fact that the patient became witty was a sure sign of the imminence of an attack of frenzy.'*

Still more graphic is the description given by Krafft-Ebing.† 'The content of consciousness is here [in 'maniacal exaltation'] pleasure, psychical well-being. It is just as little induced by events of the external world as the opposite state of psychical pain in melancholia, and is, therefore, referable to an inner organic cause only. The patient literally revels in feelings of pleasure, and declares, after recovery, that never, when in good health, has he felt so contented, so buoyant, so happy, as during his illness. This spontaneous pleasure undergoes powerful increments . . . through the perception by the patient of the facilitated processes of ideation . . . through the intensive accentuation of ideas by feelings of pleasure and by agreeable cœnæstheses, especially in the domain of muscular sensation. . . . In this way the cheerful mood temporarily exalts itself to the height of pleasurable emotions (gay extravagance, exuberance), which find their motor exteriorization in songs, dances, leaps. . . . The patient becomes more plastic in his diction . . . his faculties of conception act more rapidly, and, in accelerated association, he is at once more prompt in repartee, witty and humorous to the point of irony. The plethora of his consciousness supplies him with inexhaustible material for talk, and the enormous acceleration of his ideation, in which there spring up complete intermediate forms with the rapidity of thought, without undergoing exteriorization in speech, causes his current of ideas, in so far as they find expression, to seem rambling. . . . He continually exercises criticism in respect of his own condition, and proves that he is himself aware of his abnormal state by . . . claiming, among other things, that he is only a fool, and that to such everything is permissible. . . . The invalid cannot find words enough to depict his maniacal well-being, his "primordial health."'

And now every individual feature of this picture of disease shall be pointed out in Nietzsche's writings. (I repeat my previous remark, that I am compelled to limit myself in citing examples, but that literally on every page of Nietzsche's writing examples of the same kind are to be found.)

His cœnæstheses, or systemic sensations, continually inspire

* Dr. Wilhelm Griesinger, *op. cit*, p. 77.

† Dr. von Krafft-Ebing, *Lehrbuch der Psychiatrie auf klinischer Grundlage für praktische Aertze und Studirende.* Vierte theilweise umgearbeitete Auflage. Stuttgart, 1890, p. 363 *ff.*

him with presentations of laughter, dancing, flying, buoyancy, generally of movement of the gayest and easiest kind—of rolling, flowing, plunging. 'Let us guard ourselves from immediately making gloomy faces at the word "torture" . . . even there something remains for laughter.' 'We are prepared for a carnival in the grand style, for the most spiritual carnival-laughter and exuberance, for the transcendental height of the most exalted idiocy and Aristophanic derision of the universe. . . . Perhaps if nothing else of to-day has a future, our very laughter still has a future.' 'I would even permit myself to classify philosophers according to the quality of their laughter —up to those capable of golden laughter [!] . . . The gods are jocular. It seems as if, even in sacred deeds, they could not forbear laughing.' 'Ah! what are ye then, ye written and painted thoughts of mine? It is not long since ye were so fantastic, so young and naughty . . . that ye made me sneeze and laugh.' 'Now the world laughs, the dismal veil is rent.' 'It is laughter that kills, not wrath. Come, let us kill the spirit of heaviness!' 'Truly there are beings chaste by nature; they are milder in heart; they laugh more agreeably and copiously than ye. They laugh as well over chastity, and ask, What is chastity?' 'Had He [Jesus Christ] remained in the desert, perhaps He would have learned to live and to love the earth—and to laugh besides.' 'The tension of my cloud was too great; between the laughters of the lightnings I will cast hail-showers into the deep.' 'To-day my shield quivered gently and laughed at me; that is the holy laughter and tremor of beauty.'

It will be seen that in all these cases the idea of laughter has no logical connection with the real thought; it is far rather an accompaniment of his intellection as a basic state, as a chronic obsession, having its explanation in the maniacal excitation of the centres of ideation. It is the same with the presentations of dancing, flying, etc. 'I should only believe in a god who knew how to dance.' 'Truly, Zarathustra is no hurricane and whirlwind; and if he is a dancer, yet is he by no means a dancer of the tarantella.' 'And once upon a time I wished to dance, as I never yet have danced; away over the whole heaven did I wish to dance. . . . Only in the dance do I know of parables for the highest things.' 'I found this blessed security in all things also: that on the feet of chance they preferred—to dance. O thou heaven above me, O pure! O sublime! thy purity is now for me . . . that thou art a dancing-floor for divine chances.' 'Ask of my foot . . . truly after such a rhythm, such a tick-tack, it likes neither to dance nor rest.' 'And, above all, I learned to stand and walk and run and leap and climb and dance.' 'It is a fine fool's jest this, of speech; thanks to it, man dances over all things.' 'O my soul, I taught thee to say "to-day," as well as "once" and "formerly," and to dance thy measure over all the "here" and "there" and "yonder." Thou castest thy glance at my foot crazy for the dance.' 'If my virtue is a dancer's virtue, and I often bounded with both feet into a rapture of golden emerald,' etc.

(' A state of mind he experienced with horror:') 'A perpetual movement between high and deep, and the feeling of high and deep, a constant feeling as if mounting steps, and at the same moment as if reposing on clouds.' 'Is there, indeed, one thing alone that remains uncomprehended by it . . . that only in flight is it touched, beheld, lightened upon?' 'All my will would fly alone, would fly into thee.' 'Ready and impatient to fly, to fly away; that is now my nature.' 'My wise longing cried out from me, and laughed also . . . my great longing, with rushing wings. And often it dragged me forth, and away in the midst of my laughter; then, indeed, I flew shuddering . . . thither, where gods dance, ashamed of all clothes.' 'If I ever spread still heavens above me, and with my own wings flew in my own heavens. . . . If my malice is a laughing malice . . . and if my Alpha and Omega is that all heaviness may become light, all body a dancer, all spirit a bird; and verily that is my Alpha and Omega,' etc.

In the examples hitherto cited the insane ideas are mainly in the sphere of movement. In those that follow it is excitations of the sensorial centres that find expression. Nietzsche has all sorts of illusions of skin-sensibility (cold, warmth, being breathed upon), of sight (lustre, lightning, brightness), of hearing (rushing, roaring), and of smell, which he mixes up in his fugitive ideation. 'I am too hot and burnt with my own thoughts.' 'Ah! ice surrounds me; my hand is burnt by iciness.' 'The sun of my love lay brooding upon me; Zarathustra was stewing in his own juice.' 'Take care that there be honey ready to my hand . . . good, icy-fresh, golden honeycomb.' 'Into the coldest water I plunged with head and heart.' 'There I am sitting . . . lusting for a maiden's round mouth, but still more for maidenly, icy-cold, snow-white, cutting, biting teeth.' 'For I deal with deep problems as with a cold bath—soon into it, soon out of it. . . . Ho! the great cold quickens.' 'Over thy surging sea I blew with the storm that is called spirit; I blew from it all clouds.' 'To their bodies and to their spirits our happiness would be as ice-caverns! and, like strong winds, we will live above them . . . and like a wind will I once blow among them.'

'I am light . . . but this is my loneliness, that I am engirdled with light. . . . I live in my own light; I drink back into myself the flames that break forth from me.'

'Mute over the roaring sea art thou this day arisen for me.' 'They divine nothing from the roaring of my happiness.' 'Sing, and riot in roaring, O Zarathustra!' 'Almost too fiercely for me thou dost gush forth, well-spring of joy . . . too violently doth my heart gush forth to meet thee.' 'My desire now breaks forth from me like a fountain.'

'There is often an odour in her wisdom, as if it came forth from a swamp.' 'Alas! that I should have so long lived in the midst of their noise and foul breath. O blessed stillness around me!' O pure odours around me! 'That was the falsehood in my pity, that in each I saw and smelt what was mind enough for him. . . . With blissful nostrils again I breathed the freedom of the mountain! My nose is at length redeemed from the odour of all that is human!' 'Bad air! bad air! . . . Why must I smell the entrails of a misguided soul?' 'This workshop, where ideals are manufactured, meseems it stinks of nothing but lies.' 'We avoided the rabble . . . the stink of shopkeepers . . . the foul breath.' 'This rabble, that stinks to heaven.' 'O odours pure around me! . . . These crowds of superior men—perhaps they do not smell nice,' etc.

As these examples show, Nietzsche's thought receives its special colouring from his sense illusions, and from the excitation of the centres forming motor presentations, which, in consequence of a derangement of the mechanism of co-ordination, are not transformed into motor impulses, but remain as mere images, without influence on the muscles.

In respect of form, Nietzsche's thought makes the two characteristic peculiarities of madness perceptible: the sole domination of the association of ideas, watched over and restrained by no attention, no logic, no judgment; and the giddy rapidity of the course of ideation.

As soon as any idea whatsoever springs up in Nietzsche's mind, it immediately draws with it into consciousness all presentations related to it, and thus with flying hand he throws five, six, often eight, synonyms on paper, without noticing how overladen and turgid his literary style is thereby rendered: 'The force of a mind measures itself . . . by the degree to which it is obliged to attenuate, veil, sweeten, damp, falsify the truth.' 'We are of the opinion that severity, violence, slavery, danger in the street and in the heart, concealment, stoicism, the tempter's art and devilry of every kind; that all things wicked, fearful, tyrannical, bestial, and serpent-like in man, are of as much service in the elevation of the species "man" as their opposites. He knows . . . on what miserable things the loftiest Becoming has hitherto been shattered,' snapped off, has fallen away, become miserable.' 'In man there is material, fragment, surplus, clay, mud, nonsense, chaos; but in man there is also creator, constructor, hammer-hardness, divinity-of-the-beholder, and the seventh day. . . . That which for this one must be formed, broken, forged, torn, burnt, made red-hot, purified.' 'It would sound more courteous if . . . an unrestrained honesty were related, whispered, and praised (*nachsagte, nachraunte, nachrühmte*) of us.' 'Spit upon the town . . . where swarms all that is rotten, tainted, lustful, gloomy, worm-eaten, ulcerous, seditious.' 'We forebode that it is ever growing downwards into the more attenuated, more debonnaire, more artful, more easy-going, more mediocre, more indifferent, more Chinese, more Christian.' 'All these pallid Atheists, Anti-Christians, Immoralists, Nihilists. Sceptics, Ephectics, Hectics of the mind,' etc.

From these examples, the attentive reader must have already remarked that the tumultuous rush of words frequently results from the merest resemblance in sound. Not seldom does the riot of words degenerate into paltry quibbling, into the silliest pun, into the automatic association of words according to their sound, without regard to their meaning. 'If this turn (*Wende*) in all the need (*Noth*) is called necessity (*Nothwendigkeit*).' 'Thus ye boast (*brüstet*) of yourselves—alas! even without breasts (*Brüste*).' 'There is much pious lick-spittle-work (*Speichel - Leckerie*), baking - of - flattery (*Schmeichel - Bäckerei*) before the Lord of Hosts.' 'Spit upon the great town, which is the great slum (*Abraum*), where all the scum (*Abschaum*) froths together (*zusammanschäumt*).' 'Here and there there is nothing to better (*bessern*), nothing to worsen (*bösern*).' 'What have they to do there, far-seeing (*weitsichtige*), far-seeking (*weit-süchtige*) eyes?' 'In such processions (*Zügen*) goats (*Ziegen*) and geese, and the strong-headed and the wrong-headed (*Kreuz und Querköpfe*), were always running on before. . . . O, Will, turn of all need (*Wende aller Noth*)! O thou my necessity (*Nothwendigkeit*)!' 'Thus I look afar over the creeping and swarming of little gray waves (*Wellen*) and wills (*Willen*).' 'This seeking (*Suchen*) for my home was the visitation (*Heimsuchung*) of me.' 'Did not the world become perfect, round and ripe (*reif*)? O for the golden round ring (*Reif*)!' 'Yawns (*Klafft*) the abyss here too? Yelps (*Kläfft*) the dog of hell here too?' 'It stultifies, brutalizes (*verthiert*), and transforms into a bull (*verstiert*).' 'Life is at least (*mindestens*), at the mildest (*mildestens*), an exploiting.' 'Whom I deemed transformed akin to myself (*verwandt-verwandelt*),' etc.

Nietzsche, in the wild hurry of his thought, many a time fails to comprehend the scintillating word-images elaborated in his centres of speech; his consciousness, as it were, hears wrongly, misses its aim in interpreting, and invents wondrous neologisms, which sound like known expressions, but have no sort of fellowship in meaning with these. He speaks, for example, of *Hinterweltlern* (inhabitants of remote worlds) from *Hinterwäldlern* (backwoodsmen), of a *Kesselbauche* (kettle's belly) when he is thinking of *Kesselpauche* (kettledrum), etc.; or he even repeats, as his centres of speech prompt, wholly incomprehensible, meaningless sounds. 'Then I went to the door: Alpa! I cried, who is carrying his ashes to the mountain? Alpa! Alpa! who is carrying his ashes to the mountain?'

He frequently associates his ideas, not according to the sound of the word, but according to the similarity or habitual contiguity of the concepts; then there arise 'analogous' intellection and the fugitive ideation, in which, to use Griesinger's expression, he 'rambles incoherently from one topic to another.' Speaking of the 'ascetic ideal,' *e.g.*, he elaborates the idea that strong and noble spirits take refuge in the desert, and, without any connection, adds: 'Of course, too, they would not want for camels there.' The representation of the desert has irresistibly drawn after it the representation of camels, habitually associated with it. At another time he says: 'Beasts of prey and men of prey, *e.g.*, Cæsar Borgia, are radically misunderstood; Nature is misunderstood so long as a fundamental diseased condition is sought for in these healthiest of all tropical monsters and growths. It seems that there is among moralists a hatred against the primeval forest and against the tropics, and that the tropical man must, at any price, be discredited. But why? For the benefit of the temperate zone? For the benefit of the temperate (moderate) men? Of the mediocre?' In this case the contemplation of Cæsar Borgia forces upon him the comparison with a beast of prey; this makes him think of the tropics, the torrid zone; from the torrid zone he comes to the temperate zone, from this to the 'temperate' man, and, through the similarity of sound, to the 'mediocre' man (in German, *gemässigt* and *mittelmässig*).

'In truth nothing remains of the world but green twilight and green lightnings. Do as it pleases ye, ye wantons . . . shake your emeralds down into the deepest depth.' The quite incomprehensible 'emeralds' are called up into consciousness by the representation of the 'green' twilight and lightnings.

In this and hundreds of other cases the course of ideation can, to a certain extent, be followed, because all the links in the chain of association are preserved. It often happens, however, that some of these links are suppressed, and then there occur leaps of thought, incomprehensible, and, consequently, bewildering to the reader: 'It was the body who despaired of the earth, who heard the belly of being speaking to itself.' 'More honestly and more purely speaks the healthy body, the perfect and rectangular.' 'I am polite towards them as towards all petty vexation; to be prickly against pettiness seems to me wisdom for hedgehogs.' 'Deep yellow and hot red; so would my taste have it. This one mixes blood in all colours. He who whitewashes his house betrays to me his whitewashed soul.' 'We placed our seat in the midst—so their smirking tells me—and as far from dying gladiators as from contented pigs. But this is mediocrity.' 'Our Europe of to-day is . . . sceptic . . . at one time with that mobile scepticism which leaps impatiently and wantonly from branch to branch, at another gloomy as a cloud overladen with notes of interrogation.' 'Let us grant that he [the 'courageous thinker'] has long enough hardened and pricked up his eye for himself.' (Here the representation of 'ear' and 'pricked-up ears' has evidently crossed with confusing effect the associated idea of 'eye.') 'It is already too much for me to keep my opinions to myself, and many a bird flies away. And sometimes I find flown into my dovecot an animal that is strange to me, and that trembles when I lay my hand on it.' 'What matters my justice? I do not see that I should be fire and coal.' 'They learned from the sea its vanity, too; is the sea not the peacock of peacocks?' 'How many things now go by the name of the greatest wickedness, which are only twelve feet wide and three months long! But greater dragons will one day come into the world.' 'And if all ladders now fail thee, then must thou understand how to mount on thine own head; how wouldst thou mount otherwise?' 'Here I sit, sniffing the best air, the very air of Paradise, luminous, light air, rayed with gold; as good an air as ever yet fell from the moon.' 'Ha! up dignity! Virtue's dignity! European dignity! Blow, blow again, bellows of virtue! Ha! roar once more, morally roar! As a moral lion roar before the daughters of the desert! For virtue's howl, ye dearest maidens, is more than all European fervour, European voraciousness! And here am I, already a European; I cannot otherwise, God help me! Amen! The desert grows, woe to him who hides deserts!'

The last passage is an example of complete fugitive ideation. Nietzsche often loses the clue, no longer knows what he is driving at, and finishes a sentence which began as if to develop into an argument, with a sudden stray jest. 'Why should the world, which somewhat concerns us, not be a fiction? And to him who objects: "But a fiction must have an author," could not the reply be roundly given: Why? Does not this "must" perhaps belong also to the fiction? Is it not permissible to be at last a little ironical towards the subject as well as towards the predicate and object? Ought not the philosopher to rise above a belief in grammar? With all respect for governesses [!], is it not time that philosophy should renounce its faith in governesses?' '"One is always too many about me," so thinks the hermit. One times one to infinity at last makes two!' 'What, then, do they call that which makes them proud? They name it culture; it distinguishes them from the goat-herds.'

Finally, the connection of the associated representations suddenly snaps, and he breaks off in the midst of a sentence to begin a new one: 'For in religion the passions have once more rights of citizenship, provided that.' 'The psychologists of France . . . have not yet enjoyed to the full their bitter and manifold pleasure in *la bêtise bourgeoise*, in a manner as if —enough; they betray something thereby.' 'There have been philosophers who knew how to lend yet another seductive . . . expression to this admiration of the people . . . instead of adducing the naked and thoroughly obvious truth, that disinterested conduct is very interesting and interested conduct, provided that—— And love?'

This is the form of Nietzsche's intellection, sufficiently explaining why he has never set down three coherent pages, but only more or less short 'aphorisms.'

The content of this incoherent fugitive ideation is formed by a small number of insane ideas, continually repeating themselves with exasperating monotony. We have already become acquainted with Nietzsche's intellectual Sadism, and his mania of contradiction and doubt, or mania for questioning. In addition to these he evinces misanthropy, or anthropophobia, megalomania, and mysticism.

His anthropophobia expresses itself in numberless passages: 'Knowledge is no longer sufficiently loved as soon as it is communicated.' 'Every community leads somehow, somewhen, somewhere—to vulgarity.' 'There are still many void places for the lonesome and twosome [!] around which wafts the odour of tranquil seas.' 'Flee, my friend, into thy lonesomeness!' 'And many a one who turned away from life, only turned away from the rabble . . . and many a one who went into the desert and suffered thirst with the beasts of prey, only wished not to sit with filthy camel-drivers about the tank.'

His megalomania appears only exceptionally as monstrous self-conceit; but it is, nevertheless, clearly conceivable; as a rule it displays a strong and even predominant union of mysticism and supernaturalism. It is pure self-conceit when he says: 'In that which concerns my "Zarathustra," I accept no one as a connoisseur whom each of his words has not at some time deeply wounded and deeply enraptured; only then can he enjoy the privilege of reverentially participating in the halcyon element out of which every work is born, in its sunny brightness, distance, breadth, and certainty.' Or when, after having criticised and belittled Bismarck, he cries, with transparent allusion to himself: 'But I, in my happiness and my "beyond," pondered how soon the stronger becomes master of the strong.' On the other hand, the hidden, mystic, primary idea of his megalomania already distinctly comes out in this passage: 'But at some given time . . . must he nevertheless come, the redeeming man of great love and contempt, the creative spirit who his impulsive strength is ever driving away out of all that is apart and beyond, whose loneliness is misunderstood by the people as if it were flight from reality. It is only his immersion, interment, absorption [three synonyms for one concept!] into reality, in order that at some time, if he again comes into the light, he may bring home the redemption of this reality.'

The nature of his megalomania is betrayed by the expressions 'redeeming man' and 'redemption.' He imagines himself a new Saviour, and plagiarizes the Gospel in form and substance. *Also Sprach Zarathustra* is a complete stereotype of the sacred writings of Oriental nations. The book aims at an external resemblance to the Bible and Koran. It is divided into chapters and verses; the language is the archaic and prophetic language of the books of Revelation ('And Zarathustra looked at the people, and was astonished. Then he spake and said thus:'); there frequently appear long enumerations and sermons like litanies ('I love those who do not seek a reason only behind the stars . . .; I love him who lives to know . . .; I love him who labours and invents . . .; I love him who loves his virtue . . .; I love him who withholds for himself not one drop of mind,' etc.), and individual paragraphs point *verbatim* to analogous portions of the Gospel, *e.g.*: 'When Zarathustra had taken leave of the city . . . there followed him many who called themselves his disciples and bore him company. Thus they came to a cross-road; then said Zarathustra unto them, that thenceforth he would go alone.' 'And the happiness of the spirit is this: to be anointed by tears and consecrated as a beast of sacrifice.' 'Verily, said he to his disciples, yet a little and there comes this long twilight. Ah! how shall I save my light?' 'In this manner did Zarathustra go about, sore at heart, and for three days took no food or drink. . . . At length it came to pass that he fell into a deep sleep. And his disciples sat around him in long night-watches,' etc. Many of the chapters have most expressive titles: 'On Self-Conquest;' 'On Immaculate Knowledge;' 'On Great Events;' 'On the Redemption;' 'On the Mount of Olives;'

'On Apostates;' 'The Cry of Sore Need;' 'The Last Supper;' 'The Awakening,' etc. Sometimes, it is true, it befalls him to say, atheistically: 'If there were gods, how could I endure to be no god? *Hence*' (italics his) 'there are no gods;' but such passages vanish among the countless ones in which he refers to himself as a god. 'Thou hast the power and thou wilt not reign.' 'He who is of my nature escapes not such an hour—the hour which says to him: Only now art thou going the way of thy greatness. . . . Thou art entering on the way of thy greatness; that which has hitherto been thy last danger has now become thy last resource. Thou art entering on the way of thy greatness; now must thy best courage be, that there is no longer any way behind thee. Thou art going on the way of thy greatness; here shall no one slink behind thee,' etc.

Nietzsche's mysticism and megalomania manifest themselves not only in his somewhat more coherent thought, but also in his general mode of expression. The mystic numbers, three and seven, frequently appear. He sees the external world, as he does himself—vast, distant, deep; and the words expressing these concepts are repeated on every page, almost in every line: 'The discipline of suffering, of great suffering . . .' 'The South is a great school of healing.' 'These last great searchers . . .' 'With the signs of great destiny.' 'Where together with great compassion he has learnt great contempt—to learn, at their side, great reverence.' 'Guilt is all great existence.' 'That I may celebrate the great noon with you.' 'Thus speaks all great love.' 'Not from you is great weariness to come to me.' 'Men who are nothing but a great eye, or a great mouth, or a great belly, or something great . . .' 'To love with great love, to love with great contempt.' 'But thou, O depth, thou sufferest too deeply.' 'Immovable is my depth, but it gleams with floating enigmas and laughters.' (It is to be observed how, in this sentence, all the obsessions of the maniac crowd together—depth, brilliancy, mania of doubt, hilarious excitation.) 'All depth shall ascend to my height.' 'They do not think enough into the deep,' etc. With the idea of depth is connected that of abyss, which recurs with equal constancy. The words 'abyss' and 'abysmal' are among the most frequent in Nietzsche's writings. His words which have the prefix 'over' are associated with his motor images, especially those of flying and hovering: 'Over-moral sense'; 'over-European music'; 'climbing monkeys and over-heated'; 'from the species to the over-species'; 'the over-hero'; 'the over-human'; 'the over-dragon'; 'the over-urgent' and 'over-compassionate,' etc.

As is general in frenzied madness, Nietzsche is conscious of his diseased interior processes, and in countless places alludes to the furiously rapid outflow of his ideation and to his insanity: 'That true philosophic reunion of a bold, unrestrained mentality, running *presto* . . . They regard thought as something slow, hesitant, almost a toil; not at all as something light, divine, and nearest of kin to the dance, to exuberance.' 'The bold, light, tender march and flight of his thought.' 'We think too rapidly. . . . It is as if we carried about in our head an incessantly rolling machine.' 'It is in impatient spirits that there breaks out a veritable pleasure in insanity, because insanity has so joyous a *tempo*.' 'All talking runs too slowly for me; I leap into thy chariot, Storm! . . . Like a cry and a huzza would I glide away over vast seas.' 'Eruptive insanity forever hovers above humanity as its greatest danger.' (He is, of course, thinking of himself when speaking of 'humanity.') 'In these days it sometimes happens that a gentle, temperate, self-contained man becomes suddenly frenzied, breaks plates, upsets the table, shrieks, rages, offends everyone, and finally retires in shame and anger against himself.' (Most decidedly 'that sometimes happens,' not only 'in these days,' but in all times; but among maniacs only.) 'Where is the insanity with which ye were forced to be inoculated? Behold, I teach you the over-man, who is . . . this insanity.' 'All things are worth the same; each is alike. He who feels otherwise goes voluntarily [?] into a madhouse.' 'I put this exuberance and this foolishness in the place of that will, as I taught; in all one thing is impossible—reasonableness.' 'My hand is a fool's hand; woe to all tables and walls, and wherever there is yet room for the embellishments of fools—scribbling of fools!' (In the original there is here a play on the words *Zierrath, Schmierrath.*)* He also, in the manner of maniacs, excuses his mental disease: 'Finally, there would remain open the great question whether we could dispense with disease even for the development of our virtue, and especially if our thirst for knowledge and self-knowledge needed the sick soul as much as the healthy soul.'

Finally, he is not even wanting in the maniacal idea of his 'primæval health.' His soul is 'always clearer and always healthier'; 'we Argonauts of the ideal' are 'healthier than one would fain allow us to be—dangerously healthy, more and more healthy,' etc.

The foregoing is a necessarily condensed summary of the special colour, form, and content of Nietzsche's thought, originating in illusions of sense; and this unhappy lunatic has been earnestly treated as a 'philosopher,' and his drivel put forward as a 'system'—this man whose scribbling is one

* Translator.

single long divagation, in whose writings madness shrieks out from every line! Dr. Kirchner, a philosopher by profession, and the author of numerous philosophical writings, in a newspaper article on Nietzsche's book, *Der Fall Wagner*, lays great stress on the fact that 'it superabounds, as it were, in intellectual health.' Ordinary university professors—such as G. Adler, in Freiburg, and others—extol Nietzsche as a 'bold and original thinker,' and with solemn seriousness take up a position in respect of his 'philosophy'—some with avowed enthusiasm, and some with carefully considered reservations! In the face of such incurably deep mental obtuseness, it cannot excite wonder if the clear-thinking and healthy portion of the young spirits of the present generation should, with hasty generalization, extend to philosophy itself the contempt deserved by its officially-appointed teachers. These teachers undertake to introduce their students into mental philosophy, and are yet without the capacity to distinguish from rational thought the incoherent fugitive ideation of a maniac.

Dr. Hermann Türck* characterizes in excellent words the disciples of Nietzsche: 'This piece of wisdom ['nothing is true; all is permissible'] in the mouth of a morally insane man of letters has . . . found ready response among persons who, in consequence of a moral defect, feel themselves to be in contradiction to the demands of society. This aforesaid intellectual proletariat of large towns is especially jubilant over the new magnificent discovery that all morality and all truth are completely superfluous and pernicious to the development of the individual. It is true that these persons have always in secret said to themselves, "Nothing is true—all is permissible," and have also, as far as possible, acted accordingly. But now they can avow it openly, and with pride; for Friedrich Nietzsche, the new prophet, has vaunted this maxim as the most exalted truth of life. . . . It is not society which is right in its estimation of morality, science, and true art. Oh dear no! The individuals who follow their egoistical personal aims only—who act only as if truth were of consequence to them—they, the counterfeiters of truth, those unscrupulous penny-a-liners, lying critics, literary thieves, and manufacturers of pseudo-realistic brummagem—they are the true heroes, the masters of the situation, the truly free spirits.'

That is the truth, but not the whole truth. Without doubt, the real Nietzsche gang consists of born imbecile criminals, and of simpletons drunk with sonorous words. But besides these gallows birds without the courage and strength for criminal actions, and the imbeciles who allow themselves to be stupefied and, as it were, hypnotized by the roar and rush of

* Dr. Hermann Türck, *op. cit.*, s. 59.

fustian, the banner of the insane babbler is followed by others, who must be judged otherwise and in part more gently. In fact, Nietzsche's ranting includes some ideas which, in part, respond to a widespread notion of the age, and in part are capable of awakening the deception that, in spite of all the exaggeration and insane distortion of exposition, they contain a germ of truth and right; and these ideas explain why many persons agree with them who can hardly be reproached with lack of clearness and critical capacity.

Nietzsche's fundamental idea of utter disregard and brutal contempt for all the rights of others standing in the way of an egoistical desire, must please the generation reared under the Bismarckian system. Prince Bismarck is a monstrous personality, raging over a country like a tornado in the torrid zone; it crushes all in its devastating course, and leaves behind as traces, a widespread annihilation of character, destruction of notions of right, and demolition of morality. In political life the system of Bismarck is a sort of Jesuitism in cuirass. 'The end sanctifies the means,' and the means are not (as with the supple sons of Loyola) cunning, obstinacy, secret trickery, but open brutality, violence, the blow with the fist, and the stroke with the sword. The end which sanctifies the means of the Jesuit in cuirass may sometimes be of general utility; but it will quite as often, and oftener, be an egoistical one. In its author this system of the most primitive barbarism had ever a certain grandeur, for it had its origin in a powerful will, which with heroic boldness always placed itself at stake, and entered into every fight with the savage determination to 'conquer or die.' In its imitators, on the contrary, it has got stunted to 'swaggering' or 'bullying,' *i.e.*, to that most abject and contemptible cowardice which crawls on its belly before the strong, but maltreats with the most extreme insolence the completely unarmed, the unconditionally harmless and weak, from whom no resistance and no danger are in any way to be apprehended. The 'bullies' gratefully recognise themselves in Nietzsche's 'over-man,' and Nietzsche's so-called 'philosophy' is in reality the philosophy of 'bullying.' His doctrine shows how Bismarck's system is mirrored in the brain of a maniac. Nietzsche could not have come to the front and succeeded in any but the Bismarckian and post-Bismarckian era. He would, doubtless, have been delirious at whatever period he might have lived; but his insanity would not have assumed the special colour and tendency now perceptible in it. It is true that sometimes Nietzsche vexes himself over the fact that 'the type of the new Germany most rich in success in all that has depth . . . fails in "swagger,"' and he then proclaims: 'It were well for us not to exchange too cheaply our ancient renown as a people of depth for Prussian "swagger," and the wit and sand of Berlin.'* But in other places he betrays what really displeases him in the 'swagger,' at which he directs his philosophical verse; it makes too much ado about the officer. 'The moment he [the 'Prussian officer'] speaks and moves, he is the most forward and tasteless figure in old Europe—unknown to himself. . . . And unknown also to the good Germans, who wonder at him as a man of the highest and most distinguished society, and willingly take their tone from him.'† Nietzsche cannot consent to that—Nietzsche, who apprehends that there can be no God, as in that case he himself must be this God. He cannot suffer the 'good German' to place the officer above him. But apart from this inconvenience, which is involved in the system of 'swagger,' he finds everything in it good and beautiful, and lauds it as 'intrepidity of glance, courage and hardness of the cutting hand, an inflexible will for dangerous voyages of discovery, for spiritualized North-Polar expeditions under desolate and dangerous skies,'‡ and prophesies exultingly that for Europe there will soon begin an era of brass, an era of war, soldiers, arms, violence. Hence it is natural that 'swaggerers' should hail him as their very own peculiar philosopher.

Besides anarchists, born with incapacity for adaptation, his 'individualism,' *i.e.*, his insane ego-mania, for which the external world is non-existent, was bound to attract those who instinctively feel that at the present day the State encroaches too deeply and too violently on the rights of the individual, and, in addition to the necessary sacrifices of strength and time, exacts from him such as he cannot undergo without destructive loss of self-esteem, viz., the sacrifice of judgment, knowledge, conviction, and human dignity. These thirsters for freedom believe that they have found in Nietzsche the spokesman of their healthy revolt against the State, as the oppressor of independent spirits, and as the crusher of strong characters. They commit the same error which I have already pointed out in the sincere adherents of the Decadents and of Ibsen; they do not see that Nietzsche confounds the conscious with the subconscious man; that the individual, for whom he demands perfect freedom, is the man, not of knowledge and judgment, but of blind craving, requiring the satisfaction of his lascivious instincts at any price; that he is not the moral, but the sensual, man.

Finally, his consequential airs have also increased the number

* *Jenseits von Gut und Böse*, pp. 198, 201.
† *Die fröhliche Wissenschaft*, p. 130.
‡ *Jenseits von Gut und Böse*, p. 147.

of his followers. Many of those marching in his train reject his moral doctrine, but wax enthusiastic over such expressions as these: 'It might some time happen that the masses should become masters . . . Therefore, O my brothers, there is need of a new nobility, the adversary of all plebeians and all violent domination, and who inscribes anew on a new tablet the word "Nobility."'*

There is at the present time a widespread conviction that the enthusiasm for equality was a grievous error of the great Revolution. A doctrine opposed to all natural laws is justly resisted. Humanity has need of a hierarchy. It must have leaders and models. It cannot do without an aristocracy. But the nobleman to whom the human herd may concede the most elevated place will certainly not be Nietzsche's 'over-man,' the ego-maniac, the criminal, the robber, the slave of his maddened instincts, but the man of richer knowledge, higher intelligence, clearer judgment, and firmer self-discipline. The existence of humanity is a combat, which it cannot carry on without captains. As long as the combat is of men against men, the herd requires a herdsman of strong muscles and ready blow. In a more perfect state, in which all humanity fights collectively against Nature only, it chooses as its chief the man of richest brain, most disciplined will and concentrated attention. This man is the best observer, but he is also one who feels most acutely and rapidly, who can most vividly picture to himself the condition of the external world, hence the man of the liveliest sympathy and most comprehensive interest. The 'over-man' of the healthy development of the species is a Paraclete of knowledge and unselfish love, not a bloodthirsty 'splendid beast of prey.' This is not borne in mind by those who believe that in Nietzsche's aristocratism they have found a clear expression of their own obscure views as to the need of noble natures of light and leading.

Nietzsche's false individualism and aristocratism is capable of misleading superficial readers. Their error may be accounted a mitigating circumstance. But even taking this into consideration, it still ever remains a disgrace to the German intellectual life of the present age, that in Germany a pronounced maniac should have been regarded as a philosopher, and have founded a school.

* *Also Sprach Zarathustra*, pt. iii., p. 74.

BOOK IV.

REALISM.

CHAPTER I.

ZOLA AND HIS SCHOOL.

It was necessary to treat in detail the two forms of degeneracy in literature and art hitherto examined, *i.e.*, mysticism and egomania, inasmuch as their career of development seems to be still in the ascendant, and they are actively at work in making themselves masters of the æsthetic conscience of our times. Concerning the third form, realism or naturalism, I can afford to be much briefer, for two reasons: one having to do with my subject, the other with myself. The former reason is that, in the land of its origin, naturalism is already wholly vanquished, and we do not kill a corpse—we bury it. The personal reason is that I have already devoted myself elsewhere to the thorough examination of naturalism.* The conclusions I there came to I continue to maintain, as regards the appreciation of its tendency, and I should only wish to limit them by a strong reservation, in so far as they greatly over-estimate M. Zola's abilities.

That naturalism in France is done with is admitted by all the world, and is really only disputed by Zola himself. 'There is no doubt whatever as to the tendencies of the new generation of literary men,' says M. Rémy de Gourmont; 'they are rigorously anti-naturalist. There has been no question of forming a party or issuing orders; no crusade was organized; it is individually that we have separated ourselves, horror-stricken, from a literature the baseness of which made us sick. Perhaps there is even less disgust than indifference. I remember, when M. Zola's last novel but one came out, that, among the eight or ten collaborators of the *Mercure de France*

* *Paris unter der dritten Republik*, Vierte Auflage. Leipzig, 1890. *Zola und Naturalismus Ausgewählte Pariser Briefe*, Zweite Auflage. Leipzig, 1887. 'Pot Bouille, von Zola.'

(a Symbolist journal), it was impossible for us to find anyone who had read through *La Bête humaine*, or anyone who would have consented to read it with sufficient care to review it. This species of book, and the method which dictates it, appears to us quite antiquated with the flavour of bygone years; more remote and more superannuated than the most truculent follies of romanticism.'*

Among the disciples of Zola, among those who collaborated in the *Soirées de Médan*, as among those who followed him later, there is scarcely one who has remained faithful to his tendency. Guy de Maupassant, before he was placed in the lunatic asylum where he died, ended by turning more and more towards the psychological novel. Joris Karl Huysmans, whom we have studied above in his new skin as a Diabolist and Decadent, cannot find words bitter enough for naturalism. J. H. Rosny writes novels now in which the scene is laid in the Stone Age, and the subject of which is the abduction of a brawny brachycephalous pre-Aryan woman by a tall, white-skinned, dolichocephalous Aryan man.† When Zola's *La Terre* appeared, five of his disciples—Paul Bonnetain, J. H. Rosny, just mentioned, Lucien Descaves, Paul Margueritte, and Gustave Guiches—deemed it necessary to protest, in a public manifesto, and with a solemnity somewhat comical, against the obscenities of this novel, and to disavow their master in proper and befitting form. If the novels of M. Zola himself still continue to find a very good and steady market, as he declares with pride, this in no way proves that his tendency is still popular. The masses persist in habits, once adopted, much longer than the leaders and creators do. If the former continue to follow M. Zola as before, the latter have already wholly left him. The success of his last novels is explained, moreover, on quite other than artistic grounds. His *flair* for what is occupying public opinion is, perhaps, the most essential part of his talent. He chooses from the outset subjects in favour of which he is assured of the positive interest of a numerous public, no matter how they may be treated. With books which relate, in the form of a novel, the story of the financial crisis of 1882, or the war of 1870, as *L'Argent* and *La Débâcle*, every known French author is sure to awaken in his own country a passionate interest even to this day. And M. Zola could equally count on a numerous connection of lovers of the obscene and nasty. This public remains faithful to him, and finds in him all it seeks. But it is a long time since he acquired any new adherents in his own country, and abroad he only obtains them among people who

* Jules Huret, *Enquête sur l'Évolution littéraire*, p. 135.

† J. H. Rosny, *Vamireh : Roman des Temps primitifs.* Paris, 1892.

anxiously follow every fashion, whether it be in neckties or books, but who are too ignorant to know as yet that M. Zola, in France itself, has long since ceased to be the last fashion.

In the opinion of his disciples, M. Zola is the inventor of realism in literature. This is a pretension which only young fellows, who are ignorant beyond all conception, could raise, and for whom the history of the world only begins at the moment when they have deigned to recognise it.

First of all, the word 'realism' itself has no æsthetic significance. In philosophy it denotes an opinion for which the general phenomenon of the world is the expression of a material reality. Applied to art and literature, it possesses no conception whatever. This I have explicitly demonstrated in another place (*Paris unter der dritten Republik*), and will confine myself here to going very briefly over the argument.

Those ale-house æsthetics, who distinguish between realism and idealism, explain the former as the effort of the artist to observe things and to reproduce them with truth. But this attempt is common to every author, whoever he may be. No one of deliberate purpose wanders from the truth in his creations; and even if he wished to do so, he could not, as this would contradict all the laws of human thought. Every one of our presentations, in fact, is based on an observation once made by us, and even when we invent *ad libitum*, we only work with the memory-images recollected from previous observations. If, in spite of this, one work gives a greater impression of truth than another, it is a question, not of this or that æsthetic tendency, but exclusively of the degree of talent. A true poet is always true; an incapable imitator can never be so. The first is true even when he disdains always to adhere closely to reality in details; the latter is not so even when he clings, with punctilious attention, and with the method of a land-surveyor, to little external details.

If one bear in mind the psychological conditions in which a work of art comes into existence, all the rhodomontade of so-called 'realism' is immediately recognised. The origin of every veritable work of art is an emotion. This is aroused either by a vital process in the internal organs of the artist, or by a sense-impression which he receives from the external world. In both cases the artist feels the necessity of giving expression to his emotion in a work of art. If this emotion is of organic origin, he will choose from among his memory-images, or his sense-impressions of the moment, those which are in harmony with his emotion, and will compose with them. If its origin is external, he will employ in his composition mainly phenomena of the external world, sensuous experiences which have evoked in him the emotion demanding objective shape, and he will combine with this, similar memory-images in accordance with the laws of association. As may be seen, the process in the two cases is absolutely the same: the artist, under the control of an emotion, welds direct sense-perceptions and memory-images into a work of art which brings him relief; only, sometimes the former, sometimes the latter, are predominant, according to whether the emotion has its origin in sense-perceptions or in organic processes. Speaking roughly, the works which result from an emotion aroused by the phenomena of the world may well be called realistic, and those expressing an organic emotion idealistic. These denominations, however, have not any really distinctive value. Among thoroughly sane individuals the emotions originate almost solely from impressions of the external world; among those whose nervous life is more or less diseased, namely, among hysterical, neurasthenic, and degenerate subjects, and every kind of lunatic, they originate much more frequently in internal organic processes. Sane artists will produce works, as a rule, in which perception will predominate; artists unhealthily emotional will produce works in which the play of association of ideas predominates—in other words, imagination working principally on memory-images. And if a false designation is absolutely adhered to, it might be said that the first, as a general rule, will produce works which are so-called realistic, and the second, works so-called idealistic. In no case is the work of art a faithful image of material reality; its genesis excludes this possibility. It is always the incarnation of a subjective emotion only. To desire to know the world by means of a work of art is a false proceeding; but the whole essence of a personality reveals itself in it to him who knows how to read. The work of art is never a document in the sense attached by naturalistic cant to this word, *i.e.*, a reliable objective presentation of external facts; but it is always a confession of the author; it betrays, consciously or unconsciously, his way of feeling and thinking; it lays bare his emotions, and shows what ideas fill his consciousness, and are at the disposal of the emotion which strives for expression. It is not a mirror of the world, but a reflection of the soul of the artist.

It might be thought, perhaps, that at least the mainly imitative arts, painting and sculpture, are capable of a faithful reproduction of reality, and thus are realisms properly so called. Even this is an error. It would never occur to a painter or a sculptor to place himself before a phenomenon, and reproduce it without selection, without accentuations and suppressions. And why does he do this? If he imitates an aspect, it is evidently because something in that aspect captivates or pleases him—a harmony of colours, an effect of light, a line of motion. Involuntarily he will accentuate and throw into relief the feature which has inspired him with the desire to imitate the aspect in question, and his work, consequently, will no more represent the phenomenon such as it really was, but as he saw it; it will only be a fresh proof, therefore, of his emotion, not the cast of a phenomenon. To work absolutely in the method of a camera obscura and a sensitive plate would be only possible to a very obtuse handicraftsman, who, in the presence of the visible world, had no feeling for anything, no pleasure, no disgust, no aspirations of any kind. However, it is not at all probable that so atrophied a being will ever have had the inclination to become an artist, and could acquire, even in a moderate degree, the technical skill necessary for such a profession.

And if literal realism, the positive actual imitation of the phenomenon, be interdicted even in the plastic arts by their intrinsic nature, with how much greater reason is it forbidden to imaginative writing! The painter can, after all, if he wishes to debase himself and his art to the lowest degree, reduce the co-operation of his personality in a work of art (or, to be more exact, to the *work*, for then there can be no question of art) to an extremely feeble, a scarcely perceptible point; he can reduce himself to the condition of a mere camera obscura, transmit his visual impressions in the most mechanical manner possible to his motor organs, and compel himself to think and feel nothing during the progress of the work. His picture is furnished for him by Nature itself: it is his optical horizon. If, then, he wishes to exercise no choice, to express nothing of his own, not even to compose, still there remains the possibility of copying the phenomena which are enclosed within the limits of his field of vision. His so-called picture is then no more than an expressionless fragment of the world, in which the artist's personality is only represented by the frame which encloses it, not because the phenomena of Nature really terminates at that point, but because the eye of the painter only embraces that portion, and no more; nevertheless, it is a picture in a technical sense, *i.e.*, a picture that can be hung upon the wall and looked at. The imaginative writer (dichter), on the contrary, does not find his work ready in this way. It is not provided for him by Nature itself. His subjects are not developed in space, but in time. They are not arranged by the side of one another in such a way that the eye perceives them and can retain all it sees; but they succeed each other, and the imaginative writer must by his own intellect assign them their limits, he must himself decide what he ought to seize upon and what he must let go; where the phenomenon begins which he wishes to utilize in his work, and where it ends. He cannot begin or end a conversation in the middle of a word, in imitation of M. Jean Béraud, for example, who in a well-known picture has made the frame cut off the wheels of a waggon in the middle. He may not produce an inexpressive photograph of the uniform course of events of life and the world. He must fence round and dam up certain places in the course of events. In doing this he clearly affirms himself and his personality. He betrays his original stamp. He allows his intentions, views, and sentiments to be recognised. If amongst a million of contemporary human destinies he relates one only, it is that for some reason or other this particular one has interested him more than the rest of the million. If he transmits to us only some few features, ideas, conversations, and actions of the person he has selected (not even a millionth part of all that makes up his actual life) it is because, for some reason or other, these seemed to him more important and more characteristic than all the rest; because in his opinion they prove something, they express an idea not conceived by things as they are, but which he believes he can deduce from reality, or which he desires to read into it. Thus, his 'realistic' work always reproduces his thoughts only, his interpretation of reality, his interest in it, and not reality itself. If the imaginative writer wished to transcribe the world phonographically or photographically, his work would no longer be a poem, even in a purely technical sense; it would not even be a book, to the extent that the work of the painter who only photographs still continues, in a purely technical sense, to be a picture; it would be something with neither form, sense, nor name; for, in reproducing the existence of a single human being during one day only, thousands of pages could be filled if all his sensations, thoughts, words, and actions were treated as of equal value. That selection is therefore made among them which is the subjectivity of the imaginative writer, *i.e.*, the reverse of 'realism.'

Besides, the work of the painter addresses itself to the same senses as the phenomenon of Nature itself, and reproduces it with the help of the same means by which the world itself is revealed to the senses, viz., with light and colour. Of course the lights, colours, and lines of the painter are not exactly those of the real phenomenon, and it is only in consequence of an illusion that, in his imitation, the phenomenon is recognised; but this illusion is the work of such inferior cerebral centres that even animals are capable of it, as is demonstrated by the classical anecdote so well known of the birds wishing to peck at the bunch of grapes painted by Zeuxis. The imaginative writer, on the contrary, does not address himself to the senses; to be more exact, he appeals by hearing or sight, to which he presents spoken or written words, not to the centres of perception, as the plastic artist does in the first instance, but to the higher centres of conception, judgment, and reasoning. Nor has he the means for directly reproducing the sensible phenomenon itself, but he must first translate the phenomenon into concepts under a linguistic, *i.e.*, a conventional, form. This is, however, an excessively complicated and highly differentiated activity, which bears completely the impress of the personality exercising it. If even two eyes do not see in the same manner, how much less can two brains perceive and interpret in the same way what the eye has seen, class it with pre-existing concepts, associate it with feelings and representations, and clothe it in traditional forms of language? The activity of the imaginative writer, therefore, is incomparably more than that of the artist, essentially personal; the elaboration of sense-impressions into representations, and the translation of representations into words, are so peculiarly individual, so exclusively subjective, that for this cause also imaginative writing can never be reality itself, *i.e.*, 'realistic.'

The notion of so-called 'realism' cannot withstand either psychological or æsthetic criticism. We might, perhaps, attempt an external, superficial, practical conception of it, and say, for example, Realism is the method in the application of which the imaginative writer starts from his perceptions and observations, and seeks his subjects in the environment he knows personally; idealism is the opposite method, which that writer employs who, in creating, yields to the play of imagination, and who, in order not to impede its free energy, borrows his materials from remote times and countries, or from social strata of which he has no direct knowledge, but which he conceives only in the visions of aspiration, intuition, or surmise. Reasonable and plausible as this explanation appears, it, too, nevertheless, dissolves into blue mist when more closely examined. For, in fact, the choice of subject-matter, the surroundings from which it is borrowed, or in which it is placed, have no decisive signification; no method is therein manifested, but merely the author's personality. One in whom observation predominates will be 'realistic,' *i.e.*, will express experiences, even if he pretends to speak of men and things placed wholly beyond the reach of his observation; and the other in whom the mechanical association of ideas prevails will be 'idealistic,' *i.e.*, he will simply follow the wanderings of his imagination, even when he desires to represent circumstances which may be personally familiar to him.

Let us give one example only of the two cases. What is more 'idealistic' than fairy-stories? Very well, here are some passages from the best-known fairy-tales of the brothers Grimm: 'There was once upon a time a king's daughter who went into the forest and seated herself on the brink of a cool fountain' (*The Frog Prince; or, Iron Henry*). 'But the little sister at home [he is speaking of the daughter of a king who had driven away his twelve sons] grew up, and remained the only child. Once there was a great washing-day, and amongst the washing were twelve men's shirts. "For whom are these shirts?" demanded the princess; "they are much too small for my father." Then the laundress told her that she had had twelve brothers,' etc.; 'and as the little sister sat in the meadow in the afternoon bleaching the linen, the words of the laundress came into her mind,' etc. (*The Twelve Brothers*). 'The woodcutter obeyed; he fetched his child, and gave her to the Virgin Mary, who carried her up into heaven. There the child lived happily; she ate nothing but sweet cakes, and drank new milk,' etc. 'So fourteen years went by in heaven. Then the Virgin Mary had to take a long journey; but before she went away, she called the girl to her, and said, "Dear child, I entrust you with the keys of the thirteen doors of Paradise,"' etc. (*Mary's Child*). The unknown writer of these fairy-tales transports his stories into royal palaces, or even into heaven—*i.e.*, into surroundings which he certainly does not know; but he endows beings and things, and even the Virgin Mary, with such traits as are known and familiar to him by observation. From the royal palace one enters a wood or a meadow as one might on leaving a farm; the princess runs to the fountain in the forest quite alone, looks after the linen, and bleaches it on the grass, just like a domestic servant. The Holy Virgin undertakes a journey, and confides the keys of the household to her adopted daughter, as a rich châtelaine might do. These fairy-tales are composed from a peasant's own experience, who describes his own world with honest realism, and simply gives other names to the figures and circumstances with which he is familiar. M. Edmond de Goncourt, on the contrary, the great pioneer 'realist,' relates, in his novel *La Faustin*, the love-story of a Lord Annandale and an actress of the Théâtre Français, which elicits from M. F. Brunetière, the critic, these observations: 'I should much like to hear M. Zola's opinion on M. de Goncourt's novel. What can M. Zola, who has jested so eloquently on the subject of novels of adventure—of those novels in which princes walked about incognito with their pockets full of diamonds—think in his inmost heart of this Lord Annandale throwing handfuls of gold out of the windows, and ruling from one day to another over fifty English servants in his mansion in Paris, without counting the retainers of his lady? What can M. Zola, who has made merry so comfortably over the idealistic novel, as he calls it, think of this one in which love triumphant carries off the lovers into the adorable world of dreams—what can he think to himself concerning this passionate tenderness which M. de Goncourt's Englishman has for the tragedienne, this almost deified gallantry, this sensual liaison *dans le bleu,* this physical love in ideality, and all the rest of the jargon which I spare the reader?'* M. Edmond de Goncourt professes to depict a contemporary Englishman, an actress also of our own times, events in Parisian life—*i.e.*, all of them mattershe might have observed, and with which he ought to be familiar; but what he does relate is so incredible, so impossible, unprecedented, that one can only shrug one's shoulders over the childish fable. Thus, the German story-teller who conducts us into a society of angels, saints, and kings, really shows us healthy, robust peasants and lasses whose living reality is in no way diminished by the carnival crowns and gilded-paper halos playfully placed on their heads; while the French realist who would transport us into Parisian life among Parisians, floats before our eyes fleshless phantoms moving in clouds of cigar-smoke, marsh-mists, and punch-flames, and who remain just as unreal, for all the effort of the author to conjure into them a distant resemblance to an Englishman in a frock-coat, and a hysterical lady in a lace-trimmed négligée. The author of the fairy-tales is a realist in the sense of the explanation given above; the novelist of Parisian manners, Edmond de Goncourt, is an idealist of the most aggravating type.

From whatever side we approach this pretended realism, we never succeed in seeing in it a concept, but only an empty word. Every method of investigation leads us to the same result—viz., that there is no realism in poetry, *i.e.*, no impersonal, actual copy of reality; there are only the various personalities of the poet. The only decisive thing is the individuality of the poet. One of them draws from the phenomenon of Nature, another from his internal organic processes, those emotions which incite them to create. One is capable of attention, and observes; another is the slave of an unbridled association of ideas. In one the presentation of the 'not-self' predominates in consciousness, in another the 'self.' I do not hesitate to express the matter in a single word—one is healthy and in an evolution of growth; the other is changed more or less pathologically — has more or less fallen into degeneracy. The healthy poet mingles knowledge with every one of his works, whether it be Dante's *Inferno* or Goethe's *Faust;* and if held desirable, this element of knowledge, which it is not possible to acquire except by attention and observation, may be called realism. The degenerate poet never

* Ferdinand Brunetière, *Le Roman naturaliste*, nouvelle édition. Paris, 1892, p. 285.

fashions anything but empty soap-bubbles of knowledge, even when he maintains, and is himself convinced, that he is giving out what he has observed; and this confused ebullition of ideas, shot in the best cases with changing hues, but most frequently simply dirty froth, is very often called, by a misnomer, idealism.

Still another and the latest meaning has been applied to realism; it stands for the systematic treatment of the lower ranks of life, and commonplace men and things. According to this definition, the works in which labourers, peasants, petty bourgeois, etc., appear, would be realistic, and those in which gods, heroes, kings, etc., take part, idealistic. Louis XIV., according to the well-known anecdote when Teniers' tavern-scenes were exhibited before him, let fall the indignant and disdainful comment, 'Take away these grotesque things!' He would not have condemned an artistic method and manner of representation, but the baseness of the subject only would have offended his Olympian eye. This explanation of the term 'realism' is a little more comprehensible than the others; but I have no need to show how grossly external and how philosophically and æsthetically worthless it is. We have seen, in fact, above, how the simplest feelings and ideas of peasants may be attributed to gods and to kings; and, conversely, there is no lack of works in which a royal crown or a saintly halo hovers invisibly over the heads of human beings in the lowest social position. In Gregory Samarow's novels, emperors and kings disport themselves who feel, think, and speak like the commercial travellers of a third-rate wine business; in Berthold Auerbach's village stories we see peasants who in heart and head are of the highest nobility, sometimes even semi-divine. The one kind is as unreal as the other, only in the first we discern the craft of the sensation-monger, in the second there speaks to us the refined and tender-souled poet. In *The Mill on the Floss*, by George Eliot, we find a farm-servant, Luke, and a miller's daughter, Maggie, who would do honour to any Pantheon in the grandeur of their character and morals; in Thackeray's *Vanity Fair* we are shown a Marquis of Steyne, very magnificent and very proud, and another such, Earl Bareacres, with neither of whom would any decent man shake hands. Those are as true as these; but whereas the former betray the heart of a poet full of love and pity, the latter reveal the soul of an artist overflowing with bitterness and wrath. Which, now, is noble—the emperors and kings of Samarow or the Black Forest peasants of Auerbach? Which is plebeian—the farming men of George Eliot or the powerful English peers of Thackeray? And which of these works must be qualified as realistic, which as idealistic, if realism signifies being occupied with inferior persons and conditions, idealism with those that are superior?

Hence to serious investigation, which does not stop at the mere jingle of words, the expressions 'realism' and 'idealism' convey no meaning. We will now see what the partisans of M. Emile Zola give out as his originality, in what he himself claims to be a model and a pioneer, and how he justifies his pretension of impersonating a totally new epoch in the history of literature.

M. Zola's disciples boast of his art of description and his 'impressionism.' I make a great difference between the two. Description endeavours to seize upon the characteristic features of the phenomenon by all the senses at once, and convey them in words; impressionism shows the conscious state of a person receiving impressions in the domain of one sense only, seeing things only, hearing them only, feeling them only, etc. Description is the work of a brain which comprehends the things it perceives in their connection and their essence; impressionism is the work of a brain which receives from the phenomenon only the sensuous elements—and by a one-sided aspect—of knowledge, but not knowledge itself. The describer recognises in a tree, a tree, with all the ideas which this concept includes. The impressionist sees before him merely a mass of colour composed of spots of different greens, on which the sun flashes here and there points and rays of light. Description for its own sake, as well as impressionism, are, in poetry, an æsthetic and psychological error, as will be demonstrated as briefly as possible; but even this error was not invented by M. Zola, for long before him the romanticists, and Théophile Gautier particularly, cultivated the broad style of description, inorganically interpolated into literary composition; and, on the subject of impressionism, the brothers De Goncourt showed M. Zola the way.

The purely objective description of objects is science, when it is worth anyone's while to acquire of them as clear a representation as may be communicated by words without the assistance of image or number. Such description is simply child's play and waste of time, when no one is interested to pause and look at the things described, either because they are too well known or because they are without importance.*

* Thirty years before realism began to create a disturbance in Germany, with its mania for description, the Swiss novelist, Gottfried Keller, with a curious premonition, ridiculed it. See *Die Leute von Seldwyla*, Auflage 12, Berlin, 1892, Band II., p. 108. (The hero of the story entitled *Die missbrauchten Liebesbriefe* [the misused love-letters] suddenly conceives the notion of becoming an author.) 'He laid aside the book of commercial notes, and drew forth a smaller one provided with a little steel lock. Then he placed himself before the first tree he came to, examined it attentively,

Finally, it rises into art while remaining of an inferior species, when it chooses words so well that it follows the most delicate peculiarities of the objects, and at the same time calls out the emotions that the observer experiences during his observations, *i.e.*, when the words employed have not only the value of a just portrayal of sensuously perceptible properties, but have an emotional colouring, and appear accompanied by images and metaphors. We may cite as examples of art of portrayal all good descriptions of travel, from the *Voyage to the Equinoxial Regions of the New Continent*, by Alexander Humboldt, to *Sahara and Soudan*, by Nachtigal, *Im Herzen Afrikas*, by Schweinfurth, or Edmond de Amicis' books on *Constantinople*, *Morocco*, *Spain*, *Holland*, etc. But these have nothing in common with imaginative writing, which always has for its object man, with his ideas and sentiments, not excepting fables of animals, parables, allegories, fairy-tales, all the hybrid forms in which the human element of all imagination appears disguised as an anthropomorphism applied to animals, and even to inanimate objects. The material frame, the scene and surrounding, have no importance in an imaginative work, except in so far as they affect the person or persons of whom it treats. The imaginative writer may be regarded either as a spectator who narrates human events as they develop before his eyes, or as an actor in these events, which he looks upon and feels with the consciousness of one of the personages concerned. In both cases he can naturally only perceive in the material surroundings whatever plays a part in the events themselves. If he is a spectator, he will certainly not let his eyes wander over the field of vision indifferently, but will pause before a scene which attracts his attention, and for which he seeks to arouse our interest. If he has himself adopted the disguise of one of the actors, he will be even more completely absorbed by the human events in which he himself co-operates, and will preserve still less any inclination to stroll indifferently by the side of scenes which have nothing to do with his given state of mind, and divert him from acts and feelings with which he is preoccupied at the moment. Hence an imaginative work

---

and wrote: "A beech-trunk. Pale gray, with still paler flecks and transverse stripes. Two kinds of moss cover it, one almost blackish, and one of a sheeny, velvety green. In addition, yellowish, reddish and white lichen. which often run one into another. . . . Might perhaps be serviceable in scenes with brigands." Next he paused before a stake driven into the earth, on which some child had hung a dead slow-worm. He wrote: "Interesting detail. A small staff driven into the ground. Body of a silver-gray snake wound round it. . . . Is Mercury dead, and has he left his stick with dead snakes sticking here? This last allusion serviceable, above all, for commercial tales. N.B.—The staff or stake is old and weather-beaten; of the same colour as the snake; in places where the sun shines upon it it is covered with little silver-gray hairs. (This last observation might be new, etc.),"' etc.

which is true to human nature will only contain descriptions of such material surroundings as a spectator (absorbed in the actual events which form the subject of the work, or as one of its actors) is in a state to perceive, *i.e.*, only what is directly connected with the events. If the description includes extraneous matter, it is psychologically false; it disturbs moods, interrupts events, diverts the attention from what ought to be the essential point in the work of art, and transforms the latter into a patchwork; showing signs that its author lacked artistic earnestness, that the work is not born from the need to give poetic expression to a genuine emotion.

A very much worse error than desultory, cold-blooded description in imaginative writing is impressionism. In painting it has its authorization. The latter reproduces the impressions of the visual senses, and the painter is within the limits of his art when he presents his purely optical perceptions without composing, or without relating a story, *i.e.*, without introducing any idea into the scene he reproduces, without combining any activity of his highest centres of ideation with the activity of the centres of perception. The picture produced according to this method will be very inferior from an æsthetic point of view, but it will be a picture, and can be defended as such. Poetical impressionism, on the other hand, is a complete misconception of the essence of imaginative work; it is the negation and suppression of it. The medium of poetry is language. Now this is an activity, not of the centres of perception, but of the centres of ideation and judgment. The immediate phonetic reaction upon sensory excitations is merely an exclamation. Without the co-operation of the highest centres a perception cannot express itself phonetically except by an 'Ah!' or an 'Oh!' But in the same ratio that the purely emotional cry of an animal rises to the height of intelligible grammatically articulated human speech, the purely sensuous perception rises also to the height of concept and judgment, and it is psychologically quite false so to depict the language of the external world as if it set free only a sensation of colour or of sound, and provoked neither ideas, concepts, not judgments. Impressionism in literature is an example of that atavism which we have noticed as the most distinctive feature in the mental life of degenerates. It carries back the human mind to its brute-beginnings, and the artistic activity of its present high differentiation to an embryonic state; that state in which all the arts (which were later to emerge and diverge) lay side by side inchoate and inseparate. Consider, as an example, these impressionist descriptions by the brothers De Goncourt: 'Above it a great cloud lowered, a heavy mass of a sombre purple, a scud from the north. . . . This cloud rose and ended in sharp rents against a brightness where pale green merged into rose. Then the sky became dull, of the colour of tin, swept by fragments of other gray clouds. . . . Beyond the softly-swaying pinetops, under which the broad garden walk could be seen bare, leafless, red, almost carmine, . . . the eye took in the whole space between the dome of the Salpêtrière and the mass of the Observatory; first, a great plane of shadow resembling a wash of Indian ink on a red ground, a zone of warm bituminous tones, burnt with those frost-touched reds and those wintry glows that are found on an English artist's water-colour palette; then, in the infinite delicacy of a degraded tint, a whitish streak arose, a milky nacreous vapour, pierced by the bright tones of new buildings.' 'The delicate tones of an old man's complexion played on the yellowish and bluish pink of his face. Through his tender, wrinkled ears—ears of paper interwoven by filaments—the day in passing became orange.' 'The air, streaked with water, had an over-wash of that violet blue with which the painter imitates the transparency of thick glass. . . . The first vivid smile of green began on the black branches of the trees, where, like strokes from a brush, touches of spring could be discerned leaving behind it light coatings of green dust.'*

Such is the procedure of impressionism. The writer gives himself the air of a painter; he professes to seize the phenomenon, not as a concept, but to feel it as simple sense-stimulation. He writes down the names of colours as an artist lays on his washes, and he imagines that he has herewith given the reader a particularly strong impression of reality. But it is a childish illusion, for the reader, nevertheless, comes to see no colours, but merely words. He has to transform these names of colours, like every other word, into images, and with the same mental effort he would procure himself a much livelier impression if, instead of heavily enumerating to him one after another of the optical elements of the phenomenon, the phenomenon were presented to him ready elaborated into a concept. M. Zola has borrowed this absurdity from the De Goncourt brothers with some exactitude, but it was not he who invented it.

Another of his originalities is said to be the observation and reproduction of the *milieu*, the environment, human and material, of the persons represented. Coming after the indulgence in useless description, and after impressionism, the theory of the 'milieu' produces a most comical effect, since it is the exact contrary of the psychological theory which forms the point of departure of impressionism and of the mania for

* Edmond et Jules de Goncourt, *Manette Solomon*. Paris, 1876, pp. 3, 145, 191.

description. The impressionist places himself over against some phenomenon as a mere sense, as photographer or phonographist, etc. He registers the nerve-vibrations. He denies himself all higher comprehension, the elaboration of perceptions into concepts, and the classification of the concepts in the experiences which, as general knowledge, pre-exist in his consciousness. The theorist of the 'milieu,' on the contrary, systematically attributes the chief importance, not to the phenomenon, but to its causal connection; he is not a sense which perceives, but a philosopher who endeavours to interpret and explain according to a system. What, in fact, does the theory of the 'milieu' mean? It means that the imaginative writer asserts that the individuality and mode of conduct of any person are a consequence of the influences that his environment, living or dead, exert upon him, and that he is trying to discover these influences, and the nature of their action on that person. The theory in itself is right, but, again, it is not M. Zola who invented it, for it is as old as philosophic thought itself. In our own times, Taine has distinctly conceived and established it, and, long before M. Zola, Balzac and Flaubert sought to introduce its operation into their novels. And yet this theory, extremely fertile as it is in anthropology and sociology, and giving, as it does, an impulse to meritorious research, is in imaginative writing but another error, and constitutes a confusion of kinds engendered by vague thought. The task of the man of science is to investigate the causes of phenomena. Sometimes he finds them, frequently he does not; often he believes he has discovered them, till more exact observation subsequently tells him he has deceived himself and must rectify his hypotheses. The investigation of the conditions under which man acquires his various physical and mental qualities is in full progress, but is only at its commencement, and has as yet furnished extremely few positive facts. We do not even know why one human race is tall or another short in stature; why this one has blue eyes and fair hair, that one dark eyes and hair; and yet these are incomparably simpler, more external and more accessible properties than the subtle peculiarities of mind and character. On the causes of these peculiarities we know nothing definite. We can make conjectures on this subject, but, meanwhile, even the most plausible of these have still the character of hypotheses, of probable, but not of verified, truth. And here the imaginative writer would like to come upon the scene, carry off unfinished scientific hypotheses, complete them by means of his own fantastic conceits, and teach: 'Do you see? this man whom I show you has become what he is because his parents have had such and such attributes, because he has lived here or there, because when a child he received such and such impressions, because he has been thus nurtured, thus educated, has had such and such intercourse, etc.' He is here doing what is not his office. Instead of an artistic creation he attempts to give us science, and he gives us false science, since he has no suspicion of the influences which really form the man, and the details of the 'milieu' which he throws into relief as being the causes of individual peculiarities are probably the least essential, and, in any case, only a minimum portion of what, in the formation of the personality, has played a really determining part. Think of it for a moment. The one question as to the origin of the criminal has produced in these last twenty years thousands of books and pamphlets; hundreds of medical men, jurists, economists, and philosophers of the first rank, have devoted to it the most profound and assiduous research, and we are still far from being able to indicate with certainty what share heredity social influences (*i.e.*, the 'milieu,' properly so called) and unknown biological peculiarities of the individual, have in the formation of the criminal type. And then there comes a wholly ignorant writer, who, quite by himself, with the sovereign infallibility claimed for himself by the author in his own province, decides a question which the combined ten years' labour of a whole generation of professional investigators has brought but very little nearer to a solution! This is an audacity only explicable by this fact, that the writer has not the very smallest idea of the weight of the task which he undertakes with so light a heart.

If, in spite of this, Balzac and Flaubert seem to have produced excellent works with this theory of the 'milieu,' it is an optical illusion. They have devoted great attention and detailed descriptions to the environment of their characters (especially Flaubert in *Madame Bovary*), and the superficial reader thereby receives the impression that there exists a connection of causality between the environment and the being and doing of the personages, it being one of the most elementary and tenacious peculiarities of human thought to link causally one with another all phenomena which present themselves simultaneously or successively. This peculiarity is one of the most fruitful sources of defective conclusions, and it cannot be overcome except by the most attentive observation, often even only with the help of experiment. In the novels of Balzac and Flaubert, where the 'milieu' plays so great a part, the 'milieu,' in fact, explains nothing. For the personages who move in the same 'milieu' are, notwithstanding, wholly different. Everyone reacts on the influences of the 'milieu' in his own particular way. This distinctive character must be the datum, it cannot be the result, of the 'milieu.' The latter has, at most, the significance of an immediate proximate cause, but the most remote causes of the effect in question are found in the distinctive character of the personality, and on the latter, the 'milieu' that the poet depicts gives us no real enlightenment.

On the pretension of M. Zola and his partisans, that his novels are 'slices from real life' (*tranches de vie*), it is useless to linger. We have seen above that M. Zola is far from being capable of transcribing in his novels life as real and as a whole. Like all the imaginative writers before him, he also makes a choice; from a million thoughts of his personages, he reproduces one only; from ten thousand functions and actions, one only; from years of their life, some minutes, or merely seconds; his supposed 'slice from life' is a condensed and rearranged conspectus of life, artificially ordered according to a definite design, and full of gaps. Like all other imaginative writers, he also makes his choice according to his particular personal inclinations, and the only difference is that these inclinations, which we shall at once recognise, are very dissimilar from those of other writers.

M. Zola calls his novels 'human documents' and 'experimental novels.' I have already, thirteen years ago, expressed myself so fully on this double pretension, that I have now nothing more to add to what I said then. Does he think that his novels are serious documents from which science can borrow facts? What childish folly! Science can have nothing to do with fiction. She has no need of invented persons and actions, however *ben trovati* they may be; but she wants beings who have lived, and actions which have taken place. The novel treats of individual destinies, or at most those of families; science has need of information on the destinies of millions. Police reports, lists of imposts, tables of commerce, statistics of crimes and suicides, information on the prices of provisions, salaries, the mean duration of human life, the marriage rate, the birth rate, legitimate and illegitimate—these are 'human documents.' From them we learn how people live, whether they progress, whether they are happy or unhappy, pure or corrupt. The history of civilization, when it wants facts, puts M. Zola's entertaining novels aside as of no account, and has recourse to tedious statistical tables. And a very much more singular whim still is his 'experimental novel.' This term would prove that M. Zola, if he employs it in good faith, does not even suspect the nature of scientific experiment. He thinks he has made an experiment when he invents neuropathic personages, places them in imaginary conditions, and makes them perform imaginary actions. A scientific experiment is an intelligent question addressed to Nature, and to which Nature must reply, and not the questioner himself. M. Zola also puts questions. But to whom? To Nature?

No; to his own imagination. And his answers are to have the force of proof. The result of scientific experiment is constraining. Every man in possession of his senses can perceive it. The results at which M. Zola arrives in his pretended 'experiment' do not exist objectively; they exist only in his imagination; they are not facts, but assertions, in which every man can believe, or not, at his pleasure. The difference between experiments, and what M. Zola calls such, is so great that it is difficult for me to impute the abusive application of the term to ignorance only, or to incapacity for thought. I believe rather in a conscious premeditated snare. The appearance of M. Zola occurred at a time when mysticism was not yet the fashion in France, and when the favourite catch-words of the writing and gossiping gang were positivism and natural science. In order to recommend himself to the masses, a man had to represent himself as a positivist and as scientific. Grocers, hotel-keepers, small inventors, etc., have everywhere and always the habit of decorating their sign-boards or their produce with a name which is connected with an idea dominant with the public. At the present day a hotel-keeper or a tradesman recommends his house or his shop by such titles as 'The Progress' or 'International Commerce;' and a manufacturer extols his goods as 'Electric' braces or 'Magnetic' ink. We have seen that the Nietzscheans designate their tendency as 'psycho-physiological.' In the same way Zola long before them hung out the catch-word sign to his novels—'Y^e^ scientificke experimente.' But his novels had no more visible connection with natural science and experiment than the ink above mentioned with magnetism, and the braces with electricity.

M. Zola boasts of his method of work; all his books emanate from 'observation.' The truth is that he has never 'observed;' that he has never, following Goethe, 'plunged into the full tide of human life,' but has always remained shut up in a world of paper, and has drawn all his subjects out of his own brain, all his 'realistic' details from newspapers and books read uncritically. I need only recall a few cases in which his sources have been placed within his reach. All the information on the life, manners, habits, and language of the Parisian workmen in *L'Assommoir* are borrowed from a study by M. Denis Poulot, *Le Sublime*. The adventure of *Une Page d'Amour* is taken from the *Mémoires de Casanova*. Certain features in which the masochism or passivism of Count Muffat is declared in *Nana*, M. Zola found in a quotation from Taine relative to the *Venice Saved* of Thomas Otway.* The scene of the confinement, in *La Joie de Vivre*, the description of the

* F. Brunetière, *op. cit.*, p. 153.

Mass, in *La Faute de l'Abbé Mouret*, etc., are copied word for word from an obstetric manual and a Mass-book. One reads sometimes in the newspapers very pretentious statements of the 'studies' to which M. Zola gives himself up when he undertakes a new novel. These 'studies' consist, on his part, in making a visit to the Bourse when he wishes to write on speculation, in undertaking a trip on a locomotive when he desires to describe the working of a railway, in once casting a glance round some available bedroom when he means to depict the mode of life of the Parisian *cocottes*. Such a manner of 'observation' resembles that of a traveller who passes through a country in an express train. He may perceive some external details, he may notice some scenes and arrange them later in descriptions rich in colour, if wholly inaccurate; but he learns nothing of the real and essential peculiarities of the country, and the life and ways of its inhabitants. Like all degenerates, M. Zola, too, is a complete stranger to the world in which he lives. His eyes are never directed towards nature or humanity, but only to his own 'Ego.' He has no first-hand knowledge of anything, but acquires, by second or third hand, all that he knows of the world or life. Flaubert has created, in *Bouvard et Pécuchet*, the characters of two blockheads, who, with unsuspecting ingenuousness, attack all the arts and sciences, and imagine they have acquired them when they have dipped into, or, more correctly, have skimmed through, the first book on the subject which falls into their hands. Zola is an 'observer' of the Bouvard et Pécuchet species, and on reading Flaubert's posthumous novel one is tempted to believe in places that when describing the 'studies' of his heroes he was thinking, at least amongst others, of Zola.

I think I have shown that M. Zola has not the priority in any one of the peculiarities which constitute his method. For all of them he has had models, and some few are as old as the world. The supposed realism, mania for description, impressionism, the emphasis on the 'milieu,' the human document, the slices of life—all these are so many æsthetic and psychological errors, but Zola has not even the doubtful merit of having conceived them. The only thing he has invented is the word 'naturalism,' substituted by him for 'realism' (the sole term in vogue till then), and the expression 'experimental novel,' which means absolutely nothing, but possesses a piquant little smattering of science which Zola's public, at the period when this novelist made his appearance, felt as an agreeable seasoning.

The only real and true things contained in M. Zola's novels are the little traits borrowed by him from the items of news in the daily papers and from technical works. But these also become false from the lack of criticism and taste with which he employs them. In fact, in order that the borrowed detail should remain faithful to reality, it must preserve its right relation to the whole phenomenon, and this is what never happens with M. Zola. To quote only two examples. In *Pot-Bouille*, among the inhabitants of a single house in the Rue de Choiseul, he brings to pass in the space of a few months all the infamous things he has learnt in the course of thirty years, by reports from his acquaintances, by cases in courts of law, and various facts from newspapers about apparently honourable bourgeois families; in *La Terre*, all the vices imputed to the French peasantry or rustic people in general, he crams into the character and conduct of a few inhabitants of a small village in Beauce; he may in these cases have supported every detail by cuttings from newspapers or jottings, but the whole is not the less monstrously and ridiculously untrue.

The self-styled innovator who, it is asserted, has invented hitherto unknown methods of construction and exposition in the province of the novel, is in reality a pupil of the French romanticists, from whom he has appropriated and employed all the tricks of the trade, and whose tradition he carries on, walking in the straight road of historical continuity, without interruption and without deviation. This is what is most clearly proved by the descriptions, which reflect not the world, but the view that the poet is capable of taking of the world. I will quote, for the sake of comparison, some characteristic passages from *Notre Dame de Paris*, by Victor Hugo, and from different novels by Zola, which will show the reader that both could be very easily confounded, the self-styled inventor of 'naturalism' and the extreme romanticist. 'The broom ransacked the corners with an irritated growling.' 'The Kyrie Eleison ran like a shiver into this kind of stable.' 'The pulpit . . . stood in front of a clock with weights, enclosed in a walnut wood case, and the hollow vibrations of which shook the whole church, like the beatings of an enormous heart, hidden somewhere beneath the flag-stones.' 'The rays [of the sun], more and more horizontal, withdraw slowly from the pavement of the square, and mount perpendicularly along the gabled front, making its thousand bas-reliefs spring out from their shadow, while the great central rose-window blazes like a Cyclop's eye inflamed by the glow of the forge.' 'When the priest . . . quitted the altar . . . the sun remained sole master of the church. It had rested in its turn on the altar cloth, illuminated the door of the tabernacle with splendour, celebrating the fruitful promise of May. A warmth arose from the flag-stones. The whitewashed walls, the great Virgin, the great Christ himself, took on a shiver of vital sap [!], as if death had been vanquished by the eternal youth of the earth.' 'In a crevice of this spout two pretty gilliflowers in blossom, shaken and animated by the breath of the air, made sportive salutations to each other.' 'At one of the windows a great service-tree reared itself, throwing its branches across the broken panes, extending its shoots as if to look within.' 'Towards the east, the morning breeze chased some white flocks of down across the sky, torn from the foggy fleece of the hills.' 'The closed windows slept. Some few, here and there, brightly lit, opened their eyes, and seemed to make certain corners squint.' 'Already some whiffs of smoke were disgorged here and there over all that surface of roofs, as by the fissures of an immense sulphur-kiln.' 'A miserable guillotine, furtive, uneasy, ashamed, which seems always afraid of being caught *in flagrante delicto*, so quickly does it disappear after having given its blow.' 'The alembic went on dully, without a flame, or any gaiety in the extinct reflexions of its coppers, letting flow its alcoholic sweat, like a slow and obstinate spring, which should end by invading the rooms, spreading over the boulevards without inundating the immense hollow of Paris.' 'At the barrier, the herd-like trampling went on in the cold of the morning. . . . This crowd, from a distance, was a chalky blur, a neutral tone, in which a faded blue and dirty gray predominated. Occasionally, a workman stopped short . . . while around him the others walked on, without a smile, without a word to a comrade, with cadaverous cheeks, faces turned towards Paris, which, one by one, devoured them by the gaping street of the Faubourg Poissonnière.' 'And then, as he dived farther into the street, legless cripples, blind and lame men multiplied around him; the one-armed and the one-eyed, and the lepers with their wounds, some coming from the houses, some from the adjacent small streets, some from the air-holes of cellars, howling, bellowing, screaming, all limpingly, lamely, rushing towards the light, and wallowing in the mire like snails after rain.' 'The square . . . presented . . . the appearance of a sea, in which five or six streets, like so many mouths of rivers, discharged new waves of heads at every instant. . . . The great stairs, ascended and descended without intermission by a double stream . . . flowed incessantly into the square, like a cascade into a lake.' 'The flickering brightness of the flames made them appear to move. There were serpents which had the appearance of laughing, gargoyles that one seemed to hear yelping, salamanders which breathed in the fire, dragons which sneezed in the smoke.' 'And the steam-engine, ten paces off, went on steadily breathing, steadily spitting from its scorched metal throat.' 'These were no longer the cold windows of the morning; now they appeared as if warmed and vibrating with internal tremor. There were people looking at them, women, standing still, squeezing against the plate-glass, quite a crowd brutalized by covetousness. And the stuffs seemed alive in this passion of the pavement: the laces shivered, fell back and hid the depths of the shop, with a disquieting air of mystery.' It would be easy to extend these comparisons to some hundreds of pages. I have indulged in the little joke of not adding the author's name to the passages quoted. By the nature of the object described the specially attentive reader will perhaps be able to guess in one or another of these quotations, whether they are from Victor Hugo or from Emile Zola; I have tried to facilitate the matter by borrowing the passages by Victor Hugo from the *Notre Dame de Paris* alone; but the greatest number he will certainly not know to whom to attribute until I tell him that examples three, five, seven, nine, ten, thirteen, fourteen, and fifteen, are from Victor Hugo, and all the others from Zola.

This is because the latter is an out-and-out romanticist in his way of envisaging the world and in his artistic method. He constantly practises in the most extensive and intensive fashion that atavistic anthropomorphism and symbolism, consequent on undeveloped or mystically confused thought, which is found among savages in a natural form, and among the whole category of degenerates in an atavistic form of mental activity. Like Victor Hugo, and like second-class romanticists, M. Zola sees every phenomenon monstrously magnified and weirdly distorted. It becomes for him, as for the savage, a fetish to which he attributes evil and hostile designs. Machines are horrible monsters dreaming of destruction; the streets of Paris open the jaws of Moloch to devour the human masses; a *magasin de modes* is an alarming, supernaturally powerful being, panting, fascinating, stifling, etc. Criticism has long since declared, though without comprehending the psychiatrical significance of this trait, that in every one of M. Zola's novels some phenomenon dominates, like an obsession, forms the main feature of the work, and penetrates, like an appalling symbol, into the life and actions of all the characters. Thus, in *L'Assommoir*, the still; in *Pot-Bouille*, the 'solemn staircase'; in *Au Bonheur des Dames*, the draper's shop; in *Nana*, the heroine herself, who is no ordinary harlot, but '*je ne sais quel monstre géant à la croupe gonflée de vices, une enorme Vénus populaire, aussi lourdement bête que grossièrement impudique, une espèce d'idole hindoue qui n'a seulement qu' à laisser tomber ses voiles pour faire tomber en arrêt les viellards et les collégiens, et qui, par instants, se sent elle-même planer sur Paris et sur le monde.*'* This

* F. Brunetière, *op. cit.*, p. 156.

symbolism we have encountered among all degenerates, among symbolists properly so called, and other mystics, as well as among diabolists, and principally in Ibsen. It never fails in the madness of doubt or negation.* The would-be 'realist' sees the sober reality as little as a superstitiously timid savage, or a lunatic afflicted by hallucinations. He puts into it his own mental dispositions. He disposes of phenomena arbitrarily, so that they appear to express an idea which is dominating him. He gives to inanimate objects a fantastic life, and metamorphoses them into so many goblins endowed with feeling, will, cunning and ideas; but of human beings he makes automata through whom a mysterious power declares itself, a fatality in the ancient sense, a force of Nature, a principle of destruction. His endless descriptions delineate nothing but his own mental condition. No image of reality is ever obtained by them, for the picture of the world is to him like a freshly varnished oil-painting to which one stands too close in a disadvantageous light, and in which the reflection of one's own face may be discerned.

M. Zola calls his series of novels 'The Natural and Social History of a Family under the Second Empire,' and he seeks in this way to awaken the double idea that the Rougon-Macquarts are a typical average family of the French middle class, and that their history represents the general social life of France in the time of Napoleon III. He expressly asserts, as the fundamental principle of art, that the novelist should only relate the everyday life observed by himself.† I allowed myself for thirteen years to be led astray by his swagger, and credulously accepted his novels as sociological contributions to the knowledge of French life. Now I know better. The family whose history Zola presents to us in twenty mighty volumes is entirely outside normal daily life, and has no necessary connection whatever with France and the Second Empire. It might just as well have lived in Patagonia, and at the time of the Thirty Years' War. He who ridicules the 'idealists' as being narrators of 'exceptional cases,' of that which 'never happened,' has chosen for the subject of his *magnum opus* the most exceptional case he could possibly have

* 'Everything is a mystery. Everything is a semblance. Nothing really exists.' The saying of one of Arnaud's patients afflicted with the mania of negation. See F. L. Arnaud, 'Sur le Délire des Négations,' *Annales médico-psychologiques*, 7e série, t. xvi., p. 387 *et seq.*

† 'I would lay humanity on a white page, all things, all beings, a work which would be a vast ark.'—E. Zola, preface to *La Faute de l'Abbé Mouret*, edition of 1875. 'Throw yourself into the commonplace current of existence.' 'Choose for your hero a person in the simplicity of daily life.' 'No hollow apotheoses, no grand false sentiments, no ready-made formulæ.' —E. Zola, *Le Roman expérimental*, *passim.*

found—a group of degenerates, lunatics, criminals, prostitutes, and 'mattoids,' whose morbid nature places them apart from the species; who do not belong to a regular society, but are expelled from it, and at strife with it; who conduct themselves as complete strangers to their epoch and country, and are, by their manner of existence, not members of any modern civilized people whatever, but belong to a horde of primitive wild men of bygone ages. M. Zola affirms that he describes life as he has observed it, and persons he has seen. He has in reality seen nothing and observed nothing, but has drawn the idea of his *magnum opus*, all the details of his plan, all the characters of his twenty novels, solely from one printed source, remaining hitherto unknown to all his critics, a characteristic circumstance due to the fact that not one of them possesses the least knowledge of the literature of mental therapeutics. There is in France a family of the name of Kérangal, who came originally from Saint-Brieuc, in Brittany, and whose history has for the last sixty years filled the annals of criminal justice and mental therapeutics. In two generations it has hitherto produced, to the knowledge of the authorities, seven murderers and murderesses, nine persons who have led an immoral life (one the keeper of a disorderly house, one a prostitute who was at the same time an incendiary, committed incest, and was condemned for a public outrage on modesty, etc.), and besides all these, a painter, a poet, an architect, an actress, several who were blind, and one musician.* The history of this Kérangal family has supplied M. Zola with material for all his novels. What would never have been afforded him in the life he really knows he found ready to his hand in the police and medical reports on the Kérangals, viz., an abundant assortment of the most execrable crimes, the most unheard-of adventures, and the maddest and most disordered careers, permeated by artistic inclinations which make the whole particularly piquant. If any common fabricator of newspaper novels had had the luck to discover the treasure he would probably have made a hash of the subject. M. Zola, with his great power and his sombre emotionalism, has known how to profit very effectively by it. Nevertheless, the subject he broaches is the *roman du colportage*, *i.e.*, of a perishing romanticism which transports his dreams into no palaces like the flourishing romanticism, but into dens, prisons, and lunatic asylums, which are quite as far from the

* The family of Kérangal has been the subject of many works, and is well known in technical literature. The last published work on them is due to Dr. Paul Aubry: 'Une Famille de Criminels,' *Annales médico-psychologiques*, 7e séries, t. xvi., p. 429 (reproduced in *La Contagion du Meurtre*, by the same author; Paris, 1894). See especially, pp. 432, 433, the curious genealogical tree of the family, in which Zola's celebrated genealogical tree of the Rougon-Macquart and the Quenu-Gradelle can be immediately recognised.

middle stratum of sane life as the latter, only in an opposite direction, tending not upwards, but downwards. But if M. Zola has infinitely more talent than the German romanticists, to whom we owe such works as *Rinaldo Rinaldini, Die blutige Nonne um Mitternacht, Der Scharfrichter vom Schreckenstein*, etc., he has, on the other hand, infinitely less honesty than they. For they, at least, admit that they relate the most marvellous and unique horrors of their kind, while Zola issues his chronicles of criminals and madmen, the fruits of his reading, as a normal account of French society, drawn from the observation of daily life.

By choosing his subject in the domain of the most extraordinary and most exceptional, by the childish or crazy symbolism and anthropomorphism displayed in his extremely unreal survey of the world, the 'realist' Zola proves himself to be the immediate descendant in a direct line of the romanticists. His works are distinguished from those of his literary ancestors by only two peculiarities, which M. Brunetière has well discerned, viz., by 'pessimism and premeditated coarseness.'* These peculiarities of M. Zola furnish us finally with a characteristic sign also of so-called realism or naturalism, which we should have in vain attempted to discover by psychological, æsthetic, historical, and literary inquiries. Naturalism, which has nothing to do with Nature or reality, is, taken all in all, the premeditated worship of pessimism and obscenity.

Pessimism, as a philosophy, is the last remains of the superstition of primitive times, which looked upon man as the centre and end of the universe. It is one of the philosophic forms of ego-mania. All the objections of pessimist philosophers to Nature and life have but one meaning, if their premise be correct as to the sovereignty of man in the Cosmos. When the philosopher says, Nature is irrational, Nature is immoral, Nature is cruel, what is this, in other words, but: I do not understand Nature, and yet she is only there that I may understand her; Nature does not consider what is for my utility alone, and yet she has no other task than to be useful to me; Nature grants me but a short period of existence, often crossed by troubles, and yet it is her duty to make provision for the eternity of my life and my continual joys? When Oscar Wilde is indignant that Nature makes no difference between himself and the grazing ox, we smile at his childishness. But have Schopenhauer, Hartmann, Mainländer, Bahnsen, done anything more than inflate into thick books Oscar Wilde's ingenuous self-conceit? and that with terrible seriousness. Philosophic pessimism has the geocentric conception of the world as its postulate. It stands and falls with the Ptolemaic

* Brunetière, *op. cit.*, p. iii.

doctrine. As soon as we recognise the Copernican point of view we lose the right, and also the desire to apply to Nature the measure of our logic, our morals, and our own advantage, and there ceases to be any meaning in calling it irrational, immoral, or cruel.

But what is also true is that pessimism is not a philosophy, but a temperament. 'The systemic or organic sensations which arise from the simultaneous states of the several organs, digestive, respiratory, etc.,' says Professor James Sully, 'appear, as Professor Ferrier has lately pointed out, to be the basis of our emotional life. When the condition of these organs is a healthy one, and their functions vigorous, the psychical result is an undiscriminated mass of agreeable feeling. When the state of the organs is unhealthy, and their functions feeble or impeded, the psychical result is a similar mass of disagreeable feeling.'* Pessimism is always the form under which the patient becomes conscious of certain morbid conditions, and first and foremost of his nervous exhaustion. *Tædium vitæ*, or disgust of life, is an early premonition of insanity, and constantly accompanies neurasthenia and hysteria. It is evident that a period which suffers from general organic fatigue must necessarily be a pessimistic period. We recognise also the constant habit which consciousness has of inventing, *post facto*, apparently plausible motives, borrowed from its store of representations, and in conformity with the rules of its formal logic, to justify the emotional states of which it has acquired the knowledge. Thus, for the datum of the pessimistic disposition of mind, which is the consequence of organic fatigue, there arises the pessimist philosophy as an ulterior creation of interpretative consciousness. In Germany, in conformity with the speculative tendency and high intellectual culture of the German people, this state of mind has sought expression in philosophical systems. In France it has adopted an artistic form in accordance with the predominating æsthetic character of the national mind. M. Emile Zola and his naturalism are the French equivalent of the German Schopenhauer and his philosophical pessimism. That naturalism should see nothing in the world but brutality, infamy, ugliness, and corruption, corresponds with all that we know of the laws of thought. We know that the association of ideas is strongly influenced by emotion. A Zola, filled from the outset with organically unpleasant sensations, perceives in the world those phenomena alone which accord with his organically fundamental disposition, and does not notice or take into consideration those which differ from or contradict it. And from the associated

* James Sully, *Pessimism: A History and a Criticism.* London, 1877, p. 411.

ideas which every perception awakens in him, consciousness likewise only retains the disagreeable, which are in sympathy with the fundamentally sour disposition, and suppresses the others. Zola's novels do not prove that things are badly managed in this world, but merely that Zola's nervous system is out of order.

His predilection also for coarseness is a well-known morbid phenomenon. 'They' (the imbeciles), says Sollier, 'love to talk of obscenities. . . . This is a peculiar tendency of mind observable specially among degenerates; it is as natural to them as a wholesome "tone" is to normal minds.'* Gilles de la Tourette has coined the word 'coprolalia' (mucktalk) for obsessional explosions of blasphemies and obscenities which characterize a malady described most exhaustively by M. Catrou, and called by him 'disease of convulsive tics.'† M. Zola is affected by coprolalia to a very high degree. It is a necessity for him to employ foul expressions, and his consciousness is continually pursued by representations referring to ordure, abdominal functions, and everything connected with them. Andreas Verga described some years ago a form of onomatomania, or word-madness, which he called *mania blasphematoria*, or oath-madness. It is manifested when the patient experiences an irresistible desire to utter curses or blasphemies. Verga's diagnosis applies completely to Zola. It can only be interpreted as *mania blasphematoria*, when in *La Terre* he gives the nickname of Jesus Christ to a creature afflicted with flatulency, and that without any artistic necessity or any aiming thereby at æsthetic effect either of cheerfulness or of local colour. Finally, he has a striking predilection for slang, for the professional language of thieves and bullies, etc., which he does not only employ when making personages of this kind speak, but makes use of himself, as an author, in descriptions or reflections. This inclination for slang is expressly noticed by Lombroso as an indication of degeneration in the born criminal.‡

The confusion of thought which is shown in his theoretic writings, in his invention of the word 'naturalism,' in his conception of the 'experimental novel,' his instinctive inclination to depict demented persons, criminals, prostitutes, and semi-maniacs,§ his anthropomorphism and his symbolism, his

* Dr. Paul Sollier, *Psychologie de l'Idiot et de l'Imbécile.* Paris, 1891, p. 95.

† Catrou, *Étude sur la Maladie des Tics convulsifs* (Jumping, Latah, Myriachit). Paris, 1890.

‡ Lombroso, *L'Uomo delinquente*, etc., pp. 450-480.

§ His descriptions of impulsive criminals are not really exact. The laity have greatly admired his description of the assassin Lantier in *La Bête humaine.* The most competent judge in such matters, however, Lombroso, pessimism, his coprolalia, and his predilection for slang, sufficiently characterize M. Zola as a high-class degenerate. But he shows in addition some peculiarly characteristic stigmata, which completely establish the diagnosis.

That he is a sexual psychopath is betrayed on every page of his novels. He revels continually in representations from the region of the basest sensuality, and interweaves them in all the events of his novels without being able in any way to assign an artistic reason for this forced introduction. His consciousness is peopled with images of unnatural vice, bestiality, passivism, and other aberrations, and he is not satisfied with lingering libidinously over human acts of such a nature, but he even produces pairing animals (see *La Terre*, pp. 9, 10). The sight of a woman's linen produces a peculiar excitation in him, and he can never speak without betraying, by the emotional colouring of his descriptions, that representations of this kind are voluptuously accentuated in him. This effect of female linen on degenerates affected by sexual psychopathy is well known in mental therapeutics, and has often been described by Krafft-Ebing, Lombroso, and others.*

Connected with the sexual psychopathy of M. Zola is the part played in him by the olfactory sensations. The predominance of the sense of smell and its connection with the sexual life is very striking among many degenerates. Scents acquire a high importance in their works. Tolstoi (in *War and Peace*) represents to us Prince Pierre suddenly deciding on marrying the Princess Hélène when he smells her fragrance at a ball.† In the narrative entitled *The Cossacks* he never

says of this character, which has been inspired in M. Zola, according to his own declaration, by *L'Uomo delinquente*: 'M. Zola, in my opinion, has never observed criminals in real life. . . . His criminal characters give me the impression of the wanness and inaccuracy of certain photographs which reproduce portraits, not from Nature, but from pictures.'—*Le piu recenti scoperte ed applicazioni della psichiatria ed antropologia criminale. Con 3 tavole e 52 figure nel testo.* Torino, 1893, p. 356.

* Dr. R. von Krafft-Ebing, *Psychopathia Sexualis*, etc., 3e Auflage; Stuttgart, 1888. Beobachtung 23, Zippes Fall, s. 55; Beobachtung 24, Passow's Fall, s. 56; Aum. zu s. 57, Lombroso's Fall.

Cæsare Lombroso, *Le piu recenti scoperte*, etc., p. 227: 'He always had voluptuous sensations on seeing animals killed, or in perceiving in shops feminine under-garments and linen.' The case of which Lombroso here speaks is that of a degenerate of fifteen years old, who had been observed by Dr. MacDonald, of Clark University.

† Léon Tolstoi, *Œuvres complètes*, p. 385: 'He smelt the warmth of her body, inhaled the odour of her perfumes . . . and at this moment Pierre understood that not only *might* Hélène become his wife, but that she *must* become so—that nothing else was possible.' It is related that the King of France, Henri III., married Marie of Cleves because, at the wedding of the King of Navarre and his sister, Marguerite of Valois, wishing to dry his face in the chemise wet with the perspiration of the young princess, he was so

mentions the uncle Ieroschka without speaking of the smell he emitted.* We have seen in the previous chapters with what satisfaction the Diabolists and Decadents, Baudelaire, Huysmans, etc., lingered on odours, and especially on bad odours. M. Barrès makes his little princess say, in *L'Ennemi des Lois*: 'I go every morning to the stables. Oh, that little stabley smell, so warm and pleasant! And she inhaled with a pretty [!] sensual expression. . . .'† M. de Goncourt describes, in *La Faustin*, how the actress lets her Lord Annandale smell her bosom: '"Smell! What do you smell?" she asked Lord Annandale. "Why, carnations!" he replied, tasting it with his lips. "And what else?" "Your skin!"'‡ M. A. Binet declares that 'it is the odours of the human body which are the causes responsible for a certain number of marriages contracted by clever men with female subordinates belonging to their households. For certain men, the most essential thing in a woman is not beauty, mind, or elevation of character; it is her smell. The pursuit of the beloved odour determines them to pursue some ugly, old, vicious, degraded woman. Carried to this point, the pleasure in smell becomes a malady of love'§—a malady, I will add, from which only the degenerate suffer. The examples that Binet quotes in the course of his work, and which can be there referred to, as I have no inclination to repeat them here, prove this abundantly; and Krafft-Ebing, while insisting on the 'close connection between the sexual and the olfactory sense,' nevertheless expressly declares: 'At all events, the perceptions of smell play a very subordinate part within the physiological limits (*i.e.*, within the limits of the healthy life).‖ Even after the abstraction of its sexual significance, the development of the sense of smell among degenerates, not only of the higher, but even of the lowest type, has struck many observers. Séguin speaks of 'idiots who discriminated species of woods and stones merely by smell without having recourse to sight, and who, nevertheless, were not disagreeably affected by the smell and taste of human ordure, and whose sense of touch was obtuse and unequal.'¶

---

intoxicated by the scent which emanated from it, that he had no rest till he had won her who had borne it. See Krafft-Ebing, *Psychopathia Sexualis*, p. 17.

* Léon Tolstoi, *Œuvres complètes*, t. ii., p. 385: 'With him there had come into the room a strong, but not disagreeable, smell,' etc.

† Maurice Barrès, *L'Ennemi des Lois*, p. 47.

‡ Edmond de Goncourt, *La Faustin*. Paris, 1882, p. 267.

§ Alfred Binet, *Le Fétichisme dans l'Amour*, etc., p. 26. This passage will make the German reader think of the sniffer of souls, G. Jaeger; I have no occasion to mention him here.

‖ Dr. R. von Krafft-Ebing, *Psychopathie Sexualis*, p. 15, foot-note, p. 17.

¶ E. Séguin, *Traitement morale, Hygiène et Education des Idiots*. Paris, 1846.

M. Zola's case belongs to this series. He shows at times an unhealthy predominance of the sensations of smell in his consciousness, and a perversion of the olfactory sense which make the worst odours, especially those of all human excretions, appear to him particularly agreeable and sensually stimulating. The inspector of the Montpellier Academy, Leopold Bernard, has taken the trouble, in an elaborate work—which, curiously, has remained almost unknown*—to bring together all the passages in Zola's novels which touch on the question of odours, and to show that men and things do not present themselves to him as to normal individuals, viz., in the first instance as optical and acoustic phenomena, but as olfactory perceptions. He characterizes all his personages by their smell. In *La Faute de l'Abbé Mouret,* Albine appears 'like a great nosegay of strong scent.' Serge, at the seminary, was 'a lily whose sweet scent charmed his masters' (! !) Désirée 'smells of health.' Nana '*dégage une odeur de vie, une toute-puissance de femme.*' In *Pot-Bouille,* Bachelard exhales 'une odeur de débauche canaille'; Madame Campardon has 'a good fresh perfume of autumn fruit.' In *Le Ventre de Paris,* Françoise 'smells of earth, hay, the open air, the open sky.' In the same novel the 'cheese-symphony' occurs, as celebrated among Zola's enthusiasts as the minute description of the variety of offensive smells of the dirty linen in *L'Assommoir.*

To the 'comprehensives' whom we have learnt to know, this insistence on the odours emitted by men and things is naturally one more merit and perfection. A poet who scents so well and receives through the nose such rich impressions of the world, is 'a more keenly vibrating instrument of observation,' and his art in representing things is more many-sided than that of poets who reproduce their impressions from fewer senses. Why should the sense of smell be neglected in poetry? Has it not the same rights as all the other senses? And thereupon they rapidly built an æsthetic theory which, as we have seen, induces Huysmans' Des Esseintes to compose a symphony of perfumes, and prompts the Symbolists to accompany the recital of their compositions on the stage with odours, which they pretend are assorted to the contents of the verses. The 'comprehensive' drivellers do not for a moment suspect that they are simply fencing with the march of organic evolution in the animal kingdom. It does not depend on the good pleasure of a being to construct for himself his idea of the external world with the help of a group of such or such sense-perceptions. In this respect he is completely subservient to the conformation of his nervous system. The senses which predominate are those which his being utilizes in acquiring

* L. Bernard, *Le Odeurs dans le Romans de Zola.* Montpellier, 1889.

knowledge. The undeveloped or insufficiently developed senses help the brain little or not at all, to know and understand the world. To the vulture and condor the world is a picture; to the bat and the mole it is a sound and a tactile sensation; to the dog it is a collection of smells. Concerning the sense of smell in particular, it has its central seat in the so-called olfactory lobe of the brain, which diminishes in proportion as the frontal lobe is developed. The more we descend in the vertebrates the greater is the olfactory, the smaller the frontal, lobe. In man the olfactory lobe is quite subordinated, and the frontal lobe, the presumable seat of the highest mental functions, including language, greatly predominates. The consequence of these anatomical relations, which evade our influence, is that the sense of smell has scarcely any further share in man's knowledge. He obtains his impressions of the external world no longer by the nose, but principally by the eye and ear. The olfactory perceptions only furnish a minimum contribution to the concepts which are formed out of ideational elements. It is only in the most limited degree that smells can awaken abstract concepts, *i.e.*, a higher and complex mental activity, and stimulate their accompanying emotions; a 'symphony of perfumes' in the Des Esseintes sense can, therefore, no longer give the impression of moral beauty, this being an idea which is elaborated by the centres of conception. In order to inspire a man with logical sequences of ideas and judgments, with abstract concepts by scents alone; to make him conceive the phenomenon of the world, its changes and causes of motion, by a succession of perfumes, his frontal lobe must be depressed and the olfactory lobe of a dog substituted for it, and this, it must be admitted, is beyond the capacity of 'comprehensive' imbeciles, however fanatically they may preach their æsthetic folly. Smellers among degenerates represent an atavism going back, not only to the primeval period of man, but infinitely more remote still, to an epoch anterior to man. Their atavism retrogrades to animals amongst whom sexual activity was directly excited by odoriferous substances, as it is still at the present day in the muskdeer, or who, like the dog, obtained their knowledge of the world by the action of their noses.

The extraordinary success of Zola among his contemporaries is not explained by his high qualifications as an author, that is, by the extraordinary force and power of his romantic descriptions, and by the intensity and truth of his pessimistic emotion, which makes his representation of suffering and sorrow irresistibly impressive; but by his worst faults, his triviality and lasciviousness. This can be proved by the surest of methods, that of figures. Let us consult as to the diffusion of his different novels, the printed indications, for example, at the beginning of the last edition of *L'Assommoir* (bearing the date 1893). They have been put down as follows: Of *Nana*, 160,000; *La Débâcle*, 143,000; *L'Assommoir*, 127,000; *La Terre*, 100,000; *Germinal*, 88,000; *La Bête humaine* and *Le Rêve*, each 83,000; *Pot-Bouille*, 82,000; as a contrast, *L'Œuvre* 55,000; *La Joie de Vivre*, 44,000; *La Curée*, 36,000; *La Conquête de Plassans*, 25,000; of the *Contes à Ninon* not even 2,000 copies, etc. Thus, the novels which have had the greatest sale are those in which lust and bestial coarseness appear most flagrantly, and the demand diminishes with mathematical exactitude in proportion as the layer of obscenity, spread by Zola over his work as with a mason's trowel, becomes more thin and less ill-smelling. Three novels appear as an exception to this rule: *La Débâcle*, *Germinal*, and *Le Rêve*. Their high position as regards the number of the editions is explained by the fact that the first treats of the war of 1870, the second of socialism, the third of mysticism. These three works appeal to the frame of mind of the period. They swim with the fashionable current. But all the rest have owed their success to the lowest instincts of the masses, to its brutish passion for the sight of crime and voluptuousness.

M. Zola was bound to make a school—first, because of his successes in the book trade, which drove into his wake the whole riff-raff of literary intriguers and plagiarists, and then because of the facility with which his most striking peculiarities can be imitated. His art is accessible to every bungler of the day who dishonours the literary vocation by his slovenly hand. An empty and mechanical enumeration of completely indifferent aspects under the pretext of description exacts no effort. Every porter of a brothel is capable of relating a low debauch with the coarsest expressions. The only thing which might offer some difficulty would be the invention of a plot, the construction of a frame of action. But M. Zola, whose strength does not lie in the gift of story-telling, boasts of this imperfection as a special merit, and proclaims as a rule of art that the poet must have nothing to relate. This rule suits excellently the noxious insects who crawl behind him. Their impotence becomes their most brilliant qualification. They know nothing, they can do nothing, and they are on that account particularly adapted to '*die Moderne*,' as they say in Germany. Their so-called 'novels' depict neither human beings, nor characters, nor destinies; but, thou poor Philistine who canst not see it, it is precisely this which constitutes their value!

Moreover, justice exacts that among Zola's imitators two groups should be distinguished. The one cultivates chiefly his pessimism, and accepts his obscenities into the bargain, though without enthusiasm, and often even with visible embarrassment and secret repugnance. It consists of hysteric and degenerate subjects who are *bonâ fide*, who, in consequence of their organic constitution, actually feel pessimistic, and have found in Zola the artistic formula which corresponds most truly with their sentiments. I place in this group some dramatic authors of the 'Théâtre-Libre' in Paris, directed by M. Antoine; and the Italian 'Verists.' The naturalistic theatre is the most untrue thing that has been seen hitherto, even more untrue than the operetta and the fairy-play. It cultivates the so-called 'cruel terms,' *i.e.*, phrases in which the persons openly make a display of all the pitiable, infamous and cowardly ideas and feelings which surge through their consciousness, and systematically neglect this most primitive and palpable fact, that by far the most widespread and tenacious characteristic of man is hypocrisy and dissimulation. The forms of customs survive incalculably longer than morality, and man simulates the greater honesty, and hides his baseness under appearances so much the more seeming-pious, as his instincts are more crafty and mean. The Verists, among whom are many powerful literary natures, are one of the most surprising and distressing phenomena in contemporary literature. One understands pessimism in sorely-tried France; one comprehends it also in the insupportable narrowness of social life in the crepuscular North, with its cloudy gray skies and its scourge of alcoholism. Eroticism, too, is comprehensible among the over-excited and exhausted Parisian population, and in the Scandinavian North, as a kind of revolt against the zealous discipline and morose constraint of a bigotry without joy, and mortifying to the flesh. But how could pessimism spring up under the radiant sunshine and eternally blue sky of Italy, in the midst of a handsome and joyous people who sing even in speaking (invalids like Leopardi might naturally appear as exceptions everywhere)? and how did Italians arrive at insane lubricity, when in their country there still exists, living in the temples and in the fields, a souvenir of the artlessly robust sensuality of the pagan world, with its symbols of fecundity; where also natural and healthy sexuality has always preserved through centuries the right to express itself innocently in art and literature? If Verism is anything else but an example of the propagation of intellectual epidemics by imitation, the task devolves upon the scientific Italian critic to explain this paradox in the history of manners.

The other group of Zola's imitators is not composed of superior degenerates, unhealthy persons who sincerely give themselves out for what they are, and express often with talent what they feel; but of people who morally and mentally stand on a level with supporters of evil, who, instead of the trade of night-birds, have chosen the less dangerous and hitherto more esteemed vocation of authors of novels and dramas, when the theory of naturalism had made it accessible to them. This brood has only taken immodesty from M. Zola, and conformably with the degree of culture has carried it into obscenity without circumlocution. To this group belong the professional Parisian pornographers, whose daily and weekly papers, stories, pictures, and theatrical representations in M. de Chirac's style, continually give employment to the correctional tribunals; the Norwegian authors of novels on street-walkers; and, unhappily, also a portion of our 'Young German' realists. This group stands outside of literature. It forms a portion of that riff-raff of great towns who professionally cultivate immorality, and have chosen this trade with full responsibility, solely from horror of honest work and greed for lucre. It is not mental therapeutics, but criminal justice, which is competent to judge them.

CHAPTER II.

THE 'YOUNG-GERMAN' PLAGIARISTS.

THIS chapter is not, properly, within the scope of this book. It must not be forgotten that I did not wish to write a history of literature, nor to indulge in current æsthetic criticism, but to demonstrate the unhealthy mental condition of the imitators of fashionable literary tendencies. It does not enter into my plan to deal with those degenerates or lunatics who evolve their works from their own morbid consciousness, and themselves discover the artistic formula for their own eccentricities—in other words, with those leaders who go their own way because they choose or because they must. Mere imitators I have neglected on principle throughout the whole of my inquiry, first because the genuine degenerates only form a feeble minority among them, while the great majority is a perfectly responsible rabble of swindlers and parasites, and next because even the few diseased persons who are found in their ranks do not belong to the class of 'higher' degenerates, but are poor weak minds who, taken separately, possess no importance whatever, and at most only deserve a fleeting mention in so far as they testify to the influence of their masters on ill-balanced minds.

If, then, in spite of this, I devote a special chapter to the so-called 'Young-German' 'realists,' while I have despatched in a few words the Italian and Scandinavian Zolaists, it is verily and by no means because the former are any more worthy than the latter. On the contrary, some of the Italian 'Verists,' the Dane, J. P. Jakobsen, the Norwegian, Arne Garborg, the Swede, Auguste Strindberg, devoid as they are of real originality, possess, nevertheless, more vigour and talent in their little finger than all 'Young-Germany' put together. I only dwell on the latter because the history of the propagation of a mental contagion in his own country is not without importance for the German reader, and also because the way in which this group has appeared and permeated shows up certain traits in which we can detect the neurosis of the age, and, lastly, because some few of their members are good examples of intensive hysteria, having, in addition to complete incapacity and a general feebleness of mind, that malicious and anti-social ego-mania, that moral obtuseness, that irresistible need of attracting attention to themselves, no matter by what means, that facetious vanity and self-approbation, which characterizes the complaint.

I will not deny that when I turn towards the 'Young-German' movement I can scarcely maintain the cool equanimity with which, according to scientific method, I have hitherto observed any given phenomena. As a German writer I feel deep shame and sorrow at the spectacle of the literature which has been so long and so brutally proclaimed, with flourish of trumpets, and with systematic disdain of all that did not bear its seal, as the unique and exclusively German literature of the present time, and even that of the future.*

Since genius was congregated at Weimar, German literature has ever taken the lead in civilized humanity. We were the inventors, foreigners were the imitators. We provisioned the world with poetic forms and ideas. Romanticism originated among us, and only became a literary and artistic

* *Le Temps*, N° du 13 Février, 1892: 'Current literature . . . is, at present, at an inconceivably low ebb in Germany. From one end of the year to the other it is becoming an impossibility to discover a novel, a drama, or a page of criticism worthy of notice. The *Deutsche Rundschau* itself recently admitted this in despair. It is not only the talent and the style which are deficient—all is poor, weak and flat; one might imagine one's self in France, in the time of Bouilly. . . . Even the desire to rise above a certain level of ordinary writing seems wanting. One ends by being thankful to any contemporary German author who is seen to be making . . . the simplest effort not to write like a crossing-sweeper.' Every German who observes all the literary productions of his contemporaries will see that this is the opinion of a spiteful enemy. This opinion, nevertheless, is explained and justified by the fact that at the present day it is only the 'realists' who make enough stir to be heard in certain places abroad, and that there the natives are delighted to be able to consider them as representing all the German literature of the day.

fashion in France a good many years later, whence it passed on into England. Görres, Zacharias Werner, Novalis, and Oscar Von Redwitz, created lyric mysticism and neo-Catholicism among us, and these have only just reached France. Our poet-precursors of the revolution of 1848, Karl Beck, George Herwegh, Freiligrath, Ludwig Seeger, Friedrich von Sallet, R. E. Prutz, etc., had even then sung of the misery, the uprisings, and the hopes of the disinherited, before the Walt Whitmans, the William Morrises, and the Jules Jouys, were born, men whom to-day people in America, England, and France, would like to consider as the discoverers of the Fourth Estate for lyric poetry. Pessimism was embodied almost at the same time in Italy (in Leopardi) and among us in Nicholas Lenau, more than a generation before French naturalism built its art upon it. Goethe created symbolic poetry in the second part of *Faust* half a century before Ibsen and the French Symbolists parodied this tendency. Every healthy current and every pathological current in contemporary poetry and art can be traced back to a German source, every progress and every decadence in this sphere have their point of departure in Germany. The philosophical theory of every novel method of thought, as well as of every new error, which, during a hundred years, have gained a hold over civilized humanity, has been furnished by the Germans. Fichte gave us the theory of romanticism; Feuerbach (almost at the same time as Auguste Comte), that of the mechanical conception of the world; Schopenhauer, that of pessimism; the Hegelians, Max Stirner, and Karl Marx, that of the most rigid ego-mania and the most rigid collectivism, etc. And now we suffer the humiliation of seeing a heap of contemptible plagiarists hawking about the dullest and coarsest counterfeit of French imitations (which all the clever men in France have already abandoned and repudiated) as 'the most modern' production offered by Germany, as the flower of German literature, present and future. We even permit foreign critics to say: 'Ancient fashions disdained in France even by village beauties, are to be seen exhibited in German shop-windows as the greatest novelties, and credulously accepted by the public.' The realists naturally deny that they are mere repeaters and limping belated followers.* But he who knows

* Arno Holz—Johannes Schlaf, *Die Familie Selicke*, 3e Auflage; Berlin, 1892, p. vi.: 'In fact, nothing so provokes us to smile . . . as when they, in their anxiety to find models, label us as plagiarists of the great foreign authors. Let them say it, then. . . . It will be acknowledged some day that there has never yet been in our literature a movement less influenced from without, more strongly originated from within—in one word, more *national*—than this movement, even at the further development of which we look to-day, and which has had for its visible point of departure our *Papa*

a little more of art and poetry than is learnt in a Berlin tavern frequented by realists, or in a low newspaper informed by this sort of company; he who contemplates in its entire range the contemporary movement of thought without stopping on the frontiers of his own country, can have no doubt whatever that German realism, as a local phenomenon, may have for Germany itself a melancholy importance, but does not exist at all for universal literature, because all trace of personal or national originality is lacking. To the chorus in which the voices of humanity express its feelings and thoughts, not the faintest new note has been added by it.

Plagiarists so low down in the scale as the German realists are not in the least entitled to a detailed individual examination. To do this would be to make one's self both ridiculous in the eyes of competent judges and of a piece with strolling players, to whom it is a matter of small importance whether they are praised or blamed, provided they are mentioned. Other motives also warn me to be prudent in the choice of examples I propose to lay before the reader. I am firmly convinced that in a few years all this movement will be forgotten even to the name itself. The lads who now pretend to be the future of German literature will discover little by little that the business to which they have devoted themselves is less agreeable and lucrative than they had imagined.* Those among them who yet possess a last remnant of health and strength will find the way to their natural vocation, and become restaurant-waiters or servants, night-watchmen or peddlers, and I should fear to injure their advancement in these honest professions if I nailed here the remembrance of their aberration of past days, which would otherwise be forgotten by all. The feebler and weaker among them, who could not manfully resolve to earn their bread by a decent occupation, will disappear probably as drunkards, vagabonds, beggars, perhaps even in a house of correction, and if, after the lapse of years, a serious reader happened to come across their names in this book, he would be right in exclaiming, 'What sort of bad joke is this? What

---

Hamlet. Die Familie Selicke is the most thoroughly German piece of writing our literature possesses,' etc. This passage may serve the reader as a model both of the style in which these lads write, and of the tone in which they speak of themselves and their productions.

* The complaint of want of money is a constant refrain among the 'Young Germans.' Listen to Baron Detlev von Liliencron: 'You had nothing to eat again to-day; as a set-off, every blackguard has had his fill.' 'The terror of infernal damnation is—A garden of roses under the kisses of spring,—When I think of how heart and soul fret,—To be hourly bitten by the need of money.' And Karl Bleibtreu: 'Brass reigns, gold reigns,—Genius goes its way a-begging.' 'To call a ton of gold one's own,—Sublime end, unattainable to man!' etc.

does the author want to make me believe? There never have been such men!' Finally, an absolutely incapable pseudo-writer is individually deprived of all importance, and only acquires it as one of a number. He cannot therefore be treated critically, but merely statistically. For all these reasons I shall only draw from the whole number a few characters and works, to show with their help what German 'realism' really is.

The founder of the realist school is Karl Bleibtreu. He accomplished this work of foundation by publishing a brochure of which the principal feature was a cover of brilliant red furrowed by black lightning in zigzags, and which bore this title like the roll of a kettle-drum, *Revolution in Literature.* In this literary 'tout' Bleibtreu, without the slightest attempt at substantiation, but with a brazen brow, depreciated a whole series of esteemed and successful authors, swore with great oaths that they were dead and buried, and announced the dawn of a new literary epoch, which already counted a certain number of geniuses, at the head of whom he himself stood.

As an author Bleibtreu, in spite of the many and various works he has already published, does not yet count for much. It would, however, be unjust to ignore his great ability as a book-maker. In this respect *Revolution in der Literatur* is a model production. With skilful address, he mingled authors of repute whom he hacked into sausage-meat with a few shallow scribblers in vogue, whom it was no doubt rather foolish to fight, with the grand airs of a gladiator, but whom no one would have defended against a smiling disdain. The presence of these unwarranted intruders into the group whom he undertook to extirpate from literature, may give to his raising of the standard a semblance of reason in the eyes of superficial readers. Not less cleverly chosen were the people whom he presented to readers as the new geniuses. With the exception of two or three decent mediocrities, for whom there is always a little modest corner in the literature of a great people, these were complete nullities from whom he himself never had to fear a dangerous competition. The greatest of his geniuses is, for example, Max Kretzer, a man who writes, in the German of a Cameroon-Negro, some professedly 'Berlin' novels, of which the best known, *Die Verkommenen,* is 'Berlinish' to such a degree that it simply dilutes the history of the widow Gras and the workman Gaudry, which took place in Paris in 1877. This event, celebrated as the first adventure with cocottes in which vitriol played a part, could only happen in Paris, and under the conditions of Parisian life. It is specifically Parisian. But Kretzer calmly removed the Paris trade-mark, replacing it with that of Berlin, and he thus created a 'Berlin' novel, vaunted by Bleibtreu as the ideal of a 'genuine' and 'true' exposition. He reclothes his newly-discovered 'geniuses,' who recall Falstaff's recruits, Mouldy, Shadow, Wart, Feeble, and Bullcalf (*King Henry IV.*, Part II.), in a uniform which he could not have chosen more effectively. He dressed them out in the costume of Schiller's brigands in the Bohemian forests; he pronounced them to be a troop of rebels, fighters at barricades, Lützow huntsmen in the struggle for freedom against hypocrisy perukes, and pig-tails, and all obstructionists; and he hoped that youth and the friends of progress would take him for something serious, on seeing him march at the head of his poor, infirm cripples and knockknees, thus disguised.

His plan, although excellently contrived and conducted, was only partially successful. Scarcely had he in a certain measure organized and drilled his little troop, when it mutinied and drove him away. It did not choose another captain, for each private soldier wished himself to be chief, and the feeblest and most timid of the band alone recognised any other genius outside his own. Bleibtreu has not to this day got over the ingratitude of the people who had taken his mystification seriously, and had really looked upon themselves as the geniuses he had proclaimed them to be, without, as he thought, running any risks; and in his last publication he still utters his sorrow in these bitter verses (*Aus einem lyrischen Tagebuch*):

> 'For what purpose this long struggle? 'Tis vain! And my hand is paralyzed. Long live falsehood, stupidity, folly! Adieu, thou German piggery! The earth of the tomb will extinguish the conflagration. I have been, as long as I could think, a veritable booby. I was no honest German, I was a wounded swan.'

Bleibtreu could not give any talent to the realists invented by him, but the latter borrowed from him a few of his turns of expression. To make an impression on the ignorant, they have associated with themselves as honorary members some respectable authors whom one is surprised to meet with *dans ce galère*. Thus the realists include among their numbers, for example, Théodore Fontane, a true poet, whose novels honourably hold their place among the best productions of the kind in any literature of Europe; H. Heiberg, of vigorous although unequal talent; unfortunately compelled, as it would seem, by external circumstances to hasty and excessive work, against which, perhaps, his artistic conscience vainly protests; and Detlev von Liliencron, who is by no means a genius, but a good lyric poet with a sense of style, and who may rank by the side of *epigoni* such as a Hans Hopfen, a Hermann Lingg, a Martin Greif. Considering the high level that

German lyric poetry—the first in the world even in the judgment of foreign nations—has occupied uninterruptedly since Goethe, it is giving a German poet no small praise if one can say he is not inferior to the average of the last seventy years. Liliencron, however, does not surpass it, and I do not see how he can be fairly placed above Rudolf Baumbach, for example, whom the realists affect to despise, probably because he has disdained to join their gang. It is not incomprehensible that a Fontane or a Heiberg should consent to suffer the importunate promiscuousness of the realists. The Church, too, admits sometimes to serve in the Mass young rogues from the street, who have only to swing the censer. The sole thing that is demanded of them as realists *honoris causâ*, is to bear silently and smilingly this compromise of an honourable name. Liliencron alone thinks himself obliged to make some concessions to his new companions, in using here and there in his last poems, not his own language, but theirs.

Besides the smuggling in of some esteemed names among theirs, the realists have carefully practised and cultivated another business-trick of Bleibtreu's—that of effective disguise. They assumed (in the collection of lyric poetry entitled *Young Germany*, Friedenau and Leipzig, 1886) the name of 'Young Germany,' which calls up a faint remembrance of the great and bold innovators of 1830, as well as ideas of blooming youth and spring, with a false nose of modernism tied on. But let us here at once remark that the realists, plagiarists to the backbone, do not even possess sufficient independence to find a name peculiarly their own, but have quietly plagiarized the denomination under which the Heine-Boerne-Gutzkow group has become renowned.

As the first specimen of 'realist' literature of 'Young Germany,' I will quote the novel by Heinz Tovote, *Im Liebesrausch*.* He relates the history of a landed proprietor and former officer, Herbert von Düren, who makes the acquaintance of a certain Lucy, formerly a waitress at an inn, and the mistress of quite a number of young men in succession. He makes her his mistress, and indulges in his passion until, being unable to live without her, he induces her to marry him. Herbert, who is only partially acquainted with Lucy's past, presents her to his mother. The latter, who very soon perceives the relations existing between her son and this person, nevertheless gives her consent, and the marriage takes place. In the aristocratic and military society of Berlin, in which the couple move for a time, Lucy's antecedents soon

* Heinz Tovote, *Im Liebesrausch*, Berliner Roman, 6e Auflage. Berlin, 1893.

become known, and she is 'cut' by all the world. Herbert himself remains faithfully attached to her, until he discovers one day by accident, at the house of one of his friends—of course a 'realist' painter—a picture representing the nude figure of Lucy bathing in the sea! He very logically concludes that his wife had posed as a model to the painter, and he drives her away. As a matter of fact, however, the 'realist' had painted the nude figure from imagination, and involuntarily given it Lucy's features, because of the respectful admiration he secretly cherishes for her. (Judge for a moment how that could be if she had been disreputable!) Then Herbert, smitten with remorse, seeks the vanished Lucy, whom he discovers, after heart-breaking efforts, in his own house, where she has lived for months unknown to him. The reconciliation of husband and wife takes place amid general pathos, and the young wife dies in giving birth to a child, and uttering affecting sentiments.

I will not waste time by pointing out the silliness of this story. The essential part in a novel, moreover, is not the plot, but the form, in both the narrower and the broader sense—language, style, composition—and these I will examine a little later.

The very first thing we have a right to expect of a man who assumes to write for the public, *i.e.*, for the educated people of his own nation, is evidently that he should be master of his own language. Now, Heinz Tovote has no idea whatever of German. He commits the grossest errors every moment—solecisms, mistakes of syntax, ignorance of the value of words—which make one's hair stand on end. Some few of these abominable faults of language are tolerably widespread, others belong to the jargon of the roughest class of the people; but there are some that Tovote could never have heard. They are the result of his personal ignorance of German grammar.

Next as to his style. When Tovote writes a description, in order to determine and strengthen the substantive, he chooses, on principle, the adjective naturally contained in that substantive. Here are some examples of this intolerable tautology: 'An icy January storm.' 'In the Friedrichstrasse light elegant equipages were crowded.' 'Incarnation of the most lovable grace.' 'A slowly creeping fever. 'A lazy somnolence.' 'They glowed fiery in the last light.' 'She suffered cruel torments,' etc. I doubt if any author, having but little respect for himself, his vocation, his maternal tongue or his readers, would put such words together. There is no necessity, in hunting for the 'rare and precious epithet,' to go so far as the French stylists, but such a sweeping together of the stalest, most useless, and most inexpressive adjectives is not literature; it is properly, to echo the French critic, the work of scavengers. Another characteristic of this style is its silliness. The author relates that Herbert von Düren was 'keenly interested, from its first appearance,' in Sullivan's operetta *The Mikado*. 'Now that it had cast off its English garb, it seemed to him still more indigenous.' Thus he seriously declares that an English operetta has seemed to a German more indigenous in the German language than in English. 'Suddenly he was seized with a senseless fury against this man who saluted him so politely, whereby he, who was habitually politeness itself to everyone, did not return the salute, and turned away.' Not to respond to a salute by way of expressing his 'senseless fury' is truly not very ferocious on the part of an old officer. 'The horses were hanging their heads sadly, and sleeping.' That it is possible to sleep sadly or gaily is a discovery by Tovote. 'Like walls, the colossi of houses stood crowding against each other.' Like walls? One would think that houses really have walls. It is exactly as if Tovote had said: 'Like men, the people stood crowding against each other.'

When Tovote strives to write in a sublime and beautiful style, the result we get is as follows: 'Yet there lay in the slender perfectly levelled lines a slumbering strength.' (What can the lines be which are 'slender,' *i.e.*, not thick and 'perfectly levelled'?) 'She was already smiling through her tears, and her face resembled a summer landscape which, while the rain still falls on the corn, is bathed again in the bright rays of the sun emerging from clouds.' Thus, what we are first to think of when contemplating a face is a summer landscape. 'He felt how her lips clung [*sich klammerten!*] to his.' 'It must be granted that, considering his youth, he has the incontestable genius of a lively conception,' etc.

Tovote seeks to plagiarize the diffuse descriptions of the French naturalists, and unfolds pictures the novelty, clearness, and vigour of which the following quotations will enable us to admire. (End of a theatrical representation:) 'In the stalls the seats clapped back with a muffled sound. . . . The audience rose, doors were opened, curtains were drawn back, and the theatre emptied slowly, while a few isolated spectators alone remained in their places.' 'Unceasingly, the whole night the snowflakes fell. In thick bales [!] it lay on the bare branches of the trees, which threatened to break down in winterly weakness. The pines and low bushes were enveloped in a thick mantle of snow. To the straw, wound round the standard roses, the snow clung, and formed strange figures; it lay a foot high on the walls, and delicately veiled the points of the iron railings. All tracks were effaced. The wind, which drove the flakes before it, threw them into all the hollows, so that all the corners and all the unevennesses disappeared.' 'They stood high above the sea, which spread around them like an infinite plain.' 'The sun had set. . . . The clouds, heavily encamped on the horizon, still glowed with flaming crimson purple; then they passed into violet, which changed into a colourless gray [so there is a coloured gray also?] until night descended, and all colours gradually died out.' (Compare this pitiable attempt to counterfeit 'impressionism' with the French models quoted in the preceding chapter.) 'The night had completely closed in—a dark, profoundly black night.' (Consider the juxtaposition of these two adjectives.) 'The moon alone hung mournfully above the waters [the moon in a night both 'dark' and 'profoundly black!'], and the lighthouse threw its flood of light into the distance. Deep at their feet the sea raved with muffled roar in the spite of a thousand years [!], and licked the creviced rocks.' A 'raving spite' which 'licks' does not appear to be a very dangerous spite. 'She retained the deep wound over her eye as a little scar all her life long.' If she had a 'little scar,' she did not therefore keep a deep wound 'all her life long.' 'Above them, in the blue sky, a vulture wheeled in circles with outspread wings, lost like a black point in this sea of light.' In a vulture which is only seen as 'a black point,' it is not possible to distinguish the 'outspread wings.' Here is the description of a face: 'Two full fresh lips, chaste [!], bright red, a graceful little nose, imperceptibly tilted, but parting in a narrow straight line from the forehead.' We will leave the reader the trouble of imagining for himself this 'little nose imperceptibly tilted' in 'the narrow straight line.' 'The engine of the express train panted across the level plain which stretched all round like a burning desert. Right and left, field after field of corn, fruitful orchards and verdant meadows.' Fields, orchards, meadows, and yet a 'burning [?] desert'? 'The half-closed eyes, with their white membranes, look at him so steadily.' This does not mean, as one might suppose, the eyes of a bird, but those of a human being, in which our novelist professes to have discovered these incomprehensible 'white membranes.'

We have seen what impressionism and the descriptive *tic* of naturalism have become in the hands of Tovote. I will now show how this 'realist' can observe and reproduce reality in the smallest as in the greatest things. Herbert, the first evening of his acquaintance with Lucy, takes her to a restaurant and orders, among other things, a bottle of burgundy. 'The waiter placed the pot-bellied bottle on the table, in a flourishing curve.' Burgundy in 'pot-bellied' bottles! They eat soup, served in 'silver bowls' (!), green peas and a capon, the excellence of which forms the subject of their incredible conversation at table, and when this repast is disposed of, and Lucy has lighted a cigarette, she asks for oysters, which are brought and eaten by her 'served according to the rules of art.' I should certainly not reproach anyone for not knowing a bottle of burgundy by sight, nor at which stage of a repast one eats oysters. I myself did not grow up amongst oysters and burgundy, but it would be more honest not to speak of these good things till one knows something of them. Let us give a passing notice to the unconscious respect, mingled with envy, for the difficult and distinguished occupation of eating oysters, deliciously revealed in this admiring declaration, that Lucy has oysters 'served' (?) 'according to the rules of art,' and the backwoodsman's ignorance of the most elementary good breeding which Tovote betrays in making a man of the world talk incessantly at table about the food. To continue. Lucy's lover has travelled, viâ Brussels, 'from Havre to Egypt.' In that case he must have chartered a steamer on his own account, as there is no regular line of steamers between Havre and Egypt. For some months Herbert has had on his writing-table some unfinished manuscripts. 'He rummaged through this heap of yellow manuscripts.' Under shelter the worst ligneous fibre paper itself would certainly not turn yellow in the space of a few months. The bed-chamber, arranged with all possible care by Herbert for his Lucy, has 'blue silk curtains,' and 'pale pink satin' seats. Such a wild combination of colours would be avoided by the better secondhand dealers even in their shop windows.

I grant that all these blunders, although amusing, are insignificant. They must not be passed over, however, when committed by a 'realist,' who boasts of 'observation' and 'truth.' Graver still are the impossible actions and characters of the men. In a moment of grief Lucy lets 'fall her arms on the table-napkin in her lap, and looks vacantly before her, biting her under lip.' Has anyone ever seen or done such a thing in this state of mind? Wild ecstasy of love Lucy expresses thus: '"Kiss me," she implored, and her whole being seemed to wish to lose itself in him—"kiss me!"' Herbert had made her acquaintance in Heligoland, where she lived with an Englishman named Ward, and had taken her to be Ward's betrothed. A German officer of good family, being considerably over thirty, was actually able to look upon a woman living with a rich young foreigner alone at a watering-place as his betrothed! The latter, an absolutely neglected child of the working class, learnt English with Ward in less than a year so perfectly that she was everywhere mistaken for an Englishwoman, and played the piano so well that she could execute pieces from operettas, etc.

I do not consider it a crime when Tovote, in using French words, confounds *tourniquet* with *moulinet,* and speaks of *cabinets séparés* instead of *cabinets particuliers.* A German does not require to know French. It would be a good thing indeed if he knew German. Good taste, however, would prevent his making a display of scraps of a language of which he knows absolutely nothing.

The obscenities with which the novel swarms are incomparably weaker than in analogous passages by Zola, but they are peculiarly repulsive because, in spite of the absolute incapacity of Tovote to rise above the coarseness of commercial travellers relating their love adventures in hotels, they, nevertheless, betray his determination to be violently sensational and subtly sensual.

If I have lingered thus long over this bungling piece of work, so far below the level of literature, it is because of its being thoroughly typical of German realism. The language transgresses the simplest rules of grammar. Not one expression is accurately chosen, and really characterizes the object or the concept that is brought before the reader. That an author should speak not only accurately, but expressively, that he should be able to reproduce impressions and ideas in an original and powerful way, that he must have a feeling for the value and delicate sense of words; of this Tovote has not the slightest idea. His descriptions are shabby enough to raise a blush on the cheek of the police reporter of a low class paper. Nothing is seen, nothing is felt; the whole is but a droning echo of reading of the worst sort. 'Modernism' consists finally in this, that a pitiable commonplace is partly located in Berlin, with here and there vague talk of socialism and realism. German criticism in the seventies demanded, very justly, that the German novel should rest on a solid basis, that it should be worked out in some well-known period, amid real surroundings, in the German capital of our day. This demand has produced the 'Berlinese' novel of the plagiarists. The especial and characteristic Berlinism of this novel consists in this, that the author whenever he has to mention a street, displays the boundless astonishment of a Hottentot at the 'Panoptikum' (the Grévin Museum in Berlin), because he finds the street full of people, carriages, and shops, and seeks opportunities to quote the names of the streets in this capital. This method is within the reach of every hotel porter. In order to introduce such Berlinism into a bad novel, the author need only possess a plan of the town, and perhaps a guide-book. The peculiarities of life in the capital are represented by passages such as this: 'On both sides of the pavement [he meant to say, on the pavement on both sides of the street] a dense crowd of people surged, and in the middle of the avenue, under the trees, just bursting into leaf, a scattered multitude, resembling the irregular [?] waves of a flood, pushed on to get out of the town.' Or: 'On all the pavements people walking and pushing against each other in confusion and haste, which increased to a run, in order to avoid falling under the wheels, while escaping to a place of refuge from the deafening clatter of cabs, tramways, and large heavy omnibuses, with their roofs fully occupied,' etc. Thus, the only thing Tovote sees in Berlin is what a peasant from Buxtehude would remark, who has left his village for the first time, and cannot recover from his astonishment in finding more people and carriages than in his own village street. This is just the view which a resident in a town no longer notices, and which need not be specially described, because it is implied in the concept of a 'town,' and, above all, of a 'large town,' and is, notably, in no way characteristic of Berlin, since Breslau, Hamburg, Cologne, etc., present exactly the same sight.

Socialism enters into the 'modern' novel like Pilate into the Creed. Tovote relates, *e.g.*, how Herbert seeks for Lucy, who has disappeared; he arrives at last at the workman's quarter in Berlin, which supplies the author with this fine picture: 'Everywhere the blue and gray-red blouse of the workman, which is never seen *Unter den Linden*, who stands, day after day, near the panting machine, at the work-table, where he carries on, during long years, as if asleep, the same manual labours, until the callosities on his hands become as hard as iron.' Either Herbert, despairingly seeking his mistress, or the narrator, wishing to awaken our interest in these events, has thought of the callosities of the workmen!

The automata who in the 'realist' novel execute mock-movements, and between whom the dullest and most miserable back-stair sentimentality is played off, are always the same: a gentleman, an ex-officer whenever possible, who, we are assured, is engaged upon 'works on socialism' (of what kind we never learn, it is simply asserted that they are 'very important'); a waitress at an inn, as the embodiment of the *ewig-Weibliche;* and a realist painter who plans or executes pictures destined to regenerate humanity, and to establish the millennium on earth. Here is the recipe for the 'modernism' of the 'Young-German' realism: quotation of the names of the Berlin streets, rapture at the sight of some cabs and omnibuses, a little Berlinese dialect in the mouth of the characters, coarse and stupid eroticism, unctuous allusions to socialism and phrases on painting, such as a goose-fattener grown rich might make if she wished to pass herself off as a lady. Of the three persons who are always the supporters of this 'modernity' the waitress is the only really original one. The merit of this treasure belongs to Bleibtreu, who first presented her to the admiration and imitation of his little band in his collection of novels entitled *Schlechte Gesellschaft.* She is a conglomeration of all the fabulous beings that have hitherto been imagined in poetry: a winged chimæra, a sphinx with lion's claws, and a siren with a fish's tail, all at one and the same time. She contains in herself every charm and every gift, love and wisdom, virtue and love-glowing paganism. It is by the waitress at the inn that the talent for observation and creative power of the German 'realist' can be most accurately gauged.

If Tovote is a representative type—by no means diseased, but merely incapable beyond conception—of intruders into literature with which they will at most be connected as peddling hawkers of trashy novels, we meet in Hermann Bahr with a clearly pathological individuality. Bahr is an advanced hysteric who wants at all hazards to get himself talked about, and has had the unfortunate idea of achieving this result by books. Devoid of talent to an almost impossible degree, he seeks to captivate attention by the maddest eccentricities. Thus, he calls the book most characteristic of his method among those he has hitherto published, *Die gute Schule; Seelenstände.** *Seelenstände* literally means 'states of soul.' He had read and not understood the term *états d'âme* in the new French authors, *état* having been used in the political sense which it has in *tiers-états.*

In the story related in the *Seelenstände*, a part at least of the recipe previously mentioned is utilized. The hero is an Austrian painter living in Paris. One day, weary of living alone, he picks up a girl in the street, who, contrary to the orthodox procedure, is not a waitress, but a dressmaker, possessing, nevertheless, all the mythical excellence of the 'Young German' barmaid; he lives with her for a time, then wearies of her, and torments her to such a degree that she leaves him one fine day and goes off with a rich negro, whom she induces to buy pictures at a high price from her abandoned lover.

This fine story is the frame in which Bahr reveals the 'state' of his hero's 'soul.' This author is a plagiarist of an inveterate type, such as is only met with in serious cases of hysteria. Not a single author of any individuality who has passed before his eyes has been able to escape his rage for servile imitation.

* Hermann Bahr, *Die gute Schule; Seelenstände.* Berlin, 1890.

The principle of the 'Good School'—the misery of a painter who struggles with the conception of a work of art intended to express his whole soul, and who recognises with despair his impotence to realize it—is subtilized from Zola's *L'Œuvre*, All the details, as we shall see, he has taken from Nietzsche, Stirner, Ibsen, the Diabolics, Decadents, and French Impressionists. But all he plagiarizes becomes, under his pen, a parody of inimitably exquisite absurdity.

The painter's distress of mind is 'the lyrism of red. His whole soul was steeped in red, all his feelings, all his aims, all his desires, in sonnets of lament and hope; and in general a complete biography of red, what took place in him and usually whatever could happen to him. . . . But this lofty canticle of the red fulfilled itself in the real, simple tones of daily life. . . . It was a large well-boiled lobster, in which he embodied the masterful spirit and the violence of the red, his languor in a salmon on one side, and his mischievousness and gaiety of disposition in many radishes in cheerful variations. But the great and supreme confession of his whole soul hung on a purple tablecloth with heavy folds, on which the sun shone, a narrow shaft, but with all the more fiery glow.' If the struggle with the 'biography of the red' was a torture to him, even worse things were about to happen. One day 'the curse struck him behind, coming from an excellent salmon, juicy and sweet, which one would never have suspected of perfidy as it lay cradling itself in a rosy shimmer in its rich herb sauce.' (A cooked salmon cradling itself! This must have produced a ghostly effect. And this uncanny salmon struck him 'behind,' although it was on the table before him!) But it was precisely this sauce, this sauce of green herbs, the pride of the cook—yes, it was this that did it. It was this that conquered him. He had never seen anything like it—never before, as far back as he could remember, a softer and sweeter green, at once so languishing and so joyous that one could have sung and shouted for joy. The whole rococo was in it, only in a much more gracious, yearning note. It had to go into his picture. But he could never hit off that green sauce, and this was the tragedy of his life. He 'kept the truth locked up cowardly and idle, he who alone could grant it; he did not give it to them to assuage thirst, this healing and redeeming work of his breast,' namely, the green sauce! 'He would have liked to make a gigantic gimlet revolve in his flesh with a burning screw . . . deep, very deep, till there was a great hole . . . an immense triumphal gate of his art, through which the internals could spit it out.'

What makes this struggle with the green sauce, for the purpose of overcoming it in a 'healing and redeeming' work of art, so irresistibly comic is that the whole passage is written in an entirely serious view, and without the least idea of joking!

Bahr describes his own style in these words: 'A wild, feverish, tropical style, which calls nothing by its usual name in the ordinary idiom, but which racks itself in the hope of finding unheard-of, obscure, and strange neologisms, in a forced and singular combination.'

The painter's mistress must have been a superb creature, to judge by the description. When a stranger spoke to her in the street 'she slightly quickened her steps, and with eyelids haughtily raised, and her little head thrown back sideways, she began to hum softly, sharply snapping her fingers with impatience, in such a way as to rouse his desire to persevere in his useless suit.' This behaviour induces Bahr to call her a 'majestically inaccessible young lady.' But she is far more remarkable at her morning toilet at home than she is in the street. 'Often, when under the greetings of the morning, which enamelled with gold [!] her hyacinthine flesh, she plaited her hair while standing before her mirror, surrounded by his desires, and stretched, moistened, and slowly curved, with twitching fingers which glittered like swift serpents, quite gently and persistently, her tangled [!] eyelashes, her dishevelled eyebrows, while her lips grew round with silent whistling, between which the rapid, restless tongue hissed, shot out, and clacked, and then, with closed eyelids, leant forward as in submissive adoration, the powder-puff passed slowly, cautiously, fervently, over the bent cheeks, while the little nose, fearful of the dust, turned aside,' the painter, as may be imagined, became so amorous that 'he licked the soap from her fingers to refresh his fevered gums.' 'Suddenly standing upright on one leg, with a swing of the other she kicked her shoe into the air, to catch it again by a nimble, firm movement. In this graceful attitude she remained.' 'Sometimes she bent down languorously towards herself, very gently, very slowly, remaining voluptuously in the curve of her breasts, deep into her knees, while her lips moved; sometimes, while her hips turned in a circle, her neck glided lasciviously into swan-like [!] curves towards her obsequious image.' This sight filled her lover with such enthusiasm that it seemed to him 'as if from a thousand springs blasted [!] torrents blazed through his veins.'

It is not necessary, I think, to multiply specimens of this style, which simulates insanity, and which is not German, either in formation, use of terms, or construction. I wish merely to show to what degree Bahr is a plagiarist. Here we see a copy of Nietzsche: 'Always the same. He ought to do this, and not to do that; the same litany from his first infancy—always and only; he should and he shouldn't. What he would was the only thing never demanded of him; and thus, in this frightful servitude, he felt himself possessed by an immense desire to be for once himself at last, and an immense anguish at being always someone else eternally.' 'To say that everyone only came out of himself to penetrate into another . . . to dominate him! That a man could never, should never, be himself, not have one hour of bliss, but everlastingly renounce, transform, annihilate himself for another's gratification. . . . Alone—alone; why would they not leave one alone?' . . . 'To make a desert for himself—a still silent desert.' 'Others had not this sentiment of the "I" to such an exuberant and immeasurable extent.' 'The joyous hatred of men and the world.' Here we have Ibsen: 'He wished to go into the country—he himself, precisely as proposed by the other, certainly. But he wished to go into the country in virtue of his free resolve, because it was his will, and not the proposal of another. . . . And rather than bend to another's will he renounced his own. Moreover, since another wished it, the pleasure of wishing it himself was lost to him.' Here the De Goncourts: 'There was around her out of the sorrowful violet and bright gold a misty shimmer.' 'His feeling was always something inconceivable, and also on a yellow ground —dirty yellow—gasping, ecstatic, faint, pining away with a death-rattle, and with violet tones, but very soft.' 'It was chaste voluptuousness. He had it there in his brain, pearly gray, melting into faint violet.' Villiers de l'Isle-Adam: 'He was bound to establish the new love. . . . The question was of doing it in the style of electricity and steam. An Edison-love . . . yes, a machine-like love.' A mixture of Baudelaire and Huysmans: 'In the undulating silver dust of the light a lovely quivering sheen, woven of blue-black and pale green vapour, bathed her rosy flesh, exhaled by its soft down. . . . He wished utterly to destroy and flay her. Nothing but blood—blood. He only felt at ease when it streaked [!] down. . . . He established a theory according to which this was the way towards the new love, viz., by torture.' 'There lay the meadows red as fire spread out in lovely slopes . . . and hopes, the blue vampires, grew listless. But upright in its pride and with imperial mourning walked a huge gray sunflower, silent and pale, on the arm of an awkward fat stinking thistle, which trailed noisily afar with large rough gold.' 'This now became for him true art, the art which alone could redeem and make happy—the art of odours. . . . From pale and moaning fumes of the white rose, in which the suicide triumphs, he awakened the eternal doctrine of Buddha,' etc. The remainder is better expressed in the original, in Huysmans' novel, *A Rebours*. As to the passages full of a heat which clamours for a strait-jacket, and simulates satyriasis and Sadism; as to the quaint confusions and orthographical errors in French names which the author, who poses as a Parisian, commits at every step; and as to his frequent manifestation of megalomania, it is enough to refer to them. These things are not essential, but they contribute to make Bahr's book the only product of hysterical mental derangement hitherto existing in German literature.

The greater number of Young-German plagiarists have not yet risen to the monumental productions of a Tovote or a Bahr, and have stopped at short pieces of lyric poetry.

Special mention ought to be accorded to Gerhart Hauptmann, who has, unfortunately, permitted himself to be enrolled among the 'Young Germans.' It is difficult to confuse him with them, for if he makes concessions to their æsthetics of the commonplace with a carelessness which of itself betrays a disquieting obtuseness of artistic taste and conscience, he nevertheless may be distinguished from them by some great qualities. He possesses a luscious, vivid vocabulary, full of expression and feeling, even though it is a dialect. He knows how to see reality, and he has the power to render it in poetry.

It will not occur to anyone to pronounce any final judgment on this author of thirty years of age. As yet only his début can be mentioned, and hopes be formed for his future development. What he has hitherto produced has been surprisingly unequal. Side by side with originality his works present a barren imitation; with high artistic insight, a schoolboy's awkwardness and ingenuousness; with flights of genius, the most afflicting commonplaces. One scarcely knows if he is a novelist or a dramatic writer. In two of his pieces, in fact, *Vor Sonnenaufgang* and *College Crampton*, there is such a complete absence of progressive action, a condition of things so purely stationary and devoid of development, that even the instinct of a natural talent for the stage could never have so forgotten itself. Perhaps Hauptmann is only temporarily under the spell of an æsthetic theory, from which he will free himself later. He desires, indeed, to describe the 'milieu' faithfully and closely, and loses sight in so doing of the principal thing in poetry—of the characters and their fate. His dramas frequently fall asunder for this reason into a series of episodes, in themselves well observed and characteristic, but only distantly, or it may be not at all, connected with the plot, as, *e.g.*, in the play *Vor Sonnenaufgang*, the appearance of Hopslabär, the servant Mary who is leaving, the coachman's wife stealing the milk, etc. All are pictures of manners, but at the same time cease to form united compositions.

If Hauptmann has borrowed from the French realists the excessive and useless accentuation of the 'milieu,' he has taken from Ibsen the charlatanism of 'modernity' and the affectation of the 'thesis.' On the model of the Norwegian poet he suddenly inserts into some commonplace history belonging exclusively to no particular period or locality, some intrusive phrase containing an obscure allusion to 'the great times in which we live,' or the 'mighty events which are coming to pass,' etc. For example, *Einsame Menschen* (Lonely Folk) is the needlessly pretentious title of a drama in which we are shown a really Ibsenian idiot, who fancies himself misunderstood by his excellent wife, and becomes enamoured of a Russian girl-student, who is their visitor. As is generally the case with such feeble wights, he desires to possess the Russian, while not losing his wife; he has neither the courage to wound his wife by openly separating from her, nor the strength to conquer his guilty passion for the stranger. In his torment he tries to deceive himself, to persuade himself that his feelings towards the Russian are only those of friendship and of gratitude, that she has understood him and intellectually stimulated him. The Russian, however, is more clear-sighted, and is about to leave the house. The end of the story is that the idiot drowns himself. The conception of a weak man vacillating between two women, of whom one is the embodiment of duty, and the other of presumptive happiness, is as old as the theatre itself. It has nothing to do with the times. It can only be made to pass as 'modernism' by prevarication. And in this feeble drama Hauptmann makes his characters hold learned conversations full of allusions, such as the following:

FRÄULEIN ANNA (*the Russian*). These are, indeed, great times in which we are living. I seem to feel as if something close and oppressive were gradually lifting off from us. Do you not agree with me, Doctor?

JOHANNES (*the idiot*). In what way?

FRÄULEIN ANNA. On one side, a stifling dread was mastering us; on the other, a gloomy fanaticism. The excessive strain seems now to be straightened. Something like a breath of fresh air, let us say from the twentieth century, has come in upon us.*

The same swagger of modernity made the author decide on this title, *Vor Sonnenaufgang* (Before Sunrise), for his first work, and to qualify it as a 'social drama.' It is no more 'social' than any other drama, and has no connection whatever with 'sunrise' in a metaphorical sense. It reveals the state of affairs in a Silesian village, where the discovery of

* *Einsame Menschen;* Drama. 1891, p. 84.

coal-mines on their land has made the peasants millionaires. The contrast between the coarseness of the rustics and their opulence furnishes good scenes for a farce; but what has it to do with the age and its problems? A fragment of thesis is dovetailed into the farce. The peasant millionaire is a drunkard. The daughter may have inherited her father's vice. And so a man who has become attached and engaged to her leaves her with sorrowful determination on learning that the old man drinks. This thesis is an absurdity. A drunkard can transmit his vice to his children, but is not bound to do so, and, in the instance in point, the grown-up daughter does not betray the slightest inclination to drink. His thesis is worked out on the model of Ibsenian maunderings, and is as little taken from life as the lover who subordinates his love to a very uncertain theory. In this man we recognise our old friend, the type of the recipe for realist novels, who makes vague allusions to socialistic studies which he is reputed to pursue,* and proves himself, by these shadowy indications, to be a 'modern' man.

Hauptmann is true and strong only when he makes the poor of the lowest class speak in their own dialect. The maid-servants in *Vor Sonnenaufgang* are excellent. The nurse, who sings the baby to sleep; the laundress, Frau Lehmann, who laments her domestic troubles, are by far the most successful characters in *Einsame Menschen*. And if *Die Weber* is the best work he has hitherto produced, it is because only the poorest people, speaking only their own dialect, appear in it. But as soon as he has to deal with more complex human beings of the educated classes—beings who are not perishing with hunger nor suffering from poverty, who speak high German, and have a wider intellectual horizon—he becomes uncertain and flat, and catches up the pattern-album of realism instead of taking reality as his model.

Die Weber (The Weavers) is the only real drama among the five which Hauptmann has hitherto written.† There is

* Gerhart Hauptmann, *Vor Sonnenaufgang*, Soziales Drama, 6e Auflage; Berlin, 1892, p. 14: 'During the two years of my imprisonment, I wrote my first book on political economy.' P. 42: 'The Icarians . . . share equally all work and all desert. No one is poor; there are no poor among them.' P. 47: 'My fight is a fight for the happiness of all. . . . Moreover, I must say that the fight in the interest of progress brings me great satisfaction.' (Let it be understood that not the smallest trace of this famous 'fight' is to be seen in the piece!) P. 63: 'I should like to study the state of things here. I shall study the position of the miners here. . . . My work must be pre-eminently descriptive,' etc.

† Since this book has been published, Hauptmann has put on the stage two new pieces: *The Beaver Pelisse*, which was an utter fiasco, and *Hannele, a Dream Poem*, much discussed on account of its strange mysticism.

not much action in this piece; but it is sufficient, and it progresses. First, we see the profound misery in which the weavers are perishing; then we behold the rousing of their fury at their intolerable condition, and then their passion gradually developed before our eyes in ever-deepening intensity, rising into frenzy, destructive madness, tumults and riots, with all their tragic consequences. The extraordinary part of this drama is that the author has triumphed, with a genius which entitles him to our respect, over the enormous difficulty of captivating and stirring our human feelings, without making any individual character the centre-point of his piece, and of distributing the action between a great number of persons and a multitude of individual traits, without its ever ceasing to be a united and compact whole. These features, revealing a painfully minute observation, necessarily belong to individuals; nevertheless, they excite a very lively interest, sympathy and pity, not for the person, but for a whole class of men. We reach through emotion a generalization which usually is only a work of the intellect, through a poetic composition to a feeling which usually is excited only by history. In making this possible, Hauptmann rises infinitely above the bog of barren imitation, and creates a truly new form, viz., the drama in which the hero is not an individual, but the crowd; he succeeds, by artistic means, in presenting us with the hallucination that we are constantly seeing before us the nameless millions, while naturally there are never more than a few persons in the scene who suffer, speak, and act. Besides this great and radical innovation, other burning æsthetic questions are solved in the piece with overpowering beauty and sobriety. We have here a drama without love, and at the same time a proof that other sentiments besides the one instinct of sex can powerfully stir the soul of the reader. The piece is, moreover, a curious contribution to the wholly new 'psychology of the masses,' with which Sighele, Fournial, and others have been occupied,* and it gives an absolutely exact picture of the delirium and hallucinations which take possession of the individual in the midst of an excited crowd, and transforms his character and all his instincts after the model of the usually criminal leaders. It comprises, finally, this demonstration, which I have nowhere found so fully in all the international literature with which I am acquainted, viz., that beautiful effects, when rightly employed, can be obtained even with repulsive subjects. A poor weaver, who has not touched meat for two years, asks a comrade—not having the heart to do it

* Scipio Sighele, *La Folla delinquente*, Turin, 1892; translated into French, *La Foule criminelle*, Paris, 1893. Fournial, *Essai sur la Psychologie des Foules*. Lyon, 1892.

himself—to kill a pretty little dog which had run up to him, and his wife roasts it for him. He cannot control his craving, and begins dipping into the saucepan almost before the meat is done. His stomach, however, cannot bear the dainty, and to his great despair he is forced to reject it.* The incident in itself is not appetizing. But here it becomes beautiful and deeply affecting, for it describes with incomparably tragic power the misery of these woebegone starving people.

This piece, apparently so realistic in the sense attached to this word by superficial talkers, is, on the whole, the most convincing refutation of the theory of realism. For it is incredible that all the incidents which mark the dreadful position of the weavers could have been condensed into exactly one hour of the day, and into one single room of the workman Dreissiger's house; it is, if not wholly impossible, at all events very improbable, that the soldier's murderous bullet should happen to kill the weaver Hilse, the only man trusting in God and resigned to his fate, who remained quietly at his work when all the others rushed out to pillage and riot in the streets. The poet has not depicted 'real' life here, but has freely utilized the materials which he has gained through his observation of life in order to give artistic expression to his personal ideas. His desire was to excite our pity as vividly as that felt by himself for a definite form of human misery. With this object he collected with the sure hand of an artist, into a narrow compass, events which in life would be distributed over months or years, and at long intervals, and he has guided the flight of a blindly unconscious bullet in such a way that it commits, like a villain endowed with reason, a peculiarly dastardly crime, thus raising our compassion for the poor weavers to the height of indignation. The piece, then, shows us the ideas and designs of the poet, his manner of viewing and interpreting reality; it enables us to discern the sentiments aroused in him by the drama of life. It is, then, in the highest degree a 'subjective' work, *i.e.*, the opposite of a 'realistic' copy of fact, which would have to be photographically objective.

* Gerhart Hauptmann, *Die Weber*, Schauspiel aus den vierziger Jahren, 2e Auflage; Berlin, 1892, p. 39:

BERTHA. Where is father, then? [Old Baumert has gone silently away.]

MOTHER BAUMERT. I don't know where he can have gone.

BERTHA. Could it be that he's no longer used to meat?

MOTHER BAUMERT (*beside herself, in tears*). There now, you see—you see for yourself, he can't even keep it down. He'll throw up all the little good food he has had.

OLD BAUMERT (*returns, crying with vexation*). Well, well, 'twill soon be all over with me. They'll soon have done for me. If one do chance to get something good, one isn't able to keep it. (*He sits down on the bench by the stove, weeping.*) [All this conversation is written in Silesian dialect.]

How does it happen that an artist, who applies his means with so fine a taste and with so skilful a calculation of the effect, can commit at the same time such naïvetés as, for example, these stage-directions in *Vor Sonnenaufgang*: 'Frau Krause, at the moment of seating herself, remembers [!] that grace has not yet been said, and mechanically folds her hands, though without otherwise controlling her malice.' 'It is the peasant Krause who, as always [!], is the last to leave the inn.' 'He embraces her with the awkwardness of a gorilla,' etc. How is an actor to set to work by his awkwardness to make a spectator think precisely of a gorilla, or to show him that, 'as always,' he is the last to leave the inn? More especially, how is it to be explained that this same Hauptmann, who has created *Die Weber*, should after this lofty composition have written the novels *Der Apostel* and *Bahnwärter Thiel*?* Here we fall back into the lowest depths of Young-German incapacity. The idea is nonsensical and a plagiarism, the story has not a ray of truth, and the language (so original and lifelike, and so exactly rendering the lightest shades of thought when the author has recourse to patois) is commonplace and slipshod enough to make one weep. No words must be wasted on *Der Apostel*. A dreamer, manifestly touched by insanity, perambulates the streets of Zurich in the costume of an Oriental prophet, and is taken to be Christ by the crowd who worship him. This is the whole story. It is represented in such a way that we never know whether the narrative is telling what the Apostle dreamed or what really happened. His ideas and sentiments are an echo of Nietzsche. *Zarathustra* has incontestably got into Hauptmann's head, and left him no peace till he had himself produced a second infusion of this idiocy. The railway signalman, Thiel, has lost his wife at the birth of their first child. Constantly away from home on duty, he is obliged to marry again that his child may be cared for. The second wife, who soon gives her husband a child of her own, ill-treats the motherless one. In spite of Thiel's warnings, she one day leaves her stepchild on the rails untended, and it is crushed by a train. The signalman then murders his wife and her child with a hatchet in the most horrible manner at night, and is shut up in a lunatic asylum as a furious madman. Let me quote just a few of his descriptions: 'In the obscurity . . . the signalman's hut was transformed into a chapel. A faded photograph of the dead woman on the table before him, his Psalm-book and Bible open, he read and sang alternately the whole night through, interrupted only by the trains tearing past at intervals, and fell into an

* Gerhart Hauptmann, *Der Apostel*, *Bahnwärter Thiel*, Novellistische Studien. Berlin, 1892.

ecstasy so intense that he saw visions of the dead woman standing before his eyes.' 'The [telegraphic] pole, at the southern extremity of the section, had a particularly full and beautiful chord. . . . The signalman experienced a solemn feeling—as at church. And then in time he came to distinguish a voice which recalled to him his dead wife. He imagined that it was a chorus of blessed spirits in which her voice was mingled, and this idea awakened in him a longing, an emotion amounting to tears.' The 'Young German' speaks with contempt of Berthold Auerbach, because he depicts sentimental peasants. Is there a single one of Auerbach's Black Forest folk impregnated with such a rose-watery sentimentality as this signalman of the 'realist' Hauptmann, who leans against a telegraph-pole, and is moved to tears at its sound? Again, the passage (pp. 22, 23) which shows us Thiel in amorous excitement at the sight of his wife ('from the woman an invincible, inevitable power seemed to emanate, which Thiel felt himself impotent to resist') Hauptmann has drawn from Zola's novels, and not from the observations of German signalmen. Or has he rather desired to depict in a general way a madman who has always been such long before his furious insanity broke out? In this case he has drawn the picture very falsely.

And the style of this unhappy book! The Scotch firs . . . rubbed their branches squeaking against each other,' and 'a noisy squeaking, rattling, clattering, and clashing [of a train with the brake on] broke upon the stillness of the evening.' One and the same word to describe the noise of branches rubbing each other, and of a train with the brake on! 'Two red round lights [those of a locomotive] pierced the darkness like the fixed and staring eyes of a gigantic monster.' 'The sun . . . sparkling at its rising like an enormous blood-red jewel.' 'The sky which caught, like a gigantic and stainlessly blue bowl of crystal, the golden light of the sun.' And once again: 'The sky like an empty pale-blue bowl of crystal.' 'The moon hung, comparable to a lamp, above the forest.' How can an author who has any respect for himself employ comparisons which would make a journeyman tailor who dabbled in writing blush? Besides, what countless slovenlinesses! 'Before his eyes floated pell-mell little yellow points like glow-worms.' Glow-worms do not give out a yellow, but a bluish, light. 'His glassy pupils moved incessantly.' This is a phenomenon which no one has yet seen. 'The trunks of the fir-trees stretched like pale decayed bones between the summits.' Bones are that part of the body which does not decay. 'The blood which flowed was the sign of combat.' Truly a reliable sign! Even great faults in grammar are not wanting, but I consent to take these as printer's mistakes. If Gerhart Hauptmann has true friends, their imperative duty is to rouse his conscience. Having shown what excellent things he is capable of producing, he has not the right to scribble carelessly like the first paltry 'Young-German' writer. He must be strict with himself, and endeavour always to remain the artist he has shown himself in *Die Weber*.

Hauptmann's successes have not let Arno Holz and Johannes Schlaf rest, and both have joined to imitate his *Vor Sonnenaufgang*. Their united efforts produced the *Familie Selicke*, a drama in which nothing happens, of which alcohol is likewise the subject, and where the personages also speak in dialect. For 'modernity's' sake they have introduced a theological candidate who has become a freethinker, yet none the less wishes to obtain an incumbency. I mention this insignificant patchwork play only because the realists usually quote it as one of their *magna opera*.

Such are the Young-German realists, among whose number I will not include, as I said before, a sterling author like Gerhart Hauptmann. They do not know German, are incapable of even observing life, still more of understanding it; they know nothing, learn nothing, and experience nothing whatsoever; have nothing to say, have neither a true sentiment nor a personal thought to express, yet never cease writing; and their scribbling, in the eyes of a great number, passes as the sole German literature of the present and future. They plagiarize the stalest of foreign fashions, and call themselves innovators and original geniuses. They append on the signboard before their shops, 'At the Sign of Modernity,' and nothing is to be found in them but the discarded breeches of bygone poetasters. If the few lines in which they mutter about the obscure Socialistic 'studies' and 'works' of the hero be excluded from all they have published up to the present time, there will remain a miserable balderdash, without colour, taste, or connection with time and space, and which a tolerably conscientious editor of a newspaper even half a century ago would have thrown into the waste-paper basket as altogether too musty. They know that very well, and to be beforehand with those who would reproach them with their charlatanism, they audaciously attribute it to those respectable authors whom they cover with their slaver. Thus, Hans Merian dares to say: 'Spielhagen makes it appear as though he had drawn the fundamental ideas and conflicts in his novels from the great questions which are stirring the present time. But closely examined, all this magnificence evaporates into a vain phantasmagoria.' And: 'To the fabricators of novels *à la* Paul Lindau, recently dealing with realism, we address the reproach of false realism.'* And this same Hans Merian finds that the realism of Max Kretzer and of Karl Bleibtreu is genuine, and that their Parisian cocotte-stories, transported contraband into Berlin, and their adventures of mythical waitresses, are 'drawn from the great questions of the day'! Is not this the practice of thieves who scamper away at full speed before a policeman, shouting as they run louder than anyone else, 'Stop thief!' The movement of the Young German is an incomparable example in literature of that tendency to form cliques which I described in the first volume of this work. It began by a foundation in due form. A man arrogated to himself the rank of captain, and enrolled armed companions in order to repair with them into the Bohemian forests. The purpose was the same as that of every other band of criminals—the 'Maffia,' the 'Mala Vita,' the 'Mano negra,' etc., viz., that of living well without working, by plundering the rich, by blackmailing the poor, by favouring acts of vengeance by the members on persons whom they envy, hate, or fear, by satisfying with impunity the leaning to license and crime, kept down by custom and law. Like the 'Mala Vita' and analogous associations, this band palliates its acts and deeds by stock phrases intended to secure the favour, or at least the indulgence, of the crowd, incapable of judgment and easy to move. Brigands always profess that they are guided by the desire to repair, to the utmost of their power, the injustice of fate, by relieving the rich of their superfluities, and by then alleviating the misery of the poor. Thus, this band asserts that it defends the cause of truth, liberty, and progress, with the indecent love adventures of tavern-maidservants and prostitutes! Membership is acquired by formal admission after predetermined tests have been undergone. He must first publicly bespatter a well-known and meritorious author with mud. With the predominance of low and bad emotions in members of the band, they experience more gratification in maligning a man they envy than in being praised themselves. Next, the candidate must worship as geniuses one or more members of the band, and finally give proof, in verse or prose, that he also is able to express, in the language of a *souteneur*, the ideas of a convict, and the sensations of a noisome beast. Having undergone these three ordeals with success, he is received into the band and declared a genius. Just as the bands of brigands have their haunts, their receivers of stolen goods, and their secret or affiliated allies among the tradespeople, so this band possesses its own newspaper, its appointed editors (who, at

* Hans Merian, *Die sogenannten 'Jungdeutschen' in unsererzeitgenössischen Literatur*, 2e Aufl ge. Leipzig, ss. 12, 14. Undated.

first at least, accepted everything from it), and secret understandings with the critics of respectable papers. Its influence extends even to foreign countries—a phenomenon frequently observed in the formation of bands, and expressly confirmed by Lombroso. 'The Mattoids,' he says, 'as opposed to geniuses and fools, are linked together by a sympathy of interests and hatred; they form a kind of freemasonry so much the more powerful that it is less regular. It is founded on the need of resistance to ridicule which is common to all, and inexorably pursues them everywhere on the necessity of uprooting, or at least combating, the natural antithesis, which, for them, is the man of genius; and, in spite of their hating each other, they stand firmly by one another.'*

He who from a height surveys a horizon of a certain extent can easily observe the labour of the apostles of this international freemasonry. M. Téodar de Wyzewa, already mentioned, who introduced to the French the insane Nietzsche as the most remarkable author that Germany has produced in the second half of this century, speaks in *La Revue bleue* and in *Le Figaro* of Conrad Alberti as the 'poet' who will dominate German literature in the twentieth century. The 'new reviews' of the Symbolists and Instrumentists, *La Revue blanche*, *La Plume*, etc., translate the 'Erlebte Gedichte' of O. J. Bierbaum. On the other hand, O. E. Hartleben offers the German public the so-called 'poetry' of the Belgian Symbolist, Albert Giraud, *Pierrot lunaire*, and H. Bahr mutters with transport over the Parisian mystics. Ola Hansson is enthusiastic before German readers over the realists of the North, and carries into Sweden the good news of Young-German realism, etc.

The actions of the band have not done much good to itself, but they have caused serious injuries to German literature. It has necessarily exerted a baneful attraction over the young who have come to the front in the last seven or eight years. If we consider the enormous difficulties to which a beginner is exposed, who without protection or influence, depending wholly on himself, enters into the *Via Crucis* leading to literary success, we shall find it quite comprehensible that the tyros should be eager to join themselves to a society possessing a powerful organization, its own periodicals and publishers, as well as a definite public, and always ready to take the part of its members with the unscrupulousness and pugnacity of cut-throats. As members of the band, they are freed from all the difficulties of beginners. The most vigorous talents alone—such, for example, as Hermann Sudermann—disdained to lighten their struggles with the help of such allies. The others

* C. Lombroso and R. Laschi, *Le Crime politique*, etc., t. ii., p. 116.

willingly allowed themselves to be affiliated. The result was, on the one hand, that wholly incompetent lads were drawn into the profession of authors, who would never have come before the public if they had not had special depôts to which they could cart all their rubbish ; and, on the other hand, that of procuring for others, who were perhaps not wholly devoid of talent, periodicals and publishers for their childish effusions, the appearance of which in print would have been inconceivable before the formation of the band. Some threw themselves into the literary profession at an age when they should have been studying for a long time to come, and thereby remained ignorant, immature, and superficial; others acquired slipshod and slovenly habits into which they would never have fallen if, in the absence of the conveniences which the organization of the band offered them, they had been obliged to submit to some discipline, and develop their capacities with care. The existence of this literary 'Maffia' assisted the plagiarists against independent minds, the common herd against the solitary, the scribbler against the artist, and the obscene against the refined, so powerfully that competition was almost out of the question. The luxuriant growth of silly, boyish, and crude book-making is the result of this fostering of incapacity and immaturity, and this premium granted to vulgarity. I will demonstrate in one instance only the disastrous effect of the band. The case of the Darmstadt Gymnasium (public school) boy may be remembered, who wrote under the pseudonym of Hans G. Ludwigs, and committed suicide in 1892 at the age of seventeen. For two years he had offered incense to the realist 'geniuses,' and published idiotic novels in the official periodicals of Young Germany, and he committed suicide because, as he wrote, 'this cursed boxed-in life,' *i.e.*, the obligation to learn and work regularly in class, 'broke down his strength.' A good many gymnasium boys write trumpery things and send them to the papers; but as these are not printed, they gradually recover their reason. Their heads do not get turned, and they do not come to imagine that they are much too good to do their lessons, and diligently prepare for their examinations. Ludwigs would perhaps have been cured of his folly; he might have lived till the present day, and become a useful man, if the criminal realist periodicals had not printed his twaddle, and thus diverted him from his studies, and intensified his unwholesome boyish vanity into megalomania.

That this invasion by main force, this revolt of slaves into literature, to use Nietzsche's expression, was to a certain extent successful, can be accounted for by the state of Germany. Its literature after 1870 had, in fact, become stagnant. It could not be otherwise. The German people had been obliged to exert their whole strength to conquer their unity in terrible wars. Now, it is not possible simultaneously to make history on a great scale and lead a flourishing artistic life; it must be one or the other. In the France of Napoleon I. the most celebrated authors were Delille, Esménard, Parseval de Grandmaison, and Fontanes. The Germany of William I., of Moltke and Bismarck, could not produce a Goethe or a Schiller. This can be explained without any mysticism. From the mighty events of which they are witnesses and collaborators the nation obtains a standard of comparison, by the side of which all works of art shrink together, and poets and artists, especially those most gifted and conscientious, feel depressed and discouraged, often even paralyzed, by the double perception that their compatriots only peruse their works distractedly and superficially, and that their creations absolutely cannot attain to the grandeur of the historical events passing before their eyes. In this critical period of transient mental collapse the Young-German band made its appearance, and profited greatly by what even honest and sensible people were obliged to acknowledge as well-founded attacks—even while they condemned the form of them—on many of the then reigning literary senators.

But another and weightier ground is the anarchy which reigns at present in German literature. Our republic of letters is neither governed nor defended. It has neither authorities nor police, and that is the reason a small but determined band of evildoers can make a great stir at their pleasure. Our masters do not concern themselves about their posterity as used to be the case. They have no sense of the duty which success and glory impose upon them. Let me not be misunderstood. Nothing is further from my thoughts than the wish to transform literature into a closed corporation, and to require the new arrivals to become apprentices and journeymen (although, in fact, every new generation unconsciously forms itself on the works of its intellectual ancestors). But they have not the right to be indifferent to what will come after them. They are the intellectual leaders of the people. They have their ear. On them is the task incumbent of facilitating the first steps of the beginner, and presenting them to the public. By this much would be obtained—continuity of development, formation of a literary tradition, respect and gratitude for predecessors, severe and early suppression of individuals of absolutely unjustifiable pretensions, economy of power, which in these days a young author must fritter away in order to come out of his shell. But our literary chiefs have no understanding for all this. Each one thinks only of himself, and is furiously jealous of his colleagues and his followers. Not one of them says that in the intellectual concert of a great people there is room enough for dozens of different artists, each one of whom plays his own instrument. Not one takes into consideration that after him new talent will be born, that this is a fact he cannot prevent, and that he is preparing for himself a better old age by levelling the paths, instead of viciously trying to close them to those who, whatever he may do, will still be his successors in public favour. Who amongst us has ever received a word of encouragement from one of our literary grandees? To whom amongst us have they testified their interest and benevolence? Not one of us owes them anything whatsoever; not one feels obliged to be just towards them, nor to make himself their champion; and when the band fell upon them like a lot of brigands, to drive them off with blows, and put themselves in their place, not a hand was raised to defend them, and they were cruelly punished for having lived and acted in isolation and secret mutual hostility, sternly repulsing the young, and indifferent to the tastes of the people whenever their own works were not in question.

And as we have no Council of Ancients, so we lack also all critical police. The reviewer may praise the most wretched production, kill by silence or drag through the mire the highest masterpiece, state as the contents of a book things of which there is not the slightest mention, and no one calls him to account, no one stigmatizes his ineptitude, his effrontery, or his falsehood. Thus a public that is neither led nor counselled by its ancients, nor protected by its critical police, becomes the predestined prey of all charlatans and impostors.

BOOK V.

THE TWENTIETH CENTURY.

CHAPTER I.

PROGNOSIS.

OUR long and sorrowful wandering through the hospital—for as such we have recognised, if not all civilized humanity, at all events the upper stratum of the population of large towns to be—is ended. We have observed the various embodiments which degeneration and hysteria have assumed in the art, poetry, and philosophy of our times. We have seen the mental disorder affecting modern society manifesting itself chiefly in the following forms: Mysticism, which is the expression of the inaptitude for attention, for clear thought and control of the emotions, and has for its cause the weakness of the higher cerebral centres; Ego-mania, which is an effect of faulty transmission by the sensory nerves, of obtuseness in the centres of perception, of aberration of instincts from a craving for sufficiently strong impressions, and of the great predominance of organic sensations over representative consciousness; and false Realism, which proceeds from confused æsthetic theories, and characterizes itself by pessimism and the irresistible tendency to licentious ideas, and the most vulgar and unclean modes of expression. In all three tendencies we detect the same ultimate elements, viz., a brain incapable of normal working, thence feebleness of will, inattention, predominance of emotion, lack of knowledge, absence of sympathy or interest in the world and humanity, atrophy of the notion of duty and morality. From a clinical point of view somewhat unlike each other, these pathological pictures are nevertheless only different manifestations of a single and unique fundamental condition, to wit, exhaustion, and they must be ranked by the alienist in the genus melancholia, which is the psychiatrical symptom of an exhausted central nervous system.

Superficial or unfair critics have foisted on me the assertion that degeneration and hysteria are the products of the present age. The attentive and candid reader will bear witness that I have never circulated such an absurdity. Hysteria and degeneration have always existed; but they formerly showed themselves sporadically, and had no importance in the life of the whole community. It was only the vast fatigue which was experienced by the generation on which the multitude of discoveries and innovations burst abruptly, imposing upon it organic exigencies greatly surpassing its strength, which created favourable conditions under which these maladies could gain ground enormously, and become a danger to civilization. Certain micro-organisms engendering mortal diseases have always been present also—for example, the bacillus of cholera; but they only cause epidemics when circumstances arise intensely favourable for their rapid increase. In the same way the body constantly harbours parasites which only injure it when another bacillus has invaded and devastated it. For example, we are always inhabited by staphylococcus and streptococcus, but the influenza bacillus must first appear for them to swarm and produce mortal suppurations. Thus, the vermin of plagiarists in art and literature becomes dangerous only when the insane, who follow their own original paths, have previously poisoned the *Zeitgeist*, weakened by fatigue, and rendered it incapable of resistance.

We stand now in the midst of a severe mental epidemic; of a sort of black death of degeneration and hysteria, and it is natural that we should ask anxiously on all sides: 'What is to come next?'

This question of eventuality presents itself to the physician in every serious case, and however delicate and rash, above all, however little scientific any prediction may be, he cannot evade the necessity of establishing a prognosis. For that matter, this is not purely arbitrary, not a blind leap into the dark; the most attentive observation of all the symptoms, assisted by experience, permits a generally just conclusion on the ulterior evolution of the evil.

It is possible that the disease may not have yet attained its culminating point. If it should become more violent, gain yet more in breadth and depth, then certain phenomena which are perceived as exceptions or in an embryo condition would henceforth increase to a formidable extent and develop consistently; others, which at present are only observed among the inmates of lunatic asylums, would pass into the daily habitual condition of whole classes of the population. Life would then present somewhat the following picture:

Every city possesses its club of suicides. By the side of this exist clubs for mutual assassination by strangulation, hanging, or stabbing. In the place of the present taverns houses would be found devoted to the service of consumers of ether, chloral, naphtha, and hashish. The number of persons suffering from aberrations of taste and smell has become so considerable that it is a lucrative trade to open shops for them where they can swallow in rich vessels all sorts of dirt, and breathe amidst surroundings which do not offend their sense of beauty nor their habits of comfort the odour of decay and filth. A number of new professions are being formed—that of injectors of morphia and cocaine; of commissioners who, posted at the corners of the streets, offer their arms to persons attacked by agoraphobia, in order to enable them to cross the roads and squares; of companies of men who by vigorous affirmations are charged to tranquillize persons afflicted with the mania of doubt when taken by a fit of nervousness, etc.

The increase of nervous irritability, far beyond the present standard, has made it necessary to institute certain measures of protection. After it has frequently come to pass that over-excited persons, being unable to resist a sudden impulsion, have killed from their windows with air-guns, or have even openly attacked, the street boys who have uttered shrill whistles or piercingly sharp screams without rhyme or reason; that they have forced their way into strange houses where beginners are practising the piano or singing, and there committed murder; that they have made attempts with dynamite against tramways where the conductor rings a bell (as in Berlin) or whistles—it has been forbidden by law to whistle and bawl in the street; special buildings, managed in such a way that no sound penetrates to the outside, have been established for the practice of the piano and singing exercises; public conveyances have no right to make a noise, and the severest penalty is at the same time attached to the possession of air-guns. The barking of dogs having driven many people in the neighbourhood to madness and suicide, these animals cannot be kept in a town until after they have been made mute by severing the 'recurrent' nerve. A new legislation on subjects connected with the press forbids journalists, under severe penalties, to give detailed accounts of violence or suicides under peculiar circumstances. Editors are responsible for all punishable actions committed in imitation of their reports.

Sexual psychopathy of every nature has become so general and so imperious that manners and laws have adapted themselves accordingly. They appear already in the fashions. Masochists or passivists, who form the majority of men, clothe themselves in a costume which recalls, by colour and cut, feminine apparel. Women who wish to please men of this kind wear men's dress, an eyeglass, boots with spurs and riding-whip, and only show themselves in the street with a large cigar in their mouths. The demand of persons with the 'contrary' sexual sentiment that persons of the same sex can conclude a legal marriage has obtained satisfaction, seeing they have been numerous enough to elect a majority of deputies having the same tendency.* Sadists, 'bestials,' nosophiles, and necrophiles, etc., find legal opportunities to gratify their inclinations. Modesty and restraint are dead superstitions of the past, and appear only as atavism and among the inhabitants of remote villages. The lust of murder is confronted as a disease, and treated by surgical intervention, etc.

The capacity for attention and contemplation has diminished so greatly that instruction at school is at most but two hours a day, and no public amusements, such as theatres, concerts, lectures, etc., last more than half an hour. For that matter, in the curriculum of studies, mental education is almost wholly suppressed, and by far the greater part of the time is reserved for bodily exercises; on the stage only representations of unveiled eroticism and bloody homicides, and to this, flock voluntary victims from all the parts, who aspire to the voluptuousness of dying amid the plaudits of delirious spectators.

The old religions have not many adherents. On the other hand, there are a great number of spiritualist communities who, instead of priests, maintain soothsayers, evokers of the dead, sorcerers, astrologers, and chiromancers, etc.

Books such as those of the present day have not been in fashion for a very long time. Printing is now only on black, blue, or golden paper; on another colour are single incoherent words, often nothing but syllables, nay, even letters or numbers only, but which have a symbolical significance which is meant to be guessed by the colour and print of the paper and form of the book, the size and nature of the characters. Authors soliciting popularity make comprehension easy by adding to the text symbolical arabesques, and impregnating the paper with a definite perfume. But this is considered vulgar by the refined and connoisseurs, and is but little esteemed. Some poets who publish no more than isolated letters of the alphabet, or whose works are coloured pages on which is absolutely nothing, elicit the greatest admiration. There are societies whose object it is to interpret them, and their enthusiasm is so fanatical that they frequently have fights against each other ending in murder.

* Dr. R. von Krafft-Ebing, *Neue Forshungen*, etc., 2 Auflage, pp. 109, 118. By the same, *Psychopathia Sexualis*, 3 Auflage, p. 65.

It would be easy to augment this picture still further, no feature of which is invented, every detail being borrowed from special literature on criminal law and psychiatria, and observations of the peculiarities of neurasthenics, hysterics, and mattoids. This will be, in the near future, the condition of civilized humanity, if fatigue, nervous exhaustion, and the diseases and degeneration conditioned by them, make much greater progress.

Will it come to this? Well, no; I think not. And this, for a reason which scarcely perhaps permits of an objection: because humanity has not yet reached the term of its evolution; because the over-exertion of two or three generations cannot yet have exhausted all its vital powers. Humanity is not senile. It is still young, and a moment of over-exertion is not fatal for youth; it can recover itself. Humanity resembles a vast torrent of lava, which rushes, broad and deep, from the crater of a volcano in constant activity. The outer crust cracks into cold, vitrified scoriæ, but under this dead shell the mass flows, rapidly and evenly, in living incandescence.

As long as the vital powers of an individual, as of a race, are not wholly consumed, the organism makes efforts actively or passively to adapt itself, by seeking to modify injurious conditions, or by adjusting itself in some way so that conditions impossible to modify should be as little noxious as possible. Degenerates, hysterics, and neurasthenics are not capable of adaptation. Therefore they are fated to disappear. That which inexorably destroys them is that they do not know how to come to terms with reality. They are lost, whether they are alone in the world, or whether there are people with them who are still sane, or more sane than they, or at least curable.

They are lost if they are alone: for anti-social, inattentive, without judgment or prevision, they are capable of no useful individual effort, and still less of a common labour which demands obedience, discipline, and the regular performance of duty. They fritter away their life in solitary, unprofitable, æsthetic debauch, and all that their organs, which are in full regression, are still good for is enervating enjoyment. Like bats in old towers, they are niched in the proud monument of civilization, which they have found ready-made, but they themselves can construct nothing more, nor prevent any deterioration. They live, like parasites, on labour which past generations have accumulated for them; and when the heritage is once consumed, they are condemned to die of hunger.

But they are still more surely and rapidly lost if, instead of being alone in the world, healthy beings yet live at their side. For in that case they have to fight in the struggle for existence, and there is no leisure for them to perish in a slow decay by their own incapacity for work. The normal man, with his clear mind, logical thought, sound judgment, and strong will, sees, where the degenerate only gropes; he plans and acts where the latter dozes and dreams; he drives him without effort from all the places where the life-springs of Nature bubble up, and, in possession of all the good things of this earth, he leaves to the impotent degenerate at most the shelter of the hospital, lunatic asylum, and prison, in contemptuous pity. Let us imagine the drivelling Zoroaster of Nietzsche, with his cardboard lions, eagles, and serpents, from a toyshop, or the noctambulist Des Esseintes of the Decadents, sniffing and licking his lips, or Ibsen's "solitary powerful" Stockmann, and his Rosmer lusting for suicide—let us imagine these beings in competition with men who rise early, and are not weary before sunset, who have clear heads, solid stomachs and hard muscles: the comparison will provoke our laughter.

Degenerates must succumb, therefore. They can neither adapt themselves to the conditions of Nature and civilization, nor maintain themselves in the struggle for existence against the healthy. But the latter—and the vast masses of the people still include unnumbered millions of them—will rapidly and easily adapt themselves to the conditions which new inventions have created in humanity. Those who, by marked deficiency of organization, are unable to do so, among the generation taken unawares by these inventions, fall out of the ranks; they become hysterical and neurasthenical, engender degenerates, and in these end their race;* but the more vigorous, although they at first also have become bewildered and fatigued, recover themselves little by little, their descendants accustom themselves to the rapid progress which humanity must make, and soon their slow respiration and their quieter pulsations of the heart will prove that it no longer costs them any effort to keep pace and keep up with the others. The end of the twentieth century, therefore, will probably see a generation to whom it will not be injurious to read a dozen square yards of newspapers daily, to be constantly called to the telephone, to be thinking simultaneously of the five continents of the world, to live half their time in a railway carriage or in a flying machine, and to satisfy the demands of a circle of ten thousand acquaintances, associates, and friends. It will know how to find its ease in the midst of a city inhabited by millions, and will be able, with nerves of gigantic vigour, to respond without haste or agitation to the almost innumerable claims of existence.

If, however, the new civilization should decidedly outstrip

* Dr. A. B. Morel, *Traité des Dégénérescences*, p. 581, note: 'The state of arrested development and *sterility* are the essential characteristics of beings arrived at the extreme limit of degeneracy.'

the powers of humanity, if even the most robust of the species should not in the long-run grow up to it, then ulterior generations will settle with it in another way. They will simply give it up. For humanity has a sure means of defence against innovations which impose a destructive effort on its nervous system, namely, 'misoneism,' that instinctive, invincible aversion to progress and its difficulties that Lombroso has studied so much, and to which he has given this name.* Misoneism protects man from changes of which the suddenness or the extent would be baneful to him. But it does not only appear as resistance to the acceptation of the new; it has another aspect, to wit, the abandonment and gradual elimination of inventions imposing claims too hard on man. We see savage races who die out when the power of the white man makes it impossible for them to shut out civilization; but we see also some who hasten with joy to tear off and throw away the stiff collar imposed by civilization, as soon as constraint is removed. I need only recall the anecdote, related in detail by Darwin, of the Fuegian Jemmy Button, who, taken as a child to England and brought up in that country, returned to his own land in the patent-leather shoes and gloves and what not of fashionable attire, but who, when scarcely landed, threw off the spell of all this foreign lumber for which he was not ripe, and became again a savage among savages.† During the period of the great migrations, the barbarians constructed block-houses in the shadow of the marble palaces of the Romans they had conquered, and preserved of Roman institutions, inventions, arts and sciences, only those which were easy and pleasant to bear. Humanity has, to-day as much as ever, the tendency to reject all that it cannot digest. If future generations come to find that the march of progress is too rapid for them, they will after a time composedly give it up. They will saunter along at their own pace or stop as they choose. They will suppress the distribution of letters, allow railways to disappear, banish telephones from dwelling-houses, preserving them only, perhaps, for the service of the State, will prefer weekly papers to daily journals, will quit cities to return to the country, will slacken the changes of fashion, will simplify the occupations of the day and year, and will grant the nerves some rest again. Thus, adaptation will be effected in any case, either by the increase of nervous power or by the renunciation of acquisitions which exact too much from the nervous system.

As to the future of art and literature, with which these

* C. Lombroso and R. Laschi, *Le Crime politique*, etc., t. i., p. 8 *et seq.*

† Charles Darwin, *A Naturalist's Voyage round the World, Journal of Researches*, etc., chap. x.

inquiries are chiefly concerned, that can be predicted with tolerable clearness. I resist the temptation of looking into too remote a future. Otherwise I should perhaps prove, or at least show as very probable, that in the mental life of centuries far ahead of us art and poetry will occupy but a very insignificant place. Psychology teaches us that the course of development is from instinct to knowledge, from emotion to judgment, from rambling to regulated association of ideas. Attention replaces fugitive ideation; will, guided by reason, replaces caprice. Observation, then, triumphs ever more and more over imagination and artistic symbolism—*i.e.*, the introduction of erroneous personal interpretations of the universe is more and more driven back by an understanding of the laws of Nature. On the other hand, the march followed hitherto by civilization gives us an idea of the fate which may be reserved for art and poetry in a very distant future. That which originally was the most important occupation of men of full mental development, of the maturest, best, and wisest members of society, becomes little by little a subordinate pastime, and finally a child's amusement. Dancing was formerly an extremely important affair. It was performed on certain grand occasions, as a State function of the first order, with solemn ceremonies, after sacrifices and invocations to the gods, by the leading warriors of the tribe. To-day it is no more than a fleeting pastime for women and youths, and later on its last atavistic survival will be the dancing of children. The fable and the fairy-tale were once the highest productions of the human mind. In them the most hidden wisdom of the tribe and its most precious traditions were expressed. To-day they represent a species of literature only cultivated for the nursery. The verse which by rhythm, figurative expression, and rhyme trebly betrays its origin in the stimulations of rhythmically functioning subordinate organs, in association of ideas working according to external similitudes, and in that working according to consonance, was originally the only form of literature. To-day it is only employed for purely emotional portrayal; for all other purposes it has been conquered by prose, and, indeed, has almost passed into the condition of an atavistic language. Under our very eyes the novel is being increasingly degraded, serious and highly cultivated men scarcely deeming it worthy of attention, and it appeals more and more exclusively to the young and to women. From all these examples, it is fair to conclude that after some centuries art and poetry will have become pure atavisms, and will no longer be cultivated except by the most emotional portion of humanity—by women, by the young, perhaps even by children.

But, as I have said, I merely venture on these passing hints as to their yet remote destinies, and will confine myself to the immediate future, which is far more certain.

In all countries æsthetic theorists and critics repeat the phrase that the forms hitherto employed by art are henceforth effete and useless, and that it is preparing something perfectly new, absolutely different from all that is yet known. Richard Wagner first spoke of 'the art-work of the future,' and hundreds of incapable imitators lisp the term after him. Some among them go so far as to try to impose upon themselves and the world that some inexpressive banality, or some pretentious inanity which they have patched up, is this art-work of the future. But all these talks about sunrise, the dawn, new land, etc., are only the twaddle of degenerates incapable of thought. The idea that to-morrow morning at half-past seven o'clock a monstrous, unsuspected event will suddenly take place; that on Thursday next a complete revolution will be accomplished at a single blow, that a revelation, a redemption, the advent of a new age, is imminent—this is frequently observed among the insane; it is a mystic delirium. Reality knows not these sudden changes. Even the great revolution in France, although it was directly the work of a few ill-regulated minds like Marat and Robespierre, did not penetrate far into the depths, as has been shown by H. Taine and proved by the ulterior progress of history; it changed the outer more than the inner relations of the French social organism. All development is carried on slowly; the day after is the continuation of the day before; every new phenomenon is the outcome of a more ancient one, and preserves a family resemblance to it. 'One would say,' observes Renan with quiet irony, 'that the young have neither read the history of philosophy nor Ecclesiastes: "the thing that hath been, it is that which shall be."'* The art and poetry of to-morrow, in all essential points, will be the art and poetry of to-day and yesterday, and the spasmodic seeking for new forms is nothing more than hysterical vanity, the freaks of strolling players and charlatanism. Its sole result has hitherto been childish declamation, with coloured lights and changing perfumes as accompaniments, and atavistic games of shadows and pantomimes, nor will it produce anything more serious in the future.

New forms! Are not the ancient forms flexible and ductile enough to lend expression to every sentiment and every thought? Has a true poet ever found any difficulty in pouring into known and standard forms that which surged within him, and demanded an issue? Has form, for that matter, the dividing, predetermining, and delimitating importance which dreamers and simpletons attribute to it? The forms of lyric

* Ernest Renan, *Feuilles détachées.* Paris, 1892, Préface, p. 10.

poetry extend from the birthday-rhyming of the 'popular poet of the occasion,' who works to order and publishes his address in the paper, to Schiller's *Lay of the Bell*; dramatic form includes at the same time the *Geschundener Raub-ritter* (The Highwayman Fleeced), acted some time ago at Berlin, and Goethe's *Faust*; the epic form embraces Kortum's *Jobsiade* and Dante's *Divina Commedia*, Heinz Tovote's *Im Liebesrauche* and Thackeray's *Vanity Fair*. And yet there are bleatings for 'new forms'? If such there be, they will give no talent to the incapable, and those who have talent know how to create something even within the limits of old forms. The most important thing is the having something to say. Whether it be said under a lyric, dramatic, or epic form is of no essential consequence, and the author will not easily feel the necessity of leaving these forms in order to invent some dazzling novelty in which to clothe his ideas. The history of art and poetry teaches us, moreover, that new forms have not been found for three thousand years. The old ones have been given by the nature of human thought itself. They would only be able to change if the form of our thought itself became changed. There is, of course, evolution, but it only affects externals, not our inmost being. The painter, for example, discovers the picture on the easel after the picture on the wall; sculpture, after the free figure, discovers high relief, and still later low relief, which already intrenches in a way not free from objection on the domain of the painter; the drama renounces its supernatural character, and learns to unfold itself in a more compact and condensed exposition; the epos abandons rhythmic language, and makes use of prose, etc. In these questions of detail evolution will continue to operate, but there will be no modification in the fundamental lines of the different modes of expression for human emotion.

All amplifications of given artistic frames have hitherto consisted in the introduction of new subjects and figures, not in the invention of new forms. It was an advance when, instead of the gods and heroes which till that time alone had peopled the epic poem, Petronius introduced into narrative poetry (*The Banquet of Trimalchio*) the characters of contemporary Roman life, or when the Netherlanders of the seventeenth century discovered for painting—which knew of naught save religious and mythological events, or great proceedings of state—the world of fairs, popular festivals, and rustic taverns. Quevedo and Mendoza, who represent the beggars in the 'Picaresque' novel—the model of the German Grimmelshausen writings—Richardson, Fielding, J. J. Rousseau, who take as the subject of their novels, instead of extraordinary adventures, the reflections and emotions of ordinary average beings; Diderot, who in *Le Fils naturel* and *Le Père de Famille* places his townspeople on the arrogant French stage, which till then had only known insignificant people as figuring in comedies and farces, but in serious drama, kings and great lords alone—all these authors invented, it is true, no new forms, but gave to old forms a different content from that of tradition. We observe also an advance of this kind in the poetry and art of our own day. They have given to the proletariat the rights of citizenship in art and literature. They show the labourer, not as a coarse or ridiculous figure, not with the object of producing a comic or coarse effect, but as a serious, frequently tragic being, worthy of our sympathy. Art is hereby enriched in the same way as it once was by the introduction of rascals and adventurers, of a Clarissa, a Tom Jones, a Julie (*Nouvelle Héloïse*), a Werther, a Constance (*Le Fils naturel*), etc., into the circle of its representations. Nevertheless, when many people in bewilderment exclaim hereupon, 'The art of to-morrow will be socialistic!' they utter unfathomable nonsense. Socialism is a conception of the laws which ought to determine the production and distribution of property. With this, art has nothing to do. Art cannot take any side in politics, nor is it its business to find and propose solutions to economic questions. Its task is to represent the eternally human causes of the socialist movement, the suffering of the poor, their yearning after happiness, their struggle against hostile forces in Nature and in the social mechanism, and their mighty elevation from the abyss into a higher mental and moral atmosphere. When art fulfils this task, when it shows the proletariat how it lives and suffers, how it feels and aspires, it awakens in us an emotion which becomes the mother of projects for alteration, transformation, and reform. It is in exciting such fruitful emotions, and by them the desire to heal the hurt, that art co-operates with progress, and not by socialist declamations, and perhaps still less by executing pictures of the state and the society of the future. Bellamy's patchwork, *Looking Backward*, is outside art, and the twentieth century will surely not favour books of this quality. The glorification of the proletariat by a Karl Henckell, who practises with regard to the fourth estate a more shocking Byzantinism than was ever displayed by a tail-wagging courtier to a king, is entirely incapable of awakening interest and sympathy for the working man. Neither is true and useful emotion to be expected either by such false nonsense as, for example, Ludwig Fulda's *Verlorene Paradies*,* or Ernst von Wildenbruch's

* Ludwig Fulda, *Das verlorene Paradies*, Schauspiel in drei Aufzügen. Stuttgart, 1892. *Cf.* p. 112:

MÜHLBERGER. Rika, Rika; come out!

FREDERIKA. Oh, Lord! will they send me back?

*Haubenlerche.** A brave woman like Minna Wettstein-Adelt,† who obtains employment as a daily workwoman in a factory, and simply relates what she experienced there; a plucky man of sound sense and a warm heart like Gœhre, who depicts the life of a factory-hand according to his own experience;‡ a Gerhart Hauptmann, too, with his closely-observed details in *Die Weber*, do more for the proletariat than all the Emile Zolas, with their empty theorizing in *Germinal* and *L'Argent*, than all the William Morrises, with their high-flown rhymings on the noble workman, who becomes under their pen a caricature of the 'noble savage' so much laughed at in the old novel-writers on the primeval forests, and yet more still than all the scribblers who strew their pottage with socialist phrases by way of 'modern' seasoning. Mrs. Beecher-Stowe's *Uncle Tom's Cabin* did not preach against slavery, nor risk projects in favour of its suppression. But this book has drawn tears from millions of readers, and caused negro slavery to be felt as a disgrace to America, and thus contributed essentially to its abolition. Art and poetry can do for the proletariat what Mrs. Beecher-Stowe has done for the

---

MÜHLBERGER. Here's my daughter. She must go into the fresh air—into the fresh air.

FREDERIKA. Father, let me be. I must work.

MÜHLBERGER (*with passionate resolution*). No. No more work—no more—no more work. You must go out into the fresh air, my child—my good sick child. (*He holds her in his embrace. Pause. No one present can escape from the impression of this episode.*)

So says the author! I do not think that these sentimental phrases produce the smallest effect on anybody. Note (in the original) how Fulda, an author of talent, in no way affiliated to the 'Young-German realists,' is himself sufficiently intimidated by their ranting to seek for 'modernity' by using the Berlin dialect.

* Ernst von Wildenbruch, *Die Haubenlerche*, Schauspiel in vier Akten. Berlin, 1891. *Cf.* p. 134:

AUGUST. Work builds the world. Therefore, it must be executed for its own sake; it must be loved! . . . And you—when I have seen you standing before your tub—with the water-scoop in your hand—in such a way that the windows flew open—then I thought, Ah! here is one who loves his tub! . . .

ILEFELD. Master August, 'tis as if I had been married to it, to my tub—that's how it's been!

AUGUST. And yet you leave it standing there so that anybody might take your place? What am I to say to the tub, should it ask after Paul Ilefeld?

ILEFELD (*sits down heavily and dries his eyes with his hand*).

All the workmen I know would be convulsed with laughing at this conversation.

† Madame Minna Wettstein-Adelt, *Three and a Half Months in a Factory*, Eine praktische Studie, 2e Auflage. Berlin, 1892.

‡ Paul Gœhre, *Three Months Factory Hand and Apprentice*, Eine praktische Studie. Leipzig, 1892.

negroes of the United States. They cannot and will not do more.

It is not unusual at present to meet this sentence: 'The art and poetry of the future will be scientific.' Those who say this assume extraordinarily conceited attitudes, and consider themselves unmistakably as extremely progressive and 'modern.' I ask myself in vain what these words can mean. Do the good people who mean so well by science imagine that sculptors will in the future chisel microscopes in marble, that painters will depict the circulation of the blood, and that poets will display in rich rhymes the principles of Euclid? Even this would not be science, but merely a mechanical occupation with the external apparatus of science. But this will surely not occur. In the past a confusion between art and science was possible; in the future it is unimaginable. The mental activity of man is too highly developed for such an amalgamation. Art and poetry have emotion for their object, science has knowledge. The former are subjective, the latter objective. The former work with the imagination, *i.e.*, with the association of ideas directed by emotion; the latter works with observation, *i.e.*, with the association of ideas determined by sense-impressions, of which the acquisition and reinforcement are the work of attention. Province, object, and method in art and science are so different, and in part so opposed, that to confuse them would signify a retrogression of thousands of years. One thing only is correct: the images issuing from the old anthropomorphic conception, the allusions to obsolete states of things and ideas which Fritz Mauthner has called 'dead symbols'—all this will disappear from art. I think that in the twentieth century it will no longer occur to any painter to compose pictures like Guido Reni's *Aurora* in the Rospigliosi Palace, and that a poet would be laughed at who should represent the moon looking amorously into a pretty girl's room. The artist is the child of his times, the conception dominant in the world is his also, and in spite of all his tendency to atavism his method of expression is that with which contemporary culture furnishes him. No doubt the art of the future will avoid more than hitherto the great errors in universally recognised doctrines of science, but it will never become science.

The feelings of pleasure which a man receives from art result from the gratification of three different organic inclinations or tendencies. He needs the incitement which the variety offers him; he takes pleasure in recognising the originals in the imitations; he represents to himself the feelings of his fellow-creatures, and shares in them. He finds variety in works transporting him into wholly different scenes from those he knows, and which are familiar to him. The pleasurable feeling of recognition he obtains by the careful imitations of familiar realities. His sympathy makes him share with lively personal emotions every strongly and clearly expressed emotion of the artist. There will always be in the future, as heretofore, amateurs of works of imagination, which transport the reader or spectator into remote times and countries, or relate extraordinary adventures; others will prefer works in which the faithful observation of the known will prevail; the most refined and the most advanced will find pleasure only in those in which a soul, with its most secret feelings and thoughts, reveals itself. The art of the future will not be wholly romantic, wholly realistic, or wholly individualistic, but will appeal from first to last as much by its story to curiosity, as by imitation to the pleasure of recognition, and by the externalism of the artist's personality to sympathy.

Two tendencies which have long been rivals will presumably contend still more violently in the future for supremacy, viz., observation and the free flight of imagination, or, to speak more briefly, though more inaccurately, realism and romanticism. Good artists, doubtless, in consequence of their higher mental development, will always be more prone and more apt accurately to perceive and accurately to interpret the phenomena of the world. But the crowd will no less certainly demand of artists in the future something different from the average reality of the world. Among creators, the desire for realism will exist, as among recipients, the need of romanticism. For—and this seems to be an important point—the task of art in the coming century, will be to exert over men that charm of variety which reality will no longer offer, and which the brain cannot relinquish. All that is called 'picturesque' will necessarily disappear more and more from the earth. Civilization ever becomes more uniform. The distinctive is felt as an inconvenience by those who are marked by it, and got rid of. Ruins delight a foreigner's eye, but they inconvenience the native, and he sweeps them away. The traveller is disgusted at seeing the beauty of Venice profaned by steamers, but for the Venetian it is a benefit to cover long distances quickly for ten centesimi. Soon the last Redskin will wear a frock-coat and tall hat; the regulation railway buildings will display their prosaic outlines and hues along the great wall of China and under the palm-trees of Tuggurt in the Sahara; and Macaulay's celebrated Maori will no longer contemplate the ruins of Westminster, but a trashy imitation of the palace at Westminster will serve as a Maori House of Parliament. The unique Yosemite Park, which the Americans in their very wise foresight wish to preserve intact in its prehistoric wildness, will not satisfy the craving for something new, different, picturesque, romantic, which humanity demands, and the latter will claim from art what civilization—clean, curled, and smart—will no longer offer.

I can now sum up in a few words my prognosis. The hysteria of the present day will not last. People will recover from their present fatigue. The feeble, the degenerate, will perish; the strong will adapt themselves to the acquisitions of civilizations, or will subordinate them to their own organic capacity. The aberrations of art have no future. They will disappear when civilized humanity shall have triumphed over its exhausted condition. The art of the twentieth century will connect itself at every point with the past, but it will have a new task to accomplish—that of introducing a stimulating variety into the uniformity of civilized life, an influence which probably science alone will be in a position to exert, many centuries later, over the great majority of mankind.

CHAPTER II.

THERAPEUTICS.

Is it possible to accelerate the recovery of the cultivated classes from the present derangement of their nervous system?

I seriously believe it to be so, and for that reason alone I undertook this work.

No one, I hope, will think me childish enough to imagine that I can bring degenerates to reason by incontrovertibly and convincingly demonstrating to them the derangement of their minds. He whose profession brings him into frequent contact with the insane knows the utter hopelessness of attempting by persuasion or argument to bring them to a recognition of the unreality and morbidness of their delusions. The only result attained is that they regard the physician either as an enemy and persecutor, and fiercely hate him, or as a blockhead devoid of reason on whom they vent their derision.

It is equally vain to preach to fanatics of the insane tendencies of fashions in art and literature, on their enthusiasm for error and foolishness. These fanatics, without being actually momentarily diseased, are yet on the border-line of insanity. They do not and cannot believe it. For the works, the madness of which is at the first glance apparent to every rational being, actually afford them feelings of pleasure. These works are an expression of their own mental derangement, and of the perversion of their own instincts. In the perusal, or contemplation of these productions, the half-witted fall into a state of excitation which they hold to be æsthetic, but which is really sensual; and this sensation is so genuine and immediate, they are so sure of it, that they can feel only annoyance at or pity for him who would make it plain to them that these works evoke no pleasure, but only disgust and contempt. To an habitual drinker it is possible to prove that absinthe is pernicious, but it is absolutely impossible to convince him that it has a disagreeable taste. To him, indeed, it tastes seductively delicious. It is in vain that the psychiatrical critic assures the patient that this book, that picture, are horrible deliriums; the invalid will in good faith reply: 'Deliriums? That may be. But abhorrent? That I can never believe. I know better. They move me deeply and delightfully, and nothing you can say can prevent their doing so!' Those whose minds are more unhinged go still further, and say bluntly: 'We feel in all our nerves the beauty of these works. You do not; so much the worse for you. Instead of perceiving that you are a barbarian, devoid of intelligence, and an obtuse Philistine, you wish to argue us out of our most positive sensations. The only delirious person here is yourself.'

The history of civilization teaches to satiety, that delusions awaken ardent enthusiasm, and during hundreds or thousands of years obtain an invincible mastery of the thought and feeling of millions, because they vouchsafe a satisfaction, unhealthy though it be, to an existing instinct. Against that which procures feelings of pleasure for man, the objections of reason are unavailing.

Those degenerates, whose mental derangement is too deep-seated, must be abandoned to their inexorable fate. They are past cure or amelioration. They will rave for a season, and then perish. This book is obviously not written for them. It is, however, possible to reduce the disease of the age 'to its anatomical necessity' (to use the excellent expression of German medical science), and to this end every effort must be directed. For in addition to those whose organic constitution irrevocably condemns them to such a fate, the present degenerate tendencies are pursued by many who are only victims to fashion and certain cunning impostures, and these misguided ones we may hope to lead back to right paths. If, on the other hand, they were to be passively abandoned to the influences of graphomaniacal fools and their imbecile or unscrupulous bodyguard of critics, the inevitable result of such a neglect of duty would be a much more rapid and violent outspread of the mental contagion, and civilized humanity would with much greater difficulty, and much more slowly, recover from the disease of the age than it might under a strong and resolute combat with the evil.

Those persons, on whose minds it is above all necessary to impress the fact that the current tendencies are a result of mental degeneration and hysteria, are the slightly affected and the healthy, who allow themselves to be deluded by cunningly-devised catch-words, or who, through heedless curiosity, flock where they see a crowd. Certain critics have thought to intimidate me into speechlessness by saying: 'If the indications cited are a proof of degeneration and mental disease, then is art and poetry in general the work of fools and degenerates, even such as has, without reservation, been hitherto admired, for in this likewise there are to be met the marks of degeneration.' To which I reply: If scientific criticism, which tests works of art according to the principles of psychiatry and psychology, should result in showing that all artistic activity is diseased, that would still prove nothing against the correctness of my critical method. It would only be the acquisition of fresh knowledge. It would, doubtless, destroy a charming delusion, and prove painful to many; but science ought not to be checked by the consideration that its results annihilate agreeable errors, and frighten the easy-going out of comfortable habits of thought. Faith, again, is another sovereign besides art; it has rendered quite other services to humanity at a certain stage of evolution, has otherwise consoled and raised it, given it other ideals, and advanced it morally in a different way from even the greatest geniuses of art. Science, nevertheless, has not hesitated to pronounce faith a subjective error of man, and would, therefore, suffer far fewer scruples in characterizing art as something morbid if facts should convince it that such was the case. Moreover, not all that is morbid is necessarily ugly and pernicious. The expectoration of a sufferer from lung disease is quite as much a diseased secretion as the pearl. Is the pearl made more ugly or the expectoration more beautiful by the fact that they have the same origin? The toxine of sausage-meat is the excretion of a bacterium, that of ethyl-alcohol the secretion from a fungus. Is the similarity of genesis the condition of equal value for enjoyment in a poisoned sausage and a glass of old Rhine wine? It would prove nothing in regard to Tolstoi's *Kreutzer Sonata* or Ibsen's *Rosmersholm* if it were of necessity admitted that Goethe's *Werther* suffers from irrational eroticism, and that the *Divina Commedia* and *Faust* are symbolic poems. The whole objection, indeed, proceeds from a non-recognition of the simplest biological facts. The difference between disease and health is not one of kind, but of quantity. There is only one kind of vital activity of the cells and of the cell-systems or organs. It is the same in disease and in health. It is sometimes accelerated, and sometimes retarded; and when this deviation from the rule is detrimental to the ends of the whole organism, we call it disease. As it is here a question of more or less, it is impossible to define their limits sharply. Extreme cases are naturally easily recognised. But who shall determine with accuracy the exact point at which deviation from the normal, *i.e.*, from health, begins? The insane brain performs its functions according to precisely the same laws as the rational brain, but it obeys these laws either imperfectly or excessively. In every human being there exists the tendency to interpret sense-impressions falsely. It is diseased only when exhibited in extraordinary strength. The traveller in a railway carriage has an illusory perception of the landscape flying by him while he is sitting still. The sufferer from the delusion of persecutions imagines that someone is wafting him evil odours, or hurling currents of electricity at him. Both of these ideas rest on sense-illusions. Are both for that reason marks of insanity? The traveller and the paranoist commit the same error of thought, and, nevertheless, the former is perfectly sane, and the latter deranged in mind. It may therefore with perfect security be affirmed that certain peculiarities—such as intense emotionalism, the tendency to symbolism, the predominance of imagination—are to be met with in all true artists. That all should be degenerates is very far from being a necessary consequence of this. It is only the exaggeration of these peculiarities which constitutes a disease. The sole conclusion justified by their regular appearance in artists would be that art, without being properly a disease of the human mind, is yet an incipient, slight deviation from perfect health; and I should raise no objection to this conclusion, the less so because it in no way helps the case of real degenerates and their distinctly diseased works. But it is not enough to prove that mysticism, ego-mania, and the pessimism of realism are forms of mental derangement. All the seductive masks must be torn from these tendencies, and their real aspect be shown in its grinning nakedness.

In opposition to healthy art, which they deride as musty and antiquated, they pretend to represent youth. An ill-advised criticism has actually been caught by their lime, and emphasizes their youth with constant irony. What clumsiness! As if any effort in the world could deprive of its charm the word 'young,' this essential notion of all that is blooming and fresh, this note of the dawn and the spring, and transform it into a term of reproach and insult! The truth is, however, that degenerates are not only not young, but that they are weirdly senile. Senile is their splenetic calumniation of the world and life; senile are their babblings, drivellings, ravings and divagations; senile their impotent appetites, and their cravings for all the stimulants of exhaustion. To be young is to hope; to be young is to love simply and naturally; to be young is to rejoice in one's own health and strength, and in that of all human beings, and of the birds of the air and the beetles in the grass; and of these qualities there is not one to be met with among the youth-simulating, decayed degenerates.

They have the name of liberty on their lips when they proclaim as their god their corrupt self, and call it progress when they extol crime, deny morality, raise altars to instinct, scoff at science, and hold up loafing æstheticism as the sole aim of life. But their invocation of liberty is shameless blasphemy. How can there be a question of liberty when instinct is to be almighty? Let us remember Count Muffat in Zola's *Nana* (p. 491): 'At other times he was a dog. She threw her scented handkerchief to the end of the room for him, and he had to run on all fours to pick it up with his teeth. "Fetch it, Cæsar! . . . Look out; I'll give it to you if you're lazy! . . . Very good, Cæsar! mind! nicely! . . . Sit up!" And as for him, he loved his abasement, revelled in the joy of being a brute. He wanted to sink still lower; he cried: "Hit harder. . . . Bow wow! I am mad; hit me then!"' That is the liberty of one who is 'emancipated' in the sense of the degenerates! He may be a dog, if his crazed instinct commands him to be a dog! And if the 'emancipated' one is named Ravachol, and his instinct commands him to perpetrate the crime of blowing up a house with dynamite, the peaceable citizen sleeping in this house is free to fly into the air, and fall again to the ground in a bloody rain of shreds of flesh and splinters of bone. Progress is possible only by the growth of knowledge; but this is the task of consciousness and judgment, not of instinct. The march of progress is characterized by the expansion of consciousness and the contraction of the unconscious; the strengthening of will and the weakening of impulsions; the increase of self-responsibility and the repression of reckless egoism. He who makes instinct man's master does not wish for liberty, but for the most infamous and abject slavery, viz., enslavement of the judgment of the individual by his most insensate and self-destructive appetites; enslavement of the inflamed man by the craziest whims of a prostitute; enslavement of the people by a few stronger and more violent personalities. And he who places pleasure above discipline, and impulse above self-restraint, wishes not for progress, but for retrogression to the most primitive animality.

Retrogression, relapse—this is in general the ideal of this band who dare to speak of liberty and progress. They wish to be the future. That is one of their chief pretensions. That is one of the means by which they catch the largest number of simpletons. We have, however, seen in all individual cases that it is not the future but the most forgotten, far-away past. Degenerates lisp and stammer, instead of speaking. They utter monosyllabic cries, instead of constructing grammatically and syntactically articulated sentences. They draw and paint like children, who dirty tables and walls with mischievous hands. They compose music like that of the yellow natives of East Asia. They confound all the arts, and lead them back to the primitive forms they had before evolution differentiated them. Every one of their qualities is atavistic, and we know, moreover, that atavism is one of the most constant marks of degeneracy. Lombroso has convincingly demonstrated that many peculiarities of the born criminals described by him are also atavisms. Over-hasty critics believed that they had discovered a very subtle objection when, with a smile of self-satisfaction, they objected: 'You assert that criminal instinct is at once degeneracy and atavism. These two dicta are mutually exclusive. Degeneracy is a pathological state; the most convincing proof of this is, that the degenerate type does not propagate itself, but becomes extinct. Atavism is a return to an earlier state, which cannot have been diseased, because the men who existed under those conditions have developed themselves and progressed. Return to a healthy, albeit remote, state cannot possibly be disease.' All this verbiage has its source in the stubborn superstition which sees in disease a state differing essentially from that of health. This is a good example of the confusion which a word is capable of producing in muddled or ignorant brains. As a matter of fact there exists no activity and no state of the living organism which can in itself be designated as 'health' or 'disease.' But they become these in respect of the circumstances and purposes of the organism. According to the time of its appearance, one and the same state may very well be at one time disease and at another health. In the human fœtus, at the sixth week, hare-lip is a regular and healthy phenomenon. In the newly-born child it is a malformation. In the first year of its life the child cannot walk. Why? Because its legs are too weak to support it? Decidedly not. The well-known experiments of Dr. L. Robinson on sixty new-born infants have proved that they are able to hang by their hands from a stick for thirty seconds, a performance implying muscular strength quite as considerable, relatively to their respective ages, as is possessed by the adult. It is not from weakness that they are unable to walk, but because their nervous system has not yet learned so to regulate and combine the activity of the different groups of muscles, as to produce a purposive movement. Infants cannot yet 'co-ordinate.' Incapacity of co-ordination of muscular activity is called by medical science ataxy. Hence in infants this is the natural and healthy condition. But ataxy precisely is a serious disease when it appears in adults, as the chief symptom of inflammation of the spinal cord. The identity of the ataxy of spinal disease with healthy infantine ataxy is so complete that Dr. S. Frenkel* was able to found upon it a treatment of spinal ataxy, which consisted, essentially, in teaching the patients anew, like children, to walk and stand. It is seen, then, that a state may be at the same time diseased and yet the mere return to what was primitively a perfectly healthy state of things; and it was with culpable frivolity that Lombroso was reproached with contradiction because he saw in criminal instincts at once degeneracy and atavism. The disease of degeneracy consists precisely in the fact that the degenerate organism has not the power to mount to the height of evolution already attained by the species, but stops on the way at an earlier or later point. The relapse of the degenerate may reach to the most stupendous depth. As, in reverting to the cleavage of the superior maxillary peculiar to insects with sextuple lips, he sinks somatically to the level of fishes, nay to that of the arthropoda, or, even further, to that of rhizopods not yet sexually differentiated; as by fistulæ of the neck he reverts to the branchiæ of the lowest fishes, the selacious; or by excess in the number of fingers (polydactylia) to the multiple-rayed fins of fishes, perhaps even to the bristles of worms; or, by hermaphrodism, to the asexuality of rhizopods —so in the most favourable case, as a higher degenerate, he renews intellectually the type of the primitive man of the most remote Stone Age; or, in the worst case, as an idiot, that of an animal far anterior to man.

This is the subject in regard to which it is our duty untiringly and by every means to enlighten the weak in judgment, and the inexperienced. The fine names appropriated to themselves by degenerates, their imitators, and their critical hirelings, are lies and deceit. They are not the future, but an immeasurably remote past. They are not progress, but the most appalling reaction. They are not liberty, but the most disgraceful slavery. They are not youth and the dawn, but the most exhausted senility, the starless winter night, the grave and corruption.

It is the sacred duty of all healthy and moral men to take

* Dr. S. Frenkel, 'Die Therapie atactischer Bewegungstörungen,' *Münchener medizinische Wochenschrift*, Nr. 52. 1892.

part in the work of protecting and saving those who are not already too deeply diseased. Only by each individual doing his duty will it be possible to dam up the invading mental malady. It is not seemly simply to shrug the shoulders and smile contemptuously. While the easy-going console themselves by saying, 'No rational being takes this idiocy seriously,' madness and crime are doing their work and poisoning a whole generation.

Mystics, but especially ego-maniacs and filthy pseudo-realists, are enemies to society of the direst kind. Society must unconditionally defend itself against them. Whoever believes with me that society is the natural organic form of humanity, in which alone it can exist, prosper, and continue to develop itself to higher destinies; whoever looks upon civilization as a good, having value and deserving to be defended, must mercilessly crush under his thumb the anti-social vermin. To him who, with Nietzsche, is enthusiastic over the 'freely-roving, lusting beast of prey,' we cry, 'Get you gone from civilization! Rove far from us! Be a lusting beast of prey in the desert! Satisfy yourself! Level your roads, build your huts, clothe and feed yourself as you can! Our streets and our houses are not built for you; our looms have no stuffs for you; our fields are not tilled for you. All our labour is performed by men who esteem each other, have consideration for each other, mutually aid each other, and know how to curb their selfishness for the general good. There is no place among us for the lusting beast of prey; and if you dare return to us, we will pitilessly beat you to death with clubs.'

And still more determined must the resistance be to the filth-loving herd of swine, the professional pornographists. These have no claim to the measure of pity which may still be extended to degenerates properly so called, as invalids; for they have freely chosen their vile trade, and prosecute it from cupidity, vanity, and hatred of labour. The systematic incitation to lasciviousness causes the gravest injury to the bodily and mental health of individuals, and a society composed of individuals sexually over-stimulated, knowing no longer any self-control, any discipline, any shame, marches to its certain ruin, because it is too worn out and flaccid to perform great tasks. The pornographist poisons the springs whence flows the life of future generations. No task of civilization has been so painfully laborious as the subjugation of lasciviousness. The pornographist would take from us the fruit of this, the hardest struggle of humanity. To him we must show no mercy.

The police cannot aid us. The public prosecutor and criminal judge are not the proper protectors of society against crime committed with pen and crayon. They infuse into their mode of proceeding too much consideration for interests not always, not necessarily, those of cultivated and moral men. The policeman is so often compelled to intervene in the service of a privileged class, of the insupportable arrogance of administrations, of the assumption of infallibility of ministers and other government officials of the most unworthy byzantism and of the most stupid superstition, that he does not dishonour the man on whose shoulder he lays his heavy hand. Hence it comes to this, that the pornographist must be branded with infamy. But the punitive sentence of a judge does not with certainty have this effect.

The condemnation of works trading on unchastity must emanate from men of whose freedom from prejudice and freedom of mind, intelligence and independence, no one entertains a doubt. The word of such men would be of great weight among the people. There already exists an 'Association of Men for the Suppression of Immorality.' Unfortunately it allows itself to be guided not only by solicitude for the moral health and purity of the multitude, and especially of the young, but by considerations which to the majority of the people seem to be prejudices. The association pursues disbelief almost more than immorality. An outspoken word against revelation or the Church inspires this association with as much horror as an act of obscenity. To this narrow-minded confessionalism is it due that its work is less rich in blessing than it might be. But in spite of this, we can take this 'Association of Men' as a pattern. Let us do what it does, but without mummeries. Here is a great and grateful task, *e.g.*, for the new 'Society for Ethical Culture' of Berlin: Let it constitute itself the voluntary guardian of the people's morality. Doubtless the pornographists will attempt to turn it into ridicule. But the scorn will soon enough stick in their own throats. An association composed of the people's leaders and instructors, professors, authors, members of Parliament, judges, high functionaries, has the power to exercise an irresistible boycott. Let the 'Society for Ethical Culture' undertake to examine into the morality of artistic and literary productions. Its composition would be a guarantee that the examination would not be narrow-minded, not prudish, and not canting. Its members have sufficient culture and taste to distinguish the thoughtlessness of a morally healthy artist from the vile speculation of a scribbling ruffian. When such a society, which would be joined by those men from the people who are the best fitted for this task, should, after serious investigation and in the consciousness of a heavy responsibility, say of a man, 'He is a criminal!' and of a work, 'It is a disgrace to our nation!' work and man would be annihilated. No respectable bookseller would keep the condemned book; no respectable paper would mention it, or give the author access to its columns; no respectable family would permit the branded work to be in their house; and the wholesome dread of this fate would very soon prevent the appearance of such books as Bahr's *Gute Schule,* and would dishabituate the 'realists' from parading a condemnation based on a crime against morality as a mark of distinction.

Medical specialists of insanity have likewise failed to understand their duty. It is time for them to come to the front. 'It is a prejudice,' Bianchi most justly says,* 'to believe that psychiatry must be enclosed within a sanctuary like that at Mecca.' It is no doubt meritorious to indurate sections of the spinal cord in chromic acid, and tint them in a neutrophyllic solution, but this should not exhaust the activity of a professor of psychiatry. Neither is it sufficient that he should in addition give a few lectures to jurists, and publish observations in technical journals. Let him speak to the mass of cultivated persons who are neither physicians nor learned in law. Let him enlighten them in general publications and in accessible conferences concerning the leading facts in mental therapeutics. Let him show them the mental derangement of degenerate artists and authors, and teach them that the works in fashion are written and painted delirium. In all other branches of medical science it is discerned that hygiene is of more importance than therapeutics, and that the public health has much more to expect from prophylactics than from treatment. With us in Germany the psychiatrist alone fails as yet to concern himself with the hygiene of the mind. It is time that he should practise his profession in this direction also. A Maudsley in England, a Charcot, a Magnan in France, a Lombroso, a Tonnini in Italy, have brought to vast circles of the people an understanding of the obscure phenomena in the life of the mind, and disseminated knowledge which would make it impossible in those countries for pronounced lunatics with the mania for persecution to gain an influence over hundreds of thousands of electoral citizens,† even if it could not prevent the coming into fashion of the degenerate art. In Germany alone no psychiatrist has as yet followed this example. It is time to atone for this negligence. Popularized expositions from the pens of experts whose

* A. G. Bianchi, *La Patologia del Genie e gli scienziati Italiani.* Milano, 1892, p. 79.

† Allusion is here made to the political influence exercised in a number of German electoral districts by the anti-Semite Passchen, a proved lunatic, with a mania for persecution.—TRANSLATOR.

prominent official status would recommend them to the reader would restrain many healthy spirits from affiliating themselves with degenerate tendencies.

Such is the treatment of the disease of the age which I hold to be efficacious: Characterization of the leading degenerates as mentally diseased; unmasking and stigmatizing of their imitators as enemies to society; cautioning the public against the lies of these parasites.

We in particular, who have made it our life's task to combat antiquated superstition, to spread enlightenment, to demolish historical ruins and remove their rubbish, to defend the freedom of the individual against State oppression and the mechanical routine of the Philistine; we must resolutely set ourselves in opposition to the miserable mongers who seize upon our dearest watchwords, with which to entrap the innocent. The 'freedom' and 'modernity,' the 'progress' and 'truth,' of these fellows are not ours. We have nothing in common with them. They wish for self-indulgence; we wish for work. They wish to drown consciousness in the unconscious; we wish to strengthen and enrich consciousness. They wish for evasive ideation and babble; we wish for attention, observation, and knowledge. The criterion by which true moderns may be recognised and distinguished from impostors calling themselves moderns may be this: Whoever preaches absence of discipline is an enemy of progress; and whoever worships his 'I' is an enemy to society. Society has for its first premise, neighbourly love and capacity for self-sacrifice; and progress is the effect of an ever more rigorous subjugation of the beast in man, of an ever tenser self-restraint, an ever keener sense of duty and responsibility. The emancipation for which we are striving is of the judgment, not of the appetites. In the profoundly penetrating words of Scripture (Matt. v. 17), 'Think not that I am come to destroy the law, or the prophets; I am not come to destroy, but to fulfil.'

FINIS.

INDEX.

THE END.